For Scott, Linda, and Paul

CONTENTS

2
READING AND UNDERSTANDING A BALANCE SHEET   31

Chapter preview; The concept of net worth; Various ways to measure the worth of items; Entity convention; The balance sheet; The balance sheet equality; Asset measurement; Balance sheet items and terminology; Balance sheet classifications; Relating to your special company; Information content of a balance sheet.

Chapter overview 51   New vocabulary and concepts; Review questions; Mini-cases and questions for discussion; Essential problems.

3
ANALYZING A BALANCE SHEET   59

Chapter preview; Extending credit to customers; Equities as sources; Importance of solvency and liquidity; Convenient measures of solvency: *current ratio, quick ratio;* Convenient measures of liquidity: *debt ratio, asset composition;* Other balance-sheet-related ratios; Net working capital; Lack of consensus; Standards for comparison; Consistency Materiality; Affirmatively misleading detail.

Chapter overview 77   New vocabulary and concepts; Review questions; Mini-cases and questions for discussion; Essential problems; Supplementary problems.

4
BALANCE SHEET CHANGES AND INCOME   85

Chapter preview; Events which change a balance sheet; Transactions and adjustments; The financial accounting system; Income; Income and certain balance sheet changes; The accrual system.

Chapter overview 104   New vocabulary and new concepts; Review questions; Mini-cases and questions for discussion; Essential problems; Supplementary problems.

5
INCOME, WORKING CAPITAL, AND FUNDS
FROM OPERATIONS   113

Chapter preview; Need for income detail; Preparing an income statement; Sales revenue; Other revenue; Operating expenses; Income from operations; Using income statement information; Temporary accounts for revenues and expenses; Net working capital; Typical transactions affecting both income and net working capital; Adjustments affecting income and net working capital; Operating income and working capital funds from operations.

6
NET INCOME—THE "BOTTOM LINE"   143

Chapter preview; What is my take-home profit? Adjustment for depreciation; Adjustments for other noncurrent items; Other revenue, gain or loss; Funds from operations; Extraordinary items; Net income—the "bottom line"; Reconciling net income with owner's equity; Reconciling net income with funds from operations; Accounting income vs. taxable income.

7
WORKING CAPITAL FUNDS FLOW AND THE STATEMENT OF CHANGES IN FINANCIAL POSITION   173

Chapter preview

PART ONE   WORKING CAPITAL FUNDS FLOW
Need for additional working capital; Capital invested in a business; Determining present capital requirements; Determining future capital requirements; Determining possible sources: *internal sources, external sources*; Long-term capital structure; Various components of overall management; The working capital funds flow statement; Checklist of possible sources and applications.

PART TWO   STATEMENT OF CHANGES IN FINANCIAL POSITION   191
Part Two preview; Keeping informed on the actions of your competitors; Resource changes not involving working capital flows; The statement of changes in financial position (SCFP); Schedule of working capital changes; Possible sources and applications on the SCFP; Reporting extraordinary items; Differences in the focus of funds being reported; The SCFP as the major link between successive balance sheets.

8

VARIATIONS IN MEASURING AND REPORTING INVENTORIES ····· 213

Chapter preview; Significance of inventory and cost of goods sold; Is my profit really profit? What is my profit this year? Income for the past or for the future? Basic facts about inventory: *components of net purchases, perpetual and periodic inventory systems;* Cost flow assumptions; FIFO cost flow assumption; Weighted average cost flow assumption; LIFO flow assumption; Strict vs. modified layers; Choice among alternative flow assumptions; Effect on reported income; Lower of cost or market (LOCM); Other aspects of inventory measurement and reporting.

Chapter overview 229   New vocabulary and concepts; Review questions; Mini-cases and questions for discussion; Essential problems; Supplementary problems; Preparer procedures; Preparer problems.

CHAPTER 8 APPENDIX   OTHER ASPECTS OF INVENTORY MEASUREMENT AND REPORTING 236
Gross profit method; Retail inventory method; Inventory for a manufacturer: *product costs and period costs, manufacturer's inventories, the cost trinity;* Consignments; Damaged goods.

9

VARIATIONS IN MEASURING AND REPORTING CERTAIN NONCURRENT ASSETS ····· 243

Chapter coverage; Chapter preview; How much capacity investment is required to compete? Objectives of noncurrent asset reporting: *capacity assets reported, off-balance-sheet financing;* Capacity information provided; Initial measurement of capacity assets: *capacity assets acquired in nonmonetary exchanges;* Special situations; Cost expirations of capacity assets: *useful life and salvage value;* Various allocation methods or alternatives: *units of production or service, accelerated depreciation, years' digits method, declining-balance method;* Income effect of different methods; Amortization of intangibles; Other items related to depreciation and amortization; Limitations of balance sheet information; Disposition of capacity assets.

Chapter overview 259   New vocabulary and concepts; Review questions; Mini-cases and questions for discussion; Essential problems; Supplementary problems; Preparer procedures; Preparer problems.

10

OWNERS' EQUITY FOR PARTNERSHIPS AND CORPORATIONS ····· 269

Chapter preview; What would be my share of the profits? Partners' owners' equity still just owner's equity; Division of partners' shares;

Partnership owners' equity classification; Multistep partnership allocations; Liability limitations; Corporations; Significance of limited liability to creditors; Contributed capital; Note on corporate equity logic;
Corporate owners' equity classification; Retained earnings and dividends; Deficits; What is my stock worth? Preferred stock; Par or
stated value; Paid-in capital; Book value; Earnings per share; Treasury
stock, restrictions, and appropriations; Other restrictions and voluntary
appropriations; Stock split; Stock dividend; Summary of changes in
stockholders' equity accounts.

Chapter overview 291   New vocabulary and concepts; Review questions; Mini-cases and questions for discussion; Essential problems;
Supplementary problems; Preparer procedures; Preparer problems.

11
SPECIAL PROBLEMS IN MEASURING CERTAIN ASSETS 301

Chapter preview; What are these items? How are they measured by
accountants? Asset measurement under GAAP; Consolidated financial
statements; Initial measurement of assets: *discount on notes receivable,
bonds acquired as investments, sinking funds or other "funds" as assets,
capital leases, goodwill, assets acquired for other than cash, review of
initial measurement basis;* Recognizing expirations and losses: *loss on
current marketable securities, allowance for uncollectibles, loss on noncurrent marketable securities and other investments, amortization of
bond premium, other expirations;* Recognizing related revenues: *recovery of loss on marketable securities, amortization of receivables discount,
sinking fund increases, equity in another's undistributed earnings, percentage completion;* Other items; Review of asset changes; Asset
changes involving funds flows.

Chapter overview 328   New vocabulary and concepts; Review questions; Mini-cases and questions for discussion; Essential problems;
Supplementary problems; Preparer procedures; Preparer problems.

12
THE MEASUREMENT OF LIABILITIES 339

Chapter preview; How much does this firm really owe to others? Objectives of liability measurement and reporting; Liability valuation
accounts; Capital-lease obligations of lessee; Maturing portion of long-
term debt; Certain, estimated, and contingent liabilities; Unearned
revenue and other deferred items; Deferred income tax; Minority interest; Early debt extinguishment: *early debt retirement, refunding, debt
conversion;* Review of liability changes; Liability changes involving
funds flows.

13
FINANCIAL STATEMENT ANALYSIS 381

14
FUNDS FLOW STATEMENT PREPARATION 417

15
ARTIFICIAL ENTITIES AND DIFFERENT REPORTING PERIODS 455

pany investment, intercompany debt, intercompany transactions and accruals; Consolidated statements for purchases: *goodwill, intercompany debt, intercompany transactions and accruals;* Implications of purchase vs. pooling treatments; Minority interest; Interpreting consolidated financial statements; Statutory mergers; Segment reporting; Identifying segments; Segment information reported; Additional disclosure; Usefulness of segment information; Who wants to read all that detail? *auditor's opinion, choice of accounting method, accounting changes, supplementary information, contingencies and commitments;* I can't wait a whole year! Time orientation of interim reporting; Interpreting interim reports.

Chapter overview 478   New vocabulary and concepts; Review questions; Mini-cases and questions for discussion; Essential problems.

16
CURRENT-VALUE FINANCIAL STATEMENTS 485

Chapter preview; Is my net income really income? Income reconsidered; Distributable income; Changing situation; Replacement cost statement; Evaluating replacement cost statements; Index adjustment; Price-level-adjusted statements; Considerations related to current-value accounting; Dual-column statements; Monetary gains and losses.

Chapter overview 502   New vocabulary and concepts; Review questions; Mini-cases and questions for discussion; Essential problems; Supplementary problems.

17
BOOKKEEPING AND THE ACCOUNTING CYCLE 507

Chapter preview; Need for standardization of procedures; The debit/credit convention; The debit/credit code; The journal(s) and the audit trail; The ledger(s) and posting; Interim trial balances; The worksheet and the pre-adjusting trial balance; Adjustments and the adjusted trial balance; Closing and the post-closing trial balance; Error corrections and opening reversals; The accounting cycle; Subsidiary and special journals, ledgers, and accounts; Machine and computer systems; Chapter supplements.

Chapter overview 523   New vocabulary and concepts; Review questions; Preparer procedures; Preparer problems.

APPENDIXES

INDEX

PREFACE
FOR INSTRUCTORS

In recent years, the objectives and the coverage of the first courses in accounting have been changing. The changes have reflected progressive awareness of two facts:

1. The majority of all students enrolling in elementary accounting courses do not intend to be accounting majors.
2. Both groups of students (future accountants and nonaccountants) have the same essential information requirements related to basic accounting.

In recognition of these facts, an increasing number of colleges and universities have moved to a more balanced emphasis at the elementary level between financial and managerial topics. This text is designed for use in a first course or courses covering financial accounting, offered at the undergraduate or MBA foundation course level. Its forthcoming companion volume, *Managerial Accounting Information*, will serve the managerial course.

This book, *Financial Accounting Information*, has certain distinctive features:

- Students are focused upon objectives throughout the text. They start with learning objectives (introduction); move to the social-economic objectives of financial accounting (Chapter 1); then to the objectives and usefulness of each financial statement; and finally to the accountant's objective in measuring and reporting economic events—how the statements should reflect the effect of each transaction.
- Ends are clearly distinguished from means throughout the book. Financial statements and their uses are emphasized; and specific bookkeeping prac-

tices and procedures are shown as of secondary importance but necessary as the means to provide the desirable statements.

- Students are continuously involved in the learning process. Each major chapter leads off with a business problem involving the use of financial accounting information. Students first perceive the need for specific accounting information as a means for solving the problem. They are encouraged to use newly introduced accounting knowledge in the solution of practical and relevant business problems.

- Students encounter new accounting topics only as they need them, and the topics are in a logical learning sequence of "building blocks" of progressively greater sophistication.

- Students can immediately relate to applications involving simple proprietorships. They start with such applications, and become involved in the more complex and unfamiliar (to them) aspects of corporations only after the essential objectives and operations of the accounting system have been covered.

- The informal and conversational tone throughout the book is less severe and potentially intimidating and further encourages involvement.

- Coverage of some topics often omitted in elementary courses is included. These topics are vital to all business students, and especially important to those nonaccounting majors, either undergraduate or graduate, planning no further exposure to financial accounting.

- A complete set of financial statements and a complete annual report are included in an appendix to provide familiarity with the total financial statement package.

- Each chapter starts with a preview of material to be covered and its relevance and concludes with a summary of behavioral skills which the student should have developed from the chapter.

- Important new common business and financial accounting terms are italicized when first introduced and then listed for review at the end of each chapter. An extensive glossary of over five hundred terms is included in an appendix for ready student reference and review.

- Chapter review questions cover all important concepts introduced in the chapter.

- Chapter problems are designated as *essential* and *supplementary,* the latter group having particular relevance to graduate MBA foundation and more rigorous undergraduate courses.

- Complete solutions to all odd-numbered problems are included in an appendix. The student therefore has available, if needed, additional examples of applications in each topic area beyond the minimal included with the chapter text material. The student also has the opportunity to solve the odd-numbered problems and have immediate reinforcement in a manner similar to that in a programmed text.

- Chapters contain mini-cases and questions for class discussion which are designed, particularly for graduate students, to highlight unresolved accounting issues and to stimulate involved interest beyond material covered in the text.
- Many chapters are divided into several sections (some also have appendixes) to facilitate instructor flexibility in selecting materials and making assignments.

These features have all proved valuable in the classroom in resolving several difficulties common to the first course in accounting. The emphasis on application or use of accounting information, and the segregation of purely procedural materials, help maintain student perspective of the difference between accounting and bookkeeping. The student readily perceives the necessity of understanding the accounting system and its measurement objectives in order to use financial statements intelligently. Yet, at the same time, he or she is deterred from falling into the common trap of perceiving that recording and summarizing data is an objective in itself.

This text introduces and reinforces understanding of the effect of transactions and adjustments in terms of increase or decrease to particular statement line items and secondarily to accounts. More sophisticated computer systems in larger firms and forthcoming hardware for smaller firms bypass the debit/credit model (language) entirely. Students whose initial understanding is in terms of increase/decrease effect will not have to translate back from the debit/credit language. Those who might still subsequently need to communicate in this language find no difficulty in coding their intentions in terms of debits and credits.

The technique of first introducing the need for accounting information in the context of solving a business problem not only induces involvement, but also reinforces the student's understanding and appreciation of the important social role filled by the accountant. Also, the inclusion of business applications in the text has proved helpful to part-time faculty and teaching assistants who are looking for additional business examples that "work" in a classroom setting to make accounting continuously relevant.

The cornerstone of this text is the premise that there is no significant dichotomy between elementary material appropriate for future accountants and that for nonaccountants. Both groups need a thorough understanding of the accounting system in terms of its outputs and their usefulness. Both need a conceptual understanding of the accountant's measurement objectives. Neither group needs, at the elementary level, any more procedure or practice than is essential to understanding the information content and usefulness of financial statements and the significance of the accountant's role.

Where, in some elementary courses, coverage of important topics such as consolidation, purchase vs. pooling, cash and funds flow, and current-value accounting is omitted to make room for detailed practice and procedure, both groups of students suffer. Unless it is covered in the elementary course, the nonaccountant may never be exposed to this important information. Possible future accounting majors may be turned away by the reinforced stereotype of an accountant as only a bookkeeper. And the accounting major is forced to wait, sometimes until the very end of his or her program, before being given the overall framework of understanding into which necessary detailed procedural knowledge may be integrated.

In this book, details of accounting procedure and procedural problems are separated into Chapter 17 and into appropriate chapter supplements identified as "Preparer Procedures" and "Preparer Problems." Classroom testing has verified that a business major can achieve a good understanding and appreciation of the value and uses of accounting information when these purely preparer materials are omitted. For those instructors who desire to incorporate these procedural materials into their courses, Chapter 17 should be assigned immediately following Chapter 4. Thereafter the chapter supplements covering preparer procedures and preparer problems may be assigned as desired.

The Instructor's Manual contains suggested course outlines together with recommended time and emphasis to be devoted to each chapter depending upon course length (quarter, semester, two quarters) and upon coverage desired. Other supplementary materials are also available.

The topical coverage as detailed in the table of contents has been developed through classroom experimentation and follows predictable generalized learning patterns. We all learn most efficiently with successive passes over similar material, with each successive exposure providing reinforcement of the old and opportunity for introduction of more depth. The reference text approach, where all course material relating to a particular area is concentrated in a particular chapter, may be effective at the intermediate or advanced levels, but it is often inefficient at the introductory level. This text is written so that students do not have to purchase a separate study guide in order to understand and use the material effectively.

We also learn most efficiently in a problem-solving situation **provided** the problem being solved is perceived as having immediate relevance, where an understandable and interesting "why" precedes the "what" and the "how." In many elementary accounting texts the immediate relevance or the "why" may only be inferred as conformance with accounting principles or practices. Many elementary accounting students have not yet identified and may never identify with an accountant's objectives. For them, relevance is therefore reduced to merely passing a forthcoming examination. This text does not ask the student to identify with accountants or their objectives. Instead the student is placed in the role of a business person observing, using, and therefore learning about information provided by accountants.

Finally, a sequencing of material which seems logical to the learned is not necessarily optimal for the uninitiate. To the learned, the income statement is of major importance. Many texts, therefore, move into income measurement as rapidly as possible. Beginning students, on the other hand, arrive with an intuitive cash flow orientation. If they are expected to focus initially on income, their existing flow concepts must be pushed aside in deference to accruals. After this new conceptualization is achieved, they are then asked to forget it and go back from income to funds flow. The logic of this traditional learning sequence has always seemed tenuous, and many students find the experience unnecessarily difficult.

In this text, the student is first introduced to a proprietorship balance sheet as the logical core of the financial accounting system. Secondary and potentially confusing details such as the components of corporate owners' equity are deferred at this stage. Income is introduced along with funds from operations, and then further developed as funds from operations adjusted for nonfund items. The funds flow statement is then presented as completing the picture. Once a thorough understanding of all three statements and their articulation has been achieved, the discussion covers the components of owners' equity for partnerships and corporations and more sophisticated measurement and reporting concepts related to assets, liabilities, income, and funds flow.

BACKGROUND AND ACKNOWLEDGMENTS

Acknowledgments are so necessary, so deserved, and so numerous. The origins of the approaches used in this book go back through fifteen years of work experience starting in 1949. During this period, as a new business analyst for a New York investment banking firm, an operations research and later materials and production control manager for a mid-Western manufacturer, a methods research manager responsible for developing a computerized accounting system for one of the nation's largest merchandisers, and finally as controller of an electronics firm, I was continuously involved with the uses and the users of accounting information. In developing and conducting accounting seminars for non-accounting managers and other employees, I learned that accounting can be more efficiently introduced by initially emphasizing involvement with outputs and their uses, rather than focusing upon the details of the recording process. Many individuals too numerous to acknowledge by name contributed to this insight and to some of the approaches and techniques developed.

My additional exposure to accounting and accounting education in the Middle Management Program at Harvard Business School and subsequently in the doctoral program at Stanford further reinforced the usefulness orientation. I am particularly indebted to Professor Charles Bliss at Harvard and to Professors Charles Horngren, Gerald Wentworth, and James Porterfield at Stanford. These men provided both inspiration and much needed push and support for me to complete the doctorate years ago.

At San Francisco State, I am indebted to George Stenberg, William Niven, Julien Wade, and Dean Arthur Cunningham for providing the scheduling opportunity over a period of eight years to validate in the classroom the somewhat distinctive approaches in this text. At State I learned that most night students learn accounting more readily than do day students. I observed this difference to result primarily from the working students' ability to make relevant connections between accounting and practical business problems with which they were already familiar, could identify, and therefore could become involved. I found that available texts assumed a student interest and identification with the goals of an accountant, and that this identification was rarely present at the elementary level. And I discovered that the student without working experience could still achieve an adequate level of understanding, identification, and involvement provided that the introduction of new accounting information was preceded by a readily understandable business problem. I am thus indebted most to my students for their patience while I learned the simple truths cited above and incorporated into this book.

I am also grateful to the many individuals who reviewed portions of earlier drafts of the manuscript for this book. Earl K. Littrell (Willamette University), James M. Weglin (North Seattle Community College), Serge Matulich (Texas Christian University), and Paul Frishkoff (University of Oregon) were identified on reviews received while the others were anonymous. I hope they all will see the benefits of their constructive comments.

I am deeply indebted to three individuals. Anthony DiFrancesco and Jonas Mittelman, both colleagues at San Francisco State University, and Lawrence A. Tomassini at the University of Texas, each has reviewed in detail the entire manuscript. Their suggestions were consistently valuable. They are not, of course, responsible for any errors or oversights contained herein.

Over a thousand undergraduate and graduate students in different courses at San Francisco State University have successfully used different portions of this book. Many have provided constructive feedback to the new approaches as they were developed. One hundred graduate students successfully used a preliminary edition of the final text; and I am particularly indebted to John Jago, Karen Stratvert, and to seventy-four others from this group for their many ideas and specific recommendations, most of which have been incorporated in this edition.

Last but by no means least I appreciate the efforts of Keith Nave, Bill Hamilton, and Mary Cafarella, my editors at the Addison-Wesley Publishing Company, who have worked so hard to bring this volume into print.

I will welcome suggestions and comments on this text and on the support materials, from both faculty and students.

San Francisco   A. T. M.
January, 1978

INTRODUCTION
FOR
STUDENTS

FINANCIAL ACCOUNTING AND FINANCIAL STATEMENTS

This text is designed for your use in an elementary financial accounting course. Financial accounting covers those activities related to the preparation of certain reports which are known as financial statements. These statements report the financial status of a firm at a particular time, the firm's activities and resulting profits or losses during the most recent period, and the flows of resources occurring within the firm during the same period.

The primary objective of this text is to help you learn how to read and understand financial statements. You cannot become an expert financial statement analyst in one course, but you can develop a working understanding of the statements themselves, what information they contain, and what they do not contain.

Business people in any position of significant responsibility need to read and understand financial statements. They need to be able to interpret financial statement information as a basis for their business decisions. They also should know how their decisions and actions may affect their firm and be reflected on future financial statements.

To be able to understand financial statements, you will need to learn both the language of accounting and the basic elements of the system followed by accountants. Understanding the accounting system will enable you to know what information the accountants include and do not include in their reports, when and where the information is included, and how it is measured and reported. You will then also appreciate the vital role accountants serve within the firm and in society.

Future accountants also need to learn the details of the practices and procedures followed by accountants as part of the accounting system. These practices and procedures are often called the bookkeeping system, and are also introduced in this book in the last chapter and in certain chapter supplements. Those who desire more exposure to the accountant's bookkeeping system should read Chapter 17 after Chapter 4 and before beginning Chapter 5, and then the chapter supplements may be covered in sequence. Whether or not you become involved with bookkeeping or preparer procedures, it is important that you maintain in your mind the distinction between essential user ideas and less essential preparer procedures. Too often, elementary accounting students let themselves focus almost entirely on bookkeeping details and thus fail to gain an overall understanding of accounting.

ACCOUNTING AS A LANGUAGE

The financial statements contain summary information covering all of the economic events affecting a business during a particular time period, usually a year. If accounting reports were prepared in narrative English (like a newspaper article), they would probably run for thousands of pages and be too long to read. Accountants have, therefore, developed a highly condensed and coded way to report, in a few pages, thousands of events and their effects.

Appendix A contains the actual financial statements for the Xerox Corporation and for the Addison-Wesley Publishing Company for the year 1976. When you first look at these statements, they may seem confusing. After you have successfully completed this course, you should be able to read them with confidence in your ability to understand these and similar statements.

Turn now to Appendix A and carefully look over the two companies' financial statements.

At first glance you can see that the statements contain many different items with dollar values. To intelligently read and interpret the information content of these statements, you must first learn the accountant's language.

As is true with other languages, the language of accounting involves both vocabulary and grammar. Learning the vocabulary involves becoming familiar with both the exact definition of accounting words and how they are used. Both parts are essential. For example, imagine you were thinking of buying a friend's business, a hi-fi record and tape store. One of the major items you would be purchasing would be your friend's inventory on hand of records and tapes. Suppose you had before you an accountant's report showing that your friend had in his business the following items:

Cash	$ 500
Merchandise inventory	8,000
Supplies	300
Total Current Assets	$8,800

What would you be buying? The accountant's definition of "merchandise inventory" is merchandise on hand for sale to customers. The definition of "supplies" is materials for use in the business and not for sale. With these definitions you would be close to knowing what you would be buying. But does the $8,000 represent the retail selling price of the records? Or does it represent the wholesale cost paid by your friend? Remember that accounting vocabulary involves knowing both the definition and how the term is used. In this case you would also need to know that accountants generally value inventory at the **business firm's cost** rather than at the selling price. With a complete understanding of the accounting term "merchandise inventory," you would know that you would be buying records and tapes which had a total cost to your friend's firm of $8,000 and, hopefully, could be sold for much more.

The grammar part of the accounting language is much simpler than other languages. Accounting "grammar" involves merely an agreed ordering of information. A telephone book also has an agreed ordering of information; subscribers are listed in alphabetic order. Suppose you were looking up the telephone number of someone named Hunter. Would you have to check every name in the phone book? Because of the known ordering, you could go right to the H's, and if you found Humble, Hunt, and Huntington, you would know that Hunter was not listed. Similarly, the financial statements have a conventional ordering. If you are looking for a specific item, you can go directly to a particular report and find the portion of that report where the item should appear. You will either find the item, or else its absence will indicate either that the firm doesn't have it or that the amount is too insignificant to separately report.

To assist you in identifying the vocabulary with which you must become familiar, when a new accounting or business term is first introduced it will be printed in *italics*. At the end of each chapter, you will find a list of the more important terms introduced in that chapter. Also included at the back of the book is a glossary of common business and accounting vocabulary. If a word or phrase is new to you and its exact meaning is not clear in the context of the chapter, be sure to use the glossary. Otherwise you could be unnecessarily confused or, even worse, might misunderstand subsequent material or problems using the term.

COMMON DIFFICULTIES IN LEARNING ACCOUNTING

Unfortunately, quite a number of students find elementary accounting a difficult course. You may avoid most difficulties if you are aware of the causes, properly diagnose the problem, and take corrective action. Experience has shown that the following items may be sources of difficulty in many courses and especially in elementary accounting:

1. Student does not choose to assume personal responsibility for learning. A text or an instructor cannot teach you accounting. They can help you **learn** accounting once you choose both to take responsibility to learn and also to put forth whatever effort is necessary for you.

2. Student does not have adequate prerequisite knowledge and skills. To learn accounting effectively and efficiently, you need three skills. You should have the ability to read the English language carefully and precisely. You should have the ability to deal with simple algebraic concepts. You also should have a general understanding of and ability to conceptualize common business language and problems. Deficiency in any of these areas will make your learning of accounting more difficult. You should seek the counsel of your instructor if you think you might have problems in these areas.

3. Student does not choose to devote sufficient time and effort to learning. Most students find that successful learning of accounting requires an investment of at least six to eight hours of intensive outside preparation per week, in the typical course. Some students find that they can read or skim over material and do minimum assigned problems in much less time. They fail to use the extra time for mastering vocabulary and concepts and for reinforcement (see items 4 and 5 below). Eventually they discover, the hard way, that many more hours than those previously "saved" are required to catch up. A few find it impossible to catch up.

4. Student does not choose to thoroughly master new vocabulary and concepts with each chapter before proceeding to the next.   Each chapter builds upon vocabulary and concepts introduced in previous chapters. To avoid great and unnecessary confusion and extra effort, you must master the material in each chapter **as assigned** and not let yourself fall behind. Chapters in this text contain checklists to test yourself before proceeding. These checklists will be described later in this introduction.

5. Student does not choose to adequately reinforce his or her new knowledge. Effective and lasting learning of new knowledge and skill requires reinforcement. Reinforcement involves both repetition and application. The amount of necessary reinforcement varies among students and among different subjects. Each student must provide himself or herself with whatever repetition is necessary. Chapters in this text have cases and problems to provide opportunities for testing and reinforcing new knowledge through application to new situations.

6. Student does not choose to seek assistance from others when required. Students may avoid asking questions of their fellow students or their instructor because they think they will appear stupid. Unless one is truly exceptional, it is very difficult to learn all introductory accounting without some assistance. If you share your confusion with your classmates and your instructor, they may help you.

7. Student does not choose to prepare properly for accounting examinations. Most elementary accounting examination questions require precise answers. Correct answers require knowledge of all the vocabulary and concepts related to the item being examined. A general, as distinct from a specific, understanding often will not suffice. Knowing **almost** all of the necessary parts is usually not enough. The missing or unclear part can be vital. Continual review and self-testing as you proceed through the course will pinpoint problem areas in sufficient time for corrective action before examinations.

8. Student chooses to merely memorize vocabulary, concepts, and example problem solutions.   Some rote memorization of accounting vocabulary and concepts is necessary, but it is not sufficient to learn elementary accounting. To be of value, accounting knowledge must also be generalized so as to be readily applicable to new problem situations.

9. Student incorrectly identifies the source of his or her difficulty.   It is important that you properly identify the source of a difficulty. Many students' problems in elementary accounting courses are caused by one or more of these nine items. If you are having trouble and the real source is one or more of these 9 items, to decide merely that the problem is accounting will be counterproductive. Only when the real cause is identified can your difficulty be readily resolved. You should seek assistance from your instructor if you experience difficulty and cannot pinpoint the cause.

ORGANIZATION OF THIS TEXT

The order of presentation of new material in this text differs from that in many other elementary accounting books. If you should have a friend in another class using a different text, do not fear that you are missing something. You will have covered all of the same important material by the end of the course. You will probably find the sequence in this book easier to grasp.

Research and probably your own past experience have shown that one learns most easily and rapidly when in a problem-solving situation. Learning is more efficient when one experiences a need to learn and an immediate benefit—when one sees the road ahead and is actively involved in the learning process. Each chapter will start with a preview of its coverage—what you can learn. Where practicable, you will then be presented with a user problem situation. The new material that will follow will relate to your understanding and solving of the problem. It will also provide many more tools for solving similar problems. The introductory user problem is designed to give you a context or objective—a reason why—for learning all of the new material.

You can choose to be actively involved in the learning process as you proceed through this book. This choice will allow you to learn accounting most rapidly and efficiently. Alternatively, you can choose to rely on your instructor to induce your involvement. The latter choice will always prove less efficient and often does not work. If you do not become actively involved, you will fail to learn accounting. If you do choose involvement, you will have a successful learning experience.

If you choose to assume responsibility for your learning and make a commitment to active involvement, you will find special opportunities in many chapters. At points where your existing intuitive knowledge can be related to accounting, you will be asked a question before being provided with an explanation. At places where it is important for you to verify the adequacy of your understanding before proceeding, the text will give you a problem and suggest you pause and work out your own solution before reading further. Appendices D and E at the back of the book contain solutions to all odd-numbered chapter problems. Chapters themselves contain a minimum of exhibits (to be faced with too many exhibits might be distracting or unnecessary for you). Should you require further examples of a particular application for better understanding, you can use the odd-numbered problems and solutions as additional clarifying exhibits. Also, you can use these problems after you have completed each chapter, to verify and reinforce your understanding of the main ideas (see below).

Also, as you know, new knowledge must be further reinforced and tested before you can be certain that it is mastered. At the end of the chapters, you will find materials intended to provide opportunity for self-checking and reinforcement:

1. *Chapter Overview.* Section reviewing the major new materials in the chapter with which you should be familiar.
2. *New Vocabulary and Concepts.* List of the important new accounting terms and concepts introduced. Definitions of terms may be found in the glossary (Appendix C) at the back of the book. New concepts may be reviewed in the chapter itself.
3. *Review Questions.* Questions designed for you to test your understanding of new major ideas.
4. *Mini-cases and Questions for Discussion.* Brief cases and questions designed to clarify issues and introduce others for consideration.
5. *Essential Problems.* Problems designed to provide opportunity for you to demonstrate proper application of the essential ideas already introduced in the text. Solutions to odd-numbered problems are provided in Appendix D at the back of the book.
6. *Supplementary problems.* Additional problems provided for further reinforcement and for extension of concepts to new or ambiguous situations not specifically covered in the text. Solutions to odd-numbered problems are provided in Appendix D.

You can only be sure that you have mastered the essential material in each chapter when you are confident that you could, if asked:

- Accurately define new vocabulary listed,
- Accurately explain new concepts listed,
- Answer all review questions,
- Intelligently discuss issues raised in the mini-cases and questions for discussion, and
- Solve all essential problems.

FOOTNOTES

You will probably notice more footnotes in this book than in other elementary texts with which you might compare it. Don't let yourself be intimidated by footnotes! You will find that, in certain topic areas, you are sufficiently interested to want more precise information, while in others elaboration could be confusing. In this book many footnotes are used to provide such additional precision. This approach is used to separate the less important material from the important main ideas.

PREVIEW AND OVERVIEW

Understanding financial accounting essentially involves your being able to read and understand three different major financial statements and to know how they are prepared by accountants. Business activities and the reports about them are sufficiently complex that the 17 chapters of this text are devoted to providing you with an essential understanding. You might find it valuable to see a highly simplified example of the entire system as a preview of the road ahead.

Assume the following facts:

1. On January 1, 19X0, you started your own trucking business by investing $10,000 cash.

2. On January 2 you purchased a used truck costing $6,000. You are paying for the truck in three payments–$2,000 down, $2,000 plus 10% interest on next January 2, and $2,000 plus 10% interest per year on January 2, 19X2.

3. During 19X0 you collected $12,000 cash from customers for trucking services you supplied.

4. During 19X0 you paid out $3,000 for fuel, oil, maintenance, license fees, and insurance.

At the end of the year, an accountant could prepare a report for your firm which would give you the following information:

STATEMENT OF YOUR FIRM'S POSITION AS OF 12/31/X0

Your firm's possessions:

Cash remaining	$17,000
Truck's cost	6,000
Less adjustment for truck wearing out	(1,000)
Total possessions	$22,000

Your firm owes others within a year:

First truck payment due	$ 2,000
One year's interest owed on each truck payment	400
Total	$ 2,400

Your firm owes others more than a year from now:

Second truck payment	$ 2,000
Total owed others	$ 4,400

Your share of the firm's possessions:

Your capital in the business	$17,600
Total owed others plus your share	$22,000

STATEMENT OF YOUR FIRM'S PROFIT FOR THE YEAR 19X0

Earned from customers	$12,000
Less: Operating costs paid	3,000
Now owed as interest on both truck payments	400
Current resources (Note A) from business operations	$ 8,600
Less adjustment for truck wearing out	1,000
Profit for year	$ 7,600

STATEMENT OF MAJOR RESOURCE FLOWS DURING THE YEAR 19X0

Resources were obtained from:	
Current resources (Note A) from business operations	$ 8,600
Owner investment in the business	10,000
Loan due several years in the future	2,000
Total resources obtained	$20,600
Resources ended up:	
Invested in truck	$ 6,000
In current resources (Note A)	14,600
Total resources applied	$20,600

Note A: In this example, current resources are defined as cash less cash owed to others within one year.

Accountants have a special vocabulary to condense these descriptions. For example, accountants would call these reports the Balance Sheet, the Income Statement, and the Statement of Changes in Financial Position, respectively. They also have abbreviated titles for each item appearing in the report. Nevertheless, these same reports are prepared for all businesses. Even the reports for a firm as large as General Motors will follow the same ideas demonstrated in the simplified example above.

As you proceed through this text, think back to this example. If you cannot see how new information is just an expansion of the ideas incorporated in this example, then either:

1. You misunderstand the new idea and should obtain clarification, or
2. You are making an essentially simple system unnecessarily complicated—you are looking for complexity that just isn't there.

YOUR SUGGESTIONS

Obviously the effectiveness of this book for you will depend on factors such as your interest and effort and your classroom experience. It also will depend on how well this book is organized and written for you personally. If you like this text, be sure to tell your instructor. Also, as the author, I am very interested in obtaining your specific comments and suggestions to incorporate in a revised edition. You may forward your ideas directly to the publisher—Addison-Wesley Publishing Company, Reading, Massachusetts 01867—or give them to your instructor for forwarding. Your ideas will be appreciated and considered.

1

FINANCIAL ACCOUNTING
INFORMATION
AND
ITS ENVIRONMENT

CHAPTER PREVIEW

The purpose of this chapter is to provide you with a perspective of the financial accounting system, the individuals and groups involved, and the role of accounting and accountants in society. In this chapter, you can learn:

- The significance of accounting information to its users and to society;
- The identity of various types of users and their information needs;
- The general information content of the four major financial statements which will be the central focus of this book;
- The system of standards applied in the United States to financial statements;
- The role of the CPA in applying these standards;
- The identity and role of the various authoritative bodies involved in setting such standards.

With an overview of the function of accounting and its environment, you will be in a better position to learn about the financial accounting system and the financial statements themselves. You will have the initial perspective which is essential to an understanding of the material in subsequent chapters and its rationale.

(If you have not already read the Introduction for Students, you should do so before proceeding with this chapter.)

SOCIETY'S NEEDS

All societies or nations must deal with the problem of rationing scarce resources. In particular, each society's economic system must appropriately direct new capital—additional wealth—to those particular producers who probably will produce most efficiently the goods and services that society wants.

Whatever the particular economic system for making this decision—free markets, partially controlled markets, or government directives—the society needs information on which to base the resource-allocation decision. Included in this necessary set of information are data concerning the amount of resources a particular producer or firm currently controls, how efficiently the firm uses its resources, and the way in which additional resources are allocated in the firm. In all societies the system for gathering and reporting this necessary information is known as the accounting system.

As an example of accounting information used as the basis for resource allocation within a society, consider the following situation. Imagine you are the benevolent dictator of a tiny island. Your loyal subjects' survival and prosperity depend on catching fish and selling them to nearby islands. All fishing is supervised and controlled by two families—Family A and Family B.

Every year each family receives the cash proceeds from the fish it catches and sells. Sale proceeds are used to cover fishing costs—maintenance and replacement of fishing boats and fishing gear, supplies, and living expenses. At year end, any excess of sales receipts over monies spent for fishing costs is considered profit. Each family is supposed to distribute all profits to you for your use.

Assume that a year has just ended, and that you have received a total of $25,000 from the two families for your use. You decide that you will need $14,000 to maintain the living style appropriate to your position. The balance you wish to apportion to the families for use in expanding fishing capacity, for additional boats and gear. So long as fish are available and salable, additional capacity will mean greater prosperity for everyone.

To produce the greatest benefit to the island as a whole, you wish to allocate the $11,000 where it will be used most efficiently. You define efficiency as the most profit earned **per fishing boat.** Other factors you would also consider relate to the recent history of each family. Have they been expanding their capacity (investment in boats and gear) while still maintaining profitability? Have they been distributing all of their profits to you? Exhibit 1.1 summarizes the information available to you for your decision. How would you allocate the $11,000 and what would be your reasoning?

Given your objective of maximum efficiency, you should allocate all $11,000 to Family B. Family B is earning $2,500 profit per boat, as compared to $2,000 per boat for A. Also note that, with twice as many boats, A is catching and selling over three times as many fish as B but not earning even

Exhibit 1.1

DATA COVERING FAMILY A AND FAMILY B
FOR PREVIOUS YEAR

	Family A	Family B
1. Resources (boats with gear) currently controlled	8	4
2. Efficiency of recent resource usage:		
Fish sale proceeds	$100,000	$30,000
Fishing costs (maintenance, supplies, living)	74,000	15,000
Fishing costs (replacement)	10,000	5,000
Profit	$ 16,000	$10,000
3. History of capacity changes:		
Cash from fishing activities	$ 26,000	$15,000
Cash from dictator allocation	0	5,000
Total	$ 26,000	$20,000
Used for new boats and gear*	$ 10,000	$10,000
Distributed to dictator	15,000	10,000
Total	$ 25,000	$20,000
4. History of Profit Distributions:		
Profit	$ 16,000	$10,000
Distributed to dictator	15,000	10,000
Retained in family	$ 1,000	0

* Note: A new (additional or replacement) boat with gear costs $5,000.

twice as much profit! Family B should also be favored because last year it expanded its fleet by one boat with gear and still maintained profitability. Also, Family A is not distributing all of its profits to you. It is holding back $1,000.

In the United States, resource-allocation decisions with the same objectives are made by millions of individuals and firms who are known as investors. Their interests and information needs will be described below. The importance of this fishing example is that it not only demonstrates the need for and use of accounting information in economic decision-making, but also provides a highly simplified model of the four basic types of financial information.

The necessary information includes:

• The resources controlled by the firm and where they came from;
• The efficiency or profitability of the firm in using up existing resources to generate new resources (sales);

- The amounts and sources of additional resources recently coming under the firm's control and where they were used;
- The amount of profits withdrawn from the firm by the owner(s) and the amount reinvested in the business.

FINANCIAL ACCOUNTING AND FINANCIAL STATEMENTS

The accounting system which provides this necessary financial information is known as *Financial Accounting*. Financial accounting is concerned with the measurement and reporting of resources—goods, services, and property—and their flows. Available resources, claims against these resources, and flows in and out of a business are measured and reported in monetary terms. In the U.S. the monetary unit for recording and reporting is the dollar.

Financial accounting describes an activity involving the preparation and use of the *financial statements* of a firm or business. The statements summarize the financial status of a firm at a particular time; and they report, for the most recent period, the firm's activities and resultant profits or losses, the flows of resources, and the distribution or retention of profits. The financial statements include a *Balance Sheet*, an *Income Statement*, a *Statement of Changes in Financial Position*, and a *Statement of Retained Earnings*, together with supporting footnotes and other data.

The Balance Sheet presents a picture, as of a specific date, of the firm's financial position—what it has, what it owes to others, and what is left for the owner(s). The Income Statement summarizes the results of the firm's activities that were directly related to earning a profit during the most recent period. The Statement of Changes in Financial Position reports any major resource changes during this period, and indicates where the resources were obtained and how they were used. The Statement of Retained Earnings discloses the amount of profit the owner(s) has (have) left in the business and the amount recently withdrawn for other use.

VARIOUS USERS OF FINANCIAL STATEMENTS

In the U.S., resource-allocation decisions are made by individuals, firms, and governments, all of whom use financial information as a basis for their decisions. Individuals or firms who invest resources in businesses are known as *investors*. Investors are the primary users of financial statements.

There are several different categories of investors who may be interested in the financial accounting information concerning a particular firm. The following descriptions of people with problems are designed to help you perceive the need for accounting information and the different categories of investors. It is not necessary that you attempt to remember their names or the details of their personal situations.

Owners

Archie Brown owns a record shop in California. He has taken a salaried position with a larger company in another state and has hired Betty Carmody to manage his store for him. Archie receives a check each month representing business profits. How can he know whether Betty is doing a really good job as his manager? Are the amounts of profit all that he can reasonably expect? Should he seriously consider selling his business and investing his money elsewhere to earn more profit?

As investors, the current owner(s) of a firm is (are) obviously interested in knowing how well the firm is doing.

Potential Owners

Betty Carmody is considering buying the business from Archie and becoming its owner rather than just the salaried manager. She thinks she is doing a good job but would like to compare the firm's performance with others. To pay for the value of a going business, she knows she will probably have to offer Archie more than he actually has invested, but, as a potential owner-investor, she would first like to know how much Archie has invested. Also, she needs to know current profits to estimate whether her possible investment would be a good choice compared to other alternatives.

Potential new owners of the firm need information to evaluate the desirability of making an ownership investment in—becoming owners of—the firm.

Existing and Potential Creditors

Charles Dalton lent $5,000 to the business owned by his friend, Dave Edwards. The loan isn't scheduled to be repaid for another few months, but Charles has heard rumors that Dave's business isn't doing too well. Charles would like to know just how safe his investment is.

Frances Gilbert has been asked to lend $3,000 a year to a business owned by an acquaintance. She wants to know how well the business is doing and whether it would be safe for her to make the loan.

Existing and potential *creditors*—those who lend resources to a firm—need information to evaluate the safety and desirability of their creditor investment.

Current and Potential Suppliers

Harriet Ingraham owns a dressmaking firm. She has been supplying dresses to a shop owned by Judy Kohler. Recently, Judy has been very slow in paying her bills for dresses purchased from Harriet. Judy always seems to have a plausible excuse and is promising to do better next month. Harriet is trying to decide whether to go along with Judy, or insist that the past-due bills be paid before any more dresses will be sold on account.

Larry Michael manufactures water skis. He has a potential new customer in a firm owned by Nate Osgood. Nate wishes to purchase $500 worth of skis on account, that is, to open an account with Larry's firm and pay for the skis within 30 days after delivery. Larry needs to decide whether to extend credit to Nate, or request cash at the time of purchase.

Current and potential suppliers of goods and services on account to customers are investing in the customer's firm. When items are supplied on account or on credit, that is, when a supplier allows a customer to have a charge account and receive items before paying cash for them, the supplier becomes a creditor and is making a short-term loan to the customer. As in the case of creditors lending money, suppliers need information, in order to evaluate the safety and desirability of their creditor investment.

Employees and Unions

Pauline Quera is working as a secretary for a real-estate firm. She likes her job well enough to stay with the business. However, she would like to know how well the firm has been doing because, if things look bad, she would like to start looking for another job.

Roger Segura is thinking of going to work for the Tilden Company. The starting pay sounds good, but Roger wants to join, if possible, a rapidly growing firm with opportunities for advancement. He wants to know how big Tilden is in comparison to its competitors and how rapidly it has been growing.

Suppliers of services to the firm, such as employees and their unions, are vitally interested in the firm's survival and possible growth, and in its ability to pay its bills—in this case, wages—when due.

Current and Potential Customers

Ursula Viaquez is the purchasing agent for a large manufacturer. She has been buying a certain part exclusively from the Weinberg firm. Price, quality, and delivery have been satisfactory. However, Ursula is concerned whether the Weinberg Company is doing well as a business. If not, the risk of having only one established supplier for the needed part might be too great. She then should consider an alternative source in case Weinberg goes out of business.

Yolanda Zachariah is a buyer for a large department store. She is thinking of placing an order with a new source or supplier. The supplier has *not been accustomed to handling large orders and would have to borrow funds for additional materials and equipment in order to fill the order and possible repeat orders. Yolanda is concerned whether this source is in a good enough financial position to be able to borrow enough money to fill this order and possible repeat orders.*

Current and potential customers of the firm may depend on the firm to supply a needed product or service. This dependency makes them interested in the firm's present and prospective economic health.

Each of these people is faced with a decision. Each needs financial accounting information or information, much of which can be obtained from financial statements. As you proceed through this text, you can learn how this needed information can be obtained or interpreted from accounting data. These people are representative of the various primary investor or user groups:

> owners
> creditors
> suppliers
> employees and unions
> customers

All of these groups who have, or are considering forming, a relationship with the firm are potential users of the firm's financial statements. In addition, financial statements are useful to researchers with diverse interests, to trade associations, to financial analysts, to government agencies concerned with the regulation and encouragement of business activity, and to business managers.

Note that managers, as distinct from owners, are not listed as primary users of financial statements. Although managers are greatly concerned about the results of the firm's activities summarized in the statements, they usually have access to a separate set of accounting reports with more extensive detail, prepared exclusively for use by those working for the firm—in other words, for "internal" use. The system involving these more detailed and more frequently prepared reports for managers is known as the *managerial accounting* system. It draws from the same basic data as does financial accounting, but its specialized reports are rarely available to those outside the firm. Managerial accounting is a distinct subject not covered in this text. We shall be concerned here with the system of summary reports prepared for those outside the firm (for those who are **not** managers with access to the managerial system).

OTHER KINDS OF ACCOUNTING SYSTEMS

Managerial accounting is just one of several other types of accounting that are beyond the scope of this text. Organizations established with the goal of making a profit have certain common objectives. Financial accounting provides reports on the status and activities of these organizations. As mentioned above, managers of a business have specialized objectives. They use managerial accounting for reporting the detailed information they require. Governments and "not-for-profit" institutions have different objectives and are also subject to different legal requirements. A different accounting system, with quite different reports, exists for these organizations. It is called *fund accounting* and is not covered in this text.

Another separate type of account is *tax accounting*, as a part of overall *tax management*. Various governments tax individuals and businesses, with the dual objectives of obtaining money and of accomplishing certain social goals. Since tax objectives and tax regulations can be unrelated to the firm's economic objectives, accounting for tax purposes may be separate and distinct from financial accounting. In learning about financial accounting, you should be careful not to assume that tax rules apply to financial accounting. Tax management involves planning, tax return preparation, and compliance with tax regulations. Good tax management is important in order for a firm to minimize its taxes within the law. Accountants are usually involved with tax accounting, but both tax management and tax accounting are beyond the scope of this book.

INFORMATION AVAILABLE FOR USERS FROM FINANCIAL STATEMENTS

Returning to financial accounting, we know that financial statements are prepared for investors to use in making economic decisions. We know that there are four different types of needed information, and each is supplied by a different financial statement.

Appendix A contains the actual financial statements for the Xerox Corporation and for the Addison-Wesley Publishing Company for the year 1976. While you read in the following paragraphs the description of each statement and its information content, study these two actual statements. Although much of the terminology may be new and strange, you should find that each statement will have some meaning for you. You should be able to see how each statement tells you something different that you might wish to know about the company. Do not expect to understand everything on these statements. Study them briefly for very general understanding and as a picture of what this book is all about. The major objective of the material in this book is to provide you with the knowledge to be able to read and fully understand these and other financial statements.

The Balance Sheet, which is also called a statement of financial position, supplies information on what resources the firm currently controls, where they came from, and who has claims against them. Among other things, the balance sheet provides you as a reader or user with information which will help you answer the following questions:

1. How large is the firm in terms of the amount of total resources that it controls?

2. What kinds of resources does the firm have? Are most of its resources committed to its present activities, or can it move rapidly into new business opportunities?

3. How much cash does the firm have? How much cash can it obtain quickly? How much cash is owed to it, and how much cash does it owe to others?

4. How heavily in debt is the firm? Will it be relatively easy or difficult for it to borrow more cash if it needs to? Does it seem to be in a good position to meet its obligations when they require payment?

5. How much do the owners currently have invested in the firm? What proportion of the owners' investment is firmly committed, and what proportion represents past profits held and accumulated in the firm as additional owner investment?

The Income Statement provides information on the efficiency of resource usage in obtaining current revenues—the current profitability of the firm. Among other things, the income statement provides you with answers to the following questions:

1. How large is the firm in terms of its total volume of sales activity?

2. How profitable has the firm been? When compared with similar firms in the same business, is it making more or less profit than other firms?

3. Is the trend of profits up or down? Are profits remaining proportionate to changes in volume of activity, or are they proportionately increasing or decreasing?

4. Compared with other similar firms, does the firm appear to be charging lower prices, that is, discounting? Are its costs of doing business proportionally the same as other similar firms, or higher or lower?

5. Since profitability is one indication of debt-paying ability, does the firm appear to be in a good position to pay its bills promptly? Are profits adequate to cover current interest costs on debt, with a comfortable margin of safety?

A third type of information concerns how the firm has been allocating resources recently obtained. The Statement of Changes in Financial Position provides information concerning what new resources were generated by the firm during the preceding year and how these resources were used. This statement can provide answers to the following types of questions:

1. How much in new resources did the firm generate or obtain during the past year?

2. Where did these resources come from? Were additional resources obtained from creditors? From owners? From profits retained in the business? Is the firm changing its extent of indebtedness?

3. What has management been doing with these new resources? Are resources being committed to the replacement or expansion of the firm's buildings, equipment, and similar items? What portion is being used to retire debt? How much is being distributed to owners?

Finally, the Statement of Retained Earnings discloses information on how profits have been used—reinvested in the business or withdrawn by owner(s). This statement can provide answers to the following types of questions:

1. How much of the profit which has been earned by the business since it started has been left/reinvested in the firm by its owner(s)?

2. How much profit has been withdrawn from the business by the owner(s) during the past year?

In subsequent chapters, after you develop an understanding of the various items on each statement, you can acquire the tools of analysis that will enable you to answer each of these questions. For the moment, it is sufficient for you to have a general idea of what each statement can tell you, of where to look, depending on what you want to know.

NEED FOR OBJECTIVITY, FAIRNESS, AND RELEVANCE

It should be obvious that, unless financial statements are reasonably accurate, resource-allocation decisions may be poorly made. Society as a whole would not be as well off if there were poor resource-allocation decisions, and some groups could benefit at the expense of others. What may not be so obvious to you is that it is virtually impossible for a firm's financial statements to be precisely accurate. You will learn that much of the data included in financial statements must be estimated. Estimated data cannot be precisely accurate. At best it can be an accurate estimate, but it is still an estimate.

Financial statements must include estimates because all of the facts are not known at the time the statements are prepared. A firm may own things which it expects to sell or use, but it can never be sure of their value until they actually have been sold or used. While some items are being sold or used, others items are being purchased. There is always unfinished business. Only when, if ever, the firm goes out of business will everything be known. But users of financial information cannot wait indefinitely; they desire data at least once a year and often more frequently. Financial statements are, therefore, like progress reports. To clarify this concept of progress reports, suppose you have a small hand calculator and are asked how much longer it will be before you will have to replace it. In other words, what is the future usefulness or useful life of the calculator to you? You may know that your type of calculator lasts five years under normal usage. You may have three years to go in college and then plan to sell it, since it will no longer be needed after you are graduated. Therefore, you may confidently respond, "Three years of useful life to me." However, you may decide, upon graduation, to keep it for use on your job. On the other hand, a year from now, a much better and more useful calculator may be available which makes yours obsolete. Therefore, your "three years of useful life to me" can only be an estimate. Later in this book you will see how financial statements necessarily contain estimates very similar to your three-year calculator life.

Financial statements need to be as accurate as feasible in order to be useful and not to mislead users. In this sense, accuracy implies that the information contained in the statements should be complete; there should be full disclosure, and the information should be relevant to the user's need. Relevance implies that information should be timely, comparable with other similar information, consistently prepared from year to year, and understandable to the user. Financial information should also be as fair and objective as possible. Fairness and objectivity imply that necessary estimates must be neutral—free from bias—and verifiable by others. In the interests of fairness and objectivity, accountants have followed a principle of *conservatism*. Known losses are recognized and reported when they occur or are reasonably certain to occur. Gains, on the other hand, are not anticipated. They are recognized only when they have actually occurred.

GENERALLY ACCEPTED ACCOUNTING PRINCIPLES

To achieve the goals of relevance, fairness, completeness, and objectivity, a reasonably uniform system of measurement and reporting is necessary. In the United States, the standardized requirements are known as *Generally Accepted Accounting Principles*, or *GAAP*.[1]

To intelligently use financial statements you will need to become familiar with GAAP. This familiarity will help you to understand the highly summarized and condensed data appearing in the various financial statements. A knowledge of GAAP allows you to understand how and when certain events are recognized and reported, and how the financial effects of these events are measured or estimated.

GAAP have evolved over many years, and are constantly being modified to reflect changes occurring in the world and in man's knowledge and interests. You may not find all of GAAP completely logical and consistent. Like our system of law, some requirements have outlived their usefulness. Yet sometimes changes must take place slowly because GAAP are tied to society's framework of conventions, expectations, regulations, and legal contracts. This social framework usually changes slowly. For example, investors may be accustomed to certain reporting practices and expect them to continue, even though others might be more useful in today's world.

---

[1]   Currently there is an attempt to replace the term GAAP with the term "financial accounting standards." However, GAAP remains the most commonly used term.

Within the U.S. financial accounting system, statements are first prepared for the firm by its own accountants, supposedly following GAAP. Statements at this stage are known as *unaudited financial statements*.[2] Note the earlier qualification, supposedly following GAAP. There is no legal or other requirement that **unaudited** financial statements actually conform to GAAP or that they fairly and objectively provide all relevant information.

As a potential user, you can rely on unaudited financial statements only if you are certain you can trust the objectivity and fairness of the firm's accountants and its management. The firm's management employs its accountants and can direct their activities. Even if there is complete fairness and no intent to deceive you, there is still a question of objectivity or lack of bias. In making the various necessary estimates from the statements, will the firm's management and its accountants necessarily be neutral and objective at all times, or might they have a tendency to be biased in favor of good news and their personal interest in the firm's future?

AUDITED STATEMENTS AND THE CPA

In an attempt to resolve the questions of fairness, objectivity, and conformance with GAAP, many financial statements and their supporting records before publication are first subjected to an independent verification or an *audit*, by a *Certified Public Accountant*, or *CPA*. The CPA examines the statements, together with the records, procedures, and controls used by the firm in their preparation. The objective of the examination is to ascertain whether the statements are complete and prepared consistently in conformance with GAAP and whether reasonable objectivity and fairness were used in making necessary estimates. Upon completion of the audit, the CPA prepares a report in which is stated a professional *opinion* on the fairness of the statements. If the audit discloses significant inconsistency, failure to follow GAAP, or lack of fairness in presentation, such exceptions will be noted in the opinion which accompanies the audited or *certified financial statements*. Exhibit 1.2 is an example of an auditor's opinion.

Note that this is a "clean" opinion; it reports no exceptions from conformity with GAAP. It also discloses that there have been no changes from prior years in how these principles have been consistently applied. Consistency of accounting methods used can be very important in comparing current statement results with those of prior years. This importance will be demonstrated in later chapters. The opinion also gives the auditor's unqualified opinion that the statements fairly present the information.

The primary social role of the CPA is to audit financial statements and to lend credibility to statements prepared under the direction of the company's management. Should a statement user suffer damages as a result of significant

---

2   Unaudited statements are those which have not been independently verified. See next section, covering Audited Statements and the CPA.

Exhibit 1.2

EXAMPLE OF AN AUDIT OPINION FOR THE XYZ COMPANY

To the Stockholders and Board of Directors of the XYZ Company:

We have examined the balance sheet of the XYZ Company as of December 31, 19X0, and the related statements of income, retained earnings, and changes in financial position for the year then ended. Our examination was made in accordance with generally accepted auditing standards, and accordingly included such tests of the accounting records and such other auditing procedures as we considered necessary in the circumstances.

In our opinion, the above-mentioned financial statements present fairly the financial position of the XYZ Company at December 31, 19X0, and the results of its operations and changes in its financial position for the year then ended, in conformity with generally accepted accounting principles applied on a consistent basis.

A, B, and C
Certified Public Accountants
Chicago

March 1, 19X1

---

departures from GAAP or lack of fair presentation **and** these shortcomings were **not** noted in the auditor's opinion, the CPA may then be personally liable. This potential exposure to legally imposed damages reinforces professionalism and tends to make the CPA careful and thorough. The CPA's careful and thorough independent verification makes audited financial statements credible and, therefore, valuable.

A CPA, especially a small practitioner, may also be retained by a client firm to maintain accounting records and prepare the financial statements. CPA's also provide services to clients in the areas of tax-return preparation and general consulting. Professional standards require that when such services so involve a CPA with the firm's interests as to preclude independence, then a **separate**, independent CPA will be engaged for the audit and the opinion.

THE ANNUAL REPORT

You can find the auditor's opinion, together with the financial statements, in the firm's published *Annual Report*. Annual reports are referred to as "published" because they are printed and distributed annually to owners (shareholders) and others by the company. In addition, annual reports often include:

- The president's letter reviewing the highlights of the recent year's activities and earnings and sometimes setting forth future plans;
- Abstracts of significant comparative data;
- Listing of directors and officers;
- Descriptions and pictures of company activities and products; and
- Other information considered beneficial to readers.

You should remember that the auditor's opinion covers <u>only the financial statements and accompanying footnotes</u>. It specifically does **not** attest to the fairness and completeness of other information, especially of forecasts, which may be included in the annual report.

IMPORTANT ASSOCIATIONS AND AUTHORITATIVE BODIES

To maintain your understanding of accounting and of GAAP after you complete this text, there are several associations and authoritative bodies with which you should become familiar. Certified Public Accountants, or CPA's, generally are members of a society in the state in which they are licensed to practice. These state societies arrange for conferences, seminars, and other instruction for the continuing education of CPA's. Although CPA's have satisfactorily completed a uniform national examination, state societies supervise other additional requirements for licensing by their individual states. The largest state societies also publish periodicals containing articles and information of interest and value to members.

In addition to the state CPA societies, many CPA's are members of the national association known as the *American Institute of Certified Public Accountants*, or *AICPA*. The AICPA performs a multitude of services. It prepares and administers, twice a year, the national uniform three-day CPA examination. It publishes the monthly *Journal of Accountancy*, which contains articles and information of immediate practical interest to members, summaries of important changes in GAAP, various pertinent changes in government regulations, and articles of significant long-range theoretical interest. The AICPA also conducts conferences and seminars for continuing member education, markets self-study materials, and represents the CPA profession before Congress, the courts, and various rule-making bodies.

Managerial accountants—those that are employed by firms issuing financial statements—have a professional association known as the *National Association of Accountants*, or *NAA*. The NAA conducts conferences and seminars for the exchange of information and training of its members. It has instituted a professional examination with the intention of motivating further professionalization and training of accountants. Persons passing this NAA examination are identified as having a *Certificate in Management Accounting*, or a *CMA*. The NAA also publishes a monthly periodical, called *Management Accounting*, which contains articles of immediate practical interest to members.

The *American Accounting Association*, or *AAA*, is an association of instructors of accounting. It also conducts conferences and seminars for the interchange of information among members and publishes a quarterly journal called *The Accounting Review*. *The Accounting Review* contains both articles and information related to accounting instruction and also journal articles of a theoretical nature.

A very important nongovernmental body is the *Financial Accounting Standards Board* (or *FASB*). Although the FASB is a private standard-setting body, it has quasi-governmental powers and its standards are enforced by government regulatory agencies (see below). The FASB has replaced the earlier Accounting Principles Board (or APB) and is currently responsible for any major modification or extension of GAAP.[3]

Three agencies of the U.S. government also have significant and growing influence over financial accounting: the *Securities and Exchange Commission* (or *SEC*), the *Cost Accounting Standards Board* (or *CASB*), and the *Internal Revenue Service* (or *IRS*). The SEC is empowered by Congress to ensure the adequacy of information disclosed in the financial statements of publicly owned firms. Until recently, the SEC has generally restricted its activities, with respect to the content of financial statements, to enforcing GAAP and supporting the GAAP standards set forth by the APB and the FASB. It has, however, been progressively more active in "pushing" the AICPA and the FASB to modify and extend auditing standards and GAAP to meet the conditions of the changing world. Recently the financial reporting system has, in a few major celebrated cases, failed to adequately identify poor management or outright fraud leading to the bankruptcy of very large corporations. Also, inadequate disclosure of improper payments by many large firms has been publicized on the heels of Watergate. The accounting system, the accounting profession, and the SEC are the objects of severe criticism. The result may be a far more active role for the government and, in particular, the SEC in the establishment and enforcing of accounting standards.

The CASB is empowered by Congress to set reporting standards on government contracts. Although the CASB is concerned with accounting standards only as applied to government contracts, such standards as it has developed can have a strong influence on the rest of GAAP. If for no other reason, for a firm to apply one set of standards for government contracts and another for private business is confusing and costly. The CASB is attempting to coordinate with both the FASB and the SEC. Whether or not these three bodies can work together and, if they compete, who will win or become the leader, are currently unanswered questions vitally affecting the future of financial accounting.

The other government agency which influences financial accounting is the Internal Revenue Service. The IRS determines the reporting standards for income-tax purposes. Although there is no intended identity or similarity between taxable income and accounting income,[4] tax requirements often are incorporated into GAAP or act as a constraint on the evolution of GAAP. Again, as in the case of the CASB mentioned above, divergence from legally required tax records can necessitate costly dual sets of records.

---

[3]   Minor modifications of GAAP also occur as a result of auditing standards developed and promulgated by the AICPA.

[4]   In many cases it is desirable for a firm to report the same event differently for tax and financial accounting purposes. Data which are legal and advantageous under tax regulations can be misleading and inappropriate in financial statements.

As a potential user of financial statements, you need not be as concerned as must the accountant with all of these associations, agencies, and publications. However, financial accounting is a dynamic and changing system. An item on a statement will mean one thing today because it is prepared a certain way. In the future, as GAAP changes, it may be prepared differently and therefore mean something different. As a user, you must keep yourself advised of major changes in GAAP so as to fully understand the resulting statements. There will probably have been changes made between the time this text is written and the time when you use it. There also may be changes while you are learning introductory accounting. Your instructor will advise you of such changes and their meaning.

CHAPTER OVERVIEW

Based upon the material introduced in this chapter, you should be able to explain:

- The three distinct types of accounting information and, generally, how each applies to the resource-allocation decision made by society or by investors;

- The essential information content of the four major financial statements —the balance sheet, the income statement, the statement of changes in financial position, and the statement of retained earnings; that is, on which statement you might find specific information you might be seeking;

- How owners, creditors, suppliers, employees and/or unions, and customers may all be thought of as investors, and the interest each has in financial statements;

- The essential difference in purpose among the various accounting systems —financial accounting, managerial accounting, fund accounting, and tax accounting;

- GAAP, the primary role of the CPA, and the system enabling you, as a user of financial statements, to rely on their fairness and completeness;

- The roles of the APB, the AICPA, the FASB, and the SEC in establishing GAAP.

NEW VOCABULARY AND CONCEPTS

Financial Accounting
Financial Statements
Balance Sheet
Income Statement
Statement of Changes in Financial
    Position
Statement of Retained Earnings
Investors
Creditors
On credit or on account

Tax Management
Conservatism
GAAP
Unaudited financial statements
Audit
CPA
Opinion (auditor's)
Certified financial statements
Annual Report
CMA

- The distinction among financial accounting, managerial accounting, fund accounting, and tax accounting;
- The objectives of GAAP;
- The objective of independent verification and the role of the CPA;
- The roles of the AICPA, NAA, AAA, FASB, SEC, CASB, and IRS.

REVIEW QUESTIONS

1. What is financial accounting? How does it differ from managerial accounting? Fund accounting? And tax accounting?

2. What four separate accounting reports are usually known as the Financial Statements?

3. What type of accounting information is provided on each of the four reports making up the Financial Statements?

4. Who are the primary users of financial statements?

5. Identify five major different kinds of existing or potential "investors" who are interested in the firm's financial statements, and briefly explain why each is interested.

6. Why aren't managers included among primary users of their firm's financial statements? Explain.

7. Why must financial statements contain estimates? Explain.

8. In addition to having GAAP, what system is practiced in the United States with the objective of ensuring fairness and objectivity in financial statements?

9. Who establishes GAAP?

10. What is the purpose of the auditor's opinion and where can it be found?

11. a) What information is always included in the annual report?
    b) What additional information may also be included?
    c) Of all the information that may be included in an annual report, which is covered by the auditor's opinion? Which is not?

12. a) How does government in the United States influence GAAP?
    b) What agencies are involved, and how does each influence GAAP?

MINI-CASES AND QUESTIONS FOR DISCUSSION

MC 1.1 The chief negotiator for the Gigantic Corporation was meeting with the bargaining agent of the union which represented Gigantic's employees. Gigantic's representative says, "I have here a preliminary set of unaudited financial statements for last year which clearly show that the corporation cannot afford any wage increases." The union bargaining agent responds, "Don't try that again; our accountant has prepared statements which show that Gigantic can clearly afford a 15-percent increase across the board."

Can either of these sets of figures be considered as clearly objective or unbiased? If the two negotiators wish to start from the same set of objective or neutral data, what would you suggest they do?

MC 1.2 Mr. John Smith owns and operates a small janitorial service. For years he has employed Mr. Fred Smart, a CPA, to keep all of his accounting records and also to prepare unaudited financial statements and his tax returns for him. Mr. Smith wants to sell his business and retire. He has found a potential buyer, who wishes to see a set of audited financial statements. Mr. Smith calls his CPA and says, "Fred, I need a set of certified financial statements. After all these years, it shouldn't be too much trouble. How soon can you get them to me?"

Mr. Smart replies, "Sorry, John, but I can't give an opinion on your statements. If you have to give your buyer certified statements, you will have to get a different CPA. If it meets with your approval, you might suggest offering your buyer access to your last five years' tax returns as a possible alternative."

Why won't Smart give an opinion on Smith's financial statements? Aren't tax returns identical with financial statements? Explain.

MC 1.3 Give an example of why each of the following investors might be interested in the financial statements of the ABC Company. Explain what they would be looking for, where they might find it, and why they might be more or less interested in certain information than other types of investors.

a) Al Bernstein, an owner looking for high profits, even if a little risk is involved.
b) Charlotte Drake, a retired widow looking for an ownership investment providing steady income.
c) Ernie Fong, a bank loan officer reviewing a loan application.
d) Mike Hamilton, a credit manager asked to approve an account for a new customer.
e) Ida Jung, a union bargaining agent preparing for wage negotiations.
f) Karen Lovejoy, a jewelry buyer in a department store seeking a new supplier.

MC 1.4 What criteria, other than profit compared to resources employed, might a potential investor wish to consider?

MC 1.5 Can a CPA who is retained/paid by the firm being audited really be an objective/neutral judge of the firm's financial statements?

MC 1.6 What would be the advantages and disadvantages of having GAAP set by government regulation, i.e., similar to the tax code and regulations?

2

READING
AND
UNDERSTANDING
A BALANCE SHEET

CHAPTER PREVIEW

The objective of this chapter is to introduce you to the balance sheet, its information content, its usefulness, and its limitations. You can learn:

- How the balance sheet is like a photograph of a firm's financial condition at one point in time;
- The various items which are included in the "picture" and some specific items which are not included and why;
- How balance sheet items are conventionally ordered or classified and the meaning of the classifications;
- The accountant's basis for measuring or "valuing" balance sheet items, and why this basis has been selected;
- Why balance sheet items naturally fall into two major groups and why the totals of these groups equal each other—why the balance sheet *balances*;
- More about the information content of balance sheets, what you should expect to find, and its usefulness to you.

In subsequent chapters, you can learn that the balance sheet, and particularly the balance sheet equality, forms the core of the financial accounting system. A clear understanding of this "core statement" gained in this chapter will provide you with the basic foundation upon which you can build all of your accounting knowledge.

THE CONCEPT OF NET WORTH

In this chapter, to clarify your understanding, you will be asked at different points to assume different roles by placing yourself in another person's situation and looking at things from his or her standpoint. First you are asked to be a close friend of Mr. Tom Jones. Tom Jones has his own mobile food service business known as the Jones Canteen Company. He owns a special food-vending truck and caters to the various small local businesses, where he sells coffee and pastries during the morning coffee break. For lunch he sells sandwiches, fruit, ice cream, soft drinks, and coffee.

Mr. Jones is applying for a personal loan at his local bank, and the loan officer, Barbara Kane, asks him for a statement of *net worth* as part of his loan application. Ms. Kane explains that his net worth means the worth of what he owns **less** what he owes to others.

Mr. Jones comes to you for help in preparing the required net worth statement. He tells you that, as of today, he has the following possessions and debts:

- Clothing and other personal effects: Estimated original cost, $1,000; estimated cost to replace with used items in similar condition, $400; estimated sale value used, $100.
- TV set and hi-fi: Estimated original cost, $700; estimated cost to replace with used items in similar condition, $200; estimated sale value used, $50.
- Balance in personal checking and savings accounts, $3,000.
- Amount owed on personal charge accounts, $150.
- Balance in business checking account, $400.
- Balance of business cash on hand, $50.
- Money owed by good customers who were short of cash until their next paycheck,* $25.
- Inventory on hand of food and supplies unused and in good condition: original cost and cost to replace, $75.
- The vending truck, which cost $10,000 two years ago and on which he still owes $3,000. Of this, $1,500 is payable to the bank within a year, and the balance is payable more than a year from now. He estimates the truck will be useful to him for four more years, and then he can sell it for $4,000. He guesses that maybe he could purchase another one now, in similar used condition, for $7,000. He also thinks he could get only $5,000 if he had to sell his present truck in a hurry.
- Amount owed by him on business charge accounts, $125.

---

* Jones keeps a little book in the glove compartment where he records these "charge sales."

- He also gives you, for guidance, the bank's sample net worth statement which he received from Ms. Kane. (See Exhibit 2.1.)

Exhibit 2.1
SAMPLE NET WORTH STATEMENT
FOR JOHN DOE

Items Owned	Value
Personal bank accounts	$ XXX
Other personal items	XXX
Business bank accounts	XXX
Business receivables	XXX
Business inventory and supplies	XXX
Business equipment	XXX
TOTAL	$ XXX
Less Amounts Owed	
Personal accounts	$ XXX
Personal loans	XXX
Business accounts	XXX
Business loans	XXX
TOTAL	$ XXX
Equals Net Worth—John Doe	$ XXX

Before reading further, stop and attempt to prepare Jones' net-worth statement from the information given. You will learn accounting much more rapidly and easily if you will first attempt to do this before looking ahead for the "correct" answer.

VARIOUS WAYS TO MEASURE THE WORTH OF ITEMS

If you determine Jones' net worth to be some amount from $5,425 up to and including $11,975, you are correct in that you understand the basic idea behind net worth—what Jones owns minus what he owes to others. Different possible "correct" answers from $5,425 to $11,975 result from a lack of precise **agreement** on how to measure the worth of what Jones owns.

Now you are asked to change roles and assume that you are the bank officer, Ms. Kane, and that Tom Jones has presented you with Exhibit 2.2. Note that there are four different columns, one for each of four different measurement assumptions. Mr. Jones has explained to you that he wasn't sure which you wanted, so, to be safe, he is giving you all four.

As the bank's loan officer, you are interested in Mr. Jones' net worth for several different reasons. First, you want to see whether or not he has so much debt that, in comparison to his possessions, he is (or will be) in trouble and will be a poor risk for an additional loan. Secondly, you desire to know

Exhibit 2.2

NET WORTH STATEMENT FOR JONES

	Column 1 Unadjusted original cost	Column 2 Adjusted original cost	Column 3 Current replacement	Column 4 Expected cash if liquidated
What Jones Has:				
Personal items:				
Clothing and effects	$ 1,000	$ 400	$ 400	$ 100
TV and hi-fi	700	200	200	50
Checking and savings	3,000	3,000	3,000	3,000
Business items:				
Checking and cash	450	450	450	450
Owed from customers	25	25	25	25
Food and supplies	75	75	75	75
Truck	10,000	8,000	7,000	5,000
TOTALS	$15,250	$12,150	$11,150	$8,700
What Jones Owes:				
Personal	$ 150	$ 150	$ 150	$ 150
Business accounts	125	125	125	125
Business truck	3,000	3,000	3,000	3,000
TOTALS	$ 3,275	$ 3,275	$ 3,275	$3,275
Jones' Net Worth	$11,975	$ 8,875	$ 7,875	$5,425

whether he has any valuable items that he could pledge as security on his requested personal loan.[1]

As Ms. Kane, study Exhibit 2.2. The first column indicates Mr. Jones' possessions at their unadjusted *original cost*. As Ms. Kane, do you think this column gives the best picture of Jones' net worth now? Remember, from Chapter 1, that some of the goals of business financial statements were that they be objective, fair, and relevant. As Ms. Kane, you find these standards equally applicable for the information you want from Jones on his personal net-worth statement. Is unadjusted original cost objective, fair, and relevant? It certainly is objective, there are no estimates, and it can be easily verified. But what about fairness and relevance? As the loan officer, you would probably conclude that to use unadjusted original cost—to value Jones' clothing now at $1,000, or his two-year-old truck at $10,000—is neither fair nor, more importantly, relevant. It is not a fair measurement of today's worth, since it reflects no adjustment or allowance for wear. It therefore is not relevant in

---

[1]   As a loan officer, you would also be very much interested in information concerning Tom Jones' income or business earnings. However, this information is not included on a net-worth statement, and is not relevant to this example.

estimating Jones' net worth as of today. For exactly these same reasons (lack of fairness and relevance), accountants do not use unadjusted original-cost measurement on financial statements, even though it is the most objective information.

Now jump to column 4 of Exhibit 2.2. In this column Jones' possessions are measured at the amount of cash that could be realized from their quick sale or *liquidation*. As Ms. Kane, do you think this column gives you the best picture of Jones' current net worth? You probably find the answer to this question more difficult. If Jones were to default on his loan or leave the area, and the bank had to arrange for a sale of his possessions to repay the loan, then these figures would be most helpful. However, as a loan officer you wouldn't be inclined to make the loan if you believed Jones' possessions would need to be liquidated to pay off the loan. You want Jones to stay in business and repay his loan painlessly. After all, as a banker you are in the business of lending or renting money, and you would like Jones as a repeat customer. Therefore, you probably reject liquidation measurement as neither fair nor relevant. Again, for exactly the same reasons, accountants do not choose liquidation measurement in preparing the financial statements. Financial statements are prepared with the assumption that the firm intends, and is able, to stay in business; it's known as the *going-concern assumption*. In the special case of a business about to be liquidated, accountants prepare different reports estimating the cash realizable in liquidation. These reports are distinct from the usual financial statements, have different titles, and will not be discussed in this text.

Turn now to column 3 of Exhibit 2.2. In this column Jones' possessions are reported at the current replacement cost of similar items in the same used condition. This measurement basis may seem the most reasonable to you. Many people would probably agree that it is both fair and relevant. The problem with current or replacement cost as a reporting basis is that, for many items, it can be very difficult and expensive to obtain an objective figure. Current costs would have to be estimated in many cases, and different estimators probably would not agree on the same figure. How accurately do you think you could estimate the current replacement cost of a 15-year-old factory built from materials no longer available? For these two reasons—the expense and questionable objectivity—accountants in the United States have not used current-replacement-cost measurements on financial statements.

Column 2 of Exhibit 2.2 is headed *adjusted original cost*. The measurements in this column are in accordance with current generally accepted accounting principles, that is, GAAP. Note that, for those possessions and debts where the amount is cash, cash to be received (from banks and customers), or cash to be paid, the same amounts appear in all four columns. These items are known as *monetary items*. Monetary items involve one of three things: cash, a legally enforceable right to receive a specific amount of cash on a given date, or an obligation to pay a specific amount of cash at a specific date. Cash can be counted and cash to be received or paid by existing agreement or contract can be determined with certainty. Therefore, there is no immediate problem to valuing monetary items at any particular date.[2] The difficult valuation problems involve the nonmonetary items, such as clothing and effects, TV and hi-fi, food and supplies, and the truck.

ENTITY CONVENTION

The Jones example properly includes Jones' personal possessions and debts as part of his personal net-worth statement. Our objective is to learn about business balance sheets, which are similar to net-worth statements. Accounting balance sheets are prepared for business firms or *business entities*. They include information concerning only the business and its activities. They do not provide information about the firm's investors, except for the amount invested, nor do they cover employees or other firms. In Jones' case, since his business is not incorporated, it is known as a *proprietorship*, or one-owner business. The bank, and the government for tax purposes, considers both Jones' business and personal items collectively. But to demonstrate financial accounting for the business, we will focus on Jones' business entity. Therefore, Jones' personal assets and personal liabilities, which are not related to the business, will be excluded from the business balance sheet.

THE BALANCE SHEET

As you learned in Chapter 1, one of the four basic types of accounting information concerns what resources a firm currently controls and who has claims against these resources. This information is provided on a balance sheet. At first you can think of a balance sheet as a report of things owned by a business and amounts owed to others. Exhibit 2.3 shows a balance sheet prepared for Jones' business for the same date as his personal net-worth statement. This exhibit introduces very important accounting vocabulary and concepts which you should study carefully.

Starting with the title, note that it specifies the name of the business entity involved—Jones Canteen Company. Also note that this particular report is called a balance sheet and is ("as of") a particular date. A balance sheet is sometimes called a statement of financial position. Its purpose is to report the firm's financial position as of the close of business on the statement date. In a going concern, things are constantly changing. A balance sheet is like a

---

[2]   There are some more complex issues involved in the measurement of certain monetary items which are not necessary to discuss now. Where payments are scheduled years in the future, discounted present value may be relevant, and this will be discussed in Chapters 11 and 12. Monetary items held over time during periods of inflation can result in holding gains or losses, and this matter will be discussed in Chapter 16.

Exhibit 2.3

JONES CANTEEN COMPANY BALANCE SHEET AS OF 12/31/XX

Assets			Equities		
Current Assets:			Current Liabilities		
Cash		$ 450	Note payable		$1,500
Accounts receivable		25	Accounts payable		125
Inventory and supplies		75	Total Current Liabilities		$1,625
Total Current Assets		$ 550	Noncurrent Liabilities:		
			Note payable		1,500
Noncurrent Assets:			Total Liabilities		$3,125
Fixed asset—truck	$10,000				
Less accumulated					
depreciation	(2,000)	8,000	Owner's Equity		5,425
Total Assets		$8,550	Total Equities		$8,550

photograph. It gives information at **one point** in time. (Even one day later things could be different.)

Now look at the left half of the balance sheet. It shows the resources of the business. In accounting, economic resources having future value to the business, that are owned or effectively controlled by the business, are known as *assets*. Assets may be tangible (touchable) properties such as cash or buildings. They may also be intangible items such as legal rights or claims to receive or use other assets. In the United States, assets are listed first on the balance sheet.

Note also that assets are divided into two groups: *current assets* and *noncurrent assets*. Current assets include cash, items which will be turned into cash, and those which will be consumed or used up within one year of the balance sheet date.[3] A business has a normal *operating cycle:*

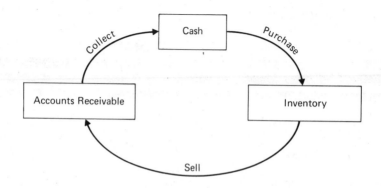

---
[3]   Some firms have an accounting (reporting) period greater than a year. For such firms, "current" would be extended to cover the entire period.

Receivables from customers, which will be collected, and inventory, which will be sold to customers and eventually collected, can be understood as convertible into cash. Examples of items which will be consumed or used up would be supplies and other so-called prepaid items, which will be discussed later in this chapter. All assets that do not fit the definition of current assets are classified as noncurrent.

Within the set of current assets, we see that Jones has *cash, accounts receivable, inventory,* and *supplies.* On a balance sheet, the amount shown for cash includes both cash on hand and in banks, for Jones a total of $450. Accounts receivable indicates those amounts of cash due from customers for sales on account: the customer has purchased the goods or services offered by the firm but has not yet paid cash for them. Such events are known as *credit sales.* (Remember that Jones allowed his good customers to purchase on credit or on account when they were short of cash, and that he kept a record of his accounts receivable in a notebook in the glove compartment of his truck.)

The term "inventory" refers to the merchandise Jones has on hand for sale to customers. His inventory might include coffee, soft drinks, and other salable food. Supplies are those items on hand that will be used up, rather than sold, in the operation of the business. For example, Jones's supplies might include cups, napkins, and so forth.

Within the set of noncurrent assets, Jones has only one type—*fixed assets.* Fixed assets include the other tangible or physical assets, owned or effectively controlled by the business and used in the business, rather than being sold to customers. Items with expected usefulness of less than a year (like Jones's cups and napkins) are classified as current supplies. Tangible assets with expected usefulness (when purchased) of more than a year (like Jones's truck) are classified as noncurrent fixed assets. Fixed assets provide the capacity to do business and, as such, are often informally referred to as capacity assets. They must be owned or effectively controlled, and they must be used in the business rather than being sold to customers. To clarify, if Jones did not own his truck and merely rented one on a month-to-month basis, it would not be shown as an asset. Also note that a firm which owned trucks but was in the business of selling trucks would classify the trucks for sale as inventory, rather than as fixed assets.

Note, on Exhibit 2.3, that Jones's truck is first shown at its original cost— $10,000. Immediately below is shown an adjustment in the amount of $2,000, which is subtracted. This adjustment is called *accumulated depreciation.* Accumulated depreciation represents an estimate of the amount of the cost that has been used up as a result of wear and obsolescence. The *undepreciated cost* —original cost less adjustment—of the truck is shown as $8,000. Remember that, on Jones's net-worth statement for the bank, there were several choices for measuring and reporting the truck. There is general agreement that to show the two-year-old truck at the full original cost of $10,000 is too high. Similarly, to show it at its liquidating resale value of $5,000 is inappropriate and probably too low.

Let us review what we know about Jones's truck. Two years ago it cost $10,000. Four years from now Jones expects to sell it for $4,000. The truck may still be useful to someone after Jones sells it, but its planned useful life to Jones is only six years. Over the six years Jones will lose $6,000 on it. That is, the truck will cost him $6,000, in addition to costs of gas, oil, and repairs. In effect, the truck's cost expires or is used up as the truck is used. Each year some of the cost is used up. Let us assume that Jones plans to use the truck equally over the six years and that his loss will be $6,000 over this period. A simple way to show the declining cost of the truck, or *cost expiration*, would be to reduce it, or *depreciate* it, by $1,000 each year. This method of allocating cost expiration evenly to years over the useful life is known as *straight-line depreciation* and is one of the methods acceptable under GAAP.

Note that for fixed assets the original cost and the amount of accumulated depreciation are shown separately. The fixed asset shown is not just directly reduced $1,000 per year. Also, it is important to understand that accumulated depreciation is just an adjustment or valuation item. It indicates the amount of costs which are estimated to have been used up or expired. It does not indicate any assets set aside like a savings account to buy a new truck. If Jones were also setting aside funds, these funds would be shown as a separate asset.

At the bottom of the lefthand side of the balance sheet is the total of the adjusted original costs of all assets in the Jones firm as of the balance sheet date. The amount $8,550 is shown as *total assets*.

Turn now to the right side of Exhibit 2.3. Items on the right side of a balance sheet are called *equities*. Equities are claims against the firm's **total assets**. Or, to put it another way, they are shares in the firm's assets. By law, creditors—those to whom the firm owes money—have first claim on the firm's assets. The owner's claim is secondary, or residual.

THE BALANCE SHEET EQUALITY

Since claims shown are against the total assets shown as available, the dollar total of equities always balances the dollar total of assets. It's just that simple; equally simple is the reason balance sheets are called balance sheets. **Total** dollar equities balance **total** dollar assets. The basic equality[4] underlying all accounting is shown in the figure on page 41.

Thus, the total dollars of equities of a going concern can be no more and no less than the total dollars of assets to be claimed.[5] If total assets increase,

---

[4]   You may hear this equality referred to as the balance sheet equation and see it written Assets = Equities. This short form can be misleading, since assets are one thing and equities another. They are not the same and can, therefore, never "equal," except in total dollar amounts. Equity claims also are not against specific assets but against all assets. Only the dollar total of all equities equals the dollar total of all assets.

[5]   It is, of course, possible that a firm's total liabilities could end up being more than its total assets. In such a situation it would be insolvent, not a going concern, and ordinary financial statements would not be prepared.

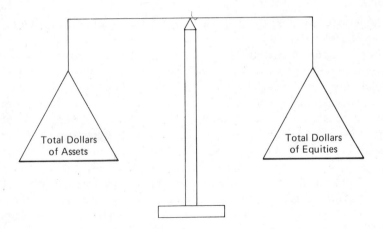

the amount available to be claimed has gone up. If there are no additional creditor claims, then the owners' residual claim increases to balance. If total assets decrease, then total claims must decrease to balance. This balance should always be maintained by accountants and is the foundation for understanding the entire accounting system. Changes affecting balance sheets will be discussed further in Chapter 4.

Note that equities are of two types: *liabilities,* or creditors' equities, and the *owner's equity.* Liabilities are the amounts owed by the firm to creditors as of the balance sheet date. Owner's equity represents the owner's residual claim against total assets. Businesses with more than one owner are known as partnerships or corporations, and will be discussed in Chapter 10.

Within the liabilities, there are two groups: *current liabilities* and *noncurrent liabilities.* Generally speaking, current liabilities are those which are payable—will use up current assets in settlement—within one year of the balance sheet date.[6] Noncurrent liabilities include those which are due **more** than one year after the balance sheet date.

Under current liabilities, Jones's balance sheet shows two items: *note payable* and *accounts payable.* The note payable represents the $1,500 due the bank on the truck within one year. When Jones purchased his truck, since he had not agreed to pay for it within a few months, by custom the amount owing was not "charged" on account. Instead Jones signed a promissory note, or I.O.U., promising to pay specific amounts on specific dates. Liabilities covered by promissory notes are classified separately on the balance sheet. Shown as accounts payable is the amount Jones owes his suppliers for goods and services already purchased but not yet paid for. When Jones buys something on account, the amount is shown on his balance sheet under accounts payable. (Note that an amount that Jones includes on his balance

---

[6]   As noted for current assets, in some cases firms use an accounting period greater than one year in length. For such firms, both the current asset and current liability classifications would extend to cover one **period** instead of only one year.

sheet under accounts payable will be included on his supplier's balance sheet under accounts receivable.)

Under noncurrent liabilities is shown the $1,500 balance of the $3,000 note payable on the truck. The $1,500 balance is not due within one year. Total liabilities as of the balance sheet date amount to $3,125. Since total assets at that date were measured at $8,550, the balance of total assets not claimed by creditors—owner's equity or net worth—amounted to $5,425. Another term used for this same residual amount is *net assets*. Net worth or net assets in this case refers to the worth of the business entity to Jones as owner. It would not refer to Jones's overall personal net worth, which would also include his personal assets and liabilities outside of the business.

The balance sheet equality—total dollar assets equal total dollar equities—can be restated as: total dollar assets equal total dollar liabilities plus total dollar owner's equity. This equality is always the same regardless of the size or complexity of the business. For proprietorships—firms owned by one person—owner's equity is usually shown on the balance sheet as one figure.

ASSET MEASUREMENT

Returning to the asset side of the balance sheet, have you wondered why this chapter has referred to the "measurement" of assets and not to their "value"? The term "worth" was used several times, and even it is potentially misleading. Value, or worth, is a subjective term. What is valuable to someone else may have little value to you. Remember that one of the goals of financial reporting is objectivity. Various alternatives exist for measuring a firm's assets. Among these alternatives are:

> Original cost
> Adjusted original cost
> Replacement cost
> Current market value
> Cash realizable from forced sale or liquidation.

Recall from the Jones Canteen example that original cost is not relevant after time has passed. Also that cash realizable from liquidation is not relevant for a going concern which does not intend to liquidate all of its assets.

What about the alternative of current market value? You may have approached accounting believing that accountants report current values. There are four reasons why current market value is not generally used by accountants as the basis for measuring assets:

1. "Current market" is an exit or sale price. It is irrelevant and unreal as a basis for measuring most assets, since the firm's intention is to use and not sell assets other than inventory. For the same reason that liquidation "value" is irrelevant, so is current market "value."

2. Current market for many assets is costly to update in the years after acquisition. Many difficult estimates would be required.

3. Current market can be too subjective.

4. Current market for many assets can be open to manipulation. Since current market often must be estimated and is subjective, it frequently cannot be objectively verified. Businesses could significantly overstate or understate assets without being provably incorrect.

For these reasons, current market is not the measurement and reporting objective for assets. Replacement cost, on the other hand, would probably be most relevant if one desired a measurement of the current position of a firm. But it can be somewhat subjective (involving difficult-to-verify assumptions and estimates); it can be costly to obtain (especially for large, special-purpose assets such as a factory); and it may be inappropriate in particular cases (the firm may not intend to replace certain assets when they wear out or become obsolete). There is also some question as to whether the proper intention of accounting is to measure current costs even if they were all objective and simple and inexpensive to obtain. Traditionally, financial accounting has been aimed at accounting for what the firm's management did with the owner's and creditors' dollars—the so-called "stewardship function." For all of these reasons, U.S. accountants have not used replacement cost as a measure of most assets.

Nevertheless, continuing high levels of inflation can make original-cost-based measures so unrealistic as to be meaningless after a few years. The SEC currently requires many large firms to disclose supplementary information on replacement costs of inventory and fixed assets. Other major countries have switched, or are seriously considering switching, to replacement-cost accounting. The issue is still very much alive in the U.S., and will be discussed further in Chapter 16.

In the Jones Canteen example, you learned that the remaining alternative—adjusted original cost—was the current GAAP choice for asset measurement. Financial accountants initially measure assets on the basis of the total of all costs incurred in their acquisition. Assets are initially reported at their *fair market value at the time of acquisition* plus other costs related to bringing the asset to its ready location and condition.[7]

BALANCE SHEET ITEMS AND TERMINOLOGY

Exhibit 2.4 lists items which may appear on many balance sheets for firms larger than Jones's. As you study it, give particular attention to the order or sequence in which items are listed, and look for the distinction both between

---

[7]   Interest cost on funds used to acquire assets is **not** included. Otherwise two identical assets could be reported differently if one was purchased with a mortgage and the other for cash.

Exhibit 2.4

TYPICAL ITEMS FOUND ON MANY BALANCE SHEETS

XYZ Company (Entity name)
Balance Sheet (Type of report)
As of X/X/XX (Period covered or date of report)

Assets	Equities
Cash	Current notes payable
Marketable securities	Accounts payable
Receivables:	Wages and salaries payable
Notes receivable	Interest payable
Accounts receivable	Taxes payable
Less allowance for	Current capital lease obligations
uncollectibles	Revenue collected in advance
Inventory	Total Current Liabilities
Supplies	
Prepaid items	Noncurrent notes payable
Total Current Assets	Bonds payable
	Noncurrent capital lease obligations
Long-term investments and funds	Total Liabilities
Fixed assets:	
Land	Owner's Equity
Buildings	(see Chapter 10 for further details)
Less accumulated depreciation	
Equipment	
Less accumulated depreciation	
Office furniture and fixtures	
Less accumulated depreciation	
Property under capital lease	
Intangible and other assets:	
Leasehold improvement	
Franchises, patents, copyrights,	
trademarks	
Deferred charges	
Total Assets	Total Equities

assets and liabilities and also between current and noncurrent items. Use your intuition to guess at the meaning of unfamiliar items before verifying their definitions listed below. Different business firms often use differing terminology for the same thing. You will need to develop the skill of "correctly guessing" the meaning of terms used by particular firms, in order to read and understand financial statements.

Statement heading   Note that a properly prepared financial statement will indicate the name of the entity reported upon, the type of report, and the period covered by (or date of) the report. Remember that, since a balance sheet is like a photograph of the firm's position at **one point** in time, a balance sheet will always be "as of" a specific date.

Assets

Assets are resources owned or controlled by the entity, which have future usefulness and which can be measured in monetary terms with reasonable objectivity. Assets may be tangible (physical) or intangible (a legal claim or right).

Cash   The total of cash on hand and in banks.

Marketable securities   This category includes securities—treasury bills and notes, bank certificates of deposit, and similar items—which are temporary investments of excess cash and are expected to be converted into cash whenever cash is needed. Marketable securities are conventionally valued at cost or current sale value, whichever is lower.

Notes receivable   Promissory notes committing a borrower or customer to pay a specific amount of cash on a specific date to the company.

Accounts receivable   Claims against customers for cash resulting from completed sales (goods or services have been supplied).

Allowance for uncollectibles   Unfortunately, not all customers always pay their bills. An estimate is made of the proportion of receivables which experience indicates will probably not be collected. This estimate is shown as a "valuation allowance." It is subtracted from accounts receivable so that "accounts receivable net" (of the allowance) will indicate the amount of cash that will probably be collectible. This allowance is sometimes called "allowance for bad debts."

Inventory   Merchandise or products on hand for sale to customers.

Supplies   Materials on hand for use rather than for sale.

Prepaid items   This category includes services which have been paid for in advance and which will normally be used up within one year. Whereas receivables are rights to receive cash, certain prepaid items are rights to receive goods and services. Examples of prepaid items would include deposits on goods or services on order, rent paid in advance, and the unexpired cost of future insurance coverage already purchased (insurance coverage is customarily paid for in advance).

Long-term investments and funds   In this category are shown securities, noncurrent receivables, and any other assets which the firm has acquired as an investment, or as "savings" segregated for a specific future purpose. These assets are not expected to be liquidated—converted to cash—within one year of the balance sheet date. Note that long-term investments and funds represent one of the three major subsets of noncurrent assets. The second is fixed assets, and the third is intangible and other assets. Investments are usually valued at cost or resale, whichever is lower. There are some exceptions to this rule that will be covered in Chapter 11.

Fixed Assets:

Land   This category includes the cost of land owned by the firm for use in its business. (A firm which regularly sold land to customers would show land for sale as **inventory**. Land purchased as purely an investment would be classified in the **investments** account.) Note that accounting assumes that land does not lose value, wear out, or become obsolete. Therefore, land is normally not adjusted for depreciation.

Buildings, equipment, office furniture and fixtures, and any other tangible fixed assets   These categories include the items (as identified) which were acquired and are being held for their future use or service potential. They are reported at their original cost before adjustment for depreciation.

Accumulated depreciation   As previously described, this is a valuation item used to reduce the book value of fixed assets to reflect use, wear and tear, potential technological or style obsolescence, or potential inadequacy.

Property under capital lease   This category includes any long-term leases, where the firm as lessee effectively, but not legally, owns and controls the leased asset. The amount is reduced directly to reflect expiration of cost rather than via an accumulated depreciation item. Appropriate accounting for capital leases will be covered in Chapter 11.

Intangible and other assets   This category is the third major subdivision of noncurrent assets. It includes all noncurrent assets not properly classified as investments or fixed assets. Intangible assets are privileges or rights acquired or developed via an identifiable expenditure. Intangibles are initially valued at original cost. As the usefulness expires, the cost initially reported is reduced directly rather than shown with a valuation account. The process of systematically and directly reducing an initial measurement to reflect expiration is called *amortization*. Intangible assets and capital leases are amortized. Tangible fixed assets other than land and capital leases are depreciated (depreciation can be thought of as the amortization of tangible fixed assets). Intangible assets include leaseholds (rent paid in advance), leasehold improvement (described below), franchises, patents, copyrights, trademarks, and similar rights and privileges. "Other" assets would include any assets that have been retired and are being held for disposition. Retired assets would be reported at their recoverable sale or salvage value, since they have no other usefulness.

Leasehold improvement   This item indicates the unexpired costs of improvements—amortizable assets—which have been physically attached by the firm to property which it does not own or effectively control. These improvements will have to be abandoned when the firm gives up the property. Note that, if such improvements had been made to owned or effectively controlled properties, or had not been physically attached, they would be included in the appropriate fixed-asset category.

Deferred charges   This category represents prepayments stretching significantly beyond one year and therefore not properly classified as "prepaid items" under current assets.

Equities

Equities are claims against total assets. There are two general classifications of equities: creditor equities (liabilities) and owner's equity. Liabilities are existing obligations to make a future payment of cash or to supply products or services.

Current payables   Current payables include Accounts Payable (accounts owed to suppliers for goods and services received) and other liabilities due within a year or a period. Most current liability categories are labeled so as to be self-explanatory. Note that it is common to separate current liabilities into subcategories by type of creditor: current notes payable to creditors who have been given promissory notes; accounts payable to suppliers of goods and services; wages payable to employees; interest payable to creditors who have loaned funds; taxes payable to governments; current *capital lease obligations; revenue collected in advance* (obligations to provide goods or services instead of cash); and so forth.

Noncurrent notes payable   Under this item are shown promissory notes due or maturing more than one year in the future.

Bonds payable   Bonds are very similar to promissory notes. They are securities exchanged for assets, usually money, loaned to the company on a long-term basis.

Noncurrent capital lease obligations   This item discloses the remaining noncurrent liability under lease contracts which have been determined to be Capital Leases, and where the item leased has been recorded as an asset.

Owner's equity   The residual claim against, or share in, total assets after subtracting all creditor claims (liabilities). Owner's equity may be referred to as "owner's capital" or "equity capital." These terms are potentially misleading, since "capital" implies something of value, such as an asset. Owner's equity is a residual share in total assets measured at cost. It does not even

Exhibit 2.5

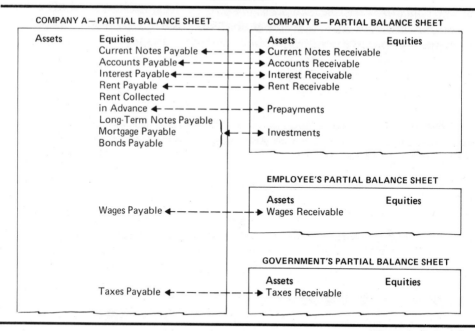

attempt to indicate value. For firms with more than one owner (partnerships and corporations), owners' equity will include further subdivisions. These will be discussed in Chapter 10.

Your understanding of balance sheets will be improved when you can clearly see that one firm's liability will always be another entity's asset. Company A's payables to Company B will be the same as Company B's receivables from A. It is important that you, as a potential user of financial statements, gain a clear perspective of the interrelationships among different firms and their statements. Exhibit 2.5 is designed to demonstrate this relationship between receivables and payables. Study Exhibit 2.5 until the relationships become obvious to you.

BALANCE SHEET CLASSIFICATIONS

The various classifications or categories of balance sheet information already introduced can be confusing. You might wish to review them.

Assets can be classified as monetary (cash or right to receive specific amount of cash at a specified time) or nonmonetary (all other assets). The monetary/nonmonetary distinction is **not** shown on the balance sheet. Assets can also be classified as current (cycling to cash, or consumable within a year) or noncurrent (all others). Noncurrent assets are further subdivided into long-term investments and funds, fixed, and intangible and other categories. Current/noncurrent classification does appear on the balance sheet.

You should memorize the conventional ordering of individual assets within the current and noncurrent classifications as shown on Exhibit 2.4. Note that the order roughly corresponds to the relative liquidity (ease of conversion into cash) of each asset.

Equities include liabilities and owner's equity, and these classifications are clearly distinct on the balance sheet. Liabilities may be monetary or nonmonetary,[8] and this distinction is not shown on the balance sheet. Liabilities can be classified as current or noncurrent, and this classification is shown.

RELATING TO YOUR SPECIAL COMPANY

One of the simplest and most effective ways for you to quickly and thoroughly understand new accounting terminology and concepts is to relate them to a firm that you personally can visualize and understand. At this point and in each subsequent chapter, you should take the time to apply your new knowledge to "your company." First, pick the business which will serve as your company throughout this book. Choose any business which would be of real interest to you. It can be a real firm where you have worked, or a real or imaginary firm you would like to own. The only thing that is important is that your company should be small enough and real enough to you so that you can easily visualize everything that goes on within the business.

The next step is to prepare on paper a balance sheet for your company as of the end of last year. Be sure to include all the assets you know are in your firm and those liabilities which would be reasonable for your business. Go ahead and fill in dollar amounts which seem reasonable and which make your balance sheet balance.

If you have taken the time to complete your balance sheet, you should experience a much clearer understanding of what balance sheets are all about. If there is anything about your firm that doesn't clearly fit, or anything in Exhibit 2.4 which you can't clearly see in your company, now is the time to find out. Review the explanations in this chapter, ask a fellow student, or seek assistance from your instructor. Don't go on to the next chapter until the ideas of a balance sheet and your company are completely clear and comfortable.

INFORMATION CONTENT OF A BALANCE SHEET

What does a balance sheet tell you about a firm? Of equal importance, what doesn't it tell you?

---

[8]   Examples of nonmonetary liabilities would include Revenue Collected in Advance and Estimated Warranty Costs, both of which represent obligations to deliver goods or perform services. Also, Deferred Income Tax could be nonmonetary, since the specific amounts and timing of tax obligations could be uncertain. These items will be discussed in a later chapter.

The balance sheet provides a picture of the company's financial position at one particular point in time. By comparing it with the firm's previous balance sheets, you can develop an understanding of the directions in which the firm is moving. Is it growing? Is the composition of its assets changing—proportionately more or less current versus noncurrent assets; proportionately more or less merchandise inventory, receivables, investments, and so forth. Also, the balance sheet tells you how heavily the company is in debt. Too much debt can be just as risky for a company as for an individual. By comparing with previous balance sheets for the same firm, you can determine the directions in which the firm's proportion of debt is moving. Is there proportionately more debt or less?

You can also gain valuable information about a firm by comparing its balance sheet with those of other firms in the same industry. The same questions would be relevant as when comparing the firm to its previous position.

Remember that one balance sheet by itself is merely a picture at one point in time. It cannot tell you where the company has been or where it is going. Remember also that the nonmonetary assets are shown at adjusted original cost and not in terms of current value. Value adjustments involve estimates. The estimates may be the best available; they may be objectively made, fair, and relevant; and they may be verified as conforming with GAAP by a CPA's audit. But they are still **estimates.** For example, remember that Jones's balance sheet showed his truck as having a current *book value* of $8,000 ($10,000 original cost less $2,000 accumulated depreciation). This is reasonable if it turns out to have the estimated six years of usefulness, and if it can be sold for the estimated $4,000 four years from now.

It is important that you understand that the balance sheet is an incomplete picture. There are several possible intangible assets which may have been acquired at considerable cost, and may have great future value, but which accountants do not report on the balance sheet as assets. These important intangibles are currently not reported because there is no generally agreed way to measure them fairly and objectively. One example would be the value of the human capital in the firm, the team of trained employees and managers who have learned to work together. Such nonreported assets will be discussed more fully in Chapter 13.

Considerable concern has also been expressed that accounting currently does not accurately reflect social benefits and costs—environmental protection or damage, and so forth. The accountant's reasoning for not attempting to report social benefits and costs has generally followed these steps:

- Society has yet to assign the responsibility for such items to particular firms.

- Financial accounting's role is to report the economic events actually affecting the entity, not what might or should affect it.

- Even known benefits or possible obligations which cannot readily be objectively quantified in monetary terms are excluded from the statements. For example, the future benefits from advertising expenditures, employee training, and research-and-development activities are too subjective to measure with any degree of reliability. How could even more nebulous social benefits and costs be fairly quantified?

- Therefore, except where they are assigned to particular firms in the form of awards or subsidies, or in the form of assessments or fines, social benefits and costs cannot properly be included in financial statements.

For the present, you may expect that the balance sheet will reveal to you all of the readily measurable resources owned or effectively controlled by the firm and all of its legally recognized liabilities. The resources you can expect to find on a balance sheet as assets will

- Be in the form of properties, rights, or claims;
- Have been acquired through an exchange transaction with others;
- Be capable of objective measurement in monetary terms;
- Represent expected future benefits to the firm.

To reinforce your new knowledge of balance sheets, turn to the Statements of Financial Position for the Xerox Corporation and for the Addison-Wesley Publishing Company reproduced in Appendix A. You have not been given an explanation of all the items shown, but you should be able to recognize the similarity to Jones's balance sheet.

CHAPTER OVERVIEW

Based upon the material presented in this chapter, you should now have a good basic understanding of the balance sheet or statement of financial position as prepared for proprietorships. You should be able to explain clearly:

- The concepts of assets and equities, and how equities include liabilities and owner's equity;
- Why the balance sheet balances;
- The various alternatives for asset measurement, which alternative accountants follow under GAAP, and why this alternative has been chosen;
- The various common specific asset and liability items which may appear on a balance sheet, what is included under each item, and generally how it is measured;
- The two valuation items so far introduced—allowance for uncollectibles and accumulated depreciation, and their function or purpose;

- The several classifications of assets and liabilities, their meaning, and their significance;
- Items that might be considered as assets and liabilities but are not included as such on the balance sheet; and the reasons why they are excluded.

You should also be able to discuss the information content of a balance sheet —what you would expect to find on a balance sheet and its usefulness and significance to you as a potential user.

NEW VOCABULARY AND CONCEPTS

Net worth
Liquidation
Going-concern assumption
Adjusted original cost
Monetary items
Business entities
Proprietorship
Asset
Current assets
Noncurrent assets
Operating cycle
Cash (on balance sheet)
Accounts receivable
Inventory
Supplies
Owner's equity/net assets
Current liabilities
Noncurrent liabilities
Note payable
Accounts payable
Fair market value at the time of
    acquisition
Marketable securities
Note receivable
Allowance for uncollectibles

Prepaid items
Long-term investments and funds
Credit sales
Fixed assets/capacity assets
Accumulated depreciation
Undepreciated cost
Cost expiration
Depreciate
Straight-line depreciation
Total assets
Equities
Liability
Land
Tangible fixed assets
Property under capital lease
Intangible and other assets
Amortization
Leasehold improvement
Deferred charges
Current capital lease obligations
Revenue collected in advance
Bonds payable
Noncurrent capital-lease obligations
Book value

- The business entity and the going concern as defining the scope of a balance sheet;
- Reported assets as distinct from all things of value;
- Equities and the balance sheet equality;
- Different kinds of equities;
- Basis for initial asset valuation;
- Adjusted cost and depreciation as basis for continuing asset valuation;

- Current vs. noncurrent classifications;
- Monetary vs. nonmonetary items.

REVIEW QUESTIONS

1. Why don't accountants use unadjusted original cost or liquidation prices as the fundamental basis for asset measurement?
2. a) What is the going-concern assumption? b) How does it affect asset measurement?
3. a) What is the entity convention? b) How does it affect the content of financial statements?
4. What is the status of current cost or replacement cost as a basis for accounting asset measurement? Why hasn't it been used?
5. What is the difference between monetary and nonmonetary assets?
6. Why are nonmonetary items more difficult to value than monetary ones?
7. a) What is meant by depreciation? b) How is it shown on a balance sheet? c) What effect does it have on assets?
8. Why does the balance sheet balance?
9. Why is owner's equity referred to as a residual claim?
10. Describe the normal operating cycle.
11. What is the difference between current and noncurrent assets? Liabilities?
12. What two items properly classified as current assets will not be normally converted into cash within one year of the balance sheet date?
13. What is an example of an item properly classified as an asset, which is not owned by the firm?
14. Current liabilities are normally broken down into separate categories on what basis?
15. What is the information content of a balance sheet? What are some of the things it can tell you?

MINI-CASES AND QUESTIONS FOR DISCUSSION

MC 2.1 Jack Silver is an elementary accounting student who, having understood the balance sheet equation to be assets = equities, maintains that it is impossible for total equities to ever be greater than total assets. Betty Hart disagrees. She says, "For a going concern, total liabilities will be less than total assets. Since owner's equity represents just the residual balance, total equities can and will equal total assets. However, many things can happen to a firm which will result in total liabilities exceeding total assets. If that happens, even with owner's equity down to zero, total equities will be greater than total assets."

"What could ever make total liabilities greater than total assets?" replied Jack. "After all, every time a firm borrows money, they have both a new asset and a new liability. How can liabilities ever become greater than assets?"

Who is correct? Could total assets ever become less than the amount of total liabilities, or, alternatively, could total liabilities be incurred in excess of total assets? If so, how? Would a usual balance sheet normally be prepared in such circumstances? Discuss.

MC 2.2 Mary Diamond, also an elementary accounting student, is enrolled in the course only because it is required. "I'm going to be a personnel major, and I can't see why or when I'll ever have to use a balance sheet after I complete this course," she says.

Prepare an explanation for Mary of how she will use balance sheets as a personnel officer and also in other required business courses. If you don't know, find out from other students or your instructor. Also you should be able to give at least one specific example of how understanding and using balance sheets will be valuable to Mary and each student in your class, once you know their intended careers. Try it.

MC 2.3 Are the following items properly included on the balance sheet as assets? Explain. If yes, at what amount should they be initially recorded and how should they be classified?

a) The firm is leasing its current office. The lease has four more years to run. Under the lease terms, the firm has given the landlord, as a security deposit, $15,000 representing the last 90 days' rent.

b) A drug manufacturer has a special-purpose machine for manufacturing Zlotz. The machine is two years old, originally had an expected useful life of nine years, and originally cost $145,000. The firm believes it could recover $20,000 if the machine were sold for parts and scrap. The firm to date has accumulated $30,000 of depreciation related to this machine. Zlotz has just been declared unsafe by the Food and Drug Administration. No more can be manufactured and sold.

c) The firm's president has just purchased a $10 "show" ticket on a particular horse in the sixth race at a local track. The race has not yet started. If the horse wins the race, the ticket will pay $50. If the horse "places," the ticket will pay $40. If the horse "shows," it will pay $25.

d) The ABC Corporation has just hired a new president for a salary of $20,000 per month. The executive recruiter who located the new president and persuaded him to consider the firm receives the equivalent of one month's presidential salary as a fee.

e) The firm has just purchased brochures costing $15,000, which it plans to distribute free as part of a major advertising campaign in two months.

f) A new building has just been purchased for $200,000. The amount of $20,000 cash and a 10-year promissory note for $180,000, plus normal interest, has been given to the seller. The note is secured by a mortgage agreement which provides that title does not pass to the buyer until the note is paid in full.

g) A milk distributor receives, from a deceased widow's estate, a painting valued at $20,000. The widow's will provided the bequest in gratitude for the firm's milk which the widow's cats had enjoyed for many years. The painting is to be hung in the company president's office.

h) As an incentive to locate in the community and provide jobs, the firm has been given title to an acre of land on which it is constructing a factory building. The land is appraised at $120,000. It would normally be assessed for property tax purposes at $40,000, and property taxes would normally be $3,000 per year, at current rates. However, part of the incentive "package" provided a forgiveness of property taxes for the first ten years.

MC 2.4 Is each of the following items monetary or nonmonetary? Explain.

a) $500 deposited with the lessee as a cleaning deposit on a one-year lease.

b) $1,000 deposit with a lessee as a security deposit, representing the last two months' rent on a three-year lease.

c) A share of common stock in the General Motors Corporation costing $60 and with a current market value of $70.

d) A $400 gift certificate good for one year at a local clothing store.

ESSENTIAL PROBLEMS

EP 2.1 Mr. Smith is applying for a bank loan and must prepare a statement of personal net worth following the format given in Exhibit 2.1. He has the following possessions and debts:

Personal possessions: Adjusted cost, $500.

Balance in personal bank account, $1,500.

Amount owed on personal bills, $300.

Balance of cash on hand in business, $100.

Business accounts receivable, $200.

Personal automobile: Original cost, $4,000;
                       estimated depreciation, $2,000.

Amount owed by business to suppliers, $400.

Cost of merchandise on hand for sale, $800.

Prepare a personal net-worth statement for Mr. Smith to give his bank using adjusted cost valuation.

EP 2.2 Referring to the data in Problem 1 above, prepare in proper form a balance sheet for Mr. Smith's business.

EP 2.3 Given the following data as of 12/31/XX, determine the amount of owner's equity in the business as of that date:

Total current assets, $400.

Total current liabilities, $200.

Total noncurrent assets, $500.

Total noncurrent liabilities, $300.

EP 2.4 For each of the following items, indicate by letter code whether it is:

    (A) A current asset item;

    (B) A current asset valuation item (subtracts from current assets);

    (C) A noncurrent asset item;

    (D) A noncurrent asset valuation item (subtracts from noncurrent assets);

    (E) A current liability item;

    (F) A noncurrent liability item.

Accounts payable	Leasehold improvement
Accounts receivable	Marketable securities
Accumulated depreciation	Notes payable (due within one year)
Allowance for uncollectibles	
Bonds payable	Notes payable (due beyond one year)
Buildings	Notes receivable (due within one year)
Cash	
Copyrights	Office furniture and fixtures
Equipment	Patents
Franchises	Prepaid items
Interest payable	Purchase leases
Inventory	Supplies
Investment	Taxes payable
Land	Wages and salaries payable

EP 2.5 What are the six most common items classified as current assets?

EP 2.6 Assume you are comparing the balance sheets of firms A and B and know that they are in the same business and that both use straight-line depreciation for fixed assets. You see, for firm A: fixed assets $200,000, accumulated depreciation $150,000, book value $50,000; and for firm B: fixed assets $70,000, accumulated depreciation $20,000, book value $50,000. Which probably is the larger firm, the firm with greater capacity? Which firm probably has the newest equipment?

EP 2.7 Given that a particular firm had current assets consisting of cash, accounts receivable, inventory, and prepaid items; and that the balances of these items were cash $100, accounts receivable $400, inventory $600, and prepaid items $200; and that total current assets equaled $1,250; how much was the amount provided as an allowance for uncollectibles?

EP 2.8 Given the following information, prepare in good form a balance sheet for the Smith Company. Include the correct amounts for prepaid items, accumulated depreciation on buildings, wages payable, owner's equity, and total equities.

    Accounts payable $125

    Accounts receivable $340

Accumulated depreciation on buildings?

Accumulated depreciation on equipment $120

Allowance for uncollectibles $40

Buildings $425

Cash $100

Equipment $570

Intangibles $50

Interest payable $35

Inventory $400

Investments $150

Land $250

Marketable securities $200

Note payable (due beyond one year) $400

Owner's equity?

Prepaid items?

Supplies $25

Taxes payable $165

Total assets $2,350

Total current assets $1,100

Total current liabilities $500

Total equities?

Total liabilities $900

Wages payable?

3

ANALYZING
A BALANCE SHEET

CHAPTER PREVIEW

The objective of this chapter is to enhance your understanding of the information content of the balance sheet and its usefulness for analyzing a firm's financial position. In this chapter, you can:

- Learn that the balance sheet indicates the sources of the resources invested in the firm;
- Understand the importance of solvency and liquidity to a business;
- Acquire several tools of balance sheet analysis, which provide information concerning a firm's solvency and potential liquidity;
- Learn to be alert to the lack of uniformity in accounting and financial-analysis terminology, concepts, and practices;
- Learn various standards of comparison useful in evaluating a company's financial position;
- Understand the importance of two more accounting standards—consistency and materiality—to financial analysis.

Additional balance sheet details provided in later chapters are essential in order for you to achieve an adequate knowledge of balance sheets and their usefulness. But, with a clear understanding of, and with the reinforcement provided by, the material contained in this chapter, you will have confidence in your knowledge of the fundamental balance sheet structure, within which you can then anchor subsequently presented details and elaborations.

EXTENDING CREDIT TO CUSTOMERS

Put yourself in the role of Jack Sargent, sales and credit manager for the Acme Wholesale Supply Company. One of your super salespersons has just come back into town with two very large orders, one from the Dilemma Company and one from the Rosy Company. Neither firm has ever purchased from you before, and each could be a valued additional regular customer. Both wish to purchase on account, and you must decide whether or not to extend credit privileges to these firms. Along with other information, you obtain recent comparative balance sheets for both companies, which are reproduced in Exhibits 3.1 and 3.2. Do these balance sheets contribute to your decision? Assume, for a moment, that all your other information was inconclusive, neither good nor bad. Would you extend credit to either or both of these firms on their large initial orders? Can you get some idea from the balance sheets as to how well managed these firms are? Do both appear to be able to pay possible future bills from you on time?

Exhibit 3.1
DILEMMA COMPANY

BALANCE SHEETS
As of 12/31/X3 and 12/31/X4

Assets	19X4	19X3
Cash	$ 5,000	$ 20,000
Accounts receivable (net)	70,000	80,000
Inventory	35,000	95,000
Supplies	10.000	5,000
Total Current Assets	$120,000	$200,000
Fixed assets	830,000	830,000
Accumulated depreciation	(340,000)	(300,000)
Total Assets	$610,000	$730,000
Equities		
Current notes payable	$280,000*	$ 25,000
Accounts payable	15,000	160,000
Other current liabilities	5,000	10,000
Total Current Liabilities	$300,000	$195,000
Long-term debt	200,000	100,000
Total Liabilities	$500,000	$295,000
Owner's Equity	110,000	435,000
Total Equities	$610,000	$730,000

* All to suppliers and all due within 60 days.

Exhibit 3.2

ROSY COMPANY

BALANCE SHEETS
As of 12/31/X3 and 12/31/X4

Assets	19X4	19X3
Cash	$ 30,000	$ 25,000
Marketable securities	80,000	60,000
Accounts receivable (net)	60,000	50,000
Inventory	55,000	60,000
Supplies	3,000	2,800
Prepaid items	2,000	2,200
Total Current Assets	$230,000	$200,000
Land	35,000	35,000
Fixed assets	70,000	70,000
Accumulated depreciation	(35,000)	(30,000)
Total Assets	$300,000	$275,000
Equities		
Accounts payable	$ 40,000	$ 75,000
Other current liabilities	10,000	25,000
Total Current Liabilities	$ 50,000	$100,000
Long-term debt	0	75,000
Total Liabilities	$ 50,000	$175,000
Owner's Equity	250,000	100,000
Total Equities	$300,000	$275,000

Before reading ahead for the answer, take the time to study Exhibits 3.1 and 3.2. You may assume, in this example, that Dilemma's order totals $40,000, Rosy's $30,000, and that both firms are in the same business and have approximately the same volume of sales. For each company, write down your decision on a piece of paper, along with notes as to your reasons. Be sure you note all of your reasons, pro and con. Give your decision significance. Assume that if you are right in both cases, you will receive a bonus, and if you are wrong in either case, you will be fired. Try it; you will probably be pleasantly surprised how much you already understand!

Before proceeding with a detailed analysis of either exhibit, you should note two things. First, the balance sheets are presented vertically, with equities below assets, rather than to the right. (This presentation is known as report or statement form.) It is often done for printing or typing layout convenience and has no significant meaning. Second, you have balance sheet data for two years for each company. This will allow you to draw some tentative conclusions about directions in which the firm may be moving. Also, be sure to note that data for the most recent year are in the first column, followed by the older data. This is quite common in financial reporting; you can make major errors if you don't check captions, but instead just assume that information runs from left to right.

What did you decide about granting credit to the Rosy Company? Given that all other information was neutral, most credit managers would find the Rosy Company picture almost too good to be true. How many of the good points did you find?

1. Even if Rosy were destroyed by fire the day after the 19X4 balance sheet date, had no insurance coverage, and lost all noncurrent assets plus inventory and even its receivable records, it could still meet all its obligations from cash and marketable securities. This would still be true if you extended credit and your $30,000 claim were also included. At the end of 19X4, Rosy was certainly in an excellent position to pay bills. At the end of 19X3 they were O.K., and 12/31/X4 was even better. Unfortunately, few real companies are as obviously "rosy."

2. Rosy could also probably borrow more long-term money if it were needed. Proportionately, it has very little total debt; that is, only about 17 percent of total assets have been financed by creditors; and there is no long-term debt. A new creditor would have very little "competition" from other creditors in claiming Rosy's assets if the business should fail. Therefore, Rosy would appear to be a good risk if it wanted a long-term loan.

3. Rosy also has a relatively small proportion of its total assets tied up or "locked in" to noncurrent items. It could move very quickly into a different line of business if it were desirable and necessary to do so. It potentially is in a favorable position to adapt to a changing world.

4. Finally, by comparison with Dilemma (which may not prove much—see below), Rosy can handle approximately the same volume of business with less than 1/10 of the investment in fixed or *capacity assets*.

The "dilemma" with respect to the Dilemma Company should not have been yours or Jack Sargent's. The dilemma faces the Dilemma Company's owner; and it appears to be simply a question of how the firm can survive more than 60 days. Clearly, even if there were favorable nonfinancial information, Dilemma appears to be a poor, if not terrible credit risk. Admittedly, Dilemma data have been made extreme, to highlight the issues for you. Even so, let us examine the information contained in its balance sheet.

1. Without obtaining a large amount of new capital (assets) quickly, Dilemma will be unable to pay its existing debt, let alone yours if you are foolish enough to extend credit to them. 19X3 was bad, but 19X4 is ridiculous!

2. Dilemma's prospects of borrowing money to meet its present crisis are probably nonexistent. The company is heavily in debt, with over 80 percent of its assets supplied by creditors. It is doubtful, in an actual business situation, whether creditors would have ever allowed things to get so bad. One thing certainly appears to have been happening; other suppliers haven't been paid on time and have demanded interest-bearing promissory notes for their claims. There's a good chance that Dilemma is favoring you with a big order because no one else would give it a cup of coffee without getting the cash first! This extreme debt situation in 19X4 is even worse than in the previous year.

3. Dilemma appears heavily committed to its present type of business. Eighty percent of its capital is "locked in" to fixed assets. This fact, in and of itself, is not necessarily undesirable; but, all other things being equal, it makes the firm less able to respond rapidly to potential changing market conditions.

4. As if things were not bad enough, it appears that Dilemma has substantial excess and unused capacity. Comparing Dilemma's investment in fixed assets to Rosy's, and knowing that both firms are doing approximately the same volume of business, something appears way out of line. Why does Dilemma have seven times as many dollars tied up in capacity assets?

5. Another signal for further investigation is the difference in inventory levels. The two firms are in the same business and doing approximately the same volume. You should be able intuitively to understand that there is an optimal (ideal) amount of merchandise to have on hand for a given level of sales. Excessive inventory requires more storage space, may result in spoilage, runs the risk that some items may go out of style, and, most importantly, ties up money in unneeded merchandise. If you have too **little** inventory, you will lose sales and customers because you are often out of stock.

As of 12/31/X4, if Rosy's inventory is about right, then Dilemma's stock is dangerously low. If Dilemma's inventory is satisfactory, then Rosy has too much. Note the drastic difference in Dilemma's inventories for both years. Remember that balance sheets cannot provide you with all the answers, but they can often raise important questions.

You should have experienced, from your own personal analysis and the one above, a significant feeling of satisfaction and perhaps amazement at the amount of information contained in the labeled numbers on Dilemma's and Rosy's balance sheets. If so, this example served its purpose. Now you may continue with some of the important usable concepts and tools for making your own analysis of balance sheets when the differences are not so obvious and extreme.

EQUITIES AS SOURCES

As a first step in preparing to analyze balance sheets, you will need to see clearly how these statements provide you with information concerning the sources of the assets invested in a business. Study the abbreviated balance sheet given below. Of the $390,000 of total capital (assets) in the business, how much was supplied by the owner? How much by long-term creditors? How much by short-term creditors?

Assets		Equities	
Total Current Assets	$150,000	Total Current Liabilities	$ 75,000
Total Noncurrent Assets		Total Noncurrent Liabilities	125,000
(net)	240,000	Owner's Equity	190,000
Total Assets	$390,000	Total Equities	$390,000

When you see that equities represent *both* claims against and sources of total assets, you will have no difficulty in answering the questions given above. Of the $390,000 of total capital invested in the business, $75,000 came from short-term creditors, $125,000 came from (or was contributed by) long-term creditors, and $190,000 represents the current owner's investment. Capital in a business can come from only four possible sources.

First, short-term creditors commit goods, services, and occasionally cash (short-term loan) to the firm for a very short period, usually 30 days. However, as accounts are being paid, new goods and services are being obtained on account. So, even though the individual investment is very short-term, the revolving effect results in the total amount of current liabilities representing a fairly stable commitment.

Long-term creditors are a second possible source of capital. Long-term creditors commit cash or noncurrent assets in exchange for interest-bearing obligations. The amount of total assets supplied through noncurrent liabilities is often fairly permanent, because maturing long-term debt is often refinanced (replaced) with new debt.

Owners provide the other two sources. An owner can commit additional resources to the firm whether or not there is any profit. As a second source, if the firm is profitable, the owner can increase the firm's capital by reinvesting profits or, more simply, by not withdrawing profits from the business. Profits and withdrawals and their effect on the balance sheet will be discussed in Chapter 4.

IMPORTANCE OF SOLVENCY AND LIQUIDITY

Have you thought that the first objective of business is to make a profit? Many firms in the United States pursue only this goal and, as a result, may fail even though they are experiencing growth while making a profit. They fail because they cannot pay their bills—meet their current obligations—and because they are unable to obtain needed cash. The ability to meet current obligations when due is known technically as *solvency*. The ability to raise cash quickly to avoid insolvency or for other purposes is known as *liquidity position*.

Your primary objective as an individual is survival. Only if you survive can you graduate from college, contribute to society, make money, and do whatever you want to do with your life. Similarly, a company's primary objective is survival. Only if it survives can it hope to make profits. Survival for you in the short run includes a supportive physical environment, oxygen, water, and food. Survival in the short run for a business also involves supportive environment, that is, an absence of new products, new legislation, or new regulation which would make its activities obsolete or illegal. Instead of oxygen, water, and food, a business needs to be solvent and remain that way. If it cannot meet its obligations with cash when due, its creditors can refuse to provide further support. They can also go to court, legally take over the business, shut it down, and liquidate all of its assets to meet their claims. Another unfortunate aspect of insolvency is that, even if your suppliers and lenders give you extra time, your employees often cannot.

Suppose today your firm's balance sheet revealed:

Assets

Cash	None
Inventory	$ 500,000
Land, buildings, and equipment	1,000,000
Accumulated depreciation	(300,000)
Total Assets	$1,200,000

Equities

Wages payable	10,000
Other current liabilities	60,000
Noncurrent liabilities	None
Owner's Equity	1,130,000
Total Equities	$1,200,000

You would be technically insolvent and could be in serious trouble. Your firm appears to have a sufficiently low proportion of debt so that you probably could raise the needed cash in a hurry, but suppose you couldn't. Even if your creditors could wait until you sold some inventory, your employees cannot eat merchandise inventory, or shares in building and equipment. If you are even temporarily insolvent and cannot meet the payroll, your employees will probably leave. They may also sue for their back wages. By then you would be in so much trouble that one more lawsuit probably would make little difference.

Try to visualize for a moment how a growing, profitable firm can become insolvent. Suppose, in 19X5, your firm is doing **Y** volume of business and has the following balance sheet:

Assets		**Equities**	
Cash	$ 10,000	Current liabilities	$ 95,000
Accounts receivable (net)	90,000	Noncurrent liabilities	105,000
Inventory	75,000	Owner's Equity	100,000
Fixed assets (net)	125,000		
Total Assets	$300,000	Total Equities	$300,000

Customers just love your products and services and you can double your business in the next six months without any significant effort. Try to project your balance sheet assets at a volume of **twice Y**:

Cash $12,000   (You would have a little more cash because of increased activity.)

Accounts receivable (net) $180,000   (Twice the sales volume would mean at least twice the receivables.)

Inventory $125,000   (You may not need to double your stock, but you would need more to facilitate doubling your sales volume.)

Fixed assets (net) $125,000   (*Note.* This projection assumes you are presently operating with considerable excess capacity. Otherwise you might have to add up to another $125,000 of capacity assets.)
Total Assets $442,000

This projection indicates that, to double your volume to twice **Y**, you would need $442,000 of capital in your business, even if you don't need more capacity assets.[1] You only have $300,000. Where, in the next six months, are you going to obtain the other $142,000? Your suppliers will be providing a small portion of this required amount by providing more goods and services on account, in response to your larger volume of purchases. But the remainder can only come from new long-term borrowings, from new capital supplied by you as owner, or from profits retained in the business. If you are making enough profit each month and can leave it in the business, and/or can raise $142,000 of new capital for the business, then doubling your volume can be accommodated.

If, on the other hand, you cannot obtain all of the necessary new capital, and you still try to double your profitable volume, you will probably run out of cash and become insolvent. Potential creditors are not eager to make loans to nearly or actually insolvent firms. If you, independently of your business, are not sufficiently liquid to be able to inject cash from the outside, you may lose your business.

Subsequent chapters will go more thoroughly into the flows of assets and liabilities which could bring about this cash shortage. For the present, just think of the fact that you probably will be required to pay for your merchandise before your customer pays you. Also, remember that your receivables are short-term loans to your customers. As you increase your volume, you will be making more loans to your customers, and you will need additional capital to do this.

---

[1]   Do not attempt to use the exact proportions of this projection as guides for any other situation. It is purely an example. In Managerial Accounting and Financial Management courses, you can learn forecasting techniques for necessary and effective cash management.

CONVENIENT MEASURES OF SOLVENCY

Now that you understand that solvency and reasonable liquidity are critically important to the survival of a firm, we can turn to several simple concepts and ratios which are commonly used to evaluate solvency. Later we will similarly cover tools for evaluating liquidity. Ratio analysis is only one of several approaches to evaluating solvency and liquidity. There are some distinct limitations to ratio analysis, especially when it is not combined with other techniques. Comprehensive analysis of solvency and liquidity is beyond the scope of this text. It is usually covered in financial management courses. Simple ratio analysis is included here and in subsequent chapters as an aid to understanding financial statements and their content.

Think of solvency as simply the ability to pay bills when due. Suppose you could determine a firm's obligations (as of today) which it would have to pay within a year. And suppose you could determine what cash it has as well as other assets that would normally be converted to cash within the same year. Wouldn't such information provide an indication of the firm's solvency? In this context, you can readily perceive the reason for the current asset and current liability groupings and subtotals on the balance sheet. It provides a convenient, quick view of the firm's current and potential solvency. Current assets and current liabilities will, of course, be changing each business day. Nevertheless, a recent balance sheet can tell you at a glance how solvent the firm apparently was on the statement date.

Trying to work with numbers of dollars and different sizes of firms can present difficulties and confusion. Suppose you were estimating the solvency of two firms, P and Q, and wanted to know which firm was more solvent. You have the following information:

	P	Q
Total Current Assets	$26,482	$512,304
Total Current Liabilities	14,876	251,793

It is more convenient and revealing to convert these absolute amounts to simple ratios or proportions, especially for comparison purposes.

Current Ratio

The first commonly used solvency ratio to learn is known as the *current ratio*.[2] It is simply calculated by dividing total current assets by total current liabilities:

$$\text{Current ratio} = \frac{\text{Total Current Assets}}{\text{Total Current Liabilities}}.$$

---

[2]   The current ratio is sometimes called the working capital ratio. This terminology is potentially confusing because of the absence of consensus on the meaning of working capital and net working capital. See elaboration later in this chapter.

Remember that, in calculating and using ratios, you are attempting to use a rough indicator rather than a precise instrument. It would serve no purpose to know that your body temperature was 101.276543°F; and a thermometer which would give you such a reading would be rather expensive. Knowing you have a fever of about 101, or perhaps 101.3, is more than adequate. P's current ratio is about 2 to 1, or closer to 1.8 to 1, and Q's is 2 to 1, or 2.0 to 1. So what? What does the ratio reveal? What is the "norm" or standard for current ratios?

Think it through rather than just memorizing an answer; then it will be easier to remember. If a current ratio is less than 1 to 1, the firm does not have enough current assets, even if they are all in cash, to cover its existing current obligations. A ratio of 1 to 1 or up to 1.6 to 1 is pretty risky, since not all current assets are usually in the form of cash, and it may take months for them to be turned into cash. A ratio of 2 to 1 is generally fairly safe. In this example, both P and Q are reasonably solvent, with Q being slightly more solvent than P. A good, safe level formerly was defined as at least 2 to 1. With today's better cash-management techniques, 1.7 or above may be satisfactory. Any generalization with respect to a desirable current ratio cannot be accurate for all types of business. Service industries with no significant inventories can have a much lower safe current ratio than industries and firms with large slow-moving inventories. If the information is available, the best standard for comparison purposes will be the current ratio of other successful firms in the same business.

Quick Ratio

The current ratio is helpful but is only a crude measure of solvency. Would you consider Company Z as being reasonably safe with the following current items?

Cash	$ 1,000	Accounts payable	$ 8,000
Marketable securities	None	Wages payable	40,000
Receivables (net)	2,000	Other current liabilities	2,000
Inventory	70,000	Total Current Liabilities	$50,000
Supplies	10,000		
Prepaid items	17,000		
Total Current Assets	$100,000		

The current ratio of Company Z is an apparently safe 2 to 1, and yet it appears to be in trouble. This example is deliberately extreme. For fun, you can make it even worse. Imagine that the balance sheet is as of January 31, that Z is in the party decorations business, and that all of the inventory represents Halloween, Christmas, and New Year's items. Would you like to be one of Z's employees? To overcome the crudity of the current ratio, another more rigorous ratio often used is called the *quick ratio* or, sometimes, the acid-test ratio. This ratio compares only the current monetary assets with current liabilities.

$$\text{Quick ratio} = \frac{\text{Current Monetary Assets}}{\text{Current Liabilities}}.$$

Remember that current monetary assets include cash and definite commitments of specific amounts of cash to be received within one year. Normally, current monetary assets consist of cash, marketable securities, and current receivables. Some analysts, to be more precise, use current monetary liabilities as the denominator. They exclude items not requiring cash in settlement, such as deferred revenue and estimated warranty costs. Usually the difference between current liabilities and current monetary liabilities is so small as not to significantly affect the quick ratio. In this text, total current liabilities will be used as the denominator.

A quick ratio of 1 to 1 or greater is generally fairly safe. Below 1 to 1 may indicate problems. The Z Company's quick ratio would be 0.06 to 1, which clearly highlights its crisis. Some analysts use the absolute amount of *net quick assets*, that is, the difference between current monetary assets and current monetary liabilities. The use of this absolute amount as a measure of solvency can be misleading when comparing firms of different overall size.

CONVENIENT MEASURES OF LIQUIDITY

Remember that liquidity refers to a firm's ability to raise more cash if it needs or wants to. Liquidity can be thought of as insurance against insolvency. It also can be considered either as providing the opportunity for a firm to quickly move into an additional new business opportunity, or as the ability to move rapidly with minimal loss out of present activities that have become undesirable. Other than new investment by the owner, or retained profit, there are two major sources of new cash for any company. Can you identify them? One would be to borrow additional cash from creditors. The second would be to convert or sell existing noncash assets for cash, that is, to voluntarily liquidate these assets. The former choice is more common, since liquidation of existing assets usually carries with it discontinuance or difficulty in continuing present activities.

Debt Ratio

A common measure of liquidity which relates to the borrowing capacity of the firm is the *debt ratio*. The debt ratio indicates the proportion of debt or creditor involvement in the company. It is determined by dividing total liabilities by total equities:

$$\text{Debt ratio} = \frac{\text{Total Liabilities}}{\text{Total Equities}}.$$

This form of the debt ratio will always turn out to be a decimal fraction and will be expressed as 0.4 to 1 in an example where total liabilities equalled 40 percent of total equities. Unfortunately, there is no agreement among analysts on the precise components of the debt ratio. Variations include: Total Noncurrent Liabilities/Total Equities, Total Noncurrent Liabilities/Owner's Equity, and Total Liabilities/Owner's Equity. Any one of these alternatives, **consistently** applied and interpreted, can signal the same proportionate debt information. In this text, Total Liabilities/Total Equities will be used.

There really is no norm or ideal debt ratio for all firms, just as there are no norms for all people. There are, however, averages for particular industries, and these industry averages serve as "norms." Even a small amount of debt with regularly required payments can be too much and too risky for a person not regularly employed. A much greater amount of debt in both absolute and relative amounts may be no problem for a high-salaried executive who is in good health and well established with his or her firm. The debt ratio is interpreted differently from other ratios in that, the higher it is, the less liquid is the firm. If it is too high, creditors will not risk additional loans. Even more so than in the case of the current ratio, the firm's debt ratio must be evaluated in terms of the specific circumstances of the particular company and the established norms for its particular industry.

Asset Composition

Another consideration related to liquidity is the composition of a firm's total assets. The debt ratio reflects the composition of equities and can have a very direct bearing on the relative ease with which a firm can raise more cash—the firm's liquidity. *Asset composition* is not usually as directly related to a company's short-term prospects for raising cash. As mentioned above, a going concern can hardly afford to sell off its capacity assets and still remain in business. Nevertheless, if current assets are a high percentage of total assets, they might provide more attractive security or collateral for a short-term loan. If you were making a short-term loan to a firm and felt it necessary to have certain assets pledged as security, wouldn't you prefer readily collectible current receivables or readily salable merchandise or supplies, instead of special-purpose fixed assets?

Asset composition can be a more important consideration in evaluating the desirability of a long-term investment, either long-term debt or owner investment. Over a period of many years, consumer tastes and industry's products change. It has been estimated that over 75 percent of items on the market today did not exist twenty years ago. A firm with a high percentage of its total assets in relatively liquid current assets can "move" more readily into new products or new lines of business. A firm with a high percentage of assets "locked in" to fixed assets is less flexible. There is no commonly recognized ratio for reflecting asset composition. The most logical ratio, and probably the one used intuitively by most analysts, would be:

$$\text{Asset composition ratio} = \frac{\text{Total Current Assets}}{\text{Total Assets}}.$$

The higher this ratio, the more liquid would be the firm's assets.

OTHER BALANCE-SHEET-RELATED RATIOS

There are several ratios (in addition to the ones given above) that are equally important in assessing solvency and liquidity. There are also other balance-sheet-related ratios and percentages that are important to the measurement of a firm's performance and efficiency. All of these additional tools of analysis incorporate data from other financial statements to which you have not yet been sufficiently exposed. Chapter 13 introduces these additional tools for your use after you have had the opportunity to become familiar with more detailed accounting information.

NET WORKING CAPITAL

Now is a convenient time to introduce you to *net working capital* as another important concept related to financial statement analysis. Net working capital is simply the amount of net current assets in the firm or the amount of total current assets *not* supplied by current creditors. It is determined by simply subtracting total current liabilities from total current assets. A business that has $80,000 of total current assets and $35,000 of total current liabilities, therefore, is said to have $45,000 of net working capital.

The concept of net working capital has several uses. It is a measure of solvency in absolute terms—the current ratio expressed as a difference in amount rather than a ratio. As such, it can be incorporated in loan agreements, where the creditor is concerned that the firm will maintain adequate solvency to protect the creditor's investment. The loan agreement will simply provide that, should net working capital fall below $XXXXX, the loan becomes immediately due and payable. In Chapter 1, the fact that changes in accounting practices were constrained by social and legal conventions was mentioned in the abstract. A concrete example would be net working capital. It would cause great difficulty if accountants were to change the rules for classification of current assets and current liabilities, or even how these items are measured, when these accounting rules have been incorporated in legal contracts.

Net working capital is also a convenient asset grouping for use in measuring and reporting resource flows related to a business. Cash flows are subject to changes in the timing of the firm's operating cycle. Net working capital flows ignore changes within the operating cycle and can then be a less volatile measurement of trend. Net working capital flows will be covered in more detail in later chapters.

LACK OF CONSENSUS

Perhaps your most difficult problem in learning to become a competent statement analyst and, for that matter, in learning financial accounting will result from the lack of consensus on terminology and concepts. As you learn accounting terminology, you will find that many different terms are used interchangeably for the same thing, and that one term may have different meanings, not just in the context of different situations, but also in the "context" of what firm or individual happens to be communicating. You will find that GAAP encompass alternative treatments of the same event as acceptable.

This lack of standardization or apparent mild chaos results from the historical fact that accounting and statement analysis had been practiced for centuries by separate firms and individuals before there was any attempt at standardization. As GAAP have evolved, accountants have been loathe to outlaw all but one equally acceptable alternative reporting practice or term when the others have been standard in different industries for many years. It is reality, and you **must** deal with reality, if you hope to be effective. You therefore must be constantly alert to alternative interpretations.

Even for such important concepts and tools as net working capital, solvency, liquidity, and ratio analysis, there exists no complete agreement. Many business people and financial analysts are not comfortable using the accounting term "current assets." Instead they use "working capital" to refer to current assets. To distinguish current assets minus current liabilities, or net current assets, they then use "net working capital." This common business terminology will be used in this text. However, you may encounter other texts or publications, especially in accounting, where working capital is used to mean current assets minus current liabilities. Such individuals, of course, do not employ the term "net working capital," as to them it would be redundant.

Similarly, you will encounter solvency used in relationship to long-term debt, and liquidity referring to debt-paying ability. There is even less standardization with respect to ratio analysis (refer to the previous definitions of the quick ratio and the debt ratio). Therefore, when you encounter words like solvency or liquidity, or when you are thinking of using ratios calculated by someone else, it is advisable that you check first on the definition being used.

STANDARDS FOR COMPARISON

Returning to statement analysis, in analyzing the balance sheet or the other financial statements, you must have a standard or basis for determining what is desirable and undesirable. Available standards for use are of two types, as already implied earlier in this chapter.

Trend analysis involves studying the same item for the same firm over a period of months or years. Here the standard is the prior year or years. In trend analysis, one is usually limited to the conclusions that conditions are either better, unchanged, or worse. A particular item could be worse than the previous year and still be the best in the industry.

To have a more adequate basis of evaluation, *comparative analysis* is desirable. Comparative analysis involves comparing data from one firm to that of other similar firms or to industry averages, where available.

Each type of analysis has its limitations and dangers. To really establish a trend, you need data for many years. But even if readily available, firms change their activities over time, and data from five years ago could be so irrelevant to today's world as to be misleading in any trend picture. To make a truly valid comparison, you need other companies in the identical business. Here again, modern firms are highly diversified. Not much of value is obtained by comparing details of company D with company E if D's business includes making tractors, making hair shampoo, and producing TV film, while E makes tractors, runs large produce farms, and owns a professional basketball team.[3] Statement analysis remains very specialized to the particular situation of the firm being analyzed. It also retains many of the characteristics of a highly specialized and intuitive art.

CONSISTENCY

It should be obvious that if certain assets are included on one balance sheet but omitted from the next, even though such assets are actually present, trend or comparative analysis could be ridiculous. Similar difficulties could exist if particular items were measured one way one year and another way the next. In Chapters 8 and 9, you will discover that GAAP allow for different approaches to measurement and reporting which can result in significantly different amounts for the identical asset, depending upon the option chosen. Inventory and fixed assets, which often together represent more than half a firm's assets, are subject to these wide measurements or, more precisely, timing electives. If a firm could readily elect one measurement option one year and a different one in the following year, the results could be worthless or misleading.

Read again both of the auditor's opinions contained in Appendix A. Note that the opinions specifically state that the standards applied were consistent with prior years. If a change became desirable, GAAP require that the change be stated in the opinion to alert you, the user. Also the effect of the change—the difference in results as between the new way and the old way if it had been continued—must be disclosed, usually in the statement footnotes. If there is a necessary departure from *consistency*, most firms will also provide important data for the prior five or ten years, restated to the new basis, to facilitate trend analysis.

Changes which occur in accounting practices do not, therefore, present much of a problem to the alert user; and changes are rare because of the overriding principle of consistency. Consistency can be understood as requiring that:

> Present accounting practices which are consistent with GAAP shall not be changed or modified without compelling reasons indicating a need for fairer disclosure, and such changes shall be infrequent and never capricious.

---

[3]   To reduce such difficulties, GAAP provide for disclosure of certain supplementary information on the separate segments of diversified firms. This segmental reporting will be discussed in Chapter 15.

Different firms, consistently following different GAAP measurement and reporting options, can dangerously mislead the unsophisticated or careless comparative analyst. In Chapter 8, for example, you can learn that it is possible for company K to report total inventory as $100,000, while company J, with a much greater quantity on hand of the same item, reports $40,000 of inventory. This situation results not from dishonest reporting but from different measurement bases. If K reported cash at $10,000 and J reported 15,000 francs, you would know you could not make a valid comparison in numbers without the current dollar–franc currency exchange rate. A potential problem in making comparative analyses between financial statements of different firms results from the fact that all assets are reported in dollars, which someone may assume are measured on the same basis. Only by reading the footnotes to the statements which disclose the measurement standards used can you determine whether a dollar or ratio comparison can be meaningful. At this stage it is important only that you realize that such a problem in comparative analysis can exist and that you must learn how to recognize and deal with it before completing your study of elementary accounting.

MATERIALITY

While being introduced to basic principles underlying all GAAP, this would be a good time for you to learn about another principle known as *materiality*. Accountants use the word "material" to mean "significant." The principle of materiality merely directs accountants' activities and reporting standards to those items which possibly will have a significant effect on the statement user's decisions and interpretations. Concurrently, it implies that trivial and inconsequential items should not clutter up the information flow.

The application of materiality can be readily perceived with an example involving thumbtacks. Suppose your firm has a bulletin board and you purchase a box of thumbtacks for 75 cents. The thumbtacks clearly are owned and have future value; therefore they qualify as an asset. Except for occasional loss or bending, the thumbtacks take a long time to lose their usefulness. Therefore, they wouldn't be a current asset. When the 75 cents is expended, should a new asset—thumbtacks—be recorded and shown on the balance sheet?

If your response is affirmative, you undoubtedly will be entitled to an award from the "Make More Work for Unemployed Accountants Association" when and if it is ever formed. Under GAAP, cash would be reduced by the 75 cents expenditure, but the new "asset" would be ignored as not material; and owner's equity would eventually be reduced to balance the reduction in total assets.

Materiality (or "don't fool around with small items") can be readily understood conceptually. Precise determinations are more difficult in practice. Would wastebaskets at $5 each be sufficiently material to be included with assets? For the firm with three, the answer would be no. For an office with

30,000 employees, each having a wastebasket, $150,000 may be material. As another example, suppose a particular small manufacturer had, in addition to land and a factory building, factory equipment costing $30,000 and office furniture and fixtures costing $25,000. Clearly, both groups are material to the small firm and probably should be separately disclosed on the balance sheet. But what if the manufacturer were very large, with factory equipment costing $17,000,000 and only $25,000 of office assets? Most accountants would probably not separately disclose the $25,000. Instead, equipment would be shown as $17,025,000. GAAP presently have no precise guidelines for materiality, although the FASB has some under consideration. Currently, materiality is a matter of judgment and is determined by the firm's accountant, further verified by the auditor.

A word about materiality and this book may be appropriate. Many of the examples and problems in prior and succeeding chapters use small, often rounded numbers. In practice, many of these would *not* be considered material. Clearly, only obviously material amounts could be used in this text. However, that would just make the arithmetic unnecessarily difficult and thus interfere with your learning the important aspects of accounting. Therefore, throughout this book, by agreement, all items will be defined as material. Now we can use small numbers and not worry.

AFFIRMATIVELY MISLEADING DETAIL

Earlier, when we were discussing current ratios, it was pointed out that computation to many decimal places was wasteful effort. Materiality would indicate that you should join the accountant and concentrate on the significant. Excessive detail may do something worse than waste time and effort; it may be *affirmatively misleading*. That is, it may imply to the user or reader, or lead him or her to infer, a false degree of accuracy. Return, for a moment, to the area of depreciation. Assume that your firm purchased for $6,113 a truck with a five-year useful life and which you expect to sell for $1,012 at the end of five years. If you elect to depreciate the truck in approximately even amounts each year, at the end of the second year the truck would be reported at:

Equipment	$ 6,113
Less accumulated depreciation	(2,040.40)[4]

---

[4]   A $6,113 cost minus $1,012 estimated recovery equals $5,101 to be allocated evenly over five years. Rounded allocation = $1,000 per year, with the extra picked up in the final year if necessary. Precise allocation would be $5,101 divided by 5, or $1,020.20 per year.

This would be arithmetically accurate but possibly misleading. Depreciation is only an estimate, and $2,040.40 implies nonexistent accuracy.

Similarly, in reporting data on financial statements, accountants always round cents to the nearest dollar even for nonestimated items such as cash. In large firms, data are rounded to the nearest thousand-dollar amount, and this practice is indicated in the heading by "(000 omitted)." Rounding does not imply sloppiness or inability to calculate. Rounding serves as a reminder to the user that he or she is dealing with estimates.

In this text, wherever practical, problems are designed to come out even in order to avoid such difficulty. If you are required to perform a specific calculation to demonstrate your competence in using a formula, carry it through all significant digits. But if you are preparing a statement, beware of excessive detail on estimated items. Be sure to ascertain your instructor's standards for any examination you may be required to take.

CHAPTER OVERVIEW

From the material covered in this chapter, you should be in a position to demonstrate that you can readily:

- Identify the various contributors of capital to a firm and the amounts of each contribution;

- Explain the meaning and importance of solvency and liquidity to a business;

- Determine and interpret analysis tools, including the current, quick, and debt ratios and the concept of asset composition;

- Define net working capital and describe several of its uses;

- Discuss with examples the difficulties inherent in the lack of uniformity in accounting and financial-analysis terminology, concepts and practices; and describe how these inconsistencies arose;

- Describe several standards of comparison which are useful for financial statement analysis;

- Define and give examples demonstrating the significance and application of the GAAP principles of consistency and materiality.

NEW VOCABULARY AND CONCEPTS

Solvency
Liquidity
Current ratio
Quick ratio
Net quick assets
Debt ratio
Asset composition

Net working capital
Trend analysis
Comparative analysis
Consistency
Materiality
Affirmatively misleading detail

- Equities disclosing both claims against and sources of assets;
- The significance of solvency and liquidity to a firm;
- The reasons that the principles of consistency and materiality are part of GAAP.

REVIEW QUESTIONS

1. What is the significant difference between "horizontal" and "vertical" presentation of balance sheets?

2. When accounting information for two successive years is shown on a financial statement, which year is usually shown first?

3. What is the first objective of a business organized with the intention of making a profit?

4. a) Why is maintaining solvency so important to a business? b) What are the risks of insolvency?

5. a) What are the advantages of liquidity? b) How does liquidity differ from solvency?

6. a) What does the current ratio measure? b) Is it a good indicator of liquidity? c) of solvency? d) How does it differ from the quick ratio?

7. a) What are two common measures of liquidity? b) Explain what each measures. c) Explain how this measurement provides an indication of liquidity.

8. Explain how a firm experiencing increasing profitable sales can involuntarily go out of business, i.e., can fail.

9. What is a reasonably safe quick ratio for the average company?

10. Explain how a current ratio can appear adequate even though a firm may be facing insolvency.

11. a) Define net working capital. b) What are two uses of net working capital? Give examples.

12. What is the difference between trend analysis and comparative analysis?

13. What is the GAAP principle of consistency?

14. How could consistency make your job of trend analysis easier, while at the same time providing no help to a possible real difficulty you may encounter in performing comparative analysis?

15. Give an example of something that might be affirmatively misleading.

16. Describe a reporting practice which accountants follow to avoid being affirmatively misleading.

MINI-CASES AND QUESTIONS FOR DISCUSSION

MC 3.1 The Sharp Company's fiscal year ended on March 31. The firm's current and quick ratios had been averaging 1.5 and 0.8, respectively. Its debt ratio had been approximately 0.6. Relevant industry "norms" were 1.8, 0.9, and 0.5 for these ratios.

During March, the firm made a concerted effort to collect receivables, with the result that they were unusually low. The firm practically stopped all purchases of new merchandise during the month and, by month end, inventory was abnormally low. Sales to customers for the first week in April were included with March data. The firm explained that these sales would have been made in March if it hadn't been for bad weather. On April 4th some equipment costing $400,000 ($50,000 down and the balance covered by a five-year promissory note) was picked up at the suppliers. This equipment had been badly needed since the first of the year. It had been available for pickup since March 10.

a) What was the company trying to accomplish?
b) Why was it taking these actions?
c) As an investor, would you like the firm's auditor to report any of these occurrences as exceptions in the opinion? Which events and why?

MC 3.2 The Klute Company had Current Assets of $200,000 and Current Liabilities of $40,000. It also had an outstanding loan agreement which provided that "$100,000 of net working capital shall be maintained." The firm considered purchasing some new equipment costing $80,000 for cash. Could it do this without violating the loan agreement? Discuss the issues.

MC 3.3 The following information is available for the Fairfax Company:

Cash	$100	Current notes payable	$100
Marketable securities	50	Accounts payable	250
Current notes receivable	25	Revenue received in advance	
Accounts receivable (net)	200	from customers	40
Total Current Assets	$375	Expected warranty costs	60
		Total Current Liabilities	$450
		Long-term debt	350
		Total Liabilities	$800
		Owner's Equity	1600
		Total Equities	$2400

a) Was the Fairfax Company's quick ratio a reasonably safe 1.07 to 1 or a potentially dangerous 0.83 to 1? Discuss the issue.
b) Four different analysts have determined Fairfax's debt ratio to be as follows:

Analyst 1: 0.33
Analyst 2: 0.5
Analyst 3: 0.15
Analyst 4: 0.22

They each claim that they are correct. Is this possible? Discuss.

MC 3.4 The current and quick ratios for the Jinx Company as of 12/31/X2 were 2.4 to 1 and 1.2 to 1. Six months later the firm was insolvent and went into receivership. How could this happen? If it could happen, what is the value of ratio analysis? Discuss.

MC 3.5 Paul and Carol were studying two balance sheets from two different companies: Company F and Company G (see summary data below). Carol says, "Company F looks as if it may have trouble staying in business. Most of the assets have been borrowed from creditors and will have to be repaid. In fact, the equivalent of 85 percent of the existing assets will have to be repaid to creditors within a year, and only 25 percent of the existing assets are readily convertible to cash within a year."

Paul replies, "I don't see it that way at all. To me, it looks as though Company F is much safer than Company G. After all, it has more than twice as many assets. Company F has $100,000 of assets which will more than cover the $85,000 of current liabilities. Also, to protect itself, I am sure Company F had arrangements long before the balance sheet date to refinance most of its current debt on a long-term basis just in case."

Balance Sheet Summary Data	Company F	Company G
Total Current Assets	$ 25,000	$30,000
Total Noncurrent Assets	75,000	10,000
Total Assets	$100,000	$40,000
Total Current Liabilities	$ 85,000	$15,000
Total Noncurrent Liabilities	5,000	15,000
Total Liabilities	$ 90,000	$30,000
Total Owner's Equity	$ 10,000	$10,000

Which of these opposing views is more nearly correct? Can you identify and clarify the misconceptions held by the person who was incorrect? Discuss.

ESSENTIAL PROBLEMS

EP 3.1 Given the following information for the Pamela Company and the Paul Company:

a) Which company was more solvent as of 19X3? Explain.

b) Did either firm have a possible solvency problem as of the end of 19X3? If so, which? Explain.

c) Which company had more apparent liquidity as of the end of 19X3? Explain.

	19X4	19X3
Pamela Company		
Current ratio	1.9:1	1.8:1
Quick ratio	1.2:1	1.1:1
Debt ratio	0.1	0.4
Asset composition ratio	0.35	0.3
Paul Company		
Current ratio	2.6:1	1.2:1
Quick ratio	1.5:1	0.5:1
Debt ratio	0.3	0.15
Asset composition ratio	0.35	0.3

EP 3.2 Using the data provided above for the Pamela Company and the Paul Company:

a) Which company was more solvent as of 19X4? Explain.

b) Which company most significantly improved its relative solvency position during 19X4? Explain.

c) Did either firm have a possible solvency problem as of the end of 19X4? If so, which? Explain.

d) Which company had more apparent liquidity as of the end of 19X4? Explain.

e) Which company improved its apparent liquidity during 19X4? Explain.

EP 3.3 Data selected from the balance sheet for the Dowd Company are presented below. Using these data, calculate the following ratios and percentages for the year 19X4:

a) Current ratio.   b) Quick ratio.

c) Debt ratio.   d) Asset composition ratio.

e) Assuming that, in Dowd's industry, a debt ratio of 0.40 is acceptable, does Dowd have some liquidity as of the end of 19X4?

f) How much cash could Dowd probably borrow without much difficulty at the end of 19X4 if all non-balance-sheet considerations were satisfactory to potential creditors?

DOWD COMPANY SELECTED BALANCE SHEET DATA

	19X5	19X4
Cash	$ 5,000	$ 15,000
Marketable securities	15,000	20,000
Receivables (net)	15,000	12,000
Inventory	20,000	15,000
Supplies	5,000	6,000
Prepaid items	3,000	2,000
Total Current Assets	$ 63,000	$ 70,000
Noncurrent assets (net)	62,000	65,000
Total Assets	$125,000	$135,000
Total Current Liabilities	$ 30,000	$ 40,000
Total Liabilities	35,000	50,000
Owner's Equity	90,000	85,000
Total Equities	$125,000	$135,000

EP 3.4 Using the data provided above for the Dowd Company, calculate the following ratios and percentages for the year 19X5:

    a) Current ratio.   b) Quick ratio.

    c) Debt ratio   d) Asset composition ratio.

    e) For each ratio, indicate whether 19X5 was better or worse than 19X4.

    f) Does Dowd appear to have a solvency problem at the end of 19X5?

    g) Assuming that, in Dowd's industry, a debt ratio of 0.45 is acceptable, does Dowd have some liquidity as of the end of 19X5?

    h) How much cash could Dowd probably borrow without much difficulty at the end of 19X5 if all non-balance-sheet considerations were satisfactory to potential creditors?

EP 3.5 Assume that you are the credit manager for the Ajax Supply Company, and you are asked for credit approval by two potential new customers, the Betty Company and the Mary Company. You have the balance sheet information given below and all other data are neutral, neither positive nor negative. Your firm follows a policy, which you recommended, and which states:

> "No credit shall be given to customers without other exceptionally favorable information unless they maintain a current ratio of at least 1.7 to 1 and a quick ratio of at least 1 to 1."

Would you approve credit for either Betty or Mary or both? Explain.

	BETTY COMPANY	MARY COMPANY
Cash	$22,100	$26,400
Receivables	29,600	2,400
Inventory	31,000	38,200
Other Current Assets	1,900	3,400
Total Current Liabilities	47,000	32,000

EP 3.6 Assume that you are a bank loan officer and the Zilch Company has applied for a six-month $50,000 loan. Your bank follows the following policy:

Where loan funds are available, loans shall be made to all applicants whose general credit information is good. However, in no case shall a loan be made to a firm whose ratios and percentages, immediately after the loan is made and when the proceeds are still in cash, depart from the following minimums: Current ratio at least 1.5 to 1, quick ratio at least 1.0 to 1, and debt ratio no greater than 0.4 to .1.

Data that do not include the anticipated loan have been supplied by the Zilch Company and are given below. You may assume that all other credit information is favorable (good), and that you have adequate available funds to loan. Would you authorize the loan? Explain your actions.

Cash	$ 15,000
Marketable securities	20,000
Receivables (net)	70,000
Inventory	40,000
Supplies	10,000
Prepaid items	5,000

Total Current Liabilities	100,000
Total Liabilities	130,000
Owner's Equity	270,000

SUPPLEMENTARY PROBLEMS

SP 3.7 The following data are taken from the PBFF Company's balance sheet as of 12/31/X1 and 12/31/X0 (000 omitted):

	12/31/X1	12/31/X0
Accounts payable	80	70
Accounts receivable (net)	38	30
Cash	42	93
Current notes payable	15	20
Inventory	94	56
Marketable securities	0	27
Noncurrent assets (net)	115	495
Noncurrent notes payable	25	177
Other current liabilities	15	25
Owner's equity	?	?
Prepaid items	12	15
Supplies	14	14

Assume that the firm had no other assets or liabilities than those shown. For 12/31/X0 determine:

a) Owner's equity.

b) Net working capital.

c) Current ratio.

d) Quick ratio.

e) Debt ratio.

f) Asset composition ratio.

SP 3.8 Determine for the PBFF Company from data given with problem SP 3.7 above the following:

a) 12/31/X1 Owner's equity.

b) 12/31/X1 Net working capital.

c) 12/31/X1 Current ratio.

d) 12/31/X1 Quick ratio.

e) 12/31/X1 Debt ratio.

f) 12/31/X1 Asset composition ratio.

g) Was the company more solvent at the end of 19X1 than at the beginning? Explain.

h) Was the company more liquid at the end of 19X1 than at the beginning? Explain.

SP 3.9 Using the balance sheets for 11/30/1975 and 11/30/1976 for the Addison-Wesley Publishing Company (Appendix A at back of book), determine the following as of 11/30/75:

a) Net working capital.

b) Current ratio.

c) Quick ratio.

d) Debt ratio.

e) Asset composition ratio.

SP 3.10 Referring to the Addison-Wesley Publishing Company (see Problem SP 3.9), determine the following as of 11/30/76:

a) Net working capital.   b) Current ratio.

c) Quick ratio.   d) Debt ratio.

e) Asset composition ratio.

f) Was the company apparently more solvent than at the beginning of its fiscal year? Explain.

g) Was the company apparently more liquid than at the beginning of its fiscal year? Explain.

SP 3.11 Using the balance sheets for the Xerox Corporation for 12/31/75 and 12/31/76 (Appendix A at back of book), determine, as of 12/31/75, the same ratios required in Problem SP 3.9 above. Note that, for Xerox, when calculating debt ratio, you should **not** include "Outside Shareholders' Interests in Equity of Subsidiaries" as a liability. This item is a form of ownership equity and is discussed in Chapter 15.

SP 3.12 Refer to Problems SP 3.10 and SP 3.11 above. For the Xerox Corporation, as of 12/31/76, give the information required in Problem SP 3.10 above, items (a) through (g).

4

BALANCE SHEET CHANGES AND INCOME

CHAPTER PREVIEW

The objectives of this chapter are to introduce you to events which change a firm's financial position, to the balance sheet effect of such events, to the double-entry accounting system for recording them, and to the concept of income as measured by accountants. You can learn:

- That certain events have no effect on a firm's financial position;
- How other events immediately or eventually affect specific items appearing on the balance sheet;
- That such effect is always dual or complementary, thus maintaining the balance sheet equality;
- That events affecting a firm's position may involve either resource exchanges with other entities or economic changes to resources already within the firm;
- That certain changes result in what accountants define as income, and how income itself is defined;
- That financial position and income are measured on what is known as the "accrual" basis rather than the cash basis.

With this fundamental knowledge, you can begin to understand how the entire financial accounting system can be conceived of as constructed upon the balance sheet as a foundation. You will see how you can always go back to the balance sheet whenever you are unsure of any event's exact economic effect. And you will have an initial insight into the meaning and significance of income to the firm and particularly to the firm's owner(s).

EVENTS WHICH CHANGE A BALANCE SHEET

Pat Ward is a business school graduate. She has always been interested in indoor plants and has had a "green thumb" since she was very young. During her senior year, she inherited $20,000 from her grandfather. She decided upon graduation to open a business specializing in the sale and care of indoor plants. She would call her firm the "Potted Planter."

Her memory of elementary accounting taken as a sophomore was somewhat indistinct, but she did know that she would require accounting information. She also clearly remembered the balance sheet, and that it always should balance. Pat obtained a large sheet of paper and drew lines on it to represent the sections of the balance sheet:

ILLUSTRATION OF BALANCE SHEET

Current Assets	Current Liabilities
	Noncurrent Liabilities
Noncurrent Assets	Owner's Equity

She then proceeded to keep records of everything that happened to her business in a daily diary. One night a week she would record the effect of the previous week's happenings on her balance sheet.

First Week

During the first week, her diary contained the following items:

Event (1): Opened a special bank account in business name and transferred $10,000 into it.

Event (2): Signed a year's lease on a store.

Event (3): Gave landlord $1,000, representing first month's rent ($500) and last month's rent as a security deposit.

Event (4): Spent $50 on cleaning and painting supplies. Used them all during the week, cleaning and fixing up interior of store.

Event (5): Met a really nice guy who likes plants. He agreed to come to work for me when I can afford help.

At the end of the week she recorded the effects of these events on the balance sheet as follows:

ILLUSTRATION OF BALANCE SHEET EFFECT

Assets		Liabilities
Cash	+ $10,000 (1)	
	− 1,000 (3)	Noncurrent Liabilities
	− 50 (4)	
Prepaid Rent	+ 1,000 (3)	
		Owner's Equity
		+ $10,000 (1)
		− 50 (4)

Note that Events (2) and (5) have no effect upon Pat's statement. They did not change the financial position of her business. They both represented *executory agreements,* one formal and one informal. Executory agreements are mutual promises to exchange money, goods, or services in the future which neither party to the agreement has yet performed. At the time of signing the lease, Pat was not obligated to the landlord unless the landlord supplied the store in usable condition. Pat was not obligated to pay her new friend wages unless she advised him to come to work, and he actually worked for her.[1]

Also note how Pat recorded the effect of Events (1), (3), and (4) and the reasoning behind such recordings:

Effect of (1): Cash in the business had increased $10,000. No other asset or liability was affected. Therefore, Pat's share (owner's equity) of total assets increased $10,000.

Effect of (3): Cash in the business had decreased $1,000. Pat now has a receivable for services—the use of the store—from the landlord (prepaid rent). One asset (cash) has merely been exchanged for another (prepaid rent). Total assets did not change. No liabilities were involved. Therefore, there was no possible change in owner's equity as a result of this one event.

---

[1]   Should one party cancel an executory agreement before performance is concluded or completed by either party, there may be damages for breach of contract. However, such damages are not determinable until the matter is settled and would depend on failure to perform in the future. At the time the agreement is made, there exists no obligation for past performance and no reason to anticipate possible future failure and damages.

Effect of (4): Cash decreased $50. Although future benefits or future cost savings would result from the cleaning and painting, this possible intangible asset had no objectively measurable benefit beyond the current year (the lease only runs for one year). The benefit is too uncertain to qualify for treatment as an asset. With cash decreased by $50, and no new asset resulting, total assets are therefore reduced by $50. Liabilities are unaffected; therefore, owner's equity must be reduced $50 to reflect the assets used and to maintain the balance.[2]

Second Week

Starting with the second week, Pat recorded in her diary only those events that affected her firm's financial position. The events recorded during the second week were:

Event (6): Inventory of plants costing $3,000 was purchased on account from a wholesale supplier.

Event (7): Supplies for use in the business costing $200—pots, dirt, fertilizer, chemicals, wrapping paper, hanging wire, and so forth— were purchased for cash.

Event (8): Two used display counters and one used cash register, together costing $2,500, were acquired. The sum of $500 cash was paid, and Pat signed a promissory note for the $2,000 balance. The note would *mature* (that is, become due and payable) in two years. The note also provided for 10 percent annual interest, payable semiannually.

(On a sheet of paper, draw the balance sheet diagram and attempt to properly record the effect of these three events, before looking below for the solution.)

ILLUSTRATION OF BALANCE SHEET EFFECT

Current Assets		Current Liabilities	
Cash	— 200 (7)	*Accounts Payable* + 3,000 (6)	
	— 500 (8)	Noncurrent Liabilities	
Inventory	+ 3,000 (6)	*Noncurrent Note Payable* + 2,000 (8)	
Supplies	+ 200 (7)		
Noncurrent Assets		Owner's Equity	
Equipment	+ 2,500 (8)		

---

[2]   Later in this chapter, you can learn that certain increases and decreases to owner's equity are separately identified and recorded for income measurement purposes. Throughout this "Potted Planter" example, all such changes will affect owner's equity directly.

Note that the effect of each event by itself is being recorded. At this point, there is no attempt to accumulate various effects. For example, events (7) and (8) both reduce cash. That is **part** of their effect. We are not now concerned with determining the remaining amount of cash on hand.

Effect of (6): Assets (inventory) increased $3,000. Liabilities (accounts payable) increased $3,000. There was no effect on owner's equity.

Effect of (7): A simple exchange of assets. Supplies increased $200 and cash decreased $200.

Effect of (8): Noncurrent assets (equipment) increased $2,500. Cash decreased $500. Noncurrent liabilities increased $2,000. Therefore there was no effect on owner's equity. Note that the future interest liability on the promissory note at the time of signing is executory, and is **not** recorded on the balance sheet. At the time of signing, no interest has as yet been **earned** by the investor holding the note, and no interest is **owed** by Pat.

Third Week

At the start of the third week, Pat opened her store for business. On the advice of other business persons, she adopted the following policies and practices:

a) All sales of plants in the store would be for cash.

b) When she delivered plants to her customer's home or provided services (watering, fertilizing, re-potting, pruning, and so forth), she would charge for her time and materials and *invoice* (send a bill to) the customer.

c) She would not attempt to record the outflow of plants or other items (inventory) sold to customers. Only the inflow of sales proceeds—cash and new accounts receivable based on invoices written—would be recorded in the diary.

The events recorded during the third week were as follows:

Event (9): Total store sales (cash sales) to customers for the week were $960.

Event (10): Total invoices for home sales and services (credit sales) for the week were $220.

Event (11): Quantities of small packages of dirt, fertilizer, and chemicals costing $500 were purchased on account. In response to customer request, these items were acquired for display and sale.

(You should attempt to record the effect of these events before proceeding, so as to reinforce your understanding.)

ILLUSTRATION OF BALANCE SHEET EFFECT

Current Assets		Current Liabilities	
Cash	+ 960 (9)	Accounts Payable + 500 (11)	
Accounts Receivable	+ 220 (10)	Noncurrent Liabilities	
Inventory	+ 500 (11)		
Noncurrent Assets		Owner's Equity	
		+ 960 (9)	
		+ 220 (10)	

Effect of (9): Assets (cash) increased $960. There was no other effect on assets (it was decided to record outflow of merchandise later). Liabilities were not affected. Therefore owner's equity is increased by $960, to reflect the additional total assets and to balance.

Effect of (10): Assets (accounts receivable) increased $220. Liabilities were unchanged; therefore, owner's equity must be increased by $220 to balance.

Effect of (11): Assets (inventory) increased $500. Liabilities (accounts payable) increased $500. Therefore there was no effect on owner's equity.

Fourth Week

The diary revealed:

Event (12): Cash sales for the week were $1,040.

Event (13): Credit sales for the week were $280.

Event (14): Purchase of additional plants on account cost $400.

Event (15): Some of the customers previously invoiced paid $150 on their accounts.

Event (16): Pat paid the plant wholesaler $2,500 on her account.

The effects of Events (12), (13), and (14) were the same (although with different dollar amounts) as events (9), (10), and (11) previously described. (See top of page 92.)

Effect of (15): A *collection of receivables* represents a simple exchange of assets. "Cash coming" has arrived. Cash is increased and accounts receivable decreased by the amount collected.

ILLUSTRATION OF BALANCE SHEET EFFECT

Assets		Liabilities	
Cash	+ 1,040 (12) + 150 (15) − 2,500 (16)	Accounts Payable + 400 (14) − 2,500 (16)	
Accounts Receivable:			
	+ 280 (13) − 150 (15)	Owner's Equity	
Inventory	+ 400 (14)		+ 1,040 (12) + 280 (13)

Effect of (16): The payment of a previously recorded liability reduces both cash and also the liability by the amount paid. There is no effect upon owner's equity.

Total Month

The balance sheet effect of each week's events has been shown separately in order to focus on the effect of each distinct event. Of course, the effect of all events is cumulative. Exhibit 4.1 shows the effect of all events during the month that changed the firm's financial position and were recorded in the diary. Remember that Events (2) and (5) are not shown, since they did not affect the firm's position at the time.

   Assume you are Pat Ward. As an owner-investor you are anxious to know where the business now stands and how well it is doing. From Exhibit 4.1, prepare a **preliminary** balance sheet as of the end of the month. Then check your result against Exhibit 4.2. Does Exhibit 4.2 fairly present the financial position of the Potted Planter, and Pat's share in its total assets, as of the end of the month? What is incorrect? Do you need any more facts before you could complete the preparation of a proper month-end statement?

Month-end Adjustments

If you have not already identified them, there are four improperly reported asset measurements: inventory, supplies, prepaid rent, and equipment.[3] Since Pat is not taking (wasting) the time to record outflows of merchandise to customers and those supplies that she has used, the amounts for these items are overstated on Exhibit 4.2. Pat will have to take a *physical inventory* of merchandise and supplies still on hand at month end before an accurate statement

---

[3]   Remember from Chapter 3 the agreement in this text that all amounts are material unless specified otherwise.

Exhibit 4.1
BALANCE-SHEET EFFECT OF FIRST MONTH'S EVENTS
POTTED PLANTER

Assets		Equities	
Cash	+$10,000 (1)	Accounts Payable	+$3,000 (6)
	− 1,000 (3)		+ 500 (11)
	− 50 (4)		+ 400 (14)
	− 200 (7)		− 2,500 (16)
	− 500 (8)		
	+ 960 (9)		
	+ 1,040 (12)	Noncurrent Note Payable	+ 2,000 (8)
	+ 150 (15)		
	− 2,500 (16)		
Accounts Receivable	+ 220 (10)		
	+ 280 (13)		
	− 150 (15)		
Inventory	+ 3,000 (6)	Owner's Equity	+10,000 (1)
	+ 500 (11)		− 50 (4)
	+ 400 (14)		+ 960 (9)
			+ 220 (10)
Supplies	+ 200 (7)		+ 1,040 (12)
			+ 280 (13)
Prepaid Rent	+ 1,000 (3)		
Equipment	+ 2,500 (8)		

Exhibit 4.2
POTTED PLANTER PRELIMINARY BALANCE SHEET
AT END OF FIRST MONTH

Assets		Equities	
Cash	$7,900	Accounts payable	$1,400
Accounts receivable	350	Total Current Liabilities	$1,400
Inventory	3,900	Noncurrent note payable	2,000
Supplies	200	Total Liabilities	$3,400
Prepaid rent	1,000		
Total Current Assets	$13,350		
Equipment	2,500		
		Owner's Equity	12,450
Total Assets	$15,850	Total Equities	$15,850

can be prepared. She will have to count the items and determine their cost. In a real situation, a physical inventory would be necessary only once a year, for the annual financial statements. Techniques for estimating these amounts in case more frequent "interim" reports are desired will be discussed in Chapter 8. Assume, for this example, that Pat wants financial statements at the end of the first month. Also assume that a physical inventory reveals ending inventory of healthy plants and merchandise costing $2,850, and unused supplies costing $75.

To complete information necessary for final balance sheet preparation, you may also assume that the equipment is expected to have a four-year useful life (Pat expects to stay in business in this store or in another one for at least four years), and that it then can be sold for $100. Also, can you think of any liabilities that Pat may have at month end which have not been recorded in the diary? What about utilities and interest? Pat owes the local power company for utilities consumed during the month and the telephone company for telephone services consumed. Neither bill has arrived in the mail and therefore nothing was recorded in the diary. You can estimate the total of both at $140 for the month. Note that this $140 is **not** executory. The utilities have supplied the service. They have earned the $140, and Pat owes it to them for services already performed. Pat also owes a few weeks' interest on the long-term promissory note. For simplicity you may assume that it is too small an amount to record, that it is not material.

You now have all necessary information to adjust the preliminary balance sheet figures. You should attempt the necessary adjustments before proceeding. Four adjustments are necessary:

Adjustment (17): Ending inventory was determined to have a cost of $2,850. From Exhibit 4.2, total merchandise available for sale (beginning inventory 0 plus net purchases $3,900) is $3,900. Therefore, the difference of $1,050 has been delivered to customers, died, or been stolen. Inventory is therefore re-

duced by $1,050. No other asset or liability is involved in this adjustment. Therefore, Owner's Equity is reduced by $1,050 to reflect this usage of assets and to balance.

Adjustment (18): Similarly, supplies is reduced by $125 to **record** supplies used. Owner's Equity is reduced by $125 to **reflect** assets used.

Adjustment (19): $500 of prepaid rent representing the first month's rental payment has been "used." It no longer represents a claim for services (store use) to be received. The service has been received. Prepaid rent is therefore reduced by $500. No other assets or liabilities are affected. Therefore Owner's Equity is reduced by $500 to reflect this *asset expiration.*

Adjustment (20): Some of the future usefulness of the equipment has been used or has expired. Over the four years of its useful life, this equipment will cost Pat $2,400 (cost $2,500, resale $100). The $2,400 will be the result of the gradual wear and possible growing obsolescence or incapacity of the equipment. Do you think Pat should reduce this asset by $2,400 at the end of the first month? Or should she ignore the eventual "loss" and only record the $2,400 reduction when the equipment is sold? Intuitively you can visualize that neither of these extremes would result in a fair picture during the four years that the equipment will be used. The $2,400 cost or "loss" is best spread (or **allocated**) over the four years of useful life. The $600 per year is $50 per month. Accumulated depreciation immediately beneath equipment should be shown as $50. Accumulated depreciation is a negative or *contra-asset* valuation item. It **subtracts** from total assets. Recording accumulated depreciation of $50 has the effect of reducing total assets by $50. Since no liabilities are affected, owner's equity is reduced by $50 to reflect this asset expiration and to balance.

Adjustment (21): The firm has an additional liability for services performed of $140, and this must be added to Accounts Payable. The benefits of the power and phone service have already been used or consumed; therefore, there is no new asset. Total assets are unchanged and liabilities are increased by $140; therefore, the owner's share of total assets (Owner's Equity) must be reduced by an equal amount to balance.

ILLUSTRATION OF BALANCE SHEET EFFECT

Current Assets		Current Liabilities	
		Accounts Payable	+ 140 (21)
Inventory	− 1,050 (17)		
Supplies	− 125 (18)	Noncurrent Liabilities	
Prepaid Rent	− 500 (19)		
Noncurrent Assets		Owner's Equity	
Accumulated Depreciation			− 1,050 (17)
on Equipment	− 50 (20)		− 125 (18)
			− 500 (19)
			− 50 (20)
			− 140 (21)

Exhibit 4.3 gives the adjusted balance sheet for Potted Planter for the end of the month. This statement gives Pat and any other investors a reasonably fair estimate of her financial position after one month of operation. Study Exhibit 4.3 and compare it to Pat's position immediately following her investment of $10,000 in the firm, which is shown below:

ILLUSTRATION OF BALANCE SHEET EFFECT

Current Assets		Current Liabilities	
Cash	$10,000		
		Owner's Equity	
		Pat Ward, Capital	$10,000
Total Assets	$10,000	Total Equities	$10,000

Is Pat better off at the end of the first month of operations than at the beginning? Her share of assets in the business has gone from $10,000 to $10,585. She is better off by $585. Later in this and subsequent chapters you can learn that *income,* or more precisely *net income,* as recorded by accountants, represents an increase in the owner's well-offness resulting from the firm's activ-

Exhibit 4.3

POTTED PLANTER ADJUSTED BALANCE SHEET
AT END FIRST MONTH

Assets		Equities	
Cash	$7,900	Accounts payable	$1,540
Accounts receivable	350	Total Current Liabilities	$1,540
Inventory	2,850	Noncurrent Note Payable	2,000
Supplies	75	Total Liabilities	$3,540
Prepaid rent	500		
Total Current Assets	$11,675		
Equipment	2,500		
Less accumulated depreciation	(50)	Owner's Equity	10,585
Total Assets	$14,125	Total Equities	$14,125

ities. In this example, Pat is shown to have $585 of net income. This result isn't too bad, considering she has only been really operating—selling to customers—for two weeks.

TRANSACTIONS AND ADJUSTMENTS

Before going any further into the concept of income and how it is measured and reported by accountants, it is important that you clearly understand how different events affecting a balance sheet are recorded. You also need to perceive clearly how each separate event affects the statement. Note that Events (1), (3), (4), and (6) through (16) in the Potted Planter example each involved an exchange of resources and/or obligations with other entities. Cash was paid out for supplies, services, and to settle obligations. Goods and services were received in exchange for an obligation to pay cash. Cash and obligations to receive cash were received in exchange for goods and services. All of these exchanges were completed during the period, and specific information concerning these events was available to Pat before the end of the period. No estimating was necessary. Completed events which involved exchanges with outsiders, and where notification is received prior to the end of the period, are known as *transactions*. The process of recording the effect of, or changes required to reflect, each separate transaction is known as making a *transaction entry*. Note that transaction entries (1), (3), (4), and (6) through (16) each had a dual or complementary effect on the Potted Planter balance sheet. Any change to a particular item required one or more complementary changes to other items, in order to maintain the balance sheet equality. Thus the origin of the term "double-entry system."

Adjustments (17) through (21) were different from transactions.[4] Along with transactions, they recorded an economic change in the firm's position and were balanced (double-entry). However, they either reflected no exchange with outsiders, or else they reflected an incomplete exchange where notification had not been received. Adjusting entries to record asset expirations—inventory, supplies, prepaid rent, and equipment used—did not reflect an exchange with outsiders.[5] The adjusting entry for the telephone and utility obligation did involve an exchange. However, this exchange was not completed, and notification had not been received. The amount owed had to be estimated. The process of recording the effect of each of these adjustments is known as making an *adjusting entry*.

---

[4]   The trend of common usage is to consider all events affecting financial statements as transactions. The distinction between transactions and adjustments herein used has been found to be an effective learning aid.

[5]   Inventory sold to customers did represent an exchange. However, Potted Planter (and many retailers) cannot afford to record the outflow of inventory as it occurs. Sale proceeds from the exchange are recorded, and the merchandise outflows are ignored until the end of the period. Periodic adjustment to reflect merchandise outflow, deterioration, and loss is then processed like an expiration not involving an exchange.

THE FINANCIAL ACCOUNTING SYSTEM

From the Potted Planter example, you can see how important it is for an accountant to record each transaction as it occurs. Otherwise one or more transactions might be forgotten, and the ending balances would be incorrect. The examples in this book involve relatively few transactions, and their effect can be recorded on a single piece of paper. Actual firms have hundreds or even thousands of transactions every month, clearly too many for a single sheet of paper.

The financial accounting system is designed to accommodate many thousands of transactions. Essentially it involves two separate records. The first is a "diary," in which each separate transaction is first recorded when it occurs in terms of its effect upon different accounts. In a sense, this first recording is an instruction regarding how much to change the balances of each account affected by the transaction. This diary of instructions is called the *journal*. Each instruction entered into the journal is called a *journal entry*.

An example of a journal entry would be the one for the Potted Planter transaction (15), where $150 receivables were collected. The journal entry could be written as:

"Increase the cash balance by $150, and decrease the balance of accounts receivable by $150, to record the collection of receivables."

To save writing long sentences each time, accountants record journal entries in a special debit/credit language or code. This code is explained in Chapter 17.

The second major record in the financial accounting system is a collection of all the firm's *accounts*. An account is a file containing a specific type of information—cash, accounts receivable, and so forth. The collection of accounts is known as the *general ledger*. Instructions from the journal are followed by changing the appropriate account balances in the general ledger. This operation is known as *posting*. Note that the ledger is organized by account name, or sometimes by account index number, whereas the journal is a chronological diary of instructions.

Each year, or each accounting period, accountants follow a regular series of steps known as the *accounting cycle*. A simplified version of the accounting cycle can be thought of as:

1. Journalizing transactions as events occur,

2. Posting from the journal to the ledger,

3. Taking a trial balance to make sure no errors in posting or journalizing have destroyed the balance sheet equality,

4. Journalizing and posting year-end adjusting entries,

5. Closing, i.e., transferring balances of any detail subaccounts into the main balance sheet account,

6. Preparing financial statements from ending account balances.

Further information on the accounting cycle may be found in Chapter 17.

INCOME

Investors are always concerned with how well a business is doing, whether or not it is earning a profit and how much. In accounting terminology, the terms income and *earnings* are synonymous with profit. Negative income and negative earnings are synonymous with loss.

Income can be defined as a **net** inflow of assets to the firm resulting from business or operating activities. Assets may flow into a business as a result of creditor or owner investment or, very rarely, from gifts or donations. Such inflows are *not* considered part of income.

Inflows of resources (assets) from customers, or from the firm's investments, in exchange for goods, services, or capital supplied by the firm are defined as *revenues*. Inflows of assets which are donations or investments in the firm are **not** revenues. For the Potted Planter, $2,000 of cash sales and $500 of credit sales represented revenues. Pat Ward's investment of $10,000 did **not** represent revenue. Revenue is usually considered to be earned when a sales transaction is made (product delivered to customer) or when a service has been rendered. There are a few exceptions to this rule, involving long-term contracts, and also situations where the risk of collecting payment is high. These exceptions are covered in later chapters.

Income is the **residual** (or **net**) amount of revenue remaining after deducting the costs of doing business, which are known as *expenses*. Expenses include:

• Current outflows of resources to suppliers or customers,
• Commitments of future resource outflows (debt),
• Expiration of assets,

all of which are intended to produce revenue.

In the Potted Planter example, the following were **expense** items:

$\begin{array}{rl} \$ & 50 \text{ of paint and cleaning materials used} \\ 1,050 & \text{of inventory sold to customers} \\ 125 & \text{of supplies used} \\ 500 & \text{of prepaid rent expiration} \\ 50 & \text{of equipment expiration (depreciation)} \end{array}$

and   140 of commitment to pay for utilities already used

$1,915

There were $1,915 of expenses during the first month. Revenues totaled $2,500. **Since income is measured as revenue minus expense,** the Potted Planter income for the period was $585.

Do you recall that $585 was the precise amount of the increase in Pat's owner's equity from the point immediately following her $10,000 initial investment to the end of the month? This is no coincidence. Income can be measured as the increase in owner well-offness (owner's equity) after **excluding** increases reflecting owner investments and any gifts or donations and assuming no owner withdrawals.

INCOME AND CERTAIN BALANCE SHEET CHANGES

To complete your understanding of the relationship between income and owner's equity, suppose Pat had also withdrawn $400 cash (or other assets) from the business for personal use. The effect on the balance sheet of a $400 *owner withdrawal* of cash would be as shown in the accompanying diagram.

ILLUSTRATION OF BALANCE SHEET EFFECT

Assets		Liabilities
Cash	$-\$400$	
		Owner's Equity
		$-\$400$

Cash would be reduced $400. There would be no other effect on assets or liabilities. Therefore, owner's equity would be reduced $400 to reflect the $400 reduction in total assets.

Had Pat withdrawn the $400, the ending balance sheet would have reported owner's equity as $10,185 instead of $10,585. The change in owner's equity during the month would then only have been an increase of $185. Would this mean that income was only $185? Intuitively, you should reject a notion of income as being dependent on whatever the owner happens to withdraw. In Pat's case, assuming the $400 withdrawal, accountants would still report that the entity—the Potted Planter—had $585 of net income. Of the $585 of increased share of total assets, $400 was withdrawn and $185 retained in the business.

With this understanding you can further understand income and its measurement to be **any change** in owner's equity **not** resulting from:

Donations,
Additional owner investment in the business, or
Owner withdrawals.

In this view, revenues would be any resource inflows which resulted in an increase (+) to owner's equity **except** donations and additional owner investment. Expenses would represent any resource outflows or resource commitments to creditors which resulted in a decrease (−) to owner's equity **except** owner withdrawals.

Exhibit 4.4 demonstrates these relationships for the Potted Planter for the first month of operation. Exhibit 4.4 summarizes all of the transactions and adjustments affecting the firm during the first month. Note especially the boxes for collecting changes to owner's equity. Accountants establish new temporary accounts each year to accumulate revenue and expense information. From these data, the income statement is prepared. At year end, the temporary revenue and expense accounts are "emptied"—closed. The net of their balances is transferred, as income or loss, to owner's equity.

THE ACCRUAL SYSTEM

GAAP requires that financial reporting follow the *accrual basis* rather than the *cash basis*. On the accrual basis, Pat Ward's first month revenue was $2,500. The $2,500 included $2,000 of cash sales plus $500 of monies earned but not yet received. Her expenses, measured on the accrual basis, totaled $1,915. What were her actual cash outflows for business purposes? You are correct if you determine her business cash outflows (not including withdrawals or payments to herself) as $4,250:

$1,000	paid to landlord
50	paid for cleaning items and paint
200	paid for supplies
500	down payment on equipment
2,500	payment on accounts payable
$4,250	

Under cash-basis accounting, Pat would recognize and report only $2,000 of cash revenue. Cash expenses would total $4,250. The Potted Planter would therefore report a $2,250 loss for the first month of operations under cash-basis accounting.

The GAAP accrual system is based on the premise that the actual timing of cash flows is not necessarily relevant to measuring when revenue is actually earned or when expense is actually incurred. Under GAAP, revenue is recognized and reported by accountants when it is earned rather than when the

Exhibit 4.4
POTTED PLANTER

Balance-Sheet Effect of All Transactions and Adjustments During First Month
(All accounts opened with zero balances)
Together with Balance Sheet as of Month End

Assets

Cash		
$ +10,000	(1)	
− 1,000	(3)	
− 50	(4)	
− 200	(7)	
− 500	(8)	
+ 960	(9)	
+ 1,040	(12)	
+ 150	(15)	
− 2,500	(16)	$ 7,900

Accounts Receivable		
+ 220	(10)	
+ 280	(13)	
− 150	(15)	350

Inventory		
+ 3,000	(6)	
+ 500	(11)	
+ 400	(14)	
− 1,050	(17)	2,850

Supplies		
+ 200	(7)	
− 125	(18)	75

Prepaid rent		
+ 1,000	(3)	
− 500	(19)	500

Total Current Assets		$11,675

Equipment	+ 2,500	(8)	2,500
Accumulated depreciation	(50)	(20)	(50)

Total Assets		$14,125

Equities

Accounts Payable		
$ + 3,000	(6)	
+ 500	(11)	
+ 400	(14)	
− 2,500	(16)	
+ 140	(21)	$1,540

Total Current Liabilities		$1,540

Noncurrent notes payable	+ 2,000	(8)	2,000
Total Liabilities			$3,540

Owner's Equity		
$ +10,000	(1)	
+ 2,500 ←		
− 1,915 ←		10,585

Revenues (+)

960	(9)
220	(10)
1,040	(12)
280	(13)

Expenses (−)

50	(4)
1,050	(17)
125	(18)
500	(19)
50	(20)
140	(21)

Total Equities		$14,125

resulting cash is collected. Earned revenue for Pat includes both $2,000 of cash sales and $500 of credit sales, where the additional cash has been earned but not yet received. Exhibit 4.5 compares Pat's expenses on a cash basis and on an accrual basis. Study this exhibit carefully. Can you discern the essential similarities and essential differences between accrual-basis expenses and those determined on a cash basis?

Exhibit 4.5

COMPARISON OF EXPENSES FOR THE POTTED PLANTER
DETERMINED ON A CASH BASIS AND ON AN ACCRUAL BASIS

Item	Cash Expense	Accrual Basis Expense	Explanation of accrual basis expense
Rent	$1,000	$ 500	Only $500 of rental payment has been earned by landlord and used by the Potted Planter.
Cleaning and painting supplies	50	50	These supplies purchased for cash have been used.
Gardening supplies	200	125	Only $125 of gardening supplies purchased for cash have been used.
Equipment	500	50	Only $50 of the cost of the equipment has expired or depreciated.
Inventory	2,500	1,050	Plants costing only $1,050 have been used (sold to customers, died or been stolen)
Utilities	0	140	Although no cash has been paid, $140 of utilities have been used. The utilities companies have earned the $140 and Pat owes it.
	$4,250	$1,915	

Under GAAP, expenses are recognized and reported when they are incurred rather than when the related cash is paid. Therefore, there are three distinct patterns to observe in comparing accrual and cash-basis expenses. These patterns correspond to the three types of expenses described above:

- Cash outflows in the current period for goods and/or services consumed during the same period are expenses under both systems ($50 for cleaning and painting items).
- Commitments to pay cash for goods and/or services already consumed during the period are expenses under the accrual system and are ignored under the cash basis system ($140 of utilities).
- Cash outflows for the acquisition of assets are treated as expenses under the cash basis. Only the portion of the asset which is deemed to have

expired is treated as an expense under the accrual system, regardless of whether cash was exchanged for the asset in the current period or in prior periods. (Prepaid rent, inventory, supplies, and equipment)

The measurement and reporting of financial (accrual basis) income and the reporting of resource flows are two distinct, separate challenges faced by accountants. They both are important as both supply important different information to financial statement users. In the following three chapters, you can investigate them further. In Chapter 5 you can learn of the similarities. Chapters 6 and 7 will cover the differences.

CHAPTER OVERVIEW

Based upon the material introduced in this chapter, you should now be able to:

- Define and describe an executory agreement;
- Distinguish between events which accountants report as changing the firm's financial position and those which do not affect balance sheet amounts;
- Distinguish between transactions and adjustments;
- Demonstrate (in terms of increases and decreases) the effect upon the balance sheet of most common transactions and adjustments;
- Explain why an entry always must have a complementary, or at least a dual, effect;
- Briefly describe the general function of: an account, a journal entry, the journal, posting, and the ledger;
- Briefly describe the accounting cycle and the significance of each step;
- Define and explain the significance of accounting income, revenue, and expense, both in terms of resource flows and also in terms of balance sheet changes;
- Explain the accrual system and how it differs from the cash-basis system.

NEW VOCABULARY AND NEW CONCEPTS

Executory agreement	Invoice
Mature	Collection of receivables

Physical inventory	Journal entry
Asset expiration	Account
Contra-asset	General ledger
Income/earnings	Posting
Net income	Accounting cycle
Transaction	Revenue
Transaction entry	Expense
Adjustment	Owner withdrawal
Adjusting entry	Accrual basis (income)
Journal	Cash basis (income)

- The role of executory agreements in accounting measurement,
- The difference between transactions and adjustments,
- The necessity of double entry,
- Expirations of costs/assets,
- The function of an account, a journal entry, the journal, posting, and the ledger,
- The several steps in the accounting cycle and their purpose,
- Income as revenue minus expense,
- Income as a change in owner's equity not resulting from donations or owner-involved transactions,
- Accrual-basis vs. cash-basis accounting.

REVIEW QUESTIONS

1. Why do accountants record transactions continually throughout the year rather than once a year when statements are prepared?

2. Conversely, why do accountants make adjustments only when necessary for statement preparation instead of continually throughout the year?

3. a) What is an executory agreement? Explain with an example.
   b) What is the effect of an executory agreement on the balance sheet? Explain.

4. What is meant by the expiration or using up of costs or assets? There are four different types of assets which are used or expire in the Potted Planter example. What are they?

5. What is meant by the statement, "This transaction represents a simple exchange of assets"? Give numerical examples of such transactions and explain the effect of each on the balance sheet.

6. What is meant by the statement, "This transaction represents a simple investment of resources in the firm by a creditor or an owner"? Give numerical examples of such transactions and explain the effect of each on the balance sheet.

7. What is meant by the statement, "This transaction represents a simple payment of a liability," or the statement, "This transaction represents a withdrawal of assets by the owner"? Give numerical examples of such transactions and explain the effect of each on the balance sheet.

8. What is meant by the statement, "This transaction represents an inflow of re-

sources from a customer and therefore represents revenue"? Give numerical examples of such transactions and explain the effect of each on the balance sheet.

9. What is meant by the statement, "This transaction or adjustment represents an expense"? Give numerical examples of such transactions demonstrating: a) asset expiration, b) a current cash outflow, c) a commitment for future cash outflow, and explain the effect of each on the balance sheet.

10. In the Potted Planter example, there were five end-of-period adjustments. Four represented adjusting the balance sheet picture for asset expirations, and one was a liability accrual. What is a liability accrual, and why was this done?

11. If, during a year, a firm had total sales all of which were made on account, totalling $100,000, revenues earned would be $100,000 even though perhaps only $80,000 of cash had been collected by year end. Why is revenue $100,000 and not just $80,000? Explain.

12. If total owner's equity is greater at the end of a period than it was at the beginning, there may have been income during the period. What could have occurred which would have resulted in increased owner's equity even if there had been no income?

13. Total owner's equity can be smaller at the end than at the beginning of a year and yet there could still be income earned during the year. Explain with an example how this could be possible.

14. Explain the following items and their function or purpose in the accounting system: a) account, b) journal entry, c) journal, d) posting, e) ledger.

15. What are the major steps in the accounting cycle and what is the purpose of each step?

16. Estimates are necessary and may be significant in the preparation of financial statements. Give two examples of adjustments which required estimates in the Potted Planter case. What exactly was being estimated in each?

MINI-CASES AND QUESTIONS FOR DISCUSSION

MC 4.1 Florence doesn't see any sense in adjusting for asset expirations. She maintains, "I don't see why adjustments have to be made each year for asset expirations. Take a company with a truck costing $10,000, which they plan to use for four years and then sell for $2,000. Why should they take off $2,000 of additional accumulated depreciation each year? Why not have it on the balance sheet as $10,000 until they get rid of it? And even if they do want to reduce the net book value of the truck each year, why should this have any effect on owner's equity? Why don't accountants just leave owner's equity alone unless the owners put more cash in or take cash out? After all, long-term loans are not changed unless there is an additional loan or a repayment. Why treat owner's equity differently?"

Can you clarify to Florence why it is desirable or necessary to record asset expirations each year? And also clarify why asset expirations must have the effect of reducing owner's equity, even though the owners don't take any cash out of the business? Discuss.

MC 4.2 Trent Jones is the manager of a small restaurant. He is concerned with reported income, especially since the restaurant owner gives him a share of profits. The annual income statement has just been prepared, and Trent is arguing with the restaurant's accountant. He says, "Charlie, we made more money than this. This income figure of yours is crazy; it's way too low. I have no quarrel with your revenue figures. Our customers all pay cash, and I know that total is correct.

"But some of these expenses are downright ridiculous. You're including stuff for which we haven't even been billed, let alone haven't paid. There are amounts included in expense for telephone and electric power. We get billed and we pay for those next month. You also are including such things as wages our employees earned between the last payday and the end of the year. Charlie, you know the next payday is next month. That's when they get paid. Those wages should be part of next month/year's expenses. It's O.K. if you want to show these things as owed on the balance sheet. But that has nothing to do with income."

As Charlie, the accountant, what could you explain to Trent to justify your financial statements?

MC 4.3 Is it possible for a firm to report $10,000 of net income, and not have enough excess cash around for the owner to withdraw the $10,000 profit? If so, where is the $10,000? Discuss.

MC 4.4 If reported profit increases owner's equity, why doesn't the owner take his profits out of owner's equity and leave the firm's assets in the business? Discuss.

MC 4.5 Why does GAAP require accrual accounting? If accountants are looking for objectivity, why do they get involved in the estimates required under the accrual system? What could be more objective and verifiable than cash-basis accounting? Cash either comes in or it doesn't; and the same for cash outflows. If everybody uniformly followed cash-basis accounting, wouldn't there be adequate comparability among different firms? In fact, under accrual accounting one firm might estimate one way and another firm another. Wouldn't cash-basis accounting be even more comparable? Discuss these issues.

ESSENTIAL PROBLEMS

EP 4.1 For each of the following events, indicate all the effects, if any, on the balance sheet, using the following codes:

IA   Increase in assets

DA   Decrease in assets

IL   Increase in liabilities

DL   Decrease in liabilities

IO   Increase or ultimately increase owner's equity

DO   Decrease or ultimately decrease owner's equity

NE   No effect on the firm's balance sheet amounts

a) Owner decides to change the name of the business.

b) Owner invests $10,000 in the business.

c) Business borrows $5,000 from the bank.

d) Owner borrows $500 from a finance company for personal use.

e) Customers purchase and receive services from the business for $2,000 cash.

f) Customers purchase and receive services from the business totaling $3,000, on account.

g) Merchandise inventory costing $1,500 is purchased on account.

h) Supplies costing $600 are purchased on account.

i) Customers pay $2,500 on their accounts.

j) Leasehold improvements costing $4,000 are made with a $500 cash payment and the balance on a current note payable.

k) The $5,000 bank loan is repaid together with $400 interest.

l) $1,000 is paid on accounts payable.

m) Owner withdraws $500 from the business for personal use.

EP 4.2 Assume you had a new company, the Easy Company, which had just been started and that events (a) through (m) in Problem EP 4.1 above were related to this company and its owner. Prepare a balance sheet for the Easy Company showing its position after event (m).

EP 4.3 For each of the following adjustments and accruals, indicate all the effects, if any, on the balance sheet using the letter codes given in Problem EP 4.1.

a) Supplies costing $600 have been purchased. At the end of the period, a physical inventory revealed $150 of supplies still unused. The supplies account needs to be adjusted for supplies which have been used.

b) $800 of leasehold improvement has expired and should be amortized.

c) The firm had been the subject (defendant) in a $6,000 lawsuit and had a contingent liability in this amount. The lawsuit has been dropped.

d) At the end of the period, it is determined that the firm owes $200 interest on its leasehold improvement note.

e) At the end of the period, it is estimated that the firm owes $75 for utilities services even though the bills have not yet been received.

EP 4.4 Assume those adjustments and accruals in Problem EP 4.3 pertain to the Easy Company described in Problem EP 4.2. Prepare a balance sheet for the Easy Company, showing its position after both events (a) through (m) and the adjustments and accruals in Problem EP 4.3.

EP 4.5 Data from Fox Company's balance sheet as of the end of the year are shown below. Since the day of the balance sheet, several events listed below have occurred. Considering each event separately, what would be the effect of this event on the firm's financial position? You need not prepare an entire new balance sheet for each event; just indicate the revised amounts for:

> Total Current Assets
> Total Assets
> Total Current Liabilities
> Total Liabilities
> Owner's Equity

BALANCE SHEET DATA AT END OF YEAR

Cash	$4,000
Notes receivable	2,000
Accounts receivable	6,000
Inventory	3,000
Supplies	800
Prepaid items	200
Investments	4,000
Land	1,500
Buildings and equipment	7,000
Less accumulated depreciation	(2,000)
Intangibles	500
Notes payable	3,500
Accounts payable	2,500
Taxes payable	1,600
Other current liabilities	1,400
Long-term note payable	4,500
Owner's equity	?

Events since End of Year

a) The company was burglarized one evening. Merchandise costing $1,200 and not covered by insurance was stolen.

b) Of the $6,000 accounts receivable net, $2,500 was owed by an old reliable customer. The customer was killed in an accident and it is discovered that he is broke and his estate cannot pay his bills.

c) The $4,000 in investments represents corporate bonds. The issuing corporation goes bankrupt and the most the Fox Company can anticipate recovering is $1,200.

d) An explosion does $4,000 worth of damage to the building and equipment. Only $3,000 of repair cost will be recovered from insurance.

e) A pending lawsuit against the company for $10,000 was settled out of court with Fox agreeing to pay $3,000 in two installments. The first installment of $1,500 is due in 90 days, and the second in two years.

EP 4.6 The Daisy Company's accountants prepared a fully adjusted balance sheet as of 12/31/XX, data from which are given below. Since then, several events have taken place. What is the combined effect of all these events on the company's financial position? To show your answer, prepare a new balance sheet reflecting the effect of all of the listed transactions.

12/31/XX BALANCE SHEET

Cash	$ 4,000	Accounts payable	$ 20,000
Accounts receivable	20,000	Other current liabilities	10,000
Inventory	30,000	Total Current Liabilities	$ 30,000
Total Current Assets	$ 54,000	Total Liabilities	$ 30,000
Equipment (net)	70,000	Owner's equity	94,000
Total Assets	$124,000	Total Equities	$124,000

Transactions

1. The company had sales to customers, all on credit, totaling $35,000.

2. The cost of the merchandise that was sold to customers for $35,000 was $20,000.

3. $15,000 is collected on accounts receivable.

4. $12,000 is paid on accounts payable.

5. $10,000 is borrowed from the bank on a note payable due in two years.

EP 4.7 Data from the George Company's balance sheet as of the end of the year are given below. (a) What was the accounting measurement of the capital invested in the company as of the balance sheet date? Who is providing this capital to the firm? (b) How much was provided by short-term creditors? (c) By long-term creditors? (d) By the owners? (e) If the owner had only actually put into the company $160,000, how much profit had the company accumulated since its beginning which the owner had not withdrawn for personal use?

Total Current Assets	$200,000
Total Assets	500,000
Total Current Liabilities	100,000
Total Liabilities	125,000

EP 4.8 Selected data from the year-end balance sheets for the years 19X1 and 19X2 for both the Able Company and the Baker Company are given below. You may assume that both firms are in the same type of business and that their capacity assets were all recently acquired.

a) Which firm has the greater amount of capital invested as of the end of 19X2?

b) Which firm, as of the end of 19X2, has the greater proportion of capital supplied by creditors, i.e., is more heavily in debt?

c) Which firm during 19X2 increased its size in terms of total capital invested?

d) Assuming no owner withdrawals or investment during 19X2, had either firm had a loss (negative profit) during the year? Explain.

Able Company	19X2	19X1
Total Current Assets	$300,000	$305,000
Total Assets	400,000	425,000
Total Current Liabilities	150,000	105,000
Total Liabilities	200,000	155,000

Baker Company

Total Current Assets	$100,000	$ 90,000
Total Assets	300,000	250,000
Total Current Liabilities	75,000	80,000
Total Liabilities	200,000	150,000

SUPPLEMENTARY PROBLEMS

SP 4.9 The Wade Company's year-end balance sheet for 19X2 is given below. During the following year—19X3—these events occurred:

- Total sales to customers amounted to $600,000, $50,000 for cash and the balance on account.
- $540,000 was collected on accounts receivable. There were no anticipated uncollectible accounts.
- An additional $10,000 of marketable securities were purchased for cash.
- The note receivable was collected together with $450 of interest.
- Inventory costing $400,000 was purchased on credit.
- Supplies costing $5,000 were purchased for cash.
- $3,000 of additional prepaid items were purchased on credit.
- All current liabilities at the beginning of the year were paid in full.
- $350,000 was paid on accounts payable.
- Other costs of operations during the year amounted to $100,000 and all were paid in cash.
- Year-end merchandise inventory amounted to $110,000.
- Year-end supplies inventory amounted to $13,000.

WADE COMPANY 19X2 YEAR-END BALANCE SHEET

Cash	$ 10,000	Notes payable	$ 15,000
Marketable securities	25,000	Accounts payable	90,000
Notes receivable	5,000	Taxes payable	14,000
Accounts receivable (net)	75,000	Other current liabilities	6,000
Inventory	100,000	Total Current Liabilities	$125,000
Supplies	28,000	Long-term notes payable	175,000
Prepaid items	7,000	Total Liabilities	$300,000
Total Current Assets	$250,000		
Investments	110,000	Owner's equity	600,000
Land	60,000		
Buildings and equipment	510,000		
Less accumulated depreciation	(70,000)		
Intangibles	40,000		
Total Assets	$900,000	Total Equities	$900,000

- Prepaid items costing $5,000 were determined to have expired.
- Buildings and equipment depreciated an additional $60,000.
- $12,000 of intangibles were determined to have expired.
- It was estimated at year end that $20,000 in current liabilities existed which had not yet been recorded, and for which the services had been used up. This $20,000 was broken down into $7,000 accounts payable, $10,000 taxes payable, and $3,000 miscellaneous.

Prepare a year-end balance sheet for the Wade Company for 19X3.

SP 4.10 Refer to the Wade Company 19X2 balance sheet in Problem SP 4.9 above. Assume that, instead of the events listed in Problem SP 4.9, a different set of events occurred during 19X3. Prepare a year-end 19X3 balance sheet based on the following different events that occurred during 19X3.

- Sales to customers were $500,000, all on credit.
- Collections on accounts receivable were $475,000, and there were no anticipated uncollectible accounts.
- $15,000 of marketable securities were sold at their cost.
- The note receivable was extended for another year. However, $600 in interest was collected.
- Inventory at a cost of $300,000 was purchased on credit.
- Supplies at a cost of $2,000 were purchased on credit.
- All current liabilities at the beginning of the year, except the current note payable, were paid in full.
- $1,200 interest was paid on the current note payable, and the note was refinanced with a new note in the same amount, due next year.
- $200,000 was paid on accounts payable.
- $50,000 of other operating costs were incurred during the year and paid in cash.
- Year-end merchandise inventory amounted to $150,000.
- Year-end supplies inventory amounted to $10,000.
- All prepaid items were determined to have expired.
- Buildings and equipment depreciated an additional $70,000.
- $10,000 of intangibles were estimated to have expired.
- Year-end accrued liabilities, with no corresponding new assets, were:

      $ 5,000   Accounts payable
       12,000   Taxes payable
        3,000   Miscellaneous

- The owner withdrew $39,400 in cash for personal use.

5

INCOME,
WORKING CAPITAL,
AND
FUNDS FROM
OPERATIONS

CHAPTER PREVIEW

The objective of this chapter is to develop further your understanding of income as measured and reported by accountants, and of the relationship both to "funds from operations" and also to change in owner well-offness. In this chapter, you can:

- Reinforce your understanding of the concepts of revenue and expense;
- See clearly that resource inflows representing revenue are reflected as an increase in owner's equity, that resource outflows representing expense are reflected as a decrease, and that the difference reflects and measures income to the owner;
- Learn how income statement information may be presented, and how this information may be interpreted and used;
- Learn why accountants establish temporary accounts each year for revenue and expense items, and how these accounts are affected by various transactions and adjustments;
- Expand your knowledge of year-end adjustments to include "accruals" and "deferrals" which are necessary to measure income appropriately;
- Develop an understanding of the various meanings of the word "funds" and of the concept of "funds from operations" referring to changes in net working capital;
- Learn of the similarities between income and funds from operations.

With this awareness, you will be in a position to acquire a full understanding of net income, the income statement, and the important articulation and interrelationships among the balance sheet, the income statement, and the statement of changes in financial position. With a clear picture of the many similarities between income and funds from operations you will have the necessary perspective to grasp readily the few possible dissimilarities and to understand how the differences between these two measurements may be reconciled.

NEED FOR INCOME DETAIL

Mike Kowalcezk is the owner-manager of a chain of five mod clothing stores. The stores are known simply as "Mike's Stores," and they carry mostly men's and women's jeans and tops. Beginning in February of 19X0, Mike decided to also make shoes, sneakers, and sandals available to his customers. Since he was not familiar with the shoe business, he arranged with a local shoe retailer to sell through his stores. The shoe company has a contract with Mike which provides that it will pay a minimum rental (for the space used) of $300 per month per store, *or* ten percent of total shoe-sales revenue, whichever is greater.

Mike's father had been in the retail clothing business. His father had suffered a major financial loss when a new freeway made it difficult for customers to come to his store, which eventually had to be closed for lack of business. The loss came from liquidation of the fixed assets in the business—land, building, equipment, and so forth—which had been owned by Mike's father. In reaction to his father's experience, Mike has a policy of *not owning any of the fixed assets involved in his business.* On a short-term basis, he rents his stores, display equipment, and even his cash registers.

Mike's business seems to be doing very well. Balance sheets for Mike's Stores for 1/31/X1 and 1/31/X2 are given in Exhibit 5.1. Exhibit 5.2 includes summary transactions and adjustments which were recorded during the year and which are cross-referenced on Exhibit 5.1. Study these two exhibits carefully. Trace the balance sheet effect of each transaction and adjustment to reinforce the material you learned in Chapter 4.

Note that the balance sheets are dated as of January 31 and not December 31. Mike's *fiscal year* is not the same as the calendar year. Many retailers' fiscal years end in January. By the end of January, the Christmas season has been completed, merchandise exchanges and returns have been processed, and any excess inventory has been reduced through post-Christmas sales. For most retailers, the end of January provides a much better time to consider one business year completed and another about to begin.

Also note, on Exhibit 5.1, that revenues, expenses, and owner withdrawals are separately grouped, and that they each affect owner's equity. If Mike had not withdrawn $135,000 of profits, owner's equity at year end would have been $422,500. The sum of $422,500 would have represented a $155,500 increase in owner's share of total assets over the beginning of the year. What was the firm's income for fiscal 19X1?

Mike has recently joined a trade association of retail clothiers. One reason for joining was that members' financial data are collected anonymously and averaged by the association. The averaged data are then supplied to members for use in comparing their individual performance with that of the hypothetical "average" firm. The most recent trade-association data are provided on Exhibits 5.3 and 5.4.

Exhibit 5.1

MIKE'S STORES

Balance Sheets as of 1/31/19X1 and 1/31/19X2
Together with Summary Transactions and Adjustments for the Year

	Beginning balance	Transactions and adjustments		Ending balance
Assets				
Cash	$100,000	(1) +450,000	(4) +850,000	
		(6) − 96,000	(9) −849,000	
		(11) −285,440	(12) − 9,500	
		(13) + 61,000	(14) −135,000	$ 86,060
Accounts receivable	120,000	(2) +1,000,000	(3) −130,000	
		(4) −850,000		140,000
Accrued rent receivable		(19) + 5,440		5,440
Inventory	130,000	(5) +815,000	(15) −800,000	145,000
Total Assets	$350,000			$376,500
Equities				
Accounts payable	$ 65,000	(5) +815,000	(7) + 17,250	
		(8) + 18,000	(9) −849,000	
		(17) + 2,000	(18) + 1,750	$ 70,000
Wages payable	18,000	(10) +267,440	(11) −285,440	
		(16) + 19,000		19,000
Owner's equity	267,000	(14) −135,000	+1,516,440	
			−1,360,940	287,500
Total Equities	$350,000			$376,500

Owner withdrawal	Revenue	Expenses
(14) −135,000	(1) +450,000	(3) −130,000
	(2) +1,000,000	(6) − 96,000
	(13) + 61,000	(7) − 17,250
	(19) + 5,440	(8) − 18,000
		(10) −267,440
		(12) − 9,500
		(15) −800,000
		(16) − 19,000
		(17) − 2,000
		(18) − 1,750

Exhibits 5.3 and 5.4 differ only in the presentation of information. Exhibit 5.3 is an income statement presented in a *single-step format*. Exhibit 5.4 is presented in a *multiple-step format*. Note that the information on Exhibit 5.4 is ordered so as to make possible an additional subtotal for trading margin or *gross profit*. Gross profit (or *gross margin*) is simply the difference between the net sales amount and total cost of the merchandise sold. It represents the amount of profit available to cover other operating expenses of running a

Exhibit 5.2

MIKE'S STORES

Summary Transactions and Adjustments
For the Fiscal Year 19X1

Transactions

(1) Cash sales $ 450,000
(2) Credit sales = Sales return 1,000,000
(3) Returns and allowances on credit sales 130,000
(4) Receivables collections 850,000
(5) Purchases of merchandise on account 815,000
(6) Payments of store rental 96,000
(7) Utilities bills received 17,250
(8) Bookkeeping fees billed 18,000
(9) Payments on accounts payable 849,000
(10) Wages earned and recorded 267,440
(11) Payments on wages payable 285,440
(12) Payments for incidental expenses 9,500
(13) Collections from shoe company 61,000 — Other revenue
(14) Owner withdrawals 135,000

Adjustments

(15) Cost of goods sold 800,000
(16) Wages earned but not recorded 19,000
(17) Bookkeeper fee earned but not yet billed to Mike 2,000
(18) Utilities used but not yet billed to Mike 1,750
(19) Shoe store rentals/profit share not yet received 5,440 — Other revenue

---

Exhibit 5.3

REPRESENTATIVE INCOME STATEMENT
FOR AVERAGE MEMBER (SINGLE-STEP FORMAT)
PUBLISHED BY TRADE ASSOCIATION FOR 19X1
(000 omitted)

GROSS SALES		$2,100
Less sales returns and allowances		100
Net Sales		$2,000
Other revenues		80
Total Revenues		$2,080
Operating Expenses:		
Cost of goods sold	$1,246	
Store depreciation	100	
Equipment depreciation	44	
Utilities	28	
Wages and salaries	320	
Bookkeeping services	30	
Incidentals	12	1,780
Income from Operations		$ 300
Funds from Operations		$ 444

Exhibit 5.4

REPRESENTATIVE INCOME STATEMENT FOR AVERAGE MEMBER
(MULTIPLE-STEP FORMAT)
PUBLISHED BY TRADE ASSOCIATION FOR FISCAL YEAR 19X1
(000 omitted)

		$	%
GROSS SALES		$2,100	
Less sales returns and allowances		100	5.0
Net Sales		$2,000	100.0
Less cost of goods sold		1,246	62.3
Gross Profit		$ 754	37.7
Less other operating expenses:			
Store depreciation	$100		5.0
Equipment depreciation	44		2.2
Utilities	28		1.4
Wages and salaries	320		16.0
Bookkeeping services	30		1.5
Incidentals	12	534	0.6
Other revenues		80	4.0
Income from Operations		$ 300	15.0
Funds from Operations		$ 444	

Exhibit 5.5

MIKE'S STORES

Income Statement for Year Ending 1/31/X1 (Fiscal year 19X0)
(000 omitted)

GROSS SALES		$1,327
Less sales returns and allowances		97
Net Sales		$1,230
Less cost of goods sold		747
Gross Profit		$ 483
Less operating expenses:		
Store rental	$ 89	
Equipment rental	0	
Utilities	17	
Wages and salaries	251	
Bookkeeping services	18	
Incidentals	9	384
Other revenues		57
Income from Operations		$ 156

business and, it is hoped, to provide an excess which will be net income to the owner. Either the single-step format or the multiple-step format is acceptable following GAAP.

Included with the trade-association data are percentages for each item based on net sales. These percentages enable members with different dollar revenue and expense amounts to readily compare the proportions of different items to a common base. For example, should one member's utilities expenses be currently 4 percent of sales while the industry average is only 2 percent, that member might wish to investigate why this expense is proportionately higher, and whether it should and could be reduced. Also included is information identified as *working capital funds from (provided by) operations*. This term will be defined later in this chapter.

Mike wishes to avail himself of the possible benefits of using the trade-association data. He wishes to compare the performance of his store both with the industry average and with his own performance last year. He asks you to make these comparisons for him, and to advise him on how well he is doing and of any specific areas that may require further investigation. Data for Mike's Stores for the fiscal year 19X0 are included as Exhibit 5.5. You will need to prepare an income statement for the fiscal year 19X1 for Mike's Stores. Then you will need to compare and analyze Mike's performance with the trade-association data for that year, and with Mike's performance in 19X0.

PREPARING AN INCOME STATEMENT

Recall, from Chapter 4, that revenues are inflows of assets from customers and other business activities, and that their balance sheet effect is to increase owner's equity. Expenses are asset expirations, outflows of assets, or commitments for future asset outflows involved in the generation of revenues. The balance sheet effect of expenses is a reduction of owner's equity. Since information relating to gross profit may be valuable for your analysis and for Mike, Exhibit 5.4 should be used as the model for comparison. Starting with the information supplied on Exhibits 5.1 and 5.2, you should first prepare an income statement for Mike for fiscal 19X1, following the format of Exhibit 5.4. Complete this income statement before proceeding with this chapter.

SALES REVENUE

Business revenue is generally referred to as *sales*. Sales refers to selling transactions that have been completed with customers, where the customers have legal title to goods or services, and the seller has acquired either cash or accounts receivable in exchange. Revenue may also take the form of commissions, fees, or interest earned, depending upon the type of business. Financial statement users are primarily interested in *net sales,* and many income statements start with this figure. Net sales represents the revenue which the firm finally ended with, after deducting any *sales returns and allowances*.

Sales returns are self-explanatory. Sales allowances usually refer to special discounts granted to customers after the sale and in settlement of the customer's account.[1]

From Exhibits 5.1 and 5.2 you can see that transactions (1), (2), and (3) pertain to gross sales revenue and sales returns and allowances. Net sales for the year for Mike's Stores would, therefore, be $1,320,000. Exhibit 5.6 gives Mike's income statement for fiscal 19X1.

Exhibit 5.6

MIKE'S STORES

Income Statement for the Year Ending 1/31/X2 (Fiscal 19X1)

GROSS SALES		$1,450,000
Less sales returns and allowances		130,000
Net Sales		$1,320,000
Less cost of goods sold:		
Beginning inventory	$130,000	
Plus purchases	815,000	
Goods available for sale	$945,000	
Less ending inventory	145,000	
Equals cost of goods sold		800,000
GROSS PROFIT		$ 520,000
Less operating expenses:		
Store rental	$ 96,000	
Equipment rental	0	
Utilities	19,000	
Wages and salaries	286,440	
Bookkeeping services	20,000	
Incidentals	9,500	430,940
Other revenue		66,440
Income from Operations		$ 155,500

OTHER REVENUE

Businesses may have revenues other than and in addition to sales. These secondary sources of revenue are normally shown separately and identified as *other revenue*, or by the specific type of revenue involved. Specific types of other revenue which you might encounter could involve revenue from secondary operations: for example, rent for use of excess capacity, gains on disposal of noncurrent assets, and so forth. "Other revenue" can also result

---

[1]   Sales allowances can include a discount for prompt payment of bills or because of damaged merchandise. These items will be covered in Chapter 8. Note that volume or trade discounts from posted or "sticker" prices, which are given at the time of sales (sales price reduced) and not afterwards, are not recorded. Sales are originally recorded net of trade and volume discounts.

from *financial activities*—lending or investing resources. Examples of such revenues would include interest earned and earnings on ownership investments. In Mike's case, transactions (13) and (19) represent "other revenue."

OPERATING EXPENSES

Business expenses are generally reported by type, and each different type that is material in amount is listed separately on the income statement. There is no standardized terminology or ordering of operating expenses on income statements. Individual firms classify expenses in the manner they feel will be most informative to the user of their statements. Often a "miscellaneous" category is shown. It will include those expenses too insignificant in amount to warrant separate disclosure. A common but not uniform practice for firms whose primary business is selling a product is to show *cost of goods sold* immediately following net sales. Cost of goods sold represents the expense of inventory transferred to customers as part of a sale. It also includes normal inventory *shrinkage*—loss through theft, spoilage, and damage.

Following cost of goods sold, many firms will show a subtotal for *gross profit*. Gross profit (or *gross margin* or *trading profit*) represents the difference between the costs and the selling prices of all the goods sold. Firms whose primary business is selling services instead of products will, of course, not report cost of goods sold or gross profit. These items would be irrelevant and meaningless to such firms.

Following gross profit will be listed all of the other *operating expenses* of the business in whatever degree of detail the firm believes appropriate. Operating expenses are all those expenses which are clearly not extraordinary.[2] In the case of Mike's Stores, transactions (6), (7), (8), (10), and (12), together with adjustments (16), (17), and (18), all represent such other operating expenses.

INCOME FROM OPERATIONS

Following ordinary revenues and expenses on the income statement, there should always be a subtotal for *income from operations*. Income from operations is sometimes called *operating income*, *operating profit*, or *operating earnings*. It represents the firm's profit for the period excluding any extraordinary gains or losses or effects of discontinued operations. Extraordinary items and discontinued-operations items will be discussed in Chapter 6. At this point it is important that you understand that income from operations reflects all revenues and expenses which are normal or which may recur.

---

2   Extraordinary items are those which are material in amount, very unusual in nature and not expected to recur in the foreseeable future. Extraordinary items will be discussed more fully in Chapter 6.

Therefore, the income-from-operations subtotal provides the user with a basis for forecasting the future.

USING INCOME STATEMENT INFORMATION

The detailed information in the income statement can be very valuable in analyzing a firm's performance. It reveals how efficiently the firm is using up resources (expenses) in order to generate new resources (revenues) from customers. The statement can be compared with those of prior years for the same firm, in order to uncover trends in revenues, expenses, and profit. It can also be used for comparison with statements of firms operating similar types of businesses, or with industry averages.

Mike asked you to give him advice on how well he was doing and what he might do to improve his profit. What are the criteria or guidelines you might use to compare his performance with the data provided by the trade association in Exhibit 5.4? To compare absolute dollar amounts between the two statements would be futile and probably meaningless, because the representative firm (industry average) has a much larger volume. To provide a meaningful basis for comparison, the data on both statements are converted to percentages. Customarily, the base (or denominator) for the percentage calculations is net sales and not gross sales. Exhibit 5.7 shows the two statements comparatively, but with the data converted to percentages. In studying this exhibit, you should be careful not to attach too much significance to minor

Exhibit 5.7

COMPARATIVE INCOME ANALYSIS

Trade Association Average and Mike's Stores

	Association average %	Mike's Stores %
GROSS SALES		
Less sales returns and allowances	5.0	9.8
Net Sales	100.0	100.0
Less cost of goods sold	62.3	60.6
Gross Profit	37.7	39.4
Less operating expenses:		
Store depreciation/rental	5.0	7.3
Equipment depreciation/rental	2.2	0
Utilities	1.4	1.4
Wages and salaries	16.0	21.7
Bookkeeping services	1.5	1.5
Incidentals	0.6	0.7
Other revenues	4.0	5.0
Income from Operations	15.0	11.8

variations. No two firms are identical, and the trade association data are for a *hypothetically* average firm. For example, Mike leases both his store and equipment together, whereas the association data shows these items separately as depreciation expense. Mike's 7.3 percent of sales for this item is practically identical with the 7.2 percent for the association figures combined. The slight difference probably represents his cost of leasing as compared to owning.

From the information presented in Exhibit 5.7, what is your evaluation of Mike's performance? Are there any items he should particularly investigate? You might give Mike the following advice:

1. Although he is making substantial profits, he does not appear to be doing as well as the industry "norm." Industry income averages 15 percent of sales. Mike is earning only 11.8 percent. Had his performance been up to industry average, fiscal 19X1 earnings would have been about $42,500 (3.2 percent of sales) greater.

2. The three areas apparently requiring further investigation are returns and allowances, gross profit, and wages and salaries expense. The high percentage for customer returns allowances (proportionately twice the industry average) could result from excessive hard selling by sales persons, poor quality of merchandise sold, or something else. It should be investigated. Higher-than-average gross profits could indicate an ideal situation where customers were just willing to pay more at Mike's Stores than at others. Mike might look into the possibility of increasing total profits by increasing sales volume with a reduced gross profit percentage. Lower prices or more price discounting might significantly increase volume. Higher-quality merchandise (and therefore greater cost) might also have this effect.

A significantly higher expense for wages of employees more than accounts for all of Mike's lower profits when compared with industry averages (5.7 percent higher wage expense vs. 3.2 percent lower income). Mike probably should first focus his attention on this item. It might indicate simple inefficiency, unnecessarily high pay scales, a reflection of excessive, work involved in processing the high volume of customer returns, or other possible causes which might be subject to corrective actions.

You need not pursue further the analysis of Mike's comparative income. Comparative analysis of funds from operations will be discussed later in this chapter. Exhibit 5.8 combines the information from Exhibits 5.5 and 5.6, to facilitate your trend analysis of the changes in revenue and expense items from prior years. Once again, these data are in percentage terms, for ease of comparison. Can you gain any further insight into the firm's operations from this exhibit? Is there anything further you would like to tell Mike?

As a result of analyzing Exhibit 5.8, you might more forcefully recommend that Mike check into sales returns and allowances and wage costs. Net

Exhibit 5.8

TREND ANALYSIS OF INCOME STATEMENTS

Mike's Stores Income Statements for the Fiscal Years 19X0 and 19X1

	19X1 %	19X0 %
GROSS SALES		
Less sales returns and allowances	9.8	7.9
Net Sales	107.3/100.0*	100.0
Less cost of goods sold	60.6	60.7
Gross Profit	39.4	39.3
Less operating expenses:		
Store rental	7.3	7.2
Equipment rental	0	0
Utilities	1.4	1.4
Wages and salaries	21.7	20.4
Bookkeeping services	1.5	1.5
incidentals	.7	.7
Other revenues	5.0	4.6
Income from Operations	11.8	12.7

* Note that net sales data provide both comparison with prior year's sales volume and the base for other items on current year's statement.

sales had increased 7.3 percent or $90,000.[3] Income had **proportionally** decreased 0.9 percent of sales or $11,880 less than might have been anticipated from increased sales. Sales returns and allowances were up 1.9 percent or $25,080 over the amount to be expected with increased sales. Wages were up 1.3 percent or $17,160, proportionally more than would be expected to result from increased sales volume. Chapter 13 will go into the analysis of income statements and the many uses of income statement information in more detail. Remember, financial statements can provide the intelligent user with directions as to which business activities might require further investigation. They do not tell you what to do.

TEMPORARY ACCOUNTS FOR REVENUES AND EXPENSES

Refer once more to Exhibit 5.1. The various revenue and expense effects on owner's equity were given as yearly summary entries. Only one entry is given for all cash sales for the year, and so forth. In Mike's Stores, entries would be made daily or weekly. There could be hundreds or thousands of "pluses" and "minuses" to owner's equity for various revenue and expense items. Imagine what it would be like to go back over thousands of such changes to owner's equity at year end to try to put together an income statement. Probably many hundreds of years ago, the first bookkeeper said, "Never again!"

---

[3] $1,320,000 of 19X1 net sales equaled 107.3 percent of 19X0 sales.

Accountants each year set up new temporary holding accounts for each revenue and expense item. Revenue pluses to owner's equity are temporarily stored in revenue accounts. Each type of expense minus is similarly accumulated in a distinct expense account. After all transactions and adjustments have been recorded at year end, the net balance in each account provides the data for the income statement.

All the temporary revenue and expense accounts are then *closed*, and their combined net effect (equivalent to net income) adjusts owner's equity at year end. "Closing" merely means to close out (or empty) one account by transferring its balance to another. Because of the use of temporary revenue and expense accounts, during the year the balance sheet accounts, by themselves, will not balance. Owner's equity will need to be updated as a result of closing all the temporary revenue and expense accounts, before the balance sheet will balance.

NET WORKING CAPITAL

Before reviewing some typical transactions and adjustments which affect income, turn for a moment to the concept of net working capital. Remember, from Chapter 3, that working capital is a term nonaccountants often use to mean current assets; and *net* working capital means *net current assets*, or current assets minus current liabilities. One of the common measures of resource flows within the firm is the *flow of working capital* or, more precisely, net working capital. A working capital flow is defined as any event (transaction or adjustment) where the balance sheet effect is a change in the balance of net working capital.

To readily identify a working capital flow, study the following diagram. The balance sheet diagram with which you are already familiar is here modified by the addition of a wavy line separating current from noncurrent assets and liabilities.

BALANCE SHEET DIAGRAM

Current Assets	Current Liabilities
Noncurrent Assets	Noncurrent Liabilities
	Owner's Equity
	Revenues (+) and Expenses (−)

Note also the dotted box shown within the Owner's Equity section. It indicates revenue and expense accounts which ultimately affect owner's equity. Can you see that **any single event** simultaneously affecting balance sheet accounts **both above and below** the wavy line **must** result in a change in the balance of net working capital? Any change in the balance of working capital is defined as a flow of working capital. Can you visualize that **any event** where **all** of the balance sheet accounts affected are either **above or below** the wavy line can have **no effect** on the balance of net working capital, and therefore, does **not** represent a working capital flow?

TYPICAL TRANSACTIONS AFFECTING BOTH INCOME AND NET WORKING CAPITAL

To see the relationships between certain income-related transactions and working capital flow, you should review some of the most common transactions occurring during the year that affect **both** income and net working capital. In Chapter 4 you reviewed many of these same types of entries for the Potted Planter in terms of their ultimate effect on owner's equity. Now you can examine the effect of similar entries on net working capital, and also on the temporary revenue and expense accounts. You know that the revenue and expense accounts, in turn, will eventually affect owner's equity.

Revenue Transactions

To record sales to customers for cash, accountants will make an entry which:

- Increases cash (an asset), and
- Increases sales (a revenue account eventually increasing owner's equity).

Credit sales are recorded by:

- Increasing accounts receivable, and
- Increasing sales.

Current revenues other than sales are similarly recorded. The appropriate current asset account is increased, together with an equal increase of a revenue account. Note that a collection of a previously recorded receivable represents merely an exchange of assets within the firm. It does not represent additional revenue. The revenue usually is recognized at the time a revenue-related receivable is first recorded.

Sales and other revenue transactions involving the receipt of cash or current receivables represent an inflow of working capital. As a result of such an event, current assets are increased. Owner's equity is equivalently increased through a revenue account. (See the accompanying diagram.)

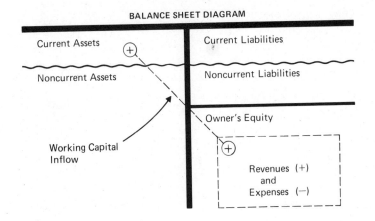

BALANCE SHEET DIAGRAM

Note that accounts are affected both above and below the wavy line. Revenue transactions involving cash or current receivables always represent a working capital inflow.

Expense Transactions

Sales returns and allowances may be considered as an expense or as contra-revenue (negative or opposite to revenue).

- Sales Returns and Allowances is increased. (This will eventually result in a **decrease** to owner's equity.) Debit
- Accounts Receivable or Cash is decreased (depending upon whether the merchandise has been paid for).

Expense transactions can follow one of two patterns. When cash or another asset is disbursed **not** for acquisition of another asset, payment of a previously recorded liability, or as a distribution (withdrawal) involving the owner, there is an expense. The accountant records:

- An increase to the appropriate expense account (which will eventually have the effect of reducing owner's equity);
- Decrease to Cash (or the other asset distributed).

Similarly, as a previously recorded asset expires, or when it becomes worthless, the accountant:

- Increases the appropriate expense account;
- Decreases the current asset account (or increases a contra-asset valuation account like Allowance for Uncollectibles, which subtracts from total assets).

Expenses which record the disbursement or expiration of current assets all represent working capital outflows. The expense reduces current assets,

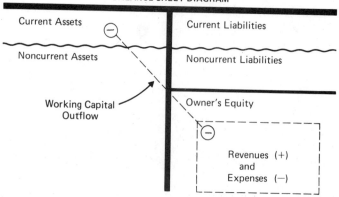

BALANCE SHEET DIAGRAM

and eventually owner's equity, via an expense account. Net working capital is reduced.

The second expense-transaction pattern involves the incurrence of an additional current liability to a creditor, where a new asset does **not** result from the exchange. For these events the accountant:

- Increases the appropriate expense account (which eventually reduces owner's equity);

- Increases the related liability account.

Expenses of this type also represent working capital outflows. Current liabilities are increased with no change to current assets. A balance of net working capital is therefore decreased, representing an outflow of net working capital.

BALANCE SHEET DIAGRAM

Current Assets	Current Liabilities ⊕
Noncurrent Assets	Noncurrent Liabilities ← Net Working Capital Outflow
	Owner's Equity
	Revenues (+) and Expenses (−) ⊖

Transactions Not Involving Revenue or Expense

Some other transactions affecting current assets or liabilities do **not** involve either revenue or expense. This group includes:

- Exchanges of current assets (receivables collections, purchase of another current asset with cash, and liquidation of current assets at accounting value with no gain or loss)—see arrow A on the diagram below;
- Payment of a previously recorded liability—see arrow B on the diagram below;
- Obtaining current assets in exchange for a short-term liability—see arrow C;
- Exchanging current liabilities (giving suppliers current notes payable in settlement of accounts)—see arrow D.

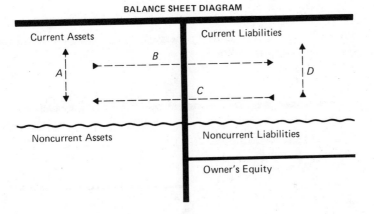

These transactions do **not** affect either the balance of net working capital or owner's equity through revenue or expense. They do **not** affect income or represent working capital flows.

ADJUSTMENTS AFFECTING INCOME AND NET WORKING CAPITAL

As you can recall, adjustments are necessary at year end to update assets and liabilities for certain events. Some of these adjustments are anticipations of information that has not yet been received. Others are for asset expirations, notification of which is never specifically received. Adjustments may also be required in order to defer recognition of revenue or expense to future years. In this chapter, we will focus upon only those adjustments affecting current assets and current liabilities. Adjustments necessary for noncurrent assets and noncurrent liabilities will be reviewed in Chapter 6.

Remember that GAAP requires use of an accrual measurement system as distinct from a cash-basis system. The term "accrual system" is commonly understood to include both *accruals* and *deferrals*. Adjustments of current assets and current liabilities for events which have transpired, and in anticipation of information not yet received, are called accruals. Common examples of accruals would include:

1. The firm, as a secondary activity, is renting an unused asset to someone. At year end, $400 of rent has been earned but not billed or paid. An accrual adjustment is necessary to:

   Increase accrued rent receivable (an asset),

   Increase rent revenue (an account for nonoperating revenue).

2. The firm has a note receivable outstanding on which $100 interest is owed but unpaid. An accrual adjustment is necessary to:

   Increase accrued interest receivable (an asset),

   Increase interest revenue (a nonoperating revenue account).

Accrued current revenue results in an increase to current assets and therefore represents a working capital inflow.

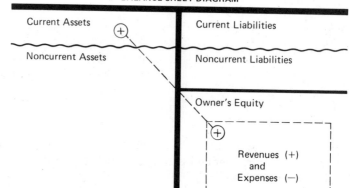

BALANCE SHEET DIAGRAM

3. The firm is renting an asset or borrowing money and there is an unpaid amount owed at year end. The other person's accrued rent or interest receivable would be your accrued rent or interest payable. His revenue would be your expense. Your accountant would record:

   • An increase to the appropriate expense account,

   • An increase to the accrued (current) liability.

4. The firm has other expenses which have been incurred but where the current liability has not yet been recorded or paid. Examples would include wages owed since the last payday, utilities consumed but not yet billed,

and so forth. The adjustment would involve increasing an accrued current liability and increasing the appropriate expense account.

Adjustments involving current liability accruals and corresponding expenses result in an increase in current liabilities with no change in current assets. Net working capital is thus reduced, and these events represent net working capital outflows.

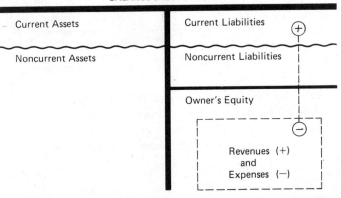

BALANCE SHEET DIAGRAM

Accruals are just one type of year-end "fine-tuning" adjustment of the financial statements. The objective is to see that all assets and liabilities are current as of the balance sheet date. Concurrently, revenues and expenses are matched in the current period. *Matching* involves making sure that all revenue earned in the current year is recorded, whether or not billed and regardless of whether or not cash has been received. Expenses are similarly matched with revenue in the same period.

In the case of Mike's Stores, there were three year-end adjustments to record accrued expenses: $19,000 of wages earned but not yet recorded or paid, a $2,000 bookkeeper fee, and $1,750 of utilities consumed. There was also an example of a revenue accrual. The sum of $5,440 of rent/profit share from the shoe store was earned but had not been recorded or received.

Year-end adjustments, other than accruals, include recording expirations of current assets and the corresponding expense. Examples would include: recording the cost of inventory delivered to customers, spoiled, damaged, or stolen; the cost of supplies used; and the expiration of prepaid items. Each of these adjustments reduces net working capital and represents a working capital outflow.

For Mike's Stores, an example of an adjustment made that was not an accrual involved the $800,000 of inventory which was determined to have been used.

Finally, adjustments could include deferrals. A sale previously recorded as revenue might not have been completed at year end. The merchandise might not have been delivered to, or the service performed for, the customer.

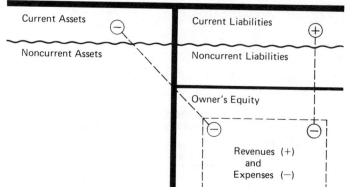

BALANCE SHEET DIAGRAM

An adjustment would be required to establish the current liability—Revenue Collected in Advance—and to reduce sales revenue.

Adjustments for deferred revenue increase current liabilities, decrease net working capital, and represent working capital outflows.

OPERATING INCOME AND WORKING CAPITAL FUNDS FROM OPERATIONS

Earlier in this chapter, operating income, or income from "ordinary operations of the business," was defined as revenues minus expenses, excluding extraordinary items. Working Capital Funds from Operations refers to the amount of net working capital generated as a result of these same "ordinary" operations. It is the difference between those nonextraordinary revenues which increase net working capital and those nonextraordinary expenses which decrease net working capital.[4]

The amount of Working Capital Funds from Operations generated during a period (usually simply identified as "Funds from Operations") provides very useful information to management and investors that is quite different from the information content of reported income or income from operations. In the next chapter you can learn that there are many reasons why a firm might desire to have additional net working capital for use in the business. Funds generated in operations is one possible source of additional net working capital (others will be introduced in Chapter 7). The amount of funds from operations discloses how much new net working capital came from this source regardless of whether the firm had a profit or a loss for the period. Funds from operations will be reported in the firm's Statement of Changes in Financial Position (SCFP).

---

[4]   In Chapter 7 you can learn that one particular nonextraordinary revenue that increases net working capital—Gains on Disposition of Noncurrent Assets—is excluded from funds from operations since it is included with another separate item reported in the SCFP.

The term "funds" must be carefully understood in this context. Some words can be deceptively simple and yet have multiple, complex meanings. They must be carefully evaluated in the context of their usage to ensure precise understanding of that which is being communicated. Examples would include "love," "cost," "value," and "funds." Funds may mean:

- Cash,
- Cash plus available credit (as in "Do we have enough funds to make the trip?"),
- Net working capital in a business,
- All business resources.

In this chapter, the term funds will be used exclusively to refer to net working capital in the firm. Used in this manner, can you see how it approximates "cash which will be available within the year"? Funds would include cash and other current assets cycling into cash (or obviating the necessity of cash outflow) within a year, less amounts already promised to creditors.

Where a firm has only current assets and current liabilities, or in those years where there are no operating revenues or operating expenses related to noncurrent assets and liabilities, then income from operations and working capital funds from operations will be identical. Mike's Stores provides such an example. All Mike's revenues and all his expenses represented working capital flows. Therefore Mike's 19X1 operating income of $155,500 (Exhibit 5.6) also represented funds from operations.

A firm can have revenues and expenses which do **not** affect working capital. Depreciation expense would be an obvious example. For such firms, income from operations and funds from operations will be different. Note that the "average"-store income statements supplied to Mike by his trade association (Exhibits 5.3 and 5.4) reported income from operations of $300,000 and funds from operations of $444,000. Can you locate the source of the difference from the information on these exhibits? The $144,000 difference arises from the two depreciation-expense items which did not involve outflows of working capital. This difference will be examined further in Chapter 6.

Mike's final request to you was that you advise him how well he was doing with respect to this different performance measurement. The industry average shows that 22.2 percent of net sales remained as new working capital generated from operations. Mike is generating only 11.8 percent. Can you see why these figures are not comparable? Since the industry funds-from-operations figure does not include deductions for capacity-asset cost, Mike's total should be adjusted for comparability. Excluding rental expenses of $96,000, Mike's funds from operations would have been $251,500, or 19.1 percent of net sales. He is still below industry average. But not to such an extreme as the unmodified figures would imply. In this example, the lower than average funds from operations would be the result of the same factors previously identified from income statement analysis.

CHAPTER OVERVIEW

From the material included in this chapter, you should now be in a position to:

- Describe, give examples of, and indicate the balance sheet effect of:
  Operating revenues,
  Other revenue,
  Adjustments involving operating and other revenue,
  Transactions representing operating expenses,
  Adjustments involving operating expenses;
- Describe and give examples of revenue and expense accruals affecting net working capital;
- Describe and give an example of a revenue deferral;
- Explain and give examples of the two approaches to income statement analysis—comparative analysis and trend analysis;
- Describe the accounting system's use of temporary accounts for revenue and expense;
- Define working capital flows and working capital funds from operations; and
- Describe and explain the circumstances when operating income and working capital funds from operations would be the same.

NEW VOCABULARY AND CONCEPTS

Fiscal year
Single-step format
Multiple-step format
Gross profit/gross margin/trading profit
Working capital funds from (provided by) operations
Sales
Net sales
Sales returns and allowances
Nonoperating revenue/other revenue
Financial activities
Cost of goods sold

Shrinkage
Operating expenses
Income from operations/operating income/operating profit/operating earnings
Net current assets
Flow of working capital
Closed/closing (account)
Accrual
Deferral
Matching
Funds

- Temporary accounts and closing;
- Accruals and deferrals and their function;
- Funds from operations and its relationship to income from operations.

REVIEW QUESTIONS

1. What is a firm's fiscal year? Can it be different from the calendar year? Why would this be desirable? Explain and give examples.

2. What is the difference between the single-step and the multiple-step format for income statements? Are they both acceptable under GAAP?

3. How does sales revenue affect owner well-offness?

4. Are sales returns and allowances expenses or revenue adjustments? Explain.

5. Do all firms report cost of goods sold? If not, why not?

6. In addition to merchandise given to customers, cost of goods sold would include what business costs?

7. (a) What is gross profit? (b) Does it include "other" revenue? (c) Explain.

8. Is all revenue considered operating revenue? If not, what would be examples of other revenues? Explain.

9. Are all expenses and losses operating expenses? If not, what would be examples of nonoperating expenses and losses?

10. Why do accountants use temporary accounts during the year for revenue and expense items? Explain.

11. To what does "closing" refer, in relation to revenue and expense accounts? Explain.

12. Is the balance sheet equality maintained among all the balance sheet accounts themselves during the year? If not, how is this equality or balance restored at year end?

13. What is income from operations? What does it mean and what is its usefulness?

14. Both comparative analysis and trend analysis can be useful in analyzing operating performance. Explain their difference, what each involves, and the distinct usefulness of each approach.

15. What are accruals and deferrals? Give examples of each.

16. What are examples of current asset expirations?

17. What are different meanings or usages for the term "funds"? Explain why working capital funds can be thought of as "available cash within the year."

18. Can income from operations and funds from operations ever be the same for a given period? If yes, in what special circumstances?

MINI-CASES AND QUESTIONS FOR DISCUSSION

MC 5.1. Mr. Grecousis, the president and former sales manager of the Belch Fire Auto Company, is having an argument with Mr. Murphy, the company comptroller. "I have a report on one of our competitors and it shows both funds from operations and income from operations as $300,000," he says. "Something must be wrong. I remember, from back in school, that income was the difference between revenue and expense. Funds from operations was the difference between working capital inflows from operations and working capital used in operations. They are two different things, aren't they?"

Mr. Murphy replies, "Yes."

"Well, if they are different, how can they be the same?"

As Mr. Murphy, try to explain to your boss how these two ostensibly different things can be the same.

MC 5.2. Ms. Prudence Struthers is an efficiency expert who has been examining your office procedures to locate areas of unnecessary activities and paperwork. She, unfortunately, knows nothing about accounting. "Have I found a really unnecessary make-work program in the accounting department?" she proclaims. "Do you know those featherbedders use a whole series of temporary holding records during the year, and then they transfer the information to where it was supposed to go anyway? They even have a fancy word for it called 'closing.' I think we should 'close down' their little make-work game."

Explain to Ms. Struthers why temporary accounts are desirable even if they are later closed.

MC 5.3. A professional sports team or club which sells season tickets defers revenue for the proportion of games remaining to be played. If season ticket sales increased dramatically this year, wouldn't the practice of deferring recognition of the revenues unfairly "hide" this good news from creditors and owners studying income statements? Discuss.

Also identify several other industries or activities where deferred revenue recognition would be commonplace.

MC 5.4. Below are listed several instances ((a) through (f)) of accounting errors. You may assume the errors are discovered only after the financial statements are published and therefore will be picked up in the subsequent year's financial statements. For each error, discuss the effect upon (understated, no effect, overstated):

   i) Quick ratio
   ii) Current ratio
   iii) Debt ratio
   iv) Current year's reported income
   v) Subsequent year's reported income

Also discuss the possible effect upon or fairness for:

   vi) Current owner, that may sell ownership interest on basis of the current incorrect statements.
   vii) New owner, that might buy ownership interest on the basis of the current incorrect statements.

   a) Inventory costing $50,000 was overlooked and therefore not included during the year-end physical inventory.
   b) A year-end purchase of $10,000 of supplies on account was not

recorded. The supplies themselves had been placed in the store-room and were included in the year-end physical inventory.

c) $120,000 of credit sales to customers made during the week following the year end were included along with the previous month's business.

d) An insurance policy costing $9,000 covering the following year had been acquired from the firm's insurance broker just prior to year end. Neither the policy nor the broker's invoice were recorded.

e) On the last day of the year, the owner withdrew merchandise costing $4,000 for personal use. The withdrawal was not recorded.

f) At year end, $600 of interest was owed to the firm on its investments. The item was not accrued.

ESSENTIAL PROBLEMS

EP 5.1. Given the following accounts and their adjusted balances for the Snow Company, select those accounts which properly appear on an income statement and list them in appropriate income-statement order.

Account	Balance
Accounts Payable	$ 75
Accounts Receivable	300
Accrued Wages Payable	25
Cash	100
Cost of Goods Sold	900
Current Notes Payable	50
Inventory	500
Other Current Liabilities	25
Other Operating Expense	225
Owner's Equity	600
Sales	1,900
Sales Returns and Allowances	100
Utilities Expense	150
Wages Expense	400

EP 5.2. Using the same data as for Problem EP 5.1 above, prepare a complete income statement in good form, showing gross profit and income from operations.

EP 5.3. Select the balance sheet accounts from Problem EP 5.1 and list them in proper order under the headings Assets and Equities.

EP 5.4. Close the revenue and expense items in Problem EP 5.1 to owner's equity and, together with the other balance sheet accounts, prepare a balance sheet in good form.

EP 5.5. From the following list of transactions and adjustments, identify by the letter R or E those which involve either revenue or expense. Indicate, for each item that represents revenue or expense, whether the eventual effect upon owner's equity is an increase or decrease.

a) Owner invests $100,000 cash in the business.
b) Merchandise costing $50,000 is purchased on account.
c) Prior month's rent of $400 is paid in cash.*
d) Customers purchase merchandise, paying $40,000 cash.
e) Customers purchase merchandise selling for $30,000, on account.
f) A utilities bill for $200 is received and recorded.
g) Wages totaling $20,000 are paid in cash.*
h) $25,000 is collected on accounts receivable.
i) $30,000 is paid on accounts payable.
j) $5,000 of supplies are purchased on account.
k) $2,000 of supplies are determined to have been used up, and an adjustment is made for the expiration.
l) $300 of interest owed to the bank is accrued.

EP 5.6. From the data given in Problem EP 5.5 above, prepare an income statement in good form with subtotals for gross profit and income from operations. You may assume that the firm had just started in business and that a physical count of inventory on hand at the end of the year revealed merchandise costing $8,000 still unsold.

EP 5.7. The following adjustments at year end are necessary for the Chowchilla Company. For each adjustment indicate:

i) The accounts first affected;
ii) Whether the account is a balance sheet (B/S), revenue (R), or expense (E) account;
iii) Whether the account balance should be increased or decreased. (*Note.* Remember that expense account balances are normally increased during the year, and that the amount of their ending balance then decreases owner's equity at closing.)

a) One of the firm's accounts receivable in the amount of $800 is determined to be uncollectible. It is removed from the books and the appropriate expense is called "bad debt expense."
b) The supplies account totals $6,000, representing supplies on hand at the beginning of the year costing $1,000, and supplies purchased for $5,000. A year-end inspection reveals that supplies with an estimated cost of $1,500 are still on hand. Adjustment is necessary for this asset expiration.
c) It is determined that $750 of interest is owed to the firm on a note receivable which has not been received or recorded.
d) $600 of rent is owed to the firm by someone leasing excess storage space. It has not been previously recorded.
e) $1,700 of accrued wages and salaries are owed to employees.
f) It is estimated that the next telephone bill will be for $500, $300 of which will be charges for the year just ended.

---

* Assume that liability not previously recorded.

EP 5.8. The Chowchilla Company's accountant mistakenly prepared its income statement without including the necessary adjustments given in Problem EP 5.7 above. Prepare a revised statement including the necessary adjustments. The statement before adjustments was as follows:

Sales		$200,000
Cost of Goods Sold		103,500
Gross Profit		$96,500
Wages and Salaries Expense	78,000	
Utilities Expense	5,000	
Interest Expense	1,500	84,500
Income from Operations		$12,000

SUPPLEMENTARY PROBLEMS

SP 5.9. An examination of the Dundee Company's income statement revealed that all revenue was in the form of cash or current receivables. All listed expenses represented either expirations of current assets, cash paid out, or current liabilities to be paid shortly. Operating income was shown as $7,000. Can you determine funds from operations for the year? Explain.

SP 5.10. The Embraceable Pillow Company's balance sheet at the beginning of the year was as follows:

Cash	$2,000		Accounts Payable	$2,500
Accounts Receivable	3,000		Other Current Liabilities	1,500
Inventory	4,000		Owner's Equity	5,000
Total	$9,000		Total	$9,000

Prepare in good form the ending balance sheet and the year's income statement, assuming that the following events took place during the year:

a) Sales amounted to $30,000, of which $5,000 were cash sales and the balance on account.

b) During the year, $24,000 was collected on accounts receivable.

c) Merchandise costing $14,000 was purchased on account.

d) At year end, $5,000 of merchandise was on hand.

e) Wages and salaries amounting to $9,000 were paid in cash.

f) At year end, $1,000 of wages were owed employees.

g) Rent and utilities bills amounting to $4,000 were paid during the year, and no more was owed at year end.

h) All beginning current liabilities were paid early in January.

SP 5.11. Using the Xerox Corporation's 1976 and 1975 income statements (in Appendix A at the back of the book), answer the following:

a) What was the amount of income from (continuing) operations before income taxes for each year?

b) How was this figure captioned on the statement?

c) In comparing operations performance (all items down to and including income from operations before income taxes) for the two years, which (if any) items were significantly better or worse? Explain.

SP 5.12. Using the Addison-Wesley Publishing Company's 1976 and 1975 income statements (in Appendix A at the back of the book), answer questions (a), (b), and (c) from Problem SP 5.11 above.

PREPARER PROCEDURES

(Chapter 17 should be completed before proceeding with this Section.)

New temporary revenue and expense accounts are set up for each year or each accounting period, and they all start with zero balances.[4] Where a transaction or adjusting journal entry would affect owner's equity and where it does not report an owner transaction (new owner investment or withdrawal or a donation), the entry is made instead to the appropriate revenue or expense account. Some journal entry examples would be:

	DR	CR
Cash	$1,000	
Accounts Receivable	3,000	
Sales		$4,000
To record cash and credit sales for the day.		
Sales Returns and Allowances	$ 200	
Accounts Receivable		$ 200
To record return of sale made on account.		
Utilities Expense	$ 75	
Accounts Payable		$ 75
To record utility bill received.		
Wages and Salaries Expense	$6,000	
Wages Payable		$6,000
To record weekly payroll (assuming no payroll taxes or deductions).		
Insurance Expense	$ 400	
Prepaid Insurance		$ 400
To record expiration of insurance.		
Interest Expense	$ 100	
Accrued Interest Payable		$ 100
To accrue interest owed on note payable.		
Accrued Rent Receivable	$ 300	
Rental Revenue		$ 300
To record rent owed on garage.		

The year-end adjustment for ending inventory involves several steps. Assume the following facts:

Beginning inventory balance	$ 40,000	DR
Net purchases for the year (recorded in separate Purchases account)	$500,000	DR
Cost of ending inventory (result of taking a physical count)	$ 49,000	

---

[4]   In some systems the first entries will be opening reversals of certain prior period accruals and deferrals (see p. 521).

The appropriate journal entries would be:

	DR	CR
Cost of Goods Sold	$540,000	
Inventory		$ 40,000
Purchases		500,000

To close inventory and purchases to cost of goods sold.*

	DR	CR
Inventory	$ 49,000	
Cost of Goods Sold		$ 49,000

To record ending inventory.†

At year end, the revenue and expense balances are determined, and these balances provide the data for the income statement.[5] These accounts are then closed to owner's equity.[6] Suppose year-end balances in representative accounts were:

Sales	$100,000	CR
Cost of Goods Sold	$ 50,000	DR
Wages and Salaries Expense	$ 20,000	DR
Rent Expense	$ 10,000	DR
Other Operating Expense	$ 5,000	DR

The appropriate journal entries would be:

	DR	CR
Sales	$100,000	
Cost of Goods Sold		$50,000
Wages and Salaries Expense		20,000
Rent Expense		10,000
Other Expense		5,000
Owner's Equity		15,000

This entry would close out (or zero-balance) the revenue and expense accounts. Their net difference of $15,000 would be transferred to increase owner's equity.

PREPARER PROBLEMS

PP 5.1. Prepare journal entries in good form for the 19 transactions and adjustments involved in the Mike's Stores example and given in Exhibit 5.2.

---

*   This entry initially assumes that all goods available for sale were sold.
†   This entry restores the excessive amount charged off to expense by the first entry.
[5]   As explained in Chapter 17, revenue and expense account balances after adjustment are usually first determined on a worksheet. The income statement data can then be drawn directly from a worksheet. Final adjusting and closing entries can then be made and posted to the accounts without delaying statement distribution.
[6]   In many systems, they are first closed to a temporary summary account appropriately called income summary. Income summary is then closed to owner's equity. In the case of a corporation, income summary would be closed to retained earnings. Retained earnings is one of the subaccounts included within corporate owners' equity (see Chapter 10). Income summary is not used in this text so that your attention will remain focused directly upon the effect on owner's equity of revenues and expenses.

PP 5.2. Prepare journal entries in good form for transactions and adjustments (a) through (l) given in Problem EP 5.5 above.

PP 5.3. Prepare an adjusted trial balance for the Snow Company, using the data given in Problem EP 5.1 above. Use two-column paper, and list the accounts with their balances as debit or credit, as appropriate. Show that total debits equal total credits.

PP 5.4. Given the appropriate journal entry closing all revenue and expense accounts for the Snow Company (Problem EP 5.1 above) to owner's equity.

PP 5.5. Prepare journal entries in good form for adjustments (a) through (f) given in Problem EP 5.7 above.

PP 5.6. Using the information supplied for the Embraceable Pillow Company in Problem EP 5.10 above, do the following:

Step 1. Prepare a worksheet with space for account descriptions and then 10 columns for amounts. Use Chapter 17, Exhibit 17.2, as a model. Label the first pair of columns as opening balance and DR/CR; the second pair as transactions and adjustments and DR/CR; the third pair as adjusted trial balance and DR/CR; the fourth pair as income statement and DR/CR; and the fifth pair as ending balance sheet and DR/CR.

Step 2. Record the opening balances and show column totals to assure debit–credit equality.

Step 3. Separately prepare journal entries for the eight transactions and adjustments given.

Step 4. Record these entries in the transactions and adjustments column. Show column totals to ensure a balance.

Step 5. Show new balances for all accounts in the adjusted columns; show totals to ensure balance.

Step 6. Record revenue and expense balances in the income statement columns. Record a closing entry on the line for owner's equity and total to ensure balance.

Step 7. Record balances of balance sheet accounts in the balance sheet columns, showing the owner's equity balance after closing, and obtain the totals to ensure balance.

6

NET INCOME —
THE "BOTTOM LINE"

CHAPTER PREVIEW

The objective of this chapter is to complete your introduction to the income statement, to the usual differences between net income and funds from operations, and to the third financial statement identified, for a proprietorship, as the Statement of Owner's Capital. In this chapter, you can:

- Learn how income taxes are reported for those entities subject to such tax;

- Learn about some of the adjustments involving noncurrent assets and liabilities that do *not* represent working capital flows;

- Develop an understanding of why they do not involve flows of funds;

- Learn how these adjustments create a difference between funds from operations and income from operations;

- Learn the meaning of income from operations and the usefulness of this subtotal;

- Develop an understanding of the logical difference between funds from operations and the normally smaller amount which the accountant identifies as net income available for owner withdrawal;

- Develop a basic familiarity with items either classified as "extraordinary" or related to "discontinued operations";

- Learn that these two classifications represent the source of possible difference between income from operations (after taxes) and net income;

- Become familiar with the Statement of Owner's Capital and how it links the Owner's Equity sections of successive balance sheets;

- Develop the ability to determine funds from operations from income-statement data and to reconcile net income and funds from operations for a given period.

With a clear understanding of the material in this and preceding chapters, you will be able to grasp the essential structure and operation of the financial accounting system and the function and purpose of three of the four financial statements. All subsequent information related to the balance sheet, the income statement, and the statement of owner's capital (or retained earnings), you will perceive as merely amplifications and additional details, all related to your existing knowledge. Finally, with a clear understanding of funds from operations, you will have already completed the more difficult part of becoming familiar with the Statement of Financial Position. You will be well prepared to complete the picture when you study Chapter 7.

WHAT IS MY TAKE-HOME PROFIT?

Imagine you are a professional management consultant to small business firms. You have a new client whose name is Sarah Washington. Sarah operates a gasoline service station. She really cares for her business and her customers, and provides them with cheerful, competent service. Her good service attracts customers and the business is doing very well.

Currently she is leasing her station and equipment on a year-to-year basis and, therefore, has no noncurrent assets. She also has no noncurrent debt. Exhibit 6.1 gives her most recent balance sheet and income statement.

Exhibit 6.1
SARAH WASHINGTON SERVICE STATION

Balance Sheet as of 12/31/X3

Assets		Equities	
Current Assets:		Current Liabilities:	
Cash	$ 3,000	Accounts payable	$ 8,000
Receivables	10,000	Wages Payable	1,000
Inventory	15,000	Other current liabilities	2,000
Supplies	300	Total Liabilities	$11,000
Prepaid insurance	1,800		
		Owner's Equity	19,100
Total Assets	$30,100	Total Equities	$30,100

Income Statement for Year Ending 12/31/X3

Gross Sales		$465,000
Cost of goods sold		372,000
Gross Profit		$93,000
Operating expenses:		
Rent expense	36,000	
Wages and salaries expense	24,000	
Supplies expense	1,200	
Insurance expense	1,800	
Other operating expense	2,000	65,000
Income from operations before taxes		28,000
Less provision for income taxes		11,200
Net Income		$16,800

Note that Sarah's income statement discloses a provision for $11,200 of income taxes. Income taxes are payable by corporations on the entity's taxable income. Net income after taxes is available to the owners of the corporation. To avoid unnecessary complexity, in this text corporate accounting is not introduced until Chapter 10. However, it is desirable to understand the treatment of income taxes on the income statement at this stage of your learning. For this chapter **only**, therefore, we will agree to assume that Sarah Washington's business entity is subject to taxes. But you should remember that in reality a nonincorporated business is normally **not** subject to income tax.

Sarah has come to you because she is considering buying the station instead of, as she says, "throwing away $3,000 a month in rent." She could buy the station and equipment for $300,000. The $300,000 would include land at $40,000, building at $180,000, and the equipment at $80,000. She plans to borrow the $300,000 from a friend and invest it in her business. The business would then buy the station and equipment. If she had done these things on the last day of the year, 12/31/X3, the balance sheet would look like Exhibit 6.2.

Exhibit 6.2
SARAH WASHINGTON SERVICE STATION

Hypothetical Balance Sheet Assuming Station Owned
As of 12/31/X3

Assets		Equities	
Current Assets:		Current Liabilities:	
Cash	$ 3,000	Accounts payable	$ 8,000
Receivables	10,000	Wages payable	1,000
Inventory	15,000	Other current liabilities	2,000
Supplies	300	Total Current Liabilities	$ 11,000
Prepaid insurance	1,800		
Total Current Assets	$ 30,100		
Fixed Assets:			
Land	$ 40,000	Owner's Equity	319,100
Building	180,000		
Equipment	80,000		
Total Assets	$330,100	Total Equities	$330,100

Property taxes on the land are $4,000 per year. They are currently paid by the present owner. If Sarah's business purchased the property, there would be an additional annual expense to the business of $4,000 in property taxes. Sarah reasons, "I think I would be 'way ahead. Think what my annual business income would be. I'd have $36,000 less in rent expense, and this would be offset by only $4,000 in additional tax expense. I'd have $32,000 more each year in profits. I could pay off the loan and still be 'way ahead."

Would her revised statement show a profit of $48,800 as she anticipates, instead of the present $16,800? If so, buying the station and equipment may be a good investment for her.

ADJUSTMENT FOR DEPRECIATION

Recall from Chapters 2 and 4 that noncurrent assets such as buildings and equipment (which are subject to wearing out or becoming obsolete) must be depreciated. Land is assumed to have infinite life, but buildings and equipment have finite lives. Assume that the equipment realistically has a 10-year useful life before requiring replacement. Also assume the building has a 30-year useful life. In both cases, for simplicity, assume that there is no resale or salvage value at the end of the useful life. Recall that allocating this cost in equal amounts over the asset's useful life is called straight-line depreciation. Each and every year during the first ten years, Sarah should record depreciation of $14,000.[1] Her business income would then be $27,600 and not the $48,800 which Sarah anticipated.

The actual decision as to whether Sarah should buy the station is too involved to analyze fully in this book. Among other things that must be taken into account are tax considerations and the full cost and the repayment schedule of Sarah's personal loan. The purpose of this example is to focus your attention on revenue and expenses related to noncurrent assets and liabilities.

Another, and perhaps the best, way to understand depreciation is to think of Sarah's income statement. Suppose she did invest the money in the business and the business, in turn, purchased the station. The business would then save $36,000 each year in cash rental payments, but would have $11,200 additional taxes to pay.[2] Funds from operations in Sarah's business would increase from $16,800 to $41,600. But can Sarah realistically take out of the firm $41,600 each year? Will the firm continue to be as well off each year if she does this?

The answer to both questions is "no." Think of 10 years hence, when the $80,000 of tools will become useless and require replacement. If Sarah had not accumulated $80,000 of funds in the business while the tools were wearing out, the firm would be unable to replace them unless new capital were obtained from outside. Exhibit 6.3 attempts to picture this concept with a **modified version** of an income statement. Note that effectively the accounting system is saying to Sarah,

> Yes, each year you have $41,600 of new funds generated from operations. But you can't consider all of that to be profit; $14,000 must be retained in the business annually to offset gradual loss of fixed assets and maintain well-offness. Otherwise, these assets could not be replaced. Your actual profit, which you could consider to be available for withdrawal, is only $27,600.

---

[1]   Building $180,000 divided by 30 years = $6,000 per year. Equipment: $80,000 divided by 10 years = $8,000 per year.
[2] $4,000 property taxes and $7,200 additional income taxes (40 percent of $18,000 of increased profit before taxes).

Exhibit 6.3

SARAH WASHINGTON SERVICE STATION

**Modified Version of Recent Income Statement Assuming
Station Owned for Year Ending 12/31/X3**

Sales		$465,000
Cost of goods sold		372,000
Gross Profit		$ 93,000
Less Operating Expenses		
Wages and salaries expense	$24,000	
Supplies expense	1,200	
Insurance expense	1,800	
Property tax expense	4,000	
Other operating expenses	2,000	
Provision for income taxes*	18,400	51,400
Funds from Operations†		$ 41,600
Less depreciation expense		14,000
Net Income		$ 27,600

* Tax computed at 40 percent of operating income after straight-
line fixed asset depreciation.
† This subtotal normally does *not* appear on an actual income
statement.

A separate account to accumulate the funds being retained in the business for asset replacement is normally **not** provided. The additional working capital is used within the operating cycle until it is required for replacement of non-current assets. To see this clearly, assume you owned a trucking business. Your business assets consist of $2,000 cash and equipment you use which cost $10,000. You collect all of your fees in cash and pay all your expenses in cash. Your business, therefore, has no liabilities and only two assets: cash and equipment. Assume your equipment has a three-year useful life and a salvage value of $1,000 at the end of the three years. Also assume that each year you earn $17,000 for your services and have $2,000 of cash expenses. Funds from operations in your business would be $15,000 each year. Your business income, after providing for depreciation of $3,000 per year, would be $12,000. Assume that each year you withdraw from the business the $12,000 of cash representing business income. What will be the financial position at the end of the third year when you will need to replace your equipment?

Assuming the factors as stated, your position after three years would be:

Cash	$11,000	Liabilities	0
Equipment	10,000	Owner's Equity	$12,000
Accumulated depreciation	(9,000)		
Total Assets	$12,000	Total Equities	$12,000

Each year, although you had $14,000 more cash, your accountant reported only $13,000 of income which you could and did withdraw. You accumulated

$1,000 of additional working capital (cash, in this simple example), exactly offsetting the reduction in noncurrent assets. You have maintained your well-offness. After three years, you can sell the old equipment for its $1,000 salvage value, purchase replacement equipment costing $10,000 and be back where you started.[3]

Returning to the Sarah Washington example, note that, in Exhibit 6.3, all revenue and expense items, except depreciation expense, involve inflows and outflows of net working capital. In this example, it is depreciation expense that makes the difference between income and funds from operations.

Recall that the adjustment for depreciation of fixed assets involves an increase of an asset valuation account called Accumulated Depreciation. This account, in turn, decreases total assets. The complementary part of the depreciation adjustment is an increase in the depreciation expense. This expense account reduces owner's equity.

Exhibit 6.4
SARAH WASHINGTON SERVICE STATION

Projected Abbreviated Balance Sheets as of 12/31/X4

Without adjusting for depreciation:

Total Currents Assets	$ 44,100	Total Current Liabilities	$ 11,000
Fixed Assets:			
Land	40,000	Owner's Equity	333,100
Building	180,000		
Equipment	80,000		
Total Assets	$344,100	Total Equities	$344,100

After adjusting for depreciation:

Total Current Assets	$ 44,100	Total Current Liabilities	$ 11,000
Fixed Assets:			
Land	40,000	Owner's Equity	319,100
Building	180,000		
Less accumulated depreciation	(6,000)		
Equipment	80,000		
Less accumulated depreciation	(8,000)		
Total Assets	$330,100	Total Equities	$330,100

[3]   Note that this example assumes no inflation. With inflation you would be as well off after three years in terms of dollars but not in terms of the purchasing power of those dollars or the ability to replace assets used. Your new equipment with inflation would probably cost more than $4,000. GAAP currently ignore this problem. Alternative measurement and reporting systems are under discussion and experimentation. They will be discussed in Chapter 16.

Exhibit 6.4 shows the firm's projected abbreviated balance sheet as of 12/31/X4, assuming that:

1. the firm owned the station;

2. operations were the same as in prior years; and

3. Sarah had withdrawn all profit.

The balance sheet is shown in two different ways—with and without the depreciation adjustment. The first balance sheet (without depreciation) is **incorrect** and **misleading** in two ways. It shows fixed assets at Sarah's unadjusted original cost after a year of wear and tear has already taken place. It also shows her equity as $14,000 greater than at the beginning, whereas she really is no better off. Note that, on the second (corrected) balance sheet, after adjusting for depreciation, Sarah's equity or well-offness is the same as at the beginning of the year on Exhibit 6.2. This second (adjusted) presentation accurately reflects her withdrawal of all profits during the year.

To see clearly why depreciation expense does **not** represent a working capital flow, refer to the balance sheet diagram introduced in the previous chapter.

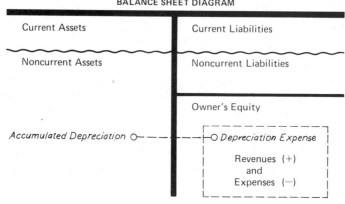

BALANCE SHEET DIAGRAM

Note that the balance sheet effect of the adjusting entry to record annual depreciation expense is to reduce items **below** the wavy line. There is no effect on the balance of net working capital. New working capital for use in replacing noncurrent assets comes from revenues. Depreciation merely "signals" owners to leave some of these new funds in the business for asset-replacement purposes—that is, not to consider all new net funds generated as **profit**, which can be withdrawn. Depreciation itself does **not** involve a flow of funds.

ADJUSTMENTS FOR OTHER NONCURRENT ITEMS

Noncurrent assets other than tangible fixed assets may also require adjustment to reflect asset expiration. Capital leases and intangible assets (such as leasehold improvements, franchises, patents, deferred charges, and so forth) all have, or are assumed to have, finite lives. Adjustments to systematically record the expiration of these assets are made to reflect the amortization, or decline in future usefulness, of these items. In the case of asset amortization, a contra-asset valuation account is not involved. Instead, the asset balance is reduced directly by an adjusting entry which:

- Increases amortization expense, and
- Decreases the asset account.

The remaining amount for such assets, which is disclosed on the balance sheet, represents the *unamortized* (not yet amortized) *cost*. You therefore know, when you are reading a balance sheet, that noncurrent assets are shown at their unamortized cost except for tangible fixed assets.

Tangible fixed assets are shown at their fair market value at the time of their acquisition by the firm (usually unadjusted original cost); and they are accompanied by a contra-asset (negative) valuation account indicating the accumulated depreciation adjustment to date. The difference between the tangible fixed asset's cost measurement and its accumulated depreciation is known as its book value. The book value of tangible fixed assets is analogous to the unamortized cost of other noncurrent assets.

Amortization of noncurrent assets reflecting expirations of cost do **not** represent working capital flows. Refer to the balance sheet diagram earlier used to portray the effect of depreciation. Noncurrent asset cost amortization has the same effect as depreciation. Only balance sheet items below the wavy line are adjusted. Net working capital is not affected.

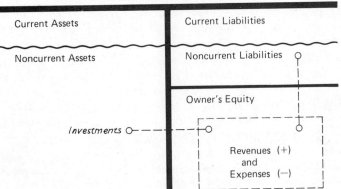

BALANCE SHEET DIAGRAM

In Chapter 11 you will be introduced to adjustments to the investments account which may be necessary. As is the case for all noncurrent assets, the effect of such adjustments is below the wavy line, and no working capital flow is involved. Similarly, in Chapter 12 you will be introduced to possible adjustments to noncurrent liability items. Would these adjustments involve a flow of working capital?

The answer is **no. No revenue or expense adjustments involving noncurrent assets or liabilities represent a working capital flow.**[4] Therefore, all such adjustments will contribute to a difference between income from operations and funds from operations. Later in this chapter, you can learn how to determine working capital funds from operations from income statement data, and how to reconcile and explain the difference between income and funds from operations.

OTHER REVENUE, GAIN OR LOSS

Other revenue and expense items that do not all involve adjustments may also contribute to a difference between income from operations and funds from operations. Recall from Chapter 5 that a firm may have revenues earned from secondary sources. "Primary" revenue for most firms is sales of goods or services to customers. The same firm may also have additional or "secondary" revenue in the form of rent on property not currently used in the generation of primary revenue, in the form of interest on notes receivable, or representing earnings on marketable securities and investments. So as not to contaminate trend analysis of primary revenue, these secondary revenues are separately disclosed on the income statement as "other revenue" or even "nonoperating revenue."

A firm may also have "revenue" or "expense" from the sale or exchange of assets other than inventory, for more or less than current book value. Such transactions are often referred to as *financial transactions* to distinguish them from primary, or operating, transactions. To minimize confusion, accountants usually identify "revenues" from financial transactions as "gains," and "expenses" related to financial transactions as "losses." If an asset (other than inventory) with a book value of $12,000 were sold for $13,500, the $1,500 "plus" affecting owner's equity would appear on the income statement as "gain from disposition (sale) of . . . $1,500." Conversely, if the same asset were sold for $10,000, a *loss* of $2,000 would be reported on the income statement.

To clarify this example, assume a firm had a fixed asset costing $30,000

---

[4]   In the case of a manufacturer, where the asset being amortized or depreciated was involved with and part of overall manufacturing cost—part of product cost— the debit would be to manufacturing overhead instead of to an amortization/depreciation expense account. See Chapter 8 appendix.

with accumulated depreciation of $18,000 and therefore a book value of $12,000. If this asset was sold for $13,500 cash, the accountant would:

> Increase cash $13,500;
> Reduce fixed assets $30,000;
> Reduce accumulated depreciation $18,000;
> Record a gain on disposition of $1,500 on the income statement (which would eventually have the effect of increasing owner's equity by this amount) to maintain the balance-sheet equality.

If this same asset had been sold for only $10,000:

> Cash would be increased by $10,000;
> Fixed assets would be reduced by $30,000;
> Accumulated depreciation would be reduced by $18,000;
> A loss of $2,000 would be recorded.

Disposition of assets will be covered in more detail in Chapter 9.

Other revenue can be considered as "nonoperating." Gains and losses from financial transactions may also be considered as nonoperating. Are you a bit confused to find that these items are included on the income statement as part of income from operations? Potential confusion arises from different definitions and interpretations of the terms "operating" and "operations." Many people think of business operations as being normal operations or primary operations. From this viewpoint, secondary revenues and gains or losses on financial transactions are nonoperating.

GAAP, on the other hand, clearly define income from operations as including all revenues, expenses, gains and losses not clearly qualifying as either *extraordinary* or related to *discontinued operations*. These two categories will be defined and discussed later in this chapter. The GAAP definition of operations is therefore much broader than just day-to-day primary business activities. Under GAAP, operations can be thought of as including **all continuing activities.** You, therefore, can visualize the income statement as including:

> \+ "Primary" revenue
> − Operating expenses
> \+ Other revenue
> \+ Gains (not extraordinary or related to discontinued operations)
> − Losses (not extraordinary or related to discontinued operations)
> ____
> = Income from (continuing) operations before taxes

GAAP do not, on the other hand, require a standardized sequencing of the elements of income from operations. Recall from Chapter 5 that a firm may elect "multiple-step" reporting and disclose a subtotal for gross profit. Firms may also elect an additional subtotal for "operating income" which is distinct from the subsequently GAAP-mandated total of income from operations. A common pattern (which is demonstrated on both statements included in Appendix A at the back of this book) of classification including this additional operating income subtotal would be:

Sales
Operating expenses
Operating income
Other revenue
Interest expense
Gains and losses on asset dispositions
Income from operations before taxes
Provision for income taxes
Income from operations after taxes

Note, in this example, that the effects of financial transactions (interest and gains and losses on asset dispositions) are segregated to reveal the results of more narrowly defined operating transactions.

Since there is no standardization "above" income from operations before taxes, you must be very careful, in making any comparisons between firms, to ensure that the data you are comparing are comparable. Exhibit 6.5 is an in-

Exhibit 6.5

ALBATROSS COMPANY

Income Statement for year ending 12/31/X7 (000 omitted)

Sales		$642
Other Revenue[1]		313	$955
Operating Expenses:		
Cost of goods sold	$270	
Wages and salaries	145	
Supplies	98	
Depreciation	177	
Amortization of assets	36	
Interest[2]	58	$784
Loss on prepaid item		22	
Loss on fixed-asset disposition		86	892
Income from operations before taxes			$ 63
Provision for income taxes			25
Income from operations			$ 38
Discontinued Operations:		
Income (net of tax)	$ 12	
Loss on asset disposition (net of tax)	19	$ (7)
Extraordinary gain (net of tax)		43	36
Net Income			$ 74

Notes:
1. Includes $40,000 not involving inflow of working capital (see Chapter 11).
2. Includes $18,000 not involving outflow of net working capital (see Chapter 12).

come statement for the Albatross Company. To avoid confusion, it does not contain subtotals for either gross profit or "operating income." Study this exhibit to become familiar with the sequencing of information starting with income from continuing operations before taxes. This sequencing is standardized.

FUNDS FROM OPERATIONS

Are all "other" revenues, gains, and losses that are included in income from operations also included in funds from operations? Recall that working capital funds from operations includes items that increase the balance of net working capital (fund inflows) and items that decrease the balance (fund outflows). Most other revenue involves inflows of working capital and is included as part of funds from operations.[5] Although gains (nonextraordinary) generally involve working capital inflows, they are excluded from funds from operations. This inconsistent treatment or exception allows for more informative reporting, in one figure, of the entire proceeds of a financial transaction on funds statements. These statements will be covered in Chapter 7.

Losses that are not extraordinary or related to discontinued operations will involve working capital outflows if they pertain to current assets. A loss affecting working capital, such as a loss on current marketable securities, would be included in funds from operations. A loss not affecting working capital, such as a loss on the sale of noncurrent assets, would **not** be included in funds from operations. The following matrix summarizes the above information relating to funds from operations:

	Included in, or affects:	
Income Statement Item	Income from operations	Funds from operations
Other revenue (involving working capital)	Yes	Yes
Other revenue (not involving working capital)	Yes	No
Nonextraordinary gains on asset dispositions	Yes	No
Nonextraordinary losses (involving working capital)	Yes	Yes
Nonextraordinary losses (not involving working capital)	Yes	No

How do I know? [handwritten annotation]

EXTRAORDINARY ITEMS

Note, on Exhibit 6.5, that neither extraordinary items nor items relating to discontinued operations are included as part of income from operations. Discontinued operations refers to a significant and separately identifiable segment of a firm's business which has been discontinued or is being phased out. Income (loss) and gain or loss on disposition of segment assets are separately reported net of tax. Net of tax means that any tax benefit or cost attributable to the discontinued operation is separately netted with the results of this operation. The applicable tax is not mingled with Provision for Income Tax. Provision for income tax is reported based on income from operations only (as if discontinued and extraordinary items did not exist).

Extraordinary items are narrowly defined. To qualify as extraordinary, an event must be material and **both** highly **unusual** in nature **and** of a **nonrecurring** type, that is, not expected to recur in the foreseeable future. Something that was merely unusual **or** infrequent would not qualify as extraordinary. Gains or losses on disposition of noncurrent assets might be material and infrequent. But differences between estimated resale value (salvage value) and actual resale proceeds are usual, and noncurrent assets can be expected to require replacement even if infrequently. A material uninsured loss of a noncurrent asset resulting from earthquake or fire would, on the other hand, clearly qualify as extraordinary. As in the case of discontinued operations, extraordinary items are disclosed net of applicable taxes.

Extraordinary gains and losses and items related to discontinued operations are excluded from income from operations on the income statement. They both are also excluded from funds from operations regardless of whether working capital is involved.

NET INCOME—THE "BOTTOM LINE"

To reinforce your understanding of the sequencing of information on the income statement, turn again to Exhibit 6.5. Starting with income from operations before taxes, note that, first, a reduction is made for income taxes applicable to the operating income for the period. Then a second subtotal—income from continuing operations—is reported. This amount represents earnings that might ordinarily be available to owners. Extraordinary items and those related to discontinued operations are reported after (below) income from operations with the final net amount designated as net income.

A common business idiom is *bottom line*. This term refers to the last line on a complete income statement, which is generally labeled net income. Net income reports the final effect on owner's equity of everything (all revenues, expenses, gains, and losses) that happened or was estimated to have happened during the year. It is the difference between all revenue and gain, on the one hand, and all expenses and losses on the other. If the difference is negative, a loss (or *net loss*) has occurred. Net income includes both the effect of normal activities—income from operations—and that of any extraordinary events or those arising from discontinued operations. Together with any effect resulting from donations to the firm, new owner investment, and owner withdrawal, net income fully explains the change in owner's equity between the beginning and the end of the year or period.

Note that net income is always the "bottom line" and many of the subtotals may not be relevant. Refer to the Albatross statement in Exhibit 6.5:

- If the firm had no discontinued operations and no extraordinary items, the "bottom line" would be Net Income $38,000 (replacing "income from continuing operations").
- If the firm was not incorporated (no income taxes applicable) and had no discontinued or extraordinary items, then the "bottom line" would be Net Income $63,000 (replacing "Income from operations before taxes").

The income statement disclosure rule can be thought of as:

Follow the classifications (as shown on Exhibit 6.5) but omit all zero items.
Label the last nonzero subtotal/total as Net Income.

RECONCILING NET INCOME WITH OWNER'S EQUITY

It is important for you to see clearly that the income statement is reporting on revenue and expenses that occur **over a period of time,** usually one year. A balance sheet, on the other hand, is like a photograph. It presents a picture of the firm's position at **one instant in time.** The income statement is one of the links between the beginning and the ending balance sheets. It reports on the earnings-related activities which resulted in a change in owner's equity. A clear demonstration of this bridge between the owner's equity sections of successive balance sheets can be seen in the third member of the financial statement set, or group. For a proprietorship or single-owner business, the third statement is known as a *Statement of Owner's Capital.* In this context, "capital" is used to mean exactly the same thing as equity. This statement is very simple and brief. It is often found printed on the bottom of the same page as the income statement.

Assume that the John Doe Company was on a calendar fiscal year. This means that its accounting period is one year in length and corresponds to the calendar. Given the following facts pertaining to the Doe Company for fiscal year 19X1:

Owner's Equity as of 12/31/X0	$75,000
Owner's Equity as of 12/31/X1	$80,000
Owner's Withdrawals during the year:	$25,000

Assuming no additional owner investment in the Doe Company during 19X1, what would be the "bottom line" of a correctly prepared income statement for

Exhibit 6.6

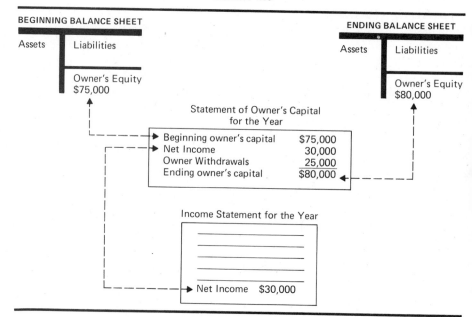

the firm? Given these facts and assumptions, net income for 19X1 would have to be exactly $30,000. The statement of owner's capital would show:

Owner's Capital 12/31/X0	$75,000
Net Income for 19X1	30,000
Owner Withdrawals	25,000
Owner's Capital 12/31/X1	$80,000

Note how this brief statement ties together and explains the changes that have occurred in owner's equity during the year. This articulation is illustrated in Exhibit 6.6. Also note how the income statement articulates with the other statements. In Chapter 10, you will find that an essentially identical statement for corporations called the Statement of Retained Earnings links the retained earnings amounts appearing within owner's equity on successive corporate balance sheets.

RECONCILING NET INCOME WITH FUNDS FROM OPERATIONS

The next chapter will introduce the fourth and final financial statement, known as the Statement of Changes in Financial Position. This statement directly articulates with the others through funds from operations and net income. To complete your introduction to and understanding of the income statement, you should be able to *reconcile* net income and funds from operations. "Reconcile" means to explain the difference in a particular situation.

First take the Sarah Washington Service Station example. Exhibit 6.7 is a *pro forma* (or projected) *income statement* for Sarah's station for 19X3, assuming she had purchased the station and equipment at the beginning of the year. Exhibit 6.7 contains the same data as Exhibit 6.3; however, the data are presented on Exhibit 6.7 in conformance with GAAP. Given the net income of $27,600 appearing as the bottom line on Exhibit 6.7, can you determine funds from operations generated during 19X3? And can you demonstrate on paper how you arrived at the correct amount? You might wish to use Exhibit 6.3 as a hint. You should attempt this reconciliation before proceeding.

Exhibit 6.7
SARAH WASHINGTON SERVICE STATION

Pro Forma Income Statement for Year Ending 12/31/X3		
Sales		$465,000
Less cost of goods sold		372,000
Gross Profit		$ 93,000
Less Operating Expenses:		
Wages and salaries	$24,000	
Supplies	1,200	
Insurance	1,800	
Property taxes	4,000	
Depreciation	14,000	
Other	2,000	47,000
Income from operations before taxes		$ 46,000
Provision for income taxes		18,400
Net Income		$ 27,600

An appropriate reconciliation would show:

Net income	$27,600
Plus depreciation	14,000
Funds from operations	$41,600

Why is depreciation added when it is not an additional source of working capital and does not even involve working capital?

Net income included a deduction of $14,000 for depreciation expense. Depreciation expense was not an outflow of net working capital. Therefore, it must be added back to obtain the total of working capital generated before nonfund deductions. Certain other expenses or losses which may appear on an income statement and which do not involve net working capital outflows similarly should be added back. These would include any amortization of a noncurrent asset to reflect cost expiration, and any other expense or loss item involving noncurrent assets or noncurrent liabilities. Also to be added back to net income would be any extraordinary loss, or loss or expense related to discontinued operations.

Conversely, the income statement might include extraordinary gains, gains or revenues related to discontinued operations, nonextraordinary gains on asset dispositions, or revenue which did not involve working capital. Since these were added in the determination of net income, they would all have to be subtracted to get back to funds from operations.

A checklist of the steps involved in determining funds from operations is provided in Exhibit 6.8. As a more complex problem to test and to reinforce your new understanding of funds from operations, on a piece of paper determine funds from operations for the Albatross Company from the information supplied on Exhibit 6.5. Do this before proceeding.

You are correct and adequately understand funds from operations if you determined the amount generated during 19X7 by Albatross as $315,000 of new net working capital. The reconciliation would be as follows:

Net Income		$ 74,000
Add back nonfund expenses and non-extraordinary losses:		
Depreciation	$177,000	
Amortization	36,000	
Interest (per statement footnote)	18,000	
Loss on fixed asset disposition	86,000	317,000
Add back loss on discontinued asset		19,000
		$410,000
Subtract nonfund revenue (per statement footnote)		40,000
Subtract extraordinary and discontinued items:		
Income from discontinued segment	$12,000	
Extraordinary gain	43,000	55,000
Funds from Operations		$315,000

A shortcut approach to deriving funds from operations involves bypassing extraordinary items and discontinued operations entirely. Taxes owed currently do represent an outflow of net working capital and you want funds generated after current tax claims. Start with income from operations after taxes. Then simply add back nonfund expenses and losses and subtract nonfund revenues and gains (if any). For Albatross, this would involve:

Income from Continuing Operations		$ 38,000
Add: Depreciation	$177,000	
Amortization	36,000	
Interest (from footnote)	18,000	
Loss on fixed-asset disposition	86,000	317,000
		$355,000
Subtract: Nonfund Revenue (per footnote)		40,000
Funds from Operations		$315,000

Exhibit 6.8

CHECKLIST FOR RECONCILING NET INCOME WITH FUNDS
FROM OPERATIONS

Start with:	Net income
Add back:	Depreciation of tangible fixed assets
	Amortization expense on other noncurrent assets
	✓ Loss on noncurrent assets
	Any other expense, or adjustments of noncurrent assets or noncurrent liabilities*
	✓ Any extraordinary losses
	✓ Any losses on discontinued operations
Subtract:	Any revenue, or adjustments to noncurrent assets or noncurrent liabilities.
	Any gains or extraordinary gains on disposition of assets
	Any income from discontinued operations
Equals:	Funds from operations

Note. These items will be discussed in Chapters 11 and 12.

ACCOUNTING INCOME VS. TAXABLE INCOME

Before leaving the discussion of income, a word of caution: In Chapter 1, you were warned not to confuse accounting income with any information you may have concerning taxable income. *Taxable income* results from tax laws and tax regulations, which incorporate many public policy considerations not related to the attempted measure of economic income for a firm. Most individuals' taxable income is determined on a cash, rather than an accrual, basis. Also, individuals have special exemptions and allowances, which are not expense-related. Even taxpayers on an accrual basis for tax purposes find the amount and timing of their taxable revenues and their tax deductions different from the requirements for matching accounting revenue and expenses under GAAP. The determination of taxable income and tax liability is not covered in this book. We will be concerned only with the proper reporting of tax liability determined by others and of actual taxes paid. The subject is mentioned once more to make sure you do not confuse tax regulations with accounting principles.

CHAPTER OVERVIEW

When you have mastered the material in this chapter, you should be able to:

- Describe the effect of any transaction (once you have a clear picture of the actual event) upon the balance sheet and the income statement;

- Distinguish, for any transaction, whether or not it involves a flow of working capital funds; and, if a flow is involved, whether it is an inflow or outflow;

- Describe the balance sheet and income statement effect of any adjustment so far introduced, and distinguish whether or not it represents a working capital flow;

- Distinguish among funds from operations, income from operations, and net income, as to: component elements included, significance or information content, and usefulness;

- Prepare an income statement in proper form, given all relevant transactions and adjustments;

- Determine funds from operations, given an income statement, and reconcile your amount with reported net income;

- Describe the only types of items that can be the source of a difference between income from operations and net income, and specify the criteria for such classification;

- Prepare a Statement of Owner's Capital, given all (or all but one) of the components; and explain clearly how this statement articulates with the beginning and ending balance sheets of the period and with the income statement for the period.

NEW VOCABULARY AND CONCEPTS

Unamortized cost	Statement of
Financial transactions	owner's capital
Extraordinary items	Reconcile
Discontinued operations	Proforma
"Bottom line"	Taxable income
Net loss	

- Adjustments that do not represent working capital flows and their purpose.

- The possible differences among funds from operations, income from operations, and net income.

- The essential logic behind the difference between funds from operations and net income.

- The articulation among two successive balance sheets, the statement of owner's capital, and the income statement.

REVIEW QUESTIONS

1. Why can't the owner of any business always consider all of working capital generated from operations as profit that can be withdrawn from the business? Explain.

2. What are the two purposes for depreciating or amortizing noncurrent assets each year?

3. If depreciation does result in funds being accumulated in the business for eventual noncurrent-asset replacement, where can these "accumulated funds" be found on the balance sheet? Explain.

4. a) Why are the expenses of depreciation and amortization of noncurrent assets added to net income in arriving at funds from operations?
   b) Are these items additional flows of funds?

5. Assume that, during a given year, a firm reported two nonextraordinary losses, one on inventory and one on fixed assets. Would both of these losses be added to net income, along with depreciation, in arriving at funds from operations? Explain.

6. In what way do the recording of depreciation and its balance sheet presentation differ from that for amortization? Explain.

7. a) What does the term "book value" mean when applied to assets in a firm?
   b) To which type of assets does this term usually refer?

8. a) What does the term "unamortized cost" mean when applied to assets in a firm?
   b) To which type of assets does this term usually refer?

9. "No revenue or expense adjustment related to noncurrent assets or to noncurrent liabilities represents a flow of net working capital." Do you agree with this statement? Explain.

10. What types of revenue or expense may be responsible for the difference between funds from operations and income from operations? Explain and give examples.

11. How would the following items be treated (added, not used, subtracted) in reconciling funds from operations and income from operations?
    a) Depreciation
    b) Amortization
    c) Gain (not extraordinary) on sale of fixed asset
    d) Loss (not extraordinary) on sale of fixed asset
    e) Loss (not extraordinary) on marketable securities

12. What is the difference between income from operations and net income?

13. What are the criteria that must be met before an item may properly be classified as extraordinary?

14. a) In what situations are the terms "gain" and "loss" often used? Explain. b) Give examples of other revenues or gains and losses that would not qualify as extraordinary.

15. Would either revenue from renting out some excess building space or a gain on the disposition of a noncurrent asset be normally classified as extraordinary? Explain.

16. Give some examples of extraordinary expenses or losses.

17. Would any of the following items normally be classified as extraordinary items?
    a) Marketable securities are sold at a loss.
    b) A receivable proves to be uncollectible.
    c) Some inventory is lost to shoplifters during normal business hours.
    d) A noncurrent asset is sold at a loss.

18. How would the following items be treated (added, not used, subtracted) in reconciling funds from operations and net income?
    a) Income from discontinued operations
    b) Net loss from discontinued operations
    c) Gain on sale of assets from discontinued segment
    d) Loss on sale of assets from discontinued segment
    e) Extraordinary gain
    f) Extraordinary loss

19. Why is net income often known as the "bottom line"?

20. a) What items may appear on the statement of owner's capital? b) What three other statements does this statement reconcile or tie together?

21. Are owner-related transactions—new owner investments and owner withdrawals—included in calculating net income? Explain.

22. a) What types of business entities are subject to income tax? b) What entities are normally not subject to income tax since the owner(s) are taxed directly?

23. Why does taxable income often differ from accounting income?

MINI-CASES AND QUESTIONS FOR DISCUSSION

MC 6.1 Mike Jones is concerned about raising some additional working capital for his firm over the next few years. He wants to make the down payment on a fixed asset he wishes to purchase. The present net working capital is just sufficient to support the present and anticipated level of operations. The firm will need $100,000 within two years. Conservatively forecast net income is $25,000 next year and $30,000 the following year. Mike, therefore, reasons that he will need to borrow on a long-term basis, or invest from his personal resources, the additional $45,000 in order to have enough operating capital.

His financial advisor suggests that, since he is forecasting depreciation expense at $10,000 per year over the next two years, he will need to obtain only an additional $25,000. The advisor refers to depreciation as a "source of funds."

Who is correct? Can depreciation be considered a source of funds? Discuss.

MC 6.2 Mary Porter and Sally Greenbaum are arguing over the importance of different information appearing on an income statement. Mary says, "I don't see why accountants bother with a subtotal for income from operations. The really important information is what actually happened to the firm last year—**everything** that happened. Net income gives the complete picture."

Sally replies, "Sure, net income gives the complete picture. But a statement user can only do something in the future. Therefore, the really important piece of information is not net income but income from operations.

You can forecast on the basis of income from operations. It can be dangerous to base a forecast on net income."

Who is right? Discuss.

MC 6.3 "Depreciation and amortization expenses are not adequate in today's world. There are many instances where total depreciation of a particular asset should far exceed 100 percent of its cost even if there was still some anticipated salvage value. Reported profits today are 'phony profits.' They can't be taken home."

Do you agree with this statement? Discuss.

MC 6.4 Why do accountants have very stringent criteria for the classification of an item as extraordinary? Why not leave this classification to the sole discretion of the firm? The firm knows its situation best. What difficulty could result if firms were just allowed to use their discretion? Discuss.

MC 6.5 Why isn't profit recognized when the merchandise or product is ready to sell? After all, it's only a matter of timing. The item will be sold eventually. Discuss.

MC 6.6 Why should income, gain on asset disposition, or loss on asset disposition be treated separately for so-called "discontinued operations"? Consider each separately. Discuss.

MC 6.7 a) Assume that, for a given firm, you could have either the net income figures for the past five years or the funds from operations figures but not both. In what circumstances might you prefer one or the other? Discuss.

b) Assume that the income from operations figure was also available for each of the five years. However, you could ask for only two of the three available sets of data. In what circumstances might you prefer one pair over another? Discuss.

ESSENTIAL PROBLEMS

EP 6.1 From the following data for the Rabbit Fur Company for the year 19X6, prepare a complete income statement in good form:

Bad debt expense	$ 7,000
Capital lease amortization	23,000
Cost of goods sold	400,000
Depreciation expense on equipment	8,000
Extraordinary fire loss	75,000
Insurance expense	5,000
Net Sales	600,000
Property tax expense	9,000
Rent expense	11,000
Supplies expense	3,000
Utilities expense	4,000
Wages and salaries expense	80,000

EP 6.2 From the following data for the Selgrave Doctors Clinic for the year, select the appropriate items and prepare a complete income statement in good form:

Accounts payable	$ 6,000
Accrued interest payable	600
Accrued rent payable	5,000
Accrued rent receivable	3,000
Accumulated depreciation	98,000
Depreciation on equipment	23,000
Extraordinary loss through accident	49,000
Insurance expense	12,000
Interest expense	2,000
Net fees billed	430,000
Prepaid insurance	24,000
Provision for income taxes	13,000
Rent expense	60,000
Rental revenue	7,000
Supplies expense	11,000
Uncollectible fees expense	3,000
Utilities expense	4,000
Wages and salaries expense	140,000
Wages and salaries payable	6,000

EP 6.3 From the following list of transactions and adjustments, identify only those that involve revenue or expense with either a (REV) or an (EXP), as appropriate:

a) Firm borrows $10,000 on a short-term loan.

b) Firm pays $2,000 interest on loans outstanding which had been previously recorded as interest payable.

c) Firm pays $114 utility bill for office. The bill had not been previously recorded.

d) A janitorial-service bill for $200 is received and recorded for office cleaning services performed during the prior month.

e) Customer purchases services at a price of $40 on account.

f) Tenant pays $150 of rent due on excess office space leased to her on a short-term basis. The receivable had already been accrued.

g) Interest of $70 is received on a note receivable. The interest receivable had not been accrued.

h) Depreciation of $800 is recorded on office equipment.

i) Wages payable of $900 for the last few days of the year are accrued at year end.

j) Adjustment is made for $400 of prepaid insurance which has expired.

k) As a secondary activity, the firm performs certain bookkeeping services for a client. The client owes $142 and this is accrued at year end.

l) A fire loss, net of insurance recovery, of $4,000 of inventory occurs.

m) Wages of $4,000 during the year are first recorded as a liability before payment.

n) $4,000 of wages are paid against previously recorded wages payable.

o) $14,000 of sales are made on account.

p) $12,000 is collected on accounts receivable.

EP 6.4 For each of the items in Problem EP 6.3 above, which involves either revenue or expense, indicate the effect upon the particular accounts involved. For example, the effect of a $7,000 cash sale would be:

Cash increased $7,000
Sales increased $7,000

EP 6.5 Identity as "EXT" the events from the following list which would be properly classified as extraordinary items:

a) The firm sells a used delivery truck with an original cost of $9,000 and accumulated depreciation of $8,000, for a gain of $3,000.

b) Firm sells a used office computer with an original cost of $95,000 and accumulated depreciation of $15,000, at a loss of $23,000.

c) During the year, merchandise costing $8,000 is pilfered by customers during selling hours.

d) In July, over the holidays, the store is damaged by a flood and merchandise costing $15,000 is destroyed.

e) A judgment for $68,000 is awarded in a law suit to a customer who was injured during a fire in the store.

f) A firm whose operating income runs about $24 million per year has a fire loss of $113.

EP 6.6 In addition to the revenue and expense items from Problem EP 6.3, assume that the firm had cost of goods sold for the year of $7,000 and anticipated no income tax liability. Prepare a multiple-step income statement in good form.

EP 6.7 Given the following data, prepare a statement of owner's capital for the Tompkins Company.

Owner's Capital 12/31/X1	$38,000
19X2 Net Income	32,000
19X2 Owner Withdrawals	20,000

EP 6.8 Given the following data, prepare a statement of owner's capital for the Grenados Company:

19X3 Income from Operations after taxes	$ 70,000
19X3 Extraordinary Loss	10,000
(the only extraordinary item during 19X3)	
19X3 Additional owner investment	112,000
19X3 Owner withdrawals	20,000
12/31/X3 Owner's capital	230,000

EP 6.9 Given the income statement below for the Bauer Company, identify those items which represented flows of net working capital, and indicate, for each, whether:

i) IFFO = Increases funds from operations

ii) DFFO = Decreases funds from operations

iii) NFFO = Funds flow but not part of funds from operations.

Sales		$500,000
Less cost of goods sold		300,000
Gross Profit		$200,000
Less Operating Expenses:		
Wages and salaries	$112,000	
Rentals	20,000	
Utilities	4,000	
Insurance	6,000	
Supplies	9,000	
Depreciation on equipment	18,000	
Amortization of leasehold improvement	22,000	191,000
Income from Operations		$ 9,000
Less extraordinary loss on noncurrent asset		18,000
Less extraordinary loss on inventory		27,000
Net Income (Loss)		$(36,000)

EP 6.10 Determine funds from operations for the Bauer Company (see Problem EP 6.9 above). Start with net income, and clearly identify each adjustment you make.

EP 6.11 For each item of operating expense on the Bauer Company income statement (see Problem EP 6.9 above), starting with cost of goods sold, determine the percentage of net sales that this expense represents.

EP 6.12 Compare the Bauer Company income statement (see Problem EP 6.9 above) to that for the Mason Company given below. For each item that is proportionately and significantly different between the two companies, list the item and indicate whether Mason appears to be doing a better job at generating revenue and controlling costs than Bauer, or vice versa. Assume a proportionately significant difference to be one which exceeded 0.5 percent of sales.

Sales		$750,000
Less cost of goods sold		412,500
Gross Profit		$337,500
Other Operating Expenses:		
Wages and salaries	$157,500	
Rentals	30,750	
Utilities	5,250	
Insurance	8,250	
Supplies	17,250	
Depreciation on equipment	27,000	
Intangibles amortization	33,000	279,000
Net Income		$ 58,500

SUPPLEMENTARY PROBLEMS

SP 6.13 The balance sheet data for the Albert Company as of 12/31/X5 (000 omitted) is given below, together with summary transactions and adjustments for 19X6.

a) Prepare in good form a balance sheet as of 12/31/X6, an income statement, and a statement of owner's capital for the year ending 12/31/X6.

b) Calculate funds from operations for the year.

Cash	$ 80	Accounts payable	$ 75
Accounts receivable	132	Taxes payable	40
Inventory	110	Other current liabilities	27
Supplies	35	Noncurrent notes payable	120
Prepaid insurance	8	Owner's equity	?
Land	40		
Buildings	200		
Accumulated depreciation on buildings	(131)		
Equipment	190		
Accumulated depreciation on equipment	(140)		
Patents	16		
Deferred Charges	6		

- Sales totaled $900,000, of which $100,000 were cash sales.
- Receivables collections totaled $782,000.
- Inventory costing $585,000 was purchased on account.
- Wages and salaries of $120,000 were earned and paid.
- Utilities costing $6,000 were consumed and paid for.
- All 12/31/X5 current liabilities were paid.
- $500,000 was paid on accounts payable.
- Inventory costing $20,000 was lost due to flood damage. Once every four or five years the firm experiences water damage.
- One of the firm's patents, with a 12/31/X5 unamortized cost of $5,000, was determined to be worthless.
- Owner withdrew $21,000 cash for personal use.
- Equipment costing $15,000, with a book value of $5,000, was sold for $7,000 cash.
- Earthquake damage to the building necessitated repairs costing $25,000, which had been paid.
- At year end, salable inventory costing $85,000 was still on hand.
- At year end, supplies costing $10,000 were unused.
- The 12/31/X5 prepaid insurance had two more years of coverage.
- Additional depreciation of $9,000 on buildings and $15,000 on equipment was determined to be appropriate.
- $2,000 of amortization on the remaining patents should be taken.
- Interest due on the noncurrent note was $12,000; $9,000 had been paid.
- Wages of $8,000 were earned but unpaid at year end.
- Income taxes were estimated at $34,000; $20,000 had been paid.

SP 6.14 The balance sheet data for the Brandywine Company as of 12/31/X2 (000 omitted) is given below, together with summary transactions and adjustments for the year 19X3.

a) Prepare in good form a balance sheet as of 12/31/X3, an income statement, and a statement of owner's capital for the year ending 12/31/X3.

b) Calculate funds from operations for the year.

Cash	$ 65	Current note payable	$ 95
Accounts receivable	184	Accounts payable	112
Inventory	147	Accrued wages payable	14
Supplies	32	Taxes payable	30
Prepaid services	11	Other current liabilities	18
Land	60		
Buildings and equipment	430	Owner's Equity	?
Accumulated depreciation	(210)		
Franchise	20		

- Net sales, all on account, totaled $800,000.
- Receivable collections totaled $850,000.
- Inventory costing $528,000 was purchased on account.
- Wages and salaries of $130,000 were earned and paid.
- Utilities costing $5,000 were consumed and paid.
- All 12/31/X2 current liabilities except the current note payable were paid.
- $450,000 was paid on accounts payable.
- The $95,000 current note was paid, plus $8,000 interest.
- $100,000 cash was borrowed on a 5-year note.
- Supplies costing $25,000 were purchased on account.
- The new supplies were stolen the day after they arrived. Unfortunately, thefts occurred quite regularly in the firm's area. There was no insurance recovery.
- The owner withdrew $15,000 of cash for personal use.
- Equipment costing $10,000, with a net book value of $6,000, was sold for $3,000 cash.
- Damages, payable within 120 days, of $40,000 were awarded to a customer injured by a flash fire in the firm's washroom. The damages have been paid.
- Year-end physical inventory disclosed inventory costing $150,000 and supplies costing $4,000 to be still on hand.
- All of the prepaid janitorial services were used.
- Additional depreciation of $30,000 was determined to be appropriate.
- The franchise was being amortized at a rate of $4,000 per year.
- Interest of $6,000 on the new noncurrent note was owed and unpaid.
- Wages of $9,000 were earned and unpaid.
- Income taxes of $6,000 applied to the year. None had been paid.

SP 6.15 The Clarke Company is planning to expand its operations at the end of
next year. It has been determined that $600,000 of additional net working
capital will be required. A pro forma income statement has been prepared
for next year. Assuming all new working capital generated in operations
would be available for expansion, what is the balance for which Clarke
must obtain outside financing?

CLARKE COMPANY
Pro Forma Income Statement for the Forthcoming Year
(000 Omitted)

Sales		$700
Other revenue		50 $750
Operating expenses:		
Wages and salaries	$300	
Supplies	30	
Interest	15	
Rent	40	
Depreciation	35	
Amortization of capital lease	21	
Insurance	8	$449
Gain on asset disposition		14
Income from operations before taxes		$315
Provision for income taxes		115
Net Income		$200

SP 6.16 The Durgin Company's pro-forma income statement is given below. The company wishes to know how much new working capital will be generated during the coming year from operations and in total. Assuming that the firm plans to continue its annual distribution of 30 percent of net income to the owner in cash:

a) How much new net working capital, after owner withdrawal, could the firm expect to have available by the end of the coming year?

b) Assume that the Durgin forecast and the Clarke forecast (Problem SP 6.15, above) turned out to be accurate. Which firm would then be doing a better job of operations management—maximizing revenues and minimizing costs? Be specific in citing apparently significant detailed differences. You may assume that Durgin's prior year sales were $545,000 and Clarke's $667,000.

c) Which firm would have been generating more working capital in proportion to sales? Explain.

DURGIN COMPANY
Pro-Forma Income Statement for the Forthcoming Year
(000 Omitted)

Sales		$600
Other revenue		12 $612
Operating Expenses:		
Wages and salaries	$140	
Supplies	26	
Interest	12	
Depreciation	66	
Amortization of capital lease	16	
Insurance	7	$267
Loss on fixed asset disposition		6
Income from operations before taxes		$339
Provision for income taxes		135
Net Income		$204

PREPARER PROCEDURES

The only preparer procedures relevant to the material introduced in this chapter concerns certain adjustments to noncurrent assets. Amortization of intangibles such as capital leases, leasehold improvement, patents, franchises, trademarks, copyrights, and deferred charges involves a direct reduction of the asset account—a credit to the asset account. The entry also involves a matching charge or debit to the appropriate expense account. For example, $140 amortization of leasehold improvement to occupancy expense would be journalized:

	DR	CR
Occupancy Expense	$140	
Leasehold Improvement		$140

To record amortization of leasehold improvement.

Since depreciation involves the contra-asset account Accumulated Depreciation, the depreciable asset account itself is not reduced. Instead, the balance in the contra-asset account is **increased.** For example, the entry to record $8,000 of depreciation on an office building would be:

	DR	CR
Depreciation Expense	$8,000	
Accumulated depreciation		$8,000

To record annual depreciation.

PREPARER PROBLEMS

PP 6.1 Prepare journal entries in good form for those transactions and adjustments given in Essential Problem EP 6.3 above, which involve either revenue or expense.

PP 6.2 Prepare journal entries in good form for all transactions and adjustments given in Essential Problem EP 6.5 above.

PP 6.3 Refer to the data supplied for the Albert Company in Supplementary Problem SP 6.13 above.

   a) Set up T-accounts for all necessary accounts for the firm.

   b) Record necessary opening balances from the beginning balance sheet.

   c) Prepare journal entries for all transactions and adjustments.

   d) Post entries, balance all accounts, close temporary accounts.

   e) Determine ending balances in balance sheet accounts and prepare post closing trim balance.

PP 6.4 Follow the instructions contained in Problem PP 6.3 above with respect to the Brandywine Company (Supplementary Problem SP 6.14 above).

7

WORKING CAPITAL FUNDS FLOW AND THE STATEMENT OF CHANGES IN FINANCIAL POSITION

CHAPTER PREVIEW

This chapter is divided into *two parts*. The objective of the first part is to complete your introduction to net working capital and its significance to the firm, the various sources from which the firm might obtain additional working capital, and the possible uses or applications of working capital within the firm. In the first part of this chapter you can:

- Learn that a certain minimum amount of working capital is necessary for the survival of a firm in a particular type of business and at a particular volume of activity;

- Learn that this minimum level differs among different types of businesses and for different levels of sales in the same firm;

- Learn the places where working capital may be needed for the firm's survival and growth—the various possible uses or applications of working capital within the firm;

- Develop an understanding of three important subdivisions of overall management—operating management, financial management, and tax management;

- Learn to distinguish operating activities from financial activities;

- Become familiar with where the firm can obtain needed additional working capital—with the several internal and external sources of additional net working capital available to the firm;

- Develop a familiarity with the Working Capital Funds Flow Statement as summarizing some or all of the significant financial management activities within the firm during the most recent period.

The objective of the second part of this chapter is to introduce you to several possible financial-management activities that may not involve working-capital flows, and to present the financial statement that summarizes all significant financial activities—the Statement of Changes in Financial Position. In the second part of this chapter, you will be able to:

- Develop an appreciation of the usefulness of information concerning the financial activities of a firm;

- Learn about the few significant resource flows within the firm which do not or may not involve net working capital, and perceive that such flows always involve "matched pairs" of resource exchanges;

- Become familiar with the fourth and final member of the financial statement "package"—the Statement of Changes in Financial Position (SCFP) —and how this statement is prepared;

- Learn of possible variations in the approach used to present financial activity on the SCFP and of the presentation of extraordinary items;
- Develop an understanding of how the SCFP explains the essential differences between two successive balance sheets and how it articulates with the income statement.

With an understanding of financial resource flows and the SCFP, you will have completed your introduction of the essential content and function of the financial statements prepared by accountants for investors. You should have the essential conceptual framework into which the important details contained in the remaining ten chapters will readily fit.

PART ONE
Working Capital Funds Flow

NEED FOR ADDITIONAL WORKING CAPITAL

Nancy Watson owns and manages a chain of seven TV, hi-fi, and small appliance outlets throughout her state. The business is called Nancy Watson Electronics and Appliances. After many years of growth, her sales volume is stabilized at an average of $125,000 per month: $13,000 of cash sales, and the balance are on account. Nancy does not offer extended financing terms to her customers. Instead she requires payment within 30 days, and competes against stores offering longer payment terms with discount pricing. Some customers do not, of course, pay on time. But, on average, her customers pay their accounts 50 days, or one and two-thirds months, after purchase.

All merchandise is sold at a 50 percent *markup*; that is, items costing $40 are sold for $80.[1] Nancy has found that she needs an average inventory on hand equivalent to two and one-half months' sales. The cash operating costs of Nancy's firm average $101,250 per month and consist of:

- $24,000 of wages and salaries;
- $62,500 for monthly purchase of merchandise;
- $14,750 covering utilities, insurance, equipment rental, supplies, merchandise, and miscellaneous.

For simplification, we will assume that Nancy's firm has no other payroll costs or payroll taxes, and no other expenses except for depreciation and income taxes at 40 percent of income from operations. We will also assume that Nancy does not have to pay tax on any assets sold at a gain.

Nancy is planning to open two new stores at the beginning of next year—19X4. She anticipates that these stores will cost $160,000 each (land $55,000 and building $105,000). At the same time, she wishes to add several new lines of merchandise. She also wishes to close and sell one existing store that is in a poor location. Nancy anticipates that, with eight stores and the new merchandise lines, she can increase her sales volume by 50 percent.

The store Nancy wishes to close cost $150,000 (land $50,000 and building $100,000) and has a net book value of $112,000. Because of inflation, she is sure she can sell it for $135,000. The firm also has a $400,000 long-term note maturing in three years. Nancy wishes to retire (pay off) this note so that

---

[1]   In retailing it is customary, even if confusing to the newcomer, to refer to "markup" as a percentage of the selling price.

she can obtain additional long-term financing. She also plans on withdrawing $20,000 from the business during the year for personal living expenses.   .

Specifically, Nancy Watson wishes to determine the answers to the following questions:

320,000

1. How much additional working capital will she require to buy the new stores, expand her business, and retire the $400,000 debt?
2. Where can she acquire these additional funds?

CAPITAL INVESTED IN A BUSINESS

You instinctively should understand that it often takes money to make money —that a certain amount of resources or capital must be invested in a firm to make it possible for the firm to operate successfully. Let us first generally review capital requirements in terms of assets. It will help if you will relate each item to your personal imaginary firm (see Introduction for Students) as we proceed.

Cash

Can your firm get along without a certain minimum amount of cash on hand? Do you want to turn away customers who do not have exact change to pay for their purchases? Will your employees and suppliers be willing to wait a few days or weeks for payment until you make a few more cash sales or collect a few more customer receivables? Obviously you must have a certain minimum amount of cash invested in your firm to cover day-to-day cash needs. And, as your business grows, your needs for cash on hand will become greater.

Receivables

Not quite so obvious as other assets is the fact that, if it is necessary for you to extend credit to your customers, you will have resources invested in your average receivables. Often you will have already paid for the merchandise sold. Now you must wait for your customer to pay you. As a short-term creditor you have invested in your customer's "business." Your receivables are your customer's payables. It should also be apparent that, as you increase your volume of credit sales, your receivables will increase, requiring more capital invested in the business.

Inventory, Supplies, and Prepaid Items

It should be intuitively obvious that, in most firms, you will need a stock on hand of merchandise to display and sell to customers. Usually you must first own these items before you can sell them. Similarly, you will also have an investment in necessary supplies on hand and in prepaid items such as rent and insurance. Again, as the volume of your business expands, you will require a larger investment of these resources in the business.

Noncurrent or Capacity Assets

Equally obvious is the necessity of having adequate facilities in which to conduct your business. If it is not economic (or otherwise undesirable, or impossible) to lease needed noncurrent assets, you will need to have funds invested in their ownership. As the volume of activity exceeds the capacity of your existing assets, you must acquire more.

You should also understand that different types of businesses have different basic capital requirements. For example, small retail firms on a cash basis have no receivables. Large retail chains often provide extended credit terms or "revolving charge accounts," which require a high investment in receivables. A small services business may lease all of its capacity assets; a large manufacturer will have a very large investment in factory and equipment. Capital requirements must be considered for a specific firm at a specific level of activity.

DETERMINING PRESENT CAPITAL REQUIREMENTS

As the first step in determining Nancy Watson's needs for additional capital, it will be desirable to determine her existing needs to maintain present operations. The result can then be compared to her existing capital investment to see whether there is any excess currently available for future use. Precise techniques of *cash management*, or cash planning, are beyond the scope of this text. They are generally covered in Managerial Accounting and Financial Management texts. Let us assume that a minimum of $75,000 of average cash on hand is required at Nancy's present level of operation.

If Nancy's receivables average one and two-thirds months' sales, her current receivables should require an investment of approximately $187,000 ($1,344,000 annual credit sales divided by 12 and multiplied by one and two-thirds). Nancy has found she requires two and one-half months' average inventory on hand. This will require an investment of $156,000 (cost of goods sold equals 50 percent of sales—$750,000 annual cost of sales divided by 12 and multiplied by 2.5). You may assume that an average investment of $5,000 is required in supplies covering all seven stores.

Therefore, Nancy's required investment at her present level of activity in current assets or working capital totals $423,000. Refer to Exhibit 7.1, which is the most recent balance sheet for Nancy Watson Electronics and Appliances dated 1/31/X3. Compared to minimum requirements, it appears that Nancy has an extra $15,000 of working capital in the business, all in cash.

Exhibit 7.1
NANCY WATSON ELECTRONICS AND APPLIANCES

Balance Sheet
As of 1/31/X3 (000 omitted)

Assets		Equities	
Cash	$ 90	Accounts payable	$ 80
Accounts receivable	187	Wages payable	12
Inventory	156	Other current liabilities	29
Supplies	5	Total Current Liabilities	$121
Total Current Assets	$438		
		Noncurrent note payable	400
Land	350	Total liabilities	$521
Buildings	700	Owner's Equity	792
Accumulated depreciation	(175)	Total Equities	$1,313
Total Assets	$1,313		

DETERMINING FUTURE CAPITAL REQUIREMENTS

How much additional working capital will Nancy require to carry out her planned changes at the end of the year? To handle a 50-percent increase in sales volume, she will need more working capital. You may assume she will need 25 percent more cash, 35 percent more inventory and supplies, and, of course, 50 percent more funds in receivables with a 50-percent sales increase. Her projected minimum requirement for working capital or current assets will total $592,000 (rounded).[2] At her present volume level, minimum requirements were determined to be $423,000. She therefore needs $169,000 of additional working capital for expanded operations. But, as the level of operations increase, so will the level of current liabilities. On a continuously revolving basis, current creditors will finance part of the additional working capital required. You may assume, for this example, that current liabilities will increase 25 percent in response to a 50-percent increase in activity. Therefore, $30,000 of new working capital will be supplied "automatically" by short-

---

[2]

	Present volume	Projected volume
Cash	$ 75,000 × 1.25	$ 93,750
Receivables	187,000 × 1.5	280,500
Inventory	156,000 × 1.35	210,600
Supplies	5,000 × 1.35	6,750
Total	$423,000	$591,600

term creditors, and only $139,000 of new **net** working capital will be required to handle increased volume.

Nancy also intends to acquire two new stores costing $160,000 apiece. You may assume she plans to purchase these properties for cash and separately obtain financing as part of her plan for new long-term debt. Recall that she also wishes to retire the existing $400,000 note, and withdraw $20,000 from the business for personal use. She therefore will need to acquire $879,-000 of additional working capital over present minimum requirements in the business to carry out her plan:

Intended Uses (Applications) of Working Capital

1. Acquire new noncurrent assets	$320,000
2. Retire noncurrent debt	400,000
3. Distribution to owner	20,000
4. Increase balance of net working capital	139,000
	$879,000

DETERMINING POSSIBLE SOURCES

Where can Nancy obtain the needed $879,000? Does all this capital have to come into the business in the form of additional resources invested by the owner? There are four other possible sources—three "internal" (involving resources over which Nancy and the business already have control) and one "external." You might guess what they are and note them on a piece of paper before proceeding.

Internal Sources

When one is looking for something, it is always best to start at home, or with what one already has. Earlier we determined that Nancy had $15,000 of excess net working capital already in the business. She can also sell any noncurrent assets that are no longer required. She is planning on closing and selling one unprofitable store. Recall that she estimated this would bring in $135,000.

Can you think of a third internal source? What about profits from customers? Exhibit 7.2 gives the income statement for the firm for fiscal 19X2. In previous chapters you have learned about working capital funds from operations, and how to determine the amount given in income statements. How much new net working capital was generated in Nancy's firm during the past year? Assuming that the current year will be the same as last year,

Exhibit 7.2

NANCY WATSON ELECTRONICS AND APPLIANCES

Income Statement
For Year Ending 1/31/X3 (000 omitted)

Sales		$1,500
Cost of goods sold		750
Gross Profit		$ 750
Operating Expenses:		
Wages and salaries	$288	
Utilities	42	
Insurance	85	
Equipment rental	12	
Supplies and miscellaneous	6	
Depreciation	35	
Interest	32	500
Income from Operations Before Taxes		$ 250
Provision for income taxes		100
Net Income		$ 150

Nancy will have $185,000 of additional working capital generated from operations.[3]

From internal sources, Nancy can look forward to $335,000 of net working capital being available in the business by the end of the year. She therefore needs to raise only $544,000 from outside sources. Did you correctly guess the following as the three possible internal sources?

1. Use of existing net working capital,
2. Funds from operations,
3. Sale of noncurrent assets.

External (Outside) Sources:

Recall from Chapters 2 and 3 that the balance sheet indicates the possible sources of all assets as being equities. There are three possible external sources when one is considering total assets. They are short-term creditors, long-term creditors, and owners. Are short-term creditors a possible source of the needed $544,000 for Nancy? The preferred answer to this question would be **no**, for several reasons. First, we have already assumed that $30,000 would be coming from short-term creditors in arriving at our initial requirement of $879,000 of **net** working capital. Any additional short-term borrowing

---

[3]

Net income	$150,000
Add: Depreciation	35,000
Funds from operations	$185,000

would not increase net working capital, and would have to be repaid within the year. Nancy is seeking additional *permanent investment*, or *long-term investment*, in net working capital and noncurrent assets to sustain a higher level of operations. Nancy could borrow, on a short-term basis, in anticipation of the following year's funds from operations. This could be risky, and will not be considered further in this example.

With the short-term creditors "out of the running," the two possible external sources of new net working capital for any firm are simply: long-term creditors and owners.

LONG-TERM CAPITAL STRUCTURE

Nancy Watson's need for a long-term commitment of assets in her firm can best be seen in terms of a *Working Capital Balance Sheet*. A Working Capital Balance Sheet is often used by financial managers to focus attention on the permanent or long-term capital invested in the firm and on the firm's *capital structure*. It does this by effectively ignoring both that portion of current assets supplied by current creditors and the current creditor's claims. It includes net working capital and noncurrent assets balanced by noncurrent debt and owner's equity. Exhibit 7.3 presents such a balance sheet for Nancy's firm as of 1/31/X3 and pro forma for 1/31/X4.

Exhibit 7.3
NANCY WATSON ELECTRONICS AND APPLIANCES

Working Capital Balance Sheets
As of 1/31/X3 and Pro-Forma for 1/31/X4
(000 omitted)

Long-Term Assets	Pro Forma 1/31/X4	Actual 1/31/X3	Long-Term Equities	Pro Forma 1/31/X4	Actual 1/31/X3
Net working capital	$441	$317	Noncurrent note	?	$400
Land	410	350	Total long-term		
Buildings	810	700	liabilities	?	$400
Accumulated depreciation	(172)*	(175)	Owner's Equity	945†	792
Total Assets	$1,489	$1,192	Total Equities	$1,489	$1,192

* Assumes reduction of $38,000 for depreciation already accumulated on assets sold and additional $35,000 of regular annual depreciation for the year.
† Assumes same net income as for fiscal 19X2 with addition of $23,000 gain on sale of old store and reduction of $20,000 representing owner withdrawal.

Note, from Exhibit 7.3, that the pro forma equities are incomplete in the amount of $544,000, the exact amount of additional investment required. The $544,000 has already been included with projected asset requirements, assuming that the funds have come from one of the two sources. Nancy's problem is to determine where, and in what proportions (creditor vs. owner) she should raise the remaining new capital. Even if she could readily borrow this amount on a long-term note, she should verify that this action would not, in the eyes of future creditors, impair a desirable capital structure. Capital structure refers to the proportion of long-term debt to total long-term capital invested. It is often measured by the *long-term debt ratio*:

$$\text{Long-term Debt Ratio} = \frac{\text{Total Noncurrent Liabilities}}{\text{Total Noncurrent Liabilities plus Owner's Equity}}$$

The long-term debt ratio is used to indicate whether a firm appears to have an optimal proportion of debt in terms of industry standards.

As an example of the use of this ratio, and of the financial planning of capital structure, assume that Nancy's industry target-ratio was 0.3 to 1. She is a little too high at the present moment with 0.34. As part of her already planned *debt refinancing* (retiring old debt and replacing with new), she would ideally obtain only $447,000 of new long-term debt (0.3 × $1,489,000). The $97,000 balance of the required $544,000 should come from additional investment on her part. Otherwise existing and future creditors might consider her firm as having proportionately too much debt.

Assuming that Nancy obtained the needed $879,000 of new net working capital from the different sources as indicated, they would have been:

1. Funds from operations	$185,000
2. Sale of noncurrent assets	135,000
3. New noncurrent debt	447,000 ✓
4. New owner investment	97,000 ✓
5. Decreased (original) balance of net working capital	15,000
Total Sources	$879,000

VARIOUS COMPONENTS OF OVERALL MANAGEMENT

The Nancy Watson case demonstrates many of the aspects of *financial management*. The overall management of any firm can be viewed as made up of three distinct components: *operating management*, financial management, and tax management. Operating management is essentially involved in using the resources already in the firm to generate revenue and, hopefully, profits. The income statement reports on the activities of operating management.

Financial management essentially involves two separate but intimately related activities: *investing activities* and *financing activities*. Investing activities involve planning the investment goals of the firm. The planning includes determining how much new capital is required in the firm and how new and existing capital should be allocated among various uses. Often investment planning is referred to as *capital budgeting*. Capital budgeting decisions would include determining:

- Whether or not to add or discontinue products, product lines, plants and equipment, and so forth;
- Whether new desired capacity should be leased or purchased;
- Which among several competing assets or groups of assets should be leased/purchased;
- How much income should be distributed to owners and how much should be retained in the business;
- How much net working capital is necessary to support planned levels of operation.

Capital budgeting is a financial management activity and its aspects are dealt with in managerial accounting and financial management texts. Financial accounting is concerned with reporting the results of investing activities—how additional resources were actually used.

The other part of financial management involves the planning of the acquisition or inflow of needed additional resources. The planning for, and the obtaining of, additional capital are known as financing activities. Financing activities involve determining:

- How much of the firm's existing resources (excess working capital and unneeded noncurrent assets) are available for investing in other areas;
- How much new capital will be generated from business operations;
- How much new capital will become available through the sale of no-longer-needed noncurrent assets;
- How much new capital can/will be raised from long-term creditors and owners, and in what proportions, to achieve a desirable long-term debt ratio.

Financing is a skilled activity involving extensive knowledge of the *capital markets*—the possible outside sources of additional capital. Financing is covered in financial management texts. Again, financial accounting is concerned with reporting the results of financing activities—where additional resources were obtained: the sources of those funds, which were then invested in the business.

THE WORKING CAPITAL FUNDS FLOW STATEMENT

A financial accounting report covering the financial-management activities during the most recent period is known as the Working Capital Funds Flow Statement. This statement quite simply reports on the results of the year's investing activities relating to working capital—where working capital is used or applied—and where it ended up. It also reports on the results of the year's financing activities involving working capital—the sources of working capital invested during the year—where it came from.

If we assume that planned operations (net income) and the planned financing and investing activities of Nancy Watson Electronics and Appliances actually took place, a Working Capital Funds Flow Statement could be prepared reporting these activities or flows in terms of their sources and uses (applications). From the information presented in the Nancy Watson example, you should attempt to prepare a "Sources and Uses" statement and an income statement before proceeding.

The working capital funds-flow statement reports on the firm's financial-management activities during the most recent period. Like the income statement, it covers a period of time. Therefore it is dated as "For the year (period) ending X/X/X" and **not** "as of." The statement lists the sources and then the applications of working capital. Exhibit 7.4 is an income statement and Exhibit 7.5 is a working capital funds-flow statement for Nancy's firm assuring the operating, financing, and investing activities took place as planned.

Exhibit 7.4

NANCY WATSON ELECTRONICS AND APPLIANCES

Income Statement for the Year Ending 1/31/X4 (000 omitted)		
Gross Sales		$1,500
Cost of goods sold		750
Gross Profit		$ 750
Operating Expenses:		
Wages and salaries	$288	
Utilities	42	
Insurance	85	
Equipment rental	12	
Supplies and miscellaneous	6	
Depreciation	35	
Interest	32	500
Gain on disposition of noncurrent asset		23
Income from Operations before Taxes		$ 273
Provision for income taxes		100
Net Income		$ 173

Study these exhibits. Note that the reconciliation of funds from operations and net income are presented as part of the funds statement itself; the statement thus ties in directly or articulates with the income statement. Also note that the transaction involving the sale of the unprofitable store is disclosed separately. Recall that the store had a net book value of $112,000, and was sold for $135,000. The $23,000 nonextraordinary gain was therefore

Exhibit 7.5

NANCY WATSON ELECTRONICS AND APPLIANCES

Working Capital Funds Flow Statement
For the Year Ending 1/31/X4
(000 omitted)

Sources		Applications	
Net Income	$173		
Plus depreciation	35		
Less gain on sale of noncurrent assets	23		
Funds from Operations	$185		
Sale of noncurrent assets	135	Acquired noncurrent asset	$320
New noncurrent debt	447	Retired noncurrent debt	400
New owner investment	97	Distributed to owner	20
		Increase in Balance of net working capital	124
Total Sources	$864	Total Applications	$864

reported on the income statement. The funds statement could have reported this gain as part of funds from operations and shown the sale proceeds as only the $112,000 book value recovered. Or it could have included the gain in funds from operations and shown the proceeds as $135,000. The first approach would have been misleading, and the second approach incorrect, because the gain would have been double-counted. Therefore, accountants break out any gain in noncurrent-asset disposition, and report it as part of the total proceeds of the sale.

Also note that the $15,000 reduction in net working capital and the $139,000 increase were netted, to show the actual change that would take place between the two balance sheets. Nancy's balance sheet as of 1/31/X4 is not shown in detail. With events assumed to have occurred as planned, it would contain the information shown pro forma on Exhibit 7.3. You can verify the further articulation among the statements by observing that the net working capital did increase by $124,000.

Exhibit 7.5 presents the statement in balanced form. This format is acceptable under GAAP and is easier for you to comprehend. (Most published statements follow the equally acceptable format shown in Exhibit 7.6.) Note that the information content of Exhibit 7.6 is identical with Exhibit 7.5. This format merely highlights the change in the firm's financial position (in terms of net working capital).

CHECKLIST OF POSSIBLE SOURCES AND APPLICATIONS

The Nancy Watson Working Capital Funds-Flow Statement provides specific examples of most of the possible sources and applications of working

Exhibit 7.6

NANCY WATSON ELECTRONICS AND APPLIANCES

**Working Capital Funds Flow Statement for the Year
Ending 1/31/X4 (000 omitted)**

Working Capital was Obtained from:		
Net income		$173
Plus depreciation	$ 35	
Less gain on noncurrent asset disposition	23	12
Funds from operations		$185
Sale of noncurrent assets	$135	
New noncurrent debt	447	
New owner investment	97	679
Total Funds Obtained		$864
Working Capital was Used to:		
Purchase noncurrent assets	$320	
Retire noncurrent debt	400	
Distribute cash to owner	20	
Total Uses		$740
Increase in Balance of Net Working Capital		$124

capital in any firm. Only two other possibilities remain: one source and one application. The other possible source actually was demonstrated in Nancy's case, but was offset by the necessary large infusion of new net working capital. During a given period, a firm may draw down its balance of net working capital and use it to acquire noncurrent assets, to retire noncurrent debt, or to distribute to the owners. Following a balanced format, an overall reduction of the balance of net working capital occurring during the period may be included as a source. Following the "unbalanced" or change-in-position format (Exhibit 7.6), uses or applications of working capital would be shown first, then sources, and finally the difference as a reduction of net working capital.

A firm may also use working capital or lose it in operations. Assume that a particular income statement showed a net loss of $500,000 for the period, and that the only nonfund expense was $140,000 of depreciation. Adding that depreciation would still result in a negative funds flow of $360,000. This would indicate that working capital outflows (expenses) in operations exceeded by $360,000 the working capital inflows (revenues) generated. Funds lost in operations would be shown as a use, or application of working capital, on the statement.

Exhibit 7.7 provides a checklist of the possible sources and applications of net working capital within any firm. Note the symmetry, which makes the list easy to remember. For each source there exists an opposite application, and vice versa. Also note that only two "pairs" are mutually exclusive. During any given period of time, funds are either obtained from or lost in operations, not both. Similarly, the balance of net working capital in the business either

Exhibit 7.7

CHECKLIST OF POSSIBLE SOURCES AND APPLICATIONS OF FUNDS*

Sources	Applications
Funds from operations	or Funds lost in operations
Sale of noncurrent assets	Purchase of noncurrent assets
Additional long-term debt	Extinguishment of long-term debt
Additional owner investment	Distribution to owner †
Reduction of net working capital balance	or Increase of net working capital balance

* Extraordinary events are omitted.
† Usually known as "withdrawals" in a proprietorship or partnership and as "dividends" in a corporation.

increases or decreases (or it doesn't change). In all the other cases, both members of a "pair" can exist in the same time period. Existing noncurrent assets can be sold and new ones purchased. An existing noncurrent loan can be paid (or retired), and another obtained. Owners can invest additional capital as well as withdraw profits. Finally, remember that if the statement is accurately prepared, the totals must always balance, just as with a balance sheet. The change in the firm's position must equal the difference between the successive balance sheets.

Perhaps you can visualize how funds-flow information often is a vital concern to anyone wishing to analyze and evaluate the performance of a particular firm. Funds-flow information provides you, as a user, with a summary of the company's principal financial activities during the period. With funds-flow information you have an indication of profitability: funds were either generated or lost in operations.[4] You can find out whether the firm has been replacing or expanding its capacity, and whether it is expanding through increased long-term capital investment other than retained profits. Or you can determine if the firm is in a "steady state," or is shrinking in size. You can also find out how the firm may be altering its proportion of long-term debt to owner's equity. And finally, you have information on funds withdrawn by the owners.

Funds-flow information is a required part of a firm's financial statement. It is provided in the Statement of Changes in Financial Position (SCFP). In Part Two of this chapter, you can learn how, in some circumstances, the SCFP can be identical to the Working Capital Funds-Flow Statement. In

---

[4]   Remember that positive funds from operations do not always indicate profit. For example:

Funds from operations	$100,000
Less depreciation and amortization	140,000
Net loss	($40,000)

other circumstances, the SCFP will contain all the working capital funds-flow information plus other significant facts.

At this point you may wish to pause and "digest" the first part of this chapter before proceeding to Part Two. So that you may use them for review, the chapter-end summary and the review questions are classified and identified to match the two parts of this chapter.

PART TWO
Statement of Changes in Financial Position

PART 2 PREVIEW

(This information is repeated from the overall chapter preview.)

The objective of the second part of this chapter is to introduce you to several possible financial-management activities that may not involve working-capital flows, and to present the financial statement that summarizes all significant financial activities—the Statement of Changes in Financial Position (SCFP). In the second part of this chapter you will be able to:

- Develop an appreciation of the usefulness of information concerning the financial activities of a firm;

- Learn about the significant resource flows within the firm which do not or may not involve net working capital, and perceive that such flows always involve "matched pairs" of resource exchanges;

- Become familiar with the fourth and final member of the financial statement "package"—the SCFP—and how this statement is prepared;

- Learn of possible variations in the approach used to present financial activity on the SCFP and of the presentation of extraordinary items;

- Develop an understanding of how the SCFP explains the essential differences between two successive balance sheets and how it articulates with the income statement.

KEEPING INFORMED
ON THE ACTIONS
OF YOUR COMPETITORS

Assume that you are the owner of an interstate regional trucking company in the Midwest. Essential to the continued successful operation of your trucking firm is "intelligence," or information, concerning all of the myriad outside factors that could significantly affect your business. You would need current information and forecasts concerning the overall economy; prices and technological changes in trucks, fuel, and tires; patterns of Teamster Union wage contracts; highway construction programs; government regulations and taxation changes, and many other similarly important factors. It would also be important for you to know what your competitors have done and are doing. Are they accelerating the replacement of equipment or just routinely replacing equipment as it wears out? Are they expanding their capacity assets; i.e., are they acquiring more trucks and more freight terminals? Is it possible that they are changing their patterns of long-term capital financing, including changing their proportion of long-term debt to total noncurrent equities?

You do not necessarily wish to just copy your competitors' actions, assuming that you could do so. At the same time you certainly want to take advantage of any new ideas discovered or developed by your competitors. You also want as much warning as possible of any potential new competitive threat, so that you can consider an appropriate response. For instance, a pattern of accelerated replacement of equipment could be a signal of a new, significantly better truck—less cost or more capacity—which you haven't heard about or considered seriously. Significant expansion of capacity could signal a potential invasion of your market. A major change in industry patterns of long-term debt proportion could indicate that, in contrast with the past, creditors are more or less willing to extend debt financing to your industry and to you.

*   *   *

In Part One you learned that some of this information could be obtained from working capital funds-flow statements. However, such statements, even if available, do not necessarily provide all the information on a firm's major resource changes. Resource changes can occur which do **not** involve working capital flows. Any changes of this type will be included in the Statement of Changes in Financial Position (SCFP). Assume that you have the following abbreviated SCFP's for the previous year for each of your two major competitors: Acme Fast Freight and Redball Express. These statements are given in Exhibit 7.8. You also have the same competitors' most recent year-end abbreviated balance sheets, which are given in Exhibit 7.9.

Exhibit 7.8

Abbreviated Statements of Changes in Financial Position
For the Year 19XX

ACME FAST FREIGHT

Sources		Applications	
Funds from operations	$310,000	Purchase of trucks	$600,000
Sale of trucks	140,000	Acquisition of land	20,000
New long-term debt	350,000	Acquisition of terminals	200,000
New owner investment	20,000	Acquisition of equipment	25,000
Decrease in net working capital	55,000		
		Withdrawals by owner	30,000
Total Sources	$875,000	Total Applications	$875,000

REDBALL EXPRESS

Sources		Applications	
Funds from operations	$250,000	Purchase of trucks	$450,000
Sale of trucks	200,000	Retire long-term debt	40,000
Decrease in net working capital	50,000	Withdrawals by owner	10,000
Total Sources	$500,000	Total Applications	$500,000

Before analyzing Exhibits 7.8 and 7.9, you should make the following assumptions:

- All significant resource changes that occur in a firm during the previous year are reported on the SCFP.
- The trucks have a five-year useful life, and depreciation is calculated to the nearest month on a straight-line (equal-amount-each-year) basis.
- The costs of capacity assets have not changed over the past several years.
- The normal long-term debt ratio in your industry has, in the past, clustered around 0.3 to 1, and creditors have effectively refused to go beyond 0.35 to 1.

What do Exhibits 7.8 and 7.9 tell you about your two major competitors? Specifically:

1. Is either firm significantly expanding its capacity?
2. Is there any evidence of significant early replacement of any fixed assets?
3. Does it appear that creditors in your industry are still holding to the 0.35 to 1 limit on possible long-term debt ratios?

From Exhibits 7.8 and 7.9 you can learn some important facts about your competitors. Apparently Acme has nearly doubled its terminal capacity. Start-

Exhibit 7.9

Abbreviated Balance Sheets as of 12/31/XX

ACME FAST FREIGHT

Net working capital	$ 200,000	Long-term debt	$ 500,000
Land	40,000		
Terminals	300,000	Owner's Equity	760,000
Less accumulated depreciation	(50,000)		
Trucks	800,000		
Less accumulated depreciation	(60,000)		
Other equipment	100,000		
Less accumulated depreciation	(70,000)		
Total Assets	$1,260,000	Total Equities	$1,260,000

REDBALL EXPRESS

Net working capital	$180,000	Long-term debt	$200,000
Land	20,000		
Terminals	150,000	Owner's Equity	635,000
Less accumulated depreciation	(100,000)		
Trucks	600,000		
Less accumulated depreciation	(50,000)		
Other equipment	75,000		
Less accumulated depreciation	(40,000)		
Total Assets	$835,000	Total Equities	$835,000

---

ing from the ending balance sheet amounts, half of Acme's land and two-thirds of its investment in terminals have been added during the past year. Redball, on the other hand, has not expanded its terminals or even replaced what has worn out. Acme is certainly expanding its capacity and might be cause for concern and counteraction on your part.

In the case of trucks, there are even more alarming signals. If trucks are being used for their full five-year useful life, on average one would expect to find 20 percent of a truck fleet replaced each year. As of 12/31/XX, 75 percent of the trucks owned by both firms are reported as having been acquired **within the previous year.** This very high rate of acquisition could represent simple expansion of trucking capacity, especially for Acme. Or it could signal the existence of a truck improvement so significant as to justify early replacement of existing equipment. You could make a better estimate by looking at the prior year's balance sheet. Nevertheless, there is ample reason for you to seek further information to make sure you understand what is happening.

Acme's long-term debt ratio is now up to approximately 0.4 to 1, which may indicate a break in the creditor's upper limit. This could mean additional potential liquidity for your firm and others, and should certainly be investigated.

This simplified example demonstrates how the Statement of Changes in Financial Position (SCFP) can provide you with much meaningful intelligence. Remember that often the statements don't provide many answers, but they can focus your attention on areas requiring further investigation through other sources, as in the situation of massive new truck acquisitions. They can similarly indicate areas of no significant change from prior years, as in the case of Redball's terminal capacity.

RESOURCE CHANGES NOT INVOLVING WORKING CAPITAL FLOWS

Remember, from Chapter 6, that certain valuation adjustments and adjustments for noncurrent-asset expirations affected balance sheet accounts below the wavy line on the diagram. Remember the diagram was introduced in Chapter 6 to help you visually distinguish events that represented working capital flows (changes) from those that did not. Such valuation and expiration adjustments are added back (or subtracted) from net income in determining funds from operations. They do not represent *discretionary resource exchanges*, i.e., exchanges of resources with those outside the firm resulting from a decision by management. The intention of the SCFP is to report significant financial-management activities or actions occurring during the recent period. Adjustments to the measured amount of noncurrent assets and liabilities do not represent current discretionary resource exchanges. Even a major loss of a noncurrent asset can be thought of as "instant depreciation or amortization" and would not represent the result of a management action. All of these **adjustments** occurring below the wavy line are **not** included on the working capital funds-flow statement, since they do not involve working capital flows. They are similarly **excluded** from the SCFP since they do not represent significant current management action.

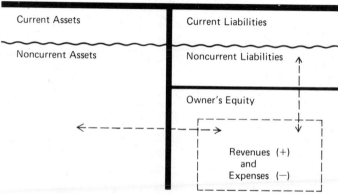

BALANCE SHEET DIAGRAM

There are, however, resource exchanges which are the result of financial management actions but which do not involve working capital flows. One example would be a noncurrent asset acquired in exchange for a down payment and a long-term note payable. Assume that a $100,000 fixed asset was acquired for $10,000 cash and a five-year note for $90,000 plus interest.

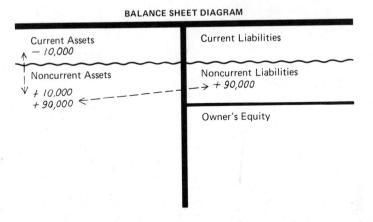

BALANCE SHEET DIAGRAM

Note that this transaction involved only a $10,000 working capital flow (change). Therefore, the $90,000 of new noncurrent debt (source) and the $90,000 of new fixed assets (application) would **not** be included on a working capital funds-flow statement.

A noncurrent asset can be acquired by direct trade for another, or with an older asset "traded-in." Only the working capital (if any) portion of this transaction would be reported on a working capital statement.

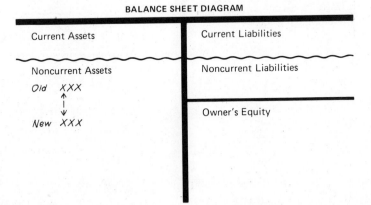

BALANCE SHEET DIAGRAM

Also, land or other noncurrent assets could be directly invested by the owner(s). Suppose land with a fair market value of $500,000 had been invested in the business by the owner. A new owner investment of $500,000 (source) would be accompanied by a new $500,000 noncurrent asset (application). Such a transaction would represent a significant discretionary resource exchange; yet it would not be included on a working capital funds-flow statement, since no working capital was involved.

BALANCE SHEET DIAGRAM

Current Assets	Current Liabilities
Noncurrent Assets	Noncurrent Liabilities
	Owner's Equity

+ 500,000 ← — — — — — — — → *+ 500,000*

Also, in the case of corporations, as will be discussed in later chapters, sometimes noncurrent creditors are allowed to exchange their creditor claim for an ownership share. Such action may significantly alter the firm's capital structure, but working capital is not involved. For example, noncurrent debt amounting to $5,000,000 could be eliminated (application) in exchange for $5,000,000 of new ownership shares (source). This *debt conversion* would not be reported on the working capital statement.

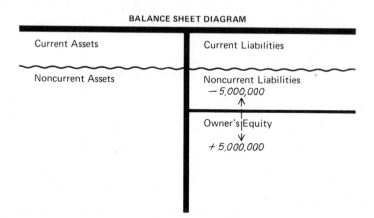

BALANCE SHEET DIAGRAM

Current Assets	Current Liabilities
Noncurrent Assets	Noncurrent Liabilities — 5,000,000
	Owner's Equity + 5,000,000

Note that, in each of these examples, the significant resource exchange, which would be omitted from the working capital funds-flow statement, involved a *"matched pair"* of a source and an application with identical amounts. The four "matched pairs" cited above are fairly common, especially the first two. To review, these four common matched pairs include:

- All or a portion of a noncurrent asset obtained (application) in exchange for additional noncurrent debt (source);

- New noncurrent asset obtained (application) in trade on the disposition of old noncurrent asset (source);
- New noncurrent asset obtained (application) as direct investment by owner(s) (source);
- Extinguishment of long-term debt (application) in exchange for additional ownership claims or shares (source) in a debt conversion.

Three less common pairs could include:

- Extinguishment of long-term debt (application) through payment of a noncurrent asset (source);
- Extinguishment of preferred stockholder claim (application) in exchange for additional common shareholder shares (source) in a stock conversion (see Chapter 10);
- Distribution to owner(s) (application) of noncurrent assets (source).

THE STATEMENT OF CHANGES IN FINANCIAL POSITION (SCFP)

Have you already guessed the difference between the SCFP and the working capital funds-flow statement? You are correct if you see that the only essential difference involves "matched pairs." The SCFP includes all working capital flows **plus** any "matched pairs" of financial transactions occurring during the period that did not involve working capital flows (changes). It presents the complete picture of major resource flows. In the case of Nancy Watson's firm in Part 1 of this chapter, her working capital funds-flow statement (Exhibit 7.5) could also properly be titled the SCFP. There were no "matched pairs" for Nancy's firm that year. Where there are no "matched pairs," the SCFP can be identical to a working capital funds-flow statement.

To see how "matched pairs" can make a difference, compare Exhibits 7.10 and 7.11. Exhibit 7.10 is an abbreviated (net income reconciliation omitted) working capital funds-flow statement for the Barry Company for the year ending 12/31/X1 presented in a balanced format. Assume that, during the year, Barry also had the following major financial transactions, none of which involved flows of working capital:

1. Acquired $50 million of new fixed assets in exchange for a ten-year note payable.
2. Acquired $40 million of new fixed assets as a direct investment by the owner(s).
3. Old long-term debt of $70 million was converted to owners' equity.

Do you see that Exhibit 7.11 picks up and incorporates these three significant "matched pairs"? The acquisition of an additional $90 million of new fixed assets is disclosed, together with the sources, i.e., $50 million of

Exhibit 7.10

BARRY COMPANY

**Abbreviated Working Capital Funds-Flow Statement
For Year Ending 19X1 (figures in millions)**

Sources of Working Capital:

Funds from operations	$100
Disposition of fixed assets	40
New long-term debt	30
New owner investment	0
Decrease in balance of net working capital	20
Total Sources	$190

Applications of Working Capital:

Acquire new fixed assets	$100
Retire old long-term debt	60
Earnings withdrawal by owner	30
Total Applications	$190

Exhibit 7.11

BARRY COMPANY

**Abbreviated Statement of Changes in Financial Position
For Year Ending 19X1 (figures in millions)**

Resources Were Obtained From (Sources):

Funds from operations	$100
Disposition of fixed assets	40
New long-term debt	80
New owner investment	110
Decrease in balance of net working capital	20
Total Sources	$350

Resources Were Applied To (Applications):

Acquire new fixed assets	$190
Retire old long-term debt	130
Earnings withdrawal by owner	30
Total Applications	$350

---

new long-term debt and $40 million of new owners' equity. Also disclosed as an application is the retirement of an additional $70 million of old long-term debt, together with its source, the $70 million of additional owner investment.

To review, the SCFP reports all major discretionary resource flows that occur during the year. Normal operating activities are summarized into a single figure—Funds from Operations. Other major flows are **not** netted but are shown separately for a maximum information disclosure. For example, on Exhibit 7.11, where Barry both retired $130 million of old debt and borrowed $80 million of new long-term funds, to have reported only a net $50 million debt decrease would provide the user with inadequate information. Instead, $80 million of new debt is reported as a source, and the extinguishment of $130 million of old debt as an application.

SCHEDULE OF WORKING CAPITAL CHANGES

Remember that the flows above the wavy line—changes in working capital items which do not result in changes to the balance of net working capital—are not shown on the working capital funds-flow statement. These same detail flows within current assets and current liabilities are omitted from the SCFP in order to focus attention on net working capital and other resource flows. In order for the financial statement user to be in a position to make a more detailed analysis, these changes are included with the SCFP on a supplementary *Schedule of Working Capital Changes*. Exhibit 7.12 is such a schedule for the Barry Company.

Exhibit 7.12
BARRY COMPANY

Schedule of Working Capital Changes
For Year Ending 12/31/X1 (figures in millions)

	12/31/X1	12/31/X0	Increase (decrease)
Current Assets:			
Cash	$105	$100	5
Accounts receivable	180	200	(20)
Inventory	300	290	10
Total Current Assets	$585	$590	(5)
Current Liabilities:			
Notes payable	$200	$200	0
Accounts payable	140	125	15
Total Current Liabilities	$340	$325	15
Net Working Capital	$245	$265	(20)

Note that this schedule merely repeats the balances in the current asset and current liability accounts from the beginning and ending balance sheets for the year. Note also that the decreases of $20 million in net working capital reconciles with the amount appearing on the SCFP, Exhibit 7.11.

POSSIBLE SOURCES AND APPLICATIONS ON THE SCFP

Exhibit 7.11 provides examples of most of the possible sources and applications on a SCFP. The only other major items which could appear would be: Funds Lost in Operations as an application instead of Funds from Operations as a source; and Increase in Balance of Net Working Capital as an application instead of Decrease as a source. Note that the five possible types of sources and applications for the SCFP are the same as those described in Part One for the working capital funds-flow statement (Exhibit 7.7). The only difference is that the SCFP also includes transactions where net working capital flows are not involved—the so-called "matched pairs."

REPORTING EXTRAORDINARY ITEMS

Occasionally a firm may have funds provided by (or used by) extraordinary items or from discontinued operations. Recall, from Chapter 6, that funds from operations is determined exclusive of extraordinary items and discontinued operations. Such items are added back (or subtracted from) net income in the determination of funds from operations. In those cases where extraordinary or "discontinued" items did generate or use funds, the amount of funds so generated or used are separately disclosed as an addition (or subtraction) on the SCFP immediately following funds from operations. This treatment effectively segregates extraordinary funds flows so that the user will not mistakenly anticipate their future recurrence.

For example, assume an income statement revealed the following:

Income from operations	$100,000
Income from discontinued operations	15,000
Extraordinary fire loss of inventory	90,000
Extraordinary fire loss of factory building	250,000
Net Loss	($225,000)

Also assume that nonfund expenses (depreciation and amortization) totaled $70,000. Can you determine funds from operations? You should attempt to do so before proceeding.

Funds from operations would be determined as follows:

Net Loss	($225,000)
Add: Depreciation and amortization	70,000
Extraordinary loss of inventory	90,000
Extraordinary loss of factory	250,000
Subtract: Income from discontinued operations	15,000
Funds from Operations	$170,000

The SCFP (and also the working capital statement) would show, in part, under sources:

Funds from Operations	$170,000
Less extraordinary fund loss (inventory)	90,000
	$ 80,000
Funds provided by discontinued operations	15,000
Net funds provided	$95,000

Note that the extraordinary factory loss did not represent an outflow of funds, and therefore is not reported on the SCFP as a separately identified source or application. The loss of a noncurrent asset is just like depreciation in that net working capital is not affected and no resources are exchanged.

DIFFERENCES IN THE FOCUS OF FUNDS BEING REPORTED

Even in the restricted context of the funds-flow statement, "funds" can be used in several different ways. Although the SCFP clearly reports all discretionary resource flows, under GAAP the focus of the report or the item being measured and reported as "funds" may be:

- Working capital from operations and changes in the balance of net working capital,
- Quick assets from operations and changes in the balance of quick assets,
- Cash and marketable securities from operations and changes in their combined balance, or
- Cash from operations and changes in the balance of cash.

As the focus narrows to a more restricted concept, the number of "pairs" of other resource flows may correspondingly increase. The basic concept remains unchanged. All major financing and investing activities are reported. An example of a cash-flow statement, and a discussion of its preparation and use, will be found in Chapter 14.

THE SCFP AS THE MAJOR LINK BETWEEN SUCCESSIVE BALANCE SHEETS

Recall from Chapter 6 that the statement of owner's capital (retained earnings) reconciles or connects the owner's equity sections of two successive balance sheets. The SCFP performs a similar role for the remainder of the balance sheet items. It explains the change in net working capital (or a possibly more narrow concept of funds—see above). It also explains all of the changes occurring to noncurrent assets and noncurrent liabilities other than expiration and amortization adjustments. A properly completed SCFP contains a reconciliation of net income and funds from operations. The statement therefore articulates with the income statement, and, through the statement of owner's capital (retained earnings), with the owner's equity portion of successive balance sheets. Exhibit 7.13 pictures the statement articulation. A series of successive SCFP's probably gives a better indicator (than does any of the other statements) of what the firm is really doing and where it is going.

Exhibit 7.13

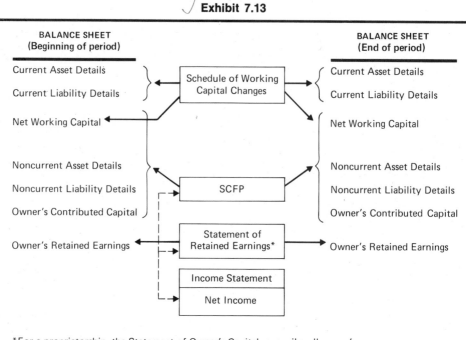

*For a proprietorship, the Statement of Owner's Capital reconciles all owner's capital, not just Retained Earnings.

CHAPTER OVERVIEW

From the material contained in Part One of this chapter, you should be able to:

- Explain, with specific examples, that a certain amount of capital is required in a business, and that the amount and composition varies with the type of business and with its level of activity;
- Describe the five possible applications of working capital within a firm, and give examples of each;
- Explain the difference between financial management and operating management, and describe investing vs. financing activities;
- Describe, with examples, the five possible sources of working capital, distinguishing between internal and external sources;
- Describe, with an example, a typical Working Capital Funds-Flow Statement and what information each item conveys.

From the material contained in Part Two you should be able to:

- Explain the usefulness of the SCFP;

- Identify at least seven different "matched pairs" of resource exchanges that might be included on the SCFP and that do not involve working capital flows;
- Describe the difference, if any, between the SCFP and the Working Capital Funds-Flow Statement;
- Describe the Schedule of Working Capital Changes and explain its function;
- Describe the appropriate treatment of extraordinary and "discontinued" items on the SCFP;
- Explain the different funds concepts acceptable under GAAP as the central focus of a SCFP;
- Explain, with examples, how the SCFP serves as a bridge between successive balance sheets, and how it articulates with the other financial statements.

NEW VOCABULARY AND CONCEPTS

Part One

Markup
Cash management
Application (Funds)
Source (Funds)
Internal source
External (outside) source
Permanent (long-term) investment
Working capital balance sheet
Capital structure
Long-term debt ratio
Debt refinancing
Financial management

Operating management
Investing activities
Financing activities
Capital budgeting
Capital markets
Working capital funds-flow statement

Part Two

Discretionary resource exchanges
Debt conversion
"Matched pair"
Schedule of working capital changes

- Capital requirements in a particular business at a particular volume level.
- Financial management and its activities as distinct from operating management.
- Possible sources and applications of working capital.
- "Matched pairs" and the possible difference between the SCFP and the working capital funds-flow statement.
- The articulation of the financial statements.

REVIEW QUESTIONS

Questions relating to Part One

1. Explain why the minimum amount of net working capital required in a business can come only from long-term creditors or owners.

2. a) Explain why a certain amount of net working capital is required for a particular kind and size of business. (b) How is working capital used in a business?

3. a) Explain why increased sales volume in a firm, whether or not profitable, is usually accompanied by needs for more capital investment in the firm. (b) Give some specific examples of asset categories requiring additional investment with increased sales volume.

4. To support increased business volume, a firm which will require $75,000 of additional working capital may need to raise only $50,000 of additional net working capital. Explain.

5. It is said that more than half of all U.S. businesses that fail do so because they are undercapitalized. If a firm starts in business with insufficient available capital, it is easy to see that it could never really get going. How can a going, successful firm become undercapitalized? Explain.

6. What are "funds from operations"?

7. What is meant by "sources of working capital"?

8. What are the three possible "internal sources" of working capital?

9. What are the two possible "external sources" of net working capital?

10. What is meant by "applications or uses of working capital"?

11. In addition to increasing the balance of net working capital on hand, there are four possible types of applications of working capital for a firm. What are these four applications?

12. Explain why, when changes in the balance of net working capital are included, sources and applications of working capital will always balance.

13. a) What is meant by the capital structure of a firm? b) How does the long-term debt ratio relate to the firm's capital structure, and how is this ratio determined?

14. How does financial management differ from operating management? Describe the two major activities of financial management.

15. What is the information content of the Working Capital Funds-Flow Statement?

Questions relating to Part Two

16. Since the working capital funds-flow statement is not usually provided along with a firm's financial statements, where, as a user, could you obtain this information?

17. a) Can the working capital funds-flow statement ever be the same as the SCFP? (b) If yes, explain the conditions when this could occur.

18. When the working capital funds-flow statement is different from the SCFP, what is the difference?

19. What are "matched pairs" of resource flows? Give examples of the three most common types of "matched pairs."

20. Certain changes in noncurrent assets and noncurrent equities are not reported on any funds statement as resource flows. Give examples of these omitted items, and explain why they are are excluded.

21. What is the Schedule of Working Capital Changes? What does it include?

22. What are extraordinary items? Give examples demonstrating how and when they are reported separately on the SCFP.

23. What are the four common definitions of funds? Explain how each relates to the other.

24. Explain how the SCFP articulates with the other financial statements.

MINI-CASES AND QUESTIONS FOR DISCUSSION

MC 7.1. Nancy Wong has been giving some hard thought to the idea that firms usually require a certain amount of net working capital provided by long-term creditors or owners. She says, "I'm still a little confused. It seems to me that some businesses could operate without net working capital. What about firms that sell only for cash? And suppose such a firm was in the business of selling services and therefore needed no inventory. Or, if it did sell merchandise, suppose it usually sold items for cash before it had to pay its suppliers?" John Miller replied, "I can't see how any firm could get by without some minimum of net working capital. After all, a firm needs some cash around, and cash is not provided by suppliers." Discuss.

MC 7.2. Angelo Bardelli is a very practical guy. "Cash from operations, I can see," he says. "But funds from operations, what good is it? So I have $60,000 in funds from operations and most of the $60,000 is in receivables and inventory. I can't pay my bills or my employees with receivables or inventory."

"You are forgetting the cycle, Angelo," replies Ilsa Mohr. "If each month your business generates $5,000 in funds from operations, each month your firm will also be generating $5,000 in cash as previous cycles are completed. So funds from operations is a good indicator of cash flow."

"Cash I can understand. Funds aren't cash," responds Angelo. Discuss.

MC 7.3. Eslita Moreno has received job offers from two firms in the same business: the Sugar Company and the Tare Company. She is interested in staying for many years with the firm she chooses, and therefore wants a company whose owner is really interested in making the business a long-run success. She has heard rumors that the owner of one of the two firms is really "milking the business for all he can get now," but she isn't sure whether this is true or to which firm the rumor applies.

You have funds-flow information for both firms for the past four years. Each year the pattern in each company essentially repeats. Below is information for each firm for a typical year. What could you tell Eslita about her concern?

SUGAR COMPANY
Working Capital Funds Flow for Year 19XX

Sources		Applications	
Funds from operations	$100,000	Withdrawal by owner	$130,000
New long-term debt	20,000		
Sale of fixed assets	10,000		
	$130,000		$130,000

TARE COMPANY
Working Capital Funds Flow for Year 19XX

Sources		Applications	
Funds from operations	$200,000	Purchase additional fixed	
Additional owner investment	30,000	assets	$140,000
		Retire long-term debt	50,000
		Withdrawal by owner	10,000
		Increase balance in net	
		working capital	30,000
	$230,000		$230,000

MC 7.4. Bob Tindel is attempting to evaluate the recent activities of the Lubbock Company. Its SCFP reports the following data in thousands of dollars:

Sources		Applications	
New long-term debt	$50	Funds lost in operations	$75
Sale of equipment	25	Owner withdrawals	20
Reduction in balance of net			
working capital	20		
	$95		$95

What can Bob infer with respect to the most recent activities of the Lubbock Company? Is it profitable? Are the owners assisting during its difficulties? Is the firm replacing or expanding its capacity? Discuss the information content of the Lubbock SCFP.

MC 7.5. Caroline Morrison believes that any effort spent to separately disclose extraordinary items on the SCFP is misdirected. She reasons that:

a) The information refers to what has already happened, not what might happen in the future. It is, therefore, irrelevant to decision-making, which must be related to the future.

b) To report funds from operations as what it would have been without extraordinary items is contrary to historical fact.

Discuss Caroline's position.

ESSENTIAL PROBLEMS

EP 7.1. With "funds" defined as net working capital, a flow of funds will, by definition, increase or decrease the balance of net working capital. Many events occurring during the year do not involve flows of funds as defined. From the list of selected events occurring to the Gismo Company during a given year, identify those that do **not** involve a flow of funds.

a) Owner invests $5,000 cash in the business.

b) Owner withdraws $1,000 cash from the business.

c) Owner withdraws merchandise costing $500, for personal use.

d) $10,000 cash is borrowed from the bank on a 90-day note.

e) $3,000 is paid on accounts payable.

f) $4,000 cash is collected from accounts receivable.

g) $6,000 cash is used to purchase securities to be held as a long-term investment.

h) $2,000 is used to purchase short-term marketable securities.

i) $20,000 is borrowed on a five-year promissory note.

j) $15,000 of principal is paid on a loan classified as a noncurrent liability.

EP 7.2. Refer to the information supplied for the Gismo Company in Problem EP 7.1 above. Assume you also knew that by year end the balance of net working capital is increased by $7,500 as compared with the beginning of the year. You may also assume that, except for funds from operations, all events involving funds flow during the year are included in the list.

a) What must have been the amount of funds from operations generated during the year?

b) If the Gismo Company's accountant prepared a working capital funds-flow statement for the year, what amount should be shown as total sources of funds?

EP 7.3. The Widget Company's Working Capital Funds-Flow Statement for the most recent year, 19XX, is given below. You may assume that statements for previous years were essentially the same.

a) Is Widget routinely replacing or expanding its capacity?

b) Is Widget's long-term capital structure expanding, contracting, or apparently in a "steady state"?

c) Is Widget's long-term debt percentage apparently increasing, decreasing, or remaining the same?

d) Is Widget becoming more or less liquid?

WIDGET COMPANY
Working Capital Funds Flow Statement for Year 19XX

Sources		Applications	
Funds from operations	$300	Purchase of noncurrent assets	$350
Sale of noncurrent assets	50	Retirement of long-term debt	75
New long-term debt	50	Withdrawals by owner	30
Additional owner investment	100	Increase in net working capital balance	45
	$500		$500

EP 7.4. Referring to information supplied for the Widget Company in Problem EP 7.3 above, assume that:

• There was and had been no inflation in the prices or costs of Widget's capacity assets,

• Widget's accountants were adjusting for depreciation in equal amounts each year over the useful life of the depreciable assets, and

• Additional accumulated depreciation for the year amounted to $200.

a) Does it appear that the Widget Company is at least replacing its capacity assets as they wear out or become obsolete?

b) Is there evidence that Widget is probably expanding its capacity?

c) What would be your responses to (a) and (b) if additional accumulated depreciation for the year amounted to $300 instead of $200? Explain any different responses.

d) What would be your responses to (a) and (b) if additional accumulated depreciation for the year amounted to $400 instead of $200? Explain any different responses.

EP 7.5. Assume you are interested in making a long-term investment in a firm in a particular industry, and one of your criteria is that it be a growth company maintaining an appropriate balance between new long-term debt and new owner's equity. You have before you the most recent working capital funds-flow statement from the Ajax Company for the year 19X2 and an abbreviated balance sheet for the end of the prior year—19X1—both of which are given below. Ajax's funds from operations are slightly above industry average. Industry average growth in terms of long-term capital structure is 20 percent per year. Ajax's 19X1 long-term debt percentage you feel represented a good balance.

a) Prepare an abbreviated balance sheet as of 12/31/X2.

b) Should you consider Ajax an active candidate for further evaluation, or should you reject Ajax as not meeting your criteria? Why?

AJAX COMPANY
Abbreviated Balance Sheet as of 12/31/X1

Net working capital	$100,000	Long-term debt	$120,000
Noncurrent assets (net)	200,000	Owner's Equity	180,000
	$300,000		$300,000

AJAX COMPANY
Working Capital Funds-Flow Statement for Year 19X2

Funds from operations	$50,000	Retire long-term debt	$15,000
New long-term debt	45,000	Acquisition noncurrent assets	50,000
New long-term owner		Withdrawals by owner	25,000
investment	20,000	Increase in net working	
		capital balance	25,000
	$115,000		$115,000

EP 7.6. As a bank loan officer, your business is the renting of money. You will earn the most for your bank with loans to established customers who readily pay one loan and then return for another. There is usually less risk of loss on loans to customers who have proved their ability to repay; and there is less cost for credit investigation for a repeat customer for whom information must merely be updated. Therefore you can assume, with all other things equal, that a bank will give preference to a repeat customer, or to a new one who can repay painlessly and therefore be a potential repeat customer.

As a bank loan officer, you have two loan applications from two potential new borrowers: the Smith Company and the Jones Company. Each is applying for a $50,000 120-day loan to purchase extra merchandise for the Christmas selling season. In each case, the merchandise will consist of Christmas items—decorations, cards, and so forth. If sales materialize as forecasted, the loans will be self-liquidating; that is, the loan principal will go into inventory and then back through receivables into cash in time to repay the loan. However, if the Christmas inventory is not sold, it will have to be held for a year; and either the loan maturity would have to be extended a year or else the loan would have to be repaid from funds generated elsewhere.

You have before you information that in the previous year Smith's funds from operations amounted to $40,000, and Jones generated $50,000. Both firms expect this year to be at least 10 percent better than last year. Assume that all other information on both firms is equally positive, and that your available loan funds will allow you to approve only one $50,000 loan.

To which firm would you grant the loan and why?

EP 7.7. Given the following partial SCFP and additional information, complete the SCFP.

Sources		Applications	
Funds from operations	?	Purchase of equipment	$30
Sale of noncurrent assets	$10	Owner withdrawals	20
New long-term debt	40	Retire noncurrent debt	?

Additional information

Net working capital at beginning of year	$170
Net working capital at end of year	180
Total noncurrent debt at beginning of year	130
Total noncurrent debt at end of year	120

EP 7.8. Given the following partial SCFP and additional information:

Sources		Applications	
Funds from operations	$75	Purchase of noncurrent assets	$25
Sales of noncurrent assets	10	Owner withdrawals	35
New owner investment	30	Retire noncurrent debt	60
New long-term debt	?		

Additional information

Total noncurrent debt at beginning of year	$200
Total noncurrent debt at end of year	160
New working capital at end of year was	240
Net working capital at beginning of year was	less than 240

a) What were total sources during the year which would appear on a completed SCFP?

b) What was net working capital at the beginning of the year?

EP 7.9. Given the SCFP's for Company A and Company B:

Sources	A	B
Funds from operations	$25	$ 5
Sale of noncurrent assets	15	0
New noncurrent debt	0	20
New owner investment	30	0
Decreased balance of Net Working Capital	NA	25
Total Sources	$70	$50

Applications		
Purchase of noncurrent assets	$35	0
Retire noncurrent debt	30	$30
Owner withdrawals	0	20
Increased balance of net working capital	5	NA
Total Applications	$70	$50

a) Which firm was neither replacing nor expanding its capacity assets?

b) Which firm's owners appear to be withdrawing prior years' retained profits?

EP 7.10. Using the information provided in Problem EP 7.9 above:

a) Which firm appears to be engaged in active replacement, if not expansion, of its capacity assets?

b) Which firm appears to be substantially reducing its long-term debt ratio?

EP 7.11. Given the following working capital funds-flow statement:

Sources		Applications	
Funds from operations	$45	Purchase new equipment	$20
		Owner withdrawals	10
		Increased balance of net working capital	15
			$45

Assuming that the new equipment had cost $100 and was purchased by paying $20 down and giving a five-year promissory note payable for the balance, prepare a SCFP in good form.

EP 7.12. Starting with the same working capital funds-flow statement given in Problem EP 7.11, assume the following differences:

• The new equipment cost $100 and was purchased by paying $60 down and giving a ten-year note payable for the balance. The balance of net working capital therefore decreased by $25.

• Land and buildings with a fair market value of $95 were acquired by the firm by direct investment on the part of the owner.

Prepare a SCFP in good form.

SUPPLEMENTARY PROBLEMS

SP 7.13. The Fong Company retails sporting goods. Its balance sheet as of 12/31/X0 and working capital funds-flow statement for the year 19X0 are given below. Fong anticipates that it can increase its business 50 percent during 19X1, and that funds from operations will increase proportionately. It expects that cash will have to be increased by 20 percent to handle the new volume; and that receivables, inventory, supplies, and accounts payable must increase in proportion to increased volume. A 20-percent increase in net fixed assets will also be required. Mr. Fong believes that he can leave only 40 percent of funds generated during next year in the business, since he must withdraw the balance for personal living expenses.

a) How much additional long-term capital should be in the business by the end of 19X1 to support the increased volume?

b) How much of this required additional capital will be in the form of net working capital and how much in noncurrent assets?

c) Will Mr. Fong have to obtain additional outside long-term investment by the end of 19X1? If so, how much?

FONG COMPANY
Balance Sheet as of 12/31/X0

Cash	$15,000	Accounts payable	$ 40,000
Accounts receivable (net)	50,000	Other current liabilities	5,000
Inventory	30,000	Total Current Liabilities	$ 45,000
Supplies	5,000		
Total Current Assets	$100,000		
Fixed Assets	200,000	Owner's Equity	180,000
Less accumulated			
depreciation	(75,000)		
Total Assets	$225,000	Total Equities	$225,000

FONG COMPANY
Data from Working Capital Funds-Flow Statement for Year 19X0

Net income	$35,000	Acquire new fixed assets	$ 5,000
Plus depreciation	15,000	Withdrawals by owner	40,000
		Increase net working	
		capital balance	5,000
Funds from operations	$50,000		$50,000

SP 7.14. The Weinstein Company's Working Capital Funds-Flow Statement for the year 19X2 is given below. During 19X3, the firm expected the following to occur:

• Funds from operations would increase 20 percent.

• Old fixed assets would be sold for $10,000.

• New fixed assets would be purchased costing $50,000.

- New long-term debt would bring in $30,000.
- Old long-term debt would be retired in the amount of $15,000.
- Owner would withdraw $60,000 from the business.

a) Prepare a projected or forecasted working capital funds-flow statement for the year 19X3.

b) What would be the expected increase or decrease in the balance of net working capital at year end?

WEINSTEIN COMPANY
Working Capital Funds Flow Statement for Year 19X2

Sources		Applications	
Funds from operations	$100,000	Acquire new fixed assets	$30,000
New owner investment	20,000	Retire long-term debt	60,000
Decrease balance of net		Owner withdrawals	40,000
working capital	10,000		
	$130,000		$130,000

SP 7.15. The following information is selected from the many items appearing on a firm's SCFP for a given year:

- Funds from operations $200
- Extraordinary inventory loss $70

What was the actual net amount of funds generated inside the business during the year?

SP 7.16. In a given year, net funds generated, including recognition of an extraordinary loss on current assets of $80, amount to $10. What amount would be reported on the SCFP as funds from operations? What other item, based on the above information, would also be reported?

PREPARER PROCEDURES AND PREPARER PROBLEMS

The details relating to the preparation of SCFP's are more readily learned after exposure to the material in Chapters 11 and 12. SCFP preparer procedures will be included under "preparer procedures" at the end of Chapter 14. Similarly, SCFP preparer problems are also included with preparer problems at the end of Chapter 14.

8

VARIATIONS IN MEASURING AND REPORTING INVENTORIES

CHAPTER PREVIEW

The objectives of this chapter are to make you aware both of the relative significance of inventory as an asset and cost of goods sold as an expense, and also of the difficulties and issues involved in measuring and reporting these items in an inflationary economy. The objectives also include introducing you to the various accounting approaches to, and systems for, measuring and reporting inventory and cost of goods sold, their effect on income, and how to identify and interpret their effect when you are analyzing financial statements for a particular firm. In this chapter you can learn:

- That inflation can cause a situation where different concepts or definitions of income may be both simultaneously needed and valuable;
- That inventory item identification costs often necessitate estimates and assumptions as alternatives;
- What items are initially included in the cost of inventory;
- The different systems used to measure and report inventory and cost of goods sold;
- The three different inventory-flow assumptions possible under GAAP, their different income effects, and the significance of consistency as applied to inventory measurement;
- Certain other important specific practices, some applicable only to certain industries and others to all firms selling products.

With this knowledge, you will be able to properly interpret the often significant inventory and cost-of-goods-sold items appearing in the financial statements. You will be aware of the need to verify the existence of common electives of inventory measurement before making direct interfirm comparisons of data. You will know where to find disclosure of the accounting method used by a particular firm and the general impact on income of the method chosen. You also have the beginning of an insight into the difficulties faced by firms and by accountants resulting from inflation. And the limitations of the financial reporting system first mentioned in Chapter 1 will become more apparent to you.

SIGNIFICANCE OF INVENTORY AND COST OF GOODS SOLD

You may be wondering why an entire chapter of this book is devoted to the single asset **inventory** and its associated expense, cost of goods sold or *cost of sales*. For a firm primarily in the business of manufacturing, distributing, or selling products or merchandise, inventory can be an extremely significant item. As an example, as of 12/31/76, inventory on hand reported by General Motors amounted to approximately six and one-third billion (not million) dollars, and amounted to 25.9 percent of total assets.[1] Of even more significance, GM's 1976 cost of goods sold was in excess of 38 billion dollars. It represented 80.6 percent of net sales and 85 percent of all the firm's cost and expenses that year! Accounting for inventory can be significant, and, as you will find out below, can present some real problems.

IS MY PROFIT REALLY PROFIT?

You may find it somewhat difficult to visualize and relate to 38 billion dollars. Try this example. Assume you own a firm which each year buys and sells one gizmo. At the beginning of this year you invested $5,000 cash in your firm. During the year you purchased one gizmo costing $5,000, paying cash. Before year end, you sold it for $7,000 cash. At year-end, your balance sheet would show:

BALANCE SHEET DIAGRAM

Current Assets	Current Liabilities
Cash $7,000	
	Noncurrent Liabilities
Noncurrent Assets	Owner's Equity
	$7,000

What was your net income or profit for the year? Would your answer be any different if the next gizmo, due in a few days from your supplier, was

---

[1]   See 1976 Annual Report for General Motors Corporation and Consolidated Subsidiaries.

going to cost $6,000 because of inflation? Accountants following GAAP will report the current year's income as $2,000. Can you withdraw your profits from the business and still be as well off as you were at the beginning? Or, for that matter, if you withdraw all of your so-called income, can you even continue in business?

The answer to these questions depends on how you precisely define "well-offness" and income. The GAAP definition of well-offness is simply the number of dollars, regardless of their purchasing power or the replacement cost of assets used. In a sense, GAAP "reasons" that your firm actually made or earned $2,000. It was $2,000 better off. The fact that inflation has occurred is an outside or *exogenous event* not resulting from the firm's activities, and therefore not reported as such. If you were starting your firm next year, you would need a start-up investment of $6,000, not $5,000.

The issues demonstrated by this simple example, and the question of what GAAP should consider and report as income, have been an active concern of accountants, academicians, and business people for decades. A further discussion, together with a description of proposed alternatives, is contained in Chapter 16. At this point, it is important only that you clearly understand the nature of the problem and its source, and that GAAP does not currently provide any adjustment for inflation.

WHAT IS MY PROFIT THIS YEAR?

A related problem, also resulting from inflation, involves the timing and proper identification of reported profits. Assume you retire from the gizmo business and, instead, decide to purchase and sell widgets. This time you started your firm with an investment of $10,000 cash. Early in the year, you purchased one widget costing $1,000. Towards the end of the year you purchased a second which, because of inflation, cost $2,000. By year end you had sold one of the widgets for $2,500. What was the amount of your ending inventory, and what was this year's income?

Study these two balance sheet diagrams carefully. Can you see that they each could be correct, depending upon which widget had been the one sold?

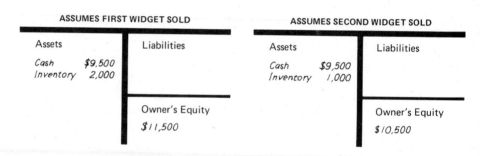

If the first widget was the one sold, your income statement would show a profit of $1,500. If the second was sold, your profit would be only $500.

Now to complete your understanding of the "timing" problem, assume that all that happened during the second year was that you sold the other widget, also for $2,500. Your ending balance sheet would show:

AT END OF SECOND YEAR

Assets		Liabilities	
Cash	$12,000		
Inventory	0		
		Owner's Equity	
		$12,000	

Looking at the entire two-year period, your total reported profit was clearly $2,000. But users wish financial information more frequently—at least yearly, and often quarterly. How much of the $2,000 was earned the first year? The second year?

Can you see that the timing of reported income depends upon which widget was **assumed** to have been sold the first year? You may find this grossly simplified example too simple; and you may be thinking that, with only two widgets, you could certainly tell which one went out to the customer first. You are right; with only two widgets, you would hardly have to make an assumption. But, without going to a more complicated example, assume you **didn't** know which widget was sold first. Think of widgets as being individual nails or washers in a hardware-store bin, or a tanker truckload of gasoline mixed with others in a large storage tank. There are a great many cases where it is impossible, or far too costly, for a firm to specifically identify different items or batches in inventory.

Returning to the widget problem with the agreement that you cannot tell physically which widget was sold, how do you determine the dollar amount of the first year's ending inventory and cost of goods sold? How do you measure the first year's profit? Obviously you, or your accountant, would have to make a cost flow or cost assignment assumption. Regardless of the actual physical flow—which widget was sold first—you would have to assign a cost ($1,000 or $2,000) to the one widget remaining. This assignment would, in turn, result in an "assignment" of cost to the widget being sold.

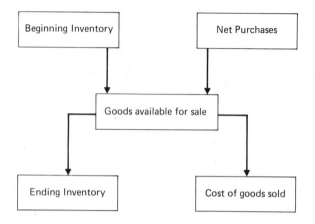

Later in this chapter, you can learn of the various assumptions acceptable under GAAP, from which accountants may choose in measuring inventory. Before proceeding, make sure you clearly see the potential significance of an inventory cost-flow assumption for reported income. In an actual firm there may be hundreds of thousands of inventoried items. Add six zeros to the widget figure and you can see the significance.

INCOME FOR THE PAST OR FOR THE FUTURE?

There is another reason for making a cost-flow assumption even when inventory could be economically identified. Remember the conceptually unresolved issue of how much profit to report for gizmos under inflation. Think of the widget case, and assume you knew that the first widget had actually been the one shipped. Would an income statement reporting a $1,500 profit provide the best information to investors? Would this much profit be repeatable in the future? Could the reporting of $1,500 profit be misleading to investors in much the same way that the inclusion of extraordinary gains as part of operating income could be misleading?

Of the $1,500 of profit in the widget example (whether or not reported as earned in the first or second year), $1,000 represented a nonrepeatable *holding gain*. If the purpose of the income statement is to report on what management has done, how well they have acted as stewards or trustees with the investors' funds, then $1,500 reported profit would be appropriate. If, on the other hand, the income statement is to serve effectively as a basis for future decisions by investors, then the $500 "repeatable" profit might be more appropriate.

GAAP allows for either flow assumption as long as it is applied consistently. Many firms have elected the *LIFO* assumption (discussed below) which would result in the cost of the most recently acquired widget being applied to the one sold, and in a reported profit of only $500. The firms elect to make this assumption even when they know the actual physical movement of merchandise may have been just the opposite. The reason for the election is that the income statement will provide more current (repeatable) cost information for investors.[2]

Another alternative that has been suggested to meet past and future income-reporting objectives simultaneously involves reporting holding gains when they occur but segregating them in a similar manner to extraordinary items. This elementary text will not explore these more advanced conceptual problems further. You should be aware of them, and you might wish to discuss them in class. What you should experience at this point is the necessity to understand fully the details concerning the accountant's current treatment of inventories under GAAP. The balance of this chapter presents the basic elements.

BASIC FACTS ABOUT INVENTORY

Regardless of possible cost-flow assumptions involved in determining ending inventory and cost of goods sold, inventory is first measured and recorded at its *full acquisition cost*. Full acquisition costs are all those costs related to making the products or merchandise available for sale at the intended selling location. The full acquisition cost does **not** include any financing (interest) costs, since these would only result in those particular circumstances where a firm was using borrowed funds rather than its own to make the purchase. Full acquisition costs of all inventory acquired during a particular period or year are collectively known as *net purchases*.

Components of Net Purchases

It is important that you understand what is included in the net-purchases figure. Net purchases are determined by adding *gross purchases* and *transportation or freight-in*, and then subtracting *purchase returns* and *purchase discounts*.

Gross purchases are the total of the invoice costs of all merchandise acquired during the year. Purchase returns represent the cost of those items acquired and subsequently returned to the supplier for whatever reason. Transportation or freight-in covers the cost of moving the merchandise from the supplier to the location where it is to be sold. Some items may be delivered by the supplier at no additional charge. For others, the purchaser may have to pay delivery costs. By including all freight-in costs, the accountant ensures that inventory is uniformly valued at the full cost of having it available for

---

2   Another reason for electing the LIFO flow assumption involves tax savings or tax postponement. LIFO may be used for tax purposes only if it is used for financial reporting. This requirement of parallel treatment is one of the only instances where financial accounting and tax accounting may not be different.

sale. Note that transportation or freight out involves part of shipping/selling expense and is **not** related to inventory measurement.

Purchase discounts require further understanding of common business practices. When a supplier sells merchandise to your firm on account, it is making a short-term investment of assets in your firm. Since the supplier's primary business is not that of making loans, it wants to motivate you to pay as soon as possible. Many orders are, therefore, shipped with payment terms such as 2/10 N 30. This code merely means you can take a two-percent discount from the invoice price if you pay within ten days of the invoice date. The full or net billed price must be paid between ten and thirty days of the invoice date. After thirty days, the supplier may charge you interest on the unpaid bill.

Suppose a particular purchase were invoiced at $500. The gross purchase would be recorded at $500. If you took advantage of the ten-day discount and settled the bill by paying only $490, the merchandise would have actually cost $10 less than had been originally recorded. Therefore any purchase discounts taken will eventually offset gross purchases, so as not to overstate inventory costs.

Perpetual and Periodic Inventory Systems

Even though a firm has but one balance sheet account for merchandise ready to sell to customers (inventory), it must maintain detailed cost records for its net purchases. The total of the inventory at the beginning of the year and net purchases is known as *goods available for sale*:

Beginning inventory plus net purchases = Goods available for sale

Some firms, and especially those using computer systems, can afford to maintain detailed separate records for each distinct inventory item. Where firms can afford to keep these detailed records for each item, and hence to record purchases and sales or shipments to this record continually throughout the year, it is said to be on the *perpetual inventory system*. Many firms cannot realistically afford the recordkeeping involved in a perpetual system. They keep records only of goods available for sale. Sales to customers at selling price are, of course, continually recorded to update the accounts for cash or accounts receivable and sales. The delivery of products to customers, that is, shipments, at cost is not continually reported. At the end of the year, such firms take a physical inventory. The physical inventory involves counting all items still on hand. The physical inventory count is "costed," that is, costs are assigned. Cost of goods sold—items shipped or missing (theft and spoilage)—is then calculated by taking the total of goods available and then subtracting the ending inventory at cost.

The firms which complete the updating of their inventory records only periodically or once a year in this fashion are said to follow the *periodic inventory system*.

In "costing" ending physical inventory under the periodic system, or in "costing" day-to-day shipments recorded under the perpetual system, a firm must be able to assign costs to items. Some firms can afford to specifically identify each unit (or batch of similar units) in inventory with that unit's cost. For example, Boeing 747 planes are large enough, and sufficiently customized, that individual cost records for each plane are both economical and necessary. Hairpins, thumbtacks, and so forth are clearly not amenable to *specific cost identification*.

COST FLOW ASSUMPTIONS

Where it is not feasible to specifically identify inventory items, or where, for other reasons previously discussed, the firm does not wish to measure inventory via the specific identification method, then a cost flow (cost assignment) assumption must be made. There are three different assumptions, one of which may be elected under GAAP. For you to see clearly the differences among these three assumptions, we will use a specific example.

John King owns a wine wholesale business. He sells to retailers domestic and imported wines by the case. The "history" of one particular wine during the year is as follows:

Beginning inventory	0
January purchase	500 cases costing $10 each
May purchase	750 cases costing $12 each
September purchase	250 cases costing $15 each
Ending inventory	250 cases costing ? $10 each →

FIFO COST FLOW ASSUMPTION

What was the proper measurement of the dollars of ending inventory for this particular wine? Regardless of the actual physical movement of wine in the warehouse, the accountant can **assume** that each lot is placed onto a conveyor belt as it arrives and that cases of wine are shipped from the opposite end of the conveyor. Most items in most firms actually physically move through inventory in this manner, in order to avoid spoilage or obsolescence. Even though they may not move on a conveyor, the first items received are generally the first items shipped. This conveyor-belt assumption is known as *FIFO*, for first-in-first-out.

Purchases ⟶ FIFO Conveyor Belt ⟶ Sales

In John King's situation, he had three lots of wine purchased at different cost. His FIFO conveyor belt would contain:

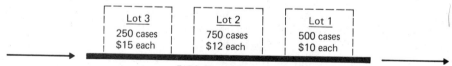

Lot 3	Lot 2	Lot 1
250 cases	750 cases	500 cases
$15 each	$12 each	$10 each

FIFO Flow Assumption

How many cases were shipped (or disappeared) during the year? Cases available for sale total 1,500. Two hundred and fifty remained on hand; therefore cost of goods sold would cover 1,250 cases. Note that the actual quantity of items leaving inventory is a physical reality and is the same regardless of the cost flow assumption.

Under the FIFO-flow assumption, what would John King report as cost of goods sold and as ending inventory for this particular wine? Calculate your answer before proceeding.

Goods available for sale, again an amount independent of any flow assumption, amounted to $17,750. If 1,250 cases were shipped under a FIFO-flow assumption, you can see that the cost of goods sold would include:

Five hundred cases at $10   = $ 5,000
Seven hundred and fifty cases at $12 = 9,000
Total $14,000

Using the FIFO-flow assumption, ending inventory of $3,750—250 cases at $15—shown on the balance sheet would be reported in terms of the most recent cost. These could be a close approximation of current market costs, depending upon how recently purchased, and make the balance sheet measurement currently relevant. On the other hand, the income statement would reflect the oldest nonrepeatable costs. Operating income could be very misleading as a basis for forecasting. It would include inflation profit or inventory holding gain along with repeatable current trading profit. To see this clearly, assume John King had received $25,000 for the 1,250 cases sold this year. His gross profit under the FIFO-flow assumption would have been $11,000. How much of this $11,000 was trading profit or repeatable profit in terms of current wine costs? In terms of current costs, John's cost of goods sold would have been $18,750 ($15 times 1,250 cases) and his trading profit only $6,250. Therefore, of his $11,000 gross profit, $4,750 represents a holding gain which he could not expect to recur unless he could raise selling prices without any further cost increases, or faster than costs increase.

To review, in periods of inflation, FIFO tends to result in ending inventory on the balance sheet reported in near-current costs. Cost of goods sold on the income statement is reported in terms of older nonrecurring costs. Therefore, gross profit in net income will include nonrepeatable holding gains. GAAP currently do not distinguish between trading profit and holding gain on the income statement.

WEIGHTED AVERAGE COST FLOW ASSUMPTION

The second common flow assumption that can be made is *weighted average cost*. For this assumption, you can visualize all items placed in a big mixing bowl and blended together. Each item shipped to customers would be a representative blend of all costs going into the mix. In the John King example, the average-cost mixing bowl would include:

$$
\begin{array}{rl}
500 \text{ at } \$10 = & \$\ 5{,}000 \\
750 \text{ at } \$12 = & 9{,}000 \\
250 \text{ at } \$15 = & 3{,}750 \\
\hline
1{,}500 & \$17{,}750
\end{array}
$$

1,500 cases costing $17,750 or $11.83 (rounded) each.

Cost of goods sold would be $14,790 and ending inventory $2,960 (dollars rounded). Note that a simple nonweighted average price of $12.33 per case would not be appropriate. 1,500 total cases at $12.33 each would equal $18,495 even though there were only $17,750 of total costs involved to begin with. The average cost must be weighted to reflect the different costs' proportions in the mix.

The weighted average cost assumption results in balance sheet inventory values which are neither the latest nor the oldest costs. A balance sheet figure for inventory is less meaningful inasmuch as it is less of an approximation of current costs than under FIFO. Inventory costs on the income statement would represent the same "blend," and profit still would include some holding gain. This "blend" of costs would be appropriate for homogenous items with reasonably stable prices. Otherwise, all the pitfalls inherent in any average could exist.

LIFO FLOW ASSUMPTION

The third cost-flow assumption for financial accounting purposes is known as LIFO, for last-in-first-out. For this assumption you can visualize a big barrel. Items purchased are placed in the barrel in layers as they arrive. Items shipped are taken out of the top of the barrel. Physically very few items are actually moved on a LIFO basis. Actual physical LIFO flow is safe only where there is no risk of spoilage or obsolescence for items at the bottom of the barrel or pile. Items physically handled on a LIFO basis would be limited to natural resources such as crude oil, coal, or sand and gravel for construction, salt, and so forth.

In the King example, the LIFO barrel would include:

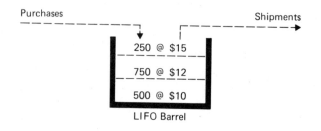

The cost of the 1,250 cases sold would be $15,250 (250 at $15.00 plus 750 at $12.00 plus 250 at $10.00). Ending inventory would be assumed to be those at the bottom of the barrel—250 cases at $10.00 or $2,500. Remember, the most recently received merchandise would probably be on hand. It would just be assumed to have the earliest cost.

Under the LIFO alternative, a firm's balance sheet could show inventory at costs 20 to 50 years old, or at least as far back as when the item was last out of stock. Balance sheet inventory data could be much less current and therefore less meaningful and relevant under LIFO. The income statement, on the other hand, would disclose the most recent costs. Very little holding gain would be mixed with trading profit, unless, of course, merchandise was not regularly replaced and the "barrel" was emptied of "old items" in a given year. LIFO is frequently used since it results in reported income that is more likely to recur and thus provides a better forecasting base.

Whether a firm follows periodic or perpetual procedures is of significance in understanding the statements if the firm also uses LIFO. LIFO amounts can be different depending upon whether the firm is using *periodic LIFO* or *perpetual LIFO*. Under periodic LIFO, information is not available regarding the time when individual shipments occurred during the year. Therefore, it must be assumed that all units sold had been shipped on the last day of the year. This would be after all purchases during the year had been received and their layers added to the barrel. The LIFO example for John King above demonstrates periodic LIFO.

Perpetual LIFO could result in different amounts of ending inventory and cost of goods sold. Suppose John King's firm followed perpetual LIFO. Under the perpetual system, information would be available on the actual dates purchases arrived and shipments were made. Exhibit 8.1 provides these additional data together with perpetual-LIFO progressive steps. Note that under perpetual LIFO, you know that only ten cases of $10-cost wine remained, together with the other layers. Under periodic LIFO, you can only assume

Exhibit 8.1

JOHN KING WINE WHOLESALER

Details of Perpetual LIFO Calculations

Data:	
Beginning inventory	Zero
January purchase	500 @ $10
Shipments February, March, and April	490 Units
May purchase	750 @ $12
Shipments June, July, and August	700 Units
September purchase	250 @ $15
Shipments October, November, and December	60 Units

Inventory just prior to the May purchase:

10 @ $10

LIFO Barrel

Inventory immediately subsequent to the May purchase:

750 @ $12

10 @ $10

LIFO Barrel

Inventory just prior to the September purchase:

50 @ $12

10 @ $10

LIFO Barrel

Ending Perpetual Inventory:

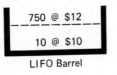

190 @ $15

50 @ $12

10 @ $10

LIFO Barrel

---

that all layers (purchases) were on hand before shipment, and therefore 250 cases of $10 wine were assumed to remain in the bottom of the inventory "barrel." Ending inventory would be $3,550 under perpetual LIFO but only $2,500 under periodic LIFO. Goods available either to be sold or to remain in inventory amounted to $17,750. Therefore, cost of goods sold would be

$14,200 under perpetual LIFO and $15,250 under periodic LIFO. This difference could become really significant if you consider a firm with hundreds or thousands of different items.

STRICT VS. MODIFIED LAYERS

Under either FIFO or LIFO, if the integrity of each layer is maintained over prior years, then the system is referred to as "strict." For example, following strict LIFO, a firm might have past layers including:

> 500 units acquired this year for $3 each
> 200 units acquired the year before for $2 each
> 400 units acquired two years ago for $0.50 each

Especially under LIFO, the maintenance of records of many different layers in prior years can be burdensome. Therefore many firms follow a "modified" rather than strict layering approach. Under the modified system, each year's ending inventory is combined into a single layer at weighted average cost. Strict layer separation is then only followed in the current year between beginning inventory and the current year's purchases, and among different purchases in the current year.

In the example above, under a modified LIFO system, the prior years' layers would be combined and the records would carry:

> 500 units acquired this year for $3 each
> 600 units of beginning inventory at $1 each.

CHOICE AMONG ALTERNATIVE FLOW ASSUMPTIONS

As mentioned earlier, GAAP allows a firm to choose among these three alternative flow assumptions if it is not following specific identification. However, GAAP also provides that, once a given alternative is elected, it must be adhered to consistently from year to year.[3] Consistency among GAAP alternatives is a fundamental principle of financial accounting. Its importance is indicated by the fact that the annual auditor's opinion is required either to attest to consistency or to note the exception.

EFFECT ON REPORTED INCOME

You should now realize why a user of financial statements needs to understand something about the accountant's choice of inventory-flow assumption and recording system. When prices are changing, two identical firms can have

---

[3]   GAAP allows a firm to change in infrequent special circumstances. However, the CPA opinion will advise you of the change in the year it occurs. The income effect of the change will also be disclosed, and prior years' published data will be restated under the new alternative.

very different income statements and balance sheets, even with identical movements of inventory. In periods of inflation, a FIFO firm is realizing and reporting inventory holding gain as part of gross profit as it goes along. A LIFO firm may postpone for many years the reporting of much of this holding gain. In the identical-firm situation, the FIFO firm during inflation would be reporting higher profits than the LIFO firm when the **only** difference would be the accountant's inventory-flow assumption.

A specific example might help you to understand and remember the income effect of electing different inventory-flow assumptions. Assume that you are in a period of significant inflation, and that your firm during the year has sold 500,000 widgets. Also assume that your goods available for sale consisted of 100,000 units costing $1 each in beginning inventory, 400,000 units costing $2 apiece purchased in April, and 500,000 units costing $3 apiece acquired in November. Following the periodic inventory system, what would be your cost of goods sold under each alternative: FIFO, average cost, and LIFO?

Flow assumption	Cost of goods sold
FIFO	$ 900,000
Avg. Cost	1,200,000
LIFO	1,500,000

In this example, as compared with FIFO, the LIFO flow assumption would result in an additional $600,000 being included in cost of goods sold, with a corresponding reduction in reported net income of $600,000.

A financial statement user must be careful not to make direct comparisons between or among companies unless he or she is certain the firms are all electing the same inventory cost-flow assumption. Similar major intercompany variations can also result from different depreciation and amortization methods. These will be discussed in Chapter 9. The financial statement user can ascertain which valuation alternatives are being followed by a particular firm by consulting the statement footnotes. GAAP requires that a firm disclose the accounting methods being used in the preparation of its financial statements.

Refer to the annual report of the Addison-Wesley Publishing Company in Appendix A at the back of this book. Note that a Summary of Significant Accounting Policies is given immediately following the SCFP. The fourth item advises you that Addison-Wesley follows FIFO. The "lower of cost or market" reference is to an overall GAAP requirement and will be discussed below.

LOWER OF COST OR MARKET (LOCM)

Regardless of the cost-flow assumption being used, there exists one overriding principle of ending-inventory measurement. Under the principle of conservatism, GAAP requires that ending inventory not be stated above its *net realizable value*. The cost of the ending inventory is first determined and recorded,

following one of the previously described methods. Then, before the bala
sheet is released, the calculated ending inventory is tested to ensure tha
meets the LOCM requirement.

LOCM means the lower of cost or market.[4] However, "market" does
mean market value in the conventional sense. LOCM would be more rea
understood as the lower of original cost or "recoverable cost." The objec
of this GAAP standard is that inventory should not be reported at any am
greater than that which could be recovered or realized from it in the fut
There is a formula for determining the "M" of LOCM or "recoverable cost

For example, given the following three sets of facts:

	Situation A	Situation B	Situatio
Net realizable value (NRV):			
Upper limit of M	$100	$100	$10
Replacement cost	90	105	6
NRV less normal profit margin:			
Lower limit of M	70	70	7

In Situation A, replacement cost is between the upper and lower limits; th
fore, M would be $90. In Situation B, replacement cost exceeds the u
limit; therefore M is the upper limit, or $100. In Situation C, replacement
is below the lower limit; therefore M is $70.

If recoverable cost (M) is equal to or greater than the already reco
inventory cost, no adjustment is made. If recoverable cost (M) is less,
an adjustment is made to reduce reported ending inventory to the recover
cost amount. The balancing reduction to owner's equity would be throug
operating expense account, possibly entitled "Inventory Revaluation Expe

As mentioned above, the LOCM standard for inventory valuation
example of the underlying accounting rule of conservatism. Conserva
simply stated, means an avoidance of unpleasant surprises. If a loss is rea
ably certain, recognize it now. Also, don't recognize expected gains or p
until they actually occur, since they may not. Suppose you had a store
an inventory of pocket calculators. These calculators previously sol
$29.95, and you paid $18.00 each for those in your inventory. If they are

---

[4]   GAAP provide exceptions for certain items having established mass ma
Examples would include agricultural commodities, precious metals, and mark
securities held as trading inventory by a broker. These items are carried in inve
at selling price, and any profit is recognized prior to sale.

[5]   "M (market)" or recoverable cost is one of three amounts:

   a) Net realizable value: expected selling price less cost of completing the
      finishing the item (if partially finished), packaging, and shipping;
   b) Replacement cost: current cost of obtaining a similar item;
   c) Net realizable value less the firm's normal gross-profit margin.

   Recoverable cost is defined as: (a) if (b) > (a); (b) if (a) > (b) > (c); and
   (c) > (b).

selling for $14.95, there is no way you are going to recover your $18.00 inventory cost for each calculator. You are going to sustain a loss, and conservatism requires that you recognize it in the current year by "writing down" your inventory.

Inventory measurement is just one example of the need for estimates and assumptions within the financial accounting system. Estimates cannot be unbiased or perfectly neutral. Also, users of financial information are not "neutral." If you knew that an actual event would necessarily be different from your expectation, you would usually prefer pleasant surprises (unexpected gains) to unpleasant surprises (unexpected losses). Accountants know that they are working with estimates and assumptions. GAAP sensibly dictates that estimates should be on the conservative side. It attempts to ensure that most "surprises" encountered by the financial statement user will not be unpleasant. In the next chapter, you will see the need for still more estimating in the measurement of noncurrent assets.

OTHER ASPECTS OF INVENTORY MEASUREMENT AND REPORTING

The most important elements relating to the accountant's measurement and reporting of inventories have already been covered above. In addition, there are special inventory-related topics with which you might wish to become familiar. They include:

- The method of estimating inventory at intervals during the year or when inventory records are lost,
- Special estimating procedures followed by many retailers,
- Inventory costing peculiar to a manufacturer,
- Reporting inventory on consignment to others, and
- Accounting for damaged and repossessed merchandise.

These specialized topics are covered in an appendix to this chapter.

CHAPTER OVERVIEW

Based on the material presented in this chapter, you should be able to:

- Describe the significance of inventory measurement to asset measurement and income reporting;

- Describe the inventory measurement problems created by inflation;
- Explain the basis for initial inventory (input) measurement;
- Describe the difference between a periodic and a perpetual inventor system, and the significance of this difference;
- Explain why cost-flow assumptions may be necessary;
- Describe the three cost-flow assumptions acceptable under GAAP, g examples of each, and explain the alternative effects of each on the bal sheet and income statement;
- Explain the importance of consistency as applied to inventory measure ment;
- Describe LOCM and how it represents an example of the accountin principle of conservatism.

NEW VOCABULARY AND CONCEPTS

Exogenous event	Periodic inventory (system)
Holding gain	Specific (cost) identification
Full acquisition cost	FIFO
Net purchases	Weighted average cost
Gross purchases	LIFO
Transportation-in/freight-in	Periodic LIFO
Purchase returns	Perpetual LIFO
Purchase discounts	Net realizable value
Goods available for sale	LOCM
Perpetual inventory (system)	

- Basis for initial measurement of inventory.
- Price changes and assumed inventory cost flows.
- Cost-flow assumption/cost-assignment assumption.
- Effects of cost-flow assumption on financial statement.
- Consistency and conservatism.

REVIEW QUESTIONS

1. a) What is the current rationale under GAAP for excluding recognition of tionary changes to existing assets, that is, for recognizing new higher prices in a transaction? (b) Exogenous specific price decreases may be recognized u the LOCM rule. Explain.

2. a) Explain why a firm might be forced to use an inventory cost-flow assump (b) Explain why a firm might elect to use a cost-flow assumption even wh did not need to.

3. a) What are the components of net purchases? (b) Explain each component and how it affects net purchases.

4. a) Once an inventory-flow assumption is adopted by a firm, can it change to another? (b) If yes, when and what must be disclosed? (c) How is the principle of "consistency" involved?

5. Describe what is meant by the specific (cost) identification system. Give an example of how it would work and a product where it rationally might be used.

6. Explain the average cost-flow assumption.

7. Explain the FIFO cost-flow assumption.

8. Explain the LIFO cost-flow assumption.

9. Regardless of the flow assumptions accountants may adopt, what are examples of items that usually **physically** follow the FIFO flow pattern? The LIFO pattern?

10. a) What is trading profit and what is inventory holding gain? (b) How are each reported under FIFO? (c) Under LIFO?

11. a) What is the difference between the perpetual and the periodic inventory systems? (b) How does this difference affect LIFO?

12. In periods of inflation, what is the effect upon reported income of using FIFO as compared with average cost and with LIFO?

13. Is the possible LOCM adjustment made as part of the initial determination of ending inventory, or is it made after the normal determination of ending inventory? Explain.

14. How does LOCM relate to the accounting principle of conservatism?

MINI-CASES AND QUESTIONS FOR DISCUSSION

MC 8.1. Becky and Lolita are discussing the income statements of the Peter Company and the Paul Company. Becky says, "Peter's net income is $100,000 and Paul's is only $50,000. That means that Peter had twice as much profit as Paul."

"Not necessarily," replies Lolita. "The statement footnotes say that Peter follows FIFO and Paul uses LIFO. In periods of inflation, that could explain the entire difference. In fact, it is possible that, if both use the same system, Paul might report more income than Peter!"

"That doesn't make sense," says Becky. "Both statements have CPA opinions that they are consistently following GAAP. How could a CPA approve Paul's statement if, as you say, Paul may be making more profit than Peter?" Discuss.

MC 8.2. Jack has read that many companies' reported earnings have been very high. "Business is not suffering," he says.

Phil disagrees. "A lot of profit during periods of inflation is 'phony profit.' Some firms with high reported profits aren't really doing well at all. It all has something to do with holding gains." Discuss.

MC 8.3. In a large corporation where the owners (stockholders) and management are different, it is possible that the owners' and management's preferences for a particular inventory cost-flow assumption might differ. Also, in any firm, it is possible for owners and creditors to have different flow assumption preferences. Explain how these differences could occur and discuss their implications.

MC 8.4. Is holding gain on inventory more like an unusual but periodically recurring gain on a noncurrent asset disposition or more like a truly extraordinary item? Discuss.

MC 8.5. Income tax is generally based on "dollar income" in the same manner as GAAP income measures "dollar value." No allowance for inflation or future replacement costs is currently incorporated in either system. Discuss.

MC 8.6. Assume that a very large piece of equipment has been sold to a customer for $850,000 on account at year end. The profit of $150,000 has been included in last year's reported income. Early this year, the customer is unable to obtain financing or has an extraordinary loss. The equipment is returned unused and the sale is cancelled. How should the equipment be recorded in inventory? At what amount? How can the sale and profit be reversed on last year's closed and published statements? If the equipment is resold to another customer this year, should the sale and profit be included in this year's totals? If it is, wouldn't this result in double counting? Discuss.

MC 8.7. The LIFO method has been criticized as enabling firms to manipulate their reported income just by purchasing or deferring purchase of inventory at year end. Is this possible? How would it work? Discuss.

ESSENTIAL PROBLEMS

EP 8.1. The Tail Ski Wholesale Company uses the average cost-flow assumption to measure its inventory and cost of goods sold. Its fiscal year runs from June 1 through May 31. At the beginning of the current fiscal year—June 1—its inventory of a particular type of ski consisted of 200 pairs, all purchased at a cost of $30 per pair. During the year, the following additional purchases were made:

> July: 300 pairs costing $35 per pair
> November: 150 pairs costing $40 per pair
> January: 200 pairs costing $50 per pair

Assume the firm used periodic inventory. At year end a physical inventory revealed 300 pairs still in stock. What amounts would properly be reported: (a) on the firm's ending balance sheet for inventory; and (b) on its income statement for cost of goods sold?

EP 8.2. Refer to the Tail Ski Company data in Problem EP 8.1 above. Suppose you knew the firm followed periodic inventory but did not know which flow assumption they were using. Their income statement showed cost of goods sold as $18,500. You cannot locate the footnote concerning inventory methods. (a) Were they using LIFO or FIFO? (b) Calculate ending inventory under the method they are using. (c) Also determine both cost of goods sold and ending inventory under the other method, which they are not using.

EP 8.3. Refer to the Tail Ski Company data in Problem EP 8.1 above. Assume that, instead of periodic inventory, the firm used perpetual inventory. The 550 units were sold and shipped as follows:

September:	250 pairs
October:	100 pairs
December:	200 pairs

Determine cost of goods sold under the average cost method.

EP 8.4. Refer to the Tail Ski Company data in Problem EP 8.1 and in EP 8.3 above. Determine cost of goods sold and ending inventory, assuming the firm used perpetual LIFO.

EP 8.5. You are trying to compare the profit performance of two firms, A and B. A's income statement showed cost of goods sold as $210,000 and reported operating income of $30,000. B's showed cost of goods sold as $160,000 and operating income as $70,000. Footnotes reveal that they are both following the same accounting methods except that A uses periodic LIFO and B follows periodic FIFO. From other information, you have calculated that B's cost of goods sold following periodic LIFO would have been $205,000. What would be B's operating income, determined on the same basis as A for comparison purposes?

EP 8.6. Referring to the situation described in Problem EP 8.5 above, suppose B's LIFO cost of goods sold was not obtainable. Instead you have the following additional information on A:

Reported ending inventory:	$70,000
Ending inventory if FIFO had been used:	95,000

What would A's operating income have been, determined on the same basis as B for comparison purposes?

EP 8.7. The following information is available for a particular firm:

Gross purchases	$473,000
Transportation in	27,000
Purchase returns	32,000
Purchase discounts and allowances taken	8,000

What are net purchases for the year?

EP 8.8. The following information is available for a particular firm:

Beginning inventory	$125,000
Ending inventory	140,000
Cost of goods sold	560,000
Gross purchases	590,000
Purchase returns	40,000
Purchase discounts and allowances taken	10,000

What was the cost of transportation in, during the year?

EP 8.9. At year end the cost of ending inventory for the Spindrift Compan~ determined to be $95,000, following periodic FIFO. An LOCM calcu~ revealed that M was $97,000. At what amount should ending inve~ be reported on the balance sheet? Explain your reasoning.

EP 8.10. Refer to the Spindrift Company in Problem EP 8.9. If M had been ~ mined to be $87,000, how should balance sheet inventory have bee~ ported and why?

SUPPLEMENTARY PROBLEMS

(Based on material contained in the chapter appendix)

SP 8.11. The Barking Seal was a retailer of jeans and shirts. At the start ~ year, the merchandise on hand was priced to sell at $34,000, and th~ had been estimated at $22,000. During the year net purchases amo~ to $140,000, and these new items had been priced to sell at $22~ Sales during the first few months were slow. Markdowns of $15,000~ taken. At year end, stock still on hand had a total selling price of $4~ Following the retail method, ending inventory at cost should be rep~ at what amount?

SP 8.12. The Cotati Manufacturing Company maintained all three of its inve~ levels on a periodic inventory system. There were no price changes d~ the year. Inventory movements were determined as follows:

Raw materials: Beginning inventory plus net purchases equaled materials available for use. Raw materials availab~ use minus ending raw materials inventory equaled ~ rials used in work in process.

Work in process: Beginning inventory plus raw materials used plus ~ labor plus factory overhead equaled cost of goods ~ ufactured. Cost of goods manufactured minus e~ work in process inventory equaled cost of items ~ ferred to finished goods.

Finished goods: Beginning inventory of finished goods plus c~ items transferred from work in process equaled ~ available for sale. Goods available for sale less e~ finished goods inventory equaled cost of goods so~

Determine net purchases of raw material for the year, given the foll~ data:

Beginning raw material inventory	$ 40,000
Ending raw material inventory	30,000
Beginning work-in-process inventory	90,000
Direct labor added during the year	260,000
Factory overhead added during the year	520,000
Ending work-in-process inventory	100,000
Beginning finished goods inventory	200,000
Cost of goods sold	950,000
Ending finished goods inventory	150,000

PREPARER PROCEDURES

Many firms on periodic inventory maintain separate temporary accounts throughout the year for the various components of net purchases. Purchases are credited to accounts payable and charged or debited to gross purchases instead of to inventory. Similarly, the other components are charged or credited throughout the year to these temporary accounts rather than to inventory.

For example, suppose, on one order, there were the following events:

Invoice cost	$1,000
Transportation in	90
Returns	150
Discount taken	17

The appropriate journal entries (without explanations) would be:

	DR	CR
Gross purchases	$1,000	
Accounts payable		$1,000
Transportation in	$ 90	
Accounts payable		$ 90
Accounts payable	$ 150	
Purchase returns		$ 150
Accounts payable	$ 17	
Purchase discounts taken		$ 17

At year end, beginning inventory, gross purchases, transportation in, purchase returns, and purchase discounts are all closed to cost of goods sold. The ending inventory information is then used to reverse out of cost of goods sold and place back into inventory the amount unsold.

PREPARER PROBLEMS

PP 8.1. Prepare journal entries for the following events. The firm uses temporary accounts for the elements making up net purchases.

a) Merchandise is purchased at an invoice cost of $50,000.

b) Defective merchandise invoiced at $4,000 is returned.

c) A freight bill for $5,000 of transportation-in is received.

d) Accounts payable of $46,000 are settled, taking a purchase discount and paying only $45,080.

PP 8.2. Assume that the events in Problem PP 8.1 above were the only elements of net purchases during a period. At the beginning of the period, inventory was $6,000. Ending inventory was determined to be $7,000. Prepare all entries to close the net purchases accounts and to record ending inventory.

CHAPTER 8 APPENDIX
Other Aspects of Inventory Measurement and Reporting

GROSS-PROFIT METHOD

Often a firm desires to determine ending inventory and the cost of goods sold at interim points throughout the year, in the process of estimating interim income. For firms on periodic inventory, accurate determination of ending inventory involves taking and costing a physical inventory. Normally a complete physical inventory takes too much time and effort to be feasible more than once a year. How can a firm estimate cost of goods sold, say, at the end of a quarter? What information is readily available? Beginning inventory, net purchases, and net sales amounts for the current year are generally available. Similarly, sales and cost of goods sold for the prior year are available.

For example, the following information may be available for the Vance Company as of 3/31/X8:

19X7 Net sales	$400,000
19X7 Cost of goods sold	280,000
12/31/X7 Inventory	65,000
Net sales for first 3 months of 19X8	115,000
Net purchases for first 3 months of 19X8	75,000
Cost of goods sold for the first 3 months of 19X8	?
3/31/X8 Inventory	?

Given these data, how could you reasonably estimate the cost of goods sold and the ending inventory for the first quarter of 19X8? If you assumed continuation of last year's gross-profit ratio, then 70 percent of $115,000 (first quarter 19X8 sales) would provide an estimate of cost of goods sold; and ending inventory could be estimated at $59,500 ($140,000 of goods available less $80,500 estimated cost of goods sold).

The *gross-profit method* involves assuming continuation of the previous profit ratio. In most circumstances, this can represent a reasonable assumption for interim-period estimating purposes. It can also be the only feasible method of estimating casualty loss (fire, major theft, and so forth) of inventory for firms following the periodic system, or for those on perpetual systems whose records have been lost or destroyed. The gross-profit method is *not* acceptable under GAAP for annual financial statement reporting.

RETAIL INVENTORY METHOD

Retail stores often use a more sophisticated version of the gross-profit method known as the *Retail Inventory Method*. This method does not involve assuming continuation of a prior period gross-profit ratio. Under the retail method, the ratio is updated before application. The retail inventory method is sufficiently accurate to be acceptable under GAAP for financial reporting purposes.

Unless retailers maintain complete computerized perpetual inventory records that are justified for other purposes, they usually cannot afford to keep, for each separate inventory item, necessary detailed purchase cost records for use in "costing" the ending inventory. For other purposes, however, they do have readily available data on markups, selling prices, and *markdowns*. Markdowns may be viewed as reductions of originally intended selling price. Inventory data are therefore maintained for the firm as a whole, or for major departments within the firm, at both cost and "selling."

For example, assume that, at the end of a quarter, the following information is available:

	Cost	Selling
Beginning inventory	$ 50,000	$ 80,000
Net purchases	250,000	425,000
Less markdowns	N.A.	(5,000)
Goods available	$300,000	$500,000

Note that markdowns are not applicable to cost. Also note that this system generates a continually updated gross-profit ratio. At the end of the quarter, the firm can, with reasonable confidence, estimate the quarter's cost of goods sold as 60 percent of sales.

The more important application of the retail method is to obtain ending inventory at cost for use in the periodic inventory equation. If you had goods available for sale for the entire year at both cost and selling, and if you knew the firm had no records for "costing" each item in a physical inventory, what could you do? In retailing, selling prices are readily available with the merchandise. A physical inventory is taken and "priced" at selling price. Then this amount is converted to cost via the goods-available ratio. Thereafter, the periodic inventory system proceeds as with any other firm.

The retail method results in a moving-average cost for inventory. It can also be adapted to LIFO or FIFO. LIFO or FIFO retail methods involve a somewhat more complicated treatment of markdowns, and are beyond the scope of this elementary text.

INVENTORY FOR A MANUFACTURER

Manufacturers have inventory-measurement problems different from those for a wholesaler or retailer. To clearly understand the essentials of inventory accounting for a manufacturer, it is first necessary that you learn to distinguish between *product costs* and *period costs.*

Product Costs and Period Costs

Study Exhibit 8.2, which is the asset side of a balance sheet for the Sommers Wholesale Company. Note that all listed assets are coded as either monetary (M) or nonmonetary (NM). All nonmonetary assets except land are further coded as DFD-PROD for deferred product costs or DFD-PER for deferred period costs.

Exhibit 8.2

SOMMERS WHOLESALE COMPANY

Balance Sheet—Assets Only

CODES*	ASSETS:	
M	Cash	$ 12,000
M	Marketable securities (U.S. Govt. bonds)	40,000
M	Accounts receivable	60,000
NM/DFD-PROD	Inventory	120,000
NM/DFD-PER	Supplies	5,000
NM/DFD-PER	Prepaid insurance	3,000
	Total Current Assets	$240,000
NM	Land	$ 12,000
NM/DFD-PER	Buildings and equipment	180,000
NM/DFD-PER	Less accumulated depreciation	(75,000)
NM/DFD-PER	Intangible assets	6,000
	Total Assets	$363,000

*M = Monetary
NM = Nonmonetary
DFD-PROD = Deferred Product Cost
DFD-PER = Deferred Period Cost

If you think about what will eventually happen to all nonmonetary assets except for land, you realize that they will be used or will expire. They will be reduced eventually to zero—*written off* with corresponding expenses which reduce owner's equity by equal amounts. Another way to think of these particular assets is that they represent future expenses which are being deferred and carried forward as assets until future years. As these assets expire, the associated expense will be recognized as a reduction of owner's equity.

One of these deferred expenses is different from the others and is coded DFD-PROD. Its asset name is inventory, and it is different because it is deferred until a sale is made. DFD-PROD stands for deferred product cost. Product costs are deferred as assets and are matched with revenues on the income statement only when sales are made.

The remaining deferred expenses are coded DFD-PER. They expire and become recognized as expenses as time periods go by, regardless of the timing of sales revenue. DFD-PER stands for deferred period costs. Period costs are deferred as assets, and then matched with future years or time periods on the income statement. The distinction between product costs and period costs is an important first step in the understanding of inventory accounting for a manufacturer.

Manufacturer's Inventories

Exhibit 8.3 lists the assets for the Jacks Manufacturing Company together with the same monetary/nonmonetary product/period codes that were used for Sommers' assets on Exhibit 8.2. In comparison with the Sommers' Company's assets, Jacks has two important differences.

Exhibit 8.3
JACKS MANUFACTURING COMPANY

Balance Sheet—Assets Only

CODES*	ASSETS:	
M	Cash	$ 40,000
M	Accounts receivable	250,000
	Inventory:	
NM/DFD-PROD	Finished goods	300,000
NM/DFD-PROD	Work in process	100,000
NM/DFD-PROD	Raw materials	50,000
NM/DFD-PROD	Factory supplies	10,000
NM/DFD-PROD	Prepaid insurance on factory	6,000
	Total Current Assets	$ 756,000
NM	Land	$ 50,000
NM/DFD-PROD	Factory building	150,000
	Less accumulated depreciation	(80,000)
NM/DFD-PROD	Factory equipment	200,000
	Less accumulated depreciation	(120,000)
NM/DFD-PER	Office building	70,000
	Less accumulated depreciation	(15,000)
NM/DFD-PER	Office furniture and fixtures	12,000
	Less accumulated depreciation	(8,000)
	Total Assets	$1,015,000

*M = Monetary
NM = Nonmonetary
DFD-PROD = Deferred Product Cost
DFD-PER = Deferred Period Cost

First, Jacks has three inventory accounts separately disclosing the cost of inventory in different states of completion. Sommers, as a wholesaler, has in inventory only merchandise ready for sale. Jacks has some inventory ready for sale, and this amount is shown as *finished goods*. As a manufacturer, Jacks also has products in the factory in various stages of completion. The cost so far accumulated in these products is shown separately as *work-in-process* inventory. Finally, Jacks has some stock of purchased raw materials, which have not yet started into production. Cost of this stock is disclosed as *raw-materials* inventory.

The second important distinction is that Jacks' coded assets show several items in addition to inventories as deferred product costs. This situation exists, as explained below, only for manufacturers. Retailers and wholesalers have only finished goods, and their deferred product costs are all in inventory.

The Cost Trinity

For a manufacturer, the total cost of a finished product includes more than the net purchase cost of the raw material used to make the product. It includes the labor cost of those workers who actually worked on the product during its manufacture. It also includes all of the other manufacturing costs necessary

Exhibit 8.4

THE TRINITIES* IN A MANUFACTURER'S INVENTORY

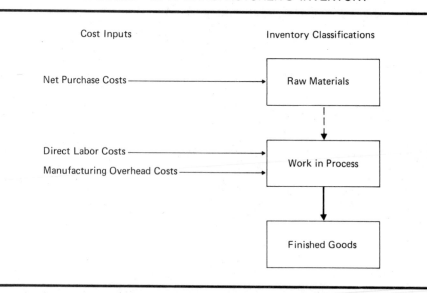

* Trinity of accounts: Raw materials, work in process, and finished goods.
  Trinity of costs: Material, labor, and overhead.

for production. Total product cost of a manufactured item can be remembered as having a trinity of costs—*material, labor,* and *overhead.* Exhibit 8.4 portrays this cost trinity. The material component includes the net purchase cost of the specific raw material used to produce this specific product. The labor component includes the wages and fringe-benefit costs for those workers and hours worked in actual production of the product.

All other manufacturing costs are accumulated and called *manufacturing overhead.* Overhead would include such items as wages and salaries of factory workers not working directly on the production of products but still necessary to support production, such as foremen, truckers, sweepers, maintenance personnel, and others. It would also include factory supplies used, cost of utilities, insurance cost for the factory, depreciation cost on the factory building and equipment, and any other cost or expenses directly related to the manufacturing activity. Overhead costs are then allocated or apportioned to all items produced.

To understand how manufacturing costs are accumulated in inventory, assume the following facts (data in thousands of dollars):

Beginning raw materials inventory	$ 40
Purchase during year of raw materials	250
Ending raw material inventory	30
Beginning work in process inventory	60
Factory direct labor expense incurred during year	780
Factory overhead expense incurred during year	390
Ending work in process inventory	70
Beginning finished goods inventory	300
Ending finished goods inventory	315

Assuming that the firm follows periodic inventory, and that there are no price/cost changes throughout the year, can you calculate cost of goods sold for the year?

If you determined cost of goods sold to be $1,405,000, you are correct and have an adequate basic understanding of a manufacturer's inventory costs. If not, refer to the data given above and proceed through each inventory level in turn:

1. The total cost of raw materials available for use during the year amounted to $290,000 ($40,000 of beginning inventory plus $250,000 purchased). With materials costing $30,000 unused at year end, materials costing $260,000 may be assumed to have been put into production during the year.

2. The cost of total products in production during the year amounted to $1,490,000. Items costing $60,000 were partially completed at the beginning of the year. Manufacturing costs of $1,430,000 were incurred/added during

the year ($260,000 of materials, per above, plus $780,000 of direct labor plus $390,000 of manufacturing overhead). With products costing $70,000 still in production and partially completed at year end, products costing $1,420,000 may be assumed to have been completed and transferred to finished goods inventory during the year.

3. The cost of goods available for sale during the year amounted to $1,720,000 (beginning inventory of $300,000 plus products completed during the year, per above, costing $1,420,000). With ending inventory of $315,000, cost of goods sold would be $1,405,000.

A manufacturer's expenses **not** directly related to manufacturing are treated as period costs. Examples would include office supplies expense, wages and salaries of all nonmanufacturing personnel, depreciation expense on office buildings,[6] depreciation on office furniture and fixtures, and other nonfactory items.

Now study Exhibit 8.3. Note that factory supplies and prepaid insurance on factory are coded as deferred product cost. They will not be written off directly to expense. They will first move into product cost through overhead as they are used or as they expire. Then, as part of product cost, they will be expenses when the sale of finished goods is made.

Similarly, the factory building and factory equipment are shown as deferred product cost. Depreciation, even though it occurs as time passes, will first be applied to inventory cost through inclusion in overhead. It will then be matched with revenue on the income statement as part of cost of goods sold when the product is sold. Depreciation of nonmanufacturing assets continues to be treated as a period cost. It is taken as a direct operating expense in future periods independently of sales.

CONSIGNMENTS

Sometimes Firm A will "loan" inventory to Firm B at its location to sell to Customers C. Firm B does not **purchase** from Firm A; it merely **sells for** A, as one of A's salespersons. Inventory "loaned" to another firm for sale is said to be *on consignment*. It remains on Firm A's balance sheet, possibly separately classified, until sale to a customer is made by Firm B. Cost of shipment to B (but not from B to C) would properly be included in the asset cost of inventory on consignment.

DAMAGED GOODS

Inventory that is damaged and merchandise that is repossessed from customers is costed at its net realizable or recoverable value.

---

[6]   Where the general selling and administrative offices are in the same building as the factory, total building depreciation is allocated between product and period cost, on the basis of space.

9

VARIATIONS IN MEASURING AND RECORDING CERTAIN NONCURRENT ASSETS

CHAPTER COVERAGE

This chapter covers the measurement and reporting of certain noncurrent assets. The noncurrent assets covered or introduced include nonmonetary fixed and intangible assets other than goodwill. These assets are often referred to as capacity assets or operational assets, since they effectively provide capacity for business operations. Other noncurrent assets are specifically covered in later chapters:

Investments and funds	Chapter 11
Goodwill	Chapter 15

CHAPTER PREVIEW

The objective of this chapter is to expand your knowledge of the accounting measurement and reporting of capacity assets. In this chapter you can:

- Learn which capacity assets are reported, which are not, and why certain intangible "assets" are not treated as such by accountants;
- Develop an understanding of "off-balance-sheet financing" and how recent changes in GAAP have modified the situation;
- Learn of the basis for initial measurement and reporting of new and improved capacity assets under differing circumstances of acquisition;
- Develop a familiarity with the most common methods of systematically recording capacity-asset expirations, the differences in the objectives of these methods, and the rationale of each;
- Learn how these differences may introduce potential distortions in comparative analysis of two or more firms' financial statements;
- Learn that GAAP standards covering methods of depreciation and amortization are very broad in scope, and that GAAP is primarily concerned with consistency of method;
- Become aware of the limitations of balance sheet information concerning capacity assets;
- Become familiar with the accountant's treatment of capacity-asset dispositions.

With this knowledge you will be able to properly interpret the often significant amounts reported as capacity assets for a firm. As in the similar case of inventory, you will be aware of the importance of verifying common measurement electives before attempting direct interfirm comparisons of data. Finally, you will know where to obtain information on the accounting method(s) being used by a particular firm, and how to interpret the significance of the method chosen, and its effect upon reported income.

HOW MUCH CAPACITY IS REQUIRED TO COMPETE?

Saul Goldman is a small West Coast wholesaler of janitorial service equipment. His industry is characterized by small local firms scattered around the country and by significantly larger firms, all of which are currently located east of the Mississippi. Smaller firms such as Saul's average an annual sales volume of approximately $750,000. The larger firms average annual sales of about $8 million. Saul has been very successful, and is considering expanding his business and moving into the "big leagues." He understands that, to compete successfully with the "majors," he would need to match their much larger investment in specially built warehouses and semi-automated material-handling equipment. He believes that, with his knowledge of the business, he could succeed as a large West Coast firm. One of the many things he needs to determine, before making a decision to proceed, is the actual amount of capacity required to be a major wholesaler in his field. Saul needs to estimate:

- The total dollars of required investment in capacity assets *fixed assets* if all were purchased at the same time, and
- The "age mix" of assets on hand at any one time in a typical established firm.[1]

Saul has operating income data and balance sheets, abbreviated to highlight noncurrent assets, for two of the major firms: Smith and Jones. This information is given in Exhibit 9.1. Saul is alarmed at the apparent disparity *a great difference* of capacity between these two firms. Study the data given for the Smith and Jones companies. As a first approximation, what would you recommend to Saul Goldman as to the minimum investment in capacity assets required to support an $8-million sales volume? Are all long-term assets being used by a firm reported on the balance sheet? How could you explain the disparity in amounts shown for the two firms? What is the accountant's intention in reporting noncurrent assets; that is, what is reported and how is it measured?

OBJECTIVES OF NONCURRENT ASSET REPORTING

The accountant's objective in reporting noncurrent assets is to disclose those properties or rights which:

- Were acquired in an exchange transaction—are owned or effectively controlled by the entity;

---

[1]   Capacity assets have different useful lives and are acquired at different times. At any one point in time a firm will have a mix of some assets near replacement with most of their useful life expired, some about half-way through their useful life, and other relatively new assets with most of their useful life ahead.

Exhibit 9.1

SMITH COMPANY AND JONES COMPANY

Selected Data from Balance Sheets As Of 12/31/XX
and from Income Statements for the Year ending 12/31/XX (000 omitted)

	SMITH	JONES
Net working capital	$ 400	$ 405
Land	100	50
Buildings	375	180
Less accumulated depreciation	(175)	(84)
Equipment	725	360
Less accumulated depreciation	(425)	(211)
Property under capital lease	0	150
Total Noncurrent Assets (Net)	$ 600	$ 445
Total Assets	$1,000	$ 850
Noncurrent mortgage notes	$ 350	$ 170
Obligations under capital leases	0	130
Total Noncurrent Liabilities	$ 350	$ 300
Owner's Equity	650	550
Total Equities	$1,000	$ 850
Sales	$7,900	$8,100
Cost of goods sold	4,740	4,860
Depreciation	95	42
Rent	0	69
Interest	31	15
Other operating expenses	2,644	2,784
Income from operations	$ 390	$ 330

- Have demonstrable future usefulness or benefit to the firm extending beyond one year; or
- Are measurable with reasonable objectivity—either expired benefit or future benefits are capable of logical objective determination.

"Exchange transactions," in this context, include self-constructed assets where the materials, labor, and services resulted from exchanges with suppliers and employees. It also includes assets donated by those outside of the entity. It specifically excludes intangibles (ideas or methods) acquired fortuitously or generated within the firm, and "value" increases resulting from such exogenous events as inflation. It also excludes those items neither owned nor effectively controlled but temporarily held under executory or simple rental agreements. Accountants view nonmonetary assets as collections of future benefits or services which have been acquired at a particular cost.

Capacity Assets Reported

Consistent with this objective and in conformance with GAAP, you may expect to find classified, under noncurrent assets, all those assets presently owned or effectively controlled by the firm which, at the time of acquisition, had future usefulness extending beyond one year and whose usefulness is measurable with reasonable objectivity.[2] Examples of capacity and other noncurrent assets that are normally included on the balance sheet are:

> Land
> Buildings
> Equipment
> Furniture and fixtures
> Capital leases
> Leasehold improvement
> Other intangibles such as patents,
>   franchises, and so forth

Capacity Assets Not Reported

As first discussed in Chapter 2, a firm may have many assets which are not reported as such by accountants. These *omitted assets* may be very significant and essential to the firm's successful operation. Omitted assets all involve intangible future benefits. They are omitted because their future benefits are uncertain or contingent on future events (assets not presently owned or effectively controlled by the firm), or because the benefits are not readily measurable. Examples of omitted assets include:

- Rights to use tangible assets under executory lease agreements where the item may be currently in the firm's possession and yet the duration of future possession and therefore the amount of benefit is uncertain;
- Benefit accruing with the firm as a result of past expenditures for public relations, advertising, employee hiring and training, and development of new products and processes (results of research and development).

Off-Balance-Sheet Financing

Some assets previously excluded, or omitted, are now included as a result of a change in GAAP. Often when a tangible asset is owned by a firm, it must

---

[2]   This statement should be understood to refer to all *material* capacity assets. Following the principle of materiality, accountants would not normally record as assets, and depreciate, wastebaskets, staplers, and so forth, even though they have future value and provide capacity. Such immaterial items would normally be charged off to supplies expense when acquired, or initially recorded under supplies and charged off when first used.

be financed, that is, acquired in exchange for a down payment and a long-term loan. In such a situation, the firm's balance sheet would reveal less liquidity as the result of the purchase. The balance sheet would disclose the nonliquid asset and a greater amount of long-term debt (higher debt ratio). The accountant's definition of an asset formerly was restricted to something legally owned. "Effectively controlled" was not part of the definition. In recent years the practice of acquiring assets under long-term lease, with the lease term often covering the entire useful life of the asset, became prevalent. Some firms may have entered into *capital leases* to appear more liquid, to escape reporting the long-term obligation because it was "executory." Others may not have been able to afford the down payment required as part of normal financing. Regardless of the reason, a situation existed where, in substance, the firm was able to effectively control the asset over most or all of its useful life. The firm also effectively had a long-term obligation. Neither used to be included in the balance sheet; hence the term *off-balance-sheet financing*.

GAAP was recently modified to significantly reduce the amount of off-balance-sheet financing. Long-term leases, which are, in substance, purchases, must now be included in the balance sheet. The asset that is effectively controlled is classified, along with fixed assets, under a caption similar to "Property held under capital lease." The associated liability is reported as "Obligations under capital leases." Capital leases will be discussed in more detail in Chapter 11. Ordinary leases which are not, in substance, purchases, are known as *operating leases*. Operating leases, since they are executory and do not represent effective control over the asset, are not reported in the balance sheet.

CAPACITY INFORMATION PROVIDED

Returning to Saul Goldman's analysis with respect to the Smith and Jones companies, one question was "Are all long-term assets being used by a firm reported on the balance sheet?" What would you tell Saul to assist him in his analysis? Saul should realize that many essential intangible assets may be present but not reported by either firm. Saul could reasonably assume that the same intangibles would be omitted from both statements, and therefore not be a source of disparity.

Saul was also concerned about the different totals for capacity assets appearing for the two firms when they both had essentially the same volume of business (sales). What is the magnitude of this difference, and how could you explain it? The book values, or original cost less depreciation and amortization, of Smith's and Jones' capacity assets were $600,000 and $445,000 respectively. Excluding the effect of accumulated depreciation, the totals would be $1,200,000 and $740,000. Smith appears to have almost twice the capacity assets of Jones. Several factors could contribute to this difference. Smith could have a significant amount of unused capacity. Smith might be able to handle $13 million of sales with no additional capacity assets required. There is another possibility. Jones could be leasing much of his capacity on a sufficiently short-term basis that it escapes capital-lease treatment, that is, under operating leases. If this were happening, Jones' income statement would reveal significant rental expense. Examine Exhibit 9.1. What would be a reasonable assumption for Saul to make regarding the disparity? Note that Jones has very high rental expense. Probably only a portion of this would relate to property under capital lease, since annual rental is $69,000 and the entire future capital-lease obligation is only $130,000. Also note that the sum of Jones' annual expenses related to capacity assets (depreciation, rent, and interest) is $126,000, which is identical to Smith's similar expenses. Later you will see how different depreciation methods could make such a comparison misleading. But even then, there appears definite evidence that the disparity results from an ownership-versus-rent difference in practice, and not from significantly different capacities.

Assuming that Jones' data do not invalidate Smith's as being representative, can Saul use the reported amounts as an indication of the investment required? What do the reported amounts represent? Do all these amounts represent cash requirements for starting a business?

INITIAL MEASUREMENT OF CAPACITY ASSETS

GAAP requires that capacity assets be initially measured and recorded at their fair market value at the date of acquisition. The initial measurement would include all reasonable necessary costs required (excluding financing—interest and cash discount—costs), to get the asset into place and ready to provide service. What the accountant uses as evidence of these costs depends upon how the asset is required and from whom. Many capacity assets are acquired from nonrelated parties as a result of an *expenditure*. An expenditure involves an outflow of monetary items—cash, or a commitment to pay cash (new debt)—in exchange for goods or services received. If the item received has measurable usefulness possibly extending beyond the current accounting period, it is *capitalized*, or recorded as an asset. If not, then the expenditure results in an expense. When capacity assets are acquired as a result of an expenditure involving nonrelated parties, the *original cost*, or *historical cost* (excluding financing charges), is considered adequate evidence of the fair market value and provides the initial basis for measurement.

For example, assume that a manufacturer had the following expenditures related to putting a new machine "on line" in the factory:

$130,000	Invoice cost from machine-tool manufacturer,
$2,000	Cost of insurance and trucking to bring machine to plant,
$2,500	Contractor's cost for concrete foundation and electrical hookup,
$500	For installation and tune-up,
$1,000	For repairing damage caused at the time of installation.

What would be the initial capitalized cost of this asset? The sum of $135,000 would be recorded as the fair value of all reasonable and necessary costs to place this equipment in service. The $1,000 would be an expense in the current period, because it was not a reasonable and necessary cost for the asset.

Capacity Assets Acquired in Nonmonetary Exchanges

Capacity assets may be acquired for nonmonetary consideration. They may be contributed (invested) by the owner. They may be donated as a gift (rare), or by government to induce activity involving a desired product or service (environmental or health research, defense, and so forth) or operation at a specific location. Where there is an exchange, and the item given up has a readily determinable fair market value (e.g., stock in a publicly traded corporation), the value of the item exchanged is assumed to indicate the value of the asset acquired. In other situations, additional evidence of fair market value, such as a professional appraisal, is required.

An asset may be acquired in exchange for a trade-in of another asset plus an additional payment. If the two assets involved are similar, then the newly acquired asset is recorded at the book value of the old plus the additional payment. If dissimilar, additional evidence (appraisal) of the fair market value of the new asset is required, and a gain or loss on the transaction may be reported.

As an example of a trade-in, assume new asset B was acquired in exchange for old asset A plus $20,000. Asset A at the time of the trade had a book value of $7,000. If A and B were similar assets—both were trucks—how would B be initially recorded? If A and B were dissimilar—a piano traded in on a truck—and B's appraised value was $24,000, what would the accountant report? In the first case, B would be recorded at $27,000. In the second case, B would be recorded at $24,000. Assets with a combined book value of $27,000 (cash plus piano) were given up. Therefore a $3,000 loss on disposition of the piano would be recorded.

SPECIAL SITUATIONS

You still need to be introduced to four special situations to complete your basic understanding of the initial measurement involved in reporting capacity assets. Assets may be acquired as part of a *basket purchase*. Usually land and any building on it are sold together at one price. Accountants must divide or allocate this single cost to two different accounts, since one is depreciated and the other is not. An appraisal of one or the other part would be required as a basis for the division of the "basket." Two or more assets with different useful lives but acquired together would be another example of a basket purchase requiring division.

Apportionment of related acquisition costs can be extended to two other common situations. In the case where a "finder's fee" or commission is paid to an agent who locates an eventually acquired property, the fee or commission may properly be apportioned between the land and building costs. Also, where a firm constructs its own asset, that portion of insurance covering the period while the asset is under construction may also be capitalized as part of the asset's cost. The logic of GAAP is consistent. All costs (**except** interest costs on borrowed funds) which are directly related to acquiring and preparing an asset for use are properly capitalized into the asset's original cost.

You may have noted the earlier qualification "nonrelated parties." If a father's firm acquired a 1956 used VW in nonrunning condition from his son, paying $20,000 cash, should this asset (?) be recorded on the firm's balance sheet at $20,000 or should it be recorded at the fair market (scrap or junk) value of $50, together with a $19,950 owner withdrawal? When a transaction is not "*arm's length*"—when it is **between related parties**—then the exchange price may not be considered adequate evidence of fair value without further external verification.

A newly acquired capacity asset may qualify for an *investment tax credit* (ITC). An ITC is a direct subsidy given by the federal government in the form of a tax reduction. It is intended to stimulate purchase of new capacity assets by business. The ITC, the several ways in which it may be reported, and some of the political aspects involved, will be discussed in Chapter 11. One method of recording the ITC acceptable under GAAP is as a direct reduction of the asset's initial cost. The initial measurement could therefore be fair market less applicable ITC, the somewhat tenuous theory being that this net amount represented the actual cost to the firm.

Additional reported capacity assets can result from *betterments*, or improvements, to existing assets. Ordinary repairs and maintenance to tangible capacity assets are treated as maintenance expense and are not capitalized. However, adding a new floor or wing to a building at a cost of $150,000 could hardly be considered maintenance or repair. The $150,000 would properly be capitalized in the building account. What if your firm incurred an $1,800 charge for truck overhaul, part of which ($800) involved installation of a rebuilt engine? The rebuilt engine would extend the previously anticipated useful life of the truck to the firm by two years. Would you still expense the entire $1,800? Assuming materiality in this situation, accountants would expense only $1,000 and would capitalize $800 as a betterment. In this situation, the individual asset's capacity or usefulness has not been increased, only its useful life. Therefore, rather than add the $800 to the fixed-asset account, accountants might subtract it from accumulated depreciation:

Before betterment:	Truck	$10,000
	Accumulated depreciation	(6,000)
After betterment:	Truck	$10,800
	Accumulated depreciation	(6,000)
or	Truck	$10,000
	Accumulated depreciation	(5,200)

Note that under either approach, the book value of the truck is increased by the $800 betterment.

COST EXPIRATIONS OF CAPACITY ASSETS

All capacity assets, except for land, are subject to wear and tear and obsolescence.[3] As described in earlier chapters, the process of systematically allocating the expiration of cost value to the years of the asset's useful life is known as **depreciation** for tangible fixed assets, and **amortization** for other assets. To provide more complete information relating to capacity assets, depreciation is accumulated in a separate negative-valuation account shown on the balance sheet immediately beneath the related asset. Annual amortization charges, rather than being accumulated in a separate account, directly reduce the unamortized balance of the intangible asset account.

Useful Life and Salvage Value

The total cost expiration of an asset to be depreciated or amortized is the difference between its initial value and the net amount that can be realized when it is disposed of. The anticipated net recovery in dollars upon disposition is known as the asset's *salvage value*. Other terms used synonymously by accountants are "residual value" or "scrap value." (The use of the word "value" is unfortunate. Net recovered dollars would be more explicit.) Salvage value is used throughout this text, because it is a generally accepted term.

The period of time over which the total cost expiration occurs—the time elapsing from the date on which the asset is first placed in use until its final disposition—is referred to as its anticipated *useful life,* or *service life.* Note carefully that useful life refers to the usefulness to the firm, that is, how long the **company** expects to use the asset. It does not refer to the total life of the asset to **all** users. The overall life of the asset itself may be many years greater than its useful life to the firm.

Are you clear on the intention of accountants with respect to depreciation and amortization? There is no intention to adjust capacity assets to reflect current market value. The intention is to match or to allocate expiring costs to the periods in which the related benefits (revenues) occur. Admittedly, such allocations are arbitrary and not very precise or scientific. They represent the accountant's best judgment.

---

[3] Land is adjusted only in the special case of extractive and natural-resource industries. In these cases, it is amortized as timber is cut, ore removed, and so forth. Amortization of land is known as *depletion.*

VARIOUS ALLOCATION METHODS OR ALTERNATIVES

Up to this point, you have been introduced only to straight-line depreciation as one of the allocation methods acceptable under GAAP. The accountant's choice of straight-line theoretically implies that the asset's usefulness or benefits will be equal in each period and that directly associated costs (fuel and maintenance costs) will also be equal. On the other hand, straight-line depreciation would theoretically imply that overall usefulness was **increasing** if related costs, and therefore total costs, were increasing over time. Many actual situations do not fit either of these two patterns; GAAP therefore provides for alternatives. GAAP actually permits any systematic and rational method deemed appropriate in the circumstances, so long as it is consistently used. Three commonly used allocation methods are given below as alternatives to the straight-line method of depreciation.

Units of Production or Service

A realistic basis for depreciation would be to directly match cost expiration with usage. For example, a truck's useful life may be estimated as 200,000 miles rather than a certain number of years. If the difference between the initial value and the salvage value—the *amount to be depreciated*, or the *depreciable base*—were $10,000, one could calculate depreciation at $0.05 per mile of use. Each year a check of the odometer would indicate the amount to be depreciated that year. This so-called *units-of-production method*, also called *units of service* or productive-output method, while appealing as logical, is not often used. Most assets do not have usage meters that are attached or readily attachable. Useful-life estimation, in terms of usage or service output units, is difficult. Finally the operation of this method could cost more than the benefit of the more precise information. Except for factory assets for manufacturers, depreciation is a *period cost*. Period costs are those charged to expense in the period incurred, as distinct from *product costs*, which are held as assets until matched with specific sales. Therefore, accountants usually associate depreciation increments with the passage of time rather than with usage.

Accelerated Depreciation

Where the usefulness of an asset is expected to decrease over time—for example, an older bus only occasionally used with discount customers—straight-line, or even units-of-service, allocation might be inappropriate. And even if benefits are uniform, the costs of operation, especially repair and maintenance costs, often increase dramatically as an asset gets older. Such situations indicate the desirability of allocating more depreciation in the early years and less in the later years, for better overall cost matching. The combined effect of the related expenses would then more uniformly match the uniform benefits. Any method of depreciation where more is allocated in the early years of useful life and less in the later years is known as an *accelerated depreciation* method.[4]

Years' Digits Method

One of the two more common accelerated-depreciation methods with which you should be familiar is known as the "sum of the years' digits" method, or simply the *years' digits* (or *SYD*) method. To understand the years' digits method, imagine an asset with a four-year life and $60,000 to be depreciated over those four years. First, obtain the sum of the digits of the useful life. One plus two plus three plus four equals ten.[5] Second, divide the total amount to be depreciated by this sum to get "depreciation shares"—$6,000 each, in this example. Then, **each year,** depreciate an amount equal to the share times the years' digit in **inverse order** (starting with the highest digit first):

	Share	Inverted digits	Amount of depreciation
First year	$6,000	4	$24,000
Second year	6,000	3	18,000
Third year	6,000	2	12,000
Fourth year	6,000	1	6,000
Total			$60,000

Assume, in the above example, that the asset had originally cost $65,000 and had an expected salvage value of $5,000 after four years of use. The amount to be depreciated would be $60,000. Book value after four years following the SYD method shown above would be $5,000. The asset would then be fully depreciated (book value equals salvage value).

Declining-Balance Method

Another commonly used accelerated method is known as *declining-balance* depreciation. Under this method, a fixed percentage rate is applied each year to the book value of the asset at the beginning of the year. In the final year, sufficient depreciation is taken to reduce the book value to, but not below, salvage value and the process is terminated. The fixed percentage rate may be

---

[4]   Accelerated depreciation is acceptable for tax purposes regardless of the pattern of other costs and benefits. It is almost always advantageous to take advantage of accelerated depreciation for tax purposes. It is not necessary or even desirable that depreciation for financial-reporting purposes be the same as tax depreciation. Nevertheless, many firms will use accelerated depreciation for both purposes rather than keep two sets of depreciation records.

[5]   For longer lives, the formula $n\frac{(n+1)}{2}$, with n as the useful life, is convenient.

calculated by a formula[6] or arbitrarily chosen. When the rate is arbitrarily chosen, declining-balance depreciation ignores salvage value until the final year when book value is arbitrarily adjusted to salvage value. The amount of declining-balance depreciation is not determined on the basis of the amount to be depreciated. It is calculated on the declining book value.

A common arbitrary rate, often also used for certain assets for tax purposes, is 200 percent of the straight-line rate, or *double-declining-balance* (or *DDB*). DDB is one of a great number of different declining balance methods. DDB is merely a declining balance method using a 200 percent rate. The application of double-declining-balance can be illustrated with an asset which cost $10,000. Assume the useful life is five years, and the estimated salvage value is $1,000. The straight-line rate would be 20 percent, and therefore the double-declining rate would be 40 percent.

Year	Beginning book value	Annual depreciation (40 percent)	Accumulated depreciation
1	$10,000	$4,000	$4,000
2	6,000	2,400	6,400
3	3,600	1,440	7,840
4	2,160	864	8,704
5	1,296	296*	9,000

* Note that, in the final year of useful life, only the amount necessary to reduce book value to salvage value is expensed ($1296 − 1000 = $296).

INCOME EFFECT OF DIFFERENT METHODS

Just as LIFO and FIFO can cause comparability problems between firms electing the different systems, straight-line and accelerated depreciation can cause similar difficulties. Compared with a firm which has elected straight-line depreciation, another firm which has elected an accelerated method would have greater depreciation expense in the early years of the asset's useful life and less in the last few years.

Exhibit 9.2 illustrates this comparability problem. Note that the exhibit assumes identical performance of the three firms over the five years—funds from operations were $5,000 each year. Note that for the first two years, both accelerated methods result in reported income being less than under straight-line. And note that, even though the firms are actually experiencing constant profits, under accelerated-depreciation methods, two are reporting **substantially increased** profits each successive year!

---

[6] Depreciation rate $(\%) = \left(1 - \sqrt[n]{\dfrac{\text{Net salvage value}}{\text{Acquisition cost}}}\right) \times 100$, where $n =$ years of useful life.

Exhibit 9.2

INCOME STATEMENT EFFECT OF DIFFERENT DEPRECIATION METHODS

This comparison assumes that each firm acquires assets costing $10,000 with a five-year useful life and $1,000 salvage value; it also assumes that each firm's operating income before depreciation equaled $5,000 each year.

	FIRM A (Straight-line)		FIRM B (Years' digits)		FIRM C (Double-declining)	
Year	Depreciation expense	Operating income	Depreciation expense	Operating income	Depreciation expense	Operating income
1	$1,800	$3,200	$3,000	$2,000	$4,000	$1,000
2	1,800	3,200	2,400	2,600	2,400	2,600
3	1,800	3,200	1,800	3,200	1,440	3,560
4	1,800	3,200	1,200	3,800	864	4,136
5	1,800	3,200	600	4,400	296	4,704

In theory, a firm would not elect accelerated depreciation with all other revenues and expenses constant. In practice, GAAP allows it. Also it could have been elected in different circumstances in the past, and continued into the present, following the GAAP principle of consistency. Can you see where a comparison of two firms' performance, when one was using straight-line and the other double-declining, could lead to disastrously incorrect conclusions?

The user of financial statements must be careful not to blindly accept reported income comparisons between two companies unless they are both using the same depreciation and amortization methods. The balance sheet footnotes should fully disclose the method(s) being used.

AMORTIZATION OF INTANGIBLES

Although the foregoing discussion and examples have focused on depreciating tangible fixed assets, the information is equally applicable to intangible assets. Intangible assets, especially capital leases, can be very significant in amount and income statement effect. Any of the various methods of depreciation may be used for amortizing capital leases and other intangible assets. The only difference from depreciation is that amortization does not involve an asset-valuation account for "accumulated amortization." Instead, remember that amortization is subtracted each year directly from the beginning unamortized balance of the asset.

OTHER ITEMS RELATED TO DEPRECIATION AND AMORTIZATION

Companies may find it expedient to account for certain capacity assets on a group (similar items) or composite (dissimilar items) basis. *Group* or *com-*

posite depreciation or amortization is merely a process where a number of assets are treated collectively as if they were a single unit. A weighted-average useful life based on cost times life of the individual assets is used to determine depreciation or amortization for the entire lot.

Also, assets are acquired throughout the year. It is customary to prorate depreciation or amortization to the nearest month from the time the asset was put in service. For example, an asset put in service on May 20 would be depreciated for seven months during the first calendar year (7/12 of annual depreciation).

Once initial estimates of useful life and salvage value have been made, consistency does **not** require that they be adhered to blindly if subsequent events indicate that they are incorrect. When new information indicates that the original estimates were incorrect, the estimates are revised for the current and subsequent years. Note that accountants do not attempt to rewrite history. If the useful life is extended over the original estimate, they will prorate remaining depreciation over the new remaining life. Similarly, revised depreciation amounts in current and subsequent years could result from a **reduction** of estimated useful life or a change in **expected salvage value.** Should an asset be *fully depreciated*—book value equals salvage value—and it turns out thereafter to have more years of useful life, no adjustment can be made. The asset continues on the books until it is disposed of.

A *change of accounting estimate* described above should be undertaken whenever new information becomes available. Note, however, that a change in **estimate** should not be confused with a *change in accounting method.* A change in accounting method would involve a changeover from straight-line to an accelerated-depreciation method, or vice versa. It would also include changing from FIFO to LIFO. Consistency requires adherence to one method once adopted. GAAP only allows for changes in infrequent cases where circumstances have clearly made an alternative method preferable. Changes in accounting method are always considered sufficiently significant to be noted in the auditor's opinion and justified in statement footnotes, together with data showing the effect of the change.

Differences in depreciation methods for a given firm between its financial statements and its tax returns can give rise to *deferred income tax.* Deferred income taxes will be discussed more completely in Chapter 12. At this point it is only necessary for you to see how they can arise in relation to different depreciation methods. Turn again to Exhibit 9.2 and imagine that the data were alternative amounts for the **same firm.** Visualize Firm A as using straight-line for financial reporting purposes and double-declining for tax purposes. The same total tax would be paid over the five-year period; but, if taxes were based on declining-balance income, taxes would be lower in the earlier years and higher in later years than they would have been had the tax been based on straight-line income. Assume taxes were 40 percent and were based on the double-declining income. Exhibit 9.3 shows the alternative effects of no tax deferral and tax deferral. What actually is happening is that declining-balance tax depreciation, as compared with straight-line, enables the firm to postpone tax payments and make them up in later years. Taxes would have been $1,280

Exhibit 9.3

ILLUSTRATION OF DEFERRED INCOME TAX EFFECTS

Year	Income before taxes	Actual taxes paid	Income after tax without deferral	Amount of deferral*	Income after tax with deferral
1	$3,200	$ 400	$2,800	$+880	$1,920
2	3,200	1,040	2,160	+240	1,920
3	3,200	1,424	1,776	−144	1,920
4	3,200	1,654	1,546	−374	1,920
5	3,200	1,882	1,318	−602	1,920

* Note. Plus (+) equals deferred tax liability accrued. Minus (−) equals reduction of deferred tax liability.

each year on a straight-line basis. In effect, the company is receiving a non-interest-bearing loan from the government, and then repaying the loan. During the five years it is better off, or at least no worse off, than had it used straight-line for tax purposes and paid $1,280 in taxes each year.

Then look at reported income after tax **without** tax deferral. It appears to indicate steadily declining profitability for a firm with stable profits and an interest-free loan. GAAP therefore requires that the "postponed" taxes be accrued as a liability which is later reduced when the taxes to be paid exceed $1,280. Tax expense is therefore shown at $1,280 each year, with after-tax income at a constant $1,920.

LIMITATIONS OF BALANCE SHEET INFORMATION

Have you forgotten Saul Goldman? Saul still wants to know how much investment in capacity assets appears to be required for an $8-million-volume level. Turn to Exhibit 9.1. Assuming Smith does not have excess capacity and is a representative firm, what can you tell Saul? How reliable would your estimate be in terms of current cost? Would your estimate have been any more or less reliable had one of the material capacity assets been an intangible asset?

Since the original cost information for all of Smith's reported capacity assets is disclosed, you could tell Saul, "Approximately $1,200,000 of capacity assets would be required." Note that you cannot tell him:

• Whether the assets were new or used when purchased, or

• How recent, and therefore relevant in an inflationary economy, these figures are.

Even with footnote information on depreciation methods employed, you have no information on useful lives or salvage values. "Roughly 55 percent depreciated" therefore doesn't mean much. The Saul Goldman questions were not designed to trick you. Instead, they should have focused your attention on the actual information available with respect to capacity assets. More importantly, you should be aware of the information **not** available and the apparent inferences that should **not** be drawn.

DISPOSITION OF CAPACITY ASSETS

To complete your general understanding of accounting for capacity assets, there is one further area to be introduced—disposition of capacity assets. A tangible asset continues to be disclosed on the balance sheet until it is disposed of, even if fully depreciated. When disposition occurs, depreciation is first updated to the date of disposition. This is necessary, since ordinarily depreciation on all assets is updated only at the close of the period, when statements are to be prepared.

The updated book value is then removed from the accounts (both the entire asset cost and its related accumulated depreciation) and the salvage-value inflow is recorded. In a sense, this is a simple exchange of assets, except that rarely is an asset sold for precisely its updated book value. If salvage value exceeds book value, total assets increase. Owner's equity is therefore increased through a gain account. Conversely, a loss on disposition is recorded as an operating loss. Note that gains and losses on disposition of noncurrent assets are operating items and **not** considered extraordinary.

Intangible assets are disclosed on the balance sheet until their unamortized cost is reduced to zero, or until they are disposed of, whichever occurs first. Disposal of intangible assets follows the same steps as for tangible assets.

As an example of a disposition, consider an asset with an original cost of $60,000. It has been depreciated at a rate of $6,000 per year. At the beginning of the current year, $36,000 of depreciation has been accumulated. It was sold for $22,000 on July 1. An additional $3,000, representing one-half of a year's depreciation, is first recorded and charged to depreciation expense. Updated book value is now $21,000. There would be a gain on disposition of $1,000.

CHAPTER OVERVIEW

From the material in this chapter, you should be able to:

- Describe the GAAP standards for recognition of a capacity asset, and explain why other intangible items with future benefits for the firm are not reported as assets;

- Precisely define the standards for the initial measurement and reporting of capacity assets under different types of acquisition;
- Explain the intention of depreciation and amortization, their different applicability, and their different balance sheet presentation;
- Describe the foremost common methods for systematically recording asset expiration, calculate depreciation or amortization by each method, and explain the rationale behind the choice of a particular method;
- Describe and contrast the different income effects of each alternative method and the significance of these differences to comparative statement analysis;
- Explain the information provided with respect to capacity assets on the balance sheet, and cite the limitations of, and possibly inappropriate inferences from, such information;
- Describe the accounting treatment of capacity-asset dispositions, and determine the gain or loss on a given disposition;
- Briefly explain the significance of such related items as: trade-ins, basket purchases, arm's-length transactions, the investment tax credit, betterments, changes in estimates, group or composite depreciation, and deferred income taxes.

NEW VOCABULARY AND CONCEPTS

Operational assets
"Omitted assets"
Capital leases
Off-balance-sheet financing
Operating lease
Expenditure
Capitalize
Original/Historical cost
Basket purchase
Arm's length
Investment tax credit (ITC)
Betterment
Salvage value
Useful life/service life
Period cost

Product cost
Amount to be depreciated/depreciable base
Units of production method/units of service method
Accelerated depreciation
Years' digits method (SYD)
Declining-balance method
Double-declining-balance method (DDB)
Group/composite depreciation
Fully depreciated
Change of accounting estimate
Change in accounting method
Deferred income tax

- Criteria for identification as capacity asset.
- Basis for initial measurement and reporting of capacity assets.
- Objective of depreciation and amortization.
- Rationale for selecting each of four standard methods.
- Income statement effect of each method.
- Rationale for income tax deferral.

REVIEW QUESTIONS

1. Something acquired by a firm and having future benefits to the firm extending beyond one year still must meet three tests or qualifications to be capitalized and reported as a capacity asset. Describe these three qualifications and the rationale for each.

2. List at least four tangible and four intangible capacity assets and explain how each meets the qualifications for asset treatment.

3. List several long-term assets which are **not** measured and reported as such by accountants, and explain why each does not "qualify."

4. a) Describe what is meant by "off-balance-sheet financing."
   b) Describe a recent change in GAAP related to items previously part of off-balance-sheet financing.
   c) How was the definition of an asset altered by this change?

5. a) How does "fair market value at the time of acquisition" relate to the initial measurement and recording of nonmonetary assets?
   b) Is fair market value always the same as "original cost"?
   c) If not, explain the possible source of the difference and which amount is used as the initial measurement of capacity assets.

6. What is an expenditure?

7. How is the basis for measurement of and recording a new capacity asset determined when:
   a) It is acquired with an expenditure?
   b) It is acquired via a nonmonetary exchange?
   c) It is acquired by donation?
   d) It is self-constructed?
   e) It is acquired as part of a basket purchase?
   f) It is acquired as part of a transaction involving a trade-in?
   g) It is acquired from a related party (non-arm's-length)?
   Give an example illustrating your reply to each question.

8. What costs are included in the initial valuation of a capacity asset?

9. What is a betterment and how is it handled by accountants?

10. Does useful life refer to the useful life of the asset? If not, to what does useful life refer?

11. A particular asset's useful life with proper care and maintenance is 18 years. The firm will not need it after seven years and will sell it to another user at that time. What is the useful life of this asset for depreciation purposes? Explain.

12. a) Define period and product costs.
    b) Explain why a wholesaler would treat merchandise purchases and capacity-asset purchases as one or the other, and why.

13. a) Explain how you would determine the amount to be depreciated/amortized or the depreciation or amortization base for any capacity asset.
    b) Would this same amount be useful for all four depreciation methods? Explain.

14. What is the difference between straight-line and accelerated depreciation?

15. Under what circumstances would straight-line depreciation be preferable to an accelerated method?

16. Under what circumstances would an accelerated method of depreciation be preferable to straight-line?

17. A firm acquires an auto costing $13,000. Salvage value is estimated at $1,000 and useful life to the firm as ten years, during which it is expected to be driven 180,000 miles. The car was driven 15,000 miles during its second year. What would second-year depreciation expense be, and why, if:
    a) straight-line depreciation were being used?
    b) units-of-production or -service depreciation were being used?
    c) years' digits depreciation were being used?
    d) double-declining-balance depreciation were being used?

18. a) Does GAAP allow for changing depreciation methods once started? (b) Does GAAP allow for changing depreciation estimates once started? (c) What is the difference between depreciation methods and depreciation estimates?

19. An asset costing $6,000 with six-year life and zero salvage was being depreciated on a straight-line basis. At the end of three years it was determined that only two more years of useful life remained. Explain if, how, and why:
    a) The first three years' depreciation expense and total accumulated depreciation would be modified following GAAP.
    b) The fourth year's depreciation expense would be modified following GAAP.
    c) The fifth year's depreciation expense would be modified following GAAP.

20. In the early years of useful life and in comparison with straight-line, will a firm using accelerated depreciation report higher or lower operating income, all other things being equal?

21. Why can't one estimate the age of noncurrent assets subject to amortization by using the balance sheet figure?

22. Why can't one estimate the age of fixed assets subject to depreciation by using the balance sheet figures?

23. Properly recording the disposition of a capacity asset may involve three steps:
    Step 1: ?
    Step 2: Eliminate the asset balance (and accumulated depreciation) from the asset accounts and record the proceeds of the sale.
    Step 3: ?
    a) What are steps (1) and (3)?
    b) When might steps (1), or (3), or both, be unnecessary? Explain.

MINI-CASES AND QUESTIONS FOR DISCUSSION

MC 9.1. Sam Fisher is very disturbed. "Who says consistent accounting?" he asks. "Look at these two statements! Two retailers with identical delivery trucks. I **know**—I sold them both to these guys less than a week apart. They cost $6,000, and would you believe it? After one year Mel's Surplus Store has it depreciated $1,000. The exclusive Maison Fifi Lingerie Shop took $2,000 depreciation the first year. How can you wear out a truck hauling around lingerie? It doesn't make sense!"

Can you explain to Sam that higher depreciation may be perfectly logical for Maison Fifi? Obsolescence may be a more important factor than wear and tear. Maison Fifi may need to have a new truck every year to maintain its image. Discuss.

MC 9.2. Colleen Murphy is skeptical about accounting terms. "How can accountants talk about a loss on disposition of a fixed asset?" she asks. "If they had estimated the useful life and salvage value accurately, there wouldn't be any so-called loss. Such a loss is just the accountant's estimating error, and should be considered extra depreciation that year. And the same thing applies to gains upon disposition. Take off too much depreciation, and you're bound to have a gain. It should be a reduction of depreciation, not a separate gain." Discuss.

MC 9.3. Can reported income be manipulated through choice of depreciation methods or estimates? Could hidden "reserves" of depreciation-expense increases and decreases be created for use in a year when the firm wanted to report lower earnings (labor-contract negotiations are going on) or higher earnings (it needs to raise more capital)? Discuss.

MC 9.4. Isn't a capital lease still an executory contract? Aren't all executory contracts off the balance sheet? Discuss.

MC 9.5. Why are financing costs (interest and cash discounts) excluded in measuring and recording capacity assets? Why are cash discounts (but not interest) included in the measurement of inventory? Discuss.

MC 9.6. A owns land originally costing $5,000 and on its books at that amount. It sells the land to B for the current fair market value of $25,000.
a) Would the $20,000 gain be reported if B were nonrelated?
b) Would the $20,000 gain be reported if B were related (a wholly owned subsidiary company)?
Discuss.

MC 9.7. Refer to MC 9.6 above. A has recorded the sale and the gain. How should the following be reported by A if, during the following year:
a) A repurchases the land from B (not related) for $25,000.
b) B completely defaults on a $20,000 note given A as part of the original sale. A takes back the property.
c) A repurchases the land from B (closely related) for $30,000.
Discuss.

MC 9.8. Assume that a firm buys an asset costing $100,000 which it intends to use for five years and then resell. It estimates that, because of rapid inflation affecting this type of asset, resale value in five years will be $105,000. Should the asset be depreciated? How much? Discuss.

MC 9.9. A firm has capacity assets costing $600,000, on which it has been regularly taking $25,000 of annual depreciation. During all of 19X4, the firm was shut down by a strike. There were no 19X4 revenues. Should the 19X4 Income Statement (loss statement?) add insult to injury by recording $25,000 of depreciation expense?

a) If yes, wouldn't inclusion be a violation of "matching"—shouldn't expenses be matched with revenues?

b) If not, wouldn't omission be a violation of "consistency"—don't costs expire (aging and obsolescence) whether or not the asset is used?

Discuss.

MC 9.10. A seasonal resort wishes to prepare interim (quarterly) income statements. During one-half of the year (off-season), funds from operations are negative. The overall yearly profit is excellent. Should 50 percent of annual depreciation be allocated to the two off-season quarterly reports? If not, how much should be allocated? If you advocate zero depreciation for these two quarters, are you being consistent with your position in MC 9.9 above? Discuss.

ESSENTIAL PROBLEMS

EP 9.1. The Sisich Bottling Company has just acquired a new bottling machine for its line of soft drinks. The machine cost $260,000 at the factory in Chicago. Related costs were:

Freight bill to truck the machine to Sisich Company	$4,000
Insurance coverage while being transported	$400
Contractor's bill for installing concrete base for machine	$500
Electrician's bill for installing power lines to machine	$1,600
Rigger's bill for unloading machine and installing in factory	$1,300
Maintenance during first year of operation	$900

Determine the amount to be added to the equipment account.

EP 9.2. The Waspin Company on January 1 purchased an old office building for refurbishing and use. The cost of the building and land was $240,000. Related events during the year were as follows:

Land was appraised at	$60,000
Real estate commission paid	$12,000
Contractor's bill for remodeling	$45,000
Landscape bill for landscaping grounds	$9,000
Insurance on premises for first year	$1,000
Watering and gardening bill last half of year after landscaping completed	$300

Assuming the building is ready for use and is occupied on July 1, what would be the appropriate total additions to the land account and to the building account?

EP 9.3. On January 1, 19X0, the McDaniel Company purchased three different fixed assets: A, B, and C. Each cost $50,000, each had an estimated five-year useful life, and each had an estimated salvage value of $5,000. The firm elected to depreciate A on straight-line, B on years' digits, and C on double-declining balance. On the 12/31/X0 balance sheet, accumulated depreciation was shown as $15,000, $20,000, and $9,000 for the three assets. Which accumulated depreciation related to which asset?

EP 9.4. Refer to the McDaniel Company in Problem EP 9.3 above. One of the firm's income statements, prepared during the life of these assets, showed combined depreciation expense for all three as $25,200. For which year was the statement prepared?

EP 9.5. On a 12/31/XX balance sheet, two particular noncurrent assets—P and Q —were shown as:

Fixed asset P	$74,000
Accumulated depreciation on P	($57,000)
Intangible asset Q	$11,000

The following day, these assets were sold at a gain of $2,000. How much did the company receive on the sale of these two assets?

EP 9.6. On a 12/31/X0 balance sheet, the Littlejohn Company had only two non-current assets, as follows:

Truck	$18,000
Accumulated depreciation	($ 6,000)
Intangible asset	$ 9,000

The truck was being depreciated at $4,000 per year and the intangible asset was being amortized at $3,000 per year. On 7/1/X1 the company sold both of these noncurrent assets at a combined net loss of $5,000. How much did the company receive on the sale of these two assets?

EP 9.7. An asset acquired on 1/1/X3 had accumulated depreciation of $30,600 on 12/31/X4. If double-declining balance was being used and the asset had a five-year life, what was the asset's original cost?

EP 9.8. An asset acquired on 1/1/X5 had accumulated depreciation of $30,000 and a book value of $20,000 on 12/31/X7. If the asset had a six-year useful life and SYD depreciation was being used, what was the expected salvage value?

EP 9.9. A recently acquired asset—1/1/?–had an accumulated depreciation of $21,875 and a book value of $28,125 on 12/31/X9. The asset was expected to have an eight-year life and double-declining balance was being used. When was the asset acquired?

EP 9.10. An asset acquired on 1/1/X2 and being depreciated on a straight-line basis was sold on 4/1/X8. The asset originally cost $40,000, and had been depreciated under the assumption of a nine-year life and a $4,000 salvage value. It was sold for $12,000. Was there a gain or a loss on the sale? Explain.

SUPPLEMENTARY PROBLEMS

SP 9.11. Bruce Hatch started his trucking business three years ago, and it is now the beginning of the fourth year. When he started, he elected straight-line depreciation as the simplest. His trucks cost $56,000, had an estimated four-year life in the business, and an anticipated salvage value of $8,000. He is trying to compare his income statement with that of a competitor of the same size. The footnotes to the competitor's statement reveal that it is using years' digits depreciation. Bruce has decided that accelerated depreciation would have been better for him. He will use it on new trucks in the future. How should he mentally adjust his third-year operating income for comparability with his competitor's statement?

SP 9.12. Refer to the data given in SP 9.11 above. Suppose instead that both Bruce's trucks and his competitor's trucks had six-year lives, and his competitor was using double-declining balance. How much of an adjustment to his operating income should Bruce mentally make for comparison purposes?

PREPARER PROCEDURES

Compound entries may be required to record acquisitions, annual depreciation, and dispositions. Examples would include:

1. Building and land costing $250,000 acquired, paying $25,000 down and giving two promissory notes—one for $25,000 plus interest, maturing in six months, and one for $200,000 plus interest, maturing in ten years. The land alone was appraised at $60,000. The journal entry (without accompanying explanation) recording the acquisition would be:

	DR	CR
Land	$ 60,000	
Buildings	190,000	
Cash		$ 25,000
Current Notes Payable		25,000
Noncurrent Notes Payable		200,000

2. An attorney's bill is received for $1,000 covering legal services related to the above acquisition. The fee is to be prorated between the loan and the building.

	DR	CR
Land	$240	
Buildings	760	
Accounts Payable		$1,000

3. Annual depreciation on buildings is $30,000, on equipment $64,000, and on office furniture and fixtures $19,000:

	DR	CR
Depreciation Expense	$113,000	
Accumulated depreciation on buildings		$30,000
Accumulated depreciation on equipment		64,000
Accumulated depreciation on O.F.F.		19,000

4. An intangible asset has an unamortized cost of $64,000 on 12/31/X4. It has been previously amortized on a straight-line basis at $8,000 per year. On 9/30/X5, it is sold for $59,000:

	DR	CR
Cash	$59,000	
Amortization Expense	6,000	
Intangible Asset		$64,000
Gain on Sale of Intangible Asset		1,000

5. A piece of equipment costing $130,000 has a book value of $45,000 on 12/31/X8. Depreciation is on a straight-line basis at $9,000 per year. On 4/30/X9, the equipment is sold for $40,000:

	DR	CR
Cash	$40,000	
Depreciation Expense	3,000	
Accumulated Depreciation	85,000	
Loss on Sale of Equipment	2,000	
Equipment		$130,000

6. Equipment costing $90,000 and with a book value of $25,000, together with $75,000 cash, is traded in on a similar piece of equipment.

	DR	CR
Equipment (New)	$100,000	
Accumulated Depreciation (Old)	65,000	
Cash		$75,000
Equipment (Old)		90,000

7. Assume in transaction 6 above that the two items of equipment were **not** similar and that the new equipment had a fair market value of $93,000:

	DR	CR
Equipment (New)	$93,000	
Accumulated Depreciation (Old)	65,000	
Loss on Equipment Disposition	7,000	
Cash		$75,000
Equipment (Old)		90,000

PREPARER PROBLEMS

Journalize the following transactions and adjustments in good form:

PP 9.1. On 5/23/X7 the firm purchased land and building in exchange for $20,000 cash and a 20-year mortgage note for $270,000 plus interest. The building was appraised at $260,000.

PP 9.2. On 3/7/X2 the firm acquired land, buildings, and equipment in exchange for $30,000 cash and a 15-year mortgage note for $270,000 plus interest. The buildings and equipment were appraised at $90,000 and $180,000 respectively.

PP 9.3. A building acquired on 1/1/X2 at a cost of $275,000 was being depreciated, assuming a 5-year life on the double-declining basis. Record the depreciation for the year 19X4.

PP 9.4. A building acquired on 12/28/X3 at a cost of $400,000 was estimated to have a 25-year life and a $20,000 salvage value. Record depreciation for the year 19X9 following the years' digits method.

PP 9.5. Equipment costing $230,000 and with a book value of $40,000 on 12/31/X6 was sold on 3/1/X7 for $40,000. Depreciation had been taken on a straight-line basis at a rate of $24,000 per year.

PP 9.6. Equipment costing $80,000 and with a book value of $6,000 on 12/31/X8 was sold on 7/5/X9 for $2,000. Depreciation had been taken on a straight-line basis at a rate of $7,400 per year.

PP 9.7. A new truck was acquired on 10/22/X6 in exchange for $6,000 cash, a $5,000 interest-bearing note, and the trade-in of an old truck. The old truck cost $15,000 and had a book value of $8,000 on 12/31/X5. The old truck was being depreciated on a straight-line basis at a rate of $1800 per year.

PP 9.8. A new machine tool with a fair market value of $135,000 was purchased on 1/8/X7 in exchange for $15,000 cash, a mortgage note for $115,000 plus interest, and the trade-in of a truck. The truck had cost $20,000 and had a book value on 12/31/X6 of $8,000. It had been depreciated on a straight-line basis at an annual rate of $3,000.

10

OWNERS' EQUITY FOR PARTNERSHIPS AND CORPORATIONS

CHAPTER PREVIEW

The objective of this chapter is to introduce you to accounting for businesses with more than a single owner—partnerships and corporations. You can:

- Learn that the basic financial accounting system is essentially the same for proprietorships, partnerships, and corporations, with the only significant difference occurring within owners' equity;

- Learn about partnership agreements and their control over the accountant's distribution of income and equity shares among partners;

- Become familiar with some of the distinctive features of corporations including limited liability, the concept of "permanent" contributed capital, and owner-withdrawal limitations designed to protect creditors;

- Learn how to interpret the stockholders' equity section of a corporate balance sheet;

- Learn how various stockholder-related transactions, including stock sale, stock splits, stock dividends, cash dividends, and the purchase and resale of treasury stock are recorded and reported;

- Become familiar with the relationships among stockholder claims, par value, book value, market values, and earnings per share.

With this knowledge you will have completed your basic understanding of financial accounting for all types of single business entities—proprietorships, partnerships, and corporations. You will be able to read intelligently financial statements prepared for any individual firm. And you will have the background necessary for the introduction in the next chapter of some of the more specialized and complex asset-measurement problems encountered by accountants.

WHAT WOULD BE MY SHARE OF THE PROFITS?

Jan Ford is thinking of going into *partnership* with Mary Schneider. Mary has a very successful hardware store in a shopping center and has been considering opening another one in a new shopping center at the other end of town. Jan would invest $30,000 cash in the business. This $30,000, together with an additional five-year loan of $60,000 from Jan's family, would provide adequate capital for the new store.

The tentative *partnership agreement* provides that, in the event of dissolution, net assets would be allocated in direct proportion to owners' equity balances at the time of dissolution. As partners might have different amounts of capital in the business, and also might be contributing different effort and skill, a simple 50–50 split of profits might not be fair compensation. The tentative agreement therefore provides that any business profits will be divided as follows:

- Profits up to an amount equal to 10 percent of yearly average owner's equity will be allocated proportionally to average annual investment of each partner (compensates for funds invested);
- Profits in excess of this amount will be apportioned on the basis of 60 percent to Mary and 40 percent to Jan (recognition of Mary's superior experience).

Projected or *pro-forma statements* have been prepared by Mary, which reflect the first year of operation and assume that no profits are withdrawn. They show partnership equity only in total and do not reflect the proposed division between partners. Mary explained that the individual shares could be determined once the two have agreed on a basis for profit division. These pro-forma statements, in abbreviated form, are shown on Exhibit 10.1.

PARTNERS' OWNERS' EQUITY STILL JUST OWNER'S EQUITY

Exhibit 10.1 deliberately does not show a projected division of owners' equity. It is important that you understand that it makes absolutely no difference how partners divide their shares. Total owners' equity for a partnership is equivalent to owner's equity for a proprietorship. Recall the basic balance sheet equality which was first introduced in Chapter 2. Total owners' equity is still simply total assets minus total liabilities.

The accounting system itself is essentially the same for a proprietorship and for a partnership. The only difference is that, instead of a single balance sheet account for the owner's equity, there would be one or more accounts

Exhibit 10.1
MARY AND JAN HARDWARE STORES

Abbreviated Pro-Forma Balance Sheets and Income Statements
Balance Sheet at Beginning of First Year of Partnership:

Total Current Assets	$150,000	Total Current Liabilities	$ 40,000
Total Noncurrent Assets (net)	20,000	Total Noncurrent Liabilities	60,000
		Total Partners' Equity	70,000
Total Assets	$170,000	Total Equities	$170,000

Income Statement for First Year of Partnership:

Sales	$540,000
Cost of goods sold	325,000
Gross Profit	$215,000
Other operating expenses	140,000
Operating Income	$ 75,000

Balance Sheet at end of First Year of Partnership:

Total Current Assets	$237,000	Total Current Liabilities	$ 50,000
Total Noncurrent Assets (net)	18,000	Total Noncurrent Liabilities	60,000
		Total Partners' Equity	145,000
Total Assets	$255,000	Total Equities	$255,000

for each partner. The sum of all partners' shares after closing would still be equal to total assets minus total liabilities. Accounting procedures will differ only with respect to transactions affecting owners' equity directly, and for closing revenue and expense accounts.

Income, instead of being closed to a single owner's equity account, will be allocated to several owners' equity accounts following the proportions specified in the partnership agreement. Note that GAAP are not involved in this apportionment. GAAP merely require the accountant to follow the partners' wishes. It is the partners' business and their equity interest to divide as they choose.

DIVISION OF PARTNERS' SHARES

The division of owners' equity makes no difference to the firm or to the accounting system. It does make a difference to the partners. They want information on where they stand.

Let us return to the example involving Mary and Jan. Owners' equity at the beginning was $70,000. This projection assumed Jan's contribution had been $30,000. Therefore Mary's share must have been $40,000. A more detailed beginning balance sheet would show owners' equity as:

Mary Schneider, Capital	$40,000
Jan Ford, Capital	30,000
Total Partners' Equity	$70,000

Assume the partnership agreement provided that the average investment of each partner would be determined from the formula:

$$\frac{\text{Beginning balance} \times 2 + \text{investments--drawings}}{2}$$

In a partnership, partner withdrawals are known as *drawings*. This formula merely ignores current year's profit or loss.

Since there were no projected additional investments or drawings by either partner during the first year, the average investment would remain $40,000 for Mary and $30,000 for Jan. Following the proposed agreement, the projected $75,000 of profits would be divided as shown on Exhibit 10.2.

Exhibit 10.2
MARY AND JAN HARDWARE STORES

Pro-Forma Statement of Change in Partners' Capital

	Mary Schneider	Jan Ford	Total
Ownership Equity 1/1	$40,000	$30,000	$ 70,000
Additional investments	0	0	0
Less withdrawals	0	0	0
10% Income allocation	4,000	3,000	7,000
60–40 balance allocation	40,800	27,200	68,000
Ownership Equity 12/31	$84,800	$60,200	$145,000

PARTNERSHIP OWNERS' EQUITY CLASSIFICATION

The ending balance sheet, still assuming no withdrawals, would disclose the same information as shown at the bottom of Exhibit 10.2. There would be one line for each partner showing the final share of total owners' equity. The ending balance sheet for Mary and Jan in the owners' equity section would disclose:

Mary Schneider, Capital	$ 84,800
Jan Ford, Capital	60,200
Total Partners' Equity	$145,000

A partnership is just a multiple proprietorship. Each partner has a share of the overall "proprietorship."

MULTISTEP PARTNERSHIP ALLOCATIONS

Mary and Jan already have a two-step allocation agreement. With an average total equity of $70,000, 10 percent of this amount, or the first $7,000 of profits, were to be allocated in proportion to average investment. The remainder, as a second step, was split 60–40. Many agreements are more complex. They may produce allocations for different contributions of capital, experience, contacts or customers, and time devoted to the business. In fact, they may provide anything the partners can agree upon that is workable.[1]

One of the reasons for partnership agreement complexity involves salaries. In the case of both proprietorships and partnerships, owners' payments to themselves or uses of assets are not treated as salaries. Wages and salaries expense for these types of firms will not include any remuneration to the owner(s). All assets taken by the owner(s) are recorded as withdrawals, or drawings. Therefore, where partner's contributions of time and skill differ, differential "salaries," which are agreed upon in advance, must be incorporated in the partnership agreement as an allocation of shares.

LIABILITY LIMITATIONS

In addition to treating salaries as withdrawals, proprietorships and partnerships have another thing in common—*unlimited liability*. Unlimited liability simply means that a proprietor and each general partner in a partnership is personally responsible for all of the obligations of business.[2] A creditor who is unable to obtain payment from the assets of the firm has legal claim on the personal assets of a proprietor or a general partner. In law, there is no distinction between the firm and the individual.

CORPORATIONS

Corporations are a third and quite distinct legal form of business. Unlike the owners of proprietorships or partnerships, corporate owners have *limited liability*. In law, a corporation is a separate legal entity distinct from its own-

---

[1]   Partnership agreements should provide for:
- Division of profits or losses,
- Limitations on drawings,
- Management responsibilities,
- Procedures in event of partner's death,
- Transfer of partner's interest,
- Division on liquidation.

[2]   A partnership may have some members who are limited partners. Limited partners may not participate in the management of the firm. Limited partners have limited liability. Usually they cannot lose more than they have invested.

ers. Corporate owners are known as *stockholders*, and their liability for the corporation's debts is essentially limited to what they have already contributed or invested.

There are many advantages and disadvantages of the corporate form of business. Most are not relevant to understanding financial accounting. In addition to owners' limited liability, ownership in a corporation is readily transferable to another. If either Jan or Mary died, were disabled, or just wished to withdraw, the partnership would have to be dissolved. The net assets might have to be sold and the proceeds divided. Any additional partners would also necessitate a new partnership agreement.

Corporate owners own shares in the corporation. These shares are known as voting *common stock*, or simply stock. Stock can be transferred—sold, given, or bequeathed—from one owner to another with no effect whatever on the corporation's continuity of operation. Holders of shares of stock in corporations are known as stockholders or *shareholders*. Under the terms of a corporation's charter and corporation law, holders of voting stock have a voice in management and share in net assets and profits in proportion to the number of shares owned. The term common stock or *voting stock* is used to designate ownership shares with the rights described above. Common stockholders vote each year to elect a *Board of Directors*.[3] The directors, as the elected representatives of the owners, oversee the management of the business. They hire the corporation president and define his and other jobs and responsibilities. They also hire or engage the independent auditor to report to them and the stockholders.[4]

SIGNIFICANCE OF LIMITED LIABILITY TO CREDITORS

The stockholders' limited-liability feature in a corporation may be advantageous to the stockholder. It is a different story for the creditor. Assume, for a moment, that you are a creditor of a business. Suppose the firm's balance sheet revealed:

		Total Liabilities	$300,000
		Owners' Equity	400,000
Total Assets	$700,000	Total Equities	$700,000

As a creditor of this business, would you feel secure? You know that, in liquidation, your claim comes first. There would have to be liquidation losses in excess of $400,000 before you would suffer any loss on your claim. Suppose the firm were a partnership or a proprietorship, and suppose the owner(s)

---

[3]   In rare cases a corporation may also have some common stock which is non-voting. Nonvoting common stock is not covered in this text.

[4]   Usually the Board of Directors recommends to the stockholders the selection of a particular CPA firm to be engaged as the firm's auditor for the forthcoming year. The stockholders then vote to ratify this selection.

withdrew $399,000 of choice assets. As long as the personal net worth of the owner(s) was adequate, you would not be concerned. You have a direct claim against the personal assets of the owner(s) in addition to the business' assets.

Now suppose this same firm were a corporation, and the owners could withdraw $399,000 of choice assets. Where would that leave you as a creditor, with no place else to go? Your answer should be obvious (and perhaps not printable). The important concept to grasp is that, for corporate creditors, corporate owners' equity provides a "cushion." The larger this "cushion," the more losses can be absorbed first by the owners, before you, as a creditor, are in trouble.

CONTRIBUTED CAPITAL

As a potential corporate creditor, you need to know how much of a "cushion" you can rely on, that is, how much cannot be withdrawn by the owners to-morrow. The various state laws provide protection to corporate creditors in this matter. Owners may not withdraw assets for their benefit if the result would be to reduce total owners' equity (the cushion) below a certain minimal amount. This minimal amount is generally equal to the amount of owners' *contributed capital,* as distinct from profits (earnings) retained in the business. The use of the word "capital" can be confusing, since capital normally implies something of value, an asset. The term "contributed capital," as used in this context, in a corporation refers to that portion of total assets not available for owners' withdrawal. It does not refer to the specific assets themselves.

NOTE ON CORPORATE EQUITY LOGIC

Throughout this text an attempt is made to explain the **why** along with the **what** of financial accounting. Unfortunately, many of the elements of cor-porate owners' equity are the result of somewhat obscure and involved law and tradition. It is recommended that you approach both the business prac-tices and the accountant's reporting as just the way it is. Finance courses and texts are devoted to understanding many of the practices that will be described in this chapter.

CORPORATE OWNERS' EQUITY CLASSIFICATION

Before proceeding, make sure that you have a clear understanding of total owners' equity. It makes no difference whether a firm is a proprietorship, a partnership, or a corporation. The total owners' equity still merely reflects that amount of total assets which is not claimed by creditors. For a partner-ship, total owners' equity is divided between or among the partners, and their individual shares are separately stated. For a corporation, total owners' equity is stated on a different basis.

Many corporations have thousands and even hundreds of thousands of separate owners. Furthermore, the roster of owners is constantly changing, as individuals buy and sell stock shares from and to one another. It would be ridiculous to try to disclose individual shares in a large corporation's balance sheet. There is, however, an important distinction within owners' equity of a different kind. Creditors wish to know the amount of contributed capital, which is their safety factor. Owners and directors also are interested in the proportion of assets that could legally be withdrawn by the owners as *dividends*. Dividends merely mean owner withdrawals by corporate stockholders.

GAAP therefore provide for this fundamental division of total corporate owners' equity. The corporate balance sheet will show:

Capital stock	$XXXX
Retained earnings	YYYY
Total Stockholders' Equity	$ZZZZ

Capital stock refers to the common stock and indicates the amount of capital contributed by the stockholders. This amount is also known as the legal capital (or stated capital) and generally cannot be used as the basis for dividends. *Retained earnings* indicates that share of total assets which represent previous profits not yet withdrawn from the business as dividends. As such, it also indicates how much could possibly be withdrawn in the future, legally.

Refer to Exhibit 10.3 on page 278. This exhibit illustrates the essential similarity and differences between balance sheets for three forms of business. The balance sheets appear in abbreviated form for Mary and Jan as a partnership (same as Exhibit 10.2), as a proprietorship (assuming one partner bought out the other), and as a corporation. Study this exhibit to obtain a clear picture of the differences within owners' equity.

RETAINED EARNINGS AND DIVIDENDS

You have probably already correctly concluded that, in the case of a corporation, revenue and expense accounts or income are closed to retained earnings (income or profit) at year end. Similarly, dividends reduce retained earnings.

Dividends are decided upon by the corporate Board of Directors by a formal directors' vote. Before a dividend can be voted or declared, two conditions must be met. There must be adequate earned resources (profits) not previously withdrawn and reflected by retained earnings. And, since most dividends are in cash, there must be adequate solvency and liquidity so that a dividend will not cause a cash shortage. Cash dividends voted, or cash dividends declared, are considered to be a current liability of the corporation

Exhibit 10.3
BALANCE SHEETS FOR THREE LEGAL FORMS OF THE SAME BUSINESS

MARY HARDWARE STORES (Proprietorship)

Total Current Assets	$237,000	Total Current Liabilities	$ 50,000
Total Noncurrent Assets		Total Noncurrent	
(Net)	18,000	Liabilities	60,000
		Mary Schneider, Capital	145,000
Total Assets	$255,000	Total Equities	$255,000

MARY AND JAN HARDWARE STORES (Partnership)

Total Current Assets	$237,000	Total Current Liabilities	$ 50,000
Total Noncurrent Assets		Total Noncurrent	
(Net)	18,000	Liabilities	60,000
		Mary Schneider, Capital	84,800
		Jan Ford, Capital	60,200
Total Assets	$255,000	Total Equities	$255,000

MARY AND JAN HARDWARE STORES, INC. (Corporation)

Total Current Assets	$237,000	Total Current Liabilities	$ 50,000
Total Noncurrent Assets		Total Noncurrent	
(Net)	18,000	Liabilities	60,000
		Capital Stock	70,000
		Retained Earnings	75,000
Total Assets	$255,000	Total Equities	$255,000

until actually paid. Therefore the accountant will treat a dividend declaration as a transaction when it occurs. Retained Earnings is reduced by the amount of the intended dividend, and Dividends Payable, as a current liability, is correspondingly increased.

As an example of a cash dividend, assume the XYZ Corporation Board of Directors declared a $30,000 cash dividend on March 15, to be paid to owners as of April 30. On March 15 the accountant would make an entry having the following effect:

Decrease retained earnings by	$30,000
Increase dividends payable by	$30,000

When the dividend was paid on April 30, the payment would be recorded with another entry. Can you state its dual effect? It would decrease cash and decrease dividends payable by $30,000 in the same way as any payment of a current liability. The declaration of a cash dividend represents a flow of funds Net working capital is reduced. The subsequent payment of a dividend liability is a cash flow, but not a flow of working capital. Whereas dividends and losses reduce retained earnings, the balance in the capital-stock account for our purposes in this text is never reduced. It would be increased only to reflect additional capital contributed by owners.

DEFICITS

You now understand that dividends cannot be declared if they would reduce total owners' equity below the amount shown as contributed capital. In other words, dividends cannot legally be declared in excess of the amount shown in retained earnings.[5] But what about losses, that is, *negative* net income?

Suppose the ABC Corporation had $400,000 in capital stock and $100,000 of retained earnings at the beginning of a year. During the year the corporation had a net loss of $135,000. Can you guess what will appear on the ending balance sheet? You are correct if you guessed:

Capital Stock	$400,000
Retained Earnings	(35,000)
Total Shareholders' Equity	$365,000

Negative retained earnings is known as a *deficit*. When a corporation is in a deficit position, it must not declare any dividends. The $35,000 deficit advises you that the company would need $36,000 of income in the future before it could consider even $1,000 of dividends. The deficit also advises creditors that the contributed capital has been impaired, that their "cushion" is reduced. The impairment was not for the benefit of the owners. Unfortunately, there are no laws to protect creditors against business losses!

WHAT IS MY STOCK WORTH?

What exactly is a share of stock worth? If you own a share of stock in a corporation, aside from having a vote for directors, what rights do you have? What can the financial statements tell you about the value of your stock?

Assume you inherited 800 shares of common stock in the Reliable Corporation. You have a copy of the corporation's most recent financial statements. The stockholders' equity section of the balance sheet is given in Exhibit 10.4. Study Exhibit 10.4. What does it tell you about your 800 shares of stock? To understand this exhibit, it will be necessary to examine each new item that appears.

---

[5] Some states restrict withdrawals that would imperil the firm's liquidity even if not reducing total owners' equity below minimums.

Exhibit 10.4

RELIABLE CORPORATION

Stockholders' Equity Section of Balance Sheet as of 12/31/X4

Preferred stock—12% $100 par (10,000 shares issued and outstanding)		$1,000,000
Capital stock—$10 par (200,000 shares issued, 196,500 shares outstanding)		2,000,000
Paid-in capital[1]		900,000
. . . .*		
Retained Earnings:		
Appropriated for self-insurance	$ 500,000	
Appropriated for treasury-stock restriction	200,000	
Unappropriated retained earnings	1,400,000	
Total Retained Earnings		2,100,000
Less treasury stock (3,500 shares)		(200,000)
Total Stockholders' Equity		$5,800,000

Note: (1) $300,000 contributed by preferred stockholders;
$600,000 contributed by donors and common stockholders.

*   Dotted line would not normally appear on balance sheet.

PREFERRED STOCK

Common stockholders in a corporation are in a relatively high-risk position, as are all business owners. Whether or not there are profits, creditors still demand and receive interest on their long-term investments. But common stockholders can receive dividends only if there have been profits, and if it is not necessary or desirable to retain cash in the business. In the event of serious trouble and liquidation, common stockholders are entitled only to anything remaining after creditors and liquidation costs are paid in full. Often this residue can prove to be little or nothing.

When a corporation wishes to obtain more capital, it may not desire or be able to incur more debt. At the same time, it may be difficult to persuade existing and potential owners to risk an additional investment in common stock. *Preferred stock* is often the compromise solution. Preferred stock is not debt and, unlike interest, preferred dividends need not be paid in good and bad years. On the other hand, preferred stock has a fixed dividend rate higher, at least at the time the preferred stock is issued, than normal debt interest; and it is entitled to receive dividends before any dividends may be paid to the common stockholders. In addition to the preference as to dividends, preferred stockholders are preferred in liquidation. If anything remains after creditors' claims and liquidation costs are paid, preferred stockholders receive their claims in full before any distribution to common stockholders. Preferred stock is normally nonvoting. It represents an ownership claim that is safer than common stock. Preferred stock is therefore shown in the stockholders' equity section above capital stock.

Preferred stock may have other features. It may be cumulative—entitled to passed or omitted dividends before common dividends; it may be convertible—exchangeable for common stock at a fixed rate; or it may have many other rarer features. All of these variations are beyond the scope of this elementary text.

Note, on Exhibit 10.4, that the preferred stock is shown at $100 par and at 12 percent. The par is a normal or base amount and will be described further below. The 12 percent indicates that the preferred stockholders are entitled to receive $120,000 in dividends on their 10,000 shares (12 percent times $100 par, times 10,000 shares) each year that directors desire to declare any common dividend.

PAR OR STATED VALUE

Note, in Exhibit 10.4, that both the preferred and common stocks are shown to have a *par value*. And note that the dollar amounts included in each account are exactly the product of the par value times the number of shares issued. You may expect to find most preferred stock to have a par value. Some corporations' common stock has par or *stated value* and some does not. The significance of par is involved and not relevant. Par is simply a base amount. If a firm elects to have par or stated-value stock, then only this amount per share will appear in the capital stock account. Par or stated-value stock may not be issued (sold) by the firm in exchange for less than the par or stated value.[6] Also, in all states, the par or stated capital represents permanent capital not providing the basis (not available) for dividends.

PAID-IN CAPITAL

Paid-in capital is an arbitrary classification and may be viewed as an "overflow" account. It is used to record any contributions by owners in excess of par or stated value. For example, if the Reliable Corporation issued and sold one more share of its common stock for $60, cash would be increased by $60. Only the par amount—$10—would be added to the capital stock account. The excess over par would be recorded in the "overflow" account—paid-in capital —to balance.

Paid-in capital is also used to record other issues of additional stock where the valuation in the exchange exceeds par or stated value. Examples would include the exchange of the firm's stock for new noncurrent assets, where either the stock or the asset is objectively valued above the stock's par

---

[6] Some states provide for exceptions to this rule.

value. Another possibility involves convertible long-term debt or *convertible debentures*. Convertible debt is debt that allows the creditor to exchange his debt for a fixed number of shares of common stock and become an owner. Where debt is converted and the book value of the exchanged debt exceeds the par value of the stock issued, the excess would go into paid-in capital. Note that these two examples—stock issue in exchange for noncurrent assets, and debt conversion—represent two common "matched pairs" of resource flows discussed in Chapter 7.

Examples of these transactions involving paid-in capital would include:

1. Stock with par value of $100,000 is sold for $130,000. Cash is increased by $130,000. Capital stock is increased by $100,000 (par value only). Paid-in capital is increased $30,000 to balance.

2. Stock with par value of $50,000 is exchanged for land with a fair market value of $75,000. Land is increased by $75,000. Capital stock is increased by $50,000 (par value only). Paid-in capital is increased $25,000 to balance.

3. Long-term debt with a book value of $400,000 is exchanged for 30,000 shares of $10 par common stock. Long-term debt is reduced by $400,000 to record its extinguishment. Capital stock is increased by $300,000 (par value only). Paid-in capital is increased $100,000 to balance. Debt conversion will be discussed further in Chapter 12.

Paid-in capital also accumulates any excess of market price over par in a stock dividend, or any excess over cost on the resale of treasury stock (see below). Finally, although they are rare, can you guess what happens to gifts made to a corporation? The asset received is added to total assets. Owners' equity reflects this increase, but how? The gift does not result in the issue of new stock. It does not reflect profit or earnings. You are correct if you understand that the "catch-all" account—paid-in capital—is increased to balance.

Note the dotted line in Exhibit 10.4. It is there to distinguish between contributed capital and retained earnings. Contributed capital reflects stockholder (and donor) investments of assets in the firm. It includes the stated capital (preferred and capital stock) and any paid-in capital.

BOOK VALUE

One measure often used by financial analysts is the *book value of common stock*. Recall that the term **book value** is also used with respect to an asset. A truck costing $15,000, with $7,000 of accumulated depreciation, is said to have a book value of $8,000. Book value can be thought of as meaning the "net amount currently assigned (reported) by accountants." What is the net amount of total assets assigned to the common stockholders on Exhibit 10.4?

The book value of the firm to all owners (stockholders) is the total owners' equity or $5,800,000. Preferred stockholders have a claim against, or share in, total assets equal to their contribution. Exhibit 10.4 shows this amount to be $1,300,000 ($1,000,000 par plus $300,000 excess over par included in paid-in capital). Preferred stockholders usually have no claim against retained earnings.[7] If Reliable's preferred stockholders have a $1,300,000 claim or share in total assets, what is the *common book value,* or book value of all the common stock of the firm?

Remember, you are assumed to own 800 shares of Reliable's common stock. The fact that, as of 12/31/X4, all common had a book value of $4,500,000 may be interesting to you in some abstract fashion. You might be more interested in the book value of your stock. From Exhibit 10.4, calculate the book value of your stock.

Book value per share is generally understood to mean "per share of common stock outstanding."

$$\text{Book value per share} = \frac{\text{Book value of common stock}}{\text{Number of shares outstanding}} \quad 196{,}500$$

or

$$\text{Book value per share} = \frac{\text{Total stockholders' equity–preferred claims}}{\text{Number of common shares outstanding}}$$

The book value of a common share of Reliable on 12/31/X4 would be $22.90 (rounded). The book value of your stock would be $18,320.

EARNINGS PER SHARE

Even though this chapter is focused on the owners' equity section of the balance sheet, you must not forget the income statement. While you are thinking about per-share calculations, there is another ratio which is given even more importance than book value per share. It is known as *earnings per share* and usually is referred to as *EPS*. If, for the year 19X4, Reliable had reported net income of $758,625, how much was "available" to the common stockholder? What was your personal share?

Exhibit 10.4 discloses that the annual **preferred** dividend, if declared and paid, would amount to $120,000 (12% × $100 × 10,000 shares). Preferred dividends must be paid before common. Of 19X4 earnings, therefore, $638,625 is "available" for the common stockholders after preferred dividends.

---

[7]   In rare or unusual circumstances where preferred stock is cumulative, preferred stockholders would have claims against retained earnings in the case where previous years' preferred dividends had not been paid in full. This claim for back dividends is called "arrearage" and would be disclosed parenthetically on the balance sheet or in the footnotes.

Remember that "available" does not mean "will be paid." Only if the firm has adequate cash to cover the dividend payment without impairing its solvency and liquidity and only if the profits need not be retained in the business as a source of needed additional working capital for the future could you anticipate that the directors will declare all or part of this $638,625 in common dividends. Even though not necessarily coming to you in cash, what is your share of this year's profits?

$$EPS = \frac{\text{Net income} - \text{preferred dividend}}{\text{Average number common shares outstanding during year}}$$

For the Reliable Corporation 19X4 EPS would be $3.25. Note that common earnings for the year are divided by simple *average* shares outstanding during the year (beginning shares plus ending shares divided by 2). In the Reliable example, it was necessary to assume that outstanding shares had not changed since 12/31/X3. Your personal share of 19X4 earnings would be $2,600 (800 shares times $3.25 per share).

EPS is considered so important that GAAP require EPS (or variations) to be disclosed on the income statement immediately below net income. The importance of EPS lies in its relationship to *market value* or *market price* (per share) of stock. The market value of your stock today is what it is worth to you if you want to sell it today. The market price is that amount you could anticipate receiving (or paying) per share if you were to sell (or buy) a small amount of a firm's stock.

When a corporation wishes to raise capital from owners, it issues (sells) stock to outsiders, usually for cash. Thereafter, it normally does not buy back its own stock whenever a stockholder wishes to sell. Instead, the stockholder who wants to sell his or her stock must find a buyer. An entire industry, including organized stock exchanges and member stockbrokers, exists to bring potential buyers and sellers together. Stock prices may go up or down daily, depending on whether there are more buyers than sellers, or vice versa. Assume Reliable's stock is traded—bought and sold—quite frequently. It would therefore be said to have a "market." Market price quotations represent the most recent price at which the stock was traded. A new transaction not involving an attempt to sell or buy a very large quantity would probably be executed at close to the previous price.

Remember that we started out attempting to determine the worth to you of your 800 shares of Reliable common. Par value is $10 per share, or $8,000. Book value is $18,320. Do either of these amounts have any immediate relevance to you? The appropriate answer is no. Par value represents an obsolescent legalistic convention. You need only remember that it is the basis for arbitrary subclassifications of contributed capital on a balance sheet. Book value per share has very little significance.[8] Your claim against the firm's total

---

[8]   In stock-price analysis, book value per share is sometimes compared to market price as a possible indication of time to buy or time to sell. Such a use can prove misleading, and does not represent a concern of this text.

assets never becomes "real" or "operational" unless the majority of stock-holders, or the creditors and courts in bankruptcy, decide to liquidate the business. Liquidating amounts are different from GAAP going-concern mea-surements. In liquidation you might receive far more or far less than your $18,320 book value. Overall book value of all common shares collectively is used in statement analysis of the firm, as distinct from one of its owners. This analysis will be discussed in Chapter 13.

Of immediate interest to you is the market price (per share) or market value (of your lot of shares) of your stock. Assume that Reliable common was quoted at $32 per share. At a market price of $32, the market value of your stock would be $25,600. This amount is probably most relevant to you as a stockholder. Along with many other factors, EPS, and especially antici-pated EPS, influences stock prices. Other things equal, the higher the ex-pected earnings, the higher will be the market price. Analysts often view a particular market price in terms of EPS. Reliable would be said to be sell-ing at "ten times earnings." The *earnings multiple* and other aspects of security analysis are not part of this book. You need only understand why certain information is provided by accountants. Also beyond the scope of this book are other vital concerns you would have as a Reliable stockholder. These would include such items as potential capital gains on your stock, when you should sell, and tax consequences of your decision.

TREASURY STOCK, RESTRICTIONS, AND APPROPRIATIONS

Continuing with those interests relevant to this course which you would have as a stockholder in Reliable, does its balance sheet provide you with any information as to possible future dividends that might be declared by your board of directors? If the firm had at least $2,100,000 of currency not needed ("excess") cash, could you anticipate all $2,100,000 being paid in dividends? What is treasury stock and why is it shown as a negative figure?

Occasionally, a corporation will need, for various reasons, to purchase from existing shareholders a small amount of its issued and outstanding common stock. A firm's own stock which it has repurchased is known as *treasury stock*. Treasury stock does not represent a claim against assets that is already recorded on the company's balance sheet. Therefore, it is not logical to include it as an additional asset. Accountants therefore record treasury stock at its cost as a contra-equity item within the corporate owner's equity section. Shares of common stock outstanding will then be less than those issued by the number of treasury shares.

It is conceivable that a company could accumulate enough treasury stock so that total owners' equity would fall below the amount of contributed cap-ital. This would subvert the protection for creditors. Consequently, a cor-poration may not legally purchase treasury stock costing more than its re-corded retained earnings. Nor can the firm subsequently declare dividends (reducing retained earnings) if such dividends plus treasury stock would impair the contributed capital. The accountant therefore discloses this limitation by indicating the amount of the restriction on retained earnings. *Retained earnings restrictions* are disclosed in one of two ways: Either they are simply footnoted, or they can be shown in a separate appropriation account. If the separate appropriation-account approach is used, the nonrestricted retained earnings are shown separately as *unappropriated retained earnings*. An example of this second approach is shown for the Reliable Corporation on Exhibit 10.4. You can see that Reliable currently holds treasury stock costing $200,000. Therefore retained earnings are restricted by $200,000. This restriction is disclosed by Reliable as an appropriation.

Before Reliable acquired the treasury stock, it would have had $200,000 more cash and $200,000 more of stockholders' equity. Retained earnings would have been $2,100,000 with only $500,000 appropriated for self-insurance. When the treasury stock was acquired, cash was reduced $200,000 and the $200,000 contra-account was included with stockholders' equity (thus reducing total stockholders' equity by $200,000) to balance. Also, an additional $200,000 appropriation of retained earnings was established to disclose the dividend restriction. This latter adjustment affected only unappropriated retained earnings. It had no effect upon total retained earnings or upon total stockholders' equity.

When treasury stock is disposed of, the restriction applicable to the stock distribution is eliminated. The treasury stock account is also reduced in proportion to the cost of the amount of stock disposed of. Proceeds received from the resale of treasury stock in excess of its purchase cost are not considered revenue or gain. Instead, they are considered additional capital contributions, like any original contributions in excess of par. Accountants would record the effect of selling 100 shares of treasury stock for $40 cash per share, when the stock had cost $25, as follows:

Increase cash by	$4,000
Decrease treasury stock by	$2,500 (increases owner's equity)
Increase paid-in capital by	$1,500

The restriction is then also eliminated where treasury stock is resold at less than cost, this "loss" is subtracted from paid-in capital.

OTHER RESTRICTIONS AND VOLUNTARY APPROPRIATIONS

In addition to treasury stock restrictions, other restrictions of a contractual nature can exist. A creditor may demand a larger safety factor than that provided by contributed capital. The company may agree, and contract to restrict dividends by a certain amount until the loan is paid.

Also, the directors may decide to publicly designate some retained earnings as not "available" in the foreseeable future to provide the basis for dividends. This voluntary appropriation of retained earnings has the same effect as a restriction. However, it differs from a restriction in that it can be removed at the will of the directors. It does not depend upon completion of some other event, as is necessary for removal of a restriction.

The term "appropriation" appears to be replacing a once common term "reserve," also used to denote retained earnings limitations. The use of reserve can be misleading, since it carries the connotation of something being held. Remember that **nothing** on the right side of a balance sheet represents an asset. The retained earnings shown, and any parts thereof, are merely a representation of a source, claim, or share in total assets.

Look again at Exhibit 10.4. What is the balance sheet telling you as a stockholder? Can you see that the accountant, in the accounting language, is providing you with the following message?

> Two million one hundred thousand dollars of our total assets came from past earnings and are presently not committed for distribution to stockholders. Of this $2,100,000 share of total assets, $200,000 cannot be distributed unless all of our treasury stock is resold. Another $500,000 we do not currently plan even to consider for distribution. We are self-insuring ourselves in certain areas, and will need to have this amount of capital readily available to cover possible losses. One million four hundred thousand dollars of assets may be considered for distribution as dividends at some time in the future.

Note the reference to assets. Retained earnings merely indicate a source and share of assets. Potential distributions of retained earnings are actually potential distributions of assets to stockholders, which then would result in a reduction of retained earnings. There are, however, two actions which Reliable's directors could take, either of which could benefit you as a stockholder and neither of which would involve use or distribution of assets (except for paperwork costs). The directors could declare a *stock split* or a *stock dividend*.

STOCK SPLIT

A stock split merely proportionally increases the number of shares held by existing shareholders, and correspondingly decreases any par or stated value per share. If Reliable's directors were to split the stock 4 for 1, you would receive an additional 2400 shares in the mail, or else exchange your 800 $10 par shares for 3200 $2.50 par shares. You would now have 3200 shares instead of 800, but would still have the same claim in liquidation, voting power, and proportionate share of any dividends. The accountant would merely change the capital stock note to read "$2.50 par—800,000 shares issued, 786,000 outstanding." Except to record the paperwork expenses, no dollar amounts on the balance sheet change as a result of a stock split.

At this point you may be wondering "Why split stock?" Think of what will happen to the market price of your Reliable stock, which was $32 per share. With the same firm and the same earnings potential but four times as many shares outstanding, the market price will drop to around $8. For the moment, assume that the market price reflected full dilution at $8. What would be your benefit? Stock is normally traded, to reduce paperwork costs, in lots or batches of 100 shares. Before the split, had you wanted to sell 100 shares of Reliable at the market price, you would have had to find a buyer willing to invest $3200 in Reliable stock. After the split, you could sell "at market" a 100-share block to anyone willing to invest $800. The minimum bet to play the game has been reduced. More players can afford to "play" with Reliable, and your liquidity (chances to sell without suffering loss) is therefore increased. This increase in liquidity for existing shareholders is generally the primary objective of a stock split in the first place.

What would be your second or other possible benefit from a stock split? If Reliable split 4 for 1, the actual market probably would not fully dilute, and the price might stop (say) at $8.50 per share. If it did, you would be $1600 ahead (800 shares at $32 vs. 3,200 shares at $8.50). Often the market does not fully dilute when a stock splits. More people able to play mean more buyers, and the price is bid up accordingly. So there is a sort of magic to a stock split—something for nothing. The fact that the market does not fully discount or dilute the price in consideration of the additional shares results in a second benefit to the stockholder.

STOCK DIVIDEND

Somewhat related to a stock split, but involving entirely different accounting treatment, is the stock dividend. Like stock splits, stock dividends involve distributions, rather than sales, of additional stock where the amount distributed is usually less than 20 percent of the amount of stock previously outstanding. A stock dividend is like a "baby" (1.2 to 1) split. However, the purpose, and therefore the reporting, are different. The intention is not to reduce or dilute the market price, although some dilution may result. The purpose is to transfer to contributed capital some past earnings not yet distributed, to *capitalize retained earnings*. Stock dividends may be thought of as a form of compulsory investment or involuntary stock sale to existing stockholders.

Rather than distribute cash dividends and require the owners to use the dividends to purchase more stock, the new stock is just issued and mailed. The par value is not split. The market value of the number of shares distributed is transferred from retained earnings to the contributed capital accounts for common stock. Preferred stock is not involved. The market value of the stock dividend is distributed with the par-value portion (number of stock dividend shares times par value) added to the capital stock account. Any excess of market value over par increases paid-in capital. Note that a stock dividend has no cost to the firm in assets distributed and no effect on **total** stockholder's equity. The individual stockholder's proportionate claim and voting power is unchanged. Yet, since the market generally doesn't dilute the stock price fully for the additional shares, the stockholder benefits immediately. Also, the firm may maintain its same cash-dividend policy on a per-share basis after the stock dividend. This would result in larger future dividends to the owners, a benefit often contributing to the market's optimism in not fully diluting for the additional stock.

If Reliable were to declare and distribute a 10-percent stock dividend on its outstanding shares with the market price at $32, then 19,650 shares would be distributed. Stock dividends are customarily **not** distributed to treasury shares. You would receive 80 additional shares. So long as the market price stayed above $29.09, you would gain. The accountants would record the earnings capitalization as follows:

Decrease unappropriated retained earnings by	$628,800
Increase $10-par capital stock by	196,500
Increase paid-in capital by	432,300

Stock dividends represent the last new topic necessary for your essential understanding of partners' and stockholders' equity sections of the balance sheet. You should not lose sight of the fact that the basic financial accounting system, and the information content of the financial statements, are essentially not affected by the legal form of the business. With different legal forms, there are differences within owners' equity. The treatment of assets, liabilities, revenue, expenses, and funds flow is basically uniform.

SUMMARY OF CHANGES IN STOCKHOLDERS' EQUITY ACCOUNTS

To assist you to bring together the various elements of corporate equity accounting introduced in this chapter, Exhibit 10.5 summarizes the various events which can alter the balances in the equity accounts. Remember that certain of these changes merely involve a reallocation of dollars among different owners' equity accounts. Stock splits, stock dividends, and changes to appropriations do not affect the total of stockholders' equity. As you study Exhibit 10.5, for each item visualize an event which would result in the specific change.

Exhibit 10.5

SUMMARY OF CHANGES WHICH MAY OCCUR IN STOCKHOLDER
EQUITY ACCOUNTS[9]

Preferred stock

Increased by:

Par-value portion of proceeds from sale of additional stock
Par-value portion of stock issued in conversion of
long-term debt[10]

Capital stock

Increased by:

Par- or stated-value portion of proceeds from sale of
additional stock
Par- or stated-value portion of stock issued as stock
dividend
Par- or stated-value portion of stock issued as part
of conversion of long-term debt[10]

Paid-in capital

Increased by:

Excess over par for new preferred stock sold or issued on debt conversion
Excess over par or stated value of new common
stock sold, distributed as stock dividend, or distributed as part of long-term debt conversion
Gifts to corporation
Excess over cost of proceeds from sale of treasury stock

Decreased by:

Amount below cost of treasury stock sold

Appropriations

Increased by:

Voluntary appropriation established or increased by
directors
Involuntary appropriation recognizing restriction of
retained earnings resulting from contractual obligation or treasury-stock purchase

Decreased by:

Reduction or elimination of voluntary appropriation
Reduction or elimination of restriction

Unappropriated
retained
earnings

Increased by:

Net income
Reduction or elimination of an appropriation

Decreased by:

Net loss (negative net income)
Declaration of cash dividend
Declaration of stock dividend
Creation of or increase in a voluntary appropriation
or restriction

---

[9]   Does not include subscribed stock, stock warrants, stock dividends declared but
not yet issued, and stock retirements, all of which are beyond the scope of this text.

[10]   Bond conversion is discussed more fully in Chapter 12.

CHAPTER OVERVIEW

Based upon an understanding of the material covered in this chapter, you should be able to:

- Explain the essential similarities in accounting for proprietorships, partnerships, and corporations;
- Describe the basic differences between proprietorship accounting and either partnership or corporate accounting;
- Define the role of the partnership agreement in the division of earnings and partner's equity, and determine such a division, given the essential facts;
- Explain the meanings of limited and unlimited liability and their effect upon GAAP for owners' equity accounting.
- Describe the essential difference between, and the intention behind, contributed capital and retained earnings.
- Explain the functions of the several accounts possibly appearing as parts of contributed capital, including preferred stock, capital stock, and paid-in capital;
- Explain the functions of the several accounts possibly appearing as parts of the retained earnings subsection, including voluntary appropriations, restrictions, unappropriated retained earnings, and treasury stock;
- Define and describe any relationships among par value, book value, market value, and earnings per share, all as applied to common stock.
- Explain the reasoning behind, and the accounting for, certain stockholder-related events, including cash dividends, stock splits, stock dividends, and the purchase and resale of treasury stock.
- Describe and explain the various possible limitations upon the distribution of assets to stockholders as dividends.

NEW VOCABULARY AND CONCEPTS

Partnership	Board of Directors
Partnership agreement	Contributed capital
Pro-forma statements	Dividend
Drawings	Capital stock
Unlimited liability	Retained earnings
Limited liability	Deficit
Stockholders/shareholders	Preferred stock
Common stock	Par value/stated value
Voting stock	Paid-in capital

Convertible debenture	Earnings multiple
Book value of common stock/	Treasury stock
common book value	Retained earnings restrictions
Book value per share	Appropriation
Earnings per share (EPS)	Unappropriated retained earnings
Market value (of stock)	Stock split
Market price (of stock)	Stock dividend

- The necessity for partnership agreements.
- The common need for multistep partnership agreements covering earnings allocations.
- The difference between contributed capital and retained earnings.
- The necessity for dividend limitations and their association with limited liability.
- The difference between book value and market value.
- Capitalization of retained earnings.

REVIEW QUESTIONS

1. A partnership agreement specifies the division of net assets upon dissolution of the partnership. What other important provisions should be included in such an agreement?

2. How does the accountant determine the basis for allocating profits and equity among partners? How do GAAP apply in this determination?

3. What are the limits of owner liability in a proprietorship? A partnership? A corporation?

4. What is the significance of limited liability to the corporation's owners? To its creditors?

5. a) What is contributed capital? (b) What is its significance to creditors? (c) Why is it segregated from retained earnings in a corporate balance sheet?

6. What three different transactions could result in an increase in the balance reported for capital stock?

7. What are the various possible limitations on dividend declarations?

8. What events can increase or decrease retained earnings?

9. If you owned 100 shares of a 12 percent $100 par-value preferred stock, and if the common stockholders were receiving a dividend this year, how much dividend must you individually receive?

10. As a preferred stockholder, how much in the way of dividends can you count on receiving in the future?

11. What effect does par or stated value for stock have on recording new issues, stock dividends, or debt conversions?

12. a) What is the function of the paid-in capital account? (b) What four different events can result in an increase in paid-in capital? (c) Under normal (going-concern) circumstances, could paid-in capital be reduced? If yes, under what conditions would this occur?

13. When a firm also has preferred stock, how does one calculate the book value per share of common stock?

14. a) Explain the differences among par value, book value, and market value? b) What is EPS? Describe its relationship to the income statement and to stock prices.

15. Why isn't treasury stock included, along with other purchased securities, in the appropriate asset accounts?

16. Why are retained earnings restricted by the cost of treasury stock acquired and not yet resold?

17. a) What is the difference between an appropriation of retained earnings and a restriction? (b) What is the common effect of both on retained earnings?

18. If a company has 20,000 shares of $10 par common stock issued and outstanding, and then splits two for one, what dollar amount after the split will appear in the capital stock account? What will appear after the split in the capital stock footnote concerning par value and shares issued?

19. A stock dividend is said to have the effect of permanently capitalizing retained earnings. Explain.

20. What is the difference between the accountants' treatment of a stock split and a stock dividend?

MINI-CASES AND QUESTIONS FOR DISCUSSION

MC 10.1. Bob, Mike, and Ted have decided to go into partnership. They are trying to work out a partnership agreement that will be fair to everyone. Bob states his position: "Look, you guys, I know I don't know much about business, and I'll only be around a few hours a week. But I'm putting up almost all of the money—$200,000. I could get 12 percent if I invested it in real estate. This partnership couldn't get off the ground without my money."

"I can see that, Bob," says Mike. "But I'm the one who really has the management experience in this business. I'll be putting in 50 to 60 hours per week. Without my knowledge and effort, the business could never make a profit. I can make $60,000 in salary working for another firm."

"Don't forget me," says Ted. "I may know only how to sell, but without customers, all of your money and management skill wouldn't generate revenue. Sixty per cent of our planned first year's sales are coming from customers that are already mine. I'll be bringing them along from my present job. I'm making $75,000 in straight commissions right now."

Assume that anticipated first-year profits are $120,000 before any remuneration to partners. Can you suggest a fair partnership agreement? Discuss.

MC 10.2 Ann Mason is considering whether to lend $200,000 to the Ajax Corporation for a three-year period. She is concerned about the safety of her loan in the event that the firm fails. A pro-forma balance sheet, projecting conditions after the loan was made, shows:

Total Current Liabilities	$100,000
Total Noncurrent Liabilities	250,000
Total Liabilities	$350,000
Capital Stock	150,000
Retained Earnings	375,000
Total Equities	$875,000

She says, "I would be comfortable with a debt-to-equity ratio of 0.5, but 0.7 is too risky. After all, the corporation could take out all $375,000 in dividends."

Is there anything Ajax could do or suggest which might reduce Ann's concern? Discuss.

MC 10.3. Sally Swallow is quite upset. She has just learned that a corporation can buy and sell its own stock in the market. "That's totally unfair," says Sally. "The company will always know good and bad news before it gets published for us in the financial statements. And it has all those internal forecasts which aren't available to me. It's like betting on a horserace after the race is over. You don't have the results yet, but one bettor does."

a) Can the company usually "win" with its insider information?
b) What prevents a company from taking unfair advantage of its "edge"?
c) Couldn't the majority of stockholders, or even an effectively controlling minority, make nice profits and receive large dividends by taking advantage of unsuspecting and unknowledgeable outsiders?

Discuss.

MC 10.4. Book value per share of common stock and market value per share are rarely if ever the same. Often market value is higher than book value. What factors cause this situation? Also, occasionally, market value will be below book value. What could bring about this situation? Discuss.

MC 10.5. Jerry Black is confused. He understands a stock split which effectively splits existing outstanding shares into smaller pieces. He sees clearly why a stock split should not, and does not, affect the dollar amounts in the balance sheet accounts.

What doesn't make sense to Jerry is the accountant's treatment of stock dividends. "Since a stock dividend is just a baby split, why shouldn't it be treated like all other splits?" Jerry asks you. "And why bring in the current market price? There is no attempt to have stock values in the owners' equity section report market values."

Discuss. See whether you can satisfy Jerry with a reason for this apparently disparate treatment.

MC 10.6. If someone has 100 shares of common stock in a corporation with 400,000 shares issued and outstanding, how significant is that person's "ownership voice"? Suppose he or she does not like what the firm is doing; what, realistically, are his or her choices? Discuss.

MC 10.7. Directors never have to declare, and often cannot declare, dividends even though large retained earnings are reported. What, then, is the significance of a voluntary appropriation, which can be eliminated by a simple resolution at the next directors' meeting? Discuss.

MC 10.8. If you owned one share of common stock in a corporation, wouldn't EPS and dividends per share, both compared to book value per share, be good measures of your return on your investment? Discuss.

ESSENTIAL PROBLEMS

EP 10.1. The Pat and Mike partnership agreement calls for profits to be distributed as follows:

Step 1: 10 percent of average investment before any remaining profit is apportioned.

Step 2: Remaining profits, up to a total of $30,000, divided 70 percent to Pat and 30 percent to Mike.

Step 3: Any remainder in excess of $30,000 to be divided equally.

Pat's capital account was $63,000 at the beginning of the year and $57,000 at year end, reflecting $6,000 of withdrawals. Mike's was constant at $20,000. Total profits were $16,000. How should they be divided?

EP 10.2. Assume the same information as for Problem EP 10.1, except that the total profits were $52,000. What should be reported in each partner's capital account at year end, after distribution of profits?

EP 10.3. An ending balance sheet revealed total assets to be $400,000, total liabilities $150,000, and contributed capital $200,000. What was the amount of retained earnings?

EP 10.4. The following information is available on a firm at year end:

Total current assets	$ 50,000
Total assets	400,000
Total noncurrent liabilities	80,000
Retained earnings	100,000
Net working capital	30,000

What was the amount of contributed capital shown in stockholders' equity?

EP 10.5. Given the following information, determine the balance of retained earnings at the end of the year:

Beginning retained earnings	$200,000
Net loss for year	50,000
Dividends declared	10,000

EP 10.6. Given the following data, calculate total dividends declared during the year:

Beginning retained earnings	$640,000
Net income during the year	120,000
Ending retained earnings	700,000

EP 10.7. Given the following data, prepare a complete corporate owners' equity section of the balance sheet in good form:

Total Assets	$312,000
Total Liabilities	220,000
Capital stock (total contributed capital)	100,000

EP 10.8. Given the following information (in thousands of dollars), prepare in proper form the complete corporate owners' equity section of the balance sheet as of 12/31/X1:

12/31/X1	Net working capital	$110,000
12/31/X1	Total noncurrent assets	260,000
12/31/X1	Total assets	450,000
12/31/X1	Total noncurrent liabilities	90,000
12/31/X0	Retained earnings	80,000
19X1	Total revenues and gains	510,000
19X1	Total expenses and losses	430,000
19X1	Dividends declared	40,000

EP 10.9. Selected data from the Able Corporation's balance sheet as of 12/31/X0 were as follows (000 omitted):

Cash	$130	Total Liabilities	$220
Other Assets	840		
		Capital Stock	400
		Paid-in Capital	50
		Retained Earnings	300
Total Assets	$970	Total Equities	$970

The capital stock consisted of $10-par common stock with 40,000 shares issued and outstanding. During 19X1, the following major events occurred:

a) Able had net income of $200,000, all ending up as cash.

b) Able declared and then paid a cash dividend of $2 per share.

c) Able declared and distributed a 10-percent stock dividend when the market price was $45 per share.

d) After the stock dividend, Able split its common stock two for one.

How would you expect the accountant to report the effects of all of these events? Prepare a balance sheet for the Able Corporation as of 12/31/X1, reflecting the events given.

EP 10.10. Selected information from the Baker Corporation's 12/31/X0 balance sheet revealed (000 omitted):

		Total Liabilities	$ 200,000
		*Capital Stock	300,000
		Paid-in Capital	100,000
		Retained Earnings	600,000
Total Assets	$1,200	Total Equities	$1,200

* $10 par, 30,000 shares issued and outstanding.

During 19X1, the following events transpired:

a) Baker sold 5,000 shares of $100-par 14-percent preferred stock at a price of $115 per share.   1,050,000

b) Baker split its common stock five for one.

c) The corporation received a gift of $50,000 cash.

d) After the stock split, the firm declared and issued a 10-percent stock dividend when the market price was $4 per share.

Prepare a balance sheet for the Baker Corporation as of 12/31/X1, reflecting these events.

EP 10.11. The Charlie Corporation's balance sheet, owners' equity section, was as follows as of 12/31/X0 (000 omitted):

Preferred stock ($100 par; 12%)	$ 500
Paid-in capital on preferred stock	20
Capital stock ($10 par; 200,000 shares)	2,000
Paid-in capital on common stock	810
Appropriation for self-insurance	900
Unappropriated retained earnings	1,670
Total Owners' Equity	$5,900

What was the total book value of the Charlie Corporation to its common shareholders?

EP 10.12. Refer to the Charlie Corporation's 12/31/X0 statement in Problem EP 10.11. If, at that time, Charlie had 500,000 shares of $4-par common stock issued and outstanding, what was the book value per share of the firm's common stock?

EP 10.13. Refer to the Charlie Corporation's 12/31/X0 statement in Problem EP 10.11. During 19X1, the following events related to retained earnings occurred:

a) The company reported net income after taxes of $400,000.

b) The company declared a preferred dividend and a cash dividend of $1.50 per share on the common stock.

c) The company declared and distributed after the cash dividend a 5-percent stock dividend when the market price was $40 per share.

d) The directors voted to reduce the self-insurance appropriation by $400,000.

What would be the 12/31/X1 balance in unappropriated retained earnings?

EP 10.14. Refer to the Charlie Corporation's 12/31/X0 statement in Problem EP 10.11. Assume the following events occurred during 19X1.

a) The preferred dividend was declared and paid.

b) The common stock was split five for one.

c) After the split, a 10-percent stock dividend was declared and distributed when the market price was $9 per share.

d) After the stock dividend, a cash dividend of $.25 per share on the common was declared.

e) Reported net income after taxes for 19X1 was $300,000.

What would be the 12/31/X1 balance in unappropriated retained earnings?

SUPPLEMENTARY PROBLEMS

SP 10.15. The Dawe Corporation's 12/31/X0 balance sheet owners' equity section was as follows (000 omitted):

Capital stock ($5 par; 40,000 shares)	$ 200
Paid-in capital	60
Reserve for treasury-stock restriction	20
Unappropriated retained earnings	330
Treasury stock (400 shares)	(20)
Total Owners' Equity	$ 590

During 19X1 the company resold the 400 shares of treasury stock at a price of $55 per share. It subsequently purchased another 500 shares of treasury stock at a cost of $57 per share. Assume that no other events affecting owners' equity occurred during the year. Give the owners' equity section of the Dawe Corporation's 12/31/X1 balance sheet, reflecting these events.

SP 10.16. Refer to the data given for the Dawe Corporation in Problem SP 10.15. Assume that in 19X1 the 400 shares of treasury stock had been resold at a price of $40 per share; and that, subsequently, 600 additional shares of treasury stock costing $38 per share had been acquired. Give the owners' equity section of the Dawe Corporation's 12/31/X1 balance sheet, reflecting these events.

PREPARER PROCEDURES

Since owners' equity is assumed to have a credit balance, all owners' equity accounts for a partnership and a corporation normally have credit balances. The contra-equity accounts—drawings in a partnership, and treasury stock in a corporation—have debit balances.

In a partnership, owner withdrawals are recorded by crediting the appropriate asset account for the item withdrawn—usually cash or inventory—and debiting the particular partner's drawing account. The drawing account at year end is then closed to the individual partner's capital account.

For a corporation, cash dividends become a current liability at the time they are formally declared by the board of directors. The entry recording the declaration of a cash dividend would be:

	DR	CR
Dividends declared	$XXX	
Dividends payable		$XXX

The dividends account at year-end is closed to unappropriated retained earnings; or just to retained earnings if there are no appropriations.

Issuance of new stock would involve credits to the capital stock account, or to both capital stock and paid-in capital in the case of par- or stated-value stock. The balancing debit will be to cash for stock sold, to the appropriate asset account for stock issued in exchange for such an asset, or to retained earnings for a stock dividend.

Acquisition of treasury stock can involve two entries—one recording the acquisition and one establishing the restriction. For example:

	DR	CR
Treasury Stock	$XXX	
Cash		$XXX
Retained Earnings	$XXX	
Appropriation for treasury stock restriction		$XXX

Disposition of treasury stock involves simple reversal of the acquisition entry(ies) in the amount of the cost of the stock resold. Proceeds in excess of cost are credited, and any amount below cost debited, to paid-in capital.[11]

PREPARER PROBLEMS

PP 10.1. Refer to Problem EP 10.9 above. Prepare journal entries as required for events (b), (c), and (d).

PP 10.2. Refer to Problem EP 10.10 above. Prepare journal entries as required for events (a) through (d).

PP 10.3. Refer to Problem EP 10.13 above. Prepare journal entries as required for events (b), (c), and (d).

---

[11]   In very rare cases, losses on treasury stock dispositions may exceed prior contributions from treasury stock transactions. Such excess losses are debited to retained earnings. Also, beyond the scope of this text is an alternative method involving the accounting for treasury stock at par rather than at cost.

PP 10.4. Refer to Problem EP 10.14 above. Prepare journal entries as required for events (b) and (c).

PP 10.5. Refer to Problem SP 10.15 above. Prepare all necessary journal entries to record the two transactions and any necessary restriction changes.

PP 10.6. Refer to Problem SP 10.16 above. Prepare all necessary journal entries to record the two transactions and any necessary restriction changes.

11

SPECIAL PROBLEMS IN MEASURING CERTAIN ASSETS

CHAPTER PREVIEW

The objective of this chapter is to complete your elementary accounting knowledge of asset measurement in conformance with GAAP. In this chapter you can:

- Become familiar with the concept of consolidation and the purpose of consolidated financial statements;
- Review the basic principles of asset measurement incorporated in GAAP;
- Learn how accountants apply these principles to the initial valuation of specific assets not covered in previous chapters;
- Learn how accountants apply these principles to the measurement of specific assets subsequent to their acquisition;
- Complete your understanding of those adjustments to assets (reflecting revenue and expenses) which are included in income from operations;
- Review all changes that can occur to all common asset accounts; and
- Complete your understanding of those adjustments to noncurrent assets that do not involve working capital flows, and therefore are not part of working capital funds from operations.

With this knowledge, you will be qualified to read and correctly interpret the asset side of most published balance sheets. You will also have the necessary background to learn about and be able to intelligently use more sophisticated tools of balance sheet analysis pertaining to assets.

WHAT ARE THESE ITEMS? HOW ARE THEY MEASURED BY ACCOUNTANTS?

Crystal Gurney has been assigned by her firm to analyze the Jedro Corporation's financial statements and additional information supplied by Jedro. Crystal's firm is considering the purchase of the Jedro Company. The current phase of her study focuses on Jedro's assets. Her firm wishes to know exactly what assets it would be acquiring, and how they are currently measured (valued) by Jedro.

Exhibit 11.1 gives the asset side of Jedro's most recent balance sheet. Exhibit 11.2 contains additional information related to Jedro's assets. Crystal understands that, on balance sheets, monetary assets are shown at or near current value. Nonmonetary items are shown at adjusted original cost. These generalized measurement and reporting objectives were first presented in Chapter 2.

Exhibit 11.1
JEDRO CORPORATION
AND CONSOLIDATED SUBSIDIARIES

Asset Portion of Consolidated Balance Sheet as of 12/31/XX

Cash		$180,000
*Marketable securities[a]		300,000
Receivables:		
Accounts receivable	$350,000	
*Less allowance for uncollectibles	(10,000)	
Notes receivable	95,000	
*Less discount on notes receivable	(5,000)	
Accrued interest receivable	15,000	445,000
Inventory[b]		720,000
Prepaid items		40,000
Total Current Assets		$1,685,000
*Investments and Funds[c]		$1,123,000
Fixed Assets:		
Land	$110,000	
*Buildings and equipment[d]	430,000	
Less accumulated depreciation	(260,000)	
*Property under capital lease	190,000	470,000
*Deferred charges		70,000
*Goodwill		115,000
Total Assets		$3,463,000

a) *Cost $316,000
b) At LOCM using FIFO
c) Investments: $780,000; Bond Sinking Fund $343,000
d) Net of $30,000 investment tax credit.

The Jedro statement doesn't seem to be quite that simple to interpret. Some items are familiar. Crystal has no difficulty understanding the accounting measurement of Cash, Accounts Receivable, Notes Receivable, Accrued Interest Receivable, Prepaid Items, and Accumulated Depreciation. The footnote for inventory tells her that the $720,000 represents the most recent acquisition costs (FIFO) adjusted for possible losses of recoverable cost (LOCM). However, the other items and footnotes are not completely familiar to Crystal. She has marked with an asterisk the twelve items requiring clarification. She wants to know:

1. What is a consolidated balance sheet? What is the difference between something consolidated and unconsolidated?

2. If Marketable Securities cost $316,000, why are they shown at $300,000, and what is their current resale value?

3. What is the Allowance for Uncollectibles? Why is it necessary?

4. What is the Discount on Notes Receivable? What does it represent?

5. Are Investments shown at cost, current market value, or some other amount? And what is a Bond Sinking Fund? Shouldn't this item be included with Bonds on the liability side of the balance sheet?

6. What is the $10,000 Premium on Acme Bonds? What does it represent?

7. What is the $30,000 discount on Buttercup Bonds? Is it like a discount on notes receivable?

8. What is the $18,000 proportionate share of Edwards Corporation's undistributed earnings? Are these dividends which may be receivable? Why aren't there similar amounts shown for the Carter and Dungeness Corporations?

9. What does "Net of $30,000 Investment Tax Credit" mean? What do taxes or tax credits have to do with buildings and equipment?

10. How is the Capital Lease measured? Does the $190,000 relate to the cost of the property or to the required payments under the lease agreement?

11. What are the $70,000 of Deferred Charges? Does the word "charges" refer to charge accounts with suppliers? If so, shouldn't these be shown as liabilities for Jedro and assets to the supplier?

12. What is Goodwill? Who has goodwill towards whom? And what does this have to do with the balance sheet?

Study Exhibits 11.1 and 11.2 carefully. Each new item will be discussed in this chapter. With what you already understand about accounting, you should be able to make a good educated guess in answer to each of Crystal Gurney's questions. Your tentative answers, and the thought process leading to them, will provide you with an excellent framework to integrate the new knowledge below.

Exhibit 11.2

JEDRO CORPORATION
AND CONSOLIDATED SUBSIDIARIES

Additional Information on Investments (supplied by company)

Acme Corporation Bonds	$190,000
*Premium on Acme Corporation Bonds	10,000
Buttercup Corporation Bonds	220,000
*Less Discount on Buttercup Corporation Bonds	(30,000)
Carter Corporation Preferred Stock	39,000
Dungeness Corporation Common Stock	41,000
Edwards Corporation Common Stock	292,000
*Equity in Edwards Corporation's Undistributed	
Earnings	18,000
	$780,000

ASSET MEASUREMENT UNDER GAAP

Remember, from previous chapters, that the accountant's basis for the initial measurement of objectively measurable assets is the fair market value of the asset at the time of its acquisition. When a new asset is acquired in an exchange transaction with an unrelated party ("arm's-length" transaction), the cost can be assumed to represent the fair value. In related-party transactions, other verification of fair value is required.

In Chapter 9 you learned that interest costs are **not** included in the initial measurement of capacity assets. GAAP excludes identifiable interest costs in the initial measurement of all assets, in order to achieve consistency of measurement. Otherwise two identical assets acquired at the same time could be recorded with different amounts if one had been "financed" and the other purchased for cash.

Subsequent to acquisition, GAAP requires that all assets be reduced to reflect expirations of usefulness or recoverable amounts. Remember that capacity assets are systematically depreciated or amortized down to their salvage (recoverable) value. And recall that, following the principle of conservatism, anticipated losses of recoverable amounts are recognized when the loss becomes reasonably certain (LOCM for inventory, for example).

Remember also that accountants, following a principle of *full disclosure*, recognize **all** measurable assets which the firm owns, has a legal claim upon, or effectively controls, as of the statement date. Adjustments at year end recognizing accrued interest receivable and accrued rent receivable are previously described examples of the implementation of this principle.

This chapter is devoted to discussing further the implementation of GAAP asset measurement and reporting objectives. In certain situations with particular assets, the way in which the accountant accomplishes these objectives may not be readily apparent to you. Therefore, in this chapter, you will have the opportunity to review each of the asterisked items in the Jedro balance sheet and its accompanying notes.

To assist you to see the consistency of rule application in different situations, this chapter will:

- First cover the initial measurement of different assets;
- Then describe the recognition of expirations and losses relating to certain assets; and
- Finally introduce the recognition of revenue associated with particular assets.

So that you can integrate and reinforce your new knowledge of initial measurement, expirations or losses, and associated revenues, with respect to each distinct asset, the chapter then contains a review of possible changes to each asset. The chapter concludes with a discussion of the relationship to funds from operations of the particular expenses and revenues introduced.

CONSOLIDATED FINANCIAL STATEMENTS

Before proceeding with particulars of asset measurement, the meaning of the terms "consolidated statement" or "and consolidated subsidiaries" requires clarification. Many of the financial statements you will be dealing with as an investor will be consolidated statements. At the outset, it is important that you understand that they differ from a single firm's statements **only** with respect to the **entity** being reported upon. Basic accounting principles of measurement and reporting are not affected.

For various reasons, many large corporations have acquired all, or at least more than half, of the voting common stock of another corporation. In such cases the acquiring corporation is known as a *parent* corporation. Another corporation which is legally controlled, through ownership of a majority of stockholder votes, by a parent is known as a *subsidiary* corporation. Sometimes a parent with 100 percent control will legally *merge* with its *wholly owned subsidiary*. Legal or statutory merger involves transferring all the assets and liabilities from the wholly owned subsidiary to the parent. The subsidiary thereafter ceases operating as a separate legal entity.[1]

Where a parent–subsidiary relationship exists, and there is no statutory merger, the parent is required by GAAP to prepare *consolidated financial statements* in addition to preparing its own regular statements. Consolidated statements can be viewed as statements showing "what we would look like

---

[1]   A statutory merger could also involve the parent and wholly owned subsidiary, transferring assets and liabilities of both into a third corporation, which would then be the surviving entity.

if we were merged." All assets owned, effectively controlled, or involving claims against those outside of the new "family," and all established legal claims from those outside of the new "family," are combined into a consolidated balance sheet. The statement reports on paper the effective "economic entity"—the parent and the subsidiaries it legally controls. The parent and its subsidiaries, however, continue as legally separate entities with independent sets of accounting records.

Actual preparation of consolidated statements is sufficiently intricate so that accounting majors often take all or part of an advanced accounting course in order to learn the techniques. For our purposes, we can assume that consolidated statements merely represent a combination of parent and subsidiary information with "intrafamily" items eliminated. An example of an "intrafamily" elimination would be a situation where Parent owed Subsidiary $50,000 at year end. Parent would have $50,000 of Accounts Payable and Subsidiary $50,000 of Accounts Receivable. On a combined balance sheet for the "family," $50,000 would be eliminated from *both* combined receivables and combined payables as part of the preparation of a consolidated statement. The $50,000 would not be collectible from, or payable to, anyone outside the "family." Consolidated statements are discussed more fully in Chapter 15. Crystal Gurney can assume that the fact that Jedro's statement is consolidated need not affect her understanding of the basic asset-measurement principles employed by accountants.[2]

INITIAL MEASUREMENT OF ASSETS

The application to new assets of the principle of fair market value at the time of acquisition should present you with no conceptual difficulties. However, the separation and reporting of related interest costs sometimes is not obvious or is not always simple. Possible difficulties arise from traditional business practices and exchanges wherein the related interest costs are not always separately identified.

Discount on Notes Receivable

Promissory notes between unrelated parties generally provide for rental charges for the borrowed funds in the form of interest. It helps to understand interest as rent for money. Promissory notes can be written in three different ways:

1. All interest separately stated from the principal (*face value*) of the note. These notes are known as *interest-bearing notes*.

---

[2]   The method of consolidation, however, could affect whether certain assets are restated to more recent costs and whether goodwill is recognized. See Chapter 15 for a discussion of this point under "Purchase vs. Pooling Treatment."

2. All interest added to the principal and included in the face value of the note. The practice of incorporating or including interest with the principal is called *capitalizing* the interest. These notes are known as *noninterest bearing notes,* since no additional interest is specified.

3. A portion of the interest is separately stated, and the remainder is capitalized into the face value.

For example, assume you were making a one-year loan of $1,000 to someone. Suppose reasonable interest rates for loans of similar risk and duration were ten percent annually. Your total expected cash receipts at the end of the year would be $1,100—$1,000 principal plus $100 interest. A promissory note covering this loan could be written in different ways:

Note A: "I owe you $1,000 (face value) payable in one year plus ten percent interest."

Note B: "I owe you $1,100 (face value) payable in one year."

Note C: "I owe you $1,075 (face value) payable in one year plus $25 interest."

Observe that Note A has no interest capitalized into the face value; Note B has all of the interest capitalized; and Note C has some of the interest capitalized and some stated separately. Assume you would be indifferent as to which note you took in exchange for the loan. How could the accountant initially record each of these notes so that unearned interest is excluded, and so that these essentially identical loans do not appear to be different?

Recall that an agreement between two parties where neither has performed its obligations is known as executory. At the time the $1,000 loan agreement is signed, the agreement is fully executory. You must provide the $1,000 and not take it back for one year; otherwise the borrower will not owe you one year's rent or interest. At the start of the loan period, you are entitled to have only your $1,000 principal returned. After one year, you have earned and are entitled to claim $1,100.

Note A, at the time of making the loan, would be recorded by the accountant as "Notes Receivable $1,000," replacing the $1,000 cash reduction—a simple exchange of assets. No unearned interest is included in this $1,000 measurement.

Note B, at the time of the loan, would be recorded and shown in two separate parts. Notes Receivable would disclose the face value of $1,100. This accounting convention of showing the face value is traditional and has very little current meaning. Since the face value is greater than the present claim or asset amount, a negative valuation contra-account–*discount on notes receivable*–of $100 is required, in order to reduce the book value of the note by the $100 of unearned interest. Note C would be initially recorded at $1,075 with a $75 contra-account representing the discount or amount of unearned interest. **Discount on notes receivable merely represents the amount of interest, capitalized into the face value, that is not yet earned.**

Note how the use of the contra-account results in all three possible notes initially recorded at the amount of their monetary claim excluding unearned interest:

Note A:	Note receivable	$1,000
Note B:	Note receivable	1,100
	Less discount on notes receivable	(100)
Note C:	Note receivable	1,075
	Less discount on notes receivable	(75)

In this example, it was assumed that all three notes covered the same one-year loan at ten percent. It was therefore easy to determine or impute the amount of interest capitalized in Notes B and C which required separate disclosure. What if you were asked to record another note receivable which was noninterest bearing, matured in one year, and had a face value of $5,400? Following GAAP, you would need to break out the capitalized interest and show it as a discount. Without other information on the specific loan, you would need to impute the interest.[3] If you knew that other loans of similar risk and maturity were being regularly made at 8 percent annual interest, how much of the $5,400 would you impute as being interest?

In the case of short-term (one year or less) receivables, compound interest is not a factor. You can assume simple annual interest. The $5,400 noninterest bearing loan, in a situation where eight percent was the "going rate," would comprise $5,000 of principal and $400 of *imputed interest.*[4]

What would be the appropriate amount of imputed interest, if any, in the case of a one-year note with a face value of $9,500, which provided for annual interest of $310? Assume, in this situation, that the "going rate" of interest was nine percent. Is this note a simple interest-bearing note or is part of the interest capitalized in the face value?

The amount of $310 represents only slightly more than three-percent annual interest. If the going rate were nine percent for similar loans, a little less than six percent must have been capitalized. What would be the exact amount of capitalized interest which should initially be recorded as a discount? The total proceeds would be $9,810. At a nine-percent annual interest rate, $9,000 would be the principal with $810 of interest. Therefore this note would be similar to Note C in the earlier example. Interest of $310 is stated and $500 of imputed interest is capitalized. The note will initially be recorded as:

Note receivable	$9,500
Less discount on notes receivable	500

In the examples of the $5,400 and $9,500 notes, the principal amounts of $5,000 and $9,000 were the *present value* of these notes *discounted* at eight

---

[3] Essentially you would be first "inferring" the existence of capitalized interest and its amount. You would then be ascribing or "imputing" this inferred interest to the note. Accountants use the term "impute" to cover the entire process.

[4] Let X equal principal. Then $X + 0.08X = \$5,400$; and $X = \$5,000$.

percent and nine percent, respectively. Present value can be viewed as the amount or "value" of something **excluding interest.** Discounted means separating or factoring out interest at the assumed or imputed appropriate rate.

What would be the present value of an interest-bearing note where the stated additional interest represents the "going rate," that is, where no interest may be reasonably imputed as capitalized into the face value? The face value would be the present value, in this situation. No discount amount would be required to be reported as part of the initial measurement. Remember the example of Note A, for $1,000 plus ten-percent interest, where the going rate was ten percent. No interest is capitalized into the $1,000 face value. The $1,000 face value represents the present value of this note.

In one sense, GAAP requires that all assets be initially recorded at their present value, that is, with all interest factored out. Note that the term "present value" (or *discounted present value*) has this very specific meaning. It should not be used in place of, or confused with, such terms as "current value." When receivables extend beyond one year, compound interest or interest earned on interest enters the picture. Discounting for, or separating out, compound interest is arithmetically more involved and will be discussed in the appendix to Chapter 12. For the moment it is only important that you see clearly that:

1. Accountants initially measure and report receivables at their present value (excluding any capitalized interest).

2. Receivables are conventionally recorded at face value.

3. Therefore, any unearned interest capitalized into the face value (face value minus present value) is shown separately in a valuation contra-account called "discount on notes receivable."

4. Any interest not capitalized and not yet earned is ignored as also executory.

Bonds Acquired as Investments

Bonds can be viewed as readily negotiable (exchangeable) promissory notes, usually with extended maturities and always interest-bearing. Where a bond is purchased as an investment, it is recorded like a note receivable at its face or par value. If the par value and the present value of the bond are the same, no additional valuation account is required.

In certain situations, bonds may sell below or sometimes above par value. When a bond sells (or is purchased) below par value, it is said to sell at a *discount.* A $1,000 bond purchased at a discount for $900 (its present value in the open market) is like a note receivable with $100 of interest capitalized in the face value. The bond costing $900 will entitle the firm to receive regular interest payments **and** $1,000 ($900 of the firm's loaned principal plus $100 interest) upon maturity. The bond, like the note, will require a valuation account for the amount of unearned interest included in the face or par value. The accountant will record this bond held as an asset as follows:

Bonds	$1,000
Less bond discount	(100)

When a bond is purchased for more than par, it is said to sell (or be purchased) at a *premium*. Bonds sell at a premium when their stated interest rate (which is printed or engraved on the bond itself, is part of the bond indenture or contract, and cannot be changed) is too high. If the competitive or "going rate" for a similar bond were six percent and a particular bond was committed to seven percent, it would command a premium. The premium can be viewed as an amount paid by the bondholder which will be returned to him as part of the higher-than-necessary interest rate to which the bond is committed. Initially, bond premium is separately recorded as part of the cost of the bond. A $1,000 bond purchased for $1,200 ($200 premium) would be first reported as:

Bonds	$1,000
Bond premium	200

Note that Bond Premium is a valuation account, but is *not* negative or contra. It adds to the measured amount of the asset.

Sinking Funds or Other "Funds" as Assets

Occasionally a firm will establish a distinct "fund," somewhat like a savings account, for a specific purpose. Note that such funds represent still another use of this readily misunderstood and overused word. Usually such funds are deposited with a trustee or escrow agent, and may be used only for their originally intended purpose. A *bond sinking fund* is a fund established for the retirement of a firm's outstanding bonds (liabilities). It is initially measured and reported at the amount of cash deposited in the fund. Note that, even though a sinking fund appears effectively to reduce the amount of remaining liability on a firm's outstanding bonds, it is **not** shown on the balance sheet as a contra-liability or offset to the firm's bond liability. GAAP has a rule of no offset.[5] The logic behind the rule is simple: In the case of a bond sinking fund, should the trustee abscond with the funds, the firm is still fully liable to its bond creditors. The existence of the fund itself does not reduce the amount of the firm's liability.

---

[5]   A single exception to the no-offset rule exists in the special case of nonnegotiable government Tax Anticipation Certificates, which are disclosed as an offset to the tax liability for which they will be used.

Capital Leases

Capital leases have previously been discussed in Chapter 9. The initial measurement of capital leases by the lessee is consistent with other assets. If you had a new capital lease on some equipment providing for payments of $3,000 per year for fifteen years, can you guess how the accountant would initially record this asset? Remember that each $3,000 payment effectively includes some interest payable to the lessor on his capital tied up or invested in the equipment. If you guessed $45,000 as the initial amount, you are on the right track and forgetting to separate out interest. If you guessed that the capital lease would be recorded at its present value (interest excluded), you understand initial asset measurement. GAAP has specific guidelines for determining the imputed interest rate to apply, and these guidelines are beyond the scope of this text. Following the guidelines, the $45,000 will be discounted to factor out interest. The present value will then be recorded. Since $45,000 is not a face or par value, tradition does not require it to be recorded along with a contra account. Property held under capital lease is initially reported at a single amount—the present value of the future stream of lease payments.

Goodwill

The final new item appearing on Exhibit 11.1 is *goodwill*. Goodwill refers to the intangible, and not readily measurable, value inherent in a successful business. It includes such items as good customer image, good supplier and other creditor relations, a trained and cooperating work-force, and so forth. Recall, from Chapter 3, that an accounting asset must be readily and objectively measurable in monetary terms. Significant time and money are spent each year by a firm in building and maintaining its goodwill. It is extremely difficult to identify such expenditures, and effectively impossible to value their carry-over, or remaining future benefits, at year end. GAAP therefore prohibits, because of its subjectivity, any attempt by a firm to capitalize its own goodwill.

However, when one firm acquires voting control of another firm, in recognition of the reality of the goodwill, it often will have to pay more than the accounting book value of the acquired firm. Such a transaction establishes an objective value for the subsidiary's goodwill, or that portion acquired by the parent. Subject to allocation to undervalued tangible assets acquired, the price paid above book value of the subsidiary's net assets may be reported as goodwill. In the case of a merger, it could be shown as "purchased goodwill."[6]

Assets Acquired for Other than Cash

In previous chapters you learned that assets acquired in an exchange for other than 100 percent cash were valued at their fair market value, or the fair mar-

---

[6]   An alternative treatment to mergers and consolidations involves the so-called pooling-of-interests approach. Under pooling treatment, goodwill does not arise. See Chapter 15.

ket value of the items given in exchange. The one exception involved a trade-in of a similar item, where the book value of the old item plus other considerations provided the measurement basis (See Chapter 9). In previous chapters, it was assumed that the face value of any new liabilities involved in an asset acquisition was their present value. GAAP does not allow this assumption in all cases.

Suppose the new asset were acquired for $10,000 cash and a five-year note for $30,000 plus five percent interest. Would the asset be initially reported at a "cost" of $40,000? The answer would be yes if five percent represented reasonable interest in the circumstances. However, if reasonable interest were greater, say seven percent, then the $30,000 face-value note could be presumed to include two percent capitalized interest. Assuming this capitalized interest amounted to $2,800, the present value of the note would be $27,200. The asset would then be initially reported at $37,200 and not $40,000.

Review of Initial Measurement Basis

To recapitulate, assets are initially measured and reported at their fair market value at the time of acquisition. Cost, or the fair value of items given in exchange, is presumed to be an adequate measurement in an exchange between unrelated parties. Interest is excluded. Where a stream of future cash payments is involved, the present value of the payment stream discounted at the reasonable or going rate of interest is used to eliminate the interest component. Notes receivable and bonds are reported at face value. Where face value differs from present value, a valuation account is employed to separately state the unearned-interest component (note or bond discount) or the amount paid for future excessive interest (bond premium).

RECOGNIZING EXPIRATIONS AND LOSSES

Now that you have been introduced to the basis for initial measurement of all assets, you can proceed to the subject of subsequent measurement of assets in succeeding periods after acquisition. GAAP requires that initial amounts recorded for assets be reduced to reflect expiration of usefulness or loss in recoverable value. Reductions of individual assets (other than cash), which are not part of an exchange or distribution to owners, result in an expense. Expirations or use of inventory, supplies, prepaid items, depreciable fixed assets, and most intangible assets, have been covered in previous chapters. As described in Chapter 9, capital leases as capacity assets are amortized by the lessee to reflect loss of usefulness just as if the leased asset were owned. The pattern of amortization is independent of the lease payment schedule. Also, possible LOCM adjustment for loss in recoverable value of inventory was discussed in Chapter 8. This section will deal individually with other possible assets not previously discussed.

Loss on Current Marketable Securities

Securities—stocks, bonds, and notes—which are readily salable are known as marketable securities. Marketable securities held by a firm as merely a short-term investment of excess idle cash (where the securities' conversion into cash could occur within one year as a normal part of business) are classified as current assets. Those securities where the intention is to hold them as a long-term investment are classified as noncurrent assets under investments (see below). Most current marketable securities are usually in the form of U.S. Treasury bills or short-term notes. These monetary assets were initially recorded at cost.

Market prices (cost and resale value) of securities vary. Suppose that, on a particular statement date, Current Marketable Securities that had cost $200,000 now had a current market value of $160,000. Following the accounting principle of conservatism, how should they be reported on the balance sheet? You are correct to assume that they will be written down to $160,000. A loss of $40,000 will be recorded as part of income from operations. The original cost of $200,000 will also be disclosed as a footnote for the statement user's information.

Note that, like inventory (LOCM), the "usefulness" of current marketable securities is in their short-term sale value (plus, of course, interest earned). Supplies, prepaid items, fixed assets, and intangibles are not normally adjusted downwards to reflect loss of recoverable cash. Their usefulness is internal and is not affected by declines in market prices. On the other hand, current marketable securities and inventory are adjusted for declining market values, since such a decline does impair their usefulness. Therefore, holding or unrealized losses are recorded **as they occur.**

Note also that marketable securities are treated as a group. Prices of some securities held may rise and others fall. Only if the recoverable value of the entire group **taken as a whole** declines below book value, is a loss recognized and recorded. A loss would directly reduce the balance reported for Marketable Securities and be reflected as "Loss on Current Marketable Securities" on the income statement. No valuation contra-account is involved.

Allowance for Uncollectibles

Usually a firm will have accounts receivable with many different customers. Unfortunately these accounts are not all collectible. When a specific receivable is deemed to be uncollectible, that is, there is no reasonable hope of future collection, it is written off. Accounts Receivable is reduced and the expense is reflected on the income statement as "Bad Debt Expense" or some similar description. Note that bad debts are so common that the term **loss** is not even used.

What about the still-active receivables at year end? Based on experience, the accountant knows that a certain portion will, in the future, prove to be uncollectible. Therefore, a statistical estimate of expected losses is made, based on experience. These anticipated losses are used to reduce Accounts Receivable indirectly via a contra or negative-valuation account known as Allowance for Uncollectibles. The balancing reduction is to Bad Debt Expense. Charging the current year's income with the anticipated losses (expenses) on the same year's sales not yet collected accomplishes the matching of these costs with related revenues in the same period. The allowance is re-evaluated and updated each year as part of the adjusting process.

In the example of the Jedro Corporation (Exhibit 11.1), Crystal Gurney can assume that Accounts Receivable–Net (of allowance for uncollectibles) of $340,000 represents the amount of cash which the accountant forecasts (with reasonable certainty) will be forthcoming.

Loss on Noncurrent Marketable Securities and Other Investments

Potential unrealized losses on noncurrent marketable securities taken as a group and on other investments are treated somewhat differently from losses on current marketable securities. Since the immediate usefulness of these non-current assets does not involve readily recoverable cash, only a *permanent holding loss* of recoverable value is recognized both as a reduction of the asset amount and on the income statement. Permanent holding losses are any that are expected to be realized at the time the asset will be sold in the future. For example, a bond purchased at $1,000 par may subsequently have a market-value decline to $875. If it is intended to hold the bond to maturity, the $1,000 maturity value will be collected and no loss will be realized. No permanent loss has occurred. On the other hand, a firm may hold stock cost-ing $6,000 in a company which has failed. If the best estimate of liquidation proceeds to the stockholders indicate that the subject firm would eventually receive $2,500, a permanent loss of $3,500 would be recorded.

Temporary holding losses on noncurrent marketable securities taken as a group are disclosed on the balance sheet. The accountant's intention is to indicate what would happen if the securities were sold earlier than expected. He or she is reporting, "A loss in cash recovery usefulness has occurred, but is not expected to be realized in the long run." Temporary losses reduce the investments account but are **not** included as an expense or loss on the income statement. They are reflected by a separate contra-account within owners' equity. For example, if a temporary loss of $95,000 occurred for noncurrent marketable securities as a group, the accountant would:

Reduce Investments by $95,000, and
Increase Securities Valuation Allowance (a contra-equity account) by 95,000.

This will act to reduce total owners' equity.

Amortization of Bond Premium (for bonds held as investments)

Remember that, when bonds selling at a premium are purchased as investments, the bond premium is separately reported as part of the cost. The face or par value of the bond is recoverable in cash at maturity. The premium is not. The premium represents the amount paid for the privilege of receiving higher-than-normal interest payments over the life of the bond "receivable." Since it "expires," bond premium is amortized each year over the life of the bond "receivable." Rather than report bond-premium amortization as a separate expense on the income statement, accountants "net" it against the higher interest revenue. Assume that bonds with a twenty-year maturity were acquired wih a $20,000 premium. Each year the accountant will:

Reduce interest revenue by $1,000
Reduce bond premium by $1,000[7]

For Jedro (Exhibit 11.2) the $10,000 unamortized (not yet amortized) bond premium on its Acme Bonds will not be realized in cash at maturity. Instead it can be viewed as "excess interest receivable" which will be part of the high Acme interest payments to be received in the future.

Other Expirations

Capital leases are originally recorded at the present value of the stream of future lease payments. Thereafter they are amortized to reflect expiration of usefulness as if the property were owned (see Chapter 9). In the Jedro example, Crystal may assume that the reported $190,000 represents the unamortized cost of the assets acquired via a capital lease.

Crystal did not mark Land with an asterisk on Exhibit 11.1. She probably was assuming that the $110,000 represented the cost of the land. In most cases she would be correct. However, where a firm extracts resources from its land —timber, mining, rock-quarrying, and similar activities—GAAP requires that the land be amortized to reflect the reduction in its usefulness. Land amortization is called *depletion*. To be more correct, therefore, you and Crystal should think of the amount reported on a balance sheet for Land as always representing the undepleted balance of the original cost.

Deferred charges can be thought of as noncurrent prepaid items. Deferred charges represent prepayments where the benefits extend significantly beyond one year. The expiration or amortization of deferred charges to match these benefits will extend over several years, making the asset noncurrent. Examples

---

[7]   Straight-line amortization (as shown) is acceptable when the amounts involved are not material. A method known as the "yield method," which takes into account compound interest considerations, is preferred for material amounts. The yield method is beyond the scope of this text.

of deferred charges would include costs involved in selling a long-term bond issue (to be spread over the life of the issue), advance payments to employee pension trusts, and the like. Deferred charges are reduced or amortized as the costs expire or the benefits are used. The reduction is reflected on the income statement as an operating expense.

The word "charge" can cause confusion. In general usage, charge can refer to "charging" something on account, which would involve a payable. In accounting, the word "charge" often refers to a cost or an expense. Hence, Deferred Charges are expenses which are deferred until future periods as assets, a long-term prepayment. As of 12/31/XX, Jedro reports $70,000 of past expenditure with benefits not yet realized.

Goodwill is recognized when its existence is objectively verified and measurable at the time control over an entire company is purchased. Since accountants are unable to verify its continued existence, goodwill on consolidation or purchased goodwill in a merger are arbitrarily amortized to zero over a period extending from ten to forty years after acquisition. Amortization of goodwill is reflected on the income statement as an operating expense. As of 12/31/XX, Jedro is reporting $115,000 of unamortized goodwill.

Although not appearing as part of the Jedro example, a firm may have assets that are a part of a discontinued segment of the business which is being liquidated. Such assets will be reclassified to the bottom of the balance sheet and identified as relating to discontinued operations. Recall, from Chapter 6, that expirations, and gains or losses on dispositions of such assets, are reflected on the income statement along with extraordinary items, below income from operations. They are reported net of related tax effect and are **not** included as part of income from operations.

RECOGNIZING RELATED REVENUES

Most asset adjustments record expirations or use as expense or loss. There are a few instances where adjustments are made to record revenues earned. In earlier chapters, adjustments for certain accruals of revenue were discussed. For example, the existence of earned but unrecorded and unpaid rent or interest at year end necessitates an adjusting entry. The entry would:

> Increase accrued rent or interest receivable,
> Increase rent or interest revenue on the income statement.

Similar accruals are necessary in other situations.

Recovery of Loss on Marketable Securities

A decline in the market value of the group of current marketable securities, which has previously been recorded as a loss, may reverse. The combined market value may subsequently increase. Any increase in the market value of current marketable securities as a group, above previously reported book value, represents a gain. Where the gain represents a recovery of previously recorded loss—that is, does not result in book value being above cost—the holding gain is recognized in the accounts. Marketable Securities is increased, and a nonextraordinary gain is reflected on the income statement. Note that GAAP and conservatism preclude any increase in marketable securities, or reflected revenue, above original cost unless and until the securities are actually sold.

For example, assume a group or portfolio of current marketable securities that originally cost $130,000 is currently reported at $105,000, reflecting a previous market loss. The market recovers, and the portfolio of current value is now $150,000. How much gain is reported? In this situation, the accountant would make a year-end adjustment:

> Increasing Marketable Securities by $25,000
> Reporting Gain on Securities at $25,000

Note that the standards for marketable securities are different from those for inventory. LOCM requires that inventory be written down for losses. Inventory may not be written back up to cost if the market recovers. Marketable securities can and must be written up (but not above cost) to record any recovery of loss.

Crystal Gurney should correctly assume that Jedro's current marketable securities measured at $300,000 reflected their current market value at the statement date. Could you tell her how she would know that the $300,000 was market value? Since the cost was noted at $316,000, and since marketable securities are valued at current value if below cost, the $300,000 must represent market value.

Noncurrent marketable securities held as investments are similarly written up to reflect recovery of any temporary loss. Such adjustments are not reported on the income statement. The adjustment increasing Investments (not above cost) is paired with a decrease of the contravaluation account in owners' equity. Decreasing the negative Securities Valuation Allowance account results in an increase of total owners' equity to balance the increase in Investments. In essence, the previously recorded temporary losses are simply partially or wholly reversed.

Amortization of Receivables Discount

Recall that interest is accrued as earned. Assume that, on July 1, 19X3, you made two one-year loans totaling $3,000, both at 10-percent annual interest. Loan A was secured by a $1,000 interest-bearing note, and Loan B by a $2,200 noninterest-bearing note. These receivables would have been initially reported together as:

Notes Receivable	$3,200
Less Discount	200

By 12/31/X3, six months' interest will have been earned. How is this fact reported on the balance sheet and income statement? The accountant would report on the 12/31/X3 balance sheet:

Notes Receivable	$3,200
Less Discount	100
Accrued Interest Receivable	50

And on the 19X3 income statement:

Interest Revenue	$150

Note that receivables-related accounts now total $3,150, showing the $150 of interest earned. On Note A, the $50 of interest is separately accrued. On Note B, the accrual is accomplished by reducing the unearned interest discount by $100. The book value of Note B is now $2,100, representing $2,000 of principal plus $100 of capitalized interest now earned.

Where interest is already capitalized into the face value of a receivable, the amount earned is accrued by a reduction of the discount. Therefore, on a balance sheet, discount on notes receivable is not necessarily the total amount of originally capitalized interest. Instead, it represents the **unamortized balance** of originally unearned interest, that is, the amount of capitalized interest remaining to be earned. On the Jedro 12/31/XX statement, $95,000 of notes receivable still included in the face value $5,000 of interest not yet earned.

Can you see that the same interpretation applies to the Buttercup Corporation bonds held by Jedro as investments? The accountant each year amortizes bond discount to reflect that portion earned, by:

Decreasing Bond Discount (which increases total assets),
Increasing Interest Revenue (which increases total equities).

Thirty thousand dollars of unamortized bond discount on Buttercup bonds represents the amount not yet earned and recognized as revenue.

Sinking-Fund Increases

The balance in a sinking fund is increased during the year as a result of two distinct events. Usually a firm each year deposits an additional predetermined amount in the fund. The amount is calculated so that, when the fund is needed, the sum of all deposits plus compound interest earned by and retained in the fund will equal the target required amount. The annual deposit is simply an asset exchange and has no effect on income. Cash is reduced, and Sinking Fund increased by the amount of the deposit.

During the year, just as in the case of a personal savings account, interest is earned on the monies already in the fund (previous deposits and accumulating interest). At year end, the current year's accrued interest is reported by an adjusting entry:

> Increasing the Fund Balance,
> Increasing Interest Revenue.

The $343,000 reported in Jedro's bond sinking fund as of 12/31/XX represents the accumulated total of all previous deposits to the fund, plus compound interest earned and retained in the fund to date.

Equity in Another's Undistributed Earnings

Imagine you are a small stockholder in a giant corporation. If you owned one percent of the common stock and the corporation had $10 million of retained earnings, could you reasonably report $100,000 of possible dividends receivable in the future as an asset? Common sense and the rule of conservatism would preclude such wishful thinking from being recorded as an asset today. Your stock should be carried at the lower of cost or current market. Only when the corporation declares a cash dividend can you recognize the additional asset and associated revenue. You would be properly accounting for your investment following the *cost method*.

Now consider the other extreme. You own 100 percent of the voting common stock of another corporation, which has $500,000 of retained earnings. What are the chances of your ever receiving a dividend? If the $500,000 had been earned by your wholly owned subsidiary since purchase of the company by you, could you properly show the $500,000 as an additional asset and report the $500,000 of revenue as being earned? Having absolute control as the sole owner of the other company, you could declare a dividend whenever you desired. Therefore the $500,000 would properly be considered an earned asset of yours today.

If a firm, which has significant influence over the timing of dividend declaration, could delay recognition of the new asset and associated revenue until the actual declaration, it could manipulate its own reported income. If it desired to understate its income (say, during renegotiation of its labor contract), it could merely hold back earnings from its controlled or significantly influenced companies. When it wanted to look good, it could bring in a whole accumulation of earnings "stored" in its subsidiary. In situations of control or significant influence, delaying asset and revenue recognition until declaration of dividends would clearly violate standards of fair, objective, and consistent reporting.

GAAP therefore provides that when an investment involves significant influence over another firm, the investor **each year** will recognize and record its proportionate share of the investee's profits or losses.[8] This "future divi-

---

[8] Significant influence always exists with legal control—more than 50 percent of the voting stock. In large publicly owned corporations with many small stockholders, effective control may exist with as little as 20 percent of the stock. Below 50 percent, the auditor will verify the existence of significant influence.

dend receivable" amount is added to (or subtracted from, to record losses) the investment account, with the balancing amount recorded as investment revenue (or loss). Accountants refer to this procedure as accounting for such investments by the *equity method,* as distinct from the cost method, where no holding gain is recognized. To record a $50,000 current year's share of earnings, the accountant would:

> Increase Investments by $50,000 (Equity in Undistributed Earnings),
> Increase Investments Revenue by $50,000.

When cash dividends are later received from such firms, where they have already been anticipated under the equity method, **no additional** revenue results. Investment is reduced, and cash is increased, in a manner similar to the collection of a receivable. To record the receipt of a $10,000 dividend when the proportionate share of earnings had already been recognized, the accountant would:

> Increase Cash $10,000,
> Decrease Investments $10,000 (Equity in Undistributed Earnings).

Where significant influence does not exist, revenue is not recognized in anticipation of dividends forthcoming. Where the proportionate share in earnings has not been previously recognized and recorded, a $10,000 dividend would be recorded as:

> Increase Cash $10,000,
> Increase Investments Revenue $10,000.

Percentage Completion

Not demonstrated in the Jedro example, but prevalent especially in the construction industry, is *percentage completion* accounting. So far in this text you have learned that revenue (and possible profit) is not recognized until a sale is completed. You can think of this form of recognition as the *completed-contract method.* In the case of long-term contracts on buildings, dams, factories, and so forth, the completed-contract method would delay recognition of profit, sometimes for many years. Where contracts do extend beyond a year, GAAP therefore allows for percentage-completion revenue and earnings recognition.

Assume you had a purchase order for 1,000 dingbats from a customer, to be delivered over three years. If you shipped 300 the first year, you would record the sale as revenue equivalent to 30 percent of the total contract. A contractor constructing a building for a total fee of $3 million over a two-year period may recognize partial completion at year end. Suppose the estimated total cost on the job was $2,800,000 and, at year end, $2 million of cost had been accumulated in construction-in-progress inventory. If the contractor was reasonably certain the building was 70 percent completed, $2,100,-

000 of revenue could be recognized together with the $2 million of cost. Only $100,000 of profit would be recognized in this case as costs are running higher than originally estimated. Percentage-completion accounting does provide for recognition of profits and losses **each year,** rather than sporadically as jobs are finished.

OTHER ITEMS

The investment tax credit (ITC) was first discussed in Chapter 9. GAAP allows the amount of the tax savings subsidy to be treated in one of two ways. It may be taken as a direct reduction in the cost of the new fixed asset. This approach is known as the *deferred method,* since the income "benefits" of the subsidy will be thus spread over the asset life through lower depreciation expenses. Footnote (d) on Exhibit 11.1 indicates that Jedro is applying this alternative. The original cost of buildings and equipment must have been $460,000, since they are reported at $430,000 net of the ITC.

In the year in which the ITC is provided (allowed) by the government, provision for income taxes on the income statement discloses the amount applicable without the ITC. Actual taxes payable are less by the amount of the ITC. Assume that, at year end, income taxes before ITC would be $200,000, and an ITC of $15,000 is allowed on new fixed assets acquired during the year. The adjusting entry to record income taxes and the ITC, following the deferred method, would be:

Increase Provision for Taxes (Income Tax Expense)	$200,000
Increase Taxes Payable	$185,000
Decrease Fixed Assets	$ 15,000

An alternative method under GAAP, which has been encouraged by the U.S. Congress, possibly for political reasons, is known as the *flow-through method.* Rather than apply the ITC as a reduction of asset cost, and thus defer the benefit recognition on the income statement, the ITC may be recognized as a reduction to the provision for income taxes all in the first year. In the above example, the $15,000 ITC would not reduce asset cost. Instead, it would be reported as reducing tax expense on the income statement. This method of reporting a "profit on a purchase" has been seriously questioned by the accounting profession. Congress, however, has effectively required GAAP to allow this alternative. You may wish to speculate on the probable political motives.

REVIEW OF ASSET CHANGES

You should now be in a position to answer all of Crystal Gurney's questions with respect to the Jedro Corporation assets. And you should be able to generalize your knowledge to other firms. Exhibit 11.3 lists the most common

Exhibit 11.3

CHANGES AFFECTING BALANCE SHEET ASSETS AND CONTRA-ASSETS

[*Note*. Does not include changes to correct for error or to record extraordinary losses.]

Accounts	Effects
Cash	Increased by:
	Cash sales to customers of goods and services (1)
	Sales of marketable securities (2)
	Collections of receivables—notes, accounts, interest, rent (3)
	Proceeds from sale of any noncurrent assets (4)
	Proceeds of loans from creditors (5)
	Deposits or advances from customers (6)
	Owner investments (7)
	Decreased by:
	Cash purchases of any other asset (8)
	Deposits or advances to suppliers (9)
	Payments of any liability (10)
	Payments for goods or services where the liability has not been previously recorded and where there is no asset acquired (11)
	Withdrawals by owner (12)
Marketable securities	Increased by:
	Acquisition of temporary investments (13)
	Adjustment reflecting recovery of market value (14)
	Decreased by:
	Sales of temporary investments (15)
	Adjustment reflecting loss of market value (16)
Notes receivable	Increased by:
	Loans made to outsiders (17)
	Notes accepted from customers in settlement of accounts receivable (18)
	Notes purchased as temporary investments (19)
	Decreased by:
	Collections of cash (20)
	Sales or "discounting" to outsiders (21)
Discount on Notes Receivable (Valuation item)	Increased by:
	Amount of interest included in note face value not yet earned (22)
	Decreased by:
	Adjustment for amount of interest earned (23)

(Continued)

Exhibit 11.3 (continued)

Accounts	Effects
Accounts receivable	**Increased by:** Sales to customers on account (24) **Decreased by:** Collections of cash (25) Determination of definite uncollectibility (26) Acceptance of promissory note receivable in settlement (27)
Allowance for Uncollectibles (Valuation item)	**Increased by:** Adjustment up to estimated amount (28) **Decreased by:** Adjustment down to estimated amount (29) Matching the removal of a specific account receivable determined to be definitely uncollectible (30)
Accrued Receivables	**Increased by:** Adjustments accruing amount firm has earned (31) **Decreased by:** Collections of cash (32)
Inventory	**Increased by:** Purchases for cash (33) Purchases on account (34) Receipt where paid for in advance (35) Manufacturing costs (36) **Decreased by:** Cost of inventory sold (37) Adjustment down to LOCM (38)
Supplies	**Increased by:** Purchases for cash (39) Purchases on account (40) **Decreased by:** Cost of supplies used (41)
Prepaid Items (rent, insurance, deposits, etc.)	**Increased by:** Payments of cash in advance for goods or services (42) Acquisitions on account of future services (43) **Decreased by:** Amortization adjustments as benefits expire or are used (44)

Exhibit 11.3 (continued)

Accounts	Effects
Investments	**Increased by:** Acquisitions of long-term investments (45) Share of "significantly influenced" investee's earnings (46) Adjustment reflecting recovery of temporary loss in market value (47) **Decreased by:** Sales of long-term investments (48) Redemption of bonds or preferred stock (49) Share of "significantly influenced" investee's losses (50) Dividends received from "significantly influenced" investees where profit share already recognized (51) Adjustment for permanent loss in market value (52) Adjustment for temporary loss in market value (53)
Investments Premium	**Increased by:** Amount of premium paid on acquisition (54) **Decreased by:** Adjustment for amount of interest "returned" by investee (55) Sales or redemption of bond (56)
Investments Discount (Valuation item)	**Increased by:** Amount of interest included in face value not yet earned (57) **Decreased by:** Adjustment for amount of interest earned (58) Sales or redemption (59)
Funds	**Increased by:** Deposits of cash (60) Adjustment accruing interest (61) **Decreased by:** Use of fund proceeds for intended purpose (62) Transferring any residual cash to cash account (63)
Land	**Increased by:** Acquisition (64) **Decreased by:** Sale (65) Depletion adjustment only in certain extractive industries (66)

(Continued)

Exhibit 11.3 (continued)

Accounts	Effects
All Other Tangible Fixed Assets	Increased by: Acquisition (67) Cost of self-constructed assets (68) Cost of improvements or betterments (69) Decreased by: Amount of investment tax credit (70) Sale or disposition (71)
Accumulated Depreciation (Valuation item)	Increased by: Depreciation adjustment as benefits expire or are used (72) Decreased by: Amount accumulated on fixed assets sold or disposed of (73) Cost of betterments (74)
Capital Leases, Intangibles, and Other Assets	Increased by: Acquisitions (75) Costs of assets developed by the firm (76) Decreased by: Amortization adjustment as benefits expire or are used (77)
Deferred Charges	Increased by: Payments of cash for services (78) Acquisition of future services on account (79) Decreased by: Amortization adjustments as benefits expire or are used (80)
Goodwill	Increased by: Actual purchase of goodwill in another firm only (81) Decreased by: Required amortization (82)

assets which you may find on a balance sheet. For each asset, the common transactions and adjustments which may affect its balance are also given. Eighty-two possible transactions and adjustments are listed. Review this exhibit carefully. For each numbered transaction or adjustment (1–82), make sure that you can:

1. Visualize a specific example;
2. Identify the other half of the entry that might be involved, that is, the other eventual balance sheet balancing effect.

ASSET CHANGES INVOLVING FUNDS FLOWS

As a final step in reviewing your understanding of asset acquisitions, changes, and dispositions, you should identify those transactions and adjustments that involve working capital funds flows and funds from operations. Exhibit 11.4 should help you clarify your understanding. It summarizes possible asset changes and their relationship to working capital flows.

Exhibit 11.4
RELATIONSHIP BETWEEN ASSET CHANGES AND
WORKING CAPITAL FLOWS

Item	How acquired/Exchange involved	Working capital flow?
New current asset acquired	Exchange for current asset or current liability	No
	Revenue from customers	Yes
	Exchange for noncurrent asset	Yes
	Exchange for new noncurrent debt	Yes
	Invested by owner	Yes
New noncurrent asset acquired	Exchange for current asset or current liability	Yes
	Exchange for noncurrent asset	No
	Exchange for new noncurrent debt	No
	Invested by owner	No
Increase in current asset measurement	Accrued revenue	Yes
	Recognition of gain	Yes
Decrease in current asset measurement	Expiration reflecting expense	Yes
	Recognition of loss	Yes
	Exchange for other current asset	No
	Disbursed to current creditors	No
	Disbursed to noncurrent creditors	Yes
	Disbursed to owners	Yes
	Exchanged for noncurrent asset	Yes
Increase in noncurrent asset measurement	Share of influenced investee's earnings	No
	Discount amortization	No
Decrease in noncurrent asset measurement	Expiration or loss of asset	No
	Loss of market value	No
Disposition of current asset	Exchange for current asset or liability	No
	Expense	Yes
	Exchange for noncurrent asset	Yes
	Retirement of noncurrent debt	Yes
	Distribution to owner	Yes
Disposition of noncurrent asset	Exchange for current asset	Yes
	Expense	No
	Exchange for noncurrent asset	No
	Retirement of noncurrent debt	No
	Distribution to owner	No

Exhibit 11.5 provides a detailed checklist of the items that do **not** involve flows of working capital, and therefore contribute to a difference between working capital funds from operations and income from operations.

Exhibit 11.5

ITEMS INVOLVED IN RECONCILING INCOME FROM OPERATIONS
AND FUNDS FROM OPERATIONS

Income from Operations (After taxes)		$ XXX
Add back:	Any depreciation on tangible fixed assets	XXX
	Any amortization of intangible assets including deferred charges and goodwill	XXX
	Any loss on noncurrent assets	XXX
	Any investments premium amortization	XXX
	Any loss share of investee's undistributed earnings	XXX
	Any noncurrent liability discount amortization (Chapter 12)	XXX
Subtract:	Any profit share of investee's undistributed earnings	YYY
	Any investments discount amortization	YYY
	Any interest revenue recognized in relation to a noncurrent "fund"	YYY
	Any noncurrent liability premium amortization (Chapter 12)	YYY
Equals:	Working Capital Funds from Operations	ZZZ

CHAPTER OVERVIEW

Based on the material covered in this chapter, you should be able to:

- Explain the purpose and significance of consolidated financial statements;
- Describe the basic standards for the initial measurement of all reported assets;
- Explain the concept of present value and how it relates to asset measurement;
- Describe and give examples of how GAAP standards are specifically applied to the initial measurement of notes receivable, bonds, capital leases, deferred charges, goodwill, and assets acquired for other than cash;
- Describe and give examples of recognition of expenses and losses related to marketable securities, accounts receivable, investments, bond premium, land, deferred charges, and goodwill;

- Describe and give examples of recognition of revenue and gains related to marketable securities, receivables and bond discounts, sinking funds, percentage-completion contracts, and the investment tax credit;
- For any asset or contra-asset introduced, describe those transactions and adjustments that can increase and decrease its reported amount on the balance sheet;
- Describe all possible asset-related items that might have to be added to or subtracted from income from operations, to obtain working capital funds from operations.

NEW VOCABULARY AND CONCEPTS

Full disclosure	Bond discount
Parent	Bond premium
Subsidiary	Bond sinking fund
Merge	Goodwill
Wholly owned subsidiary	Permanent holding loss (investments)
Consolidated financial statements	Temporary holding loss (investments)
Face value	Depletion
Interest-bearing notes	Undepleted balance
Noninterest-bearing notes	Cost method (investments)
Discount on notes receivable	Equity method (investments)
Imputed interest	Percentage-completion method
Present value	Completed-contract method
Discounted present value	Deferred method
Bond	Flow-through method

- The reason for and content of consolidated financial statements.
- Present value and the need to segregate interest.
- Significant influence and recognition of proportionate share of another's earnings.
- Temporary vs. permanent losses relating to noncurrent marketing securities.

REVIEW QUESTIONS

1. A parent and a subsidiary's balance sheets could be simply added together in a combined statement. A combined statement without further adjustment would not be a consolidated statement and would not be acceptable under GAAP. (a) What is the essential difference between a combined and a consolidated balance sheet? (b) What is the intent of adjustments or eliminations in consolidation? (c) Give an example of a possible elimination.

2. Do GAAP require that consolidated statements be prepared to include all firms where significant influence is determined to exist? If not, what are the criteria for necessary consolidation?

3. What is the difference between the standards for valuing marketable securities as a group and the LOCM valuation rule as applied to inventory?

4. a) What is the purpose of the Allowance for Uncollectibles account? (b) Why not reduce Accounts Receivable directly for anticipated uncollectibles? (c) Why does the accountant anticipate losses on receivables? Why doesn't he just wait until the losses are certain?

5. a) What is the purpose of a discount valuation account on notes receivable or on bonds owned as an investment?

   b) What does the amount of unamortized discount reported on a particular balance sheet represent?

   c) What term or concept describes the basis for the initial measurement of monetary assets? What does the initial book value of a monetary asset represent?

6. Discount on receivables and bonds owned as investments is systematically amortized. (a) What is the basis for amortization—how much and when? (b) What is the balancing adjustment and why?

7. Sometimes a bond-premium valuation account appears with bonds owned as an investment. (a) What is the purpose of this bond premium account? (b) What does the amount of unamortized premium represent? (c) Bond premium is amortized systematically to interest revenue. Why?

8. For some common-stock investments, no additional asset amount and accompanying revenue are recognized until a dividend is actually declared. For others, a proportionate share of new earnings is recognized each year, whether or not there have been any dividends declared. What is the reason behind this apparently inconsistent treatment?

9. a) What is an investment tax credit? (b) What are the two ways an accountant may recognize investment tax credit? (c) What is the differing effect upon reported net income, using these two methods?

10. Assume a particular capital-lease agreement provides for equal payments over the 20 years of the lease term. Must the firm use 20-year straight-line amortization with respect to its capital-lease asset account? If not, what standards apply to such amortization?

11. What are some common examples of deferred charges? How do deferred charges as a noncurrent asset differ from prepaid items as a current asset?

12. What are the various relationships or conditions that can result in the existence of goodwill, whether or not the goodwill is measured and reported by accountants?

13. Under GAAP it is not acceptable for a firm to capitalize its own goodwill. Why is it not acceptable?

14. a) What is goodwill arising from consolidation? (b) Purchased goodwill? (c) What does the amount so reported on a balance sheet represent? (d) What is done with this amount over future years?

MINI-CASES AND QUESTIONS FOR DISCUSSION

MC 11.1. A land development company recently acquired a large tract of undeveloped land, which it intended to subdivide into parcels and to sell. The transaction involved the firm's receiving title to 50,000 acres, in exchange for a cash payment of $100,000 and a 10-year promissory mortgage note for $400,000 at one percent annual interest. The usual interest rate for such mortgages was eight percent.

The company's accountants originally recorded the land as inventory, at a value of $500,000, and reported a noncurrent liability of $400,000. The firm's CPA would give a "clean" (no exceptions) opinion only if the land were initially valued at $312,120, and the liability shown at $400,000, together with a $187,880 discount.

What are the issues involved? Discuss.

MC 11.2. Jose Grenados is studying to be an investment analyst. He understands the primary need for consistency in the measurement and reporting of information. He has been very favorably impressed with GAAP, but now he is not so sure. "How can accountants preach consistency and then be so inconsistent?" he asks. "They use LOCM for inventory and something else for marketable securities. They pick up future dividends on some stocks and not on others. They treat some leases one way and others another. How can this be considered consistent reporting?" Discuss.

MC 11.3. Goodwill, in some cases, can represent the most valuable asset in a firm. This is regularly demonstrated by the numerous cases where a firm is sold for many times its accounting book value. If it can be so important, why don't accountants recognize a firm's own goodwill? If accountants are so dead-set against reporting goodwill, why do they then go ahead and report goodwill arising out of a purchase or consolidation? And, finally, if they do recognize and report goodwill, why do they amortize it when, in reality, it might continue to exist, or even grow?

MC 11.4. The freight-in costs on inventory, and even the insurance costs covering an asset while it is being obtained/prepared for initial use, are capitalized as part of its cost. These and similar costs are included in the initial measurement of an asset because they all represent direct ordinary and necessary expenditures to prepare the asset for its intended use. Why, then, is any interest cost excluded? There exist many situations where an asset could and would not be obtained if it could not be financed. In such situations, interest is both ordinary and absolutely necessary. Discuss.

ESSENTIAL PROBLEMS

EP 11.1. The Easy Company has a group of current marketable securities purchased during 19X1 at a cost of $90,000. The market value of this group taken together was:

$93,000 on 12/31/X1
$80,000 on 12/31/X2
$88,000 on 12/31/X3

Assume that these securities were held through 19X3, and continued to be classified as current, since they were readily available for conversion into cash. How would marketable securities be valued on the balance sheet as of 12/31/X1, 12/31/X2, and 12/31/X3? What would be the effect on operating income of the changing market values in the years 19X1, 19X2, and 19X3?

EP 11.2. Refer to the Easy Company information given in Problem EP 11.1. Assume that the market price of the group had been $85,000 as of 12/31/X4, $91,000 as of 12/31/X5, and $90,000 as of 12/31/X6. How would marketable securities be valued on the balance sheets as of 12/31/X4, 12/31/X5, and 12/31/X6? What would be the effect on operating income of the changing market values in the years 19X4, 19X5, and 19X6?

EP 11.3. The Fox Company had an account receivable of $8,000 from one of its customers, the George Company. George had requested extended time to make payment and had given Fox a six-month promissory note with a face value of $8,400, including 10 percent interest. How would this note receivable initially be reported on the balance sheet?

EP 11.4. Referring to the Fox Company data given in Problem EP 11.3, suppose a balance sheet were being prepared three months after the note had been accepted by Fox. (a) How should the note receivable be reported? (b) What, if any, effect would there be on net income related to this receivable?

EP 11.5. The George Company has just leased special equipment under a 20-year lease. Twenty years is the effective life of the equipment. At the end of the lease, George has the option of purchasing the equipment for $1. You may assume that the lease qualifies as a capital lease. The total of all 20 equal annual payments, required at the end of each year, under the lease is $200,000. The discounted present value of the total of these payments at eight percent, which you may assume is appropriate for the George Company, is $98,181 ($4,909 is the present value of the first year's payment).

In initially recording this transaction, how much will the accountant show as:

a) The asset amount?

b) The current liability amount?

c) The noncurrent liability amount?

EP 11.6. The How Company has just acquired property under a capital lease. The lease provides for total payments of $430,000, $50,000 the first year and the balance in equal payments over the remaining 19 years of the lease. The appropriate present value of the first payment is $45,870, and for the total lease is $210,092.

In initially recording the property's acquisition, how much will the accountant show as:

a) The asset?

b) The current liability?

c) The noncurrent liability?

EP 11.7. The Joy Corporation had $40,000 of expenses directly related to the cost of raising funds through a new $2,000,000, twenty-year bond issue. Should the $40,000 be treated as an operating expense in the year of issue? If not, how should it be reported on Joy's balance sheet?

EP 11.8. Refer to the Joy Corporation in Problem EP 11.7. How should the $40,000 of bond-issue cost be shown on the balance sheet five years after the original bond issue?

EP 11.9. The King Company has acquired equipment in exchange for $30,000 cash and a 5-year promissory note with a face value of $105,000. The $105,000 includes $35,000 of interest. (a) What should initially be recorded as the equipment's cost? (b) What should initially be the balancing items recorded under noncurrent liabilities?

EP 11.10. The Love Corporation has acquired a noncurrent asset in exchange for $60,000 cash, a 6-month note payable for $21,000, and a 10-year note payable for $360,000. The $21,000 face-value note includes $1,000 of interest, and the $360,000 face-value note includes $160,000 of interest. (a) What should initially be recorded as the cost of the noncurrent asset? (b) What should initially be the balancing items recorded under current and noncurrent liabilities?

SUPPLEMENTARY PROBLEMS

SP 11.11. The Mike Company owns 40,000 shares of the Nice Corporation's common stock purchased several years ago at a cost of $350,000. Nice has a total of 100,000 shares of common stock outstanding. Except for Mike's shares, the others are widely distributed. Mike is considered to have significant influence over Nice.

On 12/31/X0, Mike's balance sheet showed Nice's stock in the investment account at $412,000. During 19X1, the Nice Corporation declared and paid a cash dividend of $0.75 per share. Nice also reported $150,000 of net income for 19X1.

a) What should be the balance in Mike's investment account for Nice's stock as of 12/31/X1?

b) In Mike's 19X1 income statement, how much investment revenue should be reported attributable to the Nice Corporation?

SP 11.12. Refer to the Mike and Nice Company information in Problem SP 11.11. During 19X2, the Nice Corporation reported a net loss of $50,000. During 19X2, it also declared and paid a cash dividend of $0.25 per share.

a) What should be the balance in Mike's investment account for Nice's stock as of 12/31/X2?

b) In Mike's 19X2 income statement, investment revenue associated with the Nice Corporation should be reported as how much?

SP 11.13. The Peter Company on the first day of January, 19XX, purchased some new equipment costing $200,000. The equipment had a 10-year useful life and zero salvage value. Straight-line depreciation was appropriate for financial reporting purposes. The equipment qualified for a 10-percent investment tax credit. Peter's income taxes payable, before allowance for the credit, amounted to $33,000. Peter's net income after taxes, before allowance for the investment tax credit, amounted to $100,000.

If Peter were electing the flow-through method for reporting the investment tax credit, at the end of 19XX, how much would be reported under each of the following related items?

a) 19XX depreciation expense on the new equipment,

b) 19XX provision for income taxes,

c) 12/31/XX income taxes payable, assuming no partial payments made,

d) 19XX tax credit expense reduction,

e) 19XX net income after taxes.

SP 11.14. Assume the same information for the Peter Corporation as that given in Problem SP 11.13, except that Peter was electing the deferred method of recognizing investment tax credit. At the end of 19XX, what amounts would then be reported for each of the following related items?

a) 19XX depreciation expense on the new equipment,

b) 19XX provision for income taxes,

c) 12/31/XX income taxes payable, assuming no partial payments made,

d) 19XX tax credit expense reduction,

e) 19XX net income after taxes.

SP 11.15. The transactions and adjustments that can increase and decrease assets, as listed on Exhibit 11.3, are numbered 1–82. Considering only numbers 1–38 (down through inventory), identify by number those changes which:

a) represent revenue or gain (reportable on the income statement) at the time they occur;

b) represent expense or loss (reportable on the income statement) at the time they occur;

c) have no effect on the income statement.

SP 11.16. For transactions and adjustments 39–82 on Exhibit 11.3, make the same identifications as required in Problem SP 11.15.

SP 11.17. For transactions and adjustments 1–38 in Exhibit 11.3, identify by number those that involve a flow of working capital funds at the time they occur.

SP 11.18. For transactions and adjustments 39–82 in Exhibit 11.3, make the same identifications as those required in Problem SP 11.17.

PREPARER PROCEDURES

All asset accounts by convention normally have debit balances. Negative asset valuation accounts—known as contra-asset accounts—normally have credit balances. Examples of contra-asset accounts include discount on notes receivable, allowance for uncollectible accounts, discount on bonds owned as investments, and accumulated depreciation.

Assets are initially recorded at their fair market value excluding any unearned-interest component. Therefore, notes receivable with interest included in the face value, and bonds purchased at a discount, will be initially recorded at face value together with a contra-account effectively eliminating the unearned-interest component from total assets. For example, assume that a $6,600 note receivable, with $600 of interest included in the face value, is accepted as deferred payment for a $6,000 account receivable. This transaction would be journalized as:

	DR	CR
Notes receivable	$6,600	
Discount on notes receivable		$ 600
Accounts receivable		6,000

Similarly, equipment acquired for $30,000 cash and a 5-year note payable with a $150,000 face value, which included $20,000 of capitalized interest, would be recorded with:

	DR	CR
Equipment	$160,000	
Discount on noncurrent note payable	20,000	
Cash		$ 30,000
Noncurrent note payable		150,000

Asset expirations have previously been covered. With the exception of tangible fixed assets, expirations involve a direct credit to the asset account and a matching debit or charge to the appropriate expense account.[9]

The adjusting entry recording the matching expiration of $5,000 of financing expense previously capitalized in Deferred Charges would be:

	DR	CR
Financing Expense	$5,000	
Deferred Charges		$5,000

$8,000 of annual depreciation on buildings would be journalized:

	DR	CR
Depreciation Expense	$8,000	
Accumulated Depreciation on Buildings		$8,000

Interest receivable is accrued as earned. Where not already included in the receivable's face value, the debit is to accrued interest receivable and the credit to interest revenue. Where some or all of the interest is already included in the face value, the debit is to note or bond discount and the credit to interest revenue for the portion earned. Assume a firm has three different one-year notes receivable:

Note A: $5,000 face value (no capitalized interest) plus 8 percent interest;

Note B: $6,540 face value ($540 of interest capitalized), no additional interest;

Note C: $8,320 face value ($320 of interest capitalized) plus $240 interest.

---

[9] For a manufacturer, some assets "expire" into product cost, and the appropriate debit would be to manufacturing overhead.

To record accrual of earned revenue in these notes after six months, the following separate journal entries could be made:

	DR	CR
Accrued Interest Receivable	$200	
Interest Revenue (A)		$200
Discount on Note Receivable (B)	270	
Interest Revenue		270
Discount on Note Receivable (C)	160	
Accrued Interest Receivable	120	
Interest Revenue		280

Similar entries would be appropriate for bonds held as investments.

Premium on bonds held as investments is amortized as a reduction of interest revenue. The amortization of $15,000 of bond premium would be journalized:

	DR	CR
Interest Revenue	$15,000	
Bond Premium		$15,000

Asset revaluations reflecting external circumstances involve direct adjustments to the asset account, and a corresponding expense or revenue item. A decline in market value of current marketable securities below current book value would necessitate a charge to an operating loss account, and a credit to marketable securities. A recovery of market value would result in a debit to marketable securities, with a ceiling of cost, and a corresponding credit to gain on securities.

A $12,000 decline in the market value of a firm's portfolio of current marketable securities below their existing book value would be journalized:

	DR	CR
Loss on Marketable Securities	$12,000	
Marketable Securities		$12,000

A recovery (gain up to but not exceeding original cost) of $7,000 on marketable securities as a group during a year would be journalized:

	DR	CR
Marketable Securities	$7,000	
Gain on Marketable Securities		$7,000

A temporary loss of market value on noncurrent marketable securities (investments) and a recovery (up to cost) of temporary loss is **not** treated as expense or revenue. Instead, an owners' equity contra-valuation account—Securities Valuation Allowance —is used. A $23,000 temporary loss would be recognized with:

	DR	CR
Securities Valuation Allowance	$23,000	
Investments		$23,000

A full recovery of this temporary loss would be journalized:

	DR	CR
Investments	$23,000	
Securities Valuation Allowance		$23,000

A permanent loss on investments of $11,000 would be recognized on the income statement. Note that recovery of a permanent loss may **not** be recognized in the accounts under GAAP, since it would be considered a write-up above cost basis. The $11,000 permanent loss would be journalized:

	DR	CR
Loss on Investments	$11,000	
Investments		$11,000

In the situation where a proportionate share of an investee's earnings must be recognized because significant influence over the investee exists, the investments account is charged directly with a matching credit to investment revenue. Dividends received would be credited to investments where the proportionate share of earnings had been previously recognized, or to investments revenue where not previously recognized.

Assume a firm held voting stock in Corporations X and Y and had significant influence over X but not over Y. If X had $100,000 of earnings, paid $40,000 in dividends, and the firm held 30 percent of X's stock, the events would be journalized following the *equity method*, as follows:

	DR	CR
Investments	$30,000	
Investments Revenue		$30,000
Cash	$12,000	
Investments		$12,000

If Y paid $60,000 in dividends and the firm owned 10 percent of Y's stock, the revenue would be recognized following the *cost method*, as follows:

	DR	CR
Cash	$6,000	
Investments Revenue		$6,000

PREPARER PROBLEMS

PP 11.1. Refer to Problem EP 11.1 above. Prepare all necessary adjusting journal entries for the years 19X1, 19X2, and 19X3 to reflect appropriate revaluations of current marketable securities and associated operating revenue or expense.

PP 11.2. Refer to Problem EP 11.2 above. Prepare all necessary adjusting journal entries for the years 19X4, 19X5, and 19X6 to reflect appropriate revaluations of current marketable securities and associated operating revenue or expense.

PP 11.3. Refer to Problem EP 11.3 above; give the journal entry properly recording the acceptance of the note in settlement of the account.

PP 11.4. Refer to Problems EP 11.3 and EP 11.4, above. Give the necessary adjusting entry after three months, to record interest earned.

PP 11.5. Refer to Problem EP 11.5 above. Give the entry initially recording the acquisition of the equipment under capital lease.

PP 11.6. Refer to Problem EP 11.6, above. Give the necessary entries recording the acquisition of property by the Howe Company.

PP 11.7. Refer to Problem EP 11.9 above. Give the entry recording the equipment acquisition.

PP 11.8. Refer to Problem EP 11.10 above. Give the entry recording the noncurrent asset acquisition.

PP 11.9. Refer to Problem SP 11.11 above. Give all necessary entries during 19X1 related to the Nice investment.

PP 11.10. Refer to Problem SP 11.12 above. Give all necessary entries during 19X2 related to the Nice investment.

12

THE MEASUREMENT
OF LIABILITIES

CHAPTER PREVIEW

The objective of this chapter is to complete your elementary accounting knowledge of liability measurement and reporting in conformance with GAAP. In this chapter, you can:

- Learn of the objectives of liability measurement and reporting under GAAP;
- Discover that liability discount and premium valuation accounts are the counterpart of those for assets discussed in Chapter 11;
- Develop an understanding of the distinction among different types of liabilities and which ones are reported on the balance sheet;
- Learn that some items disclosed as liabilities do not represent obligations to creditors; and develop an understanding of what these items do represent, and why they are classified as liabilities;
- Complete your understanding of liability changes through learning of those that do not result from payment at maturity;
- Complete your understanding of those adjustments to noncurrent liabilities that do not involve flows of net working capital.

With this knowledge you will be qualified to read and interpret correctly the liability section of most published balance sheets. Together with your existing knowledge of assets (Chapter 11) and owners' equity (Chapter 10), you will be adequately equipped to analyze meaningfully more sophisticated financial statements employing the approaches and tools to be presented in the next chapter.

HOW MUCH DOES THIS FIRM REALLY OWE TO OTHERS?

Crystal Gurney is continuing her investigation of the Jedro Corporation's balance sheet. After satisfying herself that she understood the basis of valuation for the firm's reported $3,463,000 of assets (Exhibit 11.1), she turns to the firm's liabilities. Exhibit 12.1 gives Jedro's liabilities as reported in its balance sheet as of 12/31/XX. Crystal has understood liabilities to represent amounts of resources contributed by and owed to (claimed by) creditors. Again, she

Exhibit 12.1
JEDRO CORPORATION

**Liability Portion of Consolidated Balance Sheet
as of 12/31/XX**

Current Liabilities:	
Current notes payable	$200,000
*Less discount	(20,000)
Accounts payable	320,000
Accrued wages and salaries payable	40,000
Accrued interest payable	30,000
Taxes payable	135,000
*Current obligations under capital leases	20,000
*Maturing portion of 5% serial bonds	25,000
*Estimated product warranties	15,000
*Unearned revenue	50,000
Other current liabilities	25,000
Total Current Liabilities	$840,000
Noncurrent Liabilities:	
Mortgage note payable	$ 80,000
Less discount on mortgage note payable	(5,000)
7% serial bonds payable	25,000
8% bonds payable	60,000
*Less unamortized bond discount	(10,000)
9% bonds payable	100,000
*Unamortized bond premium	30,000
*Noncurrent obligations under capital leases	40,000
*Deferred income tax	90,000
Total Noncurrent Liabilities	$410,000
*Minority Interest:	$100,000

Notes:
The company is defendant in a lawsuit in the amount of $500,000.
The company has a contract to purchase 2,000,000 gizmos over
  the next four years at a price of $4 each.

* The starred items are those Gurney needs to have explained.

has marked with an asterisk the ten items about which she has questions. If her firm buys the Jedro Company, it will be assuming responsibility for Jedro's debts. She would like to be sure that all the firm's liabilities as of 12/31/XX are shown, that those liabilities shown all represent resources owed to creditors, and that she knows how the liabilities are measured. Specifically, she is interested in:

1. Are the negative valuation accounts for discount on notes payable and bonds payable related to those that would be reported along with the assets, notes receivable and bonds owned as an investment, on the creditor's balance sheet?

2. Is unamortized bond premium similar to that reported for bonds purchased at a premium as an investment?

3. Are the current and noncurrent capital-lease obligations associated with specific assets?

4. Why are estimated product warranties shown as a liability? Since they represent future costs, shouldn't they be omitted, along with future interest and future operating lease obligations? Or, if they are properly included, then why not include the $8,500,000 of potential obligations cited in the footnotes?

5. What is the maturing portion of a serial bond issue; and what are serial bonds?

6. What is deferred revenue? If it is revenue, shouldn't it be included in owners' equity or as an asset? If it is a liability, does it represent amounts actually owed to others?

7. What is deferred income tax? How can tax payments be postponed so as to be noncurrent?

8. What is minority interest? It isn't shown as a liability, and Jedro doesn't include it with stockholders' equity.

As with another exhibit in the previous chapter, you are asked in this chapter to become thoroughly familiar with Exhibit 12.1. Each asterisked item will be discussed, and the chapter will focus on this exhibit. Again you should first attempt to make an educated guess at the answers to Crystal's eight questions before proceeding. Your guesses and the thought processes involved will provide you with a valuable frame of understanding for the material that follows.

OBJECTIVES OF LIABILITY MEASUREMENT AND REPORTING

Recall, from Chapter 11, that measurement and reporting objectives for assets included reporting all measurable assets which the firm actually owned, had legal claims to, or effectively controlled as of the balance sheet date. Resources, benefits, or gains that might come in the future were specifically not included since they are either executory or represent wishful thinking. Specifically, future unearned interest was excluded in the computation of total assets.

GAAP standards for liability measurement are consistent with these objectives. All measurable obligations of the firm that legally exist as of the balance sheet date are required to be disclosed. Future obligations which are executory, or which may develop in the future, are not included on the balance sheet. Interest that is not yet owed is specifically excluded. Liabilities are measured and reported at the present value of the stream of resource payments owed. The arithmetic technique for determining present value, where a liability extends beyond one year and compound interest is involved, is covered in an appendix to this chapter.

In previous chapters, liabilities such as current notes payable, accounts payable, various accrued liabilities, noncurrent notes payable, and bonds payable have been introduced. Their measurement and reporting should now be familiar and will not be discussed further. This chapter will address other possible liabilities and liability accounts not previously covered.

LIABILITY VALUATION ACCOUNTS

The two negative liability-valuation accounts—discount on notes payable and discount on bonds payable—are the exact counterpart of discounts on notes and bonds held as assets. In fact, Jedro's $200,000 note payable with a $20,000 discount has its counterpart on the creditor's balance sheet. The creditor, as of 12/31/XX, will report as an asset the $200,000 note receivable together with a $20,000 discount. The original buyers and holders of Jedro's eight-percent bonds will be carrying them as assets, together with their associated discount.

However, the meaning and accounting treatment of these liability discounts are different from asset discounts. Discount accounts distinguish portions of interest included in face values. Liability discounts indicate that portion of interest capitalized into face values which is executory and therefore not yet owed. Liability discounts will be amortized into interest expense as the interest becomes owed and eventually payable. The holder of the note as an asset will simultaneously amortize the corresponding asset discount to interest revenue as it becomes earned and eventually receivable.

An example of a liability discount and its amortization would be a one-year, noninterest-bearing note payable with a face or maturity value of $7,630. Assuming the effective interest rate was nine percent, $630 of interest is capitalized into the face value of the note. The present value of the note at the date of issue is $7,000. The $630 of future interest is not yet earned by the creditor nor owed by the firm. As for assets, an accounting convention requires all notes and bonds to be reported at their face or par value. Therefore, initially a discount account is required to reduce the book value of the note to the amount of the existing obligation—the present value. The $7,630 note would be first recorded as:

Note Payable	$7,630
Less Discount on Note Payable	(630)

If a balance sheet were to be prepared four months later, part of the necessary adjusting process would involve accruing four months' interest now owed as a liability and representing an expense of the period. Again, as for discounts on assets (Chapter 11), the accountant will disclose the additional $210 liability by reducing or amortizing the not-yet-owed discount amount. Unamortized liability discount will then continue to report that portion of the face value not yet owed, and a third line for accrued interest payable will be unnecessary. The adjusting entry would:

Increase interest expense by	$210
Decrease note payable discount by	210

Bonds issued at a discount, and subsequent amortization of bond discount to interest expense, are handled exactly the same way as are notes payable.

Premium on bonds payable is the exact counterpart of premium on bonds held as an investment. The original buyers and holders of Jedro's nine-percent bonds will be carrying them as assets with their associated premium. Recall that, in Chapter 11, you were told that asset premiums could be viewed as cash given to the borrower, which will be returned in the future as part of interest to be received. Asset premium amortization served to reduce interest revenue to the amount earned net of "return of premium." Premium on bonds payable can be viewed as cash received from the creditor, which will be returned as part of high interest paid.[1]

The effective interest cost of the loan is less than the interest that is being paid, since part of the annual interest is a return of the premium. Liability premium is amortized over the life of the loan.[2] How will the accountant reflect this amortization on the income statement? You clearly understand liability premiums if you know that the amortization is used to reduce interest expense to the effective cost, rather than being reported as some kind of "revenue." The accountant, each year, will make an adjustment which:

Decreases bond premium, and	
Decreases interest expense.	

---

[1]   Bonds may also be sold with accrued interest to be "returned" as part of the first interest payment. In such circumstances, the amount of accrued interest is recorded as a current liability and eliminated, with a corresponding reduction to interest expense, at the time of the first interest payment. The process is nearly identical to that for bond premium.

[2]   As mentioned in Chapter 11 for amortization of asset premiums and discounts, liability premiums and discounts may be amortized on a straight-line basis if not material. Otherwise a method relating to present value known as the yield or interest method is preferred.

On the Jedro balance sheet, $20,000 of unamortized current note discount, $5,000 of unamortized mortgage note discount, and $10,000 of unamortized discount on the eight-percent bonds all represent amounts of interest included in face values, which are not yet owed as of 12/31/XX. The $30,000 of unamortized bond premium represents monies received from creditors, which will be returned to them as part of future interest payments.

CAPITAL-LEASE OBLIGATIONS OF LESSEE

As covered under capital-lease assets (Chapter 11), the lessee's *obligations under capital leases* initially represent the discounted present value (principal value) of the payments to be made. Future interest is not recorded until it is earned and owed. Capital lease obligations are segregated as to current (that is, due and payable within one year) and noncurrent portions. They mature and are satisfied by payments in accordance with the lease contract terms. The timing of current classification and subsequent payment are independent of the timing chosen for the related asset amortization. Remember also that each lease payment under a capital lease is greater than the principal (present value) portion initially recorded as the obligation. The difference represents interest expense for the year on the **total unpaid principal balance** (present value) of the capital lease "loan."

For example, assume that some equipment was leased under a 10-year capital lease calling for a $38,000 payment the first year and $18,000 per year for the next nine years. The present value of the $200,000 of total payments as scheduled would be $139,300 assuming an eight-percent interest discount rate was appropriate in this situation.[3] The balance of $60,700 represents interest costs included in the lease payments. Exhibit 12.2 reveals how this lease would be initially recorded and how it would be disclosed after the first year.

At the end of the first year, what would be the effect of the accountant's entry recording the $38,000 lease payment? Assuming the interest portion had not been accrued prior to payment, the entry would:

Reduce Current Lease Obligation by	$26,856
Increase Interest Expense by	11,144
Decrease Cash by	38,000

Note that $11,144 of interest (8 percent of the $139,000 unpaid principal balance) was no longer executory at year end. If not paid by the statement date, it would have to be accrued as part of the total payment due.

---

[3]   The appendix to this chapter explains how the present value of this stream of payments is determined.

Exhibit 12.2

EXAMPLE OF CAPITAL LEASE DISCLOSURE FOR LESSEE

Before lease:			
Cash	$300,000	Owner's Equity	$300,000

Initial recording:			
Cash	$300,000	Current capital lease obligation	$ 26,856[b]
Capital lease	139,300[a]	Noncurrent capital lease obligation	112,444
		Owner's Equity	300,000
	$439,300		$439,300

End first year:			
Cash	$262,000	Current capital lease obligation	$ 9,004[d]
Capital lease	125,370[c]	Noncurrent capital lease obligation	103,440
		Owner's Equity	274,926[e]
	$387,370		$387,370

Notes:

[a] Ten-year lease with total payments $200,000: $38,000 end first year, $18,000 per year for next 9 years. Present value, discounted at 8 percent rate appropriate to firm, equals $139,000.

[b] Present value of first year's lease payment ($38,000 total payment less $11,144 interest on outstanding "loan balance" of $139,000).

[c] Amortized 10 percent (10-year life, zero salvage, straight-line).

[d] Present value of second year's lease payment ($18,000 total payment less $8,996 interest on reduced outstanding "loan balance" of $112,444).

[e] Reduced by $13,930 asset amortization and $11,144 of interest expense.

MATURING PORTION OF LONG-TERM DEBT

All noncurrent obligations or portions thereof may eventually be reclassified as current liabilities, for the same reason that a currently maturing capital-lease obligation is reclassified. Recall that GAAP require that all liabilities which will mature within one year (period) of the balance sheet date, and which will require current assets in settlement, be classified as current. Note however, that when an agreement exists to refinance (replace) a currently maturing obligation with debt extending beyond one year, the maturing obligation will not require current assets in settlement. Therefore it will not be reclassified as current.

Note that reclassification of debt will affect the balance of net working capital, and therefore represents an "internal" working capital flow. These flows will be discussed later in this chapter. Will simple reclassification affect the balance sheet ratio? Reclassification of existing long-term debt to a current liability will reduce both the current ratio and the long-term debt ratio. It will have no effect on the overall debt ratio.

The capital-lease example given above provided for a portion of the total lease obligation to mature each year. A lease payment (principal plus interest) was required each year. Some bonds are issued with staggered maturities, based on the serial or identification numbers on the bonds. For example, bonds with serial numbers from 1 to 999 might be scheduled to mature in ten years. Those with numbers 1,000 to 1,999 might mature in eleven years, and so forth. Such bonds are known as *serial bonds*. Jedro's balance sheet discloses $25,000 of five-percent serial bonds as current liabilities. This means that $25,000 cash will be required within a year to retire bonds that have a stated interest rate of 5 percent.

CERTAIN, ESTIMATED, AND CONTINGENT LIABILITIES

Jedro's $15,000 of estimated product warranties brings up the issue of different types of liabilities which may be reported on the balance sheet. Up to this point, you have been exposed only to liabilities which have the following characteristics:

1. They were the result of a past transaction or event. Performance by the creditor has been completed.
2. They were clearly monetary. They represented an obligation to pay specific amounts of cash at specific times.

GAAP require that all of these *certain liabilities* be "booked" or recorded in the accounts. You can be assured that either all known, certain liabilities will be included on the balance sheet, or else the auditor's opinion included with the financial statements will advise you of the exception.

Recall that, in Chapter 4, an adjusting entry was required at year end to accrue the portion of utilities expense and the associated liability for the last few weeks of the year. The event was completed; the power had been consumed. The creditor—the utility company—was known. However, the actual amount was estimated. *Estimated liabilities*, where the amount of the obligation is not known precisely, and even where the payee may not be known, are still included on the balance sheet. Estimated liabilities are included because they are not executory or future-related. The event is completed and the money or service is owed.

In the situation where products are sold under warranty, the sale has been completed, and the firm has an existing obligation to the customer until the warranty period expires. In the Jedro example, based on past experience, the accountant has statistically estimated that $15,000 of warranty expenses next year will be related to sales already completed. An adjusting entry is made at year end, establishing this liability and charging warranty expense. The actual customers involved are not known, any more than actual customers who will fail to pay are known in estimating uncollectible receivables. Nevertheless, the amounts and timing can be reasonably estimated.

The accrual of estimated warranty expense is another example of the matching principle. Estimated repair or replacement costs reduce final profit on any group of warranted products sold. They represent an obligation to provide goods or services related to completed transactions and are properly matched with the revenues recognized in the year when the products are sold. If they were not matched, **next** year's profits would be reduced by expenses which would be part of **this** year's sales.

Note that estimated product warranties are nonmonetary. The obligation is to provide goods or services, and not cash. Also, it should be noted that this obligation exists as of the balance sheet date. It is not contingent or dependent upon the firm's continuing to sell the product or any other future occurrence.

Jedro's potential loss of $500,000 in a lawsuit and its $8,000,000 future purchase commitment, as footnoted, have not been booked, because they represent *contingent liabilities*. Contingent liabilities may be certain as to the amount, payee, and time, but they do not relate to a completed past event as of the balance sheet date. They are contingent or dependent on something happening in the future. As of the balance sheet date, the lawsuit had not been settled. There could be no reasonable estimate of damages to be awarded, because the plaintiff could lose. As of the balance sheet date, the purchase commitment was executory. Obligation to the supplier was contingent upon its supplying items as ordered for future delivery. This may not happen. Note that, even though not booked, material contingent liabilities must, in conformance with GAAP, be disclosed in the footnotes.

UNEARNED REVENUE AND OTHER DEFERRED ITEMS

Assume a situation where a customer has paid in advance for goods or services, and the firm has not provided them as of the balance sheet date. Does the firm have an obligation to the customer which is not contingent? Yes, the customer would have a prepaid asset and the firm would have a liability identified as unearned revenue or revenue collected in advance. Although the cash may have been received, until the company delivers the goods or services the sale or revenue has not been earned. The company has a liability to the customer to deliver the goods or services, or to refund the cash advance. Unearned revenue prepayments received from customers is classified as a current liability until the sale is completed. Jedro has a nonmonetary obligation to provide goods or services in the amount of $50,000. Common situations involving unearned revenue would include advance subscriptions for magazines or spectator tickets, and deposits on specially ordered merchandise.

You may find on balance sheets two other types of deferred or unearned items which are not present as of 12/31/XX in the Jedro example. Suppose a land-sales company was selling unimproved desert lots by mail. Often such sales involve a minimum down payment, with the balance in installments over many years. Where there is a history of a large number of defaults and repossessions, and where it is difficult, if not impossible, to compute reasonable estimates of future bad debts, do you think the accountant should recognizē and report the full sale and profit in the year the sale was made? In such situations, GAAP require that the *installment method* of revenue and profit recognition be followed. Under the installment method, the inventory of land is reduced and installment accounts receivable is increased by the sale. However, the gross profit on the sale is deferred and recognized as earned income only in proportion to cash payments received. Deferred gross profit on installment sales really represents a not-yet-realized increment increasing owners' equity or retained earnings. It does *not* represent an obligation to give resources to anyone. Therefore, it is not a liability, as previously defined.

Nevertheless, probably for the reason that it does not represent an earned increase in owner's equity and since the balance sheet traditionally has only two categories of equities, Deferred Gross Profit on Installment Sales is classified as a liability, often current. In effect, the upper portion of the right side of the balance sheet should be viewed as including liabilities and other items excluded from owners' equity. Another of these nonliability items classified as a liability relates to deferred gain on land sales where the fixed asset, land, is sold on an installment basis.

Note that, although the installment method is readily allowable for tax-reporting purposes, GAAP prohibit its use except in special circumstances similar to the ones described above. Ordinary installment sales—automobiles, appliances, and so forth—where bad debts can be reasonably estimated, and where the payments cover only a few years, are reported in full when made. Anticipated defaults are matched through allowance for uncollectibles and bad-debt expense (see Chapter 11).

DEFERRED INCOME TAX

Another deferred item more like a liability is deferred income tax. As first mentioned in Chapter 1, income-tax regulations incorporate many diverse social subsidies. These subsidies, and timing differences in the recognition of certain revenue and expense items, result in taxable income often quite different from accounting income.

Recall, from Chapter 9, that, generally, tax subsidies to business often take the form of allowing for earlier and more rapid recognition of asset expiration than would be appropriate for financial reporting purposes. When a firm takes proper advantage of these proffered tax-timing differences, the effect is to postpone tax payments. These tax payments would otherwise be required if the firm were using identical methods for financial tax-reporting purposes. The postponed taxes act as a noninterest-bearing loan, which is the form of the subsidy.

To review this effect previously referred to in Chapter 9, assume the following simplified example for a given firm:

- $100,000 asset acquired, 5-year useful life, zero salvage.

Exhibit 12.3
EXAMPLE OF APPLICATION OF DEFERRED INCOME TAX

	Years					
	1	2	3	4	5	Total
Tax Calculations:						
Taxable income before depreciation	$50,000	$50,000	$50,000	$50,000	$50,000	$250,000
Straight-line depreciation	20,000	20,000	20,000	20,000	20,000	100,000
Net taxable income	$30,000	$30,000	$30,000	$30,000	$30,000	$150,000
Tax due at 40%	12,000	12,000	12,000	12,000	12,000	60,000
Taxable income before depreciation	$50,000	$50,000	$50,000	$50,000	$50,000	$250,000
Double-declining balance depreciation	50,000	25,000	12,500	12,500	0	100,000
Net taxable income	0	25,000	37,500	37,500	50,000	150,000
Tax due at 40%	0	10,000	15,000	15,000	20,000	60,000
Balance of taxes postponed	12,000	14,000	11,000	8,000	0	
Financial Statements:						
A ⎰ Income before taxes	$30,000	$30,000	$30,000	$30,000	$30,000	$150,000
⎱ Actual tax expense	0	10,000	15,000	15,000	20,000	60,000
Net income	$30,000	$20,000	$15,000	$15,000	$10,000	$ 90,000
Income before taxes	30,000	30,000	30,000	30,000	30,000	150,000
B ⎰ Tax expense[a]	12,000	12,000	12,000	12,000	12,000	60,000
⎱ Net income	18,000	18,000	18,000	18,000	18,000	90,000
Balance of deferred income tax	12,000	14,000	11,000	8,000	0	

Note (a): Tax expense equals actual taxes due, adjusted for accrual of deferred income tax or recognition of past accrual.

- Both accounting and taxable income before depreciation was $50,000, each year for 5 years.
- Corporate income-tax rate was 40 percent.

Exhibit 12.3 indicates tax liability for each year under two different assumptions. First, depreciation for tax purposes is taken on a five-year, straight-line basis. Second, depreciation for tax purposes is taken on four-year, double-declining-balance depreciation.

Note, in Exhibit 12.3, under tax calculations, that both methods require the firm to pay $60,000 in taxes over the five years. However, using straight-line depreciation for tax purposes results in taxes of $12,000 per year. Using double-declining-balance depreciation and a shorter life for tax purposes shields income from taxes in the early years. The depreciation *tax shield* postpones taxes.

Assume that a firm followed straight-line depreciation for financial reporting purposes and took advantage of double-declining and a shorter life on its tax returns. Exhibit 12.3, subsection A, shows reported net income under this situation. In this section, reported income-tax expense is the actual amount payable in the current year. Look at the net income "bottom line" in the A section. What is the apparent trend in earnings? In reality, the firm is doing equally well each year.

GAAP provide for accruing as tax expense and deferring as deferred income tax, the amounts of postponed tax liability. The result is to normalize, or not to distort, net income. Subsection B of Exhibit 12.3 shows net income determined after provision for deferred income tax, following GAAP. Note that reported net income is $18,000 for all five years, thereby accurately reflecting level operations. Also note that reported tax expense in years 1 and 2 is the sum of actual tax plus the amount accrued. In the remaining three years, reported tax expense is actual tax less amounts previously accrued as deferred income tax.

Deferred Income Tax is another hybrid. The timing of the repayment of this "loan" is uncertain.[4] Payment in a specific year is contingent upon:

- The loan not being "extended" by acquisition of another new asset involving tax deferral;
- There being taxable income in that year (otherwise the "maturing portion" of the loan is effectively cancelled or forgiven).

Therefore, deferred income tax is not monetary. The timing of payment is not certain. Present-value measurement cannot be used to factor out the interest component, again because of uncertain timing of cash flows. Finally, it is not a liability as previously defined, since it is contingent upon future events.

Nevertheless, Jedro's $90,000 of deferred income tax is shown as a noncurrent liability in conformance with GAAP. It clearly does not represent an owner claim or investment. Only to footnote it would result in a distorted income trend, as demonstrated on Exhibit 12.3. Therefore, as the lesser of two evils, it is shown as a liability.[5]

MINORITY INTEREST

The final item appearing on Exhibit 12.1 for the Jedro Corporation is $100,000 of *minority interest*. Minority interest can appear only on a consolidated financial statement, and then only when one or more of the consolidated subsidiaries

---

4   Some tax subsidies represent permanent differences and not timing differences. Permanent differences are not involved in tax deferral.

5   Although unusual in nature and beyond the scope of this book, timing differences can result in tax liabilities in advance of recognition as tax expense with deferred taxes then a noncurrent asset. See Xerox statements in Appendix A.

is (are) less than 100 percent owned. Minority interest represents the owner-ship claim of stockholders holding less than 50 percent of the voting stock of the subsidiaries that have been consolidated. If a subsidiary is not wholly owned, some outside stockholders have owners' equity claims. When the subsidiary's assets and liabilities are combined with the parent's on a consoli-dated statement, the minority claim is included. Minority interest indicates that not all of the combined net assets are claimed, or owned, **solely** by the parent stockholders. It is sometimes included in the stockholders' or owners' equity section, in which case "owners" would mean all owners as distinct from creditors. Other firms follow Jedro's example of disclosing it between liabilities and owner's equity. Classifying minority interest outside of owners' equity has the result that reported "owners" include only Jedro stockholders. Crystal Gurney should recognize that the $100,000 minority interest repre-sents a "nonfamily claim" against certain subsidiary dividends and subsidiary assets in liquidation. It does not represent any obligation or liability.

EARLY DEBT EXTINGUISHMENT

To complete your understanding of liabilities, it is important that you recog-nize several ways that debt can be eliminated (or **extinguished**) other than through payment at maturity. Debt can be replaced by other new debt (re-financing or *refunding*). Debt can be retired in advance of the maturity date —*early debt retirement*. It sometimes can also be retired through exchange for ownership interest (stock)—debt conversion.

Early Debt Retirement

Some long-term notes and bonds carry the privilege of early repayment by the issuing firm. Early repayment can be a privilege for the issuing firm when market interest rates decline and the debt can be refinanced at a lower interest cost. It simultaneously can be a hardship or penalty for the creditor who now must locate a new, equally safe investment with perhaps a lower return.

Early debt retirement, for the foregoing reasons, often involves a prepay-ment penalty charge on loans or an early *call premium* on *callable bonds*. Upon retirement, all related items are removed from the balance sheet. These would include the book value of the liability—face value and any unamortized premium or discount—and related unamortized deferred charges. If the sum of the cash paid as part of the retirement (that is, face value plus prepayment penalty or call premium) plus the unamortized deferred charges which are eliminated, exceeds the book value of the debt eliminated, there is a loss on early debt retirement. If the sum is less than the net debt eliminated, there is a gain. Gains or losses on early debt retirement are reported as revenues or expenses in the year they occur.

Exhibit 12.4 gives an example of the balance sheet changes resulting from

Exhibit 12.4
EXAMPLE OF RESULTS OF EARLY DEBT RETIREMENT

Immediately preceding retirement

Cash	$1,500,000	Bonds payable	$1,000,000
Deferred charges	30,000	Less bond discount	(80,000)
		Owners' Equity	610,000
	$1,530,000		$1,530,000

Cash payment to retire = $1,050,000 ($1,000,000 face or maturity value, plus $50,000 call premium)

Immediately after early retirement

Cash	$ 450,000	Owners' Equity[a]	$ 450,000

Note (a):
Assets used or eliminated in retirement:

$1,050,000	Cash
30,000	Deferred charges
1,080,000	

Net liabilities eliminated in retirement:

$1,000,000	Bonds payable
(80,000)	Bond discount
$ 920,000	

Therefore, loss on retirement equals $160,000.

early debt retirement. A $1,000,000 bond issue with $80,000 of unamortized discount is retired with a payment of $1,050,000 cash. The $1,000,000 is the maturity value of the bonds, and $50,000 is the call premium or prepayment penalty. The $30,000 of deferred charges were related to the bond issue and, therefore, are also eliminated by the early retirement. The assets used or expiring exceed the net liabilities eliminated by $160,000. This amount therefore represents the loss on early retirement.

Refunding

Early retirement may be part of a replacement of old debt with new debt—a refinancing or a refunding of debt. New debt may be "sold" and the cash proceeds used to retire old debt. There also may be a direct exchange of debt instruments, new bonds or notes exchanged for old, with no cash changing hands. Regardless of the method used, GAAP require that the old debt and associated unamortized premium, or discount, and deferred charges, be treated as an independent early retirement. Therefore, a gain or loss on refunding may be realized just as for early retirement, as described above.

Debt Conversion

Some bond issues provide the bondholders with the option of exchanging their bonds for shares of stock at a fixed number of shares per bond.[6] The exchange of debt for ownership interest is called **debt conversion**. Bonds or debentures which have a conversion privilege are known as convertible debentures (or CVD's).

Where a CVD is converted, the accountant removes from the liability account(s) the amount of net liability (the book value) represented by the CVD's converted. The bonds payable liability is removed along with the associated unamortized premium or discount. Any related unamortized deferred charges are also written off.

To complete recording a CVD conversion, the accountant will restore the balance sheet equality by increasing owner's equity by the amount of the net CVD liability removed. Total equities are unchanged by conversion. Conversion represents a mere exchange of equities. In the case of a corporation with par- or stated-value stock, the net CVD claim is added to capital stock in the amount of the new par stock issued in conversion. Any excess goes to paid-in capital. Recall, from Chapter 7, that debt conversion is one of three "matched pairs" of nonfund resource flows reported in the statement of changes in financial position.

As an example of a bond conversion, assume the following facts pertain to the Mugg Company:

Bonds payable (5 percent)	$500,000	(500 $1000 par bonds)
Unamortized bond discount	(10,000)	
Capital stock	$1,000,000	($10 par, 100,000 shares issued)
Conversion ratio =		90 stock shares per bond
Current market price of Mugg Company =		$15 per share.

In response to the $15 market price, the bondholders exchange (convert) each $1,000 bond into 90 shares of stock with a market value of $1,350. Following the earlier description, and using your intuition with respect to this simple exchange of equities, you should indicate on a piece of paper the balance sheet effect if all bondholders converted. Do this before reading further.

You are correct and fully understand the balance sheet effect of conversion if you showed zero balances in the **bonds payable** and **bond discount** accounts and $450,000 and $40,000, respectively, for **capital stock** and **paid-in capital**. Of the $490,000 book value of debt extinguished by the conversion, $450,000 (500 bonds times 90 shares times $10 par) is added to capital stock,

---

[6]   In more advanced texts you may learn that preferred stock can also be convertible on a fixed conversion ratio to common stock. Convertible preferred is not very common. It will not be discussed further in this text.

representing the par value of additional shares issued. The balance of $40,000, representing an excess over par, is shown as paid-in capital.

Before leaving debt conversion, it is important that you recognize its effect upon **earnings per share** (EPS). Prior to conversion, there were 100,000 shares of common stock outstanding. After conversion, there were 145,000 shares outstanding. What effect does conversion have upon the firm's earnings? If, before conversion, EPS had been $1.50, what would EPS now be after conversion?

Conversion improves the firm's liquidity. But that has no immediate effect in net income. Annual interest expense in the amount of $25,000 is no longer required. Since interest is tax-deductible, taxable income will increase $25,000. At a 40-percent income-tax rate, taxes would increase $10,000. Therefore, the after-tax savings on conversion would be $15,000. Earnings before conversion were $150,000 ($1.50 EPS times 100,000 shares). Earnings after conversion would be $165,000. EPS after conversion would be $1.14 (rounded). EPS would be down $0.36, or 24 percent!

The actual dilution of EPS resulting from conversion, or even the potential for such dilution offered by CVD's not yet converted, is of great significance to the common stockholder and to stock prices. In Chapter 13 you will find that accountants take such potential dilution so seriously that they will report modified EPS data on the income statement.

REVIEW OF LIABILITY CHANGES

You should now be in a position to answer all of Crystal Gurney's questions with respect to the Jedro Corporation balance sheet, and you should be able to generalize your knowledge to other firms. Exhibit 12.5 lists the most common liabilities which you may find on a balance sheet. For each liability, the common transactions and adjustments that may affect its balance are also given.

Exhibit 12.5
CHANGES AFFECTING BALANCE SHEET LIABILITIES AND CONTRA-LIABILITIES*

*Note. Does not include changes to correct for error or to record extraordinary items.

Account	Effect
Current Notes Payable	Increased by: Issuing promissory note as part of loan or purchase (83) Currently maturing portion of long-term notes (84) Issuing promissory note to replace account payable (85)

(Continued)

Exhibit 12.5 (continued)

Account	Effect
	Decreased by:
	Retirement by payment of cash (86)
	Replacement with long-term note (87)
Discount on Current Notes Payable (Valuation item)	**Increased by:**
	Amount of interest included in note face value not yet owed (88)
	Decreased by:
	Adjustment for amount of interest owed (89)
	Retirement or replacement of note (90)
Accounts Payable	**Increased by:**
	Purchases of goods and services on account (91)
	Decreased by:
	Payments of cash (92)
	Taking proffered discount for early payment (93)
	Replacement with promissory note payable (94)
Current Obligation under Capital Lease	**Increased by:**
	Executing lease agreement containing current payment provision (95)
	Maturing "principal" portion of noncurrent capital-lease obligation (96)
	Accrual of current interest portion of capital-lease obligation (97)
	Decreased by:
	Payments of cash (98)
Dividends Payable	**Increased by:**
	Declaration of cash dividend (99)
	Decreased by:
	Payment of cash dividend (100)
Various Accrued or Estimated Liabilities (Rent, interest, wages, taxes, etc.)	**Increased by:**
	Adjustment accruing estimated amount owed to date (101)
	Decreased by:
	Payment of cash (102)
	Reversal to avoid double counting (103)
	Adjustment reflecting new estimate (104)
Unearned Revenue	**Increased by:**
	Receipts of customer advances or deposits (105)

Exhibit 12.5 (continued)

Account	Effect
	Decreased by:
	Delivery of goods or services to customers (106)
	Returns of advances or deposits to customers (107)
Other Current Liabilities	Increased by:
	Incurrence of liability (108)
	Maturing portion of bonds payable (109)
	Decreased by:
	Payment of cash (110)
	Replacement with noncurrent debt (111)
Noncurrent Notes and Bonds Payable	Increased by:
	Issuing debt instrument as part of loan or purchase (112)
	Issuing debt instrument as replacement for other liability (113)
	Decreased by:
	Portion maturing to current classification (114)
	Early retirement by payment of cash (115)
	Replacement by other noncurrent debt (116)
	Conversion to ownership status (117)
Premium on Bonds Payable (Valuation item)	Increased by:
	Portion of proceeds of bond issue to be returned to creditor as part of higher interest (118)
	Decreased by:
	Adjustment for amortization (119)
	Early retirement or replacement of bonds (120)
	Conversion of bonds to ownership status (121)
Discount on Noncurrent Notes and Bonds Payable (Valuation item)	Increased by:
	Amount of interest included in note or bond face value not yet owed (122)
	Decreased by:
	Adjustment for amount of interest now owed—amortization (123)
	Early retirement or replacement of note or bond (124)
	Conversion of bonds to ownership status (125)
Noncurrent Obligation under Capital Lease	Increased by:
	Executing lease agreement (126)
	Decreased by:
	Maturing "principal" portion to current classification (127)

(Continued)

Exhibit 12.5 (continued)

Account	Effect
Deferred Income Tax	Increased by: Adjustment reflecting amount of tax liability deferred (128)
	Decreased by: Adjustment for amount of previously deferred tax liability currently payable (129) Adjustment for amount of previously deferred tax liability no longer owed (130)

Possible transactions and adjustments are listed. Review this exhibit carefully. For each numbered transaction or adjustment (83–130), make sure that you can:

1. Visualize a specific example.

2. Identify the other half of the entry that might be involved—that is, the other (eventual) balance sheet balancing effect.

LIABILITY CHANGES INVOLVING FUNDS FLOWS

To complete your understanding of liability changes, you should recognize which changes involve flows of net working capital and which do not. You will need to identify those changes that are included in income from operations but that do not involve funds flows. These will contribute to a difference between income from operations and funds from operations. You will also need to know which changes are reported on the Statement of Changes in Financial Position (SCFP) and how they are reported.

Changes to Current Liabilities

All changes to current liabilities (except an exchange of one current liability for another and the payment of a current liability) involve flows of net working capital. They will be reflected in another item reported on the SCFP. The following table indicates how these changes are reflected.

Current liability change related to:	Reflected on SCFP as part of:
Expense (transaction or accrual)	Funds from operations
Expenditure for noncurrent assets	Cost of new noncurrent asset acquired
New dividend payable	Dividends
Refinancing of noncurrent debt	Additional noncurrent debt
Maturing portion of noncurrent debt	Extinguishment of noncurrent debt

Changes to Noncurrent Liabilities

Changes to noncurrent liabilities, which involve current assets or current liabilities, represent flows of working capital and are reported on the SCFP as shown on the following table:

Noncurrent liability change related to:	Reported on SCFP as:
New long-term loan (Cash)	Additional noncurrent debt
Retirement of existing loan (Cash)	Extinguishment of noncurrent debt
Refinancing of existing current liability	Both additional noncurrent debt and extinguishment of noncurrent debt
Maturing portion of long-term obligation	Extinguishment of noncurrent debt

Changes to noncurrent liabilities which involve noncurrent assets would represent what was referred to as a "matched pair" in Chapter 7. New noncurrent debt, as part of the acquisition of a new noncurrent asset, would be reported on the SCFP as Additional Noncurrent Debt (source) together with the Additional or New Noncurrent Asset Acquired (application). Changes to Noncurrent Liabilities which involve owners' equity (debt conversion) would be another matched pair. Debt conversion would be reported on the SCFP as additional owner investment—New Stock Issued (source) and Extinguishment of Noncurrent Debt (application).

Finally, there are changes to noncurrent liability valuation accounts (discount and premium) that are included in income from operations but do not involve working capital flows. Bond or Noncurrent Note Discount (liability) amortization is included as part of interest expense. The amount of liability amortization must be added back to income (along with depreciation) in arriving at funds from operations. Bond Premium (liability) amortization is included as a reduction of reported interest expense. As it also is not an inflow of funds, the amount of bond premium amortization must be subtracted from income in arriving at funds from operations. These adjustments to income, together with all others previously introduced, are included on a complete checklist that is included with SCFP Preparer Procedures at the end of Chapter 14.

CHAPTER OVERVIEW

Based upon the material contained in this chapter, you should now be able to:

- State the standards for the initial valuation of liabilities in conformance with GAAP;
- Describe the differences among certain liabilities, estimated liabilities, contingent liabilities; give examples of each; and state how and why each is disclosed in the financial statements;
- Explain the meaning of present value and how it relates to liability measurement;
- Identify those items included with liabilities which are nonmonetary or which do not represent legal obligations to give resources to an outsider, and explain why each is shown on the balance sheet together with liabilities;
- Describe how amortization of liability valuation accounts affects income and specifically interest expense, and explain the rationale for such treatment;
- Describe three different ways noncurrent debt may be extinguished or exchanged prior to maturity, and explain with examples the possible effect of each transaction on the balance sheet and income statement;
- Explain the meaning of minority interest and the reasons for disclosing it, either within or separate from owners' equity;
- Describe those liability changes that do not involve a flow of net working capital, explain which of these are involved in adjusting income to determine funds from operations, and state how the adjustment to income is made.

NEW VOCABULARY AND CONCEPTS

Obligations under capital leases	Tax shield
Serial bonds	Minority interest
"Certain liabilities"	Refunding
"Booked"	Early debt retirement
Estimated liabilities	Call premium
Contingent liabilities	Callable bonds
Installment method	CVD

- Differences among certain, estimated, and contingent liabilities and their treatment by accountants.
- Minority interest in consolidation.
- EPS dilution from convertible securities.

REVIEW QUESTIONS

1. a) What are the basic objectives/requirements of liability measurement and reporting under GAAP? (b) What are the similarities to the standards for assets?

2. What does the amount of unamortized discount on notes or bonds payable represent?

3. Discount on payables is amortized to what account? As an increase or decrease?

4. What does unamortized premium on bonds payable represent?

5. a) To what account is premium on bonds payable amortized? (b) Is the effect to increase or decrease the balance in this account? Explain.

6. a) Why doesn't the timing of maturation of noncurrent capital-lease obligation coincide with the amortization of the related leased asset? (b) What is the basis for reclassifying portions of the noncurrent capital-lease obligation to a current liability?

7. Why is there a difference between the currently maturing portion of a capital-lease obligation and the actual lease payment to be made? What does this difference represent?

8. Give examples of estimated and contingent liabilities, and explain the difference.

9. Why are estimated liabilities "booked" and contingent liabilities only footnoted?

10. a) What is unearned revenue? (b) Why isn't it an asset? (c) Give examples of deferred revenue.

11. a) What is deferred income tax? (b) What situation could bring about an increase in deferred income tax? (c) A decrease?

12. a) What is a tax shield? (b) What is its effect?

13. a) What is minority interest? (b) In what circumstances and on which financial statements does it appear?

14. a) What is a CVD? (b) What is meant by debt conversion?

15. If a corporation has, on 12/31/X0, $100,000 of long-term debt in the form of CVD's (liabilities) together with unamortized premium of $11,000, and on 1/1/X1 all of these bonds are converted, how much will be added to corporate owners' equity?

16. a) Describe "dilution of earnings" resulting from debt conversion. (b) Can such a dilution or potential dilution be significant to common stockholders? Explain.

17. Why is there often a penalty payment or a call premium given to the creditor as part of early debt extinguishment?

18. What accounts may be involved in the early retirement of bonds?

19. What are the sources of possible gain or loss on early debt extinguishment?

MINI-CASES AND QUESTIONS FOR DISCUSSION

MC 12.1. One way of viewing a bond premium is as an extra payment or gift given by the buyer to obtain the bond. The bond obligation—interest payments plus maturity principal payment—is the same with or without a premium.

Why don't accountants recognize all bond premium received as revenue or as a gift at the time of sale of the bond? After all, all of the investment tax credit—a subsidy (gift) from the government—may be recognized as revenue in the year obtained. If accountants can recognize a "profit on a purchase," why not a "profit on a loan"? Discuss.

MC 12.2. Except for deferred income tax, accountants normally disclose long-term liabilities at their present value. That is, their "principal" value excluding explicit or implicit interest at the going rate for similar obligations at the time incurred. How can this be true when:

a) Bonds and notes are shown at their face or maturity value regardless of whether interest is included therein?

b) Capital lease obligations are not shown at the sum of all payments?

c) Some notes with explicit interest have associated discount and others do not?

Discuss. Also discuss why deferred income tax is treated differently.

MC 12.3. Future-interest obligations are excluded from liability measurement, as they are executory. Why, then, is Bond Premium shown as a liability? It doesn't even represent payments which will be made, as these are already part of the bond obligation. Discuss.

MC 12.4. When a bond is subject to early extinguishment (early retirement or refunding), associated premium or discount may not be carried forward to future years. A gain or loss on early extinguishment may result. However, when a bond is converted, the book value is carried forward in owners' equity and no gain or loss is recognized. Isn't this inconsistent? Discuss.

ESSENTIAL PROBLEMS

EP 12.1. The following is a list of future real and potential obligations for a firm as of 12/31/XX. Identify each as being: "D" for definite (or certain); or "E" for estimated; or "C" for contingent or executory.

a) The monthly rental payment two months from now on an apartment for which you have just signed a two-year lease.

b) The final game of a five-game series for which you have already sold both series tickets and advance-sale game tickets.

c) A bank loan due next month taken out by a friend who had you co-sign the loan as a guarantor.

d) Possible water damage from roof leaks. You have installed the roof and have guaranteed it for two more years.

e) Possible repairs to the same roof cited in (d) above.

f) Damages awarded against you by a court in a lawsuit. You are currently appealing the decision.

g) Final installment payment on a truck that you have used for four years, and that was just destroyed by fire.

h) Payment owed to a bookmaker for a bet on a horse race. The race has been run and your horse lost.

EP 12.2. During the year, your firm recorded all customer sales in the sales revenue account as the sale was made. At year end, total sales in the account was $120,000. In making your year-end adjustments, you find out that two separate sales totaling $7,000 have not been completed. The customers have paid in full, but the merchandise was damaged in delivery, and replacement merchandise has not yet been received for delivery to the customers.

a) Sales on your firm's income statement for the year should be reported as what amount?

b) If your answer to (a) is less than $120,000, how should the difference be reported and on what statement?

EP 12.3. Eight-percent 20-year bonds with a maturity value of $300,000 are sold on 1/1/X1 at a premium. The sale proceeds are $320,000. Indicate the effect of this transaction on the selling firm's balance sheet: accounts affected, amount, and direction—increase/decrease—of the effect.

EP 12.4. Six-percent 20-year bonds with a maturity value of $300,000 are sold on 1/1/X1 at a discount. The sale proceeds are $260,000. Indicate the effect of this transaction on the selling firm's balance sheet: accounts affected, amount, and direction—increase/decrease.

EP 12.5. Refer to the bonds issued in Problem EP 12.3. Assume that full annual interest was payable annually on 12/31, and had been paid that day. Total interest expense for the year 19X1 related to the eight-percent bonds should be reported as what amount on the income statement?

EP 12.6. Refer to the bonds issued in Problem EP 12.4. Assume that annual interest is payable semiannually on 6/30 and 12/31. The 6/30 payment has been made, but the 12/31 payment will be a few days late. Give the correct balances, before closing, in each of the following accounts related to the six-percent bonds:

a) Six-percent bonds payable.

b) Discount on six-percent bonds.

c) 19X1 interest expense appearing on the income statement.

EP 12.7. The Beaver Company acquired equipment under a capital lease signed on 1/1/X2. The lease contract called for payments as follows:

Within 10 days of signing:	$50,000
At end of first year:	25,000
At end of second year:	15,000
At end of each of the remaining eight years:	10,000

The present value of these payments appropriately discounted for the Beaver Company was:

10-day payment	$ 50,000
First-year payment	18,949
Second-year payment	10,465
Third-year payment	6,302
Remaining payments	39,924
Total	$125,640

Assume that the first payment was made as scheduled, and that the second payment would be made a few days late on 1/2/X3. Also assume that the leased asset was being amortized, with the estimate of a 10-year life and zero salvage value, by the years' digits method. As of 12/31/X2, before closing, what would the appropriate balances be in the following?

a) Property under capital lease,

b) Current obligations under capital lease,

c) Noncurrent obligations under capital lease,

d) 19X2 lease interest expense.

EP 12.8. Refer to the data given for the Beaver Company in Problem EP 12.7. Assume that, as of 12/31/X3, the second and third lease payments have been made. As of 12/31/X3, before closing, what would the appropriate balances be in the following?

a) Property under capital lease,

b) Current obligations under capital lease,

c) Noncurrent obligations under capital lease,

d) 19X3 lease interest expense.

SUPPLEMENTARY PROBLEMS

SP 12.9. The Cadwallader Corporation has equipment which it is depreciating for tax purposes on the double-declining-balance method. In its financial statements, it is electing straight-line. In the first year, $50,000 depreciation is taken for tax purposes and $25,000 for financial-reporting purposes. Assume taxable and accounting income before depreciation was $175,000, and the tax rate was 40 percent. As of the end of the year before closing, the appropriate balances would be what amounts for the following accounts?

a) Taxes payable (assuming no prepayments during year),

b) Deferred income tax,

c) Provision for income taxes.

SP 12.10. Refer to the Cadwallader Corporation data given in Problem SP 12.9. At the beginning of the third year, the balance of deferred income taxes was $10,000. Third-year depreciation for tax purposes was $12,500, and third-year depreciation for financial-reporting purposes was $25,000. Assume third-year taxable and accounting income before depreciation was $240,-000, and the tax rate was still 40 percent.

As of the end of the third year before closing, the appropriate account balances would be what amounts, for the following?

a) Taxes payable (assuming no prepayments during year),

b) Deferred income tax,

c) Income tax expense.

SP 12.11. The equity portion of the Dagwood Corporation's 12/31/X0 balance sheet was as follows (000 omitted):

Total Current Liabilities	$ 150
7% convertible debentures	600
Discount on debentures	(80)
Total Liabilities	$ 670
Capital stock	1,200
Paid-in capital	400
Retained earnings	900
Total Equities	$3,170

The common stock had a par value of $10 per share. Each $1,000 face-value CVD was convertible into 25 shares of common stock.

The market price of Dagwood's stock climbed above $40 per share, and half of the bondholders converted their bonds on 1/1/X1. Give the balances in the following accounts after this conversion:

a) 7% convertible debentures;

b) Discount on debentures;

c) Capital stock;

d) Paid-in capital.

SP 12.12. Refer to the data given for the Dagwood Corporation in Problem SP 12.11. During 19X0 and previously, bond discount was being amortized on a straight-line basis at $10,000 per year. Assume that the events described in Problem SP 12.11 have transpired. It is now July 1, 19X1, and one-third of the remaining bondholders elect conversion. As part of this latest conversion:

a) How much should be added to the capital-stock account?

b) How much should be added to the paid-in capital account?

SP 12.13. Refer to the Dagwood Corporation's partial statement given in Problem SP 12.11. Assume that, instead of climbing, the market price of Dagwood's common stock was $15 per share as of 12/31/X0, and there was no reasonable expectation that it would change in the near future. The CVD's were callable at a call premium of $40 per $1,000 bond. The CVD's have been called, and all were surrendered for redemption on 1/1/X1.

a) How much cash should be given to the bondholders as part of this early debt extinguishment?

b) Would there be a gain or loss on debt extinguishment? How much?

SP 12.14. The Erstwhile Corporation, on 12/31/X0, had an outstanding issue of eight-percent bonds with a maturity value of $700,000. Associated with these bonds, as of 12/31/X0, were unamortized bond premiums of $95,000 and unamortized deferred charges of $30,000. The call premium was $50 per $1,000 bond.

Assume that the bonds have been called, and were presented for redemption on 1/1/X1. Would there be a gain or loss on this early debt extinguishment? How much?

SP 12.15. The following information is taken from the Foxwater Corporation's 12/31/X0 balance sheet and accompanying footnotes:

5% bonds payable[a]	$800,000
Capital stock[b]	$1,200,000
19X0 EPS	$1.00

[a]   Convertible—each $1000 bond entitled to receive 80 shares of common stock if converted.

[b] $10 par; issued and outstanding shares have not changed for past several years.

Assuming that income tax was assessed at 40 percent of net income before taxes, that all bondholders elect conversion on 1/1/X1, that the company has no other interest-bearing debt, and that 19X1 earnings before interest and taxes will be the same as in 19X0, what would be EPS for 19X1?

SP 12.16. The following information is taken from the Gemini Corporation's 12/31/X4 balance sheet and accompanying footnotes:

7% bonds payable[a]	$900,000
Capital stock[b]	$1,000,000
Paid-in capital	340,000
19X4 EPS	$.25

[a]   Convertible—each $1000 bond entitled to receive 900 shares of common stock if converted.

[b] $1 par; issued and outstanding shares 800,000 on 12/31/X3; on 12/31/X4, all shares issued were outstanding.

What would 19X4 EPS have been if one-half of the bondholders had converted on 1/1/X4? Assume all other 19X4 events and adjustments were the same except for interest and income taxes, and that taxes were 35 percent of net income before tax.

SP 12.17. Refer to Exhibit 12.5. For transactions and adjustments 83–100, identify by number those which:

a) Involve revenue,

b) Involve expense,

c) Do not involve either revenue or expense.

SP 12.18. For transactions and adjustments 101–130 on Exhibit 12.5, make the same identifications as required in Problem SP 12.17.

SP 12.19. Refer to Exhibit 12.5. For transactions and adjustments 83–100, identify by number those which:

a) Do not involve a flow of net working capital and do not involve either revenue or expense.

b) Do not involve a flow of net working capital but do involve either revenue or expense (are included in income from operations).

c) Involve a flow of net working capital but do not involve either revenue or expense.

d) Involve a flow of net working capital and involve revenue or expense (are included in income from operations).

SP 12.20. For transactions and adjustments 101–130 on Exhibit 12.5, make the same identifications as required in Problem SP 12.19.

PREPARER PROCEDURES

This section will cover preparer procedures related to the liabilities that were introduced in this chapter. Then a distinct subsection will be devoted to payroll accounting. Payroll procedures do not involve conceptual difficulties. The many related payroll tax regulations do, however, introduce considerable detail and complexity.

A knowledge of payroll procedure is not essential to understanding and using financial statements. It is important to understanding your own paycheck as an employee. Also, traditionally, a student who satisfactorily completes elementary accounting is supposed to at least understand payroll and cash reconciliation. Cash reconciliation will be covered in an appendix to Chapter 14.

Liabilities Involving Discounts or Premiums

A liability originally issued at a premium or discount involves a compound entry. The sale of a $1,000 bond at a premium for $1,150 would be journalized:

	DR	CR
Cash	$1,150	
Bonds Payable		$1,000
Bond Premium		150

The sale of a $1,000 bond at a discount for $900 would be journalized:

Cash	$ 900	
Bond Discount	100	
Bonds Payable		$1,000

Both bond premium and bond or note discount are amortized by adjustment to interest expense but with opposite effects. Adjustment to amortize $40 of bond premium would be journalized:

Bond Premium	$ 40	
Interest Expense		$ 40

Adjustment to amortize $50 of bond discount would be journalized:

Interest Expense	$ 50	
Bond Discount		$ 50

Note that bond premium amortization reduces annual interest expense, whereas amortization of bond discount increases it.

Capital-Lease Obligations

A capital lease is originally journalized by the lessee with the asset value equal to the sum of the discounted present value of all required lease payments (for example, $130,000). The present value of the current lease payment (for example, $30,000) is recorded as a current liability. The present value of the noncurrent payments (for example, $100,000) is recorded as a noncurrent liability:

	DR	CR
Property under Capital Lease	$130,000	
Current Capital-Lease Obligations		$ 30,000
Noncurrent Capital-Lease		
Obligations		100,000

Thereafter, the asset and liability components of capital leases are treated separately. Interest in the amount of the difference between the present value of a payment and its stated value (for example, $35,000) may be accrued to the current obligation account.

	DR	CR
Interest Expense	$ 5,000	
Current Capital-Lease Obligations		$ 5,000

Also, each year, the present value of the subsequent year's lease payment is reclassified from noncurrent obligations to current.

Estimated Liabilities

The allowance for estimated warranty expense, and for other similar liability accruals made for matching purposes, is usually a single year-end adjustment; for example:

	DR	CR
Warranty Repairs Expense	$14,000	
Estimated Product Warranties		$14,000

At the start of the next year, this entry (together with all other adjusting accruals involving anticipations) is reversed, to avoid the possibility of double-counting:

	DR	CR
Estimated Product Warranties	$14,000	
Warranty Repairs Expense		$14,000

Note that this reversal affects the next year's expense account which will thus open with a $14,000 credit, or "negative" balance. Suppose during this "next" year, total warranty repairs amounted to $89,000, of which only $75,000 related to current year's sales. The $89,000 is charged to the expense account initially having a $14,000 credit balance. The ending balance would be $75,000 debit, properly identifying the $75,000 of "additional" expense applicable to the current year. Of course, estimates are never perfect in an actual situation. The amount of the year-end accrual ($14,000 above) is determined as the balance necessary to update the accounts and compensate for the prior year's estimation error. Preferred warranty expense in any one year on the income statement is therefore understood to include:

- Actual expenses of the current year applicable to current revenues, plus
- Estimated expenses expected to occur next year but applicable to the current year's revenues, plus or minus
- Prior year's estimation error.

Unearned Revenue

Often unearned revenue is treated as a year-end exception. It is established at year end by an adjustment to sales for those sales recorded but not completed:

	DR	CR
Sales	$XXX	
Unearned Revenue		$XXX

The entry is then reversed at the start of the new year.

Deferred Income Tax

Each year, income tax is calculated on two bases:

1. Provision (amount that would be due) for taxes assuming all permanent differences between accounting income and taxable income and assuming no timing differences, and
2. Actual current tax liability after allowing for timing differences.

Assume the provision amounted to $174,000, but the actual current year's liability was only $136,000 because of tax-shield timing differences. The item $38,000 would need to be deferred as a future "liability." The entry recording taxes would be:

	DR	CR
Provision for Income Taxes	$174,000	
Income Taxes Payable		$136,000
Deferred Income Tax		38,000

In subsequent years when (if) the timing differences were reversed, the amounts previously deferred would be presumed as being paid as part of the current liability. Assume the provision amounted to $205,000 with the actual current liability in that year equaling $230,000. $25,000 of the deferred liability is now payable. The journal entry would call for:

	DR	CR
Provision for Income Taxes	$205,000	
Deferred Income Tax	25,000	
Income Taxes Payable		$230,000

Note that, each year, the provision for income taxes appearing on the income statement is normalized to include taxes temporarily postponed and to exclude previously postponed taxes now due.

Minority Interest

Procedures for accounting for minority interest in consolidation are beyond the scope of an elementary text. Minority interest is discussed further in Chapter 15.

Early Debt Retirement or Refunding

In the case of early debt retirement or refunding, we begin, as a first step, by updating all accounts related to the debt being extinguished. Then the related amounts are eliminated in conjunction with the cash payment—maturity value plus call premium—and a balancing gain or loss is recorded.

For example, assume that four hundred $1,000 six-percent bonds were called and redeemed on 4/1/X1 with a call premium of $50 each. Also assume that interest is payable semiannually on 6/30 and 12/31, and that, associated with this bond issue as of 12/31/X0, are $19,200 of unamortized bond discount and $6,400 of unamortized deferred charges. Deferred charges are being amortized at $1,600 per year, and bond discount is being amortized at $4,300 annually. Two entries—one accruing the interest liability and one updating amortization—would be required before the entry recording the extinguishment:

	DR	CR
Interest Expense	$6,000	
Accrued Interest Payable		$6,000
Interest Expense	$1,600	
Bond Discount		$1,200
Deferred Charges		400

The redemption entry would then be:

	DR	CR
Bonds Payable	$400,000	
Loss on early debt extinguishment	44,000	
Cash		$42,000
Bond Discount		18,000
Deferred Charges		6,000

Debt Conversion

Debt conversion also first involves updating amortization of debt discount or premium and any deferred charges and also accruing any interest payable through the conversion date. Then the debt and related amounts are eliminated, and the net debt amount is added to capital stock and paid-in capital.

For example, assume the same six-percent bond issue described above under debt retirement were extinguishd on 4/1/X1 by conversion to common stock. Assume the bonds or debentures are convertible into 50 shares of $10 par stock for each $1,000 bond. The two entries accruing interest and updating amortization would be the same as shown above for early retirement.

The entry recording conversion would then be as follows:

	DR	CR
Bonds Payable	$400,000	
Bond Discount		$18,000
Deferred Charges		6,000
Capital Stock		200,000
Paid-in Capital		176,000

PAYROLL ACCOUNTING

If you have been a regular employee, you are aware that your take-home pay is much less than you actually earn. The difference represents **payroll deductions** withheld from your paycheck by the employer. Payroll deductions include payroll taxes and other deductions authorized by employees (union dues, retirement contributions, stock-purchase plans, and so forth). Are you also aware that your cost to your employer is even greater than your total earnings? Employers are required to pay additional payroll taxes on the earnings of employees.

Payroll taxes and authorized deductions can make payroll accounting complex and time-consuming even for just a few employees. It is usually simpler to consider payroll accounting in two separate parts: first, the determination and recording of the actual payroll liability based on employee earnings, and then the recording of the employer's additional payroll-tax liability.

An employee's gross earnings (wage or salary plus overtime) may be subject to the following deductions:

- Federal income taxes (varies, depending upon number of employee's authorized dependents),
- State income taxes (varies, depending upon number of employee's authorized dependents),
- Federal Social Security (F.I.C.A.) taxes (apply only to certain maximum amount of employee earnings),
- State disability insurance taxes (apply only to a certain amount of earnings, different from F.I.C.A. ceilings),
- Other voluntary deductions (may be a fixed amount per payroll period, or a proportion of earnings, sometimes with a ceiling).

Can you see from the above the source of complexity? For each separate employee, the accountant must determine:

- Gross earnings for the payroll period,
- Applicable federal and state income taxes, based on the individual employee's earnings and claimed dependents,
- Applicable F.I.C.A. taxes (beyond a cumulative year's earnings ceiling, no taxes are applicable),
- Applicable state disability taxes (beyond a different cumulative year's earnings and in some states, no taxes are applicable),
- Applicable other deductions (as authorized by each employee separately).

Assume that a total weekly payroll amounted to $60,000 of wages and $30,000 of salaries earned. And assume that the totals of individually determined deductions were:

• $18,000   of federal income taxes to be withheld,
• $ 4,500   of state income taxes to be withheld,
• $ 5,400   of F.I.C.A. taxes to be withheld,
• $ 900   of state disability taxes to be withheld,
• $ 450   of union dues withheld.

The entry recording the week's payroll liability would be:

	DR	CR
Wages Expense	$60,000	
Salaries Expense	30,000	
Employee Federal Income Taxes Payable		$18,000
Employee State Income Taxes Payable		4,500
F.I.C.A. Employee Taxes Payable		5,400
State Disability Taxes Payable		900
Union Dues Payable		450
Cash (take-home pay)		60,750

The *employer's* payroll tax liability could include:

• F.I.C.A. taxes (exactly matches employee contribution),
• Federal unemployment (F.U.T.A.) taxes,
• State unemployment taxes,
• State disability taxes.

Assume, for the same weekly payroll period as above, that these taxes amounted to $5,400, $3,600, $900, and $1,800, respectively. The appropriate journal entry would then be:

	DR	CR
Payroll Tax Expense	$11,700	
F.I.C.A. Taxes Payable		$5,400
F.U.T.A. Taxes Payable		3,600
State Unemployment Taxes Payable		900
State Disability Taxes Payable		1,800

Note also that employer total payroll costs can often include expenses which are not payroll taxes as such. Examples would include costs of health insurance, supplementary unemployment benefits, pension-fund contributions, and the like. These "fringe benefit" items would be journalized in a manner similar to that for payroll taxes.

PREPARER PROBLEMS

PP 12.1. Refer to Problem 12.2 above. Prepare the necessary year-end adjusting entry deferring the unearned revenue. Also prepare the next year's opening reversal entry.

PP 12.2. Refer to Problems EP 12.3 and EP 12.4 above. Journalize both sales in good form.

PP 12.3. Refer to Problem EP 12.5 above. Give the three entries to accrue annual interest, to record subsequent payment, and to record premium amortization.

PP 12.4. Refer to Problem EP 12.6 above. Give the four entries to:
- Accrue 6/30 interest,
- Accrue 12/31 interest,
- Record payment of 6/30 interest,
- Amortize bond discount.

PP 12.5. Refer to Problem EP 12.7 above. Give all entries during the first year related to the capital lease, including:
- Acquisition,
- First payment,
- Interest accrual,
- Maturing second-year obligation,
- Asset amortization.

PP 12.6. Refer to Problem EP 12.8 above. Give all entries during the second year related to the capital lease, including:
- Delayed first-year payment,
- Second-year payment,
- Interest accrual,
- Maturing third-year obligation.

PP 12.7. Refer to Problem SP 12.9 above. Give the entry establishing deferred income tax during the first year.

PP 12.8. Refer to Problem SP 12.10 above. Give the entry reducing deferred income tax during the third year.

PP 12.9. Refer to Problem SP 12.11 above. Give the entry recording the debt conversion.

PP 12.10. Refer to Problem SP 12.12 above. Give the entry recording the debt conversion.

PP 12.11. Refer to Problem SP 12.13 above. Give the entry recording the early debt extinguishment.

PP 12.12. Refer to Problem SP 12.14 above. Give the entries updating the accounts and recording the early debt extinguishment.

PP 12.13. Prepare in good form the two journal entries necessary to record the weekly payroll and the **employer's** payroll tax and other related liabilities, given the following data:

Salaries earned	$60,000
Income taxes to be withheld	12,000
F.I.C.A. taxes to be withheld	3,600
Union dues to be withheld	300
Employer F.U.T.A. taxes	2,400
Employer health plan costs	4,800

PP 12.14. Prepare in good form the two journal entries necessary to record the weekly payroll and the employers' payroll tax and other related liabilities given the following data:

Salaries and wages earned	$35,000
Income taxes to be withheld	7,000
F.I.C.A. taxes to be withheld	2,100
State disability taxes to be withheld	350
Union dues to be withheld	300
Employee pension-fund contribution	1,050
Employer F.U.T.A. taxes	1,400
Employer state disability taxes	1,050
Employer pension-fund contribution	1,050
Employer health plan costs	1,575

CHAPTER 12 APPENDIX
Present Value

"Present value" (or "discounted present value," or "PV") is a very specific and objective business term. It should not be used interchangeably with such terms as "current value." The present value of something and its current value *can* be the same. This similarity usually occurs for an individual as a coincidence. Current value implies subjective factors involving value to whom and value for what purpose.

The present value of something is simply today's cash cost excluding any related interest costs or benefits. An asset acquired today, costing $10,000 cash plus a five-year eight-percent interest-bearing note for $50,000, has a present value of $60,000 (assuming no interest is capitalized into the face value of the note). The $20,000 of additional interest payments over the next five years are not related to *today's* cost of the item. They are rental costs on the $50,000 used to purchase the item. It could have been acquired today with a single cash payment of $60,000, its present value.

Similarly, the present value (cost) of a liability is simply the amount of cash required today to fully settle the obligation (assuming no prepayment penalty). Future executory interest is excluded from present value. If you have a current liability of $5,000 plus nine-percent interest due in one year with no early payment penalty, its present value to you is $5,000. You could settle the obligation with a cash outlay today of $5,000. What would be the present value (cost) of this same $5,000 liability due in one year if it were not interest-bearing; that is, $5,000 cash is all that would have to be paid one year from today? Assume you personally could safely invest cash for a year (perhaps in a bank or savings and loan association) and earn six-percent interest. The cash cost today of "settling" this $5,000 obligation due in one year—its present value (cost)—would be only $4,717 (rounded):

$$PV \text{ \$ plus } 0.06(PV \text{ \$}) = \$5,000$$

You could deposit $4,717 cash today, earn six-percent interest, and have the necessary $5,000 accumulated at the end of the year to pay off the debt. Assuming a six-percent interest or discount rate, $4,717 would be today's cash cost to you to settle this note—its present value.[7]

What would be the present value (benefit) to you of a $10,000 payment to be received one year from today if your opportunity interest rate (amount you could earn on money) was six percent? You are correct if you determined the present value (benefit) of the forthcoming $10,000 as only $9,434 (rounded) today:

$$PV \ \$ \ plus \ 0.06(PV \ \$) = \$10,000$$

You would be as well off receiving $9,434 in cash today as you would be receiving $10,000 a year from now (assuming a six-percent opportunity rate is appropriate). You could invest the $9,434 today and have the $10,000 (principal plus interest) in one year.

Do you see where money has a time value because of interest? A specific cash amount to be paid in the future effectively costs you less than if paid today. You would still have the interest you could earn on the delayed payment. A specific cash flow coming to you in the future would effectively be worth less than if arriving today. You would lose the interest you could have earned had the cash arrived today. Present value merely takes into account the time value of money, the opportunity cost of interest saved or lost. As normally used, PV does not attempt to allow for the effects of future inflation; only the effect of interest is included.[8]

Compound Interest

The effects of present value become more significant and dramatic as the time period involved extends beyond one year. The present value of $1,000 to be received in fifty years at a six-percent discount is only $54.30. Over the 50 years, $54.30 would only earn $162.90 of **simple** interest at six percent. The remaining $782.80 is accumulated as a result of **compound** interest—interest earned on accumulating interest.

At six percent, the present value (cost) of a $2,000 payment to be made by you in three years is only $1,679 (rounded). If you deposited $1,679 at compound interest for three years, you would accumulate the necessary $2,000 to make the payment. Your cash equivalent cost today would be only $1,679.

---

[7]   Although GAAP require present-value measurement of all assets and liabilities as they are initially recorded (see Chapters 11 and 12), it does not mandate discounting the interest component of current items unless explicitly stated, or material in amount. Discounting of small current items is used herein as an introduction to present-value measurement.

[8]   PV may also be used outside of the financial accounting system to forecast the effects of inflation, where a reasonable constant inflation rate can be assumed.

First year: 0.06 times $1,679   = $100.74
Second year: 0.06 times ($1,679 plus $100.74) = 106.78
Third year: 0.06 times ($1,679 plus $100.74
                    plus $106.78)   = 113.19
        Total Accumulated Interest   = $321 (rounded)

Present Value Table: Table A

Calculating present value can be tedious without a computer or a properly programmed calculator. The formula for the present value of $1 is

$$PV = 1/ (1 + i)^n,$$

where i = interest or discount rate per period, and n = number of periods involved. You can, of course, determine the present value of any specific number of dollars once you have the appropriate PV of $1 for the particular i and n. Appendix B at the back of this book provides, as Table A, precalculated PV's of $1 for interest rates ($i$) from 0.5 percent to 15 percent, and periods from 1 to 50.

What would be the present value discounted at nine percent of the sum of two payments, $11,000 in seven years and $19,000 in 14 years? Use Table A to determine your answer before reading further.

Table A indicates $0.5470 as the PV of $1 when i = nine percent and n = seven periods (years in this example); and $0.2992 for i = 9 and n = 14. The present value of the payments is determined as follows:

$11,000 times 0.5470   = $6,017
19,000 times 0.2992   =   5,685 (rounded)
    Total PV of both payments = $11,702

Repeated Cash Flows: Table B

Suppose you desired to determine the present value, discounted at 11 percent, of a stream of future payments including $23,000 at the end of the first year, $20,000 each year for the next 18 years, and $32,000 at the end of the 20th year. You could look up all twenty separate PV factors in Table A in Appendix B, and perform twenty separate calculations, plus summarization. An easier way is to use Table B, also in Appendix B at the back of this book. Table B assumes a flow of $1 each year and provides the cumulative PV for the same discount rates and number of periods as Table A. For the example given, you can think of it as involving a constant 20-year stream of $20,000 payments plus a $3,000 payment the first year and a $12,000 payment in year 20. Using Tables A and B, attempt a solution before proceeding.

Only three calculations are necessary if you take advantage of Table B.

$20,000 (20-year stream) times 7.9633 (Table B)	=	$159,266
3,000 (once–year 1) times 0.9009 (Table A)	=	2,701 (rounded)
12,000 (once–year 20) times 0.1240 (Table A)	=	1,488
Total PV of Payments	=	$163,455

Financial Accounting Applications

As described in Chapters 11 and 12, PV is involved in the initial measurement of all assets and liabilities. There are only two exceptions. For current items, where the unearned or not-yet-owed interest is not explicitly stated or is not material in amount, imputed interest is ignored as not significant. For deferred taxes, PV cannot be determined, since the amount and timing of the payments is not known (see discussion in this chapter.)

PV represents a particularly relevant concept and an important "tool" for measuring and reporting capital leases and for segregating imputed interest where necessary. Also, when bonds or other long-term monetary obligations are traded (sold or purchased), the market value is the PV of the future stream of payments discounted at the current market rate of interest for securities of similar risk and maturity. It is the difference between the explicit or stated rate of interest to which a bond is committed and the going market rate which "generates" a premium or discount. If the discounted present value of a $1,000 face or maturity value bond is $1150, it will sell at a $150 premium. Conversely, if the PV is $840, it will sell at a $160 discount.

PRESENT VALUE PROBLEMS

1. Determine the present value of the following items:
   a) A $3,000 payment to be made next week, discount rate nine percent.
   b) A $4,000 payment to be made in two years, discount rate eight percent.
   c) A $5,000 payment to be made in five years, discount rate seven percent.
   d) A $6,000 payment to be made in fifteen years, discount rate six percent.
   e) A $6,000 receivable due next week, discount rate five percent.
   f) A $7,000 receivable due in three years, discount rate six percent.
   g) An $8,000 receivable due in seven years, discount rate seven percent.
   h) A $9,000 receivable due in thirteen years, discount rate eight percent.

2. Determine the present value of the following items:
   a) A stream of $500 annual interest payments over five years, discount rate five percent annually.
   b) A stream of $1,500 annual interest payments over twelve years, discount rate seven percent annually.

c) A stream of $400 monthly rental payments over three years, discount rate six percent annually.

d) $500 to be received monthly starting next month for the next five years, discount rate 12 percent annually.

e) $4,000 to be received annually starting at year end for the next four years, discount rate nine percent annually.

f) $500 annual interest to be received over the next twenty years, discount rate ten percent annually.

3. Determine the present value of, and the initial discount or premium on, the following notes receivable:

a) $5,000 five-year note plus interest at eight percent, discount rate eight percent.

b) $6,000 eight-year note, no stated interest, discount rate nine percent.

c) $7,000 fourteen-year note plus interest at six percent, discount rate eight percent.

d) $8,000 twenty-year note plus interest at nine percent, discount rate six percent.

4. Determine the present value of and the initial discount or premium on the following bonds payable:

a) $10,000 twenty-year bond paying nine percent interest, discount rate nine percent.

b) $10,000 twenty-year bond paying nine percent interest, discount rate seven percent.

c) $20,000 fifteen-year bond paying six percent interest, discount rate eight percent.

5. Determine the initial asset value of a capital lease requiring the following payments (discounting at nine percent):

$50,000 on signing;
$40,000 at end of first year;
$30,000 at end of second year;
$5,000 at end of third through seventh years.

6. Determine the initial asset value of a capital lease with the following payments (discounting at ten percent):

$100,000 on signing;
$20,000 per year for ten years, starting at the end of the first year.

13

FINANCIAL STATEMENT ANALYSIS

CHAPTER PREVIEW

The objective of this chapter is to expand your awareness of the information content of financial statements, and to enhance your ability to use and analyze them intelligently. You can:

- Develop an understanding of "return on investment" as the basic criterion of economic efficiency;

- Learn how various measures incorporating both income statement and balance sheet data may be used to evaluate the efficiency of a firm's operating management;

- Learn that other measures, together with the SCFP, may be used to evaluate a firm's financial management and its recent financial activities;

- Acquire an understanding of several differing perspectives or interests of different users of accounting information, and learn the important distinction between return on investment for the firm as a whole and return for the individual investor;

- Reinforce your perspective of the limitations of financial statement analysis as being just one of several necessary parts of any investment decision.

With this knowledge, you will have a working knowledge of the major financial statements. In subsequent college courses, you will be able to read, understand, and interpret the statements with reasonable proficiency and with confidence.

IS THIS A GOOD INVESTMENT?

John Chandler is an older man, unable to work because of partial paralysis. He is financially dependent on the income from his savings. Most of his investments currently are in real estate, and presently provide an income equivalent to a ten-percent return on the monies invested. John has been advised by a friend to consider transferring some of his savings from real estate into the 12-percent preferred stock of the Columbia Corporation. He has obtained copies of Columbia's recent financial statements and is attempting to evaluate the firm as a potential investment.

John's primary objectives are safety of his capital and consistent return on investment. These factors are much more important to him than any potential for spectacular growth over the next few years in the size of the company and in its profits. In evaluating potential safety, John is considering solvency, liquidity, and the risk inherent in the firm's having excessive debt. In viewing the likelihood of consistent dividends, John essentially is evaluating the efficiency and effectiveness of the firm's management.

Exhibit 13.1 gives Columbia's balance sheets and income statements for the past two years. Exhibit 13.2 provides certain analytical ratios which John has been given for comparison purposes. Study carefully these exhibits, which are displayed on pages 384 and 385. Without any additional information, try to provide a recommendation for John Chandler.

The following questions should be answered based on the most recent (19X1) data:

1. Is the firm currently solvent?
2. Does the firm have reasonable liquidity?
3. Does the firm have too much debt?
4. Are the firm's assets being used efficiently?
5. What is the return on assets employed?
6. What is the return on the owners' investment?

However complete or imperfect your attempted replies to these questions, the required thought processes should prove to be valuable. They will give you a frame of reference for the analytical tools introduced and reviewed below.

INVESTMENT SAFETY

Although investments are not perfectly safe, some may be safer than others. There are four common tools of safety analysis: the current ratio, the quick ratio, the debt ratio, and *times interest earned*. The first three tools were discussed in Chapter 3. Columbia's current (as of 12/31/X1) ratio is 3 to 1, and

Exhibit 13.1(a)
COLUMBIA CORPORATION

Comparative Balance Sheets as of 12/31/X0 and 12/31/X1
(000 omitted)

	12/31/X1	12/31/X0
Assets:		
Cash	$ 85	$ 50
Marketable securities	55	75
Receivables:		
Notes receivable	5	15
Less discount	0	(5)
Accounts receivable	107	94
Less allowance for uncollectibles	(2)	(4)
Inventory[a]	110	100
Supplies	5	10
Prepaid items	10	5
Total Current Assets	$375	$340
Investments	35	30
Land	60	60
Fixed assets	205	200
Less accumulated depreciation[b]	(95)	(65)
Total Assets	$580	$565
Equities:		
Current notes payable	$ 10	$ 20
Accounts payable	95	85
Other current liabilities	20	10
Total Current Liabilities	$125	$115
Bonds payable	60	60
Less Bond Discount	(4)	(5)
Total Liabilities[c]	$181	$170
Preferred stock (12% $100 par)[d]	100	100
Capital stock ($10 par)[e]	150	150
Paid-in capital[f]	40	40
Retained earnings[g]	126	122
Less treasury stock	(17)	(17)
Total Stockholders' Equity	$399	$395
Total Equities	$580	$565

a) AT LOCM following FIFO.
b) Straight-line depreciation used for all fixed assets.
c) Damages amounting to $250,000 against the company have been awarded
   to an injured employee. The company is appealing the court's decision.
d) 1,000 shares issued and outstanding.
e) 15,000 shares issued.
   14,000 shares outstanding.
f) $15,000 from preferred stock.
g) $17,000 restricted by cost of treasury stock.

Exhibit 13.1(b)
COLUMBIA CORPORATION

Comparative Income Statements for Years Ending 12/31/X0 and 12/31/X1
(000 omitted)

		19X1		19X0
Sales		$ 850		$ 745
Less cost of goods sold		440		385
Gross Profit		$ 410		$ 360
Less other operating expenses:				
Wages and salaries	188		178	
Utilities	9		9	
Supplies	4		4	
Insurance	6		6	
Depreciation	35		35	
Bad debts	8		7	
Miscellaneous	3		7	
Interest	5	258	5	251
Income from operations before income taxes		$ 152		$ 109
Less provision for income taxes		61		43
Income from operations		$ 91		$ 66
Extraordinary flood damage to building		0		44
Net Income		$ 91		$ 22
Earnings per share before extraordinary items		$5.64		$3.86
Earnings per share after extraordinary items		$5.64		$0.71

Exhibit 13.2
OTHER DATA FOR COMPARATIVE EVALUATION

	Industry average 19X1	Columbia Corporation 19X0
Current ratio	2.9 to 1	3 to 1
Quick ratio	1.8 to 1	2 to 1
Debt ratio	0.3	0.3
Times interest earned	20 times	23 times
Asset turnover	1.4 times	1.4 times
Receivables turnover	9.0 times	8.4 times
Average days' receivables	41 days	43 days
Inventory turnover	3.8 times	4.0 times
Average days' sales in inventory	96 days	91 days
Return on assets employed	25%	26%

its quick ratio is 2 to 1. The previous year these ratios were the same. The company appears to be maintaining adequate solvency.

One of the risks of excessive debt is a lack of liquidity. Recall that liquidity has been defined as the ability of the firm to obtain more cash if necessary, with minimum difficulty. If a firm should need additional funds, creditors may not be willing to provide them when the firm is already too heavily in debt. The ideal and the maximum allowable debt ratios, or debt-to-equity ratios, for a firm vary by industry. Assume the normal ratios in Columbia's case are 0.3 ideal and 0.6 maximum. From Exhibit 13.1, what is your opinion of Columbia's liquidity? How much cash does it appear that the firm could borrow without exceeding its debt limits?

Columbia's debt ratios of 0.30 and 0.31, respectively, over the past two years are nearly ideal. There appears to be adequate liquidity; the firm could borrow $417,000 of additional net working capital before reaching its upper limit of debt. This amount is determined by letting X equal total equities if the firm were to borrow up to the 0.6 debt limit. $0.4X$ would equal owners' equity. With no additional owner investment, $0.4X$ would equal $399,000 (present owners' equity) and X would equal $997,000 (rounded). Maximum debt ($0.6X$) would be $598,000 (rounded). Present debt is only $181,000. Therefore the difference of $417,000 is potentially "available."

Another risk of excessive debt is the necessity of making high interest payments each year. Remember that interest must be paid whether or not the firm's operations are profitable. *Times interest earned* is the ratio used to measure the risk of interest obligations. Times interest earned is calculated by taking earnings from operations before deduction for interest expense and taxes—EBIT—and dividing by annual interest expense:

$$\text{Times Interest Earned} = \frac{\text{EBIT}}{\text{Annual Interest}}$$

Note that a firm which barely manages to cover its interest, and therefore has zero income from operations before taxes, would have a times interest earned of 1. There is no absolute standard for an adequate times interest earned rate which would indicate safety. Earnings could be reinvested in noncurrent assets and the firm could have inadequate cash to make interest payments. Furthermore, earnings could decline in the future and make coverage of interest payments difficult. Since the future ability to cover interest is of concern, the preferable definition of EBIT given above excludes the results of nonrecurring extraordinary items. Subject to these qualifications, you may consider a rate of three or more "times" as adequate safety. Does Columbia's recent performance indicate adequate safety with respect to existing interest obligations?

Columbia has $5,000 of annual interest cost and EBIT of $157,000 and $114,000, respectively, in the past two years. Times interest earned rates are therefore 31 and 23, respectively, which appear to provide adequate safety.

The company therefore does not appear to have too much debt, either in proportion to total equity or as a source of high interest requirements.

EFFECTIVENESS AND EFFICIENCY

In evaluating the company's future, John must consider many factors not revealed by the financial statements. Some of these other factors would include:

- The firm's products or services and future demand for them,
- The firm's employee relations, and
- The overall economic future.

A firm's management must be effective in choosing its objectives. Such an evaluation is beyond the scope of this book. Given the chosen objectives, management must be efficient in achieving them. Financial statements can provide information as to management's efficiency.

Efficiency measures all involve the concept of return on investment, or outputs generated by certain inputs. Efficiency, or degree of success, at only one instant in time is not really meaningful. What is meaningful is a firm's efficiency or success over a period of time. Therefore, various efficiency rates (or ratios) measure performance over a specific time period, usually a year. The numerator is the amount of a specific output generated during the year, such as sales, profit, interest, and so forth. The denominator represents resources (inputs) used or invested **during** the year to generate the output. An amount of resource assigned as of one instant in time, as reported in a balance sheet, is therefore inappropriate to use in the denominator.

EFFICIENT USE OF ASSETS

An important group of efficiency measures are known as "turnovers." First we will look at a measure of the firm's, or, more properly, its management's, efficiency of asset usage in generating revenue. The reason for, or objective of having, assets in the firm is to generate revenue and, hopefully, profit. The *asset turnover* rate indicates the degree of achievement of this objective. It is calculated by dividing sales (revenue) for the year by **average** total assets in use during the year.

$$\text{Asset turnover (times)} = \frac{\text{Sales}}{\text{Average total assets}}.$$

Note that Net Sales is commonly used, rather than total revenues. To use Gross Sales would result in including some revenues that were not actually earned, that is, some that were subsequently "cancelled" by sales returns or reduced by sales discounts. To include other secondary revenues or gains would diffuse the focus on the primary objective of the firm.

Note also that the denominator includes **average total assets** employed and **not** just the amount reported on a single balance sheet. Some analysts use more sophisticated weighted-average techniques than will be covered in this text. For our purposes, in this and all other efficiency measures, average resources employed will be determined as a simple average for the year, that is, **one-half the sum** of total assets at the beginning of the period plus those at the end of the period:

$$\binom{\text{Average}}{\text{total assets}} = \frac{\binom{\text{Total assets at be-}}{\text{ginning of period (year)}} \text{ plus } \binom{\text{Total assets at end}}{\text{of period (year)}}}{2}.$$

In assisting John Chandler to evaluate his potential investment in the Columbia Corporation, what was Columbia's asset turnover for 19X1?

For the Columbia Corporation, asset turnover would be 1.48 for 19X1. This can be interpreted as "Each dollar of average assets employed has generated $1.48 of sales." The higher the turnover, the better the efficiency of asset usage. Acceptable asset turnover varies greatly by industry. Companies requiring large investments in capacity assets may be fortunate to "turn" assets one or more times per year. Therefore, turnover can be evaluated meaningfully only in comparison with other firms, an industry standard, or as a trend indicator that compares performance to that of prior periods for the same firm.

Receivables

The turnover concept as a measure of efficiency can also be applied to specific assets or groups of assets. *Receivables turnover* is used as a measure of the timeliness of receivables collections. Note that this ratio refers to accounts receivable, and not all receivables. Accounts receivable turnover is calculated by dividing total credit sales by **average net** receivables:

$$\text{Receivables turnover (times)} = \frac{\text{Credit sales}}{\text{Average net accounts receivable}}.$$

Note that this ratio measures the number of dollars of credit sales resulting from dollars invested in receivables, that is, invested as a short-term creditor in the customer's business, through the customer's accounts payable. The numerator should therefore include only credit sales or sales made on account. In practice, information on credit sales is not always available, although most nonretail firms make substantially all sales on account. Therefore, total net sales is often used in the numerator.

$$\binom{\text{Acceptable estimator of}}{\text{receivables turnover}} = \frac{\text{Net sales}}{\text{Average net accounts receivable}}.$$

For Columbia, receivables turnover was 8.72 for 19X1. For every average dollar invested in accounts receivable, sales of $8.72 were realized. The higher the turnover, the shorter is the time during which assets were invested in customers. Desirable receivables turnover for a particular firm is influenced by industry patterns and the credit policy of the firm. In some industries, especially where cash discounts are offered, early collection is normal, and desirable turnover may be as high as 11 to 12 times. In other industries or firms, where the privilege of slow payment is part of the inducement to purchase, and early collections are not rigorously pushed, acceptable turnover might be as low as 5 to 6 times.

Rather than using receivables turnover, the efficiency of receivables collections is often evaluated in terms of *average days' receivables*. Average days' receivables is calculated by dividing receivables turnover into 365 (or sometimes 360, assuming twelve 30-day months, for simplicity), or into the number of days in the period:

$$\text{(Number of) Average days' receivables} = \frac{365}{\text{Receivables turnover}}.$$

For Columbia, in 19X1, average days' receivables was 42 (rounded). This indicates that, on the average, receivables were paid within 42 days of sale, or that the average investment involved in making a credit sale was for a period of 42 days. In the case of average days' receivables, the **lower** the number, the more rapidly receivables were being collected.

Inventories

Turnover measures are also applied to investment in inventories. *Inventory turnover* measures the cost of items delivered to customers as compared to the **average** dollars invested in inventory:

$$\text{Inventory turnover (times)} = \frac{\text{Cost of goods sold}}{\text{Average inventory}}.$$

Note that the effect of varying amounts of gross profit is excluded by using the **cost** of sales generated as the numerator, and not sales. Inventory is generally measured at cost. Therefore, both the numerator and denominator of this ratio are in terms of cost dollars.

What was Columbia's inventory turnover for 19X1? For Columbia, 19X1 inventory turnover was 4.2 times. This ratio (or rate) may be interpreted as indicating that, for each dollar invested in inventory, 4.2 dollars of sales **at cost** (before gross profit margin) were generated. Since gross profit is generated on each dollar cost of sales or each inventory "turn," a higher inventory turnover rate indicates a higher return on dollars invested in inventory. Too low an inventory turnover in a firm could indicate unnecessary dollars tied up in slow-moving inventory. Turnover could also be too high, indicating the possibility of excessive expenses of reordering in small lots or of out-of-stock conditions and lost sales.

As with other turnover measures, inventory turnover can only be evaluated against industry standards or prior years' performance. Inventory turnover in a supermarket could be 20 or more times per year. A manufacturer of giant hydroelectric turbines and other heavy equipment would be fortunate to "turn" once a year.

Recall that receivables turnover could be measured and reported in two different ways—turnover times or average days. Similarly, inventory turnover can also be expressed in terms of *average days' sales in inventory*. This is calculated by dividing 365 by inventory turnover. Columbia's 87 days indicates that average inventory during the year amounted to 87 days' sales. The smaller the number of days' sales of inventory on hand, the smaller the investment committed to inventory, and the higher the turnover.

Profitability

A different measurement of efficient asset usage relates to the ultimate objective of the firm. Companies are in business to earn the maximum return on the owners' investment, subject to legal and social constraints. Since assets are the sole source of earnings, an overall measure is *return on assets employed*. Return on assets is calculated by dividing EBIT[1] by average total assets. The ratio is then converted to a percentage through multiplying by 100:

$$\text{Return on assets employed} = \frac{\text{EBIT}}{\text{Average total assets}} \times 100.$$

Why do you think EBIT is preferred as the numerator rather than net income? Assets generate earnings regardless of who supplied the assets (creditors or owners) and regardless of how these overall "earnings" are divided among governments (taxes), creditors (interest), and owners (profits). Therefore EBIT, which indicates earnings before various distributions, is the appropriate amount to measure efficiency of asset usage. Obviously, the higher the return on assets employed, the greater will be the earnings potentially available for the owner. Columbia's 19X1 return on assets employed was 27 percent (rounded).[2]

What are your conclusions with respect to Columbia's efficient use of assets in 19X1 as compared with industry averages and with 19X0? Exhibit 13.3 includes the most recent (19X1) data as determined above. From Exhibit 13.3 you can see that Columbia is better than the industry average and has

---

[1]   Some analysts and texts define EBIT as net income before interest and taxes. As discussed previously, for calculating times interest earned, net income may include extraordinary items or inputs from discontinued operations. In such circumstances, the use of net income before interest and taxes could result in misleading inferences. Income from operations before interest and taxes is the preferred definition.

[2] $\dfrac{\$152,000 + \$5,000}{1/2\,(\$565,000 + \$580,000)} = 27.42\%.$

Exhibit 13.3

DATA FOR COMPARATIVE EVALUATION INCLUDING
MOST RECENT YEAR

	Industry average 19X1	Columbia Corporation 19X1	Columbia Corporation 19X0
Current ratio	2.9 to 1	3 to 1	3 to 1
Quick ratio	1.8 to 1	2 to 1	2 to 1
Debt ratio	0.3	0.31	0.3
Times interest earned	20 times	31 times	23 times
Asset turnover	1.4 times	1.5 times	1.4 times
Receivable turnover	9.0 times	8.7 times	8.4 times
Average days' receivables	41 days	42 days	43 days
Inventory turnover	3.8 times	4.2 times	4.0 times
Average days' sales in inventory	96 days	87 days	91 days
Return on assets employed	25%	27%	26%

improved over the previous year in all measurements except for receivables. Receivables turnover is, however, only slightly below industry average and has improved over the previous year. Columbia's management appears to be managing the firm's assets efficiently.

THREE COMPONENTS OF OVERALL MANAGEMENT

Return on assets, and the various other measures of the efficiency of asset usage, relate to the operating management of the business. Later in this chapter you will find an example of how detailed income statement analysis provides further information on operating management. Operating management refers to managing the resources available within the firm without regard to the manner in which they were financed or to the tax consequences. Overall management consists of operating management, financial management, and tax management. Efficient financial management involves obtaining necessary capital at minimal cost. It also involves maximizing the *return on owners' equity*. The objective of tax management is to minimize tax liability. This objective is achieved not only through the skilled preparation of tax returns but, more importantly, through the anticipation of tax consequences in operating and financial decisions. Similarly, operating decisions must include financial considerations, and vice versa. As all three management areas overlap, the distinction made herein is one of focus or primary attention.

Occasionally a business may be unsuccessful even with expert operating management. Many business managers are skilled in operating but naive when it comes to proper financial management. As cited in earlier chapters, a firm with profitable operations can grow too fast and possibly become insolvent. Such a failure is the result of improper (or poor) financial management.

In addition to maintaining adequate solvency and liquidity, financial management involves taking advantage of optimal *financial leverage* or *trading on equity*. Trading on equity can be understood as making money on other people's money. Since interest is tax-deductible, the "after-tax cost" of debt financing may be only 5 to 7 percent. If the funds borrowed can be used to generate EBIT of 27 percent, as in the Columbia example, these earnings, after provision for interest and taxes, are available to the owners. The benefits of trading on equity are a reward to the owner for assuming the risks of debt. Remember that interest is usually payable at least annually, and principal is payable at maturity regardless whether EBIT is positive or negative. If debt obligations cannot be met, the firm may be liquidated and the owners could lose their entire investment.

In a particular line of business or industry, it is therefore not only possible for a firm to have too much debt but also to have too little debt. The proportion of debt financing is also referred to as financial leverage.[3] A firm with too little leverage is not taking adequate advantage of trading on equity. The determination of optimal financial leverage for a given firm is a responsibility of financial management and is not covered in this text. It is cited here so that you may understand that, in financial statement analysis, you must also be concerned about excessive conservatism in financing, that is, too little debt.

EARNINGS PER SHARE

Good operating management results in optimal EBIT. Good tax management ensures minimal taxes. Efficient financial management ensures optimal leverage and therefore optimal interest with respect to achievable EBIT. The combined result is the ultimate objective of the owner, optimal return on the owner's investment.

In Chapter 10 you were introduced to several measures of ownership interest and return. Recall that the amount of "owners'" investment in a corporation is normally identified as the residual share of total assets assigned to the common stockholders. If preferred shareholders exist, even though they are legally owners rather than creditors, computations of book value of owners' investment, book value per share of stock, and earnings per share are all based on the residual **after** preferred claims.

Recall that simple EPS is determined as net income available to common stockholders, divided by the average number of common shares outstanding during the year (period):

$$\text{Simple EPS} = \frac{\text{Net income} - \text{Preferred dividend}}{\text{Average Common Shares Outstanding}}.$$

---

[3]   Leverage involves not only optimal debt, but often an optimal mix of debt, preferred stock, and common stock.

For Columbia, 19X1 EPS was $5.64 ($91,000 less $12,000, divided by 14,000 shares) and this amount is included on the income statement (see Exhibit 13.1). Also note that GAAP also require disclosure of EPS before the effect of extraordinary items or discontinued operations. For Columbia in 19X1, there was no difference, but note in Exhibit 13.1 how misleading the $0.71 19X0 EPS figure could be by itself.

For corporations with substantial amounts of convertible debentures or convertible preferred stock outstanding, the potential dilution of EPS upon conversion could be significant (see Chapters 10 and 12). Many more stock shares could be outstanding without a proportionate increase in earnings.[4] Where the potential dilution is significant, GAAP prohibit the disclosure of simple EPS, as being potentially misleading. Instead, accountants will report two earnings amounts, each **before** and **after** effects of extraordinary items. These amounts are known as *primary earnings per share* and *fully diluted earnings per share.*

Fully diluted EPS assumes that all rights, options, warrants, and conversion privileges have been exercised. It discloses the worst that could happen to EPS. Primary EPS is difficult to compute and is beyond the scope of this text. It will be equal to or greater than fully diluted EPS. It is calculated on the basis of an assumption that only certain options and debt conversions with a high probability of occurring will occur. Primary EPS discloses the dilution which probably will occur.

RETURN ON OWNERS' INVESTMENT

In evaluating the firm's performance for all common stockholders instead of on a per-share basis, earnings available for the common stockholders are compared to the average book value of the common stock:

$$\text{Return on common equity} = \frac{\text{Net income} - \text{Preferred dividend}}{\text{Average common equity}}.$$

Recall, from Chapter 10, that the book value of the common stock is total stockholders' equity less any preferred shares (preferred stock plus paid-in capital from preferred stock). The average would be one-half the sum of the beginning and ending amounts for the period.

If industry average return were 26 percent, calculate Columbia's 19X1 return, and evaluate it with respect to the industry. Columbia's *return on common equity* of 28 percent (rounded) compares very favorably with the industry average.

---

[4]   Often potential dilution can also arise from previously distributed privileges to acquire new shares known as rights, warrants, and options. A discussion of stock rights, stock warrants, and stock options and the manner in which they are disclosed in the financial statements is beyond the scope of this text. These items are more appropriately treated in texts for intermediate-level accounting or for business finance.

ASSETS NOT REPORTED AS SUCH

Often a company's return on assets or owners' equity will seem very high, possibly unreasonably high. Before making a value judgment, recall two facts from Chapter 2:

1. Not all assets involved in the earnings process are recorded on the balance sheet. Accountants do not show as assets those intangibles which they cannot fairly and objectively measure.
2. Recorded assets are shown at adjusted historical cost, which may be far below current costs.

Therefore, if all business assets could be objectively measured and recorded, and all were measured at current cost for comparison with current income, overall earnings on assets and earnings on owners' equity could be much lower.

For instance, suppose the net current cost of Columbia's average assets was $650,000 ($30,000 revaluation of FIFO inventory and $40,000 of capacity assets). Assume that excluded intangibles would cost another $150,000 to replace. On this revised basis, return on assets would be only 19.6 percent, and return on common equity would be 15.7 percent. Neither amount would represent unreasonable amounts, considering the risks involved.

RETURN FOR A PARTICULAR STOCKHOLDER

Returning to John Chandler, should he invest some of his savings in the preferred stock of the Columbia Corporation? You may assume that all the appropriate ratio and percentage data were exceptional as compared with other firms. The statements themselves provide every reason to believe the company will continue to earn 23 percent on average total owners' equity, which is more than enough to cover the 12-percent preferred stock dividend.

There are three very important questions still to be answered before you could recommend that John should seriously consider investing in Columbia:

1. What are the firm's dividend policies?
2. What would be the return to John on his investment?
3. Are there any reasons, not revealed in the statements, why John should be cautious?

Because of John's dependence on income, he is interested in dividends regardless of the firm's current earnings. You would need to find out whether the firm regularly paid preferred dividends in full. For example, did they pay preferred dividends last year despite the extraordinary loss?

Equally important would be the consideration of John's return on his possible Columbia investment. He presently is receiving 10 percent from his real-estate investments. Columbia's 12-percent preferred dividend rate is 12 percent of par value, **not** 12 percent of the market price John would have to pay for his stock. He would have to be able to acquire the preferred stock at a cost of no more than $120 per share in order to have a return of at least 10 percent. Normally, he might require an even higher return to compensate for the risk of passed or partial dividends.

Note that, if John were considering the purchase of common stock, there would be no target or fixed dividend rate. You would need to calculate *dividends per share* on the common stock for the past few years to see whether a common pattern has been established which could be projected into the future. Dividends per share is calculated by taking the total cash dividends declared during the year and dividing by average number of common shares outstanding:

$$\text{Dividends per share} = \frac{\text{Total common stock dividends declared}}{\text{Average number of common shares outstanding}}.$$

IMPORTANCE OF FOOTNOTES

Returning once again to risk analysis, is there anything about the Columbia Corporation that might indicate that John should be cautious? Footnote (c) in Exhibit 13.1 indicates that John should wait until the lawsuit is resolved. The firm has already lost its case in the first trial. It is appealing the decision. If it loses the appeal, the $250,000 of awarded damages could drastically alter the firm's financial picture and its prospects.

In analyzing financial statements, you should always study the statement footnotes carefully. Footnotes will disclose material contingent liabilities and purchase commitments. Footnotes will also inform you of the firm's measurement elections for inventory—LIFO vs. FIFO—and depreciation—accelerated vs. straight-line. Recall, from Chapters 8 and 9, how differences in accounting methods can significantly invalidate simple direct comparisons between firms using different measurement systems.

Finally, in analyzing financial statements, remember that they contain only *some* of the information relevant to an investment decision. Important factors mentioned earlier in this chapter, such as the future markets for the firm's products or services, and the overall economic picture, must be evaluated from separate information.

IS MY MANAGER DOING A GOOD JOB?

Recall from Chapter 1 that financial statement information is of interest to many people other than potential preferred and common stockholders. Statement analysis of operations is of particular interest to managers and absentee owners. For example, consider the case of Jack Jordan. Mr. Jordan owned a medium-sized motel in a resort area. He had personally built the motel and managed it when it was still small. During the last few years, he has semi-retired to a different state. He employs a resident manager whom he supervises by mail, phone, and an occasional visit.

It is early in 19X4, and Jack has just received the 19X3 income statement. He also has the average motel guidelines statement prepared for a typical firm by his trade association. He is comparing these two statements with earlier years' statements for his motel. Exhibit 13.4 gives the representative income data for 19X3 from the trade association and the actual data for Jack's motel. It also includes the motel's income statements for the years 19X2 and 19X1.

In earlier chapters, you learned that converting amounts to percentages aided in the comparison of similar data. Exhibit 13.4 also includes percentages for each reported item. Sales each year is expressed as a percentage change over the prior year. All other items are given as a percent of the current year's sales. Study Exhibit 13.4 carefully. If you were Jack Jordan, which items would you note for discussion with your manager?

Exhibit 13.4
JACK'S MOTEL

Income Statements for Years Ending 12/31/X1, 12/31/X2, and 12/31/X3 and Trade Association 19X3 Data
(000 omitted)

	Trade association data		Jack's Motel					
	19X3		19X3		19X2		19X1	
Room rentals	$960	+13%	$920	+ 5%	$880	+16%	$760	+14%
Wages and salaries	298	31%	312	34%	299	34%	251	33%
Supplies	77	8%	83	9%	70	8%	68	9%
Laundry	106	11%	56	6%	70	8%	76	10%
Utilities	86	9%	83	9%	79	9%	68	9%
Insurance	77	8%	73	8%	70	8%	61	8%
Stationery and office supplies	10	1%	10	1%	9	1%	7	1%
Landscaping	19	2%	18	2%	18	2%	15	2%
Pool maintenance	9	1%	10	1%	9	1%	7	1%
Interest	57	6%	56	6%	53	6%	46	6%
Depreciation	96	10%	101	11%	97	11%	83	11%
General maintenance	67	7%	36	4%	44	5%	38	5%
Restaurant revenue[a]	115	12%	56	6%	79	9%	91	12%
Operating income	$173	18%	$138	15%	$141	16%	$131	17%

(a) Restaurant and bar operation leased to concessionaire for a base rental plus a percentage of gross revenue.

OPERATING PERFORMANCE

Earlier in this chapter you learned that return on assets and various asset turn-overs were some of the measures of the efficiency of operating management. Detailed analysis of the income statement provides further information on the operating management of the business. To maximize return on assets employed, operating management strives to maximize revenues and to control costs. Exhibit 13.4 reveals to Jack that his manager is apparently doing an excellent job of cost control in most areas. This judgment is based both upon results reported for the past three years and upon a comparison with the trade association's data. The only expense categories requiring further investigation would appear to be wages and salaries, laundry, and general maintenance.

Of even more concern to Jack Jordan than specific expense items should be the fact that his operating income as a percent of sales is steadily declining and is substantially below the industry average—3 percent (or $27,600) under average. Jack's manager may not be doing as good a job at generating revenues as he is in controlling costs. Both revenue items are prime candidates for further investigation. Restaurant revenue is dropping sharply. If it were back at industry average, it alone would bring in $56,000 more pure profit, and would result in Jack's bottom line being above industry average.

Also note that, in 19X3, sales increased only 5 percent over the prior year. The industry average increase was 13 percent. If sales had increased 13 percent, there would be an additional $74,000 of sales revenue. And if the motel were running at the industry average of 18 percent operating income, this would have meant $13,320 in additional profit.

POSSIBLY INTERRELATED FACTORS

Although income statement analysis can only highlight items for further investigation, it is important that Jack also look for possible interrelationships among trouble spots. Let us review the items pinpointed by Exhibit 13.4.

1. Sales growth has fallen off by more than 50 percent.
2. Bar and restaurant revenues have fallen 50 percent in the past three years despite an overall 21 percent increase in room rentals.
3. Laundering expenses have dropped to almost half of the industry average in the past three years.
4. General maintenance expense is declining, and is significantly below industry average.
5. Wages and salaries are slightly higher than industry average.

Even though you certainly cannot draw firm conclusions without further investigation, can you see possible interrelationships in these factors that might merit separate investigation? The higher wages and salaries do not appear related to the other items. They may simply reflect the fact that Jack has a hired general manager, whereas most trade-association motels have owner-managers.

Cost cutting and cost control can go too far. It is possible that the significant "savings" in laundry and general maintenance are turning away customers. Sheets and towels with holes, plumbing and doors that do not work, and peeling paint are not conducive to attracting or holding guests! Jack Jordan might be well advised to make one of his periodic visits in the immediate future.

INCOME STATEMENT RATIOS

In the Jack Jordan example above, you can see the advantage of converting income statement line items to percentages of sales, for analysis purposes. Two particular items, when converted to percentages, are commonly referred to with specific titles. The *gross profit ratio* is merely a firm's gross profit or gross margin expressed as a percent of sales. A change or difference in gross profit ratio can signal:

- Different selling prices—raised prices or discounting;
- Different product costs, which may or may not indicate different quality.

The *operating ratio* is simply the firm's net income expressed as a percent of sales. It indicates the final result of management's profit-directed activities. Comparisons of operating ratios between two firms can be distorted by differing financial leverage patterns, different current tax situations, or even extraordinary items.

As an extreme example, consider two firms with the following abbreviated income statements (000 omitted):

	Firm A	Firm B
Sales	$900	$950
Operating expenses		
(except for interest)	747	797
Interest expense	3	14
Income from operations before Taxes	$150	$139
Provision for taxes	38	56
Income from operations	$112	$ 83
Extraordinary gain	40	0
Extraordinary loss	0	60
Net Income	$152	$ 23
Operating ratio	16.9%	2.4%

Firm A has practically no debt (leverage), lower proportionate taxes, and an extraordinary gain. Firm B has significantly higher debt and interest, a higher tax rate, and a large extraordinary loss. A simple comparison of operating ratios indicates that A is performing seven times as well as B. Try calculating EBIT for both firms. Most analysts will also determine EBIT and compare the ratio or percentage of EBIT to sales. EBIT to sales is a better indicator of repeatable operating performance. In the foregoing example, both firms have a similar EBIT to sales of 16 and 17 percent.

ITEMS BYPASSING THE INCOME STATEMENT

Before leaving this discussion of the income statement, it is desirable to note that there are two types of events, in addition to owner transactions and donations, which bypass the income statement. They affect owners' equity directly and are not included as revenue or expense in the determination of net income.

Both of these bypassing events reflect adjustments. The first type is known as a *prior period adjustment*. When an event that clearly should have been recognized in prior years is discovered to have been omitted from the statements, GAAP provide for direct adjustment to owners' capital or retained earnings. GAAP provide specific tests before an item can be treated as a prior period adjustment.[5] Otherwise income could be manipulated through arbitrarily treating certain items as past adjustments.

The second bypassing adjustment involves temporary revaluations of long-term investments. Recall, from Chapter 11, that a permanent loss of market or recoverable value will be recorded as a write-down of the asset and an expense on the income statement. However, where a decline in value is believed to be temporary, the write-down is not reflected in net income. Instead a contra (or negative-valuation) account is set up within owners' equity to carry the balancing adjustment. This account may be called "temporary investments revaluation." Subsequent recovery of the market or recoverable value of investments, up to but not above original cost, would result in a write-up of the asset, and a corresponding decrease or elimination of the investments revaluation account.

Except for temporary revaluation of investments, prior period adjustments, owner transactions (including treasury stock transactions), and donations, all events affecting owners' equity will be reported as revenue expense, gain, or loss, on the income statement. The income statement primarily is a report on the operating management of the business. Financial management activities are reported on the Statement of Changes in Financial Position (or SCFP). To complete your exposure to financial statement analysis, consider the following example involving analysis of a SCFP.

---

[5] An item must be clearly identifiable with activities of a specific prior year and completed then—not the result of subsequent events. Further, it must not be something essentially controlled by management, and it must not have been susceptible to reasonable estimation at the time.

HOW GOOD IS THIS SUPPLIER'S FINANCIAL MANAGEMENT? COULD THEY HANDLE REALLY LARGE ORDERS FROM US?

Becky Silverman is a purchasing agent for a large manufacturer. Her firm has just been awarded a contract for limited production of a new item. There's a very good chance that a much larger order will follow within a few months. Becky is responsible for procuring a critical component part that is to be made by one or more outside suppliers. She has obtained bids from the Giant Corporation and the Little Company. Little's bid is substantially lower, and Becky would like to give them the order.

Before committing to the Little Company, Becky wishes to evaluate the financial management activities of this supplier. Little can readily handle the first small order, but if the expected larger order comes through, Little would be required to radically expand its capacity. Becky is seeking assurance that the Little Company management could cope with the expected larger order. Could they recognize the need for, and obtain, necessary new capital? Would they maintain solvency during rapid expansion, so that there would be no risk that their creditors might interfere with production?

Becky has before her Exhibit 13.5. This exhibit includes SCFP's for the Little Company over the past three years, plus some additional selective information. Study this exhibit. See whether you can assist Becky in answering the following questions:

1. Has the firm maintained adequate solvency, especially during periods of expanding volume? Has it been increasing its net working capital to accompany increased volume? Or has it been operating with more limited solvency?

2. Has the firm maintained desirable liquidity, especially during periods of expansion?

3. Has the firm been reasonably profitable over the past few years? Little's industry standard for EBIT to total net assets is 26 percent. Profitability is essential if new owners' equity capital is to be raised for expansion.

4. Has the firm a regular practice of paying out in dividends a certain proportion of each year's earnings? What proportion of earnings are regularly retained and reinvested?

5. Has Little been expanding its capacity assets, or at least replacing assets as they have worn out?

6. Has the firm been maintaining a good proportion between debt and owners' equity as part of raising new capital? The optimal debt ratio in Little's industry is 0.4 to 1.

7. Does the firm currently generate sufficient funds from operations to significantly assist in the financing of new expansion? Becky estimates that the larger follow-up order would require Little to obtain $500,000 of additional resources for investment in net working capital and capacity assets.

Exhibit 13.5

LITTLE COMPANY

**Statements of Changes in Financial Position and Selected Data
(000 omitted)**

	19X3	19X2	19X1
SOURCES:			
Net income	$171	$119	$ 85
Plus depreciation and amortization	50	40	30
Funds from operations	$221	$159	$115
Sale of noncurrent assets	5	10	5
New long-term debt	60	140	0
New stock	37	19	104
Total Sources	$323	$328	$224
APPLICATIONS:			
Purchase of noncurrent assets	$170	$170	$120
Retirement of long-term debt	0	30	0
Dividends	68	48	34
Increase in balance of net working capital	85	80	70
Total Applications	$323	$328	$224
ADDITIONAL SELECTED DATA:			
Current ratio	2.6 to 1	2.5 to 1	3 to 1
Debt ratio	.3	.3	.2
Total assets	$900	$700	$500
Sales	$845	$595	$448
Sales growth	42%	33%	25%
EBIT	$261	$196	$135

Solvency

The Little Company has apparently managed to maintain solvency very well, especially during rapid growth. Over the past two years, sales volume has increased 89 percent and total assets have grown 80 percent. During this period, the current ratio has been held at 2.5 to 1 or above. Approximately one-third of new asset investment has been in the form of new net working capital.

Liquidity

The Little Company, again during a period of rapid growth, has managed to maintain more than adequate liquidity. If anything, the firm has been overly cautious in maintaining a 0.3 debt ratio when its industry's optimum is 0.4. Little could immediately raise $150,000 in new long-term debt, and still be within the industry standard.[6]

---

[6] To determine this amount: If debt of 0.4 is desirable, then owners' equity must be 0.6; let X equal total equity; present owners' equity of $630 equals $0.6X$; X equals $1,050; optimal debt equals $1,050 times 0.4 equals $420; $420 minus present debt of $270 equals $150 of "available" debt.

Profitability

Little has been quite profitable. Return on average assets employed has been 30 percent, 33 percent, and 33 percent, in 19X1, 19X2, and 19X3, respectively. This is well above industry averages. Return on owners' equity has been an exceptional 22 percent, 27 percent, and 31 percent, over these same three years.

Dividend Policy

Little appears to have an established policy of distributing 40 percent of earnings as dividends. This practice, coupled with high earnings (see above), should make it relatively simple for the firm to sell more stock if funds are required for expansion.

Asset Replacement/Expansion

When a firm's SCFP indicates net noncurrent capacity asset acquisition is equal to or greater than annual depreciation, the firm is probably at least regularly replacing capital assets as they wear out or become obsolescent.[7] Little is apparently replacing its capital assets as they expire. It appears also that capacity is being significantly expanded. Net noncurrent asset acquisitions exceeded annual depreciation and amortization by $85,000, $120,000, and $115,000 over the past three years.

Maintenance of Optimal Capital Structure

Little's financial managers appear to be doing an excellent job of maintaining a desirable capital structure or balance of debt to owners' equity. In 19X1, new long-term capital of $155,000 was acquired, of which $51,000 was the result of retained earnings—$85,000 net income less $34,000 of dividends. The remaining $104,000 came from the sale of new stock.

In both 19X2 and 19X3, $200,000 of new long-term capital was acquired:

	From earnings	Stock sale	New net debt	Total
1/9/X2	$ 71	$19	$110	$200
1/9/X3	103	37	60	200

Note that, in 19X2, substantially more new debt brought the debt ratio from 0.2 to 0.3. In 19X3 the proportion of new debt and new stock was controlled

---

[7]   If inflation has resulted in a significant increase in replacement costs, or if most depreciation represents the final years' charges under an accelerated method, then such a conclusion may not be accurate.

so that the debt ratio was maintained at 0.3. It appears the firm has "targeted" this more conservative leverage proportion. Given its apparent target, the firm appears to be managing its financial affairs very well.

Owners' Commitment

The Little Company's owners (stockholders) have been making a continuing significant commitment of resources to the firm in the form of **both** reinvested earnings **and** new stock. These investments have been:

	19X3	19X2	19X1
Reported income	$171,000	$119,000	$85,000
Less dividends	68,000	48,000	34,000
Income reinvested	$103,000	$71,000	$51,000
Additional (stock) investment	37,000	19,000	104,000
Total additional owner investment	$140,000	$90,000	$155,000

Potential for Raising Additional Capital

Becky Silverman is concerned whether Little could raise an additional $500,000 of new capital should the larger order materialize. An analysis of Little's current situation and recent "track record" would indicate no real difficulty in the firm's obtaining these funds. $221,000 is currently being generated from operations. As mentioned above, the company could take on $150,000 of new debt and still be at the optimal debt–equity mix. The remaining $129,000 should be readily obtainable from the sale of stock or a mix of debt and stock.

Furthermore, Little's management has demonstrated the ability to cope with rapid expansion without impairing solvency. Little's financial ability to handle the potential large forthcoming order should not be a major concern for Becky. She should, of course, satisfy herself with respect to other nonfinancial concerns that are not within the scope of this book. Such significant nonfinancial considerations could include the availability of adequate additional raw materials, skilled labor, and special tools, which might prove to be in short supply even if the funds were available to pay for them.

The Becky Silverman–Little Company example has been introduced to demonstrate the information content of financial statements and especially the SCFP. All the foregoing findings and conclusions concerning the Little Company were derived from the data appearing on Exhibit 13.5. If the origin of any of the data discussed was not readily apparent to you, you would be well advised to go back and review. When you fully understand all details of the Little Company analysis, you will be well on the road to understanding and using Statements of Changes in Financial Position.

LIMITATIONS OF FINANCIAL STATEMENT ANALYSIS

In concluding this discussion of statement analysis, it is important to review and emphasize inherent limitations. We have already pointed out the following:

1. In any investment decision, the importance of significant qualitative information not measured and reported by accountants. Examples would include, but not be limited to:

a) The quality of the firm's management and work force, and the selection and training programs needed to ensure maintenance or improvement of this quality.

b) The quality of its labor relations and its prospects for continued operation at competitive labor costs.

c) The quality of its products or services and of research directed towards new and improved products in a rapidly changing world.

d) The environment of the firm, including overall economic forecasts, industry forecasts, and the future share of the market that the firm might reasonably anticipate.

2. The difficulty in making comparisons of data between or among different firms using different options of accounting measurement. Also contributing to comparison difficulties is the diversification of firms into different markets and industries. With two firms involved in different combinations of activities, except for *overall* return on owners' investment, comparison of other data becomes relatively meaningless.

Financial statement analysis, therefore, may have limited value except for trend analysis for the same firm consistently applying the same accounting methods. Even in these situations, you should remain constantly aware that ratio analysis and the underlying data refer to history. An extrapolation of past data into a forecast has all the limitations of any prediction.

The foregoing cautions are not intended to lead to a conclusion that statement analysis is futile. Some analysis is probably better than none. You should merely remember that statement analysis can provide information which at best is only a portion of that necessary for intelligent decision making.

CHAPTER OVERVIEW

Based upon the information contained in this chapter, you should be able to demonstrate the ability to analyze a firm's financial statements and arrive at tentative conclusions and recommendations concerning the firm's:

- solvency and liquidity, employing and correctly interpreting its current, quick, and debt ratios;
- adequate but not excessive proportion of debt, employing and correctly interpreting debt and times interest earned ratios;
- efficiency of asset usage, employing and correctly interpreting: asset turnover; receivables turnover or average days' receivables; inventory turnover or average days' sales in inventory; and return on assets employed;
- degree of trading on equity and amount of financial leverage employed, assuming no preferred stock;
- adequacy of return on owners' investment, relative to the return on common equity;
- operating performance through use of income statement percentages and particularly the gross profit ratio, the operating ratio, and EBIT to sales;
- financial management activities as disclosed by the SCFP.

You should also be able to:

- calculate the return on an individual shareholder's investment in terms of simple EPS and dividends per share;
- explain the significance of primary and fully diluted EPS and when they are reported;
- describe those events or adjustments which change the balance of owners' equity but which are not included on the income statement as parts of net income;
- describe and explain some of the significant limitations of financial statement analysis.

NEW VOCABULARY AND CONCEPTS

EBIT	Financial leverage/ trading on equity
Times interest earned	Primary EPS
Asset turnover	Fully diluted EPS
Receivables turnover	Return on common equity
Average days' receivables	Dividends per share
Inventory turnover	Gross profit ratio
Average days' sales in inventory	Operating ratio
Return on assets employed	Prior period adjustment
Return on owners' equity	

REVIEW QUESTIONS

1. (a) What is EBIT? (b) Explain, with examples, why EBIT may be a more useful earnings measure than net income for certain types of financial analysis.

2. For each of the items listed below, explain: (a) its meaning and usefulness; (b) how it is calculated; and (c) whether a higher or lower figure is considered favorable in most situations:

- times interest earned
- asset turnover
- receivables turnover
- average days' receivables
- inventory turnover
- average days' sales in inventory

- return on assets employed
- return on total stockholders' equity
- return on common equity
- simple earnings per share
- dividends per share

3. What are the objectives of, and distinctions among, operating management, financial management, and tax management?

4. (a) What is financial leverage? (b) What is trading on equity? (c) How do they relate?

5. (a) What is the difference between return on owners' investment and return to a particular owner on his/her investment? (b) What causes this difference?

6. (a) What are the purposes of reporting primary and fully diluted earnings per share? (b) When would they replace simple EPS on the income statement? (c) Generally what is the difference in the meaning of primary and fully diluted EPS?

7. How can an income statement "signal" items that are probably adequately controlled and require no immediate further investigation? Give examples.

8. How can an income statement "signal" items that may be unsatisfactory and which require further investigation? Give examples.

9. (a) What is the gross profit ratio? (b) How is it calculated? (c) What are the possible factors that could lead to differences in gross profit ratios in the same firm for different periods? (d) Differences between firms in different industries?

10. What is the operating ratio and what is its significance?

11. How does the SCFP, in conjunction with the balance sheet, provide information relating to recent changes in the firm's solvency? liquidity? financial leverage?

12. (a) How can you tell from the SCFP, or preferably from several years' SCFP's, whether a firm is replacing its capacity assets as they wear out or become obsolete? (b) How can you tell whether it is expanding its capacity?

13. What is the source of working capital for investment in new or replacement assets other than sale of existing assets, new long-term debt, or additional owner investment from outside of the business?

14. How can you tell from the SCFP, or preferably from several years' SCFP's, whether the firm's owners are significantly committing funds for the future?

MINI-CASES AND QUESTIONS FOR DISCUSSION

MC 13.1. At a recent conference of financial executives, one speaker stated:

Most people really don't appreciate the value of good financial management. A good financial manager can take only average results from the operating management and transform them to very good results for the common stockholder. An absence of financial management can lead adequately operating management into insolvency.

Is this merely a meaningless self-serving declaration, or does it essentially represent the truth? Discuss.

MC 13.2. Two financial analysts are having a disagreement. One says, "I don't know why you don't use net income to average total assets as the measure of efficient asset usage. After all, net income is the final result. It represents what really happened. How can you ignore interest, taxes, and extraordinaries? They are real and they happen."

The second analyst replies, "That isn't the point. Net income represents the combined result of several different types of management, government action, and even acts of God. By using EBIT, I can somewhat pinpoint responsibility to operating management."

Who is correct? Discuss.

MC 13.3. Linda Drake is a militant looking for a cause. She has just learned about trading on equity and is bursting with righteous indignation. "This is a perfect example of capitalist exploitation," she shouts. "Making money on other people's money is a real rip-off. It is completely unfair!"

You realize that many corporations' bonds and shares of preferred stock are held by banks, insurance companies, and pension funds. You also know that common stock in the same corporations is also held by aged widows. Are these aged widows really "ripping off" big banks and insurance companies? What are the factors that make creditors and preferred stockholders content to allow common stockholders to make money on their money? Discuss.

MC 13.4. Two financial analysts are in disagreement. John maintains that the income statement of a firm or, especially a **series** of annual statements, provide the best measure of a firm's performance. Harry takes exception to this. He believes net income to be a relatively meaningless figure, and prefers to rely on funds from operation as reported on the SCFP. Harry points out that net income includes very arbitrary estimates of such things as depreciation and amortization, and therefore is not a reliable performance indicator.

Who do you think is right? Discuss.

MC 13.5. Mary is a commercial loan officer with a local bank. She believes a series of SCFP's, together with a projected (or pro-forma) SCFP, provide the best information when she is evaluating a request for a short-to-medium-term—one to five years—commercial loan. She is concerned with an applicant's ability to repay, without difficulty, any loan, with interest. She feels that in many cases net income understates the firm's debt-repayment capacity.

Do you agree with Mary? Why? Discuss.

MC 13.6. Many credit analysts do not place much reliance on the times interest earned figure. They reason that a high figure does not necessarily indicate debt safety, especially in the short run. They also know that a very low figure does not necessarily indicate inadequate funds to meet interest obligations. Discuss.

MC 13.7. Is it possible that the various turnovers in a firm—asset, receivables, and inventory—could be **too** high? Specifically, could there be any reason why a retailer might be content with—and even prefer—a relatively low receivables turnover? Are major retailers really retailers, or could they be considered financial institutions? Discuss.

ESSENTIAL PROBLEMS

EP 13.1. Exhibit 13.6 includes the recent balance sheets and income statements for the Francine Corporation. For this company, calculate the following:

a) Current ratio as of 12/31/X1,

b) Quick ratio as of 12/31/X1,

c) Debt ratio as of 12/31/X1,

d) Times interest earned during 19X1.

EP 13.2. Exhibit 13.7 includes the recent balance sheets and income statements for the Naomi Corporation. Calculate the four items required in Problem EP 13.1, for the Naomi Corporation.

EP 13.3. Determine the following data for 19X1 for the Francine Corporation (Exhibit 13.6):

a) Asset turnover,

b) Receivables turnover (assume all sales are on account),

c) Average days' receivables (based on 365-day period),

d) Inventory turnover,

e) Average days' sales in inventory (based on 365-day period),

f) Return on assets employed.

EP 13.4. Determine the six items of information required in Problem EP 13.3, for the Naomi Corporation (Exhibit 13.7).

EP 13.5. Determine the following items for 19X1 for the Francine Corporation (Exhibit 13.6).

a) Return on total owners' equity,

b) Return on common equity.

EP 13.6. Determine the following items for 19X1 for the Naomi Corporation (Exhibit 13.7).

a) Return on total owners' equity,

b) Return on common equity.

Exhibit 13.6

FRANCINE CORPORATION

Balance Sheets as of 12/31/X0 and 12/31/X1 and Income
Statement for 19X1
(000 omitted)

	12/31/X1	12/31/X0
Assets		
Cash	$ 50	$ 40
Marketable securities	60	90
Accounts receivable (net)	210	190
Inventory	280	260
Other current assets	25	30
Total Current Assets	$ 625	$ 610
Investments	75	75
Equipment	398	300
Less accumulated depreciation	(180)	(180)
Property under capital lease	95	105
Total Assets	$1,013	$ 910
Equities		
Accounts payable	$ 140	$ 120
Other current liabilities	60	50
Total Current Liabilities	$ 200	$ 170
Noncurrent notes payable	105	115
Less discount	(10)	(15)
Total Liabilities	$ 295	$ 270
Preferred stock ($100 par 14%)	100	100
Capital stock ($10 par)	300	300
Paid-in capital*	60	60
Retained earnings	258	180
Total Equities	$1,013	$ 910

* All on common stock.

Common shares outstanding	30,000 shs.	30,000 shs.

Income statement

Sales	$1,800
Cost of goods sold	1,080
Gross profit	$ 720
Interest	13
Depreciation on equipment	30
Amortization on capital lease	10
Other operating expenses	451
Operating income before taxes	$ 216
Income taxes	86
Net Income	$ 130
Dividends declared and paid	$ 52

Exhibit 13.7

NAOMI CORPORATION

Balance Sheets as of 12/31/X0 and 12/31/X1 and Income
Statement for 19X1
(000 omitted)

	12/31/X1	12/31/X0
Assets		
Cash	$ 30	$ 40
Marketable securities	80	10
Accounts receivable (net)	465	451
Inventory	325	313
Other current assets	40	30
Total Current Assets	$ 940	$ 844
Land	120	90
Fixed assets	544	400
Accumulated depreciation	(270)	(250)
Intangible assets	54	60
Total Assets	$1,388	$1,144
Equities		
Accounts payable	$ 207	$ 148
Other current liabilities	80	90
Total Current Liabilities	$ 287	$ 238
Bonds payable	250	200
Premium on bonds	18	20
Total Liabilities	$ 555	$ 458
Preferred stock ($100 par 12%)	200	200
Capital stock ($10 par)	275	265
Paid-in capital*	105	35
Retained earnings	253	186
Total Equities	$1,388	$1,144

* All on common stock

Common shares outstanding	27,500 shs.	26,500 shs.

Income statement

Sales	$2,200
Cost of goods sold	1,275
Gross profit	$ 925
Interest	14
Depreciation on fixed assets	50
Amortization of intangible assets	6
Other operating expenses	621
Operating income before taxes	$ 234
Income taxes	66
Net Income	$ 168
Dividends declared and paid	$ 101

EP 13.7. Assume that the Francine Corporation (Exhibit 13.6) regularly paid out 40 percent of its net income in dividends. Also assume that you could purchase Francine common stock on the open market for $60 per share. Calculate, for 19X1, the following:

a) Simple earnings per share,

b) Dividends per share,

c) Earnings percent return on your investment,

d) Dividends percent return on your investment.

EP 13.8. Assume that the Naomi Corporation (Exhibit 13.7) regularly paid out 60 percent of net income in dividends, and that the common stock's market price was $80 per share. Calculate, for the Naomi Corporation for 19X1, the following:

a) Simple earnings per share,

b) Dividends per share,

c) Earnings percent return to a purchaser of the stock,

d) Dividends percent return to a purchaser of the stock.

EP 13.9. Exhibit 13.8 contains income statements for the Sugarman Corporation for the years 19X0, 19X1, and 19X2.

a) Has the gross profit ratio improved?

b) Has the operating ratio improved?

c) If you were owner/manager of Sugarman, which items would you wish to investigate further and why?

Exhibit 13.8
SUGARMAN CORPORATION

Income Statements for the Years Ending 12/31/X0, 12/31/X1, and 12/31/X2
(000 omitted)

	19X2	19X1	19X0
Sales	$780	$625	$500
Less cost of goods sold	359	275	210
Gross profit	$421	$350	$290
Other operating expenses:			
Wages and salaries	101	75	65
Utilities	47	44	35
Depreciation	31	31	25
Insurance	23	25	20
Supplies	16	19	10
Maintenance	8	19	30
Interest	8	0	5
Operating income before taxes	$187	$137	$100
Income taxes	56	41	30
Net Income	$131	$ 96	$ 70

EP 13.10. Exhibit 13.9 contains income statements for the Tilamook Corporation for the years 19X0, 19X1, and 19X2.

a) What is happening to the gross profit ratio? What factors could be causing this change?

b) What is happening to the operating ratio? What factors appear to be responsible for the changing operating ratio?

c) If you were the owner-manager of Tilamook, which items would you wish to immediately investigate further, and why?

Exhibit 13.9
TILAMOOK CORPORATION

Income Statements for the Years Ending 12/31/X0, 12/31/X1, and 12/31/X2
(000 omitted)

	19X2	19X1	19X0
Sales	$505	$500	$400
Less cost of goods sold	222	230	196
Gross profit	$283	$270	$204
Other operating expenses:			
Wages and salaries	60	65	48
Utilities	51	40	24
Rent	25	25	20
Insurance	15	15	8
Supplies	10	5	4
Maintenance	20	20	16
Interest	32	25	20
Operating income before taxes	$ 70	$ 75	$ 64
Income taxes	15	15	12
Net Income	$ 55	$ 60	$ 52

EP 13.11. Exhibit 13.10 contains SCFP's for the Ultrasound Corporation for the years 19X0, 19X1 and 19X2.

a) Assuming the firm is using straight-line depreciation, does the firm appear to be regularly replacing its capacity assets as they expire? Is it expanding its capacity?

b) Do the owners appear to be making a substantial commitment to the firm's future? Is there any evidence of a fixed dividend policy?

c) Is there evidence that the firm is improving its solvency?

d) Does the firm appear to be increasing its proportion of debt, maintaining approximately the same proportion, or decreasing its indebtedness?

EP 13.12. Exhibit 13.11 contains the SCFP's in balanced form for the Victoria Corporation for the years 19X0, 19X1 and 19X2. For the Victoria Corporation, answer the same questions as those contained in Problem EP 13.11 above.

Exhibit 13.10

ULTRASOUND CORPORATION

Statement of Changes in Financial Position for the Years 19X0, 19X1, 19X2
(000 omitted)

	19X2	19X1	19X0
SOURCES:			
Net income		$300	$500
Plus depreciation		55	60
Funds from operations	$ 0	$355	$560
Sale of noncurrent assets	100	30	0
New long-term debt	150	20	0
New stock	0	0	10
Decrease balance of net working capital	100	35	0
Total Sources	$350	$440	$570
APPLICATIONS:			
Net income	$(100)		
Plus depreciation	50		
Funds lost in operations	$ 50	$ 0	$ 0
Purchase of noncurrent assets	0	40	70
Retire noncurrent debt	0	0	30
Dividends	300	400	450
Increase balance of net working capital	0	0	20
Total Applications	$ 350	$440	$570

SUPPLEMENTARY PROBLEMS

SP 13.13. Compare the income statements of the Sugarman and Tilamook Corporations (Exhibits 13.8 and 13.9) for the year 19X0. Assuming that both firms are in the same business:

a) Which firm appears to be doing a better job?

b) Which are the relatively favorable and unfavorable items in each firm?

c) What differences in accounting methods might exist which could change your conclusions?

SP 13.14. Refer to Problem 13.13 above. Answer the same questions for the years 19X1 and 19X2.

SP 13.15. Compare the SCFP's of the Ultrasound and Victoria Corporations (Exibits 13.10 and 13.11) for the year 19X0.

a) Which firm is investing more in replacement or expansion of its capacity assets?

b) Which firm is reinvesting more earnings?

Exhibit 13.11

VICTORIA CORPORATION

Statement of Changes in Financial Position for the Years 19X0, 19X1, 19X2
(000 omitted)

	19X2	19X1	19X0
SOURCES:			
Net income	$400	$300	$200
Plus depreciation	90	80	70
Funds from operations	$490	$380	$270
Sale of noncurrent assets	0	0	10
New long-term debt	0	0	20
New stock	50	30	0
Decrease balance of net working capital	0	0	5
Total Sources	$540	$410	$305
APPLICATIONS:			
Purchase of plant assets	$300	$200	$ 60
Retire noncurrent debt	100	100	205
Dividends	80	60	40
Increase balance of net working capital	60	50	0
Total Applications	$540	$410	$305

c) Which firm is doing more to improve its solvency?

d) Which firm is increasing its indebtedness more than the other?

SP 13.16. Refer to Problem SP 13.15 above. Answer the same questions for the years 19X1 and 19X2.

SP 13.17. Exhibit 13.12 includes 14 selected items of information for the Nan and Oboe Corporations for 19X0.

a) For each of the first 11 items, explain which firm has the better performance.

b) For items 12 and 13, explain which firm would be preferable for an individual first investing in the common stock today.

c) Which firm would appear a safer investment for a creditor? For an owner? Explain.

d) Which firm is doing a better job of financial management if optimal financing leverage in this industry was a debt-to-equity ratio of 0.4?

SP 13.18. For the Francine and Naomi Corporations (Exhibits 13.6 and 13.7), calculate for 19X1 items 1 through 13 as given on Exhibit 13.12. Then answer the four questions, (a) through (d), from Problem SP 13.17 above. You may assume that:

• Both firms are in the same industry;

- Francine pays 40 percent of net income in dividends, and has a current market price of $60 per share;
- Naomi pays 60 percent of net income in dividends, and the current market price of the stock is $80 per share;
- The optimal industry debt ratio is 0.4 to 1.

Exhibit 13.12

SELECTED DATA FOR 19X0 FOR THE NAN AND OBOE CORPORATIONS

		Nan	Oboe
(1)	Current ratio	3 to 1	2.5 to 1
(2)	Quick ratio	1.5 to 1	1.1 to 1
(3)	Debt ratio	.4 to 1	.2 to 1
(4)	EBIT	$500,000	$600,000
(5)	Times interest earned	40 times	60 times
(6)	Asset turnover	1.8 times	2.1 times
(7)	Receivables turnover	3 times	5 times
(8)	Inventory turnover	2 times	4 times
(9)	Return on assets employed	20%	25%
(10)	Return on owners' equity	28%	26%
(11)	Return on common equity	32%	26%
(12)	Earnings per share	$2.00	$1.80
(13)	Dividends per share	$.90	$1.20
(14)	Current market price per share of common stock	$22.00	$18.00

SP 13.19. For the Xerox Corporation and Addison-Wesley Publishing Company (Appendix A at the back of this book), calculate for 1976 items 1 through 11 from Exhibit 13.12. In the case of both firms, you may consider both classes of common stock together as if they were the same. For Xerox you may consider the minority interest ("outside shareholders' interest in equity of subsidiaries") as part of owners' equity but not common equity, Class B stock as part of Common stock, and Class B receivables may be treated like treasury stock.

SP 13.20. Assume stock prices and dividends per share for 1976 for Xerox were $57 and $1.10, and for Addison-Wesley Publishing Company were $7 and $0.40. Using this information and the data determined in Problem SP 13.19, answer questions (a), (b), and (c), from Problem SP 13.17.

14

FUNDS-FLOW STATEMENT PREPARATION

CHAPTER PREVIEW

The objective of this chapter is to provide you with the ability to prepare and interpret funds-flow statements. In the main body of the chapter, you can:

- Learn the significance and usefulness of cash flow information;
- Learn to prepare a cash flow statement from published financial statements—to convert a SCFP prepared on a working capital basis to a cash basis;
- Reinforce your understanding of funds-flow statements and particularly of the working capital statement and the SCFP prepared on a working capital basis;

and, in the chapter supplement for Preparer Procedures, you can learn how accountants prepare a working capital funds-flow statement and a SCFP from balance sheets and income statements.

With this knowledge, you will be in a position to develop, in subsequent courses, the additional skill of cash budgeting. Cash budgeting, or cash management, you will learn, is the cornerstone of successful operating and financial management.

CAN THEY MEET THE PAYROLL?

"*Meeting the payroll*" is business slang for maintaining solvency. It probably is derived from the necessity of having enough cash available on payday to pay employees. Of all creditors, employees are the least able to defer collection of their claims during a period of cash shortage for the firm.

As discussed in earlier chapters, suppliers, even though they are more able to extend their "loans" than employees, do not enjoy being asked to do so. They often will demand cash in advance on any new orders until old account balances are paid. Being "*placed on C.O.D.*" (cash on delivery) creates an even more urgent need for available cash. For these and many other reasons, successful managements closely monitor cash flow within their firms to ensure adequate solvency at all times. Cash management or cash budgeting involves planning or budgeting future cash needs and cash receipts. From continuously revised and updated cash budgets, possible shortages can be anticipated. Arrangements can then be made in advance, and not under frantic pressure, to obtain necessary new capital or to defer postponable expenditures. On the "up side," plans can be made to put excess cash to work earning interest from marketable securities.

Cash budgeting is an internal management activity. Its details are usually covered in Managerial Accounting and Finance courses and texts. Cash budgeting information is generally not made available to financial statement users. Remember that financial statements report history. Pro forma or forecasted financial statements are generally not provided to the user because of their lack of objectivity. The user, at his or her own risk, may prepare forecasts to serve as a basis for decision-making.

Financial statement users often desire to estimate the future cash flow within a firm. Assume that you are a commercial loan officer in a bank. One of your business customers wants a $100,000 seasonal loan to purchase extra Easter merchandise. You can also assume, in this example, that both you and the customer are confident that the loan will be repaid within six months. Loan security is not at issue.

As the commercial loan officer, you want the loan agreement to specify a reasonable repayment date which your customer can meet and still be able to meet his or her payroll. You do not wish to have the maturity date set unrealistically early with the then inevitable extra work of granting an extension. Your customer is thinking of total interest cost, and wants to make the loan period as short as possible.

Assume you do not have forecasted information for your customer—the Warehouse Company. However, it is early in the year, and you do have the customer's prior year SCFP. You are satisfied that, conservatively forecasting, this year will be the same as last year. If you could have last year's cash flow information, you might reasonably assume this year would be the same; or, starting with last year's cash flows, you could make modifications for events you expected would be different this year. Either way, you could arrive at an estimate of expected cash flows for the coming year.

GAAP allow a firm to prepare its SCFP on any one of several different bases—cash, cash plus marketable securities, quick assets, or net working capital. If your customer's prior year's SCFP had been prepared on a cash basis, you would already have your starting point for making a cash forecast. If not, you would need to convert the SCFP to a cash basis. In Chapter 7, you were introduced to the SCFP prepared on a net working capital basis. Since this form is very common, we will assume your customer's statement has been prepared on this basis.

From a SCFP prepared on a working capital basis, you can accurately estimate for the same year:

- Cash generated in operations,
- Cash generated from sale of noncurrent assets,
- Cash generated from new long-term debt,
- Cash generated from the sale of stock.

You can also accurately estimate:

- Cash used to acquire noncurrent assets,
- Cash used to retire long-term debt,
- Cash paid out in dividends.

These sources and applications should seem familiar because they are similar to elements of a SCFP introduced in Chapter 7. They are the elements of a *cash funds flow statement*. Instead of the broad picture of all resources, or the narrower picture of net working capital, the cash flow statement focuses on cash flows.

NET CASH INFLOW FROM OPERATIONS

For general use, or when considered over a period of several years, working capital funds from operations on the SCFP can be an adequate estimator of cash flow. Recall from Chapter 7 that "funds from operations" on the SCFP indicates new net working capital generated from the normal necessary operations of the business. Funds from operations equal fund revenue minus fund expenses. Fund revenue results in an increase in net working capital—cash sales, sales on account, and other earned revenue except equity in undistributed earnings, plus any revenue previously deferred as a current liability and now recognized. Fund expenses are those expenses which result in a decrease in net working capital (cash outflows)—the use or expiration of a current asset, or an increase in a current liability.

Subject to delays in completing the operating cycle, working capital funds inflows eventually become cash. However, at the same time, cash is being used to start new cycles. If all overlapping cycles were of the same length and all started with complete regularity—a steady-state condition—then funds from operations would equal cash from operations.

Overlapping cycles are often not identical in either length or frequency. Therefore, to obtain precise cash flows for a given period, funds from operations must be adjusted for changes in the balances of net working capital components other than cash. To see these necessary adjustments and their logic, we will follow the Trevor Company through a series of progressively more involved examples. For each example, we will assume that reported funds from operations for 19X1 exactly equaled the increase in net working capital. There were no other sources or applications of funds. All funds from operations were applied to or ended up in an increased balance of net working capital.

In the trivial case, assuming there were no current assets other than cash and no current liabilities, $75 of 19X1 funds from operations were all cash and equaled *cash generated in operations:*

	19X1	19X0
Working capital		
funds from operations	$ 75	
Cash	175	$100
Total current assets	$175	$100
Total current liabilities	0	0
Net working capital	$175	$100

Now, assume that Trevor had one other current asset besides cash. Assume it also had inventory:

	19X1	19X0
Working capital		
funds from operations	$ 75	
Cash	150	$ 75
Inventory	25	25
Total current assets	$175	$100
Total current liabilities	0	0
Net working capital	$175	$100

Did the $75 of 19X1 funds from operations equal cash generated in operations? Since the firm has no receivables, all fund revenue must have been cash. Fund expenses included cost of goods sold—a noncash item. Were all fund expenses equaled by cash outflows during 19X1? In this example for the Trevor Company, the answer is **yes**. The portion of cost of goods sold representing inventory used was exactly matched by new inventory purchased. Total dollars invested in inventory did not change. Therefore, cost of goods sold was the equivalent of cash purchases for the year. In this example, the $75 of funds from operations equals $75 of cash generated in operations.

Changes in Noncash Current Assets

Now consider a slightly different situation:

	19X1	19X0
Working capital		
funds from operations	$ 75	
Cash	165	$ 75
Inventory	10	25
Total current assets	$175	$100
Total current liabilities	0	0
Net working capital	$175	$100

In this example, $75 of reported funds from operations did not equal cash from operations. Inventory decreased during the year by $15. 19X1 fund expenses included $15 of "using up of current assets without replacement." If cost of goods sold had been $240, all $240 would, of course, have been a fund expense (outflow). But not all of the $240 could be thought of as representing cash purchases of inventory to replace inventory sold to customers. $15 of inventory was used and not replaced. Although fund expense would be $240, cash expense would be only $225. In the above example, fund revenue (all cash in this example) minus fund expenses equaled $75 (funds from operations); but total fund expenses included $15 which was a noncash expense. Therefore, with expenses reduced by $15 to a cash basis, cash from operations would be $15 more than the $75 of funds from operations. Cash generated in operations would be $90.

You can generalize on this example. In determining cash generated in operations, first **add** any **net decrease** in the balance of noncash current assets taken as a group. For items such as supplies and prepaid items, decreases can be viewed as reflecting fund expenses not representing cash outflow. These would be analogous to inventory decreases. Decreases in receivables would represent extra cash collected beyond the equivalent total of all credit sales for the period. This amount is similarly added to funds from operations in obtaining cash from operations.

Now consider the example of an increase in noncash current assets:

	19X1	19X0
Working capital		
funds from operations	$ 75	
Cash	130	$ 75
Inventory	45	25
Total current assets	$175	$100
Total current liabilities	0	0
Net working capital	$175	$100

$75 of funds from operations again does not equal the amount of cash from operations. Inventory increased by $20. $20 more cash may be thought of as flowing out for purchases than was represented by cost of goods sold. Net cash generated in operations was $55 ($75 of funds from operations minus $20 spent to more than replace inventory used).[1]

Again you can generalize. In the determination of cash generated in operations, **subtract** any **net increase** in the balance of noncash current assets taken as a group. For items such as supplies and prepaid items, increases may be thought of as cash used for their purchase beyond simple replacement. An increase in receivables represents fund revenue not yet received as a cash inflow.

To summarize, in converting funds from operations to cash generated in operations first:

Add: Any net decrease in the balance of noncash current assets
         as a group; or

Subtract: Any net increase in the balance of noncash current assets
         taken as a group.

To remember this rule, pick one noncash current asset such as inventory or accounts receivable, where you can readily see the necessary adjustment for a change in end-of-year balance. Then remember your mini-rule is applicable to all other noncash current assets.

Changes in Current Liabilities

Now let us return to the Trevor Company and allow current liabilities to enter the picture. In the trivial and extremely rare case where total current liabilities are identical at the beginning and end of the year, no adjustment to funds from operations would be necessary for liabilities. You could view this situation as one in which all fund operating expenses for the current year which were not paid for at year-end were exactly matched by cash outflows paying the prior year's ending current liabilities. Fund operating expenses were matched by cash outflows.

Suppose the total current liabilities had increased during the year by $40:

	19X1	19X0
Working capital funds from operations	$ 75	
Cash	$245	$130
Total current assets	$245	$130
Total current liabilities	70	30
Net working capital	$175	$100

---

[1]   Conceptually, in this example, you could think of $75 as being generated in operations and the $20 inventory purchase as being a distinct event. Purchases of additional inventory are really not strictly part of this year's income or funds-generating operations. To avoid many less meaningful additional breakdowns on the cash-flow statement, accountants arbitrarily define cash generated in operations to include funds from operations adjusted for any change in current liabilities and noncash current assets.

When total current liabilities increase, you can think of the amount of the increase as the portion of current year's fund operating expense not yet paid and therefore not representing cash outflows. If funds from operations were $75, and if all fund revenue was cash but $40 of fund expense did not represent cash outflow, then cash from operations would not be $75. How much would it be?

You are correct if you determined cash from operations in this example as $115. Most increases in total current liabilities are added to funds from operations in the process of determining cash generated in operations.[2]

Finally, if there is a decrease in total current liabilities during the year, the amount of the decrease is subtracted from funds from operations. A reduction of current liabilities can be viewed as cash outflow in excess of fund expenses. If total liabilities decreased $35 and funds from operations were $75, cash from operations would be only $40 (assuming no change in noncash current assets).

CONVERTING FUNDS FROM OPERATIONS TO CASH FROM OPERATIONS

The general rules for converting working capital funds from operations to cash generated in operations can be summarized as follows:

1. Start with: Funds from operations   XXX
2. Adjust for changes in noncash current assets:
       add any decrease in net noncash current assets   +XXX
   or **subtract** any increase in net noncash current assets   −XXX
3. Adjust for changes in current liabilities:
       add any increase in total current liabilities   +XXX
   or **subtract** any decrease in total current liabilities   −XXX
4. Equals: Cash generated (lost) in operations   = $XXX

Returning to your role as a commercial loan officer in a bank, can you now estimate 19X1 cash from operations for your customer—the Warehouse Company—from the information contained on Exhibit 14.1? To reinforce your understanding, or to generate necessary review, you should attempt to determine Warehouse's cash from operations before reading further.

During 19X1, Warehouse generated $280,000 cash from operations. From the SCFP, funds from operations was reported as $340,000.

---

[2]   Current liability changes that do not result from operations are excluded (ignored) in calculating cash from operations. Examples of changes that are excluded would be maturing portions of noncurrent debt and increases in dividends payable.

Funds from operations	$340,000
ADD Net increase in current liabilities	5,000
	$345,000
SUBTRACT Net increase in noncash current assets	65,000
Equals cash from operations	$280,000

In this Warehouse Company example, you can think of the necessary adjustment in two separate parts. First, the $5,000 net increase in current liabilities is added to working capital funds from operations. The $5,000 can be viewed as representing fund expenses not yet matched by cash outflows. Second, the $65,000 net increase in noncash current assets is subtracted as representing additional cash outflows related to operations but not included in funds expenses. The resultant $280,000 represents the net inflow of cash related to operating activities.

Exhibit 14.1
WAREHOUSE COMPANY

**Statement of Changes in Financial Position for the Year Ending 12/31/X1
(000 omitted)**

SOURCES	
Net income	$300
Plus depreciation	40
Funds from operations	$340
Sale of noncurrent assets	15
New long-term debt	60
New owner investment	30
Total Sources	$445
APPLICATIONS	
Purchase noncurrent assets	$200
Retire noncurrent debt	50
Dividends	150
Increase in balance of net working capital	45
Total Applications	$445

Schedule of Working Capital Changes

	Begin	End	Change
Cash	$ 40	$ 25	−15
Receivables	90	70	−20
Inventory	65	150	+85
Total Current Assets	195	245	+50
Accounts payable	70	85	+15
Other current liabilities	20	10	−10
Total Current Liabilities	90	95	+ 5
Net Working Capital	$105	$150	+45

Refer again to Exhibit 14.1. Warehouse started the year with $40,000 of cash. You have just determined that during the year it generated an additional $280,000 of cash from operations. How much cash remained at year-end? What happened to the other $295,000? Obviously this $295,000 was used somewhere, and there also may have been other sources of cash. Sources and uses of cash other than from operations will now be examined.

OTHER SOURCES OF CASH

Recall the working capital funds flow statement and the SCFP, first introduced in Chapter 7. You should remember that, in addition to operations, a firm has four possible sources of (places to obtain) funds or cash.[3] As other "inside sources," it could either sell noncurrent assets for cash, or it could draw down its balance of cash on hand for use elsewhere. As "outside sources" of additional cash, the firm could obtain cash in exchange for new long-term debt or from new owner investment of cash (sale of stock).

The SCFP will report the amounts related to each of these events occurring during the year. Recall from Chapter 7 that it is possible for a firm to have "matched pairs" of resource flows not involving flows of working capital and, therefore, certainly not cash. The most common "matched pairs" include:

- Exchange of one noncurrent asset (source) for another (application);
- Incurring of new noncurrent debt (source) in connection with purchase of noncurrent asset (application);
- New owner investment (source) of noncurrent asset (application);
- New noncurrent debt (source) in exchange for extinguishment of old noncurrent debt (application) in a debt refunding
- New ownership claims (source) in exchange for extinguishment of noncurrent creditor claims (application) in a debt conversion.

If there were any "matched pairs" during a given year, their amounts would have to be eliminated from sources or applications appearing on the SCFP in order to identify sources and applications involving cash flows. Thereafter, from the SCFP:

- Any reported disposition of noncurrent assets (after eliminating any noncurrent asset exchanges), and

---

[3]   A realized extraordinary gain could involve still another cash source. Extraordinary gains are rare. An example might include land acquired by a retail store for $50,000 for use as a parking lot. Oil or uranium is discovered under the land, and it is sold for $1,000,000 cash. To identify this $1,000,000 as cash from operations would be misleading.

- Any reported additional noncurrent debt (after eliminating debt involved as part of the purchase of noncurrent assets, or debt directly exchanged for other debt in a refunding), and

- Any reported additional owner investment (after eliminating any owner investment of noncurrent assets, and any new owner investment resulting from noncurrent debt conversion),

would each represent a distinct source of additional cash brought into the business during the period.

Referring to the data shown in Exhibit 14.1, and assuming that Warehouse had no "matched pairs" during the year, what were the total net sources of cash for the firm during the year? From "inside sources," the firm obtained:

Cash from operations	$280,000
Sale of noncurrent assets	15,000
Reduction in cash balance	15,000
	$310,000

Was any cash obtained from outside sources?

Exhibit 14.1 reveals $90,000 obtained from other outside sources. Total sources of cash during the year, assuming no "matched pairs," appear to be $400,000, as follows:

Cash from operations	$280,000
Sale of noncurrent assets	15,000
New long-term debt	60,000
New owner investment	30,000
Reduction in cash balance	15,000
Total Sources	$400,000

OTHER USES OF CASH

Earlier we were wondering what happened to $295,000 of cash. Actually we are interested in how the firm used the $400,000 identified above. Again we can look to the various possible applications on the SCFP first introduced in Chapter 7. A firm has four ordinary applications of cash other than cash lost in operations.[4] Think first of all possible uses of new cash generated by a firm. It can:

- Acquire noncash current assets;
- Pay current liabilities;

---

[4]   An extraordinary loss could involve still another cash application: A major burglary or embezzlement involving a material loss of cash could qualify as extraordinary and should be separately disclosed. Simple employee pilfering or nonmaterial cash-register robbery would normally be included under operations.

- Acquire noncurrent assets;
- Retire noncurrent debt;
- Pay dividends to owners; or
- Increase the year-end balance in its cash account.

The first two uses—acquire noncash current assets and pay current liabilities—are conventionally included as part of cash from operations (see above). The next three would be reported on the SCFP. As in the case of sources, applications might include part of a "matched pair" which would have to be eliminated. Therefore, from the SCFP:

- Any reported acquisition of noncurrent assets (after eliminating non-current asset exchanges, noncurrent asset portions obtained in exchange for new noncurrent debt, and noncurrent assets acquired directly as an owner investment), and

- Any reported retirement of noncurrent debt (after eliminating any debt conversions or direct exchanges in a refunding), and

- Any reported dividends to owners,

would each represent a distinct use of cash during the period. Finally, an increase in the balance of cash on hand revealed by the schedule of working capital changes could be included as an application (use) of cash. Cash generated elsewhere could end up being applied or "used" to increase the balance of cash on hand.

THE STATEMENT OF CASH FLOW

You now have all the steps necessary to prepare a *statement of cash flow* from the data supplied on a firm's SCFP and Schedule of Changes in Working Capital. These steps are summarized on Exhibit 14.2.

Returning to your role as a commercial loan officer, prepare a statement of cash flows for the Warehouse Company for the year 19X1 from the data given on Exhibit 14.1. Assume that the only "matched pair" during 19X1 involved $75,000 of Warehouse's new noncurrent assets which had been purchased for $35,000 down and a five-year note for the balance. You should attempt to prepare this statement before proceeding to verify the adequacy of your understanding.

Exhibit 14.3 is a statement of cash flow for the Warehouse Company for the year ending 12/31/X1. Note that the $60,000 of new noncurrent debt and the $200,000 of new noncurrent assets, as reported on the SCFP, have each been reduced by the $40,000 "matched pair" which did not involve cash flow. The earlier estimate of $400,000 of cash generated is now reduced to $360,000, recognizing a $40,000 "matched pair." Only $360,000 of cash was obtained for nonoperations use. Also note that the cash reduction of $15,000, as reported on the Schedule of Changes in Working Capital, has been included as a source, to make sources and uses balance.

Exhibit 14.2

CHECKLIST OF POSSIBLE SOURCES AND USES OF CASH

POSSIBLE SOURCES OF CASH:		
Cash generated from operations:		
Funds from operations	XXX	
Plus: any decrease in noncash current assets	+XXX	
any increase in current liabilities	+XXX	
Minus: any increase in noncash current assets	−XXX	
any decrease in current liabilities	−XXX	$XXX[a]
Disposition of noncurrent assets		XXX[b]
Additional noncurrent debt		XXX[c]
Additional owner investment		XXX[d]
Reduction during period of cash balance on hand		XXX
Extraordinary gains realized in cash		XXX[e]
Total Sources		$XXX
POSSIBLE USES (APPLICATIONS) OF CASH:		
Cash lost in operations		$XXX[f]
Acquisition of noncurrent assets		XXX[g]
Retirement of noncurrent debt		XXX[h]
Dividends		XXX[i]
Increase during period of cash balance on hand		XXX
Extraordinary losses involving cash		XXX[j]
Total Applications		$XXX

(a) Negative balance listed as use or application.

(b) Balance from SCFP after elimination of any noncurrent asset exchanges.

(c) Balance from SCFP after eliminating any new debt involved as part of a noncurrent asset purchase or involved in a direct exchange for old debt in a refunding.

(d) Balance from SCFP after eliminating owner direct investment of noncurrent assets and new owner investment resulting from noncurrent debt conversion.

(e) Proceeds of a reported extraordinary gain resulting from a sale.

(f) See (a) above.

(g) Balance from SCFP after eliminating noncurrent asset exchanges, portions of noncurrent assets acquired in exchange for new noncurrent debt, and noncurrent assets acquired by direct owner investment.

(h) Balance from SCFP after eliminating debt conversions or direct exchanges in a refunding.

(i) Full amount reported on SCFP even though some dividends are still payable which will have been picked up as cash from operations adjustment.

(j) Only amount of cash directly involved in the extraordinary loss.

Exhibit 14.3

WAREHOUSE COMPANY

Statement of Cash Flow for the Year 19X1
(000 omitted)

SOURCES OF CASH:		
Cash from operations:		
Funds from operations	$340	
Add: Net increase in current liabilities	5	
	$345	
Deduct: Net increase in noncash current assets	65	$280
Sale of noncurrent asset		15
New noncurrent debt		20
New owner investment		30
Reduction of cash balance		15
Total Sources		$360
USES OF CASH:		
Purchase of noncurrent assets		$160
Retire noncurrent debt		50
Dividends		150
Total Uses		$360

The checklist given in Exhibit 14.2 and the Cash Flow Statement given in Exhibit 14.3 are both organized to provide a balance of sources and applications. As discussed in Chapter 7 with reference to the SCFP, the balanced approach is one of the acceptable forms of presentation in conformance with GAAP. Many firms prefer to focus attention upon the change in the balance of cash on hand (or net working capital in an SCFP prepared on a working capital basis) and therefore follow an unbalanced format. Exhibit 14.4 is a cash-flow statement for Warehouse following the unbalanced format. In comparing Exhibits 14.3 and 14.4, you will note that the information content is identical. The only difference is with respect to the classification of the change in the balance of cash (or net working capital). In the balanced approach (Exhibit 14.3), the change is shown as a source (decreased balance) or application (increased balance). Following the unbalanced approach, the change is classified as a difference between total sources and total applications. You should not be confused by these different approaches to classifying the same information.

As a commercial loan officer, you can now discuss with your client his/her nonoperating plans over the next six months to raise or spend cash. Assuming that 19X2 will be the same as 19X1 and that sales revenues and collections are not seasonal, Warehouse should generate additional cash from operations of $23,000 per month. If the inventory acquired under the proposed loan is sold or turned over within two months, and collections average two months, the loan should theoretically *self-liquidate* in four months. A four-month note would appear safe, as the firm would also be generating $92,000 of cash as a backup or safety factor in the event the inventory is not all sold or collections are slow.

Exhibit 14.4
WAREHOUSE COMPANY

Statement of Cash Flow for the Year 19X1
(000 omitted)

SOURCES OF CASH:		
Cash from operations:		
Funds from operations	$340	
Add: Net increase in current		
liabilities	5	
	$345	
Deduct: Net increase in noncash		
current assets	65	$280
Sale of noncurrent asset		15
New noncurrent debt		20
New owner investment		30
Total Sources		$345
USES OF CASH:		
Purchase of noncurrent assets		$160
Retire noncurrent debt		50
Dividends		150
Total Uses		$360
Resultant decrease in balance of cash on hand		$ 15

OTHER USES OF CASH-FLOW INFORMATION

Cash-flow statements, of course, can be useful to many people other than bank loan officers. Other interested users could include:

- Suppliers and other creditors concerned about payment on their existing and future accounts, bonds, or loans;
- Owners concerned about the availability of dividends;
- Management attempting to schedule major acquisitions of new assets.

Remember that all these people need to base their decisions on a pro-forma or projected statement of cash flows. The historical statement of cash flow presented in this chapter provides a basis for such a projection or forecast.

Cash-flow information is essentially the basis for most business decisions.

In courses in Management Accounting and in Finance, you will find that cash-flow data, and not financial accounting accruals, are the basis for particular decisions such as:

- Add new product/discontinue existing product;
- Make vs. buy;
- Lease vs. buy;
- Make new investment;
- Continue operations/discontinue operations;

and many others.

Although beyond the scope of this text, it is also important that you realize that more sophisticated investment or investor's decision models are now including anticipated or expected cash flows in lieu of expected earnings. Also, as part of an overall re-evaluation of the financial accounting system, the FASB has proposed that system changes essentially be evaluated against the criterion of:

> Will the resultant financial statements provide the user with an even better ability to predict future cash flows?

CHAPTER OVERVIEW

From the material in this chapter, you should now be able to:

- Describe how changes in net noncash current assets and changes in total current liabilities may be used to determine cash from operations, given working capital funds from operations;
- Describe and give examples of four possible different "internal sources" of cash (including extraordinary items) that might appear on a balanced-format cash-flow statement;
- Describe and give examples of two possible external sources of cash;
- Describe and give examples of six possible different uses of applications of cash (including extraordinary items) that might appear on a balanced-format cash-flow statement;
- Explain the difference between a cash-flow statement or SCFP prepared following a balanced format and the same statement prepared following the unbalanced format;
- Prepare a cash-flow statement, given a SCFP prepared on a working capital flow basis.

NEW VOCABULARY AND CONCEPTS

"Meeting the payroll"   Cash funds-flow statement/
"Placed on C.O.D."   statement of cash flow
Cash from operations   Self-liquidating loan

• Difference between cash and working capital funds-flow statements.

REVIEW QUESTIONS

1. What items can cause a difference between funds from operations and cash from operations?

2. Explain how each of the following amounts are used in the determination of cash from operations:
   a) Funds from operations,
   b) Any increase in noncash current assets,
   c) Any decrease in noncash current assets,
   d) Any increase in total current liabilities,
   e) Any decrease in total current liabilities.

3. Where, in a firm's published financial statements, would you find each of the items of information cited in Question 2 above?

4. What, including cash from operations, are the six possible sources of cash that might appear on a statement of cash flow?

5. Specifically where in the financial statements could you obtain information related to the five possible sources of cash other than cash from operations?

6. What, including cash lost in operations, are the six possible uses or applications of cash that might appear on a statement of cash flow?

7. Specifically, where in the financial statements, could you obtain information related to the five possible uses of cash other than cash lost in operations?

8. Who are various potential users of cash-flow statements? Would they use the statement directly, or as a basis for another statement? Explain your answer.

MINI-CASES AND QUESTIONS FOR DISCUSSION

MC 14.1. Financial analysts, in making comparisons between firms, will sometimes cite a preferred firm as one having the higher cash flow or "cash income." The accounting profession has steadfastly opposed such "cash income" reporting and analysis. If it is true that cash flows are so basic to business decision-making, why don't accountants, at the very least, mandate a cash-flow statement as part of the audited annual report? Isn't the cash-flow statement always more objective and verifiable than all of the other statements presently prepared? Discuss.

MC 14.2. How can a cash-flow statement prepared for the past year be useful for predicting cash flows in the current year? Don't decisions have to be based on future or anticipated cash flows? Discuss.

ESSENTIAL PROBLEMS

EP 14.1. Exhibit 14.5 contains data for the Hodge Company for the year ending 12/31/X1. Determine the amount of cash generated from operations during 19X1 by the firm. Show all of your calculations starting with funds from operations.

EP 14.2. Exhibit 14.6 contains data for the Illustrious Company for the year 19X1. Determine the amount of cash generated from operations during 19X1 by the firm. Show all of your calculations, starting with funds from operations.

Exhibit 14.5(a)
HODGE CORPORATION

Balance Sheet as of 12/31/X1
(000 omitted)

ASSETS		EQUITIES	
Cash	$ 135	Accounts payable	$ 210
Receivables	220	Other current liabilities	30
Inventory	285	Total Current Liabilities	$ 240
Total Current Assets	$ 640	Long-term debt[c]	217
Investments	440	Total Liabilities	$ 457
Land	50		
Buildings[a]	270	Capital stock[d]	465
Accumulated depreciation on		Paid-in capital[d]	140
buildings	(135)	Retained earnings	355
Equipment	420	Total Owners' Equity	$ 960
Accumulated depreciation on			
equipment	(308)		
Intangibles[b]	40		
Total Assets	$1,417	Total Equities	$1,417

Notes:
[a] During the year, buildings costing $70 were acquired with the payment of $20 and the signing of a five-year note payable for the balance.
[b] Intangibles costing $5 were acquired in exchange for common stock.
[c] During the year, $50 was borrowed on a ten-year note payable and another five-year note for $50 was given as partial payment on new buildings purchased (see Note (a) above). $83 of long-term debt was retired with cash, and an additional $100 was converted to common stock.
[d] During the year, the Capital Stock and Paid-in Capital accounts were increased by $50 representing a sale of new stock, $50 representing a stock dividend, $100 representing conversion of long-term debt (see Note (c) above), and $5 issued in exchange for a new intangible asset (see Note (b) above).

Exhibit 14.5(b)
HODGE CORPORATION

**Statement of Income and Retained Earnings
for Year Ending 12/31/X1
(000 omitted)**

Sales	$2,500
Cost of goods sold	1,500
Gross profit	1,000
Other income from investments[a]	60
Operating expenses:	
Depreciation on fixed assets	30
Amortization of intangibles	15
All other	975
Gain on sale of fixed asset[b]	20
Income from operations	$ 60
Income taxes	15
Extraordinary loss on fixed asset[c]	25
Net Income	$ 20
Beginning retained earnings	$ 400
Net income	20
Cash dividend	15
Stock dividend	50
Ending retained earnings	$ 355

Notes:
[a] Consists of $20 received in dividends plus $40 representing share of undistributed earnings of investee over which Smith exerted significant influence.
[b] Equipment costing $30 with accumulated depreciation of $12 was sold for $38.
[c] An unused building costing $50 with accumulated depreciation of $25 was destroyed by an earthquake. The loss was not covered by insurance and may be assumed to qualify as extraordinary.

EP 14.3. Identify each of the "matched pairs" of resource flows contained in the Hodge SCFP (Exhibit 14.5). Eliminate the effect of these "matched pairs," and prepare a **working capital** funds-flow statement for the Hodge Company for 19X1.

EP 14.4. Exhibit 14.6 provides data for the Illustrious Corporation for 19X1. Assume you also know that the following events transpired during this year:

- $70,000 of new noncurrent assets purchased involved a down payment of $10,000 and a three-year note payable for the balance;

- $40,000 of new noncurrent debt was a direct exchange in a refunding for $40,000 of older debt, which was retired;

- $80,000 of noncurrent debt was converted to common stock during the year.

Identify each of the "matched pairs" of resource flows contained in the Illustrious SCFP. Eliminate the effect of these "matched pairs," and prepare a **working capital** funds-flow statement for the Illustrious Company for the year 19X1.

EP 14.5. From the information provided in Exhibit 14.5, prepare a statement of cash flow for the Hodge Company for the year 19X1.

EP 14.6. From the information provided in Exhibit 14.6 and that contained in Problem EP 14.4, prepare a statement of cash flow for the Illustrious Company for the year 19X1.

Exhibit 14.5(c)
HODGE CORPORATION

Statement of Changes in Financial Position for the Year Ending 12/31/X1
(000 omitted)

Resources obtained from:		
Net income		$ 20
Adjust for nonfund items:		
Share of investee's earnings	$(40)	
Depreciation	30	
Amortization	15	
Gain on sale of fixed asset	(20)	(15)
Total funds		$ 5
Adjust for extraordinary loss on fixed assets		25
Funds from operations		30
Disposition of equipment		38
New long-term debt		100
Issuance of stock		155
Total Sources		$323
Resources were applied to:		
Acquire new buildings		$ 70
Acquire new intangibles		5
Retire long-term debt		183
Pay dividends		15
Increase working capital		50
Total Applications		$323

Schedule of Changes in Working Capital for the Year Ending 12/31/X1
(000 omitted)

	Begin	End	Change
Cash	$100	$135	$35 increase
Receivables	200	220	20 increase
Inventory	300	285	15 decrease
Total current assets	600	640	40 increase
Accounts payable	200	210	10 increaes
Other current liabilities	50	30	20 decrease
Total current liabilities	250	240	10 decrease
Net working capital	350	400	50 increase

Exhibit 14.6

ILLUSTRIOUS CORPORATION

Statement of Changes in Financial Position for 19X1
(000 omitted)

SOURCES

Net income	$215	
Add: Depreciation on fixed assets	30	
Amortization of intangible assets	20	
Funds from operations		$265
Sale of noncurrent assets		15
New long-term debt		100
New stock		200
Decrease in balance of net working capital		40
Total Sources		$620

APPLICATIONS

Purchase Noncurrent Assets	$170
Retire Noncurrent Debt	300
Dividends	150
Total Applications	$620

Schedule of Working Capital Changes for 19X1
(000 omitted)

	Begin	End	Change
Cash	$ 60	$ 50	$—10
Receivables	190	170	−20
Other current assets	150	180	+30
Total Current Assets	400	400	0
Accounts payable	135	115	−20
Other current liabilities	20	80	+60
Total Current Liabilities	155	195	+40
Net working capital	$245	$205	−40

PREPARER PROCEDURES

Accountants must know how to prepare a statement of changes in financial position (SCFP). Preparer procedures relating to this statement were not included with Chapter 7. They are more readily assimilated along with material not introduced until the last few chapters. The procedures set forth below relate to the preparation of a SCFP based on flows of net working capital, the same basis as first introduced in Chapter 7.

Long-Way Approach

There are two approaches to preparing a SCFP. The first, or long-way approach, involves starting with the transactions and adjustments occurring during the year. The second, or shortcut approach, involves starting with the other three completed financial statements—the balance sheet, the income statement, and the statement of retained earnings.

The long-way approach involves identifying all transactions and adjustments occurring during the year as operating (O), financial (F), or SCFP-irrelevant (I). Operating items are all those that affect operating income, and that are not SCFP-irrelevant (see below). Operating transactions and adjustments are those which reflect fund revenue and fund expenses. Fund revenue transactions and adjustments are all of those involving current assets (cash and receivables) and current liabilities (unearned revenue). Fund expenses are those which involve cash expenditure, current asset use or expiration, or incurrence of a current liability. Once identified, operating transactions and adjustments are netted to determine working capital funds from operations.

Financing transactions are those which do not primarily involve revenue or expense, and which are not SCFP-irrelevant (see below). They include such events as:

- Acquisition and disposition of noncurrent assets,
- Issuance and extinction of concurrent debt,
- New owner investment (stock sale) and withdrawals (dividends).

Financial items are summarized by type and reported on the SCFP.

SCFP-irrelevant items are irrelevant to the objectives of the SCFP and do not affect the statement. They include the following types:

a) Any adjustment to noncurrent assets or noncurrent liabilities to reflect amortization, depreciation, or loss. Specifically included in this group are amortizations of bond premium and discount, whether the bonds represent investment or debt.

b) Any adjustment to the investments account reflecting shares of significantly influenced investee's losses or profits not matched by dividends received.

c) Any adjustment to the investments account reflecting temporary loss or recovery of market value.

d) Any accrual or expiration of deferred income tax liability.

e) Any loss on disposition of noncurrent assets.

f) Any transaction or adjustment where the effect is solely to exchange account balances within owners' equity—establishing and extinguishing reserves, stock dividends, and so forth.

All transactions and adjustments identified as SCFP-irrelevant are simply ignored in SCFP preparation via the long-way approach. The long-way approach will not be discussed further. Most accountants use some variation of the shortcut approach, which follows.

Short-cut Approach

Most transactions and adjustments throughout the year are either directly relevant to the SCFP, or else are summarized in information which is relevant. Very few items are SCFP-irrelevant. It is therefore much less work to start with the already completed statements—the balance sheet, the income statement, and the statement of retained earnings. You will then only have to back out or reverse the effect of the few SCFP-irrelevant items. Exhibit 14.7 contains statements for the Waterstreet Company, which will be used as an example.

Exhibit 14.7(a)

WATERSTREET CORPORATION

Balance Sheets as of 12/31/X0 and 12/31/X1
(000 omitted)

	12/31/X1	12/31/X0
ASSETS:		
Cash	$ 68	$ 30
Receivables (net)	120	100
Inventory	210	200
Other current assets	30	20
Total Current Assets	$428	$350
Investments	43	40
Land	100	100
Fixed assets	600	500
Less accumulated depreciation	(110)	(100)
Intangible assets	34	60
Total Assets	$1095	$950
EQUITIES:		
Accounts payable	$100	$ 80
Other current liabilities	60	70
Total Current Liabilities	$160	$150
Noncurrent notes payable	60	100
Bonds payable	300	200
Less unamortized discount	(45)	(50)
Total Liabilities	$475	$400
Capital stock	400	340
Paid-in capital	80	60
Retained earnings	140	150
Total Equities	$1095	$950

Your first step involves preparing the SCFP worksheet similar to Exhibit 14.8. This worksheet lists, in the first two columns, Waterstreet's beginning and ending balance sheet; but note two important differences from the information given on Exhibit 14.7. Net working capital, net fixed assets, net bonds, capital stock plus paid-in capital, and retained earnings plus retained earnings reserves and appropriations, are all given as single net amounts. The details are not important to SCFP preparation. Also, note that the beginning balance sheet is listed in the first column.

Your second step will be to identify all of the SCFP-irrelevant transactions and adjustments occurring during the year. You should list them in entry form on a separate piece of paper. For example, in the Waterstreet case, the following six SCFP-irrelevant entries should be apparent:

	DR	CR
1. Depreciation Expense	$25	
Accumulated Depreciation		$25

Recording annual depreciation (see Type A above)

Exhibit 14.7(b)

WATERSTREET CORPORATION

**Income Statement and Statement of Retained
Earnings for the Year 19X1
(000 omitted)**

	19X1
Sales	$800
Less cost of goods sold	500
Gross profit	$300
Operating Expenses:	
Depreciation of fixed assets	25
Amortization of intangible assets	6
Interest	29
All other operating expenses	144
Investments revenue	4[a]
Operating income before taxes	$100
Less income taxes	40
Operating income	$60
Less extraordinary loss on intangible assets	20
Net Income	$ 40
Retained earnings 12/31/X0	$150
Net income	40
Less: Cash dividends	20
Stock dividend	30
Retained earnings 12/31/X1	$140

[a] $1,000 in dividends were received.

	DR	CR
2. Amortization Expense	6	
Intangible Assets		6

Recording amortization of intangibles (see Type A above)

3. Interest Expense	5	
Unamortized Bond Discount		5

Recording amortization of bond discount (see Type A above)

4. Investments	3	
Investments Revenue		3

Recording portion of investments revenue not representing a flow of working capital (see Type B above)

5. Extraordinary Loss on Intangible Asset	20	
Intangible Asset		20

Recording loss on intangibles (see Type A above)

6. Retained Earnings	30	
Capital Stock and Paid-in Capital		30

Recording stock dividend (see Type F above)

Exhibit 14.8

WATERSTREET CORPORATION

SCFP Worksheet

	Column 1	Column 2	Column 3	Column 4	Column 5
	12/31/X0	12/31/X1	Reversals	Revised 12/31/X1	Net changes during year
Net working capital	$200	$268			
Investments	40	43			
Land	100	100			
Fixed assets (net)	400	490			
Intangible assets	60	34			
Total	$800	$935			
Noncurrent notes payable	$100	$ 60			
Bonds payable (net)	150	255			
Capital stock and paid-in surplus	400	480			
Retained earnings	150	140			
Total	$800	$935			

Step 3 involves reversing the effect on the ending balance sheet of all SCFP-irrelevant entries (see Column 3). Note that revenue and expense reversals are made directly to retained earnings. After reversal, Column 4 shows the ending balance sheet as if the SCFP-irrelevant entries had never been made. Exhibit 14.9 shows the SCFP worksheet for the Waterstreet Company after completion of the reversals.

Study Exhibit 14.9 carefully until you are confident you understand the reversing process. Recall that the objective of these reversals is to restate items on the ending balance sheet to the amounts that would have appeared if all of the SCFP-irrelevant entries had never been recorded. The SCFP-irrelevant reversals are all reference-numbered on Exhibit 14.9 to correspond to the entries given above.

The effect of Entry 1 originally was to reduce net fixed assets (by increasing accumulated depreciation) and to reduce retained earnings (by increasing depreciation expense). The amount of reduction must be restored to both of these items. Similarly, the amount of intangibles amortization (Entry 2) is restored to the asset account and to retained earnings. The effect of Entry 5 was similar to amortization. The reversal restores the amount of the loss to both the asset account and retained earnings.

The effect of Entry 3 was to increase new bond liability (by reducing bond discount) and to reduce retained earnings (by increasing interest expense). The reversal reduces net bond liability and increases retained earnings.

The effect of Entry 4 was to increase investments and to increase retained earnings (through increasing investments revenue). The reversal subtracts this nonfund revenue from both "sides" of the balance sheet.

Entry 6 originally reduced retained earnings and increased both capital stock and paid-in capital by the market value of the stock dividend. The reversal restores these accounts to their original amounts.

Exhibit 14.9

WATERSTREET CORPORATION

SCFP Worksheet

	Column 1	Column 2	Column 3	Column 4	Column 5
	12/31/X0	12/31/X1	Reversals	Revised 12/31/X1	Net changes during year
Net working capital	$200	$268		$268	
Investments	40	43	− 3(4)	40	
Land	100	100		100	
Fixed assets (net)	400	490	+25(1) +6(2)	515	
Intangible assets	60	34	+20(5)	60	
Total	$800	$935		$983	
Noncurrent notes payable	$100	$ 60		$ 60	
Bonds payable (net)	150	255	− 5(3)	250	
Capital stock and paid-in surplus	400	480	−30(6) +25(1) +6(2) +5(3) −3(4) +20(5)	450	
Retained earnings	150	140	+30(6)	223	
Total	$800	$935		$983	

Step 4 involves calculating the change between the beginning balance sheet and the restated ending balance sheet. These changes are posted in Column 5 of the worksheet. See Exhibit 14.10.

Step 5 involves completing the preparation of the SCFP, starting with information from Column 5 of the worksheet. Changes appearing in Column 5 should be interpreted and processed as follows:

Increase in Net Working Capital

An increase in the balance of net working capital may be recorded as an application. For Waterstreet, $68,000 net working capital increase is shown as an application. See Exhibit 14.11.

Decrease in Net Working Capital

A decrease in net working capital (not part of the Waterstreet example) may be recorded as a source. If this procedure is followed, total sources will equal total applications on the completed statement.

Exhibit 14.10
WATERSTREET CORPORATION

SCFP Worksheet

	Column 1	Column 2	Column 3	Column 4	Column 5
	12/31/X0	12/31/X1	Reversals	Revised 12/31/X1	Net changes during year
Net working capital	$200	$268		$268	+ 68
Investments	40	43	− 3(4)	40	0
Land	100	100		100	0
Fixed assets (net)	400	490	+25(1) + 6(2)	515	+115
Intangible assets	60	34	+20(5)	60	0
Total	$800	$935		$983	
Noncurrent notes payable	$100	$ 60		$ 60	− 40
Bonds payable (net)	150	255	− 5(3)	250	+100
Capital stock and paid-in surplus	400	480	−30(7) +25(1) + 6(2) + 5(3) − 3(4) +20(5)	450	+ 50
Retained earnings	150	140	+30(7)	223	+ 73
Total	$800	$935		$983	

Increase in Any Net Noncurrent Asset

An increase in a net noncurrent asset during the year would represent the net application of resources to the acquisition of additional assets of this type. It would be shown as an application unless you also knew that some of these same types of assets had been disposed of during the year. If you had separate information that some of these assets were also sold during the year, then the sale would be a separate source. The application would then be the amount from column 5 plus the book value of the asset sold or disposed of. For example, if you knew that Waterstreet, during 19X1, had sold fixed assets with a book value of $5,000 for $5,000, the $5,000 proceeds would be a source.[5] Applications to the purchase of new fixed assets would then be $115,000 (from Column 5) plus $5,000. In the Waterstreet example, the $115,000 net change reflected acquisition of new fixed assets with a cost of $120,000 and sale of others with a book value of $5,000. Therefore, $5,000 is shown on the SCFP as a source and $120,000 as an application.

---

[5]   If noncurrent assets were sold for more or less than book value, the actual proceeds of the sale would be shown as a source, but only the book value would be used to increase net changes in arriving at total applications.

Exhibit 14.11

WATERSTREET CORPORATION

**Statement of Changes in Financial Position for Year
Ending 12/31/X1
(000 omitted)**

Resources were obtained from:		
Net income		$40
Add:	Depreciation on fixed assets	25
	Amortization of intangible assets	6
	Amortization of bond discount	5
	Extraordinary loss on intangible assets	20
Subtract:	Investments revenue not received in the form of working capital	3
Funds from operations		$ 93
Sale of fixed assets		5
New long-term debt		100
Sale of stock		50
Total Sources		$248
Resources were applied to:		
Purchase new fixed assets		$120
Retired long-term debt		40
Dividends		20
Increased balance of net working capital		68
Total Applications		$248

Decrease in Any Net Noncurrent Asset

A decrease in net noncurrent assets in Column 5 on the worksheet (not shown in the Waterstreet example) would represent a possible net source of working capital from disposition of noncurrent assets. If you knew of no acquisitions during the year, this amount would represent the book value of assets sold. The actual proceeds of the sale would be listed as a source. If you also knew that some assets had been acquired, their cost would be a separate application.

Increase in Net Equity Item Other Than Retained Earnings

Any increase shown in Column 5 for long-term debt or capital stock would represent a net source of new resources. If you knew of no reductions during the year for the same item, it would be shown as a source on the SCFP. If you also knew of debt reductions, they would be listed separately as an application. The source would then be the amount in Column 5 plus the amount of debt reduction. In the Waterstreet example, there were no retirements of bonds and stock does not decrease. Therefore, $100,000 of new long-term debt and $50,000 of new stock are shown separately on Exhibit 14.11 as sources.

Decrease in Net Equity Item Other Than Retained Earnings

Any decrease shown in Column 5 for long-term debt would represent a net application of resources. If you knew of no additional debt of the same type during the year, the item would be shown as an application on the SCFP. If you also knew of debt additions, they would be listed separately as a source. The application would then be the amount in Column 5 plus the amount of additional debt. In the Waterstreet example, there were no additions to noncurrent notes payable. Therefore the $40,000 of net note reduction was shown as an application.

Increase or Decrease in Retained Earnings After Reversals

In column 5 of the SCFP worksheet, the amount shown as net change in retained earnings after reversals reflects the result of:

- Funds from operations (or losses),
- Any cash dividends declared,
- Any extraordinary gains or losses affecting working capital,
- Any gains on the disposition of noncurrent assets.

Each of these items is separately included on the SCFP. It is therefore necessary to separately identify the different components of the Column 5 amount.

If you have access to the statement of retained earnings, you can obtain the total of cash dividends declared. These dividends are shown as a separate application on the SCFP. In the Waterstreet example, dividends of $20,000 are shown as an application.

If the income statement indicates any extraordinary gains or losses directly affecting working capital, they would also be separately disclosed on the SCFP. Extraordinary gains directly affecting working capital would be listed as a separate source immediately beneath funds from operations. Extraordinary losses involving working capital would be shown as a reduction following funds from operations.

The amount remaining, after separating dividends and extraordinaries, would represent funds from operations plus any gains on disposition of noncurrent assets. If the income statement indicates any gain on disposition of noncurrent assets, this gain will have already been included in the sale proceeds listed as a separate source (see above). It therefore must be eliminated to avoid double counting.

The remaining amount will represent funds from operations:

- Amount of retained earnings changes after reversals (from column 5);
- Plus: Cash dividends declared,
- Minus: Gains on disposition of noncurrent assets,
- Minus: Extraordinary gains directly affecting working capital,
- Plus: Extraordinary losses directly affecting working capital,
- Equals: Funds from operations.

Funds from operations is shown as a separate source. Negative funds from operations would represent funds lost in operations, and would be disclosed as an application. In the Waterstreet example, the Column 5 amount of $73,000 plus $20,000 of dividends equals $93,000 of funds from operations. There were no gains on asset dispositions or extraordinary items in the Waterstreet example.[6]

Reconciliation of Funds from Operations with Net Income

As a final step in completing the SCFP, net income must be reconciled with funds from operations. This reconciliation is disclosed by first listing the amount of net

---

6   Preparer problem PP 14.5, and its solution, provides an example including these items.

income, and then adding all SCFP-irrelevant items which represented an expense or loss—Entries 1, 2, 3, and 5, in the Waterstreet example. Then SCFP-irrelevant entries representing revenue are subtracted—Entry 4 in the Waterstreet example.

Chapters 6 and 7 covered the determination of funds from operations, given the income statement. Exhibit 14.12 is a checklist of those steps necessary to reconcile net income with funds from operations. Note that those items to be added back and those items to be subtracted are precisely those SCFP-irrelevant transactions and adjustments cited earlier, which have an effect on the income statement.

Exhibit 14.13 is a checklist of the steps necessary to prepare a SCFP on a working capital basis, given balance sheets and an income statement. Study this exhibit carefully, to review and reinforce the preparer procedures presented in this chapter.

Exhibit 14.12

CHECKLIST FOR RECONCILING
NET INCOME WITH FUNDS FROM OPERATIONS

Start with:	Net income
Add back:	Depreciation on fixed assets
	Amortization of other noncurrent assets
	Amortization of investment premium
	Amortization of noncurrent liability discount
	Losses (not extraordinary) on disposition of noncurrent assets
	Portion of income tax expense representing increase in deferred income taxes
Subtract:	Amortization of noncurrent liability premium
	Amortization of investment discount
	Investments increase representing "significantly influenced" firm's earnings not yet received in dividends
	Gains (not extraordinary) on disposition of noncurrent assets
	Portion of income tax expense representing decrease in deferred income taxes
Equals:	Funds from both operations and extraordinary items
Separate:	By adding any extraordinary "funds losses"
	By subtracting any extraordinary "funds gains"
Equals:	Funds from operations

Exhibit 14.13

CHECKLIST FOR PREPARING A SCFP ON A WORKING CAPITAL BASIS

Step 1: Determine funds from operations and any extraordinary fund inflows or outflows, following the instructions given on Exhibit 14.12.

Step 2: Condense *beginning* and ending balance sheets through:
a) Replacing all current assets and all current liabilities with a single asset indicated as amount of net working capital;
b) Combining with their respective valuation accounts into a single net amount:
  • Investments
  • Each separate category of tangible fixed assets
  • Long-term debt

Exhibit 14.13 (continued)

CHECKLIST FOR PREPARING A SCFP ON A WORKING CAPITAL BASIS

c) Combining into single net amounts:
- Preferred stock and paid-in capital on preferred stock.
- Capital stock and remaining paid-in capital.
- Retained earnings, together with all reserves and appropriations of retained earnings.

Step 3: Identify all SCFP-irrelevant transactions and adjustments that have occurred and been recorded during the year.

Step 4: Reverse the effect of all SCFP-irrelevant items on the ending balance sheet (all revenue, gain, expense, and loss items are reversed to retained earnings).

Step 5: Determine net changes during year between beginning balance sheet and ending balance sheet after reversals.

Step 6: Identify and list as sources:
- Positive funds from operations, together with separately disclosed extraordinary gains or losses of funds (Step 1 above).
- Proceeds (net book value plus gains or minus losses) from any disposition of noncurrent assets. Remember that, if noncurrent assets were both acquired and disposed of during the year, total proceeds from disposition (not net of acquisitions) are shown in the SCFP as a source.
- Proceeds from any additional noncurrent debt incurred during the year. Remember that, if noncurrent debt was both incurred and extinguished during the year, total new debt incurred (not net of extinguishments) is shown in the SCFP as a source.
- Proceeds from any additional investment of assets (or debt replaced in conver-
- sion) by owners; new stock issued.

Step 7: Identify and list as applications:
- Negative funds from operations (funds lost in operations), together with separately disclosed extraordinary gains or losses of funds.
- Acquisitions of noncurrent assets. Remember that, if noncurrent assets were both acquired and disposed of during the year, total acquisitions (not net of dispositions) are shown in the SCFP as an application.
- Extinguishments of noncurrent debt (whether by retirement, refunding, or conversion). Remember that, if noncurrent debt was both incurred and extinguished during the year, total debt extinguished (not net of new debt incurred) is shown in the SCFP as an application.
- Total cash dividends declared.

Step 8: Determine the amount of change in the balance of net working capital during the year:
- Following the unbalanced classification, the change in net working capital is shown as a result of, or as reconciling the difference between, total sources and total applications.
- Following the balanced classification, an increase in the balance of net working capital is included on the SCFP as an application (where the otherwise unapplied working capital generated finally came to rest). A decrease is included as a source (where the otherwise unaccounted-for working capital used came from). Under the balanced classification, total sources will equal total applications.

Note that, if cash dividends information is not available, it can be derived as follows:

- First determine funds from operations (per above)
- Then derive dividends from the equation:

Funds from operations
Plus: Gains on sales of noncurrent assets
          Extraordinary gains directly affecting working capital
Minus: Extraordinary losses directly affecting working capital
          Amount of retained earnings changes after reversals (from column 5)
Equals: Cash dividends declared

Exhibit 14.14(a)
WAHOO CORPORATION

Balance Sheets as of 12/31/X0 and 12/31/X1
(000 omitted)

	12/31/X1	12/31/X0
ASSETS:		
Cash	$109	$ 40
Receivables (net)	250	200
Other current assets	40	20
Total Current Assets	$399	$260
Investments	92	90
Fixed assets:		
Land	80	105
Buildings	200	200
Less accumulated depreciation	(140)	(120)
Equipment	160	150
Less accumulated depreciation	(70)	(50)
Property held under capital lease	72	80
Total Assets	$793	$715
EQUITIES:		
Accounts payable	$100	$ 95
Current obligations under capital lease	5	5
Other current liabilities	35	30
Total Current Liabilities	$140	$130
Bonds payable	100	100
Premium on bonds	8	10
Noncurrent obligations under capital lease	35	40
Deferred income tax	20	10
Total liabilities	$303	$290
Capital stock	340	300
Paid-in capital	35	25
Investments temporary revaluation	(15)	(10)
Reserve for contingencies	65	35
Unappropriated retained earnings	65	75
Total Equities	$793	$715

The steps required to complete the SCFP may initially appear complex. Most firms do not, in any given year, have changes affecting all possible sources and all possible applications. Therefore, the preparation of a SCFP in a particular case is often reasonably simple.

PREPARER PROBLEMS

PP 14.1. From the information given for the Wahoo Corporation (Exhibit 14.14) complete the first two columns of a SCFP worksheet. Give the beginning and ending balance sheets in condensed form, as demonstrated in Exhibit 14.8.

Exhibit 14.14(b)
WAHOO CORPORATION

Income Statement and Statement of Retained Earnings
for the Year 19X1
(000 omitted)

Sales	$1200
Operating expenses:	
Wages and salaries	900
Utilities and insurance	140
Interest	7
Depreciation on buildings	20
Depreciation on equipment	25
Lease amortization	8
Investments revenue[a]	15
Loss on sale of equipment	15
Operating income before taxes	$ 100
Income taxes	30
Operating income after taxes	$ 70
Extraordinary flood loss on land	25
Net Income	$ 45
Unappropriated retained earnings 12/31/X0	$ 75
Net income	45
Dividends	25
Increase contingencies appropriation	30
Unappropriated retained earnings 12/31/X1	$ 65

[a] Of $15,000 of revenue, $8,000 was received in dividends and interest.

PP 14.2. From the information given for the Yuba Corporation (Exhibit 14.15), complete the first two columns of a SCFP worksheet. Give the beginning and ending balance sheets in condensed form, as contained in Exhibition 14.8.

Exhibit 14.15(a)
YUBA CORPORATION

Balance Sheets as of 12/31/X0 and 12/31/X1
(000 omitted)

	12/31/X1	12/31/X0
ASSETS:		
Cash	$ 35	$ 90
Receivables (net)	200	150
Other current assets	40	30
Total Current Assets	$275	$270
Investments	140	110
Fixed assets	579	420
Less accumulated depreciation	(340)	(300)
Intangible assets	40	40
Total Assets	$694	$540
EQUITIES:		
Accounts payable	$105	$ 80
Other current liabilities	20	30
Total Current Liabilities	$125	$110
Bonds payable	200	160
Less bond discount	(16)	(20)
Total Liabilities	$309	$250
Preferred stock	50	50
Capital stock	150	100
Paid-in capital	60	40
Retained earnings	125	100
Total Equities	694	$540

PP 14.3. Refer to Problem PP 14.1. Prepare a list of the ten SCFP-irrelevant entries for the year 19X1.

PP 14.4. Refer to Problem PP 14,2. Prepare a list of the SCFP-irrelevant entries for the year 19X1.

PP 14.5. Refer to Problems PP 14.1 and PP 14.3. Complete the SCFP worksheet for the Wahoo Corporation by:

- Recording the effect of SCFP-irrelevant entries to be reversed (Column 3);

- Recording the ending balance sheet after reversals of SCFP-irrelevant items (Column 4);

- Determining balance sheet changes after reversals (Column 5).

PP 14.6. Refer to Problems PP 14.2 and PP 14.4. Complete the SCFP worksheet for the Yuba Corporation.

PP 14.7. Calculate funds from operations for the Wahoo Corporation (Problems PP 14.1, PP 14.3, and PP 14.5) in two different ways:

- Starting with retained earnings changes after reversals;

- Starting with net income.

Exhibit 14.15(b)
YUBA CORPORATION

**Income Statement and Statement of Retained
Earnings for the Year 19X1
(000 omitted)**

Sales	$1000
Operating Expenses:	
Wages and salaries	695
Utilities and insurance	117
Interest	16
Depreciation on fixed assets	40
Amortization of intangibles	10
Investments revenue[a]	17
Operating income before taxes	$ 105
Income taxes	25
Net Income	$ 80
Retained earnings 12/31/X0	$ 100
Net income	80
Cash dividends	40
Stock dividend	15
Retained earnings 12/31/X1	$ 125

[a] All $17,000 of revenue was received in cash.

PP 14.8. Calculate funds from operations for the Yuba Corporation (Problems PP 14.2, PP 14.4, and PP 14.6 above) in two different ways:

- Starting with retained earnings changes after reversals;
- Starting with net income.

PP 14.9. Prepare a SCFP in good form for the Wahoo Corporation. Data are given on Exhibit 14.14.

PP 14.10. Prepare in good form a SCFP for the Yuba Corporation. Data are given on Exhibit 14.15.

PP 14.11. Prepare a SCFP in good form for the Columbia Corporation for the year 19X1 from the data given in Exhibit 13.1 (in Chapter 13).

PP 14.12. Prepare a SCFP in good form for the Francine Corporation for the year 19X1 from the data given on Exhibit 13.6 (in Chapter 13).

PP 14.13. Prepare a SCFP in good form for the Naomi Corporation for the year 19X1 from the data given on Exhibit 13.7 (in Chapter 13).

CHAPTER 14   APPENDIX
Bank Reconciliation

If you have had a bank checking account, you are already familiar with the desirability and necessity of reconciling your checkbook with your bank's statement of your account each month. A business must similarly update and correct the balance in its cash account (Cash on Hand and In Banks) each month. The process of comparing one's own records with the bank's, to explain differences and to locate any errors made by either party, is known as *bank reconciliation*.

At the start of the reconciliation process, you should have:

1. Your cash account records, indicating the amount of cash you believe you have in the bank available for drawing checks and also the amount of cash you have on hand.

2. Your bank's statement of your account, indicating beginning balance, deposits received, checks cleared, other additions and subtractions to your account, and the ending balance.

3. Cancelled checks which you have drawn and which have cleared your account at the bank during the month.

Exhibit 14.16 contains information that might appear on a typical bank statement. Note that it indicates your firm's account has been charged (reduced) $5,400.50 for six of your checks which have cleared the bank during the month. These six cancelled checks will have been returned to you by the bank with your statement. Exhibit 14.16 also indicates two other charges to your account—$3.00 identified as a bank service charge and $500.00 identified as an NSF (insufficient funds) check also being returned.

The $500.00 NSF check is an example of a check previously received from a customer and deposited at the bank. The $500.00 was originally credited (added) to your account by the bank at the time of deposit, as part of the $6,000.00 of deposits shown as received. When your bank was unable to collect on the check from the customer's bank, it charged your account and returned the check to you. You, of course, now have an additional receivable claim against your customer for this $500.00 and will be attempting to collect it, separately from the bank reconciliation process.

Exhibit 14.16

EXAMPLE OF INFORMATION CONTAINED ON
MONTHLY BANK STATEMENT

Beginning balance		$10,000.00
Deposits received:	$1,200.00	
	800.00	
	500.00	
	3,500.00	6,000.00
Note collected:		400.10
Checks paid:	$1,400.00	
	700.00	
	1,600.00	
	900.00	
	800.50	5,400.50
NSF Check		500.00
Service charge		3.00
Ending balance		$10,496.60

In addition to the $6,000.00 of deposits shown as received, Exhibit 14.16 also shows that the bank has credited your account for $400.10 representing a note which you had given the bank to collect for you (for collection). The bank indicates, on its statement, that your ending balance after all of this activity is $10,496.60.

You may assume your cash account shows a balance of $10,799.50 ($10,499.50 in the bank and $300.00 cash on hand). Your accounts show checks drawn since the last reconciliation totaling $6,300.50, and deposits sent to the bank totaling $6,800.00. How can you reconcile your books showing a balance of $10,799.50, with the bank's statement indicating $10,496.60? Is either the correct current cash balance?

Reconciling involves correcting the separate amounts for any discovered errors and updating for information (amounts) not yet received and processed. To adjust the bank's balance to the correct balance of total cash in the firm, two items may have to be added. Any cash on hand ($300.00 in this example) must be added, since the bank knows nothing about it. Similarly, any deposits in transit—recorded on the firm's books but not yet received and processed by the bank—must also be added to the bank's statement balance ($800.00 in this example). Also any outstanding checks—checks that have been drawn and deducted on the firm's books but have not yet been presented to the bank for payment—must be deducted from the bank's statement balance, since these funds are no longer available to the firm (outstanding checks totaled $900.00 in this example).

Exhibit 14.17 shows an example of a bank reconciliation incorporating the above data. Note that the $10,496.60 bank-statement balance has been adjusted for cash on hand, deposits in transit, and outstanding checks. The adjusted amount, $10,696.60, is identified as the corrected cash balance. To prove the accuracy of this amount, it is reconciled with the amount appearing in the firm's books.

Exhibit 14.17

EXAMPLE OF BANK RECONCILIATION

From bank statement		From firm's accounts	
Balance per statement	$10,496.60	Balance per books	$10,799.50
Add:		Add:	
Cash on hand	300.00	Note proceeds	400.10
Deposits in transit	800.00		
	$11,596.60		$11,199.60
Deduct:		Deduct:	
		NSF deposit	500.00
Outstanding checks	900.00	Service charge	3.00
Correct cash balance	$10,696.60	Correct cash balance	$10,696.60

The bank statement provides information concerning events not yet recorded in the firm's accounts. After reconciliation is complete, appropriate entries must be made to record this additional information. As part of the reconciliation process, additional deposits not previously recorded are added to the original book balance ($400.10 collected on a note, in this example).

Exhibit 14.17 shows this adjustment. It also shows deductions for charges (reductions) not previously recorded in the firm's books such as NSF (bad) checks received from customers and service charges assessed by the bank ($500.00 and $3.00 in this example). After these updating adjustments, the corrected cash balance equals $10,696.60. This total is identical to that previously arrived at by adjusting the bank's statement balance, and the reconciliation is complete.

The reconciliation process could also uncover errors of recording in the firm's books, which would then both be shown as an adjustment to the firm's book balance on the reconciliation and would also generate a correcting entry. Although rare, bank reconciliation can also uncover errors made by the bank. Bank errors would be shown as adjustments to the bank-statement balance on the reconciliation, and the bank would then be advised to change its records accordingly.

ARTIFICIAL ENTITIES AND DIFFERENT REPORTING PERIODS

CHAPTER PREVIEW

Many firms become involved in business combinations and publish consolidated financial statements. The objective of this chapter is to acquaint you with the several ways a business combination may occur and with the different forms it can take, and specifically to enable you to understand and properly interpret consolidated financial statements. Important financial information may also be disclosed for segments of a business and for the entire firm more frequently than once a year (period). Another objective of this chapter is to acquaint you with the availability and meaning of segment information and interim reports. In this chapter you can:

- Learn that business combinations can come about through acquisition of one firm by another or through a pooling of interests of two firms;
- Discover that the accounting treatment of a business combination is distinctly different, depending upon whether the combination is deemed a purchase or a pooling, and learn the significance of the differences;
- Develop an understanding of the objectives of consolidated financial statements and of the basic principles of consolidation involved in their preparation;
- Learn about the accountant's response to the need for information relating to individual segments of a business and to more timely reporting of financial information;
- Become familiar with the content, usefulness, and limitations of segment information and interim reports;
- Review and expand your knowledge of the importance of financial statement footnotes and of their common information content.

With this information, you should be comfortable dealing with consolidated statements and their few special accounts. You will perceive that they are essentially identical in concept to those statements prepared for an individual firm, and you will be familiar with statement footnotes, segment information, and interim reports. You will have completed your elementary knowledge of financial statements as they are currently prepared, and you will be in a position to consider some significantly different measurement proposals, under consideration in this country and abroad, which will be introduced in the following chapter.

ALL IN THE FAMILY

The Gargantuan Corporation actually is a *holding company*. It owns all or most of the voting stock of several other corporations which are engaged in various businesses. By itself, Gargantuan does little except make investments and collect interest and dividends. The balance sheet and income statements of the company are given in Exhibit 15.1.

Exhibit 15.1
GARGANTUAN CORPORATION

**Balance Sheet and Income Statement for
Year Ending 12/31/X1
(000 omitted)**

Assets:	
Cash	$ 45
Office supplies	3
Total Current Assets	48
Investments	25,412
Total Assets	$25,460
Equities:	
Accounts payable	$ 20
Other current liabilities	5
Total Current Liabilities	$ 25
Long-term debt	0
Total Liabilities	$ 25
Capital stock (no par)	23,000
Retained earnings	2,435
Total Equities	$25,460
Income Statement:	
Investments revenue	$ 6,076
Office expenses	200
Wages and salaries	1,000
Operating income	$ 4,876
Income taxes	632
Net income	$ 4,244

These statements really disclose little about the vast corporate empire which Gargantuan controls. Included in the firm's annual report, you would find a different set of statements indicated as being for the "Gargantuan Corporation and Consolidated Subsidiaries." These consolidated statements are given in Exhibit 15.2. The consolidated statements reveal the details of the combined assets and liabilities of the Gargantuan Corporation and the separate corporations it controls. You can see that Exhibit 15.2 provides the reader with much more usable information than does Exhibit 15.1.

Exhibit 15.2
GARGANTUAN CORPORATION AND
CONSOLIDATED SUBSIDIARIES

Consolidated Balance Sheet as of 12/31/X1
(000 omitted)

Assets:	
Cash	$ 2,075
Marketable securities	1,740
Accounts receivable (net)	6,300
Inventory	10,125
Supplies	3,280
Prepaid items	2,450
Total Current Assets	$25,970
Investments (unconsolidated)	5,750
Fixed Assets:	
Land	4,560
Buildings	8,230
Accumulated depreciation	(4,460)
Equipment	12,720
Accumulated depreciation	(8,380)
Property under capital lease	3,600
· Intangible and other assets:	
Patents and copyrights	1,475
Deferred charges	2,270
Consolidated goodwill	1,920
Total Assets	$53,655
Equities:	
Current notes payable	$ 2,120
Accounts payable	5,290
Other current liabilities	1,870
Total Current Liabilities	$ 9,280
Bonds payable	6,000
Less unamortized discount	(255)
Total Liabilities	$15,025
Minority interest	4,350
Capital stock	23,000
Retained earnings	11,280
Total Equities	$53,655

To read intelligently and to understand consolidated financial statements merely requires knowledge of the basic principles of consolidation, the new accounts that may arise out of consolidation, and some new vocabulary.

BUSINESS COMBINATIONS

For various reasons, two corporations and their owners may decide to work together as one. This "corporate marriage," often referred to as a business combination, merger, or acquisition, can come about in one of essentially two distinct ways. The firms may just join forces, with the owners of each company continuing as proportionate owners of the combination. This type of combination is known as a *pooling of interests*. The controlling company merely exchanges additional shares of its stock for the voting common shares of the controlled company. The second way in which corporations may merge is to have the controlling company buy the controlled company for consideration other than stock. Where one firm acquires control of another by buying out the other's owners, the merger is known as a *purchase*, or an *acquisition*.

Regardless of how the merger is accomplished, the combination may subsequently continue in one of two legal forms. The assets and liabilities of the controlled company may be transferred to the controlling corporation, and the controlled corporation extinguished; or assets and liabilities of both may be transferred to a third corporation. In either case, there is a single surviving corporation, and the merger is known as a legal or *statutory merger*. Accounting for statutory mergers will be briefly described later in this chapter.

Alternatively, the two corporations may continue to operate as separate legal entities regardless of whether the merger was accomplished via purchase or pooling. There are definite economic, legal, tax, and even operating advantages in certain situations, if the two firms continue as legally distinct operations.

Recall that, when one corporation owns more than 50 percent of the voting common stock of another corporation, the controlling corporation is known as the parent. The corporation which is legally controlled by the parent is known as the subsidiary. When a parent owns 100 percent of the voting common stock of the subsidiary, the subsidiary is known as a **wholly owned subsidiary.** When a subsidiary is not wholly owned, the stockholders other than the parent are collectively known as the minority stockholders or just the *minority*.

Note that the parent–subsidiary relationship is determined by the percentage of interest in the voting common stock. Ownership of notes, bonds, and preferred stock have no bearing on whether or not a subsidiary relationship exists. GAAP require that a parent publish financial statements, including the details of assets and liabilities of its subsidiaries.[1] These more inclusive statements are known as consolidated statements.

---

[1] Consolidation is not required in the case of certain foreign subsidiaries where local government regulations impair effective control. Consolidation is also not required where the two firms are so economically incompatible that the combined report would be meaningless. (For example, a heavy equipment manufacturer would not be consolidated with a baseball team.) On balance sheets of the parent, the investment in such cases would be disclosed as "investment in unconsolidated subsidiary."

It is important to understand that consolidated statements are prepared for an artificial entity. In a consolidation, both the parent and subsidiary are continuing as distinct legal entities. Each maintains separate accounting records and prepares separate statements. The "consolidated entity" exists only on paper. There are no accounting "books" for the consolidation. Even though the two firms are not "legally married" in the sense of living in one corporate home, they operate as one under a single top management. The artificial legal entity is a very real operating entity. Accountants, therefore, report on this operating entity. Consolidated financial statements can be viewed as a "trial marriage on paper."

CONSOLIDATED STATEMENTS FOR POOLINGS

When two firms just get together to do business, when the owners continue on together under a combined management and the merger is a pooling, accountants have not considered such action justification for a new basis of accounting. Essentially, in a pooling, the accounting book values from each firm's separate statements are combined in the consolidated statement. However, a simple combined statement—one statement added to the other line by line—may not result in a final consolidated statement. In the case of a balance sheet, further adjustment is always necessary. For income statements and SCFP's, further adjustments may be necessary, depending upon the particular circumstances.

Exhibit 15.3 presents an example of the steps necessary to arrive at a consolidated balance sheet following the pooling treatment. Study this exhibit carefully and use it as a reference for the remainder of this discussion of poolings. Note that, as a first step, the book values of the various assets and equities are simply added together on a combined statement.

Now consider the $175,000,000 of combined "family" assets, and in particular the $21,000,000 shown as investments coming from the parent's balance sheet. Remember, from Chapter 2 and 3, that reported assets are properties and rights or claims **against others.** Do all $175,000,000 of combined assets represent properties or rights or claims against others (outsiders)? Or are some claims now inside the "family"? On the parent's separate balance sheet, the $21,000,000 of investments was properly included as a claim against a separate corporation's assets. But on the combined balance sheet, does this $21,000,000 still represent a claim against other's (outsiders') assets?

On the combined balance sheet the $21,000,000 claim is now inside the family. It is against assets which are now also included on the "family balance sheet" and, if reported, would represent double-counting and result in overstatement of "family total assets." The $21,000,000 must be eliminated. In other situations where parent investments also included some portion **not** in subsidiaries, **only** the portion related to subsidiaries would be eliminated.

Exhibit 15.3

BALANCE SHEET CONSOLIDATION FOLLOWING
POOLING TREATMENT
(000 omitted)

	Parent	Subsidiary	Simple combined statement	Elimina- tions	Consolidated balance sheet
Assets					
Cash	$ 6,000	$ 4,000	$ 10,000		$ 10,000
Accounts receivable	17,000	9,000	26,000	$ 650ᶜ	25,350
Inventory	16,000	12,000	28,000		28,000
Investmentsᵃ	21,000	0	21,000	21,000ᵇ	0
Other noncurrent assets (net)	40,000	50,000	90,000		90,000
Total Assets	$100,000	$75,000	$175,000		$153,350
Equities					
Accounts payable	$ 18,000	$10,000	$ 28,000	$ 650ᶜ	$ 27,350
Noncurrent liabilities	22,000	14,000	36,000		36,000
Capital stock—$10 Par	50,000	15,000	65,000	15,000ᵇ	50,000
Paid-in capital	5,000	6,000	11,000	6,000ᵇ	5,000
Retained earnings	5,000	30,000	35,000		35,000
Total Equities	$100,000	$75,000	$175,000		$153,350

ᵃ Parent acquired 100% of voting stock of subsidiary in exchange for additional shares of parent's common stock.
ᵇ Elimination of intercompany investment at book value of subsidiary's contributed capital.
ᶜ Elimination of intercompany debt.

ELIMINATIONS IN CONSOLIDATION

The essential difference between a combined statement and a properly completed consolidated statement is simply the elimination of items which, on a family statement, are now inside the family. Note that any eliminations are made only on the consolidated working papers. Nothing is eliminated from the "books" of either company.

Continuing with necessary eliminations on Exhibit 15.3, are all equities on the combined statement claims by creditors or owners who are distinct from the combined corporations? Capital Stock and Paid-in Capital claims totaling $21,000,000 coming from the subsidiary's balance sheet do not represent outside claims on the family statement. They must also be eliminated. Elimination of *intercompany investment* from the combined total is always necessary in the preparation of a consolidated balance sheet. For subsidiaries qualifying for pooling treatment, the intercompany investment elimination is simple and straightforward, since the parent's investment is originally recorded as its share (100 percent on Exhibit 15.3) of the subsidiary's book value of contributed capital. In subsequent years following acquisition, under the equity method discussed in Chapter 11, the parent will have picked up and will be including, in its investment account, its share of the subsidiary's retained earnings **since acquisition, not** distributed in dividends. These amounts will also be eliminated from combined investments and combined retained earnings in order to avoid double counting. Note that, in a pooling, only subsidiary retained earnings since acquisition are subject to elimination. Subsidiary retained earnings **prior** to acquisition are not eliminated. They are added to parent earnings on the consolidated statement.

In essence, the parent has acquired or "bought" earnings by simply issuing stock. This makes sense if the parent is now a "partnership" of previously separate owners who are merely combining their past earnings. It is inappropriate if the parent has substantially bought out the subsidiary's owners.[2] Following the purchase treatment (see below), intercompany investment elimination can be more complicated and always involves elimination of the parent's share of subsidiary retained earnings.

Intercompany Debt

Eliminations in consolidation of balance sheets also involve elimination of any *intercompany debt*. Assume, in the case of the example in Exhibit 15.3, that parent owed subsidiary $650,000 at year end for products purchased and resold to customers. Parent's separate $18,000,000 of accounts payable properly includes this $650,000 of intercompany debt, and subsidiary's separate $9,000,000 of accounts receivable properly includes the $650,000 claim. But do $28,000,000 of combined payables all represent obligations of the family to outside creditors? Do $26,000,000 of combined receivables represent family claims for cash against outside customers?

In this example, $650,000 of receivables and payables are now "inside" the family and must be eliminated. Other common possible intercompany debts or claims necessitating elimination might include:

- Interest receivable and payable,
- Rents,
- Dividends,
- Bonds or notes of one firm held by the other.

It is only important at this stage that you understand that a consolidated balance sheet is a combined balance sheet with the elimination of certain

---

[2]   Accountants have very specific and complicated tests to determine whether a merger qualifies as a pooling of interests. If it does not qualify, GAAP require that the merger be treated as a purchase (see below).

"inside-family" items. The most common eliminations are intercompany investment and intercompany debt.[3]

Intercompany Transactions and Accruals

Eliminations may also be necessary to complete consolidated income statements and consolidated SCFP's. Here again the basic concept is unchanged. The statements are first combined (added together). Then any **transactions** and **accruals** occurring during the year between the firms must be eliminated since they do not represent events occurring between the family and outsiders. Suppose the subsidiary had sold products costing $5,000,000 during the year to the parent, and the parent had resold them to outside customers. The subsidiary would properly include the five million on its income statement as part of sales. The parent would properly include this amount on its income statement as part of its cost of goods sold. On the consolidated income statement, five million would have to be eliminated from both combined sales and combined costs of goods sold as not representing exchanges with outsiders. Other common income statement eliminations include matching revenues on one separate statement and expenses on the other for:

- services performed,
- interest earned,
- rent earned.

Similarly, on the combined SCFP, eliminations would be necessary for such items as:

- Sale or purchase of noncurrent assets within the family,
- Issuance or retirement of noncurrent debt within the family,
- Dividends within the family.

Both consolidated income statements and consolidated SCFP's, under the pooling treatment, merely involve combinations less eliminations for intercompany transactions and accruals.

CONSOLIDATED STATEMENTS FOR PURCHASES

A merger may essentially involve the parent's purchase of control of the subsidiary from the subsidiary's owners. Parent's cash, debt securities, or other considerations represent all or a substantial portion of that which is given to the subsidiary's stockholders in exchange for their controlling stock.

---

[3] Other more involved eliminations, such as intercompany profit remaining in inventory, are beyond the scope of this elementary text.

The subsidiary's original stockholders do not retain proportional voting interest in the new family. In some cases, even though only common stock is exchanged and subsidiary owners maintain proportional interest, the subsidiary is so relatively small and insignificant a factor in relation to the parent that the thought of their pooling their joint interests stretches credibility. Where mergers do not qualify as a pooling, accountants treat them as a purchase.

Purchase treatment is essentially quite different from pooling treatment, even though the accountant's procedures are similar and, in exceptional cases, the results in consolidation could appear very similar. Recall that, under pooling, no new basis for accounting is deemed to exist. Original accounting book values are carried forward in the new family. When a pooling has not occurred, the merger represents a purchase in the open market, and a restatement of assets acquired to fair market value at the time of acquisition becomes appropriate.

Remember that accounting book values may be well below market values or replacement costs after several years of inflation. Also recall, from Chapters 2 and 3, that a firm may have significant intangible assets that are not capable of objective measurement and therefore are not measured and disclosed as assets under GAAP. Remember that these intangible assets (which are not reported by a firm as its own assets) can include:

- The firm's human capital (resulting from investment in hiring and training employees),

- Customer goodwill (resulting from investment in advertising, public relations, and good customer service),

- Creditor and supplier goodwill (resulting from long-term satisfactory past relationships), and

- Technical knowledge (resulting from past investment in research and development).

Although these intangibles, collectively referred to as "goodwill," are not "booked" for a firm by its accountants, they have real value in the marketplace. A new firm starting in business would have to invest many years of time and perhaps many millions of dollars with the hope of creating similar goodwill. Therefore, when a company is sold, the selling owners seek recompense for the current market value of their assets plus recompense for any existing goodwill.

Assume your family owned all of the stock of a corporation whose balance sheet looks like Exhibit 15.4. Also assume that, in addition to the current values of the assets which are noted on the exhibit, you believe your firm's goodwill to be worth at least $100,000. Would you willingly sell all of your stock for its book value of $595,000? What amount would you try to obtain as a minimum from a potential buyer? You would be foolish, in this example, to not attempt to obtain at least $1,455,000 for your stock ($1,355,000 current value of net assets[4] plus $100,000 for goodwill).

Exhibit 15.4

YOUR CORPORATION

**Most Recent Balance Sheet Data
(000 omitted)**

Assets	
Cash	$ 95
Receivables	205
Inventory (LIFO)	190[a]
Investments	60[b]
Fixed assets (net)	300[c]
Total Assets	$850
Equities	
Total liabilities	$255
Capital stock	400
Paid-in capital	80
Retained earnings	115
Total Equities	$850

[a] Current replacement cost, $360,000.
[b] Cost $60,000; current market value, $430,000.
[c] Replacement cost of equivalent capacity, $520,000.

Most subsidiaries acquired in a purchase cost the parent more than the book value of the net assets acquired, for reasons similar to those above. Assume you were a good negotiator and sold your corporation to the Acquisition-Happy Conglomerate Corporation in exchange for $500,000 and a 5-year interest-bearing note for $1,000,000. Exhibit 15.5 shows both firms after the acquisition, and how they might be consolidated following the purchase treatment. Study Exhibit 15.5 carefully; it will form the basis for the discussion of purchase accounting below.

[4]	Current book value of total assets	$850,000
	Add inventory replacement adjustment	170,000
	Add unrecognized gain on securities	370,000
	Add fixed asset replacement adjustment	220,000
	Current (replacement) value of total assets	$1,610,000
	Less Total Liabilities	255,000
	Current (replacement) value of Net Assets	$1,355,000

Exhibit 15.5

EXAMPLE OF BALANCE SHEET CONSOLIDATION
FOLLOWING PURCHASE TREATMENT
(000 omitted)

	Parent	Sub-sidiary	Simple combina-tion	Eliminations and adjustments	Consol-idated balance sheet
Assets					
Cash	$ 140	$ 95	$ 235		$ 235
Receivables	350	205	555		555
Inventory	200	190	390	$+170[c]	560
Investments	1,500	60	1,560	−595[a]	430
				−905[b]	
				+370[c]	
Fixed assets (net)	800	300	1,100	+220[c]	1,320
Goodwill	0	0	0	+145[d]	145
Total Assets	$2,990	$850	$3,840		$3,245
Equities					
Total liabilities	$1,200	$255	$1,455		$1,455
Capital stock	1,000	400	1,400	$−400[a]	1,000
Paid-in capital	350	80	430	− 80[a]	350
Retained earnings	440	115	555	−115[a]	440
Total Equities	$2,990	$850	$3,840		$3,245

Eliminations and adjustments with 100-percent ownership:
[a] First eliminate intercompany investment at total subsidiary book value (contributed capital plus retained earnings).
[b] Balance in investments account applicable to subsidiary represents excess paid over accounting book value of net assets acquired. It is eliminated and replaced by (c) and (d) below.
[c] Any acquired assets are written up to current fair market value.
[d] Balance of excess payment identified as goodwill.

As with any consolidation of balance sheets, the first step is simple combination, and the second is elimination of intercompany investment. Following the purchase, the entire parent's share (100 percent, in this example) of the subsidiary's stockholders' equity is eliminated, not just the subsidiary's contributed capital. In Exhibit 15.5 this amount totaled $595,000 and is also eliminated from the combined investment account. The balance in the combined investment account in this example still representing intercompany investment is $905,000. Note that any other parent investments (not shown in this example) in nonvoting stock, nonsubsidiary companies, and unconsolidated subsidiaries are not involved in eliminations. Also not involved in elimination would be any subsidiary investments (unless they are in the family).

Goodwill

The $905,000 excess over book value represents payment for "undervalued assets" plus goodwill. It is eliminated and replaced by writing up subsidiary inventory by $170,000, investments of subsidiary by $370,000, and subsidiary fixed assets net by $220,000. What should be done with the remaining $145,000? The balance of $145,000 does not represent "asset understatement" and is therefore assumed to represent acquired goodwill. It is shown as such on the consolidated balance sheet.

Recall that GAAP do not allow a firm to attempt to measure and report its own self-generated or self-developed goodwill. Such a measurement would be too subjective. However, when a firm is purchased or sold, any existing goodwill which is paid for may be readily identified and estimated. GAAP therefore provides that *purchased goodwill* may be reported. GAAP also require that any such purchased goodwill must be amortized to zero over a period of not less than 10 and no more than 40 years. The requirement for arbitrary amortization of purchased goodwill reflects the inability of accountants to objectively verify its continued existence after acquisition, and the inappropriateness of writing it all off as a loss in the first few weeks or years after acquisition.

Intercompany Debt and Intercompany Transactions and Accruals

Intercompany debt (not shown in the Exhibit 15.5 balance sheet), if any exists, is eliminated in a purchase consolidation. These eliminations are the same as in the case of a pooling consolidation. Similarly, following the purchase treatment, intercompany transactions and accruals are eliminated on consolidated income statements and consolidated SCFP's in the same manner as under the pooling treatment.

The essential difference between purchase and pooling treatments with respect to the consolidated income statement does not involve eliminations. Significant difference can exist with respect to reported net income under the two treatments. To grasp this difference, think again of your own firm which was acquired by Acquisition-Happy Conglomerate, Inc.

Under a pooling treatment, consolidated net income would be the sum of the two firm's incomes. Under pooling, any gain on the sale, subsequent to merger, of your investments portfolio (realizing the difference between the $60,000 of book value and the $430,000 of current market value) would be reported as part of consolidated net income. However, under the purchase treatment, your firm's assets would have been revalued in consolidation. Any subsequent realization of gain on asset disposition up to market value at the time of acquisition would be excluded from consolidated net income as already recognized at the time of consolidation. Furthermore, consolidated net income would normally be lower in future years under purchase as opposed to pooling accounting. Can you explain why?

Under purchase accounting, consolidated assets were written up to reflect recognition of the $905,000 paid in excess of original-cost book values. The $905,000 of "additional assets" would not be reported under the pooling treatment (assuming you had received stock instead of cash plus debt for your corporation). Under purchase accounting, the additional $905,000 will be systematically written off as **additional expense** over future years on the consolidated income statement in the form of higher cost of goods, higher depreciation expense, and amortization of goodwill.

IMPLICATIONS OF PURCHASE VS. POOLING TREATMENTS

To recapitulate, under the pooling treatment, consolidated net income is maximized. Past earnings to add to the balance sheet can be acquired in exchange for stock. Future earnings, both operating and gains on historical-cost-measured assets acquired, can similarly be acquired and reported.[5]

Under purchase accounting, consolidated net income is often considerably lower than it would have been under the pooling treatment. Past subsidiary earnings are not added to consolidated retained earnings on the balance sheet. Future consolidated income does not include gains realized between the historical-cost book value of the subsidiary's assets and their fair market value at the date on which control was acquired. Future income is reduced by goodwill amortization and other expenses reflecting the difference between purchase cost and old book value.

Is it any wonder that parent corporations desiring to report high earnings prefer pooling to purchase treatment? Until recently, GAAP were loose enough so that many effective purchases could be reported as poolings. There is evidence that some mergers may have taken place to take advantage of the accountant's pooling treatment and to buy earnings: and that they would not have occurred had appropriate purchase treatment been required.

MINORITY INTEREST

A parent–subsidiary relationship exists when the parent controls 50 percent or more of the subsidiary's voting stock. A subsidiary does not have to be wholly owned in order to be consolidated. Consolidation when there are minority stockholders follows basically the same steps as in the 100-percent ownership case. The only essential differences are:

---

[5]   You may wish to explore and tentatively connect with this point the highly publicized 1972 incident involving ITT, the Hartford Fire Insurance Company (a "pooled" subsidiary), Dita Beard, Attorney-General John Mitchell, and the antitrust division of the Department of Justice, the Sheraton Hotel Corporation (another ITT subsidiary), and the original planning for the 1972 Republican National Convention.

1. Only the parent's share of the subsidiary owners' equity is eliminated as intercompany investment. Any balance remaining in the combined investments account which is applicable to the subsidiary common stock represents and is treated as excess of cost over book value of the net assets acquired. Any balance remaining in subsidiary owners' equity represents "outside of family" (minority) claims. These claims are combined into a single amount and shown along with other equities on the consolidated balance sheet as "minority interest."

2. Minority share of consolidated net income is separately stated so that the bottom line of the income statement will reflect income for parent stockholders.

The consolidated balance sheets and income statements for the Xerox Corporation, contained in Appendix A at the back of the book, adequately demonstrate the disclosure of the minority "share" of consolidated assets and consolidated income.

INTERPRETING CONSOLIDATED FINANCIAL STATEMENTS

In interpreting a consolidated balance sheet, you now know that, regardless of purchase or pooling treatment, reported consolidated assets will include only properties held or controlled (capital leases) by the "family" plus rights and claims against outsiders who are not family members. Similarly, all liabilities and minority interest shown will represent claims by outside creditors and stockholders. And the consolidated income statement and SCFP will reflect only transactions and accruals involving outsiders.

Purchase vs. pooling treatment will affect the accounting measurement of assets, retained earnings, and consolidated revenues and expenses subsequent to acquisition of control. You will find whether purchase or pooling treatment has been followed by reference to the statement footnotes.

STATUTORY MERGERS

At the beginning of this chapter, it was pointed out that a merger could take the form of assets and equities being legally combined in a single corporation. In such cases, a parent–subsidiary relationship would no longer exist and consolidated financial statements would be irrelevant. In the event of a statutory merger, the subsidiary assets and equities are transferred onto the books of the surviving corporation. If conditions for a pooling are met, the transfer is at accounting book value. Otherwise assets and liabilities are picked up at fair market values, together with possible purchased goodwill. In essence, under either treatment, the same original eliminations and adjustments are made as with a consolidation. In a statutory merger, however, they are actually made in the surviving corporation's accounts instead of only on consolidated working papers. After acquisition, the financial statements would be essentially similar except that they would not be labeled as "consolidated." They would be for a real legal entity—the surviving corporation.

SEGMENT REPORTING

Consolidated financial statements are just one example of accounting information supplied for artificial (nonlegal) entities. In this text, you first learned about accounting in terms of a proprietorship. Recall from Chapter 2 that a proprietorship is not a legal entity. The legal entity is the **proprietor,** including all his personal assets and liabilities and all of his business interests. One proprietor may have several different proprietorships, and each could be separately reported upon if they were different types of businesses.

Large corporations are often highly diversified into different lines of business through mergers and acquisitions. When data related to many different types of businesses are combined on a single set of financial statements, the aggregated amounts may have little meaning and no comparative value in relation to other firms. For instance, of what real significance would wage and salaries expense be in relation to anything else if the income statement combined an automated steel mill, a large lettuce farm, four movie companies, a football team, and a chain of hamburger stands?

GAAP now require that firms separately disclose, as supplementary information, certain key data concerning each of its major *segments* or different types of business. Segment data may also be thought of as information concerning artificial entities, since a segment of an overall business could be a part of one corporation, the sum of parts of several corporations, or even the sum of several corporations (a sort of miniconsolidation). The detailed GAAP guidelines for identification of segments for reporting purposes are beyond the scope of this text. Generalized information for your overall understanding is included below. You may think of a segment as a **distinctly different** type of business.

IDENTIFYING SEGMENTS

The FASB has defined segments in terms of related products or services provided. A *separately reportable segment* is one which:

a) Generates 10% or more of total revenue, or

b) Generates 10% or more of earnings, or

c) Uses separately identifiable assets representing at least 10% of all seg-mentable assets.[6]

Note that the segments are defined in terms of products or services pro-vided to customers. They are not based on geographical location or separate corporate entities. Think of a firm that obtained 50% of its revenue from selling tractors and the other 50% from selling diapers. Assume that it had a large French subsidiary selling tractors and home appliances, again on a 50–50 basis. Segment reporting with the consolidated statements would report the tractor, diaper, and home appliance lines separately. The tractor segment would include both U.S. and French operations.

SEGMENT INFORMATION REPORTED

The intent of segment reporting is to provide meaningful operating and financial data for distinct lines of business. For each reportable segment, GAAP require that supplementary information be provided with respect to the following:

a) revenue,

b) operating earnings,

c) book value of identifiable (with the particular segment) assets,

d) aggregate related depreciation, depletion, and amortization expense, and

e) amount of capital expenditures—additions to fixed assets.

In addition, GAAP also require the disclosure of certain other information of a technical nature, which is beyond the scope of this text and will not be dis-cussed here.

It is important to note that total segment revenue might exceed total firm revenue. This could result from the fact that each segment will be reported on the basis of including both revenue from outsiders and revenue from other segments. Total firm revenue, of course, **excludes** intersegment revenue. Total segment operating profit may not match total firm profit. This difference in profit should be expected, because overall corporate or home-office revenues and expenses and all interest expense are specifically excluded in the calcula-tion of segment profit.

---

[6]   Some assets are not readily "segmentable"; that is, they are common to several different segments of the business and therefore cannot be readily and specifically identified with one particular segment. Neither a corporate headquarters building nor a factory producing products for two or more distinct segments would be "seg-mentable" assets.

ADDITIONAL DISCLOSURE

In addition to segment information, a firm is required to separately disclose data on *foreign operations* where foreign operations generate at least 10 percent of total revenue or where they involve at least 10 percent of total assets. Where foreign operations are sufficiently great to be separately reportable, information on revenue, operating earnings, and identifiable assets must be disclosed.

Information concerning *major customers* must also be disclosed. Any single customer, foreign government, or domestic government agency providing at least ten percent of the firm's revenue is defined as a major customer. Such customers must be identified, together with revenues derived therefrom.

USEFULNESS OF SEGMENT INFORMATION

Exhibits 15.6 and 15.7 provide one example of the usefulness of segment information. Assume you are interested in the performance of the Farwell Corporation. You might be an officer of the company, a creditor, or a stockholder. Study the abbreviated statements contained in Exhibit 15.6. Can you see that a reader of these statements might find little cause for alarm? The operating ratio (net income as a percent of sales) is an apparently respectable 12 percent; and the return on long-term assets (EBIT as a percent of net working capital plus noncurrent assets) is an adequate 11 percent.

Exhibit 15.6
FARWELL CORPORATION

Abbreviated Financial Statement Data for Year Ending 12/31/X9 (000 omitted)

Net working capital	$10,000
Capacity assets (net)	50,000
Total	$60,000
Noncurrent debt (net)	$24,000
Stockholders' equity	36,000
Total	$60,000
Sales	$30,800
Operating expenses	26,200
Income from operations before taxes	$ 4,600
Provision for income taxes	900
Net income	$ 3,700
EBIT	$ 6,600

Now turn to Exhibit 15.7, which provides segment detail for the three major segments of Farwell's Business. As someone with a vital interest in Farwell's operations, are you still satisfied with all aspects of the firm's performance? Or do you think the firm should either take action to improve the performance of the "B" segment (appliances) or else discontinue this part of the business? Exhibit 15.7 reveals that the appliance segment requires 36 percent of the assets to generate only 25% of the total revenue, with a resultant $2,300,000 operating loss. Assuming that food and truck revenues were not dependent on the appliance business, discontinuation and liquidation of the appliances segment could result in an additional $2,300,000 of profit with $18,000,000 less of capital invested. Note also that Exhibit 15.7 reveals an additional $2,000,000 of investment in the appliance business during the past year!

Exhibit 15.7
FARWELL CORPORATION

Supplementary Segment Information for Year Ending 12/31/X9
(000 omitted)

	Segment A (Trucks)	Segment B (Appliances)	Segment C (Food)	Other	Total
Revenue	$12,300	$ 7,700	$10,800	0	$30,800
Operating income	3,700	(2,300) loss	3,200	0	4,600
Identifiable assets (at book value)	$13,500	$18,000	$13,500	$5,000	$50,000
Related expense (Depreciation and Amortization)	1,100	1,500	1,150	250	4,000
Additions to capacity assets	$ 1,100	$ 2,000	$ 2,400	$ 500	$ 6,000

This admittedly extreme example is designed to demonstrate how segment reporting can disclose significant information that is hidden in combined totals. The firm's management normally has such information in far more detail as a product of its internal managerial accounting system. However, the management might not wish to disclose this information to creditors or stockholders. The vice-president in charge of Segment B could be the president's son or daughter! The GAAP requirement of segment reporting is intended to ensure that all interested parties have reasonable access to important information that otherwise could be buried in overall company totals.

In addition to the relative performance of different segments in comparison to each other, segmental information can provide a limited basis for comparative analysis with other firms, or other firm's segments, in the same line of business. Furthermore, data on a firm's foreign operations and their locations can give the investor the opportunity to estimate relative potential benefits and risks in those nations and their possible significance to the firm. Certain nations may be politically stable, undergoing rapid growth, and may present great opportunities for future earnings. Others may be the opposite, and may even hold a high risk of nationalization or expropriation of the firm's assets and business. Also, a firm with a high proportion of foreign operations may be especially vulnerable to gains and losses on currency revaluations.

Information concerning major customers also reveals degrees of relative stability or vulnerability of the firm's future business. Heavy dependence for a large portion of revenue upon a government agency or another firm is significant investor information. Future prospects of the firm will be linked to an analysis and projection of the anticipated volume of activity of its major customers.

The FASB provides that segment information may be presented in one of several ways. You may find it incorporated in the financial statements and footnotes, in separate schedules included as part of the statement "package," or entirely in the statement footnotes.

WHO WANTS TO READ ALL THAT DETAIL?

Appendix A contains complete financial statements for both the Xerox Corporation and the Addison-Wesley Publishing Company. There is general agreement that financial statements are prepared for the knowledgeable reader. Business activities are often too complex to reduce to a few meaningful numbers. At this point, you should have an understanding of accounting adequate to intelligently read and understand the contents of both corporations' statements. Turn to Appendix A and take the time to study the statements. You should find it interesting, informative, and a rewarding and confidence-building experience. What may have appeared hopelessly confusing when you started this text should now fall into place and make sense.

If you have taken the time to read the two firms' financial statements, you may have skipped over the footnotes. It is only human to avoid apparently unnecessary detail. It is also very human occasionally to overlook something important and make a serious mistake.

When you have a need to study financial statements as the basis for an important decision, **study the footnotes!** Many times the statement footnotes contain significant information that is equally important as that contained in the statements themselves. Footnotes are considered an integral part of financial statements, and they are covered by the auditor's examination and opinion.

Auditor's Opinion

A prime reason for reading footnotes is that they contain the auditor's opinion or certificate. This opinion is essential to give a statement credibility for you. Of even more importance, it will highlight any significant changes, departures from GAAP, or auditor's reservations as to the adequacy of the audit or the fairness of disclosure.

Presently the auditor's opinion and the auditor's role are misunderstood by many readers of financial statements. Recall, from Chapter 1, that the firm itself (or its accountants) prepares the financial statements. The auditor's role is to make an independent examination and express a professional opinion on the propriety and adequacy of the firm's accounting system and the measurements and disclosure included in the firm's statements. Recently the AICPA established the Commission on Auditors' Responsibilities to investigate the gap in expectation and understanding of the auditor's role between actual practice and the user's conceptions. The Commission has made many significant recommendations for improvement both of the audit process and of public understanding of the process. You will undoubtedly have the opportunity to observe many of these changes as they take effect. Of particular interest may be a revision of the wording and presentation of the auditor's opinion, which will clarify the basic distinction between management's representations and the auditor's.

One of your primary uses of the auditor's opinion is to ascertain any exceptions from GAAP or any changes. Study the opinions for Xerox and Addison-Wesley in Appendix A. Note that the Xerox opinion contains no exceptions, it is a "clean opinion." The Coopers and Lybrand opinion on Addison-Wesley's financial statements calls your attention to a specific change in accounting method and directs you to the relevant footnote.

Choice of Accounting Method

Throughout this text you have learned that there are various measurement and reporting options within GAAP which can produce significantly different results. For example, a firm can elect LIFO or FIFO for inventory and cost-of-goods-sold valuation. These differences can make comparisons with other firms, which may elect different measurement options, difficult, dangerous, and occasionally meaningless. The statement footnotes will tell you exactly which GAAP option—*which accounting method*—the firm has elected.

Accounting Changes

Changes in accounting methods can make comparisons difficult, not just with other firms, but with data for the same firm from prior years. GAAP requires that significant *accounting changes* (changes in accounting methods) be made retroactive on any prior years' data included in the current report. Of course, the firm cannot retroactively change the data previously published and already in your files. The footnotes will contain details of any accounting changes so that you may take them into consideration in making comparisons to prior years' data.

Supplementary Information

Footnotes generally contain expansion of information only summarized on the report. This additional detail is often essential in evaluating statements. A single summary figure on the balance sheet can be relatively meaningless. For example, if you wish to analyze a firm's position, and a significant portion of total assets were in investments, you couldn't do much with a single line "investments $43,742,000." The footnotes will often contain a breakdown of the investments account, allowing you to evaluate the individual components.

Contingencies and Commitments

Finally, footnotes will disclose to you all material contingencies and commitments. Contingencies and commitments could radically alter your assumptions concerning the firm's future prospects. Remember, as a user making a decision, the historical information contained in the statements is valuable only as a basis for forecasting the future. The future is relevant to your decision. A firm might be currently involved with products and services that you believe are obsolescent. The existence of future contract commitments would influence your judgment as to how quickly the firm could switch to a different growing line of business. Major legal action pending against the firm could also severely impact the future.

I CAN'T WAIT A WHOLE YEAR!

The pace of change in the modern world continues to accelerate. Twenty or more years ago, investors could be content with progress reports—financial statements—on their investments only once a year. Now many investors desire more current updates on their investee's activities. Responding to this need, many larger firms now publish *interim reports*. These are essentially **abbreviated** and **estimated** financial statements for a period shorter than one year. They may be prepared semiannually, quarterly, or even monthly. Presently the quarterly reporting cycle appears to be the most common practice.

Interim reports appear to be growing in significance as a basis for investor decisions. There is even some evidence that the financial community has already made its major business decisions before the annual report is released. It is therefore important that you clearly understand the standards for interim reporting. Otherwise you could be seriously misled.

TIME ORIENTATION OF INTERIM REPORTING

Interim reports, hereafter discussed as quarterly reports, can be oriented in two quite different ways. They can focus on the events occurring in the particular quarter as if it were a distinct reporting period, like a year; or they can report the quarter as an integral part of a larger annual period. An example of statement differences resulting from these two approaches can be seen with respect to the cost of an annual major maintenance program. Assume that the firm schedules this annual maintenance each August during the firm's vacation shutdown. Following the distinct period approach, all maintenance costs would appear as expenses during the third quarter. GAAP encourage the alternative approach. Quarterly reports are considered to be just part of a picture which will eventually encompass the entire annual accounting period. In the case of the annual maintenance costs, they would be accrued or deferred, as appropriate, so as to reasonably apportion them to each of the four quarters in order to match revenue patterns. Of course, for those costs that cannot be readily identified and matched with the benefits of particular periods, GAAP require that they be charged to the period when incurred.

Of necessity, more items will require estimates on quarterly reports. If the firm is on periodic inventory, it probably would not wish, and could not afford, to take a complete physical inventory at the end of each quarter. Instead it may estimate cost of goods sold based on sales and using the prior year's average gross profit percentage.

INTERPRETING INTERIM REPORTS

Do not misinterpret the fact that quarterly reports are considered to be a part of an annual period, to mean that items are averaged evenly over the year. They are not! The same matching principle applicable to all accounting is also the objective of quarterly reporting. Revenues are reported in the quarter earned, and expenses are allocated to quarters to achieve the optimal matching with revenues.

In interpreting a firm's performance from quarterly reports, be careful of your standard of reference. Only in the rare case of a firm whose revenues are linear throughout the year (no seasonality) can you meaningfully compare just one quarter to the previous quarter. Comparisons need to be made to the same quarter in prior years. Alternatively, cumulative year-to-date amounts can be compared to similar cumulative amounts for prior years. Be sure you remember that seasonality can have a major impact on interim reports.

Exhibit 15.8 demonstrates the usefulness of interim-report information. Assume you have been an investor in Bolger Enterprises, and that the 19X7 Annual Report, which you received in March of 19X8, indicated only average performance for the previous year. Assume you were seriously considering selling your stock in Bolger and investing your funds elsewhere. Could Bolger's interim report for the first quarter of 19X8 influence your decision?

In this example, you might wish to hold your Bolger stock instead of selling it. The interim report indicates that sales increased 20 percent over the same quarter last year and net income increased 72 percent! It appears that Bolger's 19X8 performance may no longer be just "average." Without the interim data, you would have no way of knowing of the improvement until a full year had passed, and you would probably have sold your stock by then.

Exhibit 15.8
BOLGER ENTERPRISES, INC.

Selected Interim Report and Annual Report Data
(000 omitted)

	Most recent quarter (Winter 19X8)	Same quarter prior Year (Winter 19X7)	Prior quarter (Fall 19X7)	Prior Year total (19X7)
Revenue	$36,000	$30,000	$40,000	$130,000
Operating expenses	29,000	26,000	28,000	106,000
Income from operations before taxes	7,000	4,000	12,000	24,000
Provision for income taxes	1,500	800	2,500	4,900
Net income	$ 5,000	$ 3,200	$ 9,500	$ 19,100

Exhibit 15.8 also demonstrates the potential danger of the comparison of data to previous quarters. Assuming that the fall quarter is the largest and most profitable each year, and that Fall 19X7 was about the same as Fall 19X6, to compare Winter 19X8 with Fall 19X7 could be very misleading.

CHAPTER OVERVIEW

Based upon the material covered in this chapter, you should be able to:

- Explain the difference between a purchase and a pooling in terms of how a merger is effected;
- Explain the basic steps of consolidation following the pooling treatment;
- Explain the basic steps of consolidation following the purchase treatment;
- Describe the essential differences between purchase and pooling accounting, and explain the significance of these differences to future consolidated income reported for the combination;
- Describe the basic guidelines for segment, foreign operations, and major-customer information disclosure, and explain what disclosure is required for each;
- Describe the major categories or types of information you can expect to find included as part of financial statement footnotes;

- Explain the basic revenue and expense reporting objectives of interim reports, and the constraints relating to their appropriate use in trend analysis.

NEW VOCABULARY AND CONCEPTS

Holding company
Pooling of interests
Business combination
Purchase (of another company)
Statutory merger
Minority stockholders/minority
Eliminations in consolidation
Intercompany investment
Intercompany debt

Purchased goodwill
Segment (of a business)
Separately reportable segment
Foreign operations
Major customer
Accounting method
Accounting changes
Interim reports

- Requirements for consolidation.
- Purchase vs. pooling: difference as to method of acquisition and as to accounting method of consolidation.
- Necessary eliminations in consolidation.
- Segment information.
- Matching and interim reports.

REVIEW QUESTIONS

1. (a) What is a parent? (b) What is a subsidiary? (c) Explain the requirements for a parent–subsidiary relationship.
2. Can minority interest exist in the case of a wholly owned subsidiary? Explain your response.
3. (a) What is the difference between a consolidation and a statutory merger? (b) What is the difference in the accountant's treatment of each?
4. Explain two essentially different ways in which two corporations can merge.
5. In a pooling, how (at what amount) is the investment in the subsidiary originally carried on the parent's books?
6. In a pooling consolidation, is it possible to have investment in excess of book value, which would be used to revalue assets and/or become goodwill? Explain.
7. What happens to subsidiary retained earnings at the time of acquisition in a pooling consolidation? Explain.
8. Although handled differently for poolings and purchases, why is intercompany investment always eliminated in consolidation?
9. In addition to intercompany investment, what major eliminations are made in consolidation, regardless of purchase or pooling treatment? Give examples.

10. What is done in a purchase consolidation with any excess paid over the book value obtained?

11. (a) On a consolidated balance sheet, what happens to any minority share of the subsidiary's book value at the time of acquisition? (b) What happens to the minority's share of the subsidiary's earnings since acquisition, on the consolidated balance sheet? (c) On the consolidated income statement?

12. On a consolidated balance sheet, none of the subsidiary's owners' equity appears as such. Where does it go?

13. In balance sheet consolidation, there may also be eliminations affecting the following items:

a) Current notes receivable
b) Accounts receivable
c) Rent or interest receivable
d) Prepaid items
e) Investments in bonds, noncurrent notes, or preferred stock

f) Current notes payable
g) Accounts payable
h) Interest or rent payable
i) Bonds or notes payable
j) Preferred stock

For each of these possible "targets of elimination," describe the situation where an elimination would be appropriate, the amount to be eliminated, and the reason for the elimination.

14. In income statement consolidation, there may be eliminations affecting the following items:

a) Sales
b) Cost of goods sold
c) Rent revenue

d) Rent expense
e) Interest revenue
f) Interest expense

For each of these possible "targets of elimination," describe the situation when an elimination would be appropriate, the amount to be eliminated, and the reason for the elimination.

15. What is the difference in the accountant's treatment of a combination, between purchase treatment and pooling treatment? What is the potential effect of the differing treatments upon future income statements?

16. What is the basis for determining separately reportable segments of a business enterprise?

17. What are the three tests needed to qualify a reportable segment?

18. What minimum information must be reported for each reportable segment?

19. (a) When must foreign operations be separately disclosed? (b) What must be disclosed for significant foreign operations?

20. (a) When must major customers be disclosed? (b) What must be disclosed with respect to qualifying major customers?

21. What are five significant separate types of information that are included as part of statement footnotes?

22. In many firms, the comparison of two successive quarterly reports can prove misleading. Explain why this is possible.

MINI-CASES AND QUESTIONS FOR DISCUSSION

MC 15.1. Mr. Robert Curley sometimes takes things too literally. He perceives consolidated financial statements as essentially violating the underlying principles of accounting. "First of all, financial statements are prepared for business entities," he states. "A parent and its subsidiaries do not comprise an entity. Furthermore, even in the case of a wholly owned subsidiary, not all the assets on a consolidated balance sheet are either owned or controlled by the parent. Subsidiary creditors have prior claims on all subsidiary assets, and minority stockholders have a claim, too. Showing minority interest as an equity is like two wrongs trying to make a right. Minority stockholders have no claim against any assets but those in their subsidiary. A consolidated balance sheet shows them as having a claim against total consolidated assets!"

Discuss Mr. Curley's position. Is he correct? If he is correct, would it still be reasonable to prepare consolidated financial statements?

MC 15.2. Ann Jackson can see no reason for different treatments between purchase and pooling, "Take a business combination where everything actually happens the same except the composition of the surviving owners—the same sales, the same expenses, the same funds flows, the same everything," she says. "Yet if the surviving owners' names are different, the accountants will report lower net income than if the names are the same. Income is supposedly earned by the corporation independent of who its owners are. What possible justification is there for different accounting treatments?" Discuss.

ESSENTIAL PROBLEMS

[*Note.* In all Essential Problems below, the parent will be designated "P" and the subsidiary "S".]

EP 15.1. P purchases 100 percent of the voting common stock of S for $140,000. P has no other investments. The common book value and total owners' equity of S at the time of acquisition by P is $100,000. P's owners' equity immediately prior to acquiring S is $600,000. You may assume all of S's assets were on the firm's books at current costs. On the consolidated balance sheet immediately following acquisition:

a) P's investments will be included at what amount?

b) Goodwill will be what amount?

c) Consolidated owners' equity, including minority interest, will total how much?

EP 15.2. Answer the same questions as in Problem EP 15.1, assuming:

• P purchases 80 percent of S's common stock for $200,000;

- The common book value and total owners' equity of S at the time of acquisition was $187,500;

- P's owners' equity immediately prior to acquiring S was $700,000.

EP 15.3. P purchased 75 percent of the common stock of S for $150,000. P also has as an investment a 10-percent ownership in Q costing $30,000. The common book value and total owners' equity of S at the time of acquisition was $160,000. Since acquisition, S has $40,000 of accumulated retained earnings. P's current owners' equity totals $900,000. On a current consolidated balance sheet, what amounts should appear as:

a) Investments?

b) Goodwill?

c) Minority interest?

d) Consolidated owners' equity, including minority interest?

EP 15.4. Refer to Problem EP 15.3. Answer the same questions, based on the same information, but assume that P's proportional interest in S was 60 percent at a cost of $150,000.

EP 15.5. P's and S's combined balance sheets, after only the elimination of intercompany common stock investment, appeared as follows:

Cash	$ 400	Accounts payable	$ 700
Accounts receivable (net)	900	Other current liabilities	500
Inventory	800	Bonds payable	400
Investments	300	Less bond discount	(40)
Fixed Assets	1,200	Minority interest	200
Accumulated depreciation	(500)	Capital stock	1,000
Consolidated goodwill	200	Retained earnings	540
Total Assets	$3,300	Total Equities	$3,300

During the previous year, S had sold merchandise costing $300 to P for $500. All the merchandise purchased from S had been sold by P at year end. P had paid S for all merchandise delivered except for $40 not as yet paid. In P's investments account were some of S's bonds with a maturity value of $100 and a net book value of $90. Complete the preparation of the P AND S consolidated balance sheet.

EP 15.6. Refer to Problem EP 15.5, and start with the same partially finished consolidated balance sheet for P AND S given in that problem. Assume that, during the previous year, P had sold merchandise costing $300 to S for $400. S had resold all of this merchandise to customers. S had performed various services for P during the year, which were billed at $200. All but $20 of these services have been paid for at year end. In S's investments account at year end were some of P's bonds with a face value of $50 and a net book value of $45. Complete the preparation of the P AND S consolidated balance sheet.

EP 15.7. The combined income statement for P and S before any elimination was as follows:

Sales		$1,800
Cost of goods sold		1,100
Gross profit		$ 700
Other operating expenses:		
Wages and salaries	$400	
Depreciation	130	
Interest	15	
Rent	140	685
Other revenues		90
Operating income		$ 105
Less income taxes		40
Net Income		$ 65

During the year, S had sold P merchandise costing $300, for $500. S had also paid P $10 of interest on notes held by P. Complete the preparation of the P AND S consolidated income statement. You may assume S is a wholly owned subsidiary, and that P has sold all merchandise purchased from S.

EP 15.8. Refer to Problem EP 15.7, and start with the same partially completed income statement for P AND S given in that problem. During the year P had sold S merchandise costing $400 for $700. S had paid P $12 of interest on notes held by P. Warehouse space rented from S cost P a total of $68 for the year. Complete the preparation of the P AND S consolidated income statement. You may assume S is a wholly owned subsidiary, and that P has sold all merchandise purchased from S.

EP 15.9. P acquired 100 percent of the voting stock of S in exchange for 10,000 shares of additionally issued P $10-par common stock. At the time of acquisition, S's owners' equity was:

Capital stock	$100,000
Paid-in capital	70,000
Retained earnings	300,000
	$470,000

You may assume that P had no other investments, and that a consolidated balance sheet was to be prepared before S had any subsequent earnings. You may also assume that P's year-end retained earnings equaled $100,000 and that the combination with S qualified as pooling.

a) What was the balance in P's investments account immediately prior to consolidation?

b) What eliminations (amounts) in consolidation should be made from:

i) combined investments?

ii) combined capital stock?

iii) combined paid-in capital?

iv) combined retained earnings?

c) What amount of retained earnings should be reported on the consolidated balance sheet?

EP 15.10. P acquired 100 percent of the voting stock of S in exchange for 80,000 shares of P's additionally issued $5-par common stock. At the time of acquisition, S's owners' equity was:

Capital stock	$500,000
Paid-in capital	300,000
Retained earnings	200,000
	$1,000,000

You may assume that P had no other investments: that S had $100,000 of net income between acquisition and the year end when consolidated statements were to be prepared on a pooling basis; that between acquisition and year end, S paid out $40,000 in dividends; and that P's earnings at year end amounted to $750,000.

a) What was the balance in P's investments account immediately prior to consolidation?

b) What eliminations (amounts) in consolidation should be made from:

  i) combined investments?

  ii) combined capital stock?

  iii) combined paid-in capital?

  iv) combined retained earnings?

c) What amount of retained earnings should be reported on the consolidated balance sheet?

CURRENT-VALUE
FINANCIAL STATEMENTS

CHAPTER PREVIEW

The objective of this chapter is to introduce you to several different types of current-value financial statements as alternatives to historical-cost-based statements prepared in accordance with GAAP. You can learn:

- How inflation can render the information on financial statements less meaningful and possibly even misleading, depending upon one's information needs and assumptions;
- How replacement-cost accounting works, and some of the advantages and disadvantages of this alternative;
- How price-level-adjusted statements are another alternative, and some of the arguments supporting and attacking these statements;
- That the issue is of more than theoretical interest as other nations, the SEC, and the FASB have moved or are moving in the direction of current-value statements.

With the perspective available in this chapter, you will be better able to deal with the limitations of existing financial statements. You will be in a position to understand the continuing controversy in the United States over the desirability of and approach to current-value accounting. And finally, you will be able to interpret current-value information that may be included with financial statements.

IS MY NET INCOME REALLY INCOME?

Assume you are an independent trucker. Your business consists of yourself and your truck. All of your revenues are on a cash basis. Except for depreciation, all of your annual expenses are paid in cash by year end. For simplicity, assume at the beginning of the year that the necessary investment needed, in order to be successful as an independent trucker, was $10,000—$1,000 for working cash and $9,000 for a truck with a three-year life and zero salvage value. You therefore have invested $10,000 in your business.

Exhibit 16.1 includes your balance sheets and income statements for the first three years, prepared in accordance with GAAP. Note that, again for simplicity, it is first assumed that you withdrew no profits from the business. Your total reported income for the three years was $50,580. At the beginning of the fourth year, you can scrap your fully depreciated truck, buy another one, and continue your successful business.

Now include one more assumption. Assume truck *replacement costs* have increased 15 percent per year. As a result of this inflation, to replace your productive capacity at the start of the fourth year will cost you $13,688 (rounded). You have enough cash to do this, but was your three-year profit really $50,580? $4,688 of this $50,580 was necessary to replace your truck. Couldn't you also consider your profit as really only $45,892?

To see this issue more clearly, study Exhibit 16.2. This exhibit is the same as Exhibit 16.1 except it assumes you withdrew all $50,580 in profits over the three years. At the start of year four, you have your original $10,000 back into cash, but are you as well off as the day you started your company? Even if inflation had only affected truck purchase costs, you would still need $14,688 of cash ($1,000 working cash plus $13,688 for the truck), and you have only $10,000 in the business. Was the $50,580 you withdrew all profit, or did GAAP overstate your profit during this inflationary period?

This question does not represent a mere school problem. In a recent year, reported profits of U.S. industry were the highest ever.[1] Those individuals advocating different patterns of wealth distribution, and many politicians, were citing corporate profits as exorbitant. Many people believed that business should at least be subject to higher taxes on these very high profits.

At the same time, stock-market averages indicated that stock prices were less than half what they would be if earnings really were so great. Businessmen and financial managers were openly concerned about present and future difficulties in attracting additional investor capital into industry.

At the level of the individual firm, directors were advising stockholders that it was impossible to pay out in dividends 100 percent of reported income

---

[1]   See "Economic Reality in Financial Reporting," Touche Ross and Company, 1633 Broadway, New York, 10019; 1975.

Exhibit 16.1

YOUR TRUCKING COMPANY

**Ending Balance Sheets and Income Statements for the First Three Years
of Operation Assuming No Owner Withdrawals**

	First year	Second year	Third year
Assets:			
Cash	$19,000	$38,800	$60,580
Truck	9,000	9,000	9,000
Accumulated depreciation	(3,000)	(6,000)	(9,000)
Total Assets	$25,000	$41,800	$60,580
Equities:			
Liabilities	None	None	None
Owner's Equity	$25,000	$41,800	$60,580
Total Equities	$25,000	$41,800	$60,580
Income:			
Sales	$23,000	$25,300	$27,830
Depreciation expense	3,000	3,000	3,000
Other operating expenses	5,000	5,500	6,050
Net Income	$15,000	$16,800	$18,780

Exhibit 16.2

YOUR TRUCKING COMPANY

**Ending Balance Sheets and Income Statements for the First Three Years
of Operation Assuming Owner Withdraws 100 Percent of Income Each Year**

	First year	Second year	Third year
Assets:			
Cash	$ 4,000	$ 7,000	$10,000
Truck	9,000	9,000	9,000
Accumulated depreciation	(3,000)	(6,000)	(9,000)
Total Assets	$10,000	$10,000	$10,000
Equities:			
Liabilities	None	None	None
Owner's Equity	$10,000	$10,000	$10,000
Total Equities	$10,000	$10,000	$10,000
Income:			
Sales	$23,000	$25,300	$27,830
Depreciation expense	3,000	3,000	3,000
Other operating expense	5,000	5,500	6,050
Net Income	$15,000	$16,800	$18,780

if the business was to survive. In effect, they could be viewed as stating that not all reported income was really **income.**

What has been happening? Isn't income reported by financial accountants, and certified by CPA's, as measured in accordance with GAAP, really income? What is the source of the problem?

GAAP essentially ignore inflation when it comes to the replacement of capacity assets. Also, as pointed out in Chapter 8, in periods of inflation, GAAP may result in reasonably repeatable gross profit on inventory on the income statement while significantly understating current costs of inventory on the balance sheet—LIFO. On the other hand, under FIFO, GAAP can result in the reporting of near-current costs on the balance sheet, with high, not necessarily repeatable, holding gains included as part of reported income. Finally, general inflation results in a loss of purchasing power of dollars. Yet GAAP assume that all dollars of any year are the same as dollars from any other year.

INCOME RECONSIDERED

In Chapters 4, 5 and 6, you learned that income can be defined as a change in well-offness. You also learned that funds from operations cannot be considered profit without first providing for the maintenance or replacement of capacity assets—depreciation and amortization. So long as prices of goods and services are not changing, the historical-cost accounting system meets its objectives very well:

- Cash and other monetary assets from last year would be just as valuable this year;

- There would never be a holding gain on inventory. All gross profit would be repeatable trading profit. The cost of inventory still on hand (purchased last year) would continue to be the current cost (LIFO and FIFO would produce identical results);

- Annual depreciation based on original cost would signal that enough revenue be retained in the business to replace the depreciable assets at the end of their useful life.

Even though GAAP may ignore it, inflation is very real. With prices of goods and services changing, issues arise concerning how well a firm is maintaining its well-offness, holding gains vs. trading (repeatable) profits, and the adequacy of depreciation based on original cost. There continues to be general consensus that, conceptually, income should be considered as an increase in well-offness; or, stating the same idea differently, that income should be measured as the amount left over after first providing for the maintenance of capital (well-offness).

But how is the firm's well-offness, or the capital to be maintained, to be measured? Is it simply the number of dollars invested in the business, regardless of changes in general purchasing power of the dollar or changes in the specific replacement costs of specific nonmonetary assets? In the example of your trucking company, should the capital to be maintained simply be net assets of $10,000? GAAP presently define and measure capital to be maintained in this fashion.

To probe further, should maintenance of capital be considered as maintaining the physical productive capacity to continue in the same business? In the example of your trucking company, should the capital to be maintained be the replacement cost of the truck plus $1,000 of working capital—$11,350 after the first year ($9,000 times 1.15, plus $1,000); $12,902 after the second ($10,350 times 1.15 rounded, plus $1,000); and $14,688 after the third ($11,902 times 1.15 rounded, plus $1,000)? The replacement cost-accounting system to be discussed below is constructed on this premise.

Or should capital to be maintained be defined as the overall capacity to continue in the same business? This would include both physical capacity (inventory and capacity assets) and financial capacity (necessary net monetary working capital). If you were to assume a general inflation rate of ten percent a year (except for truck replacement cost) applicable to all revenues and expense in your trucking business (already incorporated in Exhibits 16.1 and 16.2), then working capital needs could be assumed to increase from $1,000 to $1,100, to $1,210, and to $1,331. Overall "capacity capital" to be maintained over the three years would then be $11,450 ($10,350 plus $1,100), $13,112, and $15,019, respectively.

Or should capacity to continue the same activity be considered irrelevant, but capacity to perform any business activity be the focus? In this last alternative, maintenance of capital would be defined in terms of maintaining the general purchasing power of the $10,000 of capital invested in the business. Allowing for a ten-percent general inflation rate, capital to be maintained at the end of each of the three years would be $11,000, $12,100, and $13,310, respectively. This alternative is known as *price-level adjusted accounting* and will also be further explored later in this chapter.

Which of the alternative concepts of capital to be maintained (before identifying increase in net assets as income) should accountants use? Exhibit 16.3 includes the income measurement results of the alternatives mentioned. Can you see that they are significantly different, especially for larger firms (with three or six zeros added to all figures)?

As an elementary accounting student, you are certainly not expected to answer authoritatively a question to which industry, accountants, academicians, and government so far have failed to agree upon the answer. Nevertheless, it is important that you understand the issues and currently proposed alternatives.

DISTRIBUTABLE INCOME

As a tool for ease of understanding alternative current-value systems, you can use a concept of *distributable income*. Distributable income may be defined as

Exhibit 16.3
YOUR TRUCKING COMPANY

Reported Net Income for First Three Years under Alternative Measurement Systems

| Capital Maintenance | Reported Net Income | | | |
Alternative	First year	Second year	Third year	Three-year total
1. Simple dollars invested (GAAP)	$15,000	$16,800	$18,780	$50,580
2. Productive capacity (replacement cost)	13,650	15,248	16,994	45,892
3. Overall productive and financial capacity	13,550	15,138	16,873	45,561
4. General purchasing power	14,000	15,700	17,570	47,270

Replacement-cost calculations are as follows (others are calculated in a similar fashion):

	Beginning capital	Ending capital	Increment necessary for maintenance[a]	Simple dollars' income less increment
First year	$10,000	$11,350	$1,350	$13,650
Second year	11,350	12,902	1,552	$15,248
Third year	12,902	14,688	1,786	$16,994

[a] Increment beyond $3,000 included in maintenance of simple $10,000 dollars.

the amount of assets that theoretically could be withdrawn each year, or paid in dividends,[2] and still have capital maintained (as defined in the particular system). Referring to Exhibit 16.3, we could ask, "What would be the result after three years under the different systems if income was viewed as distributable and had been distributed?"

After three years under the GAAP system, your company would have distributed $50,580 and would have $10,000 in the business. You would need an additional $4,688 to remain in business, if the only inflation was 15 percent per year applicable to the truck. You would need an additional $5,019 if both 15-percent specific inflation applied to the truck and 10-percent general inflation affected working cash needs. You would also have suffered a $3,310 loss in the general purchasing power of your $10,000 capital investment. At a 10-percent general inflation rate, you would need $13,310 to have the same general purchasing power you had when starting your business.

After three years under a replacement-cost system, your company would have distributed only $45,892 and would have $14,688 in the business. You

---

[2]   It will be assumed throughout this chapter that a firm has adequate solvency and liquidity to pay out 100 percent of distributable income in dividends.

would be able to replace your truck and still have $1,000 of cash for working capital needs. You would need an additional $331 if 10-percent general inflation had also occurred, increasing your working capital needs to $1,331. But note that, with $14,688, you would be $1,378 ($14,688 − $13,310) **better off** in terms of general purchasing power. Opponents of replacement-cost accounting take the position that maintenance of capital should not include improving one's well-offness in terms of general, or alternative-opportunity, purchasing power. This difference will be further discussed below.

Finally, under a price-level-adjusted system, your company would have distributed $47,270 and would have $13,310 in the business. You would need an additional $1,378 to buy a new truck and still have $1,000 of working capital. Perhaps more significantly you would need an additional $1,709 to have both the truck and $331 more working capital (reflecting 10-percent inflation). The $1709 would represent additional capital required only because truck costs had inflated more than the general rate. Of course, with $13,310, your alternative general purchasing power would be the same as on the day you started in business.

CHANGING SITUATION

In the past, owners, directors, and other financial statement users have had limited information. They have known that, in periods of inflation, not all reported net income was fully distributable; but they have had little information to use in estimating the portion that was distributable. Effective January 1, 1976, the largest corporations are required by the SEC to estimate and separately disclose current-replacement-cost information. Ending inventory, net fixed assets, cost of goods sold, and annual depreciation expense (assuming straight-line depreciation) are also to be reported at current replacement cost by supplementary or footnote disclosure.[3]

GAAP in The Netherlands have provided for the inclusion of replacement-cost data in the statements themselves for many years. In the United Kingdom, replacement costs may be required in the statements themselves effective in 1978. In the United States, debate is still going on. Probable changeover to include replacement costs as other than supplementary information appears several years away, if ever.

REPLACEMENT-COST STATEMENTS

To understand how replacement-cost information may be incorporated in financial statements, as opposed to merely being disclosed in footnotes, the first step is to define *replacement cost* more precisely. It is defined as the **low-**

---

[3]   Supplementary disclosure is required for statements filed with the SEC. It is not mandated for published financial statements. However, most firms will probably voluntarily include this information with published annual reports.

est normal business cost to obtain currently an item of equivalent capability. With technological changes, there are complexities in the determination of replacement costs that are beyond the scope of this elementary text. We will assume that replacement-cost data are available, and will focus our attention on statements prepared incorporating this information. Exhibit 16.4 presents the balance sheets and income statements for the years 19X0 through 19X3 for the Bohren Corporation, prepared in accordance with GAAP. Exhibit 16.5 presents the same statements for the same years on a replacement-cost basis. In both cases the following assumptions are made:

- 100 percent of reported net income is distributed in dividends each year;
- General inflation of 10 percent per year affects inventory and current revenues and expenses;
- Specific inflation of 15 percent per year affects fixed assets;
- The volume of activity remains constant;
- LIFO is used on Exhibit 16.4.

Exhibit 16.4
BOHREN CORPORATION

Balance Sheets and Income Statements for the Years 19X0 through 19X3
Prepared Following GAAP (000 omitted)

	12/31/X0	12/31/X1	12/31/X2	12/31/X3
Assets				
Cash	$ 90	$198	$307	$417
Inventory	70	70	70	70
Fixed assets	300	300	300	300
Less accumulated depreciation	0	(100)	(200)	(300)
Total Assets	$460	$468	$477	$487
Equities				
Current liabilities	$ 80	$ 88	$ 97	$107
Noncurrent liabilities	100	100	100	100
Contributed capital	280	280	280	280
Retained earnings	0	0	0	0
Total Equities	$460	$468	$477	$487
Income Statement				
Sales		$600	$660	$726
Cost of goods sold		300	330	363
Gross profit		$300	$330	$363
Depreciation		100	100	100
Other operating expenses		100	110	121
Net Income*		$100	$120	$142

* Assumes no income tax.

Exhibit 16.5
BOHREN CORPORATION

Balance Sheets and Income Statements for the Years 19X0 through 19X3
Prepared on a Replacement Cost Basis
(000 omitted)

	12/31/X0	12/31/X1	12/31/X2	12/31/X3
Assets				
Cash	$ 90	$213	$373	$574
Inventory	70	77	85	94
Fixed assets	300	345	397	457
Less accumulated depreciation	0	(115)	(266)	(457)
Total Assets	$460	$520	$589	$668
Equities				
Current liabilities	$ 80	$ 88	$ 97	$107
Noncurrent Liabilities	100	100	100	100
Contributed capital	280	280	280	280
Retained earnings	0	0	0	0
Holding gains	0	52	112	181
Total Equities	$460	$520	$589	$668
Income Statement				
Sales		$600	$660	$726
Cost of goods sold		300	330	363
Gross profit		$300	$330	$363
Depreciation		115	132	152
Other operating expenses		100	110	121
Operating income		$ 85	$ 88	$ 90
Retroactive depreciation		0	19	39
Distributable income		$ 85	$ 69	$ 51
Holding gains		52	60	69
Total Income and Gains		$137	$129	$120

Also, for simplicity, it is assumed, in the preparation of Exhibit 16.5, that all inflation took place **at the beginning** of each year.[4]

To understand replacement-cost statements, you should start with the already familiar elements. Compare Exhibits 16.4 and 16.5. Note that the following items are the same on both statements:

---

[4]   In the less simplified situation where inflation takes place throughout the year, operating expenses except for depreciation would reflect an average increase rather than the full increase. And sales would reflect whatever price increases the firm was able to obtain in the marketplace. Many firms are unable to immediately "pass on" price increases to maintain profit margins. This delay is often referred to as the "cost-profit squeeze."

- Current liabilities,
- Noncurrent liabilities,
- Contributed capital,
- Retained earnings,

- Sales,
- Cost of goods sold,
- Gross profit,
- Other operating expenses.

Noncurrent liabilities and contributed capital are not affected by inflation, since there were no changes during the years. Retained earnings remains at zero, because distributable income was assumed to be distributed in dividends. Current liabilities, sales, and other operating expenses reflect the 10-percent general inflation rate. Cost of goods sold on a replacement-cost basis (together with resultant gross profit) reflects most current inflated costs; it is identical to LIFO cost of goods sold in this example. Had older inventory at noncurrent costs been sold and a holding gain realized, cost of goods sold would still be reported at current replacement cost. The realized holding gain would be separately reported, in a similar manner to "other income."

Ending inventory on the replacement-cost balance sheet is reported at the latest costs, reflecting the end-of-year inflated prices. Similarly, fixed assets are appreciated to reflect the 15-percent inflation rate applicable to these items.

Depreciation is a little more involved. Annual depreciation expense is calculated by using the same proportion as under the present GAAP system—one-third each year, for the Bohren Corporation. The proportion is calculated with respect to the year-end asset replacement cost. For 19X1, one-third of $345,000 equals $115,000.

Accumulated depreciation is again determined on a proportionate basis. At the end of the year 19X2, two-thirds of the asset has expired. Therefore, two-thirds of $397,000 or $266,000 (rounded) is reported as accumulated depreciation.

Note that, on the income statement, there are two depreciation deductions starting in 19X2. $132,000 is deducted as an operating expense, representing one-third of the current replacement cost of fixed assets. The $19,000 of additional expense for *retroactive depreciation* represents "catch-up depreciation." It is the additional amount that should have been charged in prior years, based on the current year's even higher replacement costs. Beginning accumulated depreciation of $115,000 plus current year's $132,000 plus $19,000 of retroactive or "catch-up" depreciation equals the necessary $266,000 of ending accumulated depreciation. The retroactive depreciation deduction is necessary before arriving at distributable income—the amount which can be distributed in dividends without imparing future operations.

Holding gains represent the current year's increase in each asset's replacement cost. In 19X1, a 10-percent increase in the replacement cost of inventory—$7,000—plus a 15-percent increase in the replacement cost of fixed assets—$45,000—equaled $52,000 in holding gains. In 19X3, a 10-percent cost increase for inventory ($9,000) plus a 15-percent increase for fixed assets ($60,000) equaled $69,000 in holding gains. Accumulated holding gains are shown separately in owner's equity, in order to complete the balance sheet equality.

Note that holding gains are separately reported on the income statement and the balance sheet. They represent an increase in well-offness as compared to original dollars invested. Until the business is terminated, they do not represent assets that can be withdrawn as profit. Otherwise the operating and productive capacity would not be maintained.

EVALUATING REPLACEMENT-COST STATEMENTS

Are replacement-cost statements more meaningful to the user than current GAAP historical-cost statements? Is replacement-cost distributable income really all distributable without impairing operating and productive capacity? Replacement-cost statements have the following definite advantages:

1. All nonmonetary assets on the balance sheet are stated in current values;

2. Reported income from operations is stated in terms of current costs and therefore may be repeatable;

3. Trading profit and holding gain on goods sold are distinguished, thereby facilitating a forecast of repeatable gross profit;

4. Distributable income is clearly identified for the benefit of owners and directors who have to make dividend decisions.

To verify that replacement-cost accounting provides the proper signals with respect to distributable income, refer again to Exhibit 16.5. The Bohren Corporation has distributed as dividends only the amount shown as distributable. It holds $574,000 of cash as of 12/31/X3. Remember that, on 12/31/X0, it had net quick assets (cash less current liabilities) of $10,000; inventory costing $70,000; and brand new fixed assets. Was it as well off as of 12/31/X3? On 1/1/X4 it could purchase new fixed assets at their current replacement cost ($457,000), continue with the same inventory (now reported at the inflated replacement cost of $94,000), and still have net quick assets of $10,000. It is almost exactly as well off. The only difference is that the purchasing power of its $10,000 of net quick assets has not been maintained. The conventional replacement-cost system does not provide for maintaining well-offness in terms of the financial capacity of monetary assets. It focuses exclusively on maintaining capital, as measured in terms of the nonmonetary assets that provide physical capacity (inventory and fixed assets).

Replacement-cost statements have several disadvantages.

1. As mentioned above, they do not provide for maintenance of monetary capital, even though it is also subject to "capacity erosion" through inflation;

2. They may be difficult and costly to prepare because of the necessity of estimating current replacement costs instead of just using known information resulting from past transactions;

3. They may be subject to error and manipulation because of the difficulty (or impossibility) of objectively verifying replacement-cost estimates;

4. They may actually understate (or overstate) income by providing for replacement of assets whose cost is changing at a greater (or lesser) rate than general inflation. Such differences between specific and general inflation may not be appropriately considered as maintenance of capital (see discussion below).

INDEX ADJUSTMENT

As mentioned above, the details of determining replacement costs in specific situations are beyond the scope of this text. Nevertheless, you should become familiar with one simple technique with general applicability. Very often the effect of inflation is reasonably uniform for a group of items. In such cases, it would be wasteful to calculate each item separately. If you knew that representative items in a group cost $1.10 last year, and $1.18 this year, you could construct a *conversion index* to be used in adjusting the entire group. The conversion index would simply be the current price index or replacement cost divided by the original or older price index or replacement cost:

$$\text{Conversion index} = \frac{\text{Current price index (or replacement cost)}}{\text{Original or older price index (or replacement cost)}}$$

For the above example, if the original or beginning cost of the group to be adjusted was $17,500, you would first determine the conversion index: 118/110. You would then multiply the amount to be adjusted by the conversion index. $17,500 times 118/110 = $18,773 (to the nearest dollar). $18,773 would represent the current replacement cost of the group.

In the case of the Bohren Corporation (Exhibit 16.5), inflation on fixed assets was given as 15 percent per year, or a conversion index of 115/100. Fixed assets were restated each year by multiplying by this factor. General inflation on other items was given as 10 percent per year, or 110/100. Year-end balances for such items as inventory and current liabilities were adjusted by this factor.

PRICE-LEVEL-ADJUSTED STATEMENTS

A conversion index is also employed in the preparation of price-level-adjusted statements. As mentioned above, one income-capital maintenance alternative under consideration involves defining the capital to be maintained in terms of the general purchasing power of dollars invested. Under this approach, items subject to inflation are adjusted not to their specific current costs but by a conversion index representing general inflation. The Gross National Product (GNP) price deflator prepared by the U.S. Government has been suggested as the best conversion index for such purposes.

Exhibit 16.6 includes data for the Bohren Corporation disclosed on a price-level-adjusted purchasing-power basis. It assumes the same general inflation rate of 10 percent per year, all taking place at the start of each new year, that was assumed for replacement-cost adjustment. Note that the specific inflation rate of 15 percent on fixed assets is ignored. Instead, 10 percent is used to adjust **all** items subject to inflation.

Compare Exhibits 16.5 and 16.6. Note that Exhibit 16.6 is essentially similar to 16.5 and would be almost identical had the inflation rate for fixed assets been only 10 percent on a replacement-cost basis. One difference worth noting is that Exhibit 16.6 provides for maintaining the general purchasing power of all invested capital in the determination of distributable income. In 19X0 there were $10,000 of net quick assets invested in the business. With a

Exhibit 16.6
BOHREN CORPORATION

Balance Sheets and Income Statements for the Years 19X0 through 19X3
Prepared on a Price-Level-Adjusted Purchasing-Power Basis
(000 omitted)

	12/31/X0	12/31/X1	12/31/X2	12/31/X3
Assets				
Cash	$ 90	$209	$351	$519
Inventory	70	77	85	94
Fixed assets	300	330	363	399
Less accumulated depreciation	0	(110)	(242)	(399)
Total Assets	$460	$506	$557	$613
Equities				
Current liabilities	$ 80	$ 88	$ 97	$107
Noncurrent liabilities	100	100	100	100
Contributed capital	280	280	280	280
Retained earnings	0	0	0	0
Cumulative price-level adjustment	0	38	80	126
Total Equities	$460	$506	$557	$613
Income Statement				
Sales		$600	$660	$726
Cost of goods sold		300	330	363
Gross profit		$300	$330	$363
Depreciation		110	121	133
Other operating expenses		100	110	121
Purchasing-power maintenance		1	1	1
Operating income		$ 89	$ 98	$108
Retroactive depreciation		0	11	24
Distributable income		$ 89	$ 87	$ 84
Price-level adjustment		38	42	46
Total Income and Inflation Adjustment		$127	$129	$130

10-percent annual inflation rate, $11,000 of net quick assets would be needed the following year just to maintain general purchasing power. Therefore, the 19X1 income statement includes a provision for $1,000 for purchasing-power maintenance in the determination of distributable income. Similar provisions are included for subsequent years. The "adjustment for inflation" items are similar to holding gains on a replacement-cost statement, except that they also include the provision for all required additional working-capital investment and not just the amount for inventory and fixed assets.

Many price-level-adjusted statements suggested as alternatives to present statements have not provided for the complete working-capital adjustment contained in Exhibit 16.6. This example is included to enhance your understanding of overall capital maintenance on a general purchasing-power basis. With or without such a provision for the maintenance of purchasing power of net working capital, price-level-adjusted statements have both advantages and disadvantages. Proponents suggest their desirability in terms of the following:

1. They do a better job of reflecting current values, costs, and distributable income than do historical-cost-based statements.

2. Since a single uniform public index is used in their preparation, they are inexpensive to prepare and objectively verifiable. No estimates, with attendant difficulty, costs, and potential for error and manipulation, are involved. Objective historical transaction cost data are merely index-adjusted.

Opponents of simple price-level adjustment attack it as unreal, and as a meaningless or even misleading compromise. Opponents point out that, whereas both historical costs and replacement costs focus on differing realities, *price-level-adjusted cost* (PLAC) would be wholly unreal in most cases. Only where, for a particular asset, the specific price change was the **same** as the general inflation rate would the PLAC measurement approximate reality. When the specific inflation rate was greater than the general rate, assets would be understated. For example, Bohren's fixed assets as of 12/31/X3 under PLAC were reported at $399,000, whereas their actual replacement costs after 15-percent inflation were $457,000 (Exhibit 16.5). Similarly, following PLAC, an inventory of hand calculators would have been indexed upwards, following the general inflation rate, even though their cost has been subject to significant deflation in recent years.

CONSIDERATIONS RELATED TO CURRENT-VALUE ACCOUNTING

With the various alternatives and their relative strengths and weaknesses cited above, perhaps you can see why accountants have yet to arrive at a satisfactory solution to the problem of accounting for inflation. And the examples given above are vastly oversimplified. The actual problem is far more complex. At its very root is the question of the definition and measurement of income and of defining and measuring capital to be maintained.

Earlier in this chapter, various alternatives were given in terms of a hypothetical trucking company. Let us review the alternatives of historical costs (GAAP), replacement cost, and PLAC in an even simpler context, with the following assumption.

1. At the beginning of a period, the minimum investment to play a particular game (go into a particular business) is $10,000.

2. At the end of a period, the minimum investment for a new player, or an old one to continue, is $12,000 (20-percent specific inflation).

3. During the period, general inflation has been 10 percent. The cost of all other games, including just living, has gone up to $11,000.

4. Someone started playing with $10,000 at the beginning of the period and had $11,000 at the end of the period.

What would be the income of this person, assuming three different definitions of capital to be maintained: dollars invested; maintenance of well-offness in terms of general purchasing power; and maintenance of capacity to play the particular game (business)? Which income measurement would seem intuitively more valid to you?

Assuming that capital to be maintained is defined as just the number of dollars, then income would be $1,000. Income would be measured and reported as $1,000 following current GAAP. However, it may be difficult to perceive that this person is better off by $1,000, or that the $1,000 could be considered distributable income.

Assuming capital to be maintained is defined in terms of general purchasing power, then income would be zero. Following a purchasing-power-based accounting system, the individual would be reported as having just broken even. Zero distributable income would "signal" the owner that no assets could be withdrawn from the firm if the firm's invested capital was to be maintained in terms of its general purchasing power.

If capital is defined in terms of specific capacity (replacement-cost accounting), then the individual would have a reported loss of $1,000 for the period. Again it is difficult to see how this person is worse off with his $11,000 than anyone else who just stayed even with inflation and now wished to play the particular game. The individual has not lost; the "price of playing that particular game" (capital investment required to participate successfully in the particular business) has just increased for everyone wanting to play, old players and new alike.

By analogy, it would seem inappropriate for accountants to measure income on a replacement (of specific capacity) cost basis. Existing investors (players) might desire such measurement, especially if it could also be used for determination of tax liability. They would then have an advantage over other new players. However, an objective of accounting measurement has been, and should continue to be, fairness to all parties with potentially conflicting interests.

Perhaps the ideal system will evolve as a combination of replacement-cost measurement for balance sheet disclosure and maintenance of general purchasing power for income determination. Whatever new system is finally chosen, if any, it will probably first be required on a parallel basis with *dual-column statements*.

DUAL-COLUMN STATEMENTS

Initially, and perhaps for several subsequent years, financial statements could be prepared showing both traditional historical-cost data, and also data on the new basis in a parallel column. Such an approach might ease the problems of transition from one system to the other. It would allow the user to become familiar with the new without having to forego the old and familiar. It would also take into consideration those who believe that historical-cost data are most significant and essential.

MONETARY GAINS AND LOSSES

A final consideration related to inflation and current-value accounting is possible gain or loss on net monetary items. A firm with $200,000 of monetary assets at the beginning of the period, and $200,000 at the end, is **not** as well off if there has been general inflation. It cannot purchase as much goods and services at the end of the period as it could at the beginning.

Conversely, a firm with $200,000 of monetary liabilities at the beginning and end of a period of inflation is better off. The amount of the debt to be paid is fixed. At the end of the period it can be paid off with less costly or cheaper dollars—dollars with less purchasing power over goods and services. A lender's loss on monetary receivables is matched by the borrower's gain on monetary payables.

Since gains on monetary liabilities are offset by losses on monetary assets, overall gain or loss for a firm is based on net monetary assets or net monetary debt. The Bohren Corporation (Exhibit 16.4) on 12/31/X0 had $90,000 of monetary assets—all cash—and $180,000 of monetary debt. It therefore had $90,000 of net monetary debt on which it had a 10-percent purchasing power gain.

Holding gains or losses on net monetary items do not involve an actual inflow or outflow of resources. Accountants are not in agreement concerning whether such information should be incorporated in current-value financial statements. Neither the SEC supplementary-disclosure requirements nor the new accounting system in the United Kingdom provides for such reporting.

It is important that you recognize the existence of the phenomenon in periods of price changes, and of a firm's need for effective financial planning and management related to this reality of inflation. In recent years, major companies have successfully operated with quick ratios in the 0.6- to 0.7-to-1 range. Often these firms will elect greater total interest costs on a large amount of debt, and will incur the salary costs of teams of cash managers hired to avoid debt-repayment difficulties, knowing that these costs are more than offset by the inflationary gain in net monetary assets. Currently, GAAP will recognize and report the costs of the high-net-debt position (salaries, interest, and high debt ratio), but it does not report the action-determining benefit. Astute financial management accordingly is not only not recognized—it is reported as if it were inefficient. You should keep this situation in mind when evaluating historical-cost financial statements during periods of inflation.

CHAPTER OVERVIEW

Based on the material contained in this chapter, you should be in a position to:

- Describe several alternative definitions of income based on different measures of capital to be maintained;
- Define and discuss the applicability of conversion indices;
- Describe the differences among historical-cost, replacement-cost, and price-level-adjusted-cost accounting;
- Describe some of the advantages and disadvantages of each of these three accounting measurement alternatives;
- Explain the meaning and usefulness of such items as retroactive depreciation, holding gains, and price-level adjustment.

NEW VOCABULARY AND CONCEPTS

Price-level-adjusted accounting   Conversion index
Distributable income   Price-level-adjusted cost (PLAC)
Replacement cost   Dual-column statements
Retroactive depreciation

- Holding gains (or losses) on net monetary items
- Net income and distributable income
- Specific and general inflation

REVIEW QUESTIONS

1. How is the concept of maintenance of capital related to the definition of income? Explain with examples.

2. (a) What is distributable income? (b) Is net income, as defined by GAAP, all distributable income? If not, explain.

3. How is the replacement cost of a particular asset or group of assets defined?

4. Give examples of replacement-cost information required as supplementary information in the United States and in certain foreign countries.

5. Four major definitions of capital to be maintained are: number of dollars invested, physical capacity to continue in the same business, physical and financial capacity to stay in the same business, and the general purchasing power of the invested capital. Explain which of these concepts relate to the following alternative accounting systems, and the significance of the relationship:
   a) GAAP (historical or original cost),
   b) Price-level-adjusted,
   c) Replacement cost.

6. What are the advantages to the user of replacement-cost financial statements?

7. (a) What is "retroactive depreciation"? (b) How is it determined? (c) Is it an operating expense of the current year? (d) Explain its relationship to distributable income.

8. (a) What are holding gains? (b) Explain how holding gains can, at the same time, be both an increase in well-offness and also nondistributable.

9. What are the major advantages and major disadvantages of replacement-cost accounting as compared to current GAAP?

10. What are the major arguments for and against price-level-adjusted financial statements?

11. What are dual-column statements? When might they be desirable?

12. What are monetary gains or losses? How do they arise?

MINI-CASES AND QUESTIONS FOR DISCUSSION

MC 16.1. John Ridges is addressing a group of fellow accountants. He states, "I just can't see replacement-cost statements. The mission of accountants is to report things that have actually happened, and how they are. If a firm has realized a holding gain, let's report it as such. If inventory cost us $1,000, that is what it cost, not the $2,000 we might have to pay to replace it today. And why show replacement cost of an asset which we have not replaced and may never replace? How can we have a holding gain which we can't even distribute to our owners? It's illusory, and so is replacement-cost accounting. It's a nice fiction but accountants deal in fact."

You are the next speaker, and your topic is, "In Defense of Replacement-Cost Accounting." What would you say in reply to John Ridges? Explain.

MC 16.2. "Talking about someone being two-faced, what about these accountants?" asks Joan. "If they decide replacement-cost accounting or some other system is appropriate, why don't they just change over to it? What is all this nonsense of dual-column statements? It sounds to me like a make-work program that will really confuse the user."

Do you agree with Joan? Discuss.

MC 16.3. A major corporate executive is addressing a conference of business people. He opens with, "Time is running out. The U.S. is rapidly losing its competitive world position among advanced industrial nations. This nation's productive capacity—our physical plant and equipment—is definitely obsolescent and requires more rapid replacement. A primary cause of this country falling behind is our financial and tax accounting systems. Together they discourage both our recognition of the high cost of updating our capacity and our ability to do so. Financial income is overstated. Part of our revenues needed just to replace our existing capacity are reported as profit, to which our stockholders feel entitled in dividends. The media portray our supposedly high profits as exorbitant. And the government similarly includes this necessary additional capital maintenance cost in taxable income, and we must pay income tax on it.

"Replacement-cost accounting for both financial and tax purposes is essential for the survival of our nation. It is only common sense that a person doesn't have any income until after he has provided for just staying in his business. I'm not talking about expanding in business or even acquiring more advanced technology. I just mean being able to continue in the same business as last year."

Do you agree with the various issues raised? Discuss.

MC 16.4. There exists a general consensus that accountants cannot reasonably (and should not attempt to) measure opportunity cost or opportunity loss. That is, they cannot and should not attempt to measure and report what **might** have happened. For example, assume that a firm acquired marketable securities costing $100,000 at the beginning of the year. During the year the market value climbed to $200,000 and then dropped back to $120,000. Accountants do not recognize the gain of the $20,000, since it has not been **realized** through sale. They certainly do not recognize the opportunity **loss** of $80,000 resulting from the firm's not selling at the "top of the market."

Isn't loss on net monetary assets akin to an opportunity loss, and gain on net monetary debt at the very least unrealized? It would therefore appear inappropriate to include such information in financial statements. Discuss.

ESSENTIAL PROBLEMS

EP 16.1. Ending inventory originally cost $45,000 and fixed assets originally cost $250,000. Representative inventory items which cost $4 apiece have a current replacement cost of $5.50. Representative fixed assets which cost

$40,000 would currently cost $54,000 to replace. What would be the appropriate balance sheet amounts for inventory and fixed assets under GAAP? Under replacement-cost accounting? What would be the holding gain for the period?

EP 16.2. Ending inventory originally cost $175,000, and fixed assets originally cost $325,000. Replacement costs of inventory are currently 7 percent higher. Replacement costs of fixed assets have jumped 11 percent. What would be the appropriate balance sheet amounts for these two items under replacement-cost accounting? What would be the period's associated holding gain?

EP 16.3. A fixed asset at the beginning of the year under replacement-cost accounting was reported at $300,000, with $135,000 of accumulated depreciation. Replacement cost of this asset had increased 8 percent by year end. The asset was being depreciated 5 percent per year. Current year's operating profit before any depreciation was $45,000, and income taxes may be ignored. Under replacement-cost accounting:

a) What was the amount of annual depreciation expense?

b) What was the amount of "retroactive depreciation"?

c) What was the amount of current year's operating profit?

d) What was the amount of distributable income?

EP 16.4. Refer to Problem EP 16.3. Answer the same questions for a fixed asset that:

- Was disclosed at $550,000, with $165,000 of accumulated depreciation, at the beginning of the year;

- Was being depreciated at 10 percent per year;

- Had been subject to inflation of replacement cost as part of a group where the index had gone from 137 to 146;

- Was used by a company whose current year's operating profit, before depreciation on this particular asset, was $240,000.

SUPPLEMENTARY PROBLEMS

SP 16.5. Exhibit 16.7 includes data for the Progressive Corporation for the year 19X1. During the year, inventory replacement costs increased 5 percent, and the replacement cost of fixed assets rose 15 percent. For simplicity, you may assume that all of these changes occurred on 1/1/X1. Prepare the 12/31/X1 balance sheet and the 19X1 income statement in good form following replacement cost accounting.

SP 16.6. Refer to Problem SP 16.5. Prepare the replacement-cost-based statements as of 12/31/X1 and for 19X1 for the company, assuming that the inflation rates were:

Specific inflation—Inventory: 12 percent
Specific inflation—Fixed Assets: 4 percent

You may assume that all inflationary changes occurred on 1/1/X1.

Exhibit 16.7
PROGRESSIVE CORPORATION

Balance Sheets and Income Statements
(000 omitted)

	12/31/X1	12/31/X0
Assets		
Cash	$ 60	$ 50
Accounts receivable (net)	120	110
Inventory	90	70
Other current assets	30	10
Total Current Assets	$300	$240
Investments	50	35
Fixed assets	500	500
Less accumulated depreciation	(250)	(200)
Total Assets	$600	$575
Equities		
Accounts payable	$100	$ 80
Other current liabilities	25	30
Total Current Liabilities	$125	$110
Noncurrent liabilities	100	100
Total Liabilities	$225	$210
Contributed capital	300	300
Retained earnings	75	65
Total Equities	$600	$575

Income Statement

Sales	$720
Cost of goods sold	400
Gross profit	320
Depreciation	50
Other operating expenses	200
Operating income before taxes	70
Income taxes	30
Net Income	$ 40

Statement footnotes:
Inventory carried on LIFO.
Fixed assets depreciated on a straight-line basis.
19X1 dividend of $30,000.

17

BOOKKEEPING AND THE ACCOUNTING CYCLE

CHAPTER PREVIEW

The objective of this chapter is to acquaint you with the essentials of the accountant's bookkeeping system—the procedures used to classify, record, and summarize all data that become part of the financial statements. In this chapter, you can:

- Learn the value to the accountant of standardized procedures;
- Become familiar with the debit/credit system and its advantages as an error-prevention and error-checking device;
- Learn how transactions and adjustments are first recorded in the debit/credit code via a journal entry;
- Review in more detail the basic accounting records involved and the accounting cycle, which were introduced in Chapter 4;
- Become familiar with certain accounting terminology, tools, and practices including journal entries, the audit trail, the worksheet, closing and reversing entries, and subsidiary accounts.

With this information, you will be able to understand and converse with accountants in their professional language. Accountants have specific procedures which they used to accomplish the statement objectives discussed in this text. If you desire to learn these procedures, this chapter provides the foundation knowledge for you to understand and learn the preparer procedures included as chapter supplements with this chapter and Chapters 5, 6, 8, 9, 10, 11, 12, and 14.

NEED FOR STANDARDIZATION OF PROCEDURES

Imagine a typical firm with many thousands of transactions and adjustments necessary during the year. Can you visualize the chaos that would result if each one of the firm's accountants used his own individual system for processing data? And even if all accountants working in the same firm used one system, if it were unique what would be necessary when a new accountant was hired, even temporarily? Extensive specialized and costly training in the firm's own unique system would be required. And in peak-load periods, or when an employee was temporarily absent (because of illness or vacation), the firm could not take advantage of available temporary help. No one could be brought in on a short-term basis who already knew the system.

To minimize or eliminate this training problem, firms in the U.S. generally follow a uniform, conventional bookkeeping system. The underlying principle of the system is double-entry or dual-effect, which has been demonstrated in previous chapters. The conventional coding language employed is "debit/credit." The traditional debit/credit system may now be obsolescent. Where accounting records are maintained on computers, the traditional debit/credit instructions are often replaced by simple instructions to increase or decrease an account balance. And smaller desk-top computers are coming on the market programmed to maintain accounting records with inputs entirely on a plus or minus basis. For this reason, this text focuses on understanding transaction effects upon accounts and statements in terms of increase or decrease. The material in this chapter is provided so that you may comprehend accounting practices under either plus-or-minus or debit/credit coding.

THE DEBIT/CREDIT CONVENTION

In Chapter 2 you learned the basic balance sheet equality—total assets balance (equal) total equities—which is the foundation of the financial accounting system. In Chapter 4 you learned that transactions and adjustments affecting the balance sheet resulted in changes to the accounts which maintained the balance sheet equality. Back in the fifteenth century, a system was developed with the objective of maintaining this equality, even when thousands of changes (entries) needed to be recorded.

The debit/credit convention or coding system is very simple. Do not make it difficult merely because you cannot accept its simplicity. *"Debit"* comes from Latin and merely stands for "left" as on the left side. *"Credit,"* also from Latin, merely stands for "right," as on the right side. Debit is usually abbreviated "Dr" (or "DR") and credit as "Cr" (or "CR"). One form of portraying a balance sheet is to show assets on the left side of the page and equities on the right. The debit/credit system arbitrarily assumes that all asset accounts will have left-side balances and all equity accounts will have right-side balances. Given this assumption (or convention), total *debits*, which mean only left-side balances, will always equal total *credits*, which mean only right-side balances.

A common way of portraying this idea in textbooks is to show accounts in the form of a "T" or "T *accounts.*" Each "T" account then has space for left-side amounts and right-side amounts. Note the similarity of a "T" account to the balance sheet, which has left-side items (assets) and right-side items (equities). For example:

ASSET ACCOUNT

DR	CR
$100 (+)	$40 (−)
70 (+)	

Note that debit or left-side is abbreviated "DR," and the credit, or right-side, is abbreviated "CR." Note also that the balance in the above account is "130 debit"; 170 debit offset by 40 credit equals 130 debit. Accounts can also have credit balances. For example:

EQUITY ACCOUNT

DR	CR
$100 (−)	$200 (+)
	50 (+)

The above balance would be "150 credit."

An example of the operation of this system will serve to show its simplicity and beauty. Suppose a new firm, the AJAX Company, had just been started, and its only transaction so far was the owner investing $50,000 cash and merchandise costing $20,000 in the business. The balance sheet should then show:

ASSETS		EQUITIES	
Cash	$50,000	Liabilities	0
Inventory	20,000	Owner's Equity	$70,000
Total Assets	$70,000	Total Equities	$70,000

The three accounts in "T"-account form would show:

CASH

$50,000 (+) |

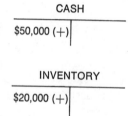

INVENTORY

$20,000 (+) |

OWNERS' EQUITY

| $70,000 (+)

Note that total debits—left-side balances—of $70,000 equal total credits—right-side balances—of $70,000.

Now let us record a few transactions following the debit/credit convention in "T"-account form. Suppose AJAX purchased an additional $5,000 of merchandise on account. To record the balance sheet effect, one would need to increase the inventory account by $5,000 and increase accounts payable by the same amount. Following the debit/credit coding, the journal entry for recording this transaction would be:

	DR	CR
Inventory	$5,000	
Accounts Payable		$5,000

Note that debit/credit positioning is similar to a programming language. This entry can be decoded as instructing: "Post $5,000 to the debit (left) side of the Inventory account (increasing this asset by $5,000), and post $5,000 to the credit (right) side of the Accounts Payable account (increasing this liability by $5,000)."

Before proceeding, try setting up the four necessary "T" accounts involved on a separate sheet of paper. Record the original owner investment as shown above. Now record the purchase on account of merchandise costing $5,000.

You are correct and are well along the road to understanding the debit/credit system if your "T" accounts show:

CASH		ACCOUNTS PAYABLE	
$50,000 (+)			$ 5,000 (+)

INVENTORY		OWNER'S EQUITY	
$20,000 (+)			$70,000 (+)
5,000 (+)			

Note that the entry itself is balanced—$5,000 in debits equal $5,000 in credits. And, after posting, the "T"-account balances still reflect the equality. Seventy-five thousand dollars of total debits equals $75,000 of total credits.

Another example involving decreases should help you get a grasp of the overall system. Suppose AJAX paid $2,000 to suppliers on its Accounts Payable. The effect would be to reduce Cash by $2,000 and reduce Accounts Payable by the same amount. What would be the journal entry to record this transaction? Write down the journal entry and follow its instructions by posting to your "T" accounts before proceeding.

The journal entry would be:

	DR	CR
Accounts Payable	$2,000	
Cash		$2,000

Immediately after posting, the accounts would show:

CASH	
$50,000 (+)	$ 2,000 (−)

ACCOUNTS PAYABLE	
$ 2,000 (−)	$ 5,000 (+)

INVENTORY	
$20,000 (+)	
$ 5,000 (+)	

OWNER'S EQUITY	
	$70,000 (+)

Note that the balance continues to be maintained in several forms. The entry itself is balanced. The total of the net balances in each of the accounts balances—$73,000 of net debits and credits. The total of all debits and credits in the system before netting each account still balances—$77,000 each of debits and credits.

THE DEBIT/CREDIT CODE

In all, there are six possible different types of accounts:

- Asset accounts
- Contra-asset accounts
- Equity accounts
- Contra-equity accounts
- Revenue and gain accounts
- Expense and loss accounts

Asset accounts normally have debit balances. To increase an asset account, you would debit it, or post to the left side. To *decrease* an asset account, you would credit it.

ASSET ACCOUNTS	
DR	CR
(Increase)	(Decrease)

Contra-asset accounts, such as Accumulated Depreciation, are negative valuation accounts. They are shown on the balance sheet along with assets, but each subtracts from its related asset. They are therefore contra, or opposite to assets, and normally have a credit balance. To increase a contra-asset account you would credit, or post on the right side. To decrease a contra-asset account, you would debit it.

CONTRA-ASSET ACCOUNT	
DR	CR
(Decrease)	(Increase)

Equity accounts normally have credit balances. How would you increase the balance in an equity account? How would you decrease it? Equity accounts are the opposite of asset accounts. They are increased by crediting and decreased by debiting or *charging*. "Charge" is often used synonymously for debit.

EQUITY ACCOUNTS

DR	CR
(Decrease)	(Increase)

Contra-equity accounts are shown on the balance sheet along with equities, but they subtract from their related equity accounts. They are therefore contra, or opposite to, equity accounts, and normally have a debit balance. Contra-equity accounts are increased by charging (debiting) and decreased by crediting.

CONTRA-EQUITY ACCOUNTS

DR	CR
(Increase)	(Decrease)

To review, asset accounts normally have debit balances and equity accounts credit balances. Contra accounts are opposites. Remember, from Chapter 4, that revenue increases owner's equity and that accountants store revenue information in temporary revenue accounts during the year. If revenue accounts are to increase owner's equity, what must be their normal balance, debit or credit? A positive balance in owner's equity is a credit. Therefore, a positive balance in a revenue account must also be a credit. Revenue accounts are increased by crediting, and decreased by debiting.

REVENUE ACCOUNTS

DR	CR
(Decrease)	(Increase)

Expense accounts are temporary accounts to store specific types of expenses during the year. At the end of the year their balance is transferred to owner's equity as a reduction. Expense accounts, therefore, normally have a debit balance. They are increased by debiting and reduced by crediting.

EXPENSE ACCOUNTS

DR	CR
(Increase)	(Decrease)

An easy way to remember the debit/credit code is to think of the accounts in terms of the balance sheet. Exhibit 17.1 is a visual summary of the various "T" accounts and the debit/credit code. All you really have to remember on the balance sheet is:

a) Asset accounts are on the left side of the balance sheet and have left-side (debit) normal or positive balances;

b) Equity accounts (liabilities and owner's equity) are on the right side of the balance sheet and have right-side (credit) normal or positive balances.

c) An increase to owner's equity is a credit; therefore revenue or gain, which increases owner's equity, must be a credit;

d) A decrease in owner's equity is a debit; therefore expense or loss, which decreases owner's equity, must be a debit;

e) Any contra accounts are just opposite.

Exhibit 17.1
VISUAL SUMMARY OF THE DEBIT/CREDIT CODE (PROGRAMMING LANGUAGE)

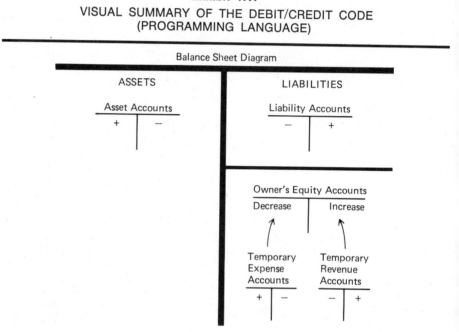

Note. Not shown are various contra-accounts which are exact opposites. For example, a contra-asset account:

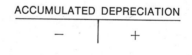

THE JOURNAL(S) AND THE AUDIT TRAIL

Transactions and adjustments are first recorded in a journal. Remember from Chapter 4 that the journal is like a diary of instructions. All transactions and adjustments are first recorded or *journalized* as an instruction, advising which accounts are to be changed and by how much. This instruction, which is made for each separate event (transaction or adjustment), is known as a journal entry. The journal entry will be accompanied by a brief written explanation such as "record purchase of inventory," "to record collection of a receivable," and so forth.

It may be desirable to check back through the accounts to the original source. Therefore, a journal entry is dated with the day journalized and also with a cross-reference code to the source document from which the accountant obtained information about the event. Thus an *audit trail* is created. If one wishes to check back on a given entry, one can go to the journal and be referred to the source document.

In larger firms with many transactions, more than one journal may be required in order to handle the volume of work. In such cases, it is common to have special journals for certain types of high-volume transactions, such as an Accounts Payable Journal or a Sales Journal.

THE LEDGER(S) AND POSTING

Separate accounts are maintained for each type of information appropriate to the particular company. For example, all firms will have a cash account, but only those firms owning equipment would have an equipment account. All open or active accounts—those having or expected to have any balance—are kept together in a combined file known as the ledger. Journal entry instructions are periodically followed by posting to the individual accounts in the ledger. When posting is completed, the entry in the journal is marked as having been posted (to avoid double recording). The amount posted to the account in the ledger is also indexed back to the original entry by date of the journal entry, thus maintaining the audit trail.

INTERIM TRIAL BALANCES

Periodically, and usually at least once a month, a *trial balance* is taken of all the accounts in the ledger. A trial balance involves totaling all the debit and credit amounts separately to see whether the totals agree. If the ledger is in balance, there could still be errors such as an amount posted to the wrong account. But if the ledger is not in balance, an error must exist. The purpose of frequent trial balances is like insurance. If an out-of-balance condition is discovered, then often only those entries and postings **since the last trial balance** need to be reviewed in order to locate the error.

THE WORKSHEET AND THE PRE-ADJUSTING TRIAL BALANCE

At the end of the year or accounting period when statements are to be prepared, the net balance in each account is recorded on a *worksheet*. Exhibit 17.2 shows a partially completed worksheet for the Potted Planter (see Chapter 4, Exhibit 4.2), with the pre-adjustment account balances recorded. All the amounts are the same as shown on Exhibit 4.2 except that:

- Items are classified as debits or credits according to the debit/credit code, and

Exhibit 17.2
POTTED PLANTER

Sample worksheet	Before adjusting		Adjustments		Adjusted		Income statement		Balance sheet	
Accounts	DR	CR	DR	CR	DR	CR	DR	CR	DR	CR
Cash	$ 7,900	$								
Accounts receivable	350									
Inventory	3,900									
Supplies	200									
Prepaid rent	1,000									
Equipment	2,500									
Accumulated depreciation										
Accounts payable		1,400								
Noncurrent note payable		2,000								
Owner's Equity		10,000								
Sales revenue		2,500								
Cleanup expense	50									
Cost of goods sold										
Supplies expense										
Rent expense										
Equipment depreciation										
Utilities expense										
Net Income										
Totals	$15,900	$15,900								

Exhibit 17.3
RECORDS IN THE FLOW OF ACCOUNTING INFORMATION

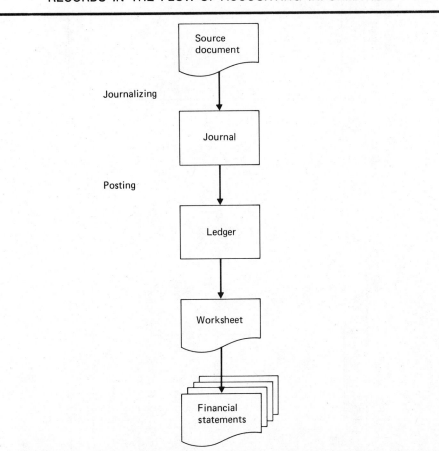

- The effects of revenue and expense transactions for the month are shown in temporary revenue and expense accounts and have not yet been combined (closed) with the $10,000 of beginning owner's equity.

Also note that debits and credits are totaled to make sure that the accounts are in balance before making adjustments.

Exhibit 17.3 shows the records in the information flow or processing stream from the source document to the final statements.

ADJUSTMENTS AND THE ADJUSTED TRIAL BALANCE

To speed up the process of completing the preparation of financial statements, year-end adjustments are first recorded directly on the worksheet. After the statements have been prepared, these adjustments are journalized and posted

Exhibit 17.4
POTTED PLANTER

Sample worksheet Accounts	Before adjusting DR	Before adjusting CR	Adjustments DR	Adjustments CR	Adjusted DR	Adjusted CR	Income statement DR	Income statement CR	Balance sheet DR	Balance sheet CR
Cash	$ 7,900	$	$	$	$ 7,900	$				
Accounts receivable	350				350					
Inventory	3,900			1,050	2,850					
Supplies	200			125	75					
Prepaid rent	1,000			500	500					
Equipment	2,500				2,500					
Accumulated depreciation				50		50				
Accounts payable		1,400		140		1,540				
Noncurrent note payable		2,000				2,000				
Owner's Equity		10,000				10,000				
Sales revenue		2,500				2,500				
Cleanup expense	50				50					
Cost of goods sold			1,050		1,050					
Supplies expense			125		125					
Rent expense			500		500					
Equipment depreciation			50		50					
Utilities expense			140		140					
Net Income										
Totals	$15,900	$15,900	$ 1,865	$ 1,865	$16,090	$16,090				

to the appropriate accounts. Exhibit 17.4 shows the Potted Planter worksheet after the adjustments have been recorded. Note that all the account balances, adjusted where required, have been carried forward to the adjusted columns. Debits and credits are again totaled to make sure that no adjustment error has destroyed the ledger balance.

CLOSING AND THE POST-CLOSING TRIAL BALANCE

Balance sheet accounts are permanent or *real accounts.* Their balances carry forward from year to year. To cite two examples, the amount of cash on hand, or the amount of debts owed to others, at year-end are the beginning balances of the next year. Other accounts are temporary or *nominal accounts.* They are used to temporarily store specific information needed for certain reports and are then "emptied" at year-end. The process of emptying these temporary accounts by transferring their balances to the appropriate permanent accounts is called **closing.**

Exhibit 17.5 shows the complete worksheet for the Potted Planter. Note that nominal accounts had been set up for all the revenue and expense items to appear on the income statement. In closing, the balance in each of these accounts has been transferred to owner's equity.[1] Note that, once again, debits and credits have been totaled to ensure that the ledger is in balance after closing.

Compare the last columns of Exhibit 17.5 with the actual Potted Planter ending balance sheet shown in Chapter 4 as Exhibit 4.3. Can you see why the balance sheet reports $14,125 of total assets whereas the worksheet shows $14,175 of total debits? The answer is in the contra account, Accumulated Depreciation; $50 of accumulated depreciation is included with other credits on the worksheet. On the balance sheet it is shown contra to equipment and therefore subtracts in determining total assets. Also note on the worksheet that income is closed to owner's equity for a total of $10,585.

ERROR CORRECTIONS AND OPENING REVERSALS

Because of the risks of additional errors and of the possibility that someone might be able to manipulate the firm's accounting records, accountants are careful to preserve the audit trail even when an error has been made. If an incorrect journal entry is discovered, or if an entry has been incorrectly posted, accountants do not use an eraser. Instead they will make the correction

---

[1]   In practice, revenue and expense accounts are first closed to a new account called Income Summary. Income Summary then is closed to Owner's Equity for a proprietorship. As discussed in Chapter 10, for a partnership, income is distributed among individual partners' shares of ownership equity according to the partnership agreement. For a corporation, Income Summary is closed to a subaccount within corporate owners' equity known as Retained Earnings.

Exhibit 17.5
POTTED PLANTER

Sample worksheet	Before adjusting		Adjustments		Adjusted		Income statement		Balance sheet	
Accounts	DR	CR	DR	CR	DR	CR	DR	CR	DR	CR
Cash	$ 7,900	$	$	$	$ 7,900	$	$	$	$ 7,900	$
Accounts receivable	350				350				350	
Inventory	3,900			1,050	2,850				2,850	
Supplies	200			125	75				75	
Prepaid rent	1,000			500	500				500	
Equipment	2,500				2,500				2,500	
Accumulated depreciation				50		50				50
Accounts payable		1,400		140		1,540				1,540
Noncurrent note payable		2,000				2,000				2,000
Owner's Equity		10,000				10,000				[10,000
Sales revenue		2,500				2,500		2,500		[+ 585]
Cleanup expense	50				50		50			
Cost of goods sold			1,050		1,050		1,050			
Supplies expense			125		125		125			
Rent expense			500		500		500			
Equipment depreciation			50		50		50			
Utilities expense			140		140		140			
Net Income							$ 585			
Totals	$15,900	$15,900	$ 1,865	$ 1,865	$16,090	$16,090	$ 2,500	$ 2,500	$14,175	$14,175

through two additional entries identified as error-correcting entries. The first entry will be a *reversing entry*. It will be designed to eliminate the incorrect posting by reversing it, or backing it out. For example, suppose the original entry had been:

	DR	CR
Accounts Payable	$100	
Cash		$100
To record payment of account		

Suppose posting had been really fouled up and that accounts **receivable** had been debited $75 and cash credited $100. The wrong **account** was posted and with the wrong **amount**, so the ledger is out of balance. The error-correcting reversing entry would be:

	DR	CR
Cash	$100	
Accounts Receivable		$75
To reverse entry of X/X/XX posted in error		

Note that this reversing entry is not balanced, but is necessary to cancel the original posting error.

After reversing out the error, the correction is completed with an additional entry in the form that should have been posted to begin with.

In some accounting systems, reversing entries are also used at the beginning of the year, to reverse the prior year's temporary year-end accrual adjustments. This is done to avoid the possibility of double-counting, when the item which was accrued subsequently arrives and is recorded normally.

For example, in the case of the Potted Planter, $140 of utilities expense was accrued at month end and is shown as a liability. The accrual was anticipating the invoice, which had not been received and journalized by the closing date. Assume that, in the following month, invoices arrived totalling $300, $140 of which represented costs of prior month's services. If the full $300 is normally recorded as a liability and as utilities expense, $140 will have been double-counted. Rather than record only part of the new invoice, the accountant will reverse the previous accrual at the start of the new accounting period. After reversal, no liability for this service will be in the accounts, and utilities expense will start with a credit (negative) balance of $140.

The $300 invoice is then recorded normally:

	DR	CR
Utilities Expense	$300	
Accounts Payable		$300

Note that the firm's total liability for these services is now correctly shown as $300. Also, the balance in Utilities Expense will be $160 ($300 debit less $140 credit), which is the correct portion applicable to the new period.

THE ACCOUNTING CYCLE

Chapter 4 first introduced you to the accounting cycle. The term accounting cycle is used to describe the several steps or stages of the accountant's activities during the year. The accounting cycle may be viewed as having eight sequential steps or phases:

1. Possible opening reversals (see above);
2. Journalizing and posting transactions throughout the year;
3. Interim trial balances;
4. Initial worksheet preparation, and the pre-adjusting trial balance;
5. Adjustments on the worksheet, and the adjusted trial balance;
6. Closing on the worksheet, and the post-closing trial balance;
7. Financial statement preparation;
8. Journalizing and posting adjusting and closing entries.

SUBSIDIARY AND SPECIAL JOURNALS, LEDGERS, AND ACCOUNTS

The financial accounting bookkeeping system can be fully understood in terms of a single journal and ledger, and with accounts only for balance sheet and income statement items. In practice, most companies keep many more detailed accounts as components of a single balance sheet account. An obvious example would be accounts receivable. If a store had several thousand charge customers, to keep all of their separate balances on one record would be impossible. In such a case, a *subsidiary ledger* is maintained with *subsidiary accounts*, one for each separate customer. The total of all of the subsidiary-account balances is carried in the single balance sheet account, which is then known as the *control account*. Some other areas where detailed accounts are often maintained include subsidiary accounts for different types of inventory, fixed assets, and accounts payable.

MACHINE AND COMPUTER SYSTEMS

In many firms, accounting records are maintained on machine or computer systems. Some smaller firms subcontract most of their bookkeeping to computer service bureaus. Regardless of the physical means employed to record, store, summarize, and report accounting information, the essential concepts are maintained, even though debit/credit programming language may not be used (as mentioned above). A discussion of the details of various machine and computer accounting systems is beyond the scope of this text.

CHAPTER SUPPLEMENTS

In the Introduction, you learned that this text separates the details of preparer procedures as being less essential and possibly even confusing in the learning of the role of accounting and the usefulness of accounting information. If you are considering becoming an accountant, or if you desire further reinforcement of your accounting knowledge, you should extend your familiarity with accounting procedures beyond the brief foregoing explanation. You will find, as supplements to this chapter, sections covering Preparer Procedures and Preparer Problems relating to the material first introduced in Chapter 4. You will also find similar supplements covering specific procedures related to the topics covered in Chapters 5 and 6, and 8 through 12.

CHAPTER OVERVIEW

Based upon the material introduced in this chapter, you should now be able to:

- Explain the debit/credit coding system and describe which types of accounts normally have debit or credit balances;
- Describe a journal entry and its function, with examples;
- Describe posting, and explain trial balances and the audit trail;
- Explain the two distinct uses of reversing entries with examples;
- Describe the worksheet and its function;
- Describe the typical accounting cycle;
- Define and describe the function of certain specific accounting practices including closing, subsidiary accounts, control accounts, and real vs. nominal accounts.

NEW VOCABULARY AND CONCEPTS

Debit/charge
Credit
"T-account"
Journalize
Audit trail
Trial balance
Worksheet

Real account
Nominal account
Reversing entry
Subsidiary ledger
Subsidiary account
Control account

- The debit/credit system
- The function of the worksheet
- The accounting cycle

REVIEW QUESTIONS

1. Why is standardization of accounting practices and procedures essential within one firm and among different firms?

2. Define the terms debit or charge and credit.

3. (a) Which accounts normally have debit balances? (b) Which accounts normally have credit balances?

4. For the following types of accounts, how are they (a) increased and (b) decreased:

Asset accounts	Owner's Equity accounts
Contra-asset accounts	Contra-equity accounts
Liability accounts	Revenue and gain accounts
Contra-liability accounts	Expense and loss accounts

5. Describe the audit trail and its purpose.

6. Describe a trial balance and its purpose.

7. (a) Describe the worksheet and its purpose. (b) Describe the sequential steps in the preparation and completion of a worksheet.

8. What are two uses of reversing entries? Explain with examples.

9. Describe the eight steps of the accounting cycle.

10. (a) What is the difference between real and nominal accounts? (b) Why does the accountant use nominal accounts? (c) What is meant by closing?

11. What is the difference between subsidiary and control accounts? (b) Why does the accountant use subsidiary accounts?

PREPARER PROCEDURES

With a general understanding of balance sheet changes, the accounting cycle, and the accountant's worksheet, you have the background to master the basic element of accounting procedure—the journal entry. Remember that, from various source documents and other information, the accountant first inputs the accounting system with an entry in the journal. Journal entries specify changes to be made in the accounts to reflect events (exchanges) occurring throughout the year, which affect the firm's balance sheet. Recall that these events are known as transactions and that entries recording transactions are known as transaction entries. Adjustments at year end to reflect accruals and asset expirations (uses) are also recorded via adjusting entries.

All journal entries (transactions and adjustments) affect the balance sheet. Some involve only changes to the real accounts appearing on the balance sheet. Others involve revenue or expense and therefore involve both a balance sheet account and also a nominal or temporary account established to store revenue or expense data.

Remember that nominal revenue and expense accounts are closed to owner's equity at year end.

Transaction Entries

To develop familiarity with specific journal entries in specific situations, return to the Potted Planter example first introduced in Chapter 4. Exhibit 17.6 lists all transactions during the first month of the firm's operations. Note that the first transaction involves an equal change in assets and owner's equity. The journal entry recording event (1) would be:

	DR	CR
Cash	$10,000	
Owner's Equity		$10,000

Exhibit 17.6
POTTED PLANTER

Transactions and Adjustments during First Month of Operations

Transactions:
(1) Owner deposits $10,000 cash in business.
(2) Signing lease—not a transaction.
(3) Paid landlord $1,000 in advance rent.
(4) $50 expenditure for supplies consumed.
(5) Tentative employment agreement—not a transaction.
(6) Purchased inventory costing $3,000 on account.
(7) Purchased supplies costing $200, paying cash.
(8) Purchased equipment costing $2,500, paying $500 cash and executing noncurrent $2,000 note at 10 percent interest for the balance.
(9) Weekly cash sales = $960.
(10) Weekly credit sales = $220.
(11) Purchased inventory costing $500 on account.
(12) Weekly cash sales = $1,040.
(13) Weekly credit sales = $280.
(14) Purchased inventory on account costing $400.
(15) Collected $150 cash on Accounts Receivable.
(16) Paid $2,500 on Accounts Payable.

Adjustments:
(17) Adjust for ending inventory, determined to be $2,850.
(18) Adjust for ending supplies, determined to be $75.
(19) Adjust for expiration of $500 of rent prepayment.
(20) Adjust for $50 of depreciation on equipment.
(21) Accrue $140 of utilities liability and related expense.

Entries which affect assets and owner's equity equally we will refer to as *Group I entries*. The effect of all Group I entries is to increase or decrease owner's equity, either directly or via a temporary revenue or expense account:

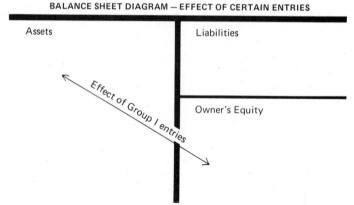

BALANCE SHEET DIAGRAM — EFFECT OF CERTAIN ENTRIES

Assets

Liabilities

Effect of Group I entries

Owner's Equity

In Exhibit 17.6, in addition to (1), there are five other transactions involving Group 1 entries. Can you identify them? Locate the five and prepare journal entries for them on a separate sheet of paper before proceeding.

Group I transactions involve assets invested by the owner (1) and assets obtained from customers (sales revenue) or as return on investments (other revenue). Exhibit 17.6 contains four revenue transactions (9), (10), (12), and (13).

		DR	CR
(9)	Cash	$960	
	Sales		$960
(10)	Accounts Receivable	220	
	Sales		220

Entries for (12) and (13) would be the same as (9) and (10) above. Group I transactions also include assets distributed to the owner and assets expended in the operations of the business. Asset withdrawal by the owner, not part of the Potted Planter example, would necessitate debiting (charging) Owner's Equity and crediting the account for the asset taken. Transaction (4) is an example of an asset expended in operations.

		DR	CR
(4)	Repair and Cleanup Expense (will eventually reduce Owner's Equity)	$50	
	Cash		$50

Another common transaction involves a simple exchange of assets. Entries involving a simple asset exchange—one asset is reduced (credited) and another increased (debited) by an equal amount—will be designated *Group 2 entries*:

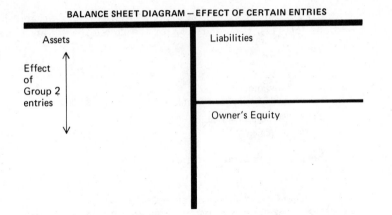

BALANCE SHEET DIAGRAM – EFFECT OF CERTAIN ENTRIES

Exhibit 17.6 contains three transactions involving a simple exchange of assets. It also contains one transaction (8) that involves both an asset exchange and another effect which will be discussed under compound entries below. You should identify and journalize the three Group 2 transactions before proceeding.

Transactions (3), (7), and (15) all involve simple exchanges of assets with no effect upon liabilities, owner's equity, revenue or expense:

		DR	CR
(3)	Prepaid Rent	$1,000	
	Cash		$1,000
(7)	Supplies	200	
	Cash		200
(15)	Cash	150	
	Accounts Receivable		150

Group 3 entries involve an exchange of assets and liabilities. Either a new asset is acquired in exchange for a new debt, or an asset (usually cash) is given to a creditor as payment on debt:

BALANCE SHEET DIAGRAM – EFFECT OF CERTAIN ENTRIES

Assets | Liabilities

Effect of Group 3 entries

Owner's Equity

Which transactions, other than (8) on Exhibit 17.6, represent Group 3 transactions? Transactions (6), (11), (14), and (16) for the Potted Planter are representative of Group 3:

		DR	CR
(6)	Inventory	$3,000	
	Accounts Payable		$3,000
(16)	Accounts Payable	2,500	
	Cash		2,500

Completing the picture of simple entries would be Group 4, involving an exchange of equities:

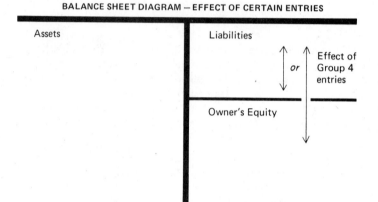

BALANCE SHEET DIAGRAM – EFFECT OF CERTAIN ENTRIES

Transactions involving exchanges of equities are not part of the Potted Planter example. In other chapters of this book, you will find examples of Group 4 transactions, which involve exchanging (refinancing) one debt with another, and even exchanging creditor claim for owner claim or vice versa (corporate debt conversion and declaration of corporate cash dividend).

Transaction (8) on Exhibit 17.6 is an example of a *compound entry*. Its effect is simply a combination of Groups 2 and 3:

		DR	CR
(8)	Equipment	$2,500	
	Cash		$ 500
	Noncurrent Note Payable		2,000

Adjusting Entries

All adjusting entries made at year (period) end fall into Groups 1 or 4, or are compound entries still involving combinations of these groups. Before proceeding, identify as being either Group 1 or 4, and then journalize, the five adjustments shown in Exhibit 17.6.

Adjustments (17), (18), (19), and (20) all involve asset expirations or use and they fall into Group 1. In the case of adjustment (17), $3,900 of merchandise inventory had been acquired during the month and $2,850 remained at month end. There-fore, $1,050 had been used (sold, stolen, or deteriorated):

		DR	CR
(17)	Cost of Goods Sold (Expense)	$1050	
	Inventory		$1050

Accountants often maintain many subsidiary accounts for inventory-related data. The usual adjustments for ending inventory are therefore more involved and are discussed under Preparer Procedures in Chapter 8.

Other Group 1 adjustments are:

		DR	CR
(18)	Supplies Expense	$125	
	Supplies		$125
(19)	Rent Expense	500	
	Prepaid Rent		500
(20)	Depreciation Expense	50	
	Accumulated Depreciation		50

Group 1 adjustments include more than asset expirations (expenses). Although not included in the Potted Planter example, Group 1 adjustments can also include revenue accruals, which are covered in Chapter 5 and elsewhere.

Adjustment (21) is an example of a Group 4 expense-accrual adjustment:

		DR	CR
(21)	Utilities Expense	$140	
	Utilities (or Accounts) Payable		$140

Other common expense accruals could involve wages, interest, and rent owed at year end but not previously recorded or paid.

Other Journal Entries

Examples of other journal entries involved in more sophisticated transactions and adjustments can be found in chapter supplements under Preparer Procedures included with Chapters 5, 6, and 8 through 12.

PREPARER PROBLEMS

PP 17.1. Prepare journal entries for each of the events given in Problem EP 4.1 (Chapter 4) which do have an effect on the firm's balance sheet accounts.

PP 17.2. Prepare journal entries for each of the adjustments given in Problem EP 4.3 which affect the firm's balance sheet accounts.

PP 17.3. Prepare journal entries for each of the events given in Problem EP 4.5.

PP 17.4. Prepare journal entries for each of the events given in Problem EP 4.6.

PP 17.5. Prepare journal entries for the transactions and adjustments given in Problem SP 4.9.

PP 17.6. Prepare journal entries for the transactions and adjustments given in Problem SP 4.10.

APPENDIXES

A

FINANCIAL STATEMENTS OF THE XEROX CORPORATION AND ANNUAL REPORT OF THE ADDISON-WESLEY PUBLISHING COMPANY, INC., FOR THE YEAR 1976

Management's Discussion and Analysis of Operating Results

Operating Results

Revenue and income results for 1976 and 1975 and the year-to-year changes follow.

(Dollars in millions, except per share data)	1976 Amount	1976 % Change from Prior Year	1975 Amount	1975 % Change from Prior Year
Total Operating Revenues	$4,403.9	+ 8.6	$4,053.8	+15.6
Operating Income	862.8	+ 3.4	834.5	− 2.5
Income before Income Taxes	804.8	+ 6.2	757.6	− 3.9
Income from Continuing Operations	358.9	+ 5.1	341.6	− 1.8
Loss from Discontinued Operations	—	—	97.3	N.M.
Net Income	358.9	+46.9	244.3	− 25.8
Income (Loss) per Common Share				
Continuing Operations	4.51	+ 5.1	4.29	− 1.8
Discontinued Operations	—	—	(1.22)	N.M.
Net Income per Common Share	$ 4.51	+46.9	$ 3.07	− 25.8

N.M. = Not Meaningful

Results of continuing operations exclude revenues and related costs of mainframe computer operations from which Xerox withdrew effective June 30, 1975. For further information on discontinued operations, refer to the Notes to Consolidated Financial Statements, page 39.

Operating Revenues

Both rentals and sales reached record levels in 1976 and 1975, with rentals increasing by 5 percent and 16 percent, respectively, over the preceding years. Sales were up by 23 percent in 1976 and 15 percent in 1975. Total operating revenues gained 9 percent in 1976 and 16 percent in 1975. Without the results of currency fluctuations, 1976 revenues would have been up by 12 percent.

Net new placements of rental machines were somewhat higher in 1976 than in 1975, but were still lower than in 1974. This decrease in machine placements reflected both unfavorable business conditions in many countries and increased competitive pressures. Increases in the volume of copies produced, however, partially offset the slower growth in the on-lease machine population. Revenues in 1975 benefited from a price increase in October 1974. However, 1976 revenues were unfavorably affected by price changes in the United States, effective early in the year, made in response to competitive pressures as well as to comply with the terms of a Federal Trade Commission consent order.

Sales were strong in both years. Outright sales of equipment, primarily copiers and duplicators and other office equipment, were up more than 80 percent in 1976 after a substantial increase in 1975. These sales, which represented under 20 percent of total sales revenues in 1975, were over 25 percent in 1976 and accounted for well over 50 percent of the year-to-year sales gain. In 1976, equipment sales benefited from lower selling prices on several copiers and duplicators and from the availability of a Xerox financing plan offered in the United States. 1976 was also the first year in which copiers and duplicators were sold in significant quantities by our subsidiaries in Western Europe and Canada. The balance of the year-to-year increase resulted from higher sales of consumable supplies, reflecting the increased volume of copies, and from increased sales of other products.

Cost of Rentals and Cost of Sales

Cost of rentals decreased 4 percent in 1976 after a 1975 increase of 30 percent. A major reason for this swing was that 1975 cost of rentals was impacted by inventory write-downs and the adoption of more conservative inventory valuation techniques both in the United States and in our international operations. These inventory-related adjustments had significantly less effect on 1976 results. In each year, cost of rentals reflected higher depreciation charges on a larger base of rental equipment.

Cost of sales increased 21 percent in 1976 after an increase of 13 percent in 1975. In each year the increase was due primarily to the higher volume of sales.

Research and Development Expenses

Research and development expenses increased 14 percent to $226 million in 1976 compared to $199 million in 1975, approximating 5 percent of operating revenues in both years. These expenses were for basic research in new technologies, for new product development and engineering and for improvements in existing products. In addition to the impact of inflation, the year-to-year increase in research and development costs reflects the Company's continued emphasis on new products which we expect to announce over the next several years.

Selling, Service, Administrative and General Expenses

These expenses increased by 12 percent in 1976 and by 22 percent in 1975. The increased expense levels reflect the costs associated with the higher level of revenues worldwide, the effect of worldwide inflationary conditions and the continued intro-ductory marketing costs of two major new products, the 9200 duplicating system and the 800 electronic typing system. In 1976, these factors were partially offset by savings achieved through the cost reduction programs instituted in 1975.

Other Income

Other income increased by $17 million in 1976 and by $29 million in 1975. The 1976 increase was the result of significantly higher income from short-term invest-ments. In 1975, the increase was due in large part to increased exchange gains resulting from the adoption of the Financial Accounting Standards Board's State-ment No. 8 relating to the translation of foreign currency financial statements and transactions. Higher income from short-term investments was also a contributing factor in the 1975 increase.

Other Deductions

Other deductions decreased by 1 percent in 1976 after increasing by 37 percent in 1975. These fluctuations relate primarily to interest expense which decreased to $120 million in 1976, reflecting lower borrowings worldwide. Partly offsetting the effect of reduced interest expense in 1976 were one-time payments, totalling $10 million, made in connection with the settlement of two disputes concerning patents and other issues. The decrease in 1976 followed an increase to $137 million in 1975 from $101 million in 1974. The increase in 1975 over 1974 reflected the full-year effect of 1974 borrowings.

Consolidated Statements of Income

Xerox Corporation and Subsidiaries

Year Ended December 31 (Dollars in thousands, except per share data)	1976	1975
Operating Revenues		
Rentals	$3,408,944	$3,242,587
Sales	994,953	811,173
Total operating revenues	4,403,897	4,053,760
Costs and Expenses		
Cost of rentals	642,359	670,280
Cost of sales	486,348	401,801
Research and development expenses	225,650	198,550
Selling, service, administrative and general expenses	2,186,691	1,948,589
Total costs and expenses	3,541,048	3,219,220
Operating Income	862,849	834,540
Other Income	81,562	64,710
Other Deductions (includes interest: 1976—$119,822; 1975—$136,959)	139,605	141,629
Income before Income Taxes	804,806	757,621
Income Taxes	377,400	342,600
Income before Outside Shareholders' Interests	427,406	415,021
Outside Shareholders' Interests	68,500	73,389
Income from Continuing Operations	358,906	341,632
Loss from Discontinued Operations, Net of Income Tax Benefit and Outside Shareholders' Interests	—	97,325
Net Income	$ 358,906	$ 244,307
Average Common Shares Outstanding	79,560,521	79,550,021
Income (Loss) per Common Share		
Continuing operations	$4.51	$4.29
Discontinued operations	—	(1.22)
Net Income per Common Share	$4.51	$3.07

Consolidated Balance Sheets
Xerox Corporation and Subsidiaries

Assets December 31 (Dollars in thousands)	1976	1975
Current Assets		
Cash	$ 70,882	$ 60,554
Bank time deposits, interest bearing	241,748	109,624
Marketable securities,		
at cost which approximates market	359,671	124,908
Trade receivables (less allowance for doubtful		
receivables: 1976—$39,109; 1975—$36,754)	613,952	617,351
Accrued rentals	177,209	179,749
Inventories, at lower of average cost or market	470,960	464,856
Prepaid expenses and other current assets	118,903	129,482
Total current assets	2,053,325	1,686,524
Assets of Discontinued Operations, at estimated		
realizable value	57,435	99,137
Rental Equipment and Related Inventories		
At cost (less accumulated depreciation:		
1976—$2,386,158; 1975—$2,058,143)	1,414,341	1,516,084
Land, Buildings and Equipment		
At cost (less accumulated depreciation:		
1976—$486,751; 1975—$400,304)	870,001	845,187
Investment in Fuji Xerox Co., Ltd., at equity	65,592	68,948
Other Assets		
Deferred income taxes	21,911	99,537
Other	129,777	140,232
Total other assets	151,688	239,769
Total Assets	$4,612,382	$4,455,649

The accompanying notes are an integral part of the consolidated financial statements.

Liabilities and Shareholders' Equity December 31 (Dollars in thousands)	1976	1975
Current Liabilities		
Notes payable	$ 71,745	$ 144,763
Payments due within one year on long-term debt	71,399	107,177
Accounts payable	187,284	227,453
Salaries, profit sharing and other accruals	401,268	342,736
Income taxes	288,060	232,003
Dividends payable	23,761	19,710
Deferred rentals and subscriptions	36,122	41,655
Total current liabilities	1,079,639	1,115,497
Deferred Investment Tax Credits	51,598	44,242
Long-Term Debt	1,000,140	1,129,242
Outside Shareholders' Interests in Equity of Subsidiaries	302,045	259,711
Shareholders' Equity		
Common stock, par value $1.00 Authorized 90,000,000 shares	79,204	79,187
Class B stock, par value $1.00 Authorized 600,000 shares	339	385
Additional paid-in capital	254,361	256,854
Retained earnings	1,867,086	1,595,698
Total	2,200,990	1,932,124
Deduct Class B stock receivables and deferrals	22,030	25,167
Total shareholders' equity	2,178,960	1,906,957
Total Liabilities and Shareholders' Equity	$4,612,382	$4,455,649

Consolidated Statements of Common and Class B Shares, Additional Paid-In Capital and Retained Earnings
Xerox Corporation and Subsidiaries

Year Ended December 31 (Dollars in thousands, except per share data)	1976	1975
Common and Class B Shares		
Common Stock		
Shares outstanding at beginning of year	79,187,249	79,092,224
Stock options exercised	16,958	94,997
Debentures converted	16	3
Exchanged for Class B stock	77	25
Shares outstanding at end of year	79,204,300	79,187,249
Class B Stock		
Shares outstanding at beginning of year	385,270	484,325
Issued	—	8,000
Repurchased	(46,205)	(107,030)
Exchanged for common stock	(77)	(25)
Shares outstanding at end of year	338,988	385,270
Additional Paid-In Capital		
Balance at beginning of year	$256,854	$262,497
Stock options exercised	448	1,227
Debentures converted	2	—
Class B stock issued	—	457
Class B stock repurchased	(2,943)	(7,327)
Balance at end of year	$254,361	$256,854
Retained Earnings		
Balance at beginning of year	$1,595,698	$1,430,615
Net income	358,906	244,307
Total	1,954,604	1,674,922
Deduct		
Cash dividends declared on common and Class B stocks (1976—$1.10 per share; 1975—$1.00 per share)	87,518	79,214
Class B stock repurchased	—	10
Total	87,518	79,224
Balance at end of year	$1,867,086	$1,595,698

The accompanying notes are an integral part of the consolidated financial statements.

Consolidated Statements of Changes in Financial Position
Xerox Corporation and Subsidiaries

Year Ended December 31 (Dollars in thousands)	1976	1975
Working Capital Provided by		
Operations		
Income from continuing operations	$ 358,906	$ 341,632
Charges (credits) not affecting working capital		
Depreciation of rental equipment	501,682	460,017
Depreciation of buildings and equipment	121,452	102,315
Outside shareholders' interests in income	68,500	73,389
Noncurrent deferred income taxes	12,940	(34,613)
Other	30,707	3,404
Working capital provided by continuing operations	1,094,187	946,144
Working capital used by discontinued operations	—	(91,769)
Disposals of discontinued operations' assets	41,702	—
Deferred income taxes becoming current	64,686	—
New long-term debt	71,994	245,145
Other	23,126	(33,710)
Working capital provided	1,295,695	1,065,810
Working Capital Used for		
Additions to rental equipment and related inventories	455,445	581,550
Additions to land, buildings and equipment	140,780	208,273
Payments made or due within one year on long-term debt	181,047	129,057
Dividends declared—Xerox Corporation shareholders	87,518	79,214
Dividends declared—outside shareholders	28,246	33,682
Reclassification of discontinued operations' current assets to noncurrent assets	—	58,598
Working capital used	893,036	1,090,374
Working Capital Increased (Decreased)	402,659	(24,564)
Working Capital at Beginning of Year	571,027	595,591
Working Capital at End of Year	$ 973,686	$ 571,027

Notes to Consolidated Financial Statements
Xerox Corporation and Subsidiaries

Summary of Significant Accounting Policies

Basis of Consolidation

All subsidiaries are consolidated in the financial statements. The accounts of Latin American subsidiaries are included for their fiscal years ended November 30. The accounts of Rank Xerox Limited and its subsidiaries and Rank Xerox Holding B.V. and its subsidiaries, referred to as Rank-Xerox Companies, are included for their fiscal years ended October 31.

Rank Xerox Limited owns 50% of the outstanding stock of Fuji Xerox Co., Ltd., a corporate joint venture whose fiscal year ends October 20; this investment is accounted for by the equity method.

In 1975, the Company acquired two companies which were accounted for by the pooling of interests method.

Net Income per Common Share

Net income per common share is computed by dividing consolidated net income by the average number of shares of common and Class B stocks outstanding during each year. Common stock equivalents (outstanding stock options, incentive stock rights and the 5% convertible subordinated debentures) and the 6% convertible subordinated debentures are excluded as the potential dilution upon assumed exercise, vesting or conversion thereof is less than 3%.

Revenues from Rental Equipment

Revenues from rental equipment, which are accounted for by the operating lease method, vary each month based on the number of copies produced.

Depreciation

The cost of rental equipment, buildings and equipment is depreciated over the estimated useful lives of the assets (five to seven years for rental equipment). Declining balance methods of computing depreciation are generally used in the U.S. and in Canada (the double declining balance method is used for rental equipment); the straight line method of computing depreciation is generally used in other countries. Significant improvements are capitalized; maintenance and repairs are charged to income. The cost and accumulated depreciation of assets retired or otherwise disposed of are eliminated from the accounts and any resulting gain or loss is credited or charged to income.

Deferred Investment Tax Credits

Investment tax credits are deferred and amortized to income over the periods during which they are earned.

International Operations

A summary of the operating results and financial position of the Company's international operations is set forth below:

(Dollars in millions)	Rank-Xerox Companies 1976	1975	Other 1976	1975	Total 1976	1975
Operating Results						
Total operating revenues	$1,396	$1,358	$531	$450	$1,927	$1,808
Income before outside shareholders' interests	$ 182	$ 199	$ 48	$ 29	$ 230	$ 228
Outside shareholders' interests	64	70	5	3	69	73
Income from continuing operations	$ 118	$ 129	$ 43	$ 26	$ 161	$ 155
Financial Position						
Current assets	$ 631	$ 623	$224	$198	$ 855	$ 821
Rental equipment	599	657	229	275	828	932
Other assets	410	370	93	67	503	437
Total assets	$1,640	$1,650	$546	$540	$2,186	$2,190
Current liabilities	$ 500	$ 534	$128	$119	$ 628	$ 653
Other liabilities	294	369	70	64	364	433
Outside shareholders' interests	285	247	17	13	302	260
Xerox Corporation interest	561	500	331	344	892	844
Total liabilities and shareholders' interests	$1,640	$1,650	$546	$540	$2,186	$2,190

Certain adjustments, including conforming deferred tax accounting to the U.S. method, have been made in the above summary.

The consolidated statements of income include aggregate exchange gains of $17,100,000 in 1976 and $27,000,000 in 1975.

In the consolidated statements of income, other income includes Rank Xerox Limited's share of Fuji Xerox Co., Ltd.'s net income of $6,397,000 in 1976 ($8,997,000 in 1975).

Working Capital

The increase (decrease) in working capital shown in the consolidated statements of changes in financial position consists of:

(Dollars in thousands)	1976	1975
Increases (decreases) in current assets		
Cash	$ 10,328	$ 4,104
Bank time deposits	132,124	55,031
Marketable securities	234,763	8,968
Trade receivables	(3,399)	(1,423)
Accrued rentals	(2,540)	15,062
Inventories	6,104	(50,706)
Prepaid expenses and other current assets	(10,579)	23,059
Net increase in current assets	366,801	54,095
Increases (decreases) in current liabilities		
Notes payable	(73,018)	(171,897)
Payments due within one year on long-term debt	(35,778)	69,471
Accounts payable	(40,169)	24,986
Salaries, profit sharing and other accruals	58,532	71,630
Income taxes	56,057	73,352
Dividends payable	4,051	21
Deferred rentals and subscriptions	(5,533)	11,096
Net increase (decrease) in current liabilities	(35,858)	78,659
Working capital increased (decreased)	$402,659	$ (24,564)

33

Inventories

Inventories consist of:

(Dollars in thousands)	1976	1975
Finished products	$354,645	$332,263
Work in process	49,986	60,862
Raw materials and supplies	66,329	71,731
Total inventories	$470,960	$464,856

Inventories used in the computation of cost of sales were $470,960,000, $464,856,000 and $458,979,000 at December 31, 1976, 1975 and 1974, respectively.

Land, Buildings and Equipment

A summary of land, buildings and equipment and accumulated depreciation follows:

(Dollars in thousands)	Estimated Useful Lives	1976	1975
Assets			
Land		$ 71,829	$ 68,598
Buildings and building equipment	20 to 50 years	371,031	323,437
Leasehold improvements	Term of lease	93,609	81,496
Plant machinery	8 to 12 years	474,911	414,870
Office furniture and fixtures	5 to 10 years	182,025	159,271
Other	3 to 5 years	118,087	105,233
Construction in progress		45,260	92,586
Total		1,356,752	1,245,491
Less accumulated depreciation		486,751	400,304
Net land, buildings and equipment		$ 870,001	$ 845,187

Notes Payable

Notes payable generally represent short-term borrowings by foreign subsidiaries, principally from banks, in local currencies.

A summary of information relating to notes payable follows:

(Dollars in thousands)	1976	1975
Maximum amount outstanding at any month end	$236,000	$342,600
Month-end average balance	$163,800	$288,300
Weighted average interest rate at year end	15⅝%	10⅜%
Weighted monthly average interest rate	11¾%	12%

At December 31, 1976, the Company had unused short-term lines of credit aggregating $200,000,000 with U.S. banks at prime interest rates. The Company maintains compensating balances of 10% of the lines of credit plus 10% of any amounts borrowed. Foreign subsidiaries had unused lines of credit aggregating $294,000,000 in various currencies at the best available interest rates.

Profit Sharing Retirement and Pension Plans

The cost of contributions to profit sharing retirement and pension plans amounted to $105,823,000 and $66,681,000 for 1976 and 1975, respectively.

Major retirement plans of the Company are noncontributory, trusteed, profit sharing retirement plans to which annual contributions are made, based upon a formula related to return on assets. Under these plans, eligible employees may elect to receive a portion of their share of the annual contribution in cash or in Xerox common stock, or to invest such amount in various funds of the profit sharing trusts. The portion of the contributions shown above subject to these elections amounted to $33,535,000 in 1976 and $10,389,000 in 1975.

There are also retirement plans for foreign employees, substantially all of which are contributory and trusteed. The market value of foreign pension funds as of December 31, 1976 exceeded the actuarially computed value of vested benefits. Past service costs under foreign plans are substantially funded.

Income Taxes

Income tax expense consists of the following:

(Dollars in thousands)	1976	1975
Federal income taxes		
Current	$108,456	$119,996
Deferred	23,139	(4,164)
Investment tax credits		
Received and deferred	25,242	24,543
Amortized	(17,886)	(14,232)
Foreign income taxes		
Current	231,200	213,723
Deferred	(20,727)	(26,651)
State income taxes		
Current	24,158	30,356
Deferred	3,818	(971)
Total income taxes	$377,400	$342,600

As a result of the tax effects of timing differences between financial statement and tax reporting, income taxes currently payable by continuing operations were less than the amount charged to income by $6,230,000 in 1976 and exceeded the amount charged to income by $31,786,000 in 1975.

The nature and tax effects of timing differences follow:

(Dollars in thousands)	1976	1975
U.K. inventory allowance deducted for tax purposes not included in financial statements	$ 33,164	$ —
Depreciation and amortization provided for tax purposes in excess of amounts in financial statements	1,900	34,280
Profits on intercompany sales included in tax returns and deferred in financial statements	(24,708)	(44,673)
U.K. Advance Corporation Tax payments	2,345	(19,878)
Other	(6,471)	(1,515)
Total	$ 6,230	$(31,786)

The effective income tax rate in 1976 was 46.9% (45.2% in 1975) as compared to the U.S. Federal income tax rate of 48%. Individual reconciling items were less than 5% of the U.S. Federal income tax rate.

Deferred income taxes have not been provided on the Company's share of undistributed earnings of subsidiaries and Fuji Xerox Co., Ltd. The Company has reinvested these earnings and does not plan to initiate any action which will precipitate the payment of income taxes thereon. Should such earnings be distributed, the additional taxes payable by the Company would not be significant.

Long-Term Debt

A summary of long-term debt follows:

(Dollars in thousands)	1976	1975
Debt of Xerox Corporation (a)		
8.20% notes due 1982 (b)	$ 200,000	$ 200,000
8⅝% sinking fund debentures due 1999 (c)	200,000	200,000
5⅜% notes due 1991—payable in annual installments	73,000	77,500
4¾% to 5¾% notes and mortgages due at various dates to 1983	13,158	14,494
6% convertible subordinated debentures due 1995 (d)	155,486	155,486
5% convertible subordinated debentures due 1988 (e)	74,998	75,000
Total	716,642	722,480
Debt of Rank-Xerox Companies		
5¾% to 9¹¹⁄₁₆% notes (7¼% to 10⅝%—1975) due at various dates to 1981—payable in U.S. dollars (f)	91,878	99,297
7% to 15% notes and mortgages (7% to 13%—1975) due at various dates to 1996—payable in pounds sterling (f)	62,989	129,347
6¼% to 10% notes and mortgages due at various dates to 1990—payable in Dutch guilders	108,741	103,228
6⅛% note (4⅝% to 7½%—1975) due 1978—payable in German marks	4,167	41,017
8½% to 12½% notes (8¼% to 11½%—1975) due at various dates to 1986—payable in French francs (f)	22,256	13,553
7½% to 21% notes and mortgages (7¼% to 14%—1975) due at various dates to 2008—payable in other currencies (f)	19,842	38,747
Total	309,873	425,189
Debt of Latin American and Canadian Subsidiaries		
6% to 10% notes (6% to 11%—1975) due at various dates to 1986—payable in U.S. dollars (f)	41,148	81,724
9% to 18% notes (8% to 18%—1975) due at various dates to 1981—payable in other currencies (f)	3,876	7,026
Total	45,024	88,750
Parallel loan financings (f) (g)	—	—
Total (h) (i)	1,071,539	1,236,419
Less payments due within one year	71,399	107,177
Long-term debt	$1,000,140	$1,129,242

(a) Among the provisions of the several loan agreements are restrictions relating to the payment of cash dividends on common and Class B stocks. At December 31, 1976, $940,000,000 of consolidated retained earnings was unrestricted.

(b) The 8.20% notes are redeemable beginning November 1, 1980 at 100%.

(c) The 8⅝% sinking fund debentures are redeemable during the twelve-month period which began November 1, 1976 at 107.54% and at reducing percentages thereafter. However, the debentures may not be redeemed prior to November 1, 1984 from moneys borrowed at an interest cost to the Company of less than 8.65% per annum. Commencing in 1984, the Company must redeem a minimum of $12,000,000 annually.

(d) The 6% convertible subordinated debentures are convertible at $92 a share and 1,690,066 shares of unissued common stock were reserved for this purpose at December 31, 1976. The debentures are redeemable during the twelve-month period which began November 1, 1976 at 104.2% and at reducing percentages thereafter. Commencing in 1981, the Company must redeem a minimum of $8,000,000 annually.

(e) The 5% convertible subordinated debentures are convertible at $148 a share and 506,743 shares of unissued common stock were reserved for this purpose at December 31, 1976. The debentures are redeemable during the twelve-month period beginning December 1, 1978 at 102% and at reducing percentages thereafter. If certain conditions occur, the debentures may be redeemed during the two-year period which began December 1, 1976 at 103% during the first twelve months and at 102.5% during the second twelve months.

(f) The interest rates on notes are subject to periodic adjustment.

(g) The Company and certain subsidiaries have entered into three parallel loan agreements with non-affiliated organizations whereby the Company's subsidiaries borrowed the equivalent of $89,905,000 in pounds sterling, and concurrently, that amount of U.S. dollars was loaned to these organizations. The Company's sub-sidiaries' borrowings amounted to the equivalent of $71,059,000 at December 31, 1976, at interest rates of 9% to 11½% ($82,355,000 at December 31, 1975, at interest rates of 9¾% to 11½%). Interest rates on related receivables were 7½% to 9¾% and 8¼% to 9¾% at December 31, 1976 and 1975, respectively. These parallel loans, which mature between 1984 and 1987, have been netted in the consolidated balance sheets. The terms of the agreements provide for offset of principal and interest in the event of default by the respective parties.

(h) Payments due on long-term debt for the next five years are: 1977—$71,399,000; 1978—$65,220,000; 1979—$59,936,000; 1980—$58,410,000; and 1981—$78,088,000.

(i) Interest on long-term debt amounted to $91,725,000 in 1976 and $96,298,000 in 1975. Interest expense for 1976 and 1975 is net of $7,736,000 and $5,223,000, respectively, of interest income on amounts loaned under parallel loan agreements.

Stock Option and Long-Term Incentive Plans

The Company has an executive long-term incentive plan approved by shareholders in 1976 under which approximately 3,700,000 shares of common stock were reserved for issue. These shares included approximately 2,000,000 shares reserved under the 1973 plan. Under the 1976 plan eligible employees may be granted incentive stock rights, non-qualified stock options, stock appreciation rights and performance unit rights.

There are outstanding non-qualified and qualified options and stock apprecia-tion rights under prior plans. These are similar in nature to comparable awards under the 1976 plan. There are also outstanding options under a merger agreement. No options were granted under plans of acquired companies subsequent to the dates of acquisition. With the adoption of the executive long-term incentive plan in 1976, no further options will be granted under prior plans.

Incentive stock rights entitle the employee to receive, without payment to the Company, shares of common stock in consideration for services performed during specified incentive periods ranging up to five years from the date of grant. The compensation expense of incentive stock rights is equivalent to the fair value of the common stock on the date of grant.

Non-qualified options are granted for the purchase of common shares at not less than 100% of the fair value of the common stock on the date of grant. Non-qualified options may be exercised within seven or ten years from the date of grant and are exercisable in installments varying from 20% to 25% per year after a specified waiting period. Qualified options, which were granted for the purchase of common shares at not less than 100% of the fair value of the common stock on the date of grant, may be exercised within five years from the date of grant, and are exercisable in installments of 20%, 30% and 50% per year after a one- or two-year waiting period.

Stock appreciation rights, which relate to specific non-qualified options, entitle the employee to receive, without payment to the Company, the value of the stock appreciation right in cash, shares of common stock, or a combination of the two at the Company's discretion, in lieu of exercise of the option. The value of the stock appreciation right is related to the increase in market value of the Company's common stock. Stock appreciation rights become exercisable and expire on the same dates as the related options.

Performance unit rights entitle the employee to receive the value of the perform-ance unit in cash, shares of common stock, or a combination of the two at the Company's discretion. The value of a performance unit is determined by a formula based upon the achievement of specific performance goals. When granted in conjunc-tion with a non-qualified stock option, payment of the performance unit right is in

37

lieu of exercise of the option. Performance unit rights are payable at the end of a three- or five-year award period.

During 1976, 436,000 incentive stock units were granted with an average value of $54; 2,000 incentive stock units were cancelled and none vested during the year. During 1976, 483,000 performance units were granted with a maximum unit value of $26; 1,000 performance units were cancelled during the year. No cash payments or share distributions were made during 1976 relating to the performance unit rights.

A summary of option and stock appreciation right transactions under all plans during 1976 and 1975 is shown below:

(Shares in thousands)	Non-Qualified Options		Stock Appreciation Rights		Qualified Options	
	1976	1975	1976	1975	1976	1975
Outstanding at beginning of year	2,469	2,423	1,312	1,188	573	859
Granted	334	188	124	179	–	6
Cancelled	(164)	(142)	(59)	(55)	(362)	(197)
Exercised	(13)	–	–	–	(4)	(95)
Outstanding at end of year	2,626	2,469	1,377	1,312	207	573
Initially exercisable during the year	453	445	244	209	42	167
Exercisable at end of year	1,146	767	622	396	199	520
Average price of outstanding options and rights	$ 90	$ 95	$111	$117	$140	$121
Average price of exercises						
Xerox Corporation	$ 58	$ –	$ –	$ –	$ –	$ 68
Acquired companies	$ 22	$ –	$ –	$ –	$ 18	$ 12
Average market price at dates of exercise	$ 62	$ –	$ –	$ –	$ 60	$ 51

The number of shares issuable under outstanding options and rights is 3,078,390 because non-qualified and qualified options and rights which have been granted concurrently will be proportionately reduced in relation to the options or rights which are exercised. Compensation expense related to incentive stock, performance unit and stock appreciation rights is charged to income over periods earned and amounted to $9,771,000 in 1976.

The number of shares available for grant of option or rights under all plans at the end of the year was: 1976—1,281,264; 1975—430,280; and 1974—537,458.

Shareholders' Equity

The Company has 80,000 shares of cumulative preferred stock, par value $100 per share, authorized but unissued.

Class B stock has equal rights with common stock as to voting, dividends and liquidation but does not have preemptive rights. Class B stock was sold to key executives under the Company's Restricted Stock Purchase Plan at a price which is 50% of the market value of the Company's common stock. The Class B stock is subject to restrictions. The Company is obligated to either repurchase the Class B shares on which restrictions have lapsed, or exchange them for the same number of shares of common stock. No further awards will be made under this plan.

Under the plan, participants had loans from the Company at December 31, 1976 of $16,309,000 ($18,534,000 at December 31, 1975) at an interest rate of 4% and have pledged the shares as collateral.

The difference between the fair market value of the Class B stock and the purchase price represents compensation which is deferred and amortized to income.

The outstanding shares of Class B stock are net of 261,012 treasury shares at December 31, 1976 (214,730 shares at December 31, 1975) which are carried at par value.

Commitments

The minimum rental commitments under noncancelable leases, substantially all for plant and office facilities, are: 1977—$96,159,000; 1978—$80,863,000; 1979—$54,682,000; 1980—$42,615,000; 1981—$35,582,000; 1982 to 1986—$119,166,000; 1987 to 1991—$85,695,000; 1992 to 1996—$59,445,000; and thereafter—$68,825,000.

Included in the above are minimum rental commitments for noncapitalized financing leases, which are not significant.

Rental expense amounted to $130,818,000 in 1976 and $116,973,000 in 1975.

Discontinued Operations

Effective June 30, 1975, the Company decided to discontinue its mainframe computer business and provided $84,375,000, net of income tax benefit of $77,477,000 and outside shareholders' interests of $4,248,000, for estimated loss on disposition of assets and for estimated operating losses and other expenses to be incurred for such discontinuance.

The assets of discontinued operations consist of:

(Dollars in thousands)	1976	1975
Current assets	$36,137	$ 58,598
Noncurrent assets	34,361	73,267
Total assets	70,498	131,865
Less reserve for estimated loss on disposition of assets	13,063	32,728
Total assets at estimated realizable value	$57,435	$ 99,137

Charges to the reserve for estimated loss on disposition of assets amounted to $32,265,000 in 1976 ($66,872,000 in 1975).

The reserve for estimated operating losses and other expenses to be incurred during the phase-out period amounted to $9,800,000 at December 31, 1976 ($37,700,000 at December 31, 1975). Charges to this reserve were $15,300,000 in 1976 ($28,800,000 in 1975). The reserve is included in salaries, profit sharing and other accruals in the consolidated balance sheets.

During 1976, $12,600,000 was reclassified from the reserve for estimated operating losses and other expenses to the reserve for estimated loss on disposition of assets. In 1975, $14,400,000 was reclassified from the reserve for estimated loss on disposition of assets to the reserve for estimated operating losses and other expenses.

The revenues, costs and expenses of discontinued operations have been excluded from the respective captions and the loss from discontinued operations is reported separately in the 1975 consolidated statement of income. During the six months ended June 30, 1975 the mainframe computer business had revenues of $40,272,000 and incurred a loss from operations of $12,950,000 after income tax benefit and outside shareholders' interests.

Under long-term agreements with affiliates of Honeywell Inc., maintenance and marketing support services are provided to the Company's mainframe computer customers. It is anticipated that these agreements will not affect the provision made in connection with discontinued operations.

Litigation

SCM Corporation has commenced an action against the Company alleging, among other things, monopolization of the plain paper office copier market and xerographic technology and acquisition of patents and technology in violation of the antitrust laws. SCM's pretrial statement expands its claim for treble damages from at least $435,000,000 to $1,764,000,000. SCM also seeks injunctive relief.

Van Dyk Research Corporation has filed a complaint against the Company alleging violations of the antitrust laws. Van Dyk seeks injunctive relief and treble damages of no less than $1,485,000,000.

A class action has been filed purporting to be on behalf of customers of the Company in California and alleging violations of federal and state antitrust laws, seeking injunctive relief and treble damages of $250,000,000.

In five other actions, claims have been asserted against the Company alleging violations of antitrust laws and seeking injunctive relief and damages. In four of the actions, treble damages of $51,000,000 in the aggregate have been claimed and in the remaining action, treble damages in an unspecified amount have been alleged.

The Company has commenced patent infringement actions against International Business Machines Corporation in the United States and Canada. In addition to asserting the invalidity of the Company's patents involved in the actions, IBM has collaterally attacked the enforceability of the patents by alleging misuse thereof.

IBM has commenced patent infringement actions against the Company in the United States and Canada. IBM seeks injunctive relief and damages (trebled in the U.S. action) in an unspecified amount.

The Company has denied any wrongdoing in all of the foregoing proceedings and is engaged in preparing its defenses.

Replacement Cost Information (Unaudited)

In accordance with Accounting Series Release No. 190 issued by the Securities and Exchange Commission, the Company's 1976 annual report on Form 10-K contains selected financial data relating to the replacement cost of buildings and equipment, rental equipment and inventories at December 31, 1976. Also presented is the approximate amount of cost of rentals and sales and depreciation expense for the year ended December 31, 1976 based on replacement cost.

The cost of replacing plant, machinery and equipment in manufacturing, marketing and administrative operations is generally greater than the original capital investment required. Similarly, increased cost factors also result in higher manufacturing costs of rental equipment and related inventories. The Company will continually strive to modify its pricing structure in recognition of rising costs, considering competitive conditions as well as government restrictions.

Quarterly Results of Operations (Unaudited)

Interim financial information for the year ended December 31, 1976 follows:

(Dollars in thousands, except per share data)	First Quarter	Second Quarter	Third Quarter	Fourth Quarter
Total operating revenues	$1,032,742	$1,089,460	$1,138,634	$1,143,061
Cost of rentals and sales	264,763	264,550	304,272	295,122
Expenses, net of other income	582,984	593,551	622,423	671,426
Income taxes	87,500	106,600	101,800	81,500
Outside shareholders' interests	15,542	22,059	15,132	15,767
	950,789	986,760	1,043,627	1,063,815
Net income	$ 81,953	$ 102,700	$ 95,007	$ 79,246
Net income per common share	$1.03	$1.29	$1.19	$1.00

Report of Independent Accountants

Peat, Marwick, Mitchell & Co.
Certified Public Accountants
White Plains, New York 10601

To the Board of Directors
and Shareholders of Xerox Corporation:

We have examined the consolidated balance sheets of Xerox Corporation and
subsidiaries as of December 31, 1976 and 1975 and the related statements of income,
common and Class B shares, additional paid-in capital, retained earnings and
changes in financial position for the years then ended. Our examination was made in
accordance with generally accepted auditing standards, and accordingly included
such tests of the accounting records and such other auditing procedures as we
considered necessary in the circumstances.

In our opinion, the aforementioned consolidated financial statements present
fairly the financial position of Xerox Corporation and subsidiaries at December 31,
1976 and 1975 and their results of operations and changes in financial position for the
years then ended, in conformity with generally accepted accounting principles
applied on a consistent basis.

Peat, Marwick, Mitchell & Co.

January 17, 1977

ANNUAL REPORT 1976

⩯ ADDISON-WESLEY
PUBLISHING COMPANY

READING, MASSACHUSETTS

Financial Highlights

	Year Ended November 30	
	1976	1975
Net Sales	$53,478,000	$55,012,000
Net Income	$3,043,000	$4,633,000
Net Income Percent of Net Sales	5.7%	8.4%
Net Income per Share	$1.14	$1.74
Dividends per Share	$.40	$.40
Working Capital	$18,736,000	$18,608,000
Shareholders' Equity	$29,217,000	$27,240,000
Average Shares Outstanding	2,669,870	2,667,241

1

DONALD R. HAMMONDS
PRESIDENT

TO OUR SHAREHOLDERS:

Sales and earnings in 1976 were a disappointment to all of us at Addison-Wesley. Good performances in certain of our operating areas were offset by mediocre or simply poor results in others. Total sales were $53.5 million, as against $55 million in 1975, while after-tax income dropped to $3 million ($1.14 per share) from $4.6 million ($1.74 per share) in the previous year.

Total sales of textbooks and scholarly works from the various sections of our Higher Education Publishing Group were slightly ahead of the prior year, although not what we had hoped for. Margins suffered because sales gains were insufficient to offset higher operating costs and the increased investment requirements of an active organization with sound but ambitious plans for the future. We are confident that stronger sales of new publications will provide the overall increases we seek in the years ahead.

The School Publishing Group, which publishes elementary and high school texts and provides tests and other materials to the school market, experienced another difficult year. In addition to encountering extremely weak markets as a whole

(overall industry sales were down), this Group found itself at the low end of the sales cycle of one of its main products, our elementary mathematics series. The result was a decline in both sales and earnings. A major revision of the mathematics program, now nearing completion, is expected to revitalize this product. We are continuing to increase market penetration in other subject areas and, in particular, we can report good progress in the development of our promising new reading series, scheduled for publication no later than 1979. All of this augurs well for the future of the School Group.

In spite of an extremely difficult and complex operating environment, the International Publishing Group (which includes our Canadian company) came through with another fine performance in both sales and earnings. This Group, which markets throughout the world products developed by our domestic divisions as well as products developed in its own centers abroad, has long been recognized by the industry as one of the leading operations of its kind. This year, despite severe foreign economic dislocations (including sharp currency devaluations in key areas), the International Group again lived up to its reputation.

Finally, we are most pleased with developments in our new General Books Division. This division offers books to the general public, both children and adults, through retail bookstores and libraries. Although held back by somewhat weak library demand for hardcover children's books, progress in sales and profits and, equally important, in our manuscript acquisition program, was extremely gratifying. The future here looks promising.

It is with mixed feelings that I offer you my first message as President. Surely it is never pleasant to report lower sales and earnings. On the other hand, organizations are tested not in times of prosperity but in times of adversity, and I am proud that during an extremely trying year Addison-Wesley people met the test. Expenses have been carefully scrutinized and frequently cut, and some difficult and painful decisions have been made; this process will continue as necessary. All this has been accomplished in good

spirit by people who are professional in their work and confident of the future.

I take great pride in being associated with Addison-Wesley and with the many sound programs initiated by my predecessors. We look forward to a bright and important future, not just in sales and earnings, but in terms of our total contribution to the educational community and information-oriented public at large. Because forecasts of educational enrollments are mixed, and because of the uncertainties of the economic climate, both foreign and domestic, it is difficult to anticipate what sales and earnings for 1977 might be. However, despite these obstacles, you may be assured that all of us at Addison-Wesley will make every effort to further achievement of our goals.

Sincerely yours,

Donald R. Hammonds

PRESIDENT

3

Addison-Wesley publishes and distributes educational materials for use in elementary and high schools, universities and industry, covering essentially all the major disciplines, and also publishes professional, reference, and nonfiction trade books. The Company's operations are conducted through four Groups: the Higher Education Publishing Group, the International Publishing Group, the School Publishing Group, and the General Books Division.

The Higher Education Publishing Group is comprised of the Science and Mathematics Division and the Social Science and Humanities Division (formerly, in combination, the College Division), the Business and Professional Division, the Advanced Book Program, and two wholly-owned subsidiaries of Addison-Wesley, W. A. Benjamin, Inc. and Cummings Publishing Company, Inc. The International Publishing Group is comprised of the Canadian company and the International Division; the latter oversees the operation of all the other foreign subsidiaries of the Company. The School Publishing Group consists of the School Division, the Innovative Publishing Program, and the new Testing Services Division. The General Books Division publishes and markets adult trade books (nonfiction) and children's books.

THE HIGHER EDUCATION PUBLISHING GROUP

Although sales in 1976 were not as strong as we had hoped, significant progress was made during the year in strengthening our organization, especially in marketing, where new sales management positions were created and a number of new salespersons were added. Considerable emphasis was placed on our manuscript acquisition program, and the number of promising titles signed makes us quite optimistic about the prospects for this Group for the next several years.

In 1976 the Science and Mathematics Division maintained its strong position in these important disciplines. Among our 1976 publications, Bittinger's *Calculus: A Modeling Approach* and the Fifth Edition of Sears, Zemansky, Young's *University Physics* were very well received. An excellent list of new publications and revisions is scheduled for 1977, including a Third Edition of the successful *Study of Biology* by Baker and Allen.

The Social Science and Humanities Division enjoyed an excellent sales increase in 1976; some of the Higher Education Group's most successful books were in the fields of economics, sociology, psychology, and education. In 1977 revised editions of important titles in educational psychology and statistics; publication of a promising book, *Exploratory Data Analysis* by John Tukey; and the introduction of the first of a five-volume encyclopedia sponsored by the American Association of Health, Physical Education, and Recreation should contribute to a further gain in sales.

While the Business and Professional Division sales in 1976 were about level with 1975, there is considerable optimism for the coming years. Major books in the fields of introduction to business, structured FORTRAN programming, and business statistics will be prominent on the 1977 list. In 1976, contracts to publish many important manuscripts were signed, among which are basic textbooks in management, marketing, cost accounting, and computer programming. Our strong manuscript acquisition program will continue in 1977.

Decline of the backlist was especially evident in the Cummings Publishing Company operation, therefore it is particularly encouraging that in 1976 Cummings signed more author contracts for new books than in any other year in its history. Agreements were con-

4

cluded for new titles in anthropology, sociology, career education, business, and economics; and in 1977 Cummings will publish its first book in the field of business, an introduction to management text. This year, effort will continue to be focused on building up a strong new list.

W. A. Benjamin, Inc. sales for 1976 showed only a modest gain. An outstanding text on the 1976 list was the Third Edition of *Molecular Biology of the Gene*, by Nobel laureate Dr. James Watson. As expected, its sales were excellent. Two key revisions head the Benjamin 1977 list: *Basic Principles of Organic Chemistry* by Roberts and Caserio, and *Basic Psychology: Brief Version* by Kendler. Books in biology, anthropology, and mathematics will round out Benjamin's 1977 program.

The Advanced Book Program showed a slight increase in sales in 1976. A highlight of its 1976 list was publication of the first volume, *Integral Geometry and Geometric Probability* by L. A. Santalo, of the Ency-

clopedia of Mathematics and Its Applications (Gian-Carlo Rota, Editor). Inasmuch as this book appeared in the last month of fiscal 1976, its sales will not be reflected until this year. Back-orders and new orders for the several additional volumes of the Encyclopedia that will appear in 1977, as well as new books in biochemistry, physics, and computation, should contribute to a more successful year.

In 1976 our newest professional section, the Medical-Nursing Division, concluded contracts for twenty texts, and in 1977 will publish books in pediatrics, anesthesiology, and medical terminology, as well as a nursing examination review text.

In 1977 the Higher Education Group will concentrate on refining sales techniques for increased market penetration, and upon building its manuscript acquisition program. We have many unusually fine books under contract which, if completed in time for 1978 publication, could make that year a strong one.

THE SCHOOL PUBLISHING GROUP

In a year in which the industry experienced generally disappointing sales results, the School Division was no exception. Not only did mathematics sales, which still represent a substantial part of our total sales, decrease, but the rest of our list, except for Innovative Program publications, showed decreases also.

The STEM elementary science series, which benefited from large state adoptions in 1975, suffered from the cyclical nature of such adoptions; there were few states adopting elementary science texts in 1976. Social studies and language arts sales were also down, especially for those programs in multimedia format, because this was where the school district budget crunch had its heaviest impact. One item of good news for

1976: our brand new Addison-Wesley Testing Service met sales projections and should show an increase in 1977.

Several steps were taken during the year to minimize the negative impact of decreased sales. The decrease necessitated substantial cuts in personnel and in other operating expenses, and improved inventory control procedures resulted in an inventory reduction of nearly 25 percent. These measures should help the Group's performance in 1977, and there are other favorable indications for the coming year:

We have several new state adoptions in science and in mathematics. We are in a position to compete for some of the "back to basics" market in language arts through the sale of such new junior high school prod-

5

ucts as *Target Mechanics, Target Usage, Target Spelling, Language Is You,* and the *Top Flight Readers.* Social studies adoptions in Detroit and Chicago and a state adoption in Georgia are encouraging.

While 1977 may not show dramatic improvement, the School Division is optimistic about the long-range future. A major revision of our Elementary Mathematics Series is in process and we are in the final developmental phase of an entry into the basal reading field, which represents the largest single market in the elementary area.

These are difficult years for school publishing, but we have a highly motivated, experienced professional team which is committed to increasing Addison-Wesley's share of the elhi markets in the years ahead.

THE INTERNATIONAL PUBLISHING GROUP

Last year our writeup in the Annual Report concluded by saying, "barring unforeseen major political upheavals, 1976 should be a good year for the International Publishing Group."

As it turned out, 1976 did produce unexpected political and economic upheavals. Currency losses in the United Kingdom, Australia, and Mexico eroded our profit margins in those areas. The crisis in Lebanon effectively shut down our major distributor in that part of the world and turned a thriving market into near chaos. (We eventually managed to salvage our book inventories in Beirut, which were returned to Amsterdam by fishing boat via Cyprus!) Nevertheless, as the months wore on, we mended our distribution network and made substantial sales to the Arab world.

In spite of these serious and unusual problems, our international operations proved their strength by managing a respectable increase in sales over 1975. They once again turned in a profitable performance.

Latin America, despite Mexico's devaluation of its currency and other weak spots, produced the greatest gains; Asia did well in 1976; both the United Kingdom and Continental Europe increased sales over 1975. In Africa, against strong international competition, we won our first contract to publish an elementary series for an African nation. In Latin America, we gained our first major sale to the government of Venezuela.

Our editorial, sales, and marketing organizations expanded again in 1976. We are developing strong, new international publishing programs for 1977: new school products in Australia, the United Kingdom, and Latin America; and the addition of many promising college titles to the lists of our Latin American companies and our French, Italian, and German publishing programs (the latter are still in the early stages of development).

The Canadian company continues to thrive. It is dominant in the elementary mathematics market in Canada, and is on the threshold of a major penetration of the elementary science market. Even though sales volume grew only modestly in Canada in 1976, the company continues at a profitable pace.

We are presently making a major effort to broaden our editorial base in Canada and to develop a strong editorial team in Toronto. At least one major indigenous editorial project, started last year, is progressing satisfactorily; several more are under consideration. As in other parts of the world, we see a strong future for local editorial projects. We are further encouraged by the beginnings of close editorial and marketing cooperation between Canada and the Australian and United Kingdom companies.

6

1977 is a year for which we have budgeted with care; we are intent on holding down expenses. We expect to have new product to sell from our domestic divisions, and increasingly from our own international publishing programs. One of the latter, *New Horizons in English*, increased in sales by 41% in 1976, including substantial sales in the United States and Canada.

With a little help from friendly governments, including our own, in holding down inflation and creating some semblance of order out of the international currency chaos, we hope for another good year in 1977.

THE GENERAL BOOKS DIVISION

In its second full year of operation, the General Books Division registered an impressive sales gain of over 20 percent and a strong net profit. Two new books, both "trade" paperbacks, achieved sales of more than 60,000 copies each in the first six months of publication: *Take Care of Yourself: A Consumer Guide to Medical Care* by Drs. Vickery and Fries, and *Women As Winners* by Jongeward and Scott. Our all-time trade bestseller, *Born to Win* by James and Jongeward, passed the 1.3 million copy mark for sales in the English language; it also enjoys excellent sales in Spanish, Dutch, and German versions.

The Vickery-Fries and Jongeward-Scott books are continuing their strong sales pattern into early 1977, and another late 1976 publication, *Married, Etc.: A Sourcebook for Couples* by Suid et al., promises to become a strong seller. Our small and select 1977 list will include a handbook for consumer action, spon-sored by Ralph Nader's National Public Interest Research Group; a book on Shyness by prominent Stanford psychologist Philip Zimbardo; an important book on the humanization of work by Pehr Gyllenhammar, the President of VOLVO; and new books by Fries and Vickery and by Muriel James.

While public and school libraries continue to represent by far the largest segment of the market for children's books, sales are growing in general bookstores. We published 24 children's books in 1976, and we expect to add about 20 in 1977. Many of these will be the first fruits of a new editorial program, commenced nearly two years ago; we believe they will be distinguished additions to our juvenile list, both in content and in excellence of design and appearance. A line of juvenile paperbacks, one of the fastest growing segments of the industry, will be launched in the fall of 1977.

ADDISON-WESLEY PUBLISHING COMPANY
CONSOLIDATED STATEMENT OF FINANCIAL POSITION

| | November 30 | |
	1976	1975
ASSETS		
Current assets:		
Cash	$ 2,597,000	$ 1,451,000
Accounts receivable, less allowance for returns and doubtful		
accounts of $2,157,000 in 1976 and $1,920,000 in 1975	12,423,000	13,494,000
Inventories	13,592,000	16,252,000
Deferred income tax benefits	1,348,000	983,000
Prepaid expenses	247,000	460,000
Total current assets	30,207,000	32,640,000
Property and equipment, less accumulated depreciation		
and amortization	8,133,000	6,948,000
Prepublication costs, less accumulated amortization	8,096,000	7,928,000
Advances and other assets	1,143,000	1,674,000
	$47,579,000	$49,190,000
LIABILITIES AND SHAREHOLDERS' EQUITY		
Current liabilities:		
Current installments of long-term debt	1,180,000	226,000
Notes payable to banks	1,000,000	3,600,000
Accounts payable	2,328,000	1,759,000
Royalties	3,996,000	3,882,000
Federal and foreign income taxes	87,000	1,668,000
Other current liabilities	2,880,000	2,897,000
Total current liabilities	11,471,000	14,032,000
Long-term debt	4,565,000	5,745,000
Deferred federal and foreign income taxes	2,326,000	2,173,000
Shareholders' Equity		
Common Stock, no par value		
Class A, authorized and issued 752,682 shares	424,000	424,000
Class B, authorized 3,000,000 shares and issued 2,019,156 shares		
in 1976 and 2,018,744 shares in 1975	7,698,000	7,696,000
Retained earnings	21,673,000	19,698,000
	29,795,000	27,818,000
Less cost of 101,904 shares of common stock in treasury	578,000	578,000
Total shareholders' equity	29,217,000	27,240,000
	$47,579,000	$49,190,000

The accompanying notes are an integral part
of the consolidated financial statements.

8

ADDISON-WESLEY PUBLISHING COMPANY

CONSOLIDATED STATEMENT
OF INCOME AND RETAINED EARNINGS

	Year Ended November 30	
	1976	1975
CONSOLIDATED STATEMENT OF INCOME		
Net sales	$53,478,000	$55,012,000
Cost of sales	23,439,000	22,574,000
Selling and administrative expenses	23,564,000	22,078,000
Operating costs and expenses	47,003,000	44,652,000
Operating income	6,475,000	10,360,000
Interest expense	773,000	1,084,000
Income before provision for income taxes	5,702,000	9,276,000
Provision for income taxes	2,659,000	4,643,000
Net Income	$ 3,043,000	$ 4,633,000
Net income per share	$1.14	$1.74
CONSOLIDATED STATEMENT OF RETAINED EARNINGS		
Retained earnings at beginning of year as previously reported	$20,454,000	$16,859,000
Sales returns adjustment	(756,000)	(727,000)
Retained earnings at beginning of year as restated	19,698,000	16,132,000
Net income	3,043,000	4,633,000
Cash dividends ($.40 per share)	(1,068,000)	(1,067,000)
Retained earnings at end of year	$21,673,000	$19,698,000

The accompanying notes are an integral part of
the consolidated financial statements.

9

ADDISON-WESLEY PUBLISHING COMPANY

CONSOLIDATED STATEMENT
OF CHANGES IN FINANCIAL POSITION

	Year Ended November 30	
	1976	1975
Source:		
Net income	$3,043,000	$4,633,000
Charges to income not requiring expenditure of funds:		
Depreciation and amortization:		
Property and equipment	596,000	580,000
Prepublication costs	4,581,000	3,930,000
Deferred federal and foreign income taxes	153,000	186,000
Funds provided from operations	8,373,000	9,329,000
Decreases in advances and other, net	553,000	85,000
Total funds provided	8,926,000	9,414,000
Application:		
Additions to prepublication costs	4,749,000	5,212,000
Additions to property and equipment	1,801,000	393,000
Decrease in long-term debt	1,180,000	227,000
Cash dividends	1,068,000	1,067,000
Total funds applied	8,798,000	6,899,000
Increase in working capital	$ 128,000	$2,515,000
Increase (decrease) in working capital:		
Cash	1,146,000	(414,000)
Accounts receivable	(1,071,000)	498,000
Inventories	(2,660,000)	2,194,000
Deferred income taxes	365,000	128,000
Current installments of long-term debt	(954,000)	(14,000)
Notes payable to banks	2,600,000	—
Accounts payable	(569,000)	1,037,000
Royalties	(114,000)	(224,000)
Federal and foreign income taxes	1,581,000	236,000
Other, net	(196,000)	(926,000)
Increase in working capital	$ 128,000	$2,515,000

The accompanying notes are an integral part
of the consolidated financial statements.

10

ADDISON-WESLEY PUBLISHING COMPANY

NOTES TO CONSOLIDATED FINANCIAL STATEMENTS

---

1. Summary of Significant Accounting Policies:

Principles of Consolidation
The consolidated financial statements include the accounts of the parent company and its wholly-owned domestic and foreign subsidiaries. All material intercompany transactions have been eliminated. Certain accounts in the 1975 financial statements have been reclassified to conform to the 1976 presentation.

Sales Returns (see Note 2)

Translation of Foreign Currencies
Net assets of foreign subsidiaries are translated into United States dollars at year-end rates except for non-current assets, which are translated at historical rates. Net sales, cost of sales, and expenses are translated at the average rates prevailing during the year except for depreciation and amortization of property and equipment and prepublication costs, which are translated at the rate of exchange prevailing at the time the related assets were acquired. Net exchange losses of $149,000 are included in 1976 net income.

Inventories
Inventories are stated at lower of cost (first-in, first-out) or market.

Depreciation and Amortization
The Company provides for depreciation primarily on accelerated methods by charges to expense which are sufficient to write off the costs of the assets over their estimated useful lives as follows: buildings and improvements, 20–40 years; furniture and equipment, 3–10 years. Amortization of leasehold interest in land is computed on a straight-line basis over the life of the related lease.

Prepublication Costs
Prepublication costs include copy editing, art, composition, and camera work necessary to prepare a book for publication and are amortized over three years from publication date.

Income Taxes
Deferred income taxes arise from income tax and financial reporting differences principally with respect to prepublication costs, inventory revaluations and sales returns.

The Company does not provide for federal income taxes on the accumulated undistributed earnings of its DISC subsidiary ($2,200,000 in 1976 and $1,800,000 in 1975) since the Company intends to permanently invest such earnings in a manner that will permit the indefinite postponement of federal income taxes. Federal income taxes which would be payable upon distribution of the undistributed earnings of the Company's Canadian subsidiary would be offset by foreign tax credits. The Company intends to permanently invest undistributed earnings of its other foreign subsidiaries.

2. Change In Accounting — Sales Returns:
In late 1976 the Company adopted the policy of providing an allowance for estimated sales returns. This change was adopted retroactively in accordance with the provisions of Statements No. 5 and 11 of the Financial Accounting Standards Board. The Company believes that this new method of accounting results in a more accurate matching of revenues with related sales returns. The effect of this change on net income for 1976 and 1975 is not material. Retained earnings at December 1, 1974 and 1975 have been adjusted to reflect this change.

3. International Operations:
Net assets, net sales and net income of international operations (approximately one-half in Canada) included in the financial statements are:

	1976	1975
Net assets	22%	22%
Net sales	31%	28%
Net income	54%	41%

4. Inventories:
Inventories consist of the following:

	November 30	
	1976	1975
Finished goods	$12,013,000	$13,944,000
Work in process	861,000	1,703,000
Paper	718,000	605,000
	$13,592,000	$16,252,000

11

5. Property and Equipment:

Property and equipment consist of the following:

| | November 30 | |
	1976	1975
Land	$ 355,000	$ 355,000
Leasehold interest in land	627,000	627,000
Buildings and improvements	10,235,000	8,629,000
Furniture and equipment	2,882,000	2,712,000
	14,099,000	12,323,000
Less accumulated depreciation and amortization	5,966,000	5,375,000
	$ 8,133,000	$ 6,948,000

6. Notes Payable and Compensating Balances:

The Company has lines of credit (interest at prime) of which $1,000,000 and $3,600,000 were outstanding at November 30, 1976 and 1975 respectively. The monthly average amount of notes payable outstanding during 1976 was $5,300,000; $8,100,000 in 1975; and the monthly average interest rate on these borrowings in 1976 was 6.8%; 7.9% in 1975. The maximum amount of notes payable outstanding at any month end during 1976 was $8,000,000; $12,750,000 in 1975.

The Company maintains compensating balances under informal arrangements which approximate 15% of the loans outstanding during the year.

7. Long-Term Debt:

At November 30, 1976, long-term debt consisted of the following:

5⅝% mortgage note, payable $59,000 quarterly, including interest, through March 1987	$1,850,000
6½% mortgage note, payable $11,000 monthly, including interest, through October 1986	1,058,000
5¾% mortgage note, payable $10,000 quarterly, including interest, through October 1986	319,000
5½% mortgage note, payable $2,000 monthly, including interest, through August 1985	168,000
8% note, payable in declining annual installments 1977 through 1979 ($940,000–$353,000)	2,350,000
	5,745,000
Less current installments	1,180,000
	$4,565,000

Certain of the Company's land and buildings are pledged as collateral for the mortgage notes.

8. Income Taxes

The provision for income taxes consists of:

	1976	1975
Federal — current	$1,606,000	$2,946,000
State — current	300,000	500,000
Foreign — current	965,000	1,139,000
Deferred	(212,000)	58,000
	$2,659,000	$4,643,000

Investment tax credits which are recognized on the "flow-through method" reduced the current federal provision by $48,000 in 1976 and $24,000 in 1975.

Deferred income taxes arise principally from the following sources:

	1976	1975
Prepublication costs	$ 33,000	$ 190,000
Inventory revaluations	(324,000)	(102,000)
Sales returns	(41,000)	(26,000)

Following is a reconciliation of the statutory federal income tax rate and the effective income tax rate:

	1976	1975
Federal statutory income tax rate	48%	48%
State income taxes, net of federal tax benefit	3	3
Undistributed earnings of DISC subsidiary	(2)	(2)
Adjustments resulting from Internal Revenue Service examination, principally investment tax credits on prepublication costs	—	2
Other, net	(2)	(1)
Effective income tax rate	47%	50%

9. Common Stock:

Class B common stock is entitled to elect three directors and has such other limited voting rights as are given it by law. Class A common stock has full voting rights and elects five to seven directors. Except as to voting, the rights of the two classes are equal, share for share.

12

10. Stock Options:

The Company's qualified stock option plan, which expired in July 1974, provided for the granting of options to key employees at 100% of market price on the date of grant and such options are exercisable over a five-year period. No options have been granted since July 1974. During the year options for 412 shares were exercised at an option price of $4.87, aggregating $2,008. At November 30, 1976 options for 38,062 shares were outstanding at $4.87 per share, of which 34,062 shares were exercisable.

The Company's nonqualified stock option plan provides for the granting of options to key employees at 100% of market price on the date of grant and such options are exercisable over a four-year period. There were no new options granted during 1976. At November 30, 1976, options for 2,000 shares were outstanding at $8.80 per share and 26,803 shares were available for future options.

11. Retirement and Profit Sharing Plans:

In 1976 the Company adopted a pension plan covering substantially all employees, and entered into individual retirement agreements with certain officers/directors. The Company also has a profit-sharing plan which has been in effect for many years.

The Company's policy is to fund pension costs accrued. The actuarially computed value of vested benefits exceeded the value of the pension accrual by approximately $823,000 as of November 30, 1976. Unfunded past service costs approximated $4,325,000 at December 1, 1975 and are being amortized over 30 years.

Total expense for all plans amounted to $804,000 in 1976 and $808,000 in 1975.

12. Net Income per Share:

Net income per share is based upon the weighted average number of Class A and Class B common shares outstanding during each year. The weighted average shares were 2,669,870 in 1976 and 2,667,241 in 1975.

13. Fourth Quarter Adjustments:

During the fourth quarter the Company made several adjustments relating principally to prepublication costs and income taxes which, in the aggregate, decreased earnings by $218,000 ($.08 per share).

14. Litigation:

In October 1976, a complaint was brought against the Company in the Federal District Court of Massachusetts by one present and one former female employee, alleging sex discrimination in employment in violation of various Federal and Massachusetts laws. The suit was filed as a class action on behalf of the named plaintiffs by the Attorney General of Massachusetts and on behalf of "all past, present and future female applicants and employees." No specific amount of monetary damages is requested; the Complaint asks the Court to require the Company to make whole any person adversely affected by policies and practices found to be unlawful and that the Court issue appropriate declaratory and injunctive relief. The Complaint also seeks plaintiffs' attorney fees.

The proceeding is still in a preliminary stage. The Company's position is that its employment practices are in compliance with the applicable laws, and the Company has filed an answer denying all of the allegations of discrimination set forth in the Complaint and intends to defend this matter vigorously.

REPORT OF INDEPENDENT CERTIFIED PUBLIC ACCOUNTANTS

To the Board of Directors and Shareholders of
  Addison-Wesley Publishing Company, Inc.:

We have examined the consolidated statements of financial position of Addison-Wesley Publishing Company, Inc. as of November 30, 1976 and the related consolidated statements of income, retained earnings and changes in financial position for the year then ended. Our examination was made in accordance with generally accepted auditing standards and, accordingly, included such tests of the accounting records and such other auditing procedures as we considered necessary in the circumstances. We previously examined and reported upon the financial statements for the year ended November 30, 1975.

In our opinion, the aforementioned consolidated financial statements present fairly the financial position of Addison-Wesley Publishing Company, Inc. as of November 30, 1976 and 1975, and the results of its operations and the changes in its financial position for the years then ended, in conformity with generally accepted accounting principles applied on a consistent basis, after giving retroactive effect to the change, with which we concur, in the method of accounting for sales returns as described in Note 2 to the financial statements.

Boston, Massachusetts
January 31, 1977

Coopers & Lybrand

13

ADDISON-WESLEY PUBLISHING COMPANY
FIVE YEAR FINANCIAL SUMMARY

SUMMARY OF OPERATIONS (1)	Fiscal Year Ended November 30		
	1976	1975	1974
Net sales	$53,478,000	$55,012,000	$50,163,000
Cost of sales	23,439,000	22,574,000	20,871,000
Selling and administrative expenses	23,564,000	22,078,000	21,504,000
Operating costs and expenses	47,003,000	44,652,000	42,375,000
Income from operations	6,475,000	10,360,000	7,788,000
Interest expense	773,000	1,084,000	1,125,000
Income before income taxes	5,702,000	9,276,000	6,663,000
Provision for income taxes	2,659,000	4,643,000	2,668,000
Net income	$ 3,043,000	$ 4,633,000	$ 3,995,000
Net income per share (2)	$1.14	$1.74	$1.48
Dividends per share	$ .40	$ .40	$ .30

(1) Restated for change in accounting for sales returns
   as described in Note 2 of the financial statements.
   This change decreased net income for each of the
   four years ended November 30, 1975, as follows:

Net income		$ 29,000	$192,000
Net income per share		$ .01	$ .07

(2) Based on the weighted average number of shares
   outstanding

OTHER FINANCIAL DATA

	1976	1975	1974
Net income as percent of sales	5.7%	8.4%	8.0%
Working capital	$18,736,000	$18,608,000	$15,808,000
Shareholders' equity	$29,217,000	$27,240,000	$23,649,000
Average number of shares outstanding	2,669,870	2,667,241	2,695,085

CLASSES OF SIMILAR PRODUCTS	Net Sales (Worldwide)		
Higher Education	$23,218,000	$22,462,000	$19,195,000
School	27,767,000	30,505,000	28,905,000
General Books	2,493,000	2,045,000	2,063,000
	$53,478,000	$55,012,000	$50,163,000

MANAGEMENT'S ANALYSIS OF SUMMARY OF OPERATIONS

1973	1972
$37,008,000	$32,980,000
15,518,000	14,209,000
15,974,000	14,759,000
31,492,000	28,968,000
5,516,000	4,012,000
744,000	662,000
4,772,000	3,350,000
2,100,000	1,318,000
$ 2,672,000	$ 2,032,000
$ .97	$ .74
$ .20	$ .20
$108,000	$ 58,000
$ .04	$ .01
7.2%	6.2%
$11,034,000	$ 8,535,000
$21,024,000	$18,874,000
2,760,085	2,752,405
$15,576,000	$14,097,000
19,852,000	17,766,000
1,580,000	1,117,000
$37,008,000	$32,980,000

Fiscal 1976 Compared with 1975

In 1976 the Higher Education Group sales increased 3% worldwide, the School Group sales decreased 9%, and General Books Division sales rose 22%. Combined, total sales decreased approximately 3%, from $55,012,000 to $53,478,000. Total operating costs and expenses were up about 5% over 1975: cost of sales increased as a percentage of sales largely because of increased amortization of prepublication costs, and selling and administrative expenses increased about 7% due to normal inflationary pressures. The combination of the 3% decrease in net sales and the 5% increase in operating costs and expenses resulted in a 37.5% decline in operating income, from $10,360,000 in 1975 to $6,475,000 in 1976; and despite the fact that lower borrowing levels and interest rates reduced interest expense substantially, net income per share declined 34% from $1.74 to $1.14.

Fiscal 1975 Compared with 1974

Sales increased 10% in 1975 to $55,012,000, and net income was $4,633,000, or 8.4% of sales. Net income per share was up 18% from $1.48 to $1.74. Dividends were increased to 40¢ per share in 1975 from 30¢ in 1974. On a worldwide basis, Higher Education sales were up 17% and School sales rose 5% in 1975. Cost of sales, operating expenses, and interest costs decreased slightly in proportion to sales. The effective income tax rate in 1975 was 50%, as compared with 40% in 1974, principally because of investment tax credits related to prepublication costs and, to a lesser extent, because of higher state income taxes and lower earnings from the DISC subsidiary.

The Company deems that it is engaged in one line of business, that of publishing and distributing educational materials.

Stock Market and Dividend Information

The Company's Class B Common Stock is traded in the over-the-counter market. The Company understands that there is virtually no public market in its Class A Common Stock. The following table shows the high bid and the low asked quotations as reported in the *Wall Street Journal* for shares of Class B Common Stock with respect to each quarterly period of the Company's two most recent fiscal years, and the amount of dividends per share paid on outstanding shares of both the Class A and Class B Common Stock for the same periods.

	Market Quotations*				Dividends per Share	
	Fiscal 1976		Fiscal 1975			
	High Bid	Low Asked	High Bid	Low Asked	Fiscal 1976	Fiscal 1975
1st Quarter	$10.38	$7.75	$9.75	$6.75	$.10	$.10
2nd Quarter	10.13	8.25	9.75	7.75	.10	.10
3rd Quarter	7.75	7.00	10.63	8.50	.10	.10
4th Quarter	6.88	6.38	8.88	7.75	.10	.10
For the Year	$10.38	$6.38	$10.63	$6.75	$.40	$.40

*These are interdealer prices, without retail markups, markdowns, or commissions, and do not reflect actual transactions.

A copy of the Company's Form 10-K Report for fiscal 1976, as filed with the Securities and Exchange Commission, is available without charge to any shareholder upon written request to the Treasurer, Addison-Wesley Publishing Company, Inc., Reading, Massachusetts 01867.

Equal Employment Opportunity Policy

It continues to be Addison-Wesley's policy to recruit, hire, and promote for all job classifications without regard to race, creed, religion, color, national origin, sex, or age, except where sex or age is a bona fide occupational qualification; and to evaluate each applicant seeking employment with the company on the basis of the applicant's experience, training, and ability to perform the work to be assigned. All other personnel actions, such as compensation, employee benefits, transfers, and layoffs, are administered on a similarly nondiscriminatory basis.

PRESENT-VALUE
TABLES

Table A: Present Value of a Single Payment/Receipt of $1,

$$PV_A = \frac{1}{(1 + i)^n}$$

where i = interest rate per period and n = number of periods.

$i = 01$ to 06; $N = 01$ to 50

N	1%	1.25%	1.5%	2%	3%	4%	5%	6%
1	0.9901	0.9877	0.9852	0.9804	0.9709	0.9615	0.9524	0.9434
2	0.9803	0.9755	0.9707	0.9612	0.9426	0.9246	0.9070	0.8900
3.	0.9706	0.9634	0.9563	0.9423	0.9151	0.8890	0.8638	0.8396
4	0.9610	0.9515	0.9422	0.9238	0.8885	0.8548	0.8227	0.7921
5	0.9515	0.9398	0.9283	0.9057	0.8626	0.8219	0.7835	0.7473
6	0.9420	0.9282	0.9145	0.8880	0.8375	0.7903	0.7462	0.7050
7	0.9327	0.9167	0.9010	0.8706	0.8131	0.7599	0.7107	0.6651
8	0.9235	0.9054	0.8877	0.8535	0.7894	0.7307	0.6768	0.6274
9	0.9143	0.8942	0.8746	0.8368	0.7664	0.7026	0.6446	0.5919
10	0.9053	0.8832	0.8617	0.8203	0.7441	0.6756	0.6139	0.5584
11	0.8963	0.8723	0.8489	0.8043	0.7224	0.6496	0.5847	0.5268
12	0.8874	0.8615	0.8364	0.7885	0.7014	0.6246	0.5568	0.4970
13	0.8787	0.8509	0.8240	0.7730	0.6810	0.6006	0.5303	0.4688
14	0.8700	0.8404	0.8119	0.7579	0.6611	0.5775	0.5051	0.4423
15	0.8614	0.8300	0.7999	0.7430	0.6419	0.5553	0.4810	0.4173
16	0.8528	0.8197	0.7880	0.7284	0.6232	0.5339	0.4581	0.3936
17	0.8444	0.8096	0.7764	0.7142	0.6050	0.5134	0.4363	0.3714
18	0.8360	0.7996	0.7649	0.7002	0.5874	0.4936	0.4155	0.3503
19	0.8277	0.7898	0.7536	0.6864	0.5703	0.4746	0.3957	0.3305
20	0.8195	0.7800	0.7425	0.6730	0.5537	0.4564	0.3769	0.3118
21	0.8114	0.7704	0.7315	0.6598	0.5375	0.4388	0.3589	0.2942
22	0.8034	0.7609	0.7207	0.6468	0.5219	0.4220	0.3419	0.2775
23	0.7954	0.7515	0.7100	0.6342	0.5067	0.4057	0.3256	0.2618
24	0.7876	0.7422	0.6995	0.6217	0.4919	0.3901	0.3101	0.2470
25	0.7798	0.7330	0.6892	0.6095	0.4776	0.3751	0.2953	0.2330
26	0.7720	0.7240	0.6790	0.5976	0.4637	0.3607	0.2812	0.2198
27	0.7644	0.7150	0.6690	0.5859	0.4502	0.3468	0.2678	0.2074
28	0.7568	0.7062	0.6591	0.5744	0.4371	0.3335	0.2551	0.1956
29	0.7493	0.6975	0.6494	0.5631	0.4243	0.3207	0.2429	0.1846
30	0.7419	0.6889	0.6398	0.5521	0.4120	0.3083	0.2314	0.1741
31	0.7346	0.6804	0.6303	0.5412	0.4000	0.2965	0.2204	0.1643
32	0.7273	0.6720	0.6210	0.5306	0.3883	0.2851	0.2099	0.1550
33	0.7201	0.6637	0.6118	0.5202	0.3770	0.2741	0.1999	0.1462
34	0.7130	0.6555	0.6028	0.5100	0.3660	0.2636	0.1904	0.1379
35	0.7059	0.6474	0.5939	0.5000	0.3554	0.2534	0.1813	0.1301
36	0.6989	0.6394	0.5851	0.4902	0.3450	0.2437	0.1727	0.1227
37	0.6920	0.6315	0.5764	0.4806	0.3350	0.2343	0.1644	0.1158
38	0.6852	0.6237	0.5679	0.4712	0.3252	0.2253	0.1566	0.1092
39	0.6784	0.6160	0.5595	0.4619	0.3158	0.2166	0.1491	0.1031
40	0.6717	0.6084	0.5513	0.4529	0.3066	0.2083	0.1420	0.0972
41	0.6650	0.6009	0.5431	0.4440	0.2976	0.2003	0.1353	0.0917
42	0.6584	0.5935	0.5351	0.4353	0.2890	0.1926	0.1288	0.0865
43	0.6519	0.5862	0.5272	0.4268	0.2805	0.1852	0.1227	0.0816
44	0.6454	0.5789	0.5194	0.4184	0.2724	0.1780	0.1169	0.0770
45	0.6391	0.5718	0.5117	0.4102	0.2644	0.1712	0.1113	0.0727
46	0.6327	0.5647	0.5042	0.4022	0.2567	0.1646	0.1060	0.0685
47	0.6265	0.5577	0.4967	0.3943	0.2493	0.1583	0.1010	0.0647
48	0.6203	0.5509	0.4894	0.3865	0.2420	0.1522	0.0961	0.0610
49	0.6141	0.5441	0.4821	0.3790	0.2350	0.1463	0.0916	0.0575
50	0.6080	0.5373	0.4750	0.3715	0.2281	0.1407	0.0872	0.0543

$$i = 07 \text{ to } 14; \ N = 01 \text{ to } 50$$

N	7%	8%	9%	10%	11%	12%	13%	14%
1	0.9346	0.9259	0.9174	0.9091	0.9009	0.8929	0.8850	0.8772
2	0.8734	0.8573	0.8417	0.8264	0.8116	0.7972	0.7831	0.7695
3	0.8163	0.7938	0.7722	0.7513	0.7312	0.7118	0.6931	0.6750
4	0.7629	0.7350	0.7084	0.6830	0.6587	0.6355	0.6133	0.5921
5	0.7130	0.6806	0.6499	0.6209	0.5935	0.5674	0.5428	0.5194
6	0.6663	0.6302	0.5963	0.5645	0.5346	0.5066	0.4803	0.4556
7	0.6228	0.5835	0.5470	0.5132	0.4817	0.4523	0.4251	0.3996
8	0.5820	0.5403	0.5019	0.4665	0.4339	0.4039	0.3762	0.3506
9	0.5439	0.5002	0.4604	0.4241	0.3909	0.3606	0.3329	0.3075
10	0.5083	0.4632	0.4224	0.3855	0.3522	0.3220	0.2946	0.2697
11	0.4751	0.4289	0.3875	0.3505	0.3173	0.2875	0.2607	0.2366
12	0.4440	0.3971	0.3555	0.3186	0.2858	0.2567	0.2307	0.2076
13	0.4150	0.3677	0.3262	0.2897	0.2575	0.2292	0.2042	0.1821
14	0.3878	0.3405	0.2992	0.2633	0.2320	0.2046	0.1807	0.1597
15	0.3624	0.3152	0.2745	0.2394	0.2090	0.1827	0.1599	0.1401
16	0.3387	0.2919	0.2519	0.2176	0.1883	0.1631	0.1415	0.1229
17	0.3166	0.2703	0.2311	0.1978	0.1696	0.1456	0.1252	0.1078
18	0.2959	0.2502	0.2120	0.1799	0.1528	0.1300	0.1108	0.0946
19	0.2765	0.2317	0.1945	0.1635	0.1377	0.1161	0.0981	0.0829
20	0.2584	0.2145	0.1784	0.1486	0.1240	0.1037	0.0868	0.0728
21	0.2415	0.1987	0.1637	0.1351	0.1117	0.0926	0.0768	0.0638
22	0.2257	0.1839	0.1502	0.1228	0.1007	0.0826	0.0680	0.0560
23	0.2109	0.1703	0.1378	0.1117	0.0907	0.0738	0.0601	0.0491
24	0.1971	0.1577	0.1264	0.1015	0.0817	0.0659	0.0532	0.0431
25	0.1842	0.1460	0.1160	0.0923	0.0736	0.0588	0.0471	0.0378
26	0.1722	0.1352	0.1064	0.0839	0.0663	0.0525	0.0417	0.0331
27	0.1609	0.1252	0.0976	0.0763	0.0597	0.0469	0.0369	0.0291
28	0.1504	0.1159	0.0895	0.0693	0.0538	0.0419	0.0326	0.0255
29	0.1406	0.1073	0.0822	0.0630	0.0485	0.0374	0.0289	0.0224
30	0.1314	0.0994	0.0754	0.0573	0.0437	0.0334	0.0256	0.0196
31	0.1228	0.0920	0.0691	0.0521	0.0394	0.0298	0.0226	0.0172
32	0.1147	0.0852	0.0634	0.0474	0.0355	0.0266	0.0200	0.0151
33	0.1072	0.0789	0.0582	0.0431	0.0319	0.0238	0.0177	0.0132
34	0.1002	0.0730	0.0534	0.0391	0.0288	0.0212	0.0157	0.0116
35	0.0937	0.0676	0.0490	0.0356	0.0259	0.0189	0.0139	0.0102
36	0.0875	0.0626	0.0449	0.0323	0.0234	0.0169	0.0123	0.0089
37	0.0818	0.0580	0.0412	0.0294	0.0210	0.0151	0.0109	0.0078
38	0.0765	0.0537	0.0378	0.0267	0.0190	0.0135	0.0096	0.0069
39	0.0715	0.0497	0.0347	0.0243	0.0171	0.0120	0.0085	0.0060
40	0.0668	0.0460	0.0318	0.0221	0.0154	0.0107	0.0075	0.0053
41	0.0624	0.0426	0.0292	0.0201	0.0139	0.0096	0.0067	0.0046
42	0.0583	0.0395	0.0268	0.0183	0.0125	0.0086	0.0059	0.0041
43	0.0545	0.0365	0.0246	0.0166	0.0112	0.0076	0.0052	0.0036
44	0.0509	0.0338	0.0226	0.0151	0.0101	0.0068	0.0046	0.0031
45	0.0476	0.0313	0.0207	0.0137	0.0091	0.0061	0.0041	0.0027
46	0.0445	0.0290	0.0190	0.0125	0.0082	0.0054	0.0036	0.0024
47	0.0416	0.0269	0.0174	0.0113	0.0074	0.0049	0.0032	0.0021
48	0.0389	0.0249	0.0160	0.0103	0.0067	0.0043	0.0028	0.0019
49	0.0363	0.0230	0.0147	0.0094	0.0060	0.0039	0.0025	0.0016
50	0.0339	0.0213	0.0134	0.0085	0.0054	0.0035	0.0022	0.0014

$i = 15$ to 50; $N = 01$ to 50

N	15%	20%	25%	30%	35%	40%	45%	50%
1	0.8696	0.8333	0.8000	0.7692	0.7407	0.7143	0.6897	0.6667
2	0.7561	0.6944	0.6400	0.5917	0.5487	0.5102	0.4756	0.4444
3	0.6575	0.5787	0.5120	0.4552	0.4064	0.3644	0.3280	0.2963
4	0.5718	0.4823	0.4096	0.3501	0.3011	0.2603	0.2262	0.1975
5	0.4972	0.4019	0.3277	0.2693	0.2230	0.1859	0.1560	0.1317
6	0.4323	0.3349	0.2621	0.2072	0.1652	0.1328	0.1076	0.0878
7	0.3759	0.2791	0.2097	0.1594	0.1224	0.0949	0.0742	0.0585
8	0.3269	0.2326	0.1678	0.1226	0.0906	0.0678	0.0512	0.0390
9	0.2843	0.1938	0.1342	0.0943	0.0671	0.0484	0.0353	0.0260
10	0.2472	0.1615	0.1074	0.0725	0.0497	0.0346	0.0243	0.0173
11	0.2149	0.1346	0.0859	0.0558	0.0368	0.0247	0.0168	0.0116
12	0.1869	0.1122	0.0687	0.0429	0.0273	0.0176	0.0116	0.0077
13	0.1625	0.0935	0.0550	0.0330	0.0202	0.0126	0.0080	0.0051
14	0.1413	0.0779	0.0440	0.0254	0.0150	0.0090	0.0055	0.0034
15	0.1229	0.0649	0.0352	0.0195	0.0111	0.0064	0.0038	0.0023
16	0.1069	0.0541	0.0281	0.0150	0.0082	0.0046	0.0026	0.0015
17	0.0929	0.0451	0.0225	0.0116	0.0061	0.0033	0.0018	0.0010
18	0.0808	0.0376	0.0180	0.0089	0.0045	0.0023	0.0012	0.0007
19	0.0703	0.0313	0.0144	0.0068	0.0033	0.0017	0.0009	0.0005
20	0.0611	0.0261	0.0115	0.0053	0.0025	0.0012	0.0006	0.0003
21	0.0531	0.0217	0.0092	0.0040	0.0018	0.0009	0.0004	0.0002
22	0.0462	0.0181	0.0074	0.0031	0.0014	0.0006	0.0003	0.0001
23	0.0402	0.0151	0.0059	0.0024	0.0010	0.0004	0.0002	0.0001
24	0.0349	0.0126	0.0047	0.0018	0.0007	0.0003	0.0001	0.0001
25	0.0304	0.0105	0.0038	0.0014	0.0006	0.0002	0.0001	0.0000
26	0.0264	0.0087	0.0030	0.0011	0.0004	0.0002	0.0001	0.0000
27	0.0230	0.0073	0.0024	0.0008	0.0003	0.0001	0.0000	0.0000
28	0.0200	0.0061	0.0019	0.0006	0.0002	0.0001	0.0000	0.0000
29	0.0174	0.0051	0.0015	0.0005	0.0002	0.0001	0.0000	0.0000
30	0.0151	0.0042	0.0012	0.0004	0.0001	0.0000	0.0000	0.0000
31	0.0131	0.0035	0.0010	0.0003	0.0001	0.0000	0.0000	0.0000
32	0.0114	0.0029	0.0008	0.0002	0.0001	0.0000	0.0000	0.0000
33	0.0099	0.0024	0.0006	0.0002	0.0001	0.0000	0.0000	0.0000
34	0.0086	0.0020	0.0005	0.0001	0.0000	0.0000	0.0000	0.0000
35	0.0075	0.0017	0.0004	0.0001	0.0000	0.0000	0.0000	0.0000
36	0.0065	0.0014	0.0003	0.0001	0.0000	0.0000	0.0000	0.0000
37	0.0057	0.0012	0.0003	0.0001	0.0000	0.0000	0.0000	0.0000
38	0.0049	0.0010	0.0002	0.0000	0.0000	0.0000	0.0000	0.0000
39	0.0043	0.0008	0.0002	0.0000	0.0000	0.0000	0.0000	0.0000
40	0.0037	0.0007	0.0001	0.0000	0.0000	0.0000	0.0000	0.0000
41	0.0032	0.0006	0.0001	0.0000	0.0000	0.0000	0.0000	0.0000
42	0.0028	0.0005	0.0001	0.0000	0.0000	0.0000	0.0000	0.0000
43	0.0025	0.0004	0.0001	0.0000	0.0000	0.0000	0.0000	0.0000
44	0.0021	0.0003	0.0001	0.0000	0.0000	0.0000	0.0000	0.0000
45	0.0019	0.0003	0.0000	0.0000	0.0000	0.0000	0.0000	0.0000
46	0.0016	0.0002	0.0000	0.0000	0.0000	0.0000	0.0000	0.0000
47	0.0014	0.0002	0.0000	0.0000	0.0000	0.0000	0.0000	0.0000
48	0.0012	0.0002	0.0000	0.0000	0.0000	0.0000	0.0000	0.0000
49	0.0011	0.0001	0.0000	0.0000	0.0000	0.0000	0.0000	0.0000
50	0.0009	0.0001	0.0000	0.0000	0.0000	0.0000	0.0000	0.0000

Table B: Present Value of a Stream of Payments/Receipts
of $1 Each Period,*

$$PV_B = \frac{1 - \dfrac{1}{(1 + i)^n}}{i}$$

where i = interest rate per period and n = number of periods.

---

* Also known as present value of ordinary annuity of one dollar.

$i = 01$ to 06; $N = 01$ to 50

N	1%	1.25%	1.5%	2%	3%	4%	5%	6%
1	0.9901	0.9877	0.9852	0.9804	0.9709	0.9615	0.9524	0.9434
2	1.9704	1.9631	1.9559	1.9416	1.9135	1.8861	1.8594	1.8334
3	2.9410	2.9266	2.9122	2.8839	2.8286	2.7751	2.7233	2.6730
4	3.9020	3.8781	3.8544	3.8077	3.7171	3.6299	3.5460	3.4651
5	4.8534	4.8179	4.7826	4.7135	4.5797	4.4518	4.3295	4.2124
6	5.7955	5.7460	5.6972	5.6014	5.4172	5.2421	5.0757	4.9173
7	6.7282	6.6628	6.5982	6.4720	6.2303	6.0021	5.7864	5.5824
8	7.6517	7.5682	7.4859	7.3255	7.0197	6.7327	6.4632	6.2098
9	8.5660	8.4624	8.3605	8.1622	7.7861	7.4353	7.1078	6.8017
10	9.4713	9.3456	9.2222	8.9826	8.5302	8.1109	7.7217	7.3601
11	10.3676	10.2179	10.0711	9.7868	9.2526	8.7605	8.3064	7.8869
12	11.2551	11.0794	10.9075	10.5753	9.9540	9.3851	8.8632	8.3838
13	12.1337	11.9302	11.7315	11.3484	10.6350	9.9856	9.3936	8.8527
14	13.0037	12.7706	12.5433	12.1062	11.2961	10.5631	9.8986	9.2950
15	13.8650	13.6006	13.3432	12.8492	11.9379	11.1184	10.3796	9.7122
16	14.7179	14.4204	14.1312	13.5777	12.5611	11.6523	10.8378	10.1059
17	15.5622	15.2300	14.9076	14.2918	13.1661	12.1657	11.2741	10.4773
18	16.3983	16.0296	15.6725	14.9920	13.7535	12.6593	11.6896	10.8276
19	17.2260	16.8194	16.4261	15.6784	14.3238	13.1339	12.0853	11.1581
20	18.0455	17.5994	17.1686	16.3514	14.8775	13.5903	12.4622	11.4699
21	18.8570	18.3698	17.9001	17.0112	15.4150	14.0292	12.8211	11.7641
22	19.6604	19.1307	18.6208	17.6580	15.9369	14.4511	13.1630	12.0416
23	20.4558	19.8821	19.3308	18.2922	16.4436	14.8568	13.4886	12.3034
24	21.2434	20.6243	20.0304	18.9139	16.9355	15.2470	13.7986	12.5504
25	22.0232	21.3574	20.7196	19.5234	17.4131	15.6221	14.0939	12.7834
26	22.7952	22.0814	21.3986	20.1210	17.8768	15.9828	14.3752	13.0032
27	23.5596	22.7964	22.0676	20.7069	18.3270	16.3296	14.6430	13.2105
28	24.3164	23.5026	22.7267	21.2812	18.7641	16.6631	14.8981	13.4062
29	25.0658	24.2001	23.3760	21.8443	19.1885	16.9837	15.1411	13.5907
30	25.8077	24.8890	24.0158	22.3964	19.6004	17.2920	15.3724	13.7648
31	26.5423	25.5694	24.6461	22.9377	20.0004	17.5885	15.5928	13.9291
32	27.2696	26.2415	25.2671	23.4683	20.3888	17.8735	15.8027	14.0840
33	27.9897	26.9052	25.8789	23.9886	20.7658	18.1476	16.0025	14.2302
34	28.7027	27.5606	26.4817	24.4986	21.1318	18.4112	16.1929	14.3681
35	29.4086	28.2080	27.0756	24.9986	21.4872	18.6646	16.3742	14.4982
36	30.1075	28.8475	27.6607	25.4888	21.8322	18.9083	16.5468	14.6210
37	30.7995	29.4790	28.2371	25.9695	22.1672	19.1426	16.7113	14.7368
38	31.4847	30.1027	28.8050	26.4406	22.4925	19.3679	16.8679	14.8460
39	32.1631	30.7187	29.3645	26.9026	22.8082	19.5845	17.0170	14.9491
40	32.8347	31.3271	29.9158	27.3555	23.1148	19.7928	17.1591	15.0463
41	33.4997	31.9280	30.4589	27.7995	23.4124	19.9930	17.2944	15.1380
42	34.1581	32.5215	30.9940	28.2348	23.7014	20.1856	17.4232	15.2245
43	34.8100	33.1077	31.5212	28.6616	23.9819	20.3708	17.5459	15.3062
44	35.4555	33.6866	32.0406	29.0800	24.2543	20.5488	17.6628	15.3832
45	36.0945	34.2584	32.5523	29.4902	24.5187	20.7200	17.7741	15.4558
46	36.7273	34.8231	33.0565	29.8923	24.7754	20.8847	17.8801	15.5244
47	37.3537	35.3808	33.5532	30.2866	25.0247	21.0429	17.9810	15.5890
48	37.9740	35.9317	34.0425	30.6731	25.2667	21.1951	18.0772	15.6500
49	38.5881	36.4758	34.5246	31.0521	25.5017	21.3415	18.1687	15.7076
50	39.1962	37.0131	34.9997	31.4236	25.7298	21.4822	18.2559	15.7619

$i = 07$ to 14; $N = 01$ to 50

N	7%	8%	9%	10%	11%	12%	13%	14%
1	0.9346	0.9259	0.9174	0.9091	0.9009	0.8929	0.8850	0.8772
2	1.8080	1.7833	1.7591	1.7355	1.7125	1.6901	1.6681	1.6467
3	2.6243	2.5771	2.5313	2.4869	2.4437	2.4018	2.3612	2.3216
4	3.3872	3.3121	3.2397	3.1699	3.1025	3.0374	2.9745	2.9137
5	4.1002	3.9927	3.8897	3.7908	3.6959	3.6048	3.5172	3.4331
6	4.7665	4.6229	4.4859	4.3553	4.2305	4.1114	3.9976	3.8887
7	5.3893	5.2064	5.0330	4.8684	4.7122	4.5638	4.4226	4.2883
8	5.9713	5.7466	5.5348	5.3349	5.1461	4.9676	4.7988	4.6389
9	6.5152	6.2469	5.9953	5.7590	5.5371	5.3283	5.1317	4.9464
10	7.0236	6.7101	6.4177	6.1446	5.8892	5.6502	5.4262	5.2161
11	7.4987	7.1390	6.8052	6.4951	6.2065	5.9377	5.6869	5.4527
12	7.9427	7.5361	7.1607	6.8137	6.4924	6.1944	5.9177	5.6603
13	8.3577	7.9038	7.4869	7.1034	6.7499	6.4236	6.1218	5.8424
14	8.7455	8.2442	7.7862	7.3667	6.9819	6.6282	6.3025	6.0021
15	9.1079	8.5595	8.0607	7.6061	7.1909	6.8109	6.4624	6.1422
16	9.4467	8.8514	8.3126	7.8237	7.3792	6.9740	6.6039	6.2651
17	9.7632	9.1216	8.5436	8.0216	7.5488	7.1196	6.7291	6.3729
18	10.0591	9.3719	8.7556	8.2014	7.7016	7.2497	6.8399	6.4674
19	10.3356	9.6036	8.9501	8.3649	7.8393	7.3658	6.9380	6.5504
20	10.5940	9.8182	9.1286	8.5136	7.9633	7.4694	7.0248	6.6231
21	10.8355	10.0168	9.2923	8.6487	8.0751	7.5620	7.1016	6.6870
22	11.0612	10.2007	9.4424	8.7715	8.1757	7.6447	7.1695	6.7429
23	11.2722	10.3711	9.5802	8.8832	8.2664	7.7184	7.2297	6.7921
24	11.4693	10.5288	9.7066	8.9847	8.3481	7.7843	7.2829	6.8351
25	11.6536	10.6748	9.8226	9.0770	8.4218	7.8431	7.3300	6.8729
26	11.8258	10.8100	9.9290	9.1610	8.4881	7.8957	7.3717	6.9061
27	11.9867	10.9352	10.0266	9.2372	8.5478	7.9426	7.4086	6.9352
28	12.1371	11.0511	10.1161	9.3066	8.6016	7.9844	7.4412	6.9607
29	12.2777	11.1584	10.1983	9.3696	8.6501	8.0218	7.4701	6.9830
30	12.4090	11.2578	10.2737	9.4269	8.6938	8.0552	7.4957	7.0027
31	12.5318	11.3498	10.3428	9.4790	8.7332	8.0850	7.5183	7.0199
32	12.6466	11.4350	10.4062	9.5264	8.7686	8.1116	7.5383	7.0350
33	12.7538	11.5139	10.4644	9.5694	8.8005	8.1354	7.5560	7.0482
34	12.8540	11.5869	10.5178	9.6086	8.8293	8.1566	7.5717	7.0599
35	12.9477	11.6546	10.5668	9.6442	8.8552	8.1755	7.5856	7.0701
36	13.0352	11.7172	10.6118	9.6765	8.8786	8.1924	7.5979	7.0790
37	13.1170	11.7752	10.6530	9.7059	8.8996	8.2075	7.6087	7.0868
38	13.1935	11.8289	10.6908	9.7327	8.9186	8.2210	7.6183	7.0937
39	13.2649	11.8786	10.7255	9.7570	8.9357	8.2330	7.6269	7.0998
40	13.3317	11.9246	10.7574	9.7791	8.9511	8.2438	7.6344	7.1050
41	13.3941	11.9672	10.7866	9.7991	8.9649	8.2534	7.6410	7.1097
42	13.4525	12.0067	10.8134	9.8174	8.9774	8.2619	7.6469	7.1138
43	13.5070	12.0432	10.8380	9.8340	8.9887	8.2696	7.6522	7.1173
44	13.5579	12.0771	10.8605	9.8491	8.9988	8.2764	7.6568	7.1205
45	13.6055	12.1084	10.8812	9.8628	9.0079	8.2825	7.6609	7.1232
46	13.6500	12.1374	10.9002	9.8753	9.0161	8.2880	7.6645	7.1256
47	13.6916	12.1643	10.9176	9.8866	9.0236	8.2928	7.6677	7.1277
48	13.7305	12.1891	10.9336	9.8969	9.0302	8.2972	7.6705	7.1296
49	13.7668	12.2122	10.9482	9.9063	9.0362	8.3010	7.6730	7.1312
50	13.8007	12.2335	10.9617	9.9148	9.0417	8.3045	7.6752	7.1327

$i = 15$ to 50; $N = 01$ to 50

N	15%	20%	25%	30%	35%	40%	45%	50%
1	0.8696	0.8333	0.8000	0.7692	0.7407	0.7143	0.6897	0.6667
2	1.6257	1.5278	1.4400	1.3610	1.2894	1.2245	1.1653	1.1111
3	2.2832	2.1065	1.9520	1.8161	1.6959	1.5889	1.4933	1.4074
4	2.8550	2.5887	2.3616	2.1662	1.9970	1.8492	1.7195	1.6049
5	3.3522	2.9906	2.6893	2.4356	2.2200	2.0352	1.8755	1.7366
6	3.7845	3.3255	2.9514	2.6428	2.3852	2.1680	1.9831	1.8244
7	4.1604	3.6046	3.1611	2.8021	2.5075	2.2628	2.0573	1.8829
8	4.4873	3.8372	3.3289	2.9247	2.5982	2.3306	2.1085	1.9220
9	4.7716	4.0310	3.4631	3.0190	2.6653	2.3790	2.1438	1.9480
10	5.0188	4.1925	3.5705	3.0915	2.7150	2.4136	2.1681	1.9653
11	5.2337	4.3271	3.6564	3.1473	2.7519	2.4383	2.1849	1.9769
12	5.4206	4.4392	3.7251	3.1903	2.7792	2.4559	2.1965	1.9846
13	5.5832	4.5327	3.7801	3.2233	2.7994	2.4685	2.2045	1.9897
14	5.7245	4.6106	3.8241	3.2487	2.8144	2.4775	2.2100	1.9932
15	5.8474	4.6755	3.8593	3.2682	2.8255	2.4839	2.2138	1.9954
16	5.9542	4.7296	3.8874	3.2832	2.8337	2.4885	2.2164	1.9970
17	6.0472	4.7746	3.9099	3.2948	2.8398	2.4918	2.2182	1.9980
18	6.1280	4.8122	3.9279	3.3037	2.8443	2.4941	2.2195	1.9987
19	6.1982	4.8435	3.9424	3.3105	2.8476	2.4958	2.2203	1.9991
20	6.2593	4.8696	3.9539	3.3158	2.8501	2.4970	2.2209	1.9994
21	6.3125	4.8913	3.9631	3.3198	2.8519	2.4979	2.2213	1.9996
22	6.3587	4.9094	3.9705	3.3230	2.8533	2.4985	2.2216	1.9997
23	6.3988	4.9245	3.9764	3.3254	2.8543	2.4989	2.2218	1.9998
24	6.4338	4.9371	3.9811	3.3272	2.8550	2.4992	2.2219	1.9999
25	6.4642	4.9476	3.9849	3.3286	2.8556	2.4994	2.2220	1.9999
26	6.4906	4.9563	3.9879	3.3297	2.8560	2.4996	2.2221	2.0000
27	6.5135	4.9636	3.9903	3.3305	2.8563	2.4997	2.2221	2.0000
28	6.5335	4.9697	3.9923	3.3312	2.8565	2.4998	2.2222	2.0000
29	6.5509	4.9747	3.9938	3.3317	2.8567	2.4999	2.2222	2.0000
30	6.5660	4.9789	3.9951	3.3321	2.8568	2.4999	2.2222	2.0000
31	6.5791	4.9825	3.9960	3.3324	2.8569	2.4999	2.2222	2.0000
32	6.5905	4.9854	3.9968	3.3326	2.8570	2.5000	2.2222	2.0000
33	6.6006	4.9878	3.9975	3.3328	2.8570	2.5000	2.2222	2.0000
34	6.6091	4.9898	3.9980	3.3329	2.8570	2.5000	2.2222	2.0000
35	6.6166	4.9915	3.9984	3.3330	2.8571	2.5000	2.2222	2.0000
36	6.6231	4.9930	3.9987	3.3331	2.8571	2.5000	2.2222	2.0000
37	6.6288	4.9941	3.9990	3.3331	2.8571	2.5000	2.2222	2.0000
38	6.6338	4.9951	3.9992	3.3332	2.8571	2.5000	2.2222	2.0000
39	6.6381	4.9959	3.9993	3.3332	2.8571	2.5000	2.2222	2.0000
40	6.6418	4.9966	3.9995	3.3332	2.8571	2.5000	2.2222	2.0000
41	6.6450	4.9972	3.9996	3.3333	2.8571	2.5000	2.2222	2.0000
42	6.6479	4.9976	3.9997	3.3333	2.8571	2.5000	2.2222	2.0000
43	6.6503	4.9980	3.9997	3.3333	2.8571	2.5000	2.2222	2.0000
44	6.6524	4.9984	3.9998	3.3333	2.8571	2.5000	2.2222	2.0000
45	6.6543	4.9986	3.9998	3.3333	2.8571	2.5000	2.2222	2.0000
46	6.6559	4.9989	3.9999	3.3333	2.8571	2.5000	2.2222	2.0000
47	6.6573	4.9991	3.9999	3.3333	2.8571	2.5000	2.2222	2.0000
48	6.6585	4.9992	3.9999	3.3333	2.8571	2.5000	2.2222	2.0000
49	6.6596	4.9993	3.9999	3.3333	2.8571	2.5000	2.2222	2.0000
50	6.6605	4.9995	3.9999	3.3333	2.8571	2.5000	2.2222	2.0000

C

GLOSSARY OF
BUSINESS AND
ACCOUNTING TERMS

[*Note:* For those terms discussed in greater depth in the main body of the text, the number of the chapter wherein the term was first introduced is shown in parentheses.]

AAA (1)   American Accounting Association.

Accelerated depreciation (9)   Any method of calculating depreciation where the charges become progressively smaller. *See* **Double-declining-balance** and **Years' digits** methods.

Account (4)   A file for the accumulation of data on an item or group of similar items.

Accounting changes (15)   Changes in accounting method, accounting estimate, or the accounting entity.

Accounting cycle (4)   The sequence of steps followed by accountants, throughout the year (period).

Accounting entity   *See* **Entity.**

Accounting estimate (9)   An estimate incorporated in a particular accounting measurement such as the period of useful life and the salvage value for a fixed asset.

Accounting method (15)   A procedure for measuring and reporting financial information in conformance with GAAP.

Accounts payable (2)   A current liability representing obligations to creditors for goods and services purchased.

Accounts receivable (2)   A current asset representing claims against customers for goods or services sold on account.

Accrual (5)   An amount recorded by an adjusting entry in recognition of a claim earned or obligation owed for which formal invoicing or payment has not occurred.

Accrual basis (income) (4)   Income measured on the basis of revenues earned less expenses, matched to related revenues independent of the timing of cash receipts and payments.

Accumulated depreciation (2)   A contra-asset reporting the sum of all depreciation charges since an asset was acquired.

Acid-test ratio   *See* **Quick ratio.**

Acquisition (of a firm)   *See* **Business combination.**

Adjusted original cost (2)   A description of the current GAAP basis for measuring and reporting nonmonetary assets. These assets are originally recorded at cost and subsequently adjusted downwards to reflect expiration of usefulness or loss of recoverable value.

Adjusted trial balance The trial balance taken after completion of adjustments and before closing.

Adjusting entry (4) An entry made at the end of an accounting period to record an event not previously recorded or recorded improperly. Examples include accruals, asset expirations, loss of recoverable values, discount or premium amortizations, revenue deferrals, and so forth.

Adjustment (4) The change in account balances resulting from an adjusting entry.

Affirmatively misleading detail (3) Reported amounts with such detail that an impression of accuracy (which is not realistic) is given to the reader. An example would be depreciation calculated and reported to the *nearest cent*.

Aging accounts receivable The classification of accounts on the basis of the time passed since the date of sale.

AICPA (1) American Institute of Certified Public Accountants.

Allowance for depreciation. *See* **Accumulated depreciation.**

Allowance for uncollectibles (2) A contra-asset indicating the amount of active receivables that are expected to prove uncollectible.

Amortization (2) The general process of systematically reducing an account balance to reflect asset expiration or the allocation of premiums and discounts to time periods. Known as *depletion* for wasting assets, and as *depreciation* for tangible fixed assets.

Amount to be depreciated (9) *See* **Depreciable base.**

Annual report (1) A report prepared once a year by a corporation for its stockholders and other interested parties. It contains the year's financial statements, footnotes, auditor's opinion, and such other nonaudited information as management desires to disseminate.

Application of funds (7) Five possible uses of additional working capital other than funds lost in operations may be considered *applications*. They include working capital lost as an extraordinary loss, working capital used to acquire noncurrent assets, working capital used to retire noncurrent debt, dividends declared, and, finally, working capital generated elsewhere and used to increase the year-end balance of net working capital on hand.

Appropriation (10) In financial accounting, the segregation of a portion of retained earnings by action of the Board of Directors, to reflect a legal restriction of retained earnings available for dividends, or to reflect an intention to withhold future dividends. In government accounting, the authorization for a specific expenditure.

"Arm's length" (9) Refers to transactions between unrelated parties which may be used as evidence of fair market value.

Asset (2)   A property, right, or claim with future objectively measurable value that is owned or effectively controlled by the firm.

Asset composition (3)   A term used in financial analysis referring to the mix of more liquid current assets as compared with less liquid noncurrent assets.

Asset expiration (4)   The decline in future service potential of an asset as a result of deterioration and obsolescence.

Asset turnover (13)   The ratio of net sales to average total assets.

Audit (1)   An examination of accounting records, procedures, and controls to ensure their adequacy in conformance with GAAP and company objectives.

Audit trail (17)   A system of cross-referencing information throughout accounting records, from original source document to final account posting.

Auditor's opinion (1)   The auditor's statement accompanying the financial statements indicating the extent of the audit and giving an evaluation of the adequacy and fairness of the financial statements in conformance with GAAP.

Authorized stock   The maximum number of shares of stock that a corporation may issue without obtaining further authorization from the state in which it is incorporated.

Average cost (inventory) (8)   One of several possible inventory cost-flow assumptions. Weighted average cost assumes that the cost of items shipped represented a proportional sample of the cost of all items available for sale. Ending inventory and cost of goods sold are priced at the same average cost per unit under this method. The average cost per unit is calculated by taking the sum of the products of [quantity times cost] for beginning inventory and net purchases, and then dividing by the quantity of items available for sale.

Average days' receivables (13)   A measure of the average time necessary to collect accounts receivable. Calculated by dividing *receivables turnover* into 365.

Average days' sales in inventory (13)   A measure of inventory turnover, or the average amount of inventory on hand in terms of sales. Calculated by dividing *inventory turnover* into 365.

Bad debt   An account receivable that is not deemed collectible.

Bad-debt expense   The sum of all accounts receivable determined to be uncollectible during the year, plus an allowance for still-active receivables at year end expected to become uncollectible.

Balance sheet (1)   The financial statement reporting assets and equities as of a specific date. Also known as a Statement of Financial Position.

"Basket-purchase" (9)   The acquisition of a group of assets for a single price where the cost must be allocated to different members of the group for accounting purposes.

Beginning inventory   The amount of inventory on hand at the start of the accounting period.

Betterment (9)   An improvement to a capacity asset which is properly capitalized as an additional asset.

Board of directors (10)   A group of individuals elected by the voting stockholders of a corporation to govern the company.

Bond (11)   A negotiable certificate as evidence of debt.

Bond conversion   See Debt conversion.

Bond discount (11)   A contra-account representing the amount of interest capitalized into the face value of a bond and not yet earned/owed.

Bond premium (11)   An account representing the amount of cash given by the bond buyer in excess of face value for the privilege of receiving greater-than-"normal" future interest payments.

Bond sinking fund (11)   See Sinking fund.

Bonds payable (2)   A liability reporting the face value of outstanding bond indebtedness.

Book value (2)   The amount recorded in the firm's accounts. For particular assets and liabilities, refers to the item net of valuation accounts. For common stock, refers to share of total assets not claimed by creditors and preferred stockholders. For the firm as a whole, equals net assets (total assets minus total liabilities).

Book value of common stock (10)   The amount of assets not claimed by creditors or preferred stockholders—common shareholders' equity. See Book value per share.

Book value per share (of common stock) (10)   Total stockholders' equity less preferred claims, divided by number of common shares outstanding.

"Booked" (12)   Slang for "recorded in the firm's accounts."

"Bottom line" (6)   Commonly used term referring to reported net income, the bottom line of the income statement.

Business combination (15)   The joining of two previously separate firms into a single accounting entity, whether by consolidation or statutory merger. Will be accounted for by following either the pooling or the purchase method.

Business entities (2)   See Entity.

Call premium (12)   The amount of excess over par which a firm will pay if it elects to retire debt before maturity.

Callable bonds (12)   Bonds that may be called (or *retired*) in advance of maturity.

Capacity assets (2)   *See* **Fixed assets.**

Capital-lease obligations (2)   A liability. The present value of remaining obligations under leases qualifying as capital leases. Capital-lease obligations may be both current and noncurrent.

Capital budgeting (7)   Refers to the process of evaluating, selecting, and scheduling acquisition of long-term assets, and of planning the financing of such acquisitions.

Capital invested   Refers to resources (assets) invested in a firm by creditors and owners.

Capitalize (9)   To record the effect of an expenditure as an asset rather than as an expense.

Capital lease (9)   A lease which, in substance, is effectively a purchase with 100-percent financing. Leases which qualify as capital leases under specific FASB criteria are capitalized and shown as fixed assets and as debt.

Capital markets (7)   Refers to various markets to which a firm may turn to raise additional invested capital. Examples would be the bond markets and the stock markets.

Capital stock (10)   The ownership shares of a corporation.

Capital structure (7)   The composition of a firm's equities. The mix of current debt, noncurrent debt, and owners' equity.

Capital surplus   An inferior term for *paid-in capital.*

Capitalized interest   Interest incorporated into the face value of a debt instrument (note or bond).

CASB (1)   Cost Accounting Standards Board.

Cash (2)   Currency, checks, and bank-account balances.

Cash-basis (income) (4)   Income measured on the basis of cash revenues received less cash expenditures occurring in the same period.

Cash budgeting (7)   *See* **Cash management.**

Cash discount   A reduction in sales or purchase price provided for prompt payment.

Cash from operations (14)   The amount of cash generated from ordinary business revenues, less expenses for the period, and including any changes within net working capital involving cash flows.

Cash funds-flow statement (14)   *See* **Statement of cash flow.**

Cash management (7)   The planning and control of cash receipts and disbursements within the firm. The objective is to avoid cash shortage and to temporarily invest excess cash.

Cash sales   Sales to customers for cash. Customer pays cash at time of purchase.

"Certain" liabilities (12)   Liabilities which exist as a result of past transactions, where the amount and date of payment are specifically known.

Certified financial statements (1)   Statements which are accompanied by an independent auditor's (CPA's) certificate or opinion.

Change in accounting method (9)   *See* **Accounting method.**

Change of accounting estimate (9)   *See* **Accounting estimate.**

Charge (17)   Generally used to mean purchase on account. In accounting, also used synonymously with *debit*.

Close/closing (accounts) (5)   The process, at year end, of transferring the balances in all nominal or temporary accounts to the real or permanent balance sheet accounts. For example, all revenue, gain, expense, and loss accounts at year end are closed to retained earnings (owner's capital).

CMA (1)   Certificate in Management Accounting awarded by the National Association of Accountants.

Collection of receivable (4)   The receipt of cash in partial or full settlement of a claim that is evidenced by a receivable.

Common book value (stock) (10)   *See* **Book value.**

Common stock (10)   Shares in a corporation, usually voting shares, and representing a residual claim against assets after settlement of creditors' and preferred stockholders' prior claims.

Comparative analysis (3)   In financial-statement analysis, the comparison of one firm's statements with those of other firms or with industry norms.

Completed-contract method (11)   Refers to the timing of revenue and expense recognition for a particular job order. Under completed-contract recognition, revenues and expenses are normally included in income determination only after the job is finished. Alternative to *percentage completion* method.

Composite depreciation (9)   *See* **Group depreciation.**

Compound entry   A journal entry affecting more than two accounts concurrently.

Compound interest   Interest based on principal and accumulated prior-period interest.

Comptroller   *See* **Controller.**

Conglomerate   A parent corporation with subsidiaries in different and dissimilar lines of business.

Conservatism (1)   A measurement principle under GAAP, wherein expenses and losses are recognized and reported when incurred or expected, but revenues and gains are not recognized and reported until they are realized or earned.

Consignment   Refers to inventory transferred from the owner (consignor) to another (consignee) for sale to third parties.

Consistency (3)   A measurement principle under GAAP providing for continued use by a firm of the same accounting method or procedure once adopted. Consistency requires that changes in accounting method be infrequent and be justified by changing circumstances.

Consolidated financial statements (11)   Statements prepared for an economic entity comprised of several legal entities—a parent and its subsidiaries.

Contingent liability (12)   A potential liability, such as a pending lawsuit, which is dependent upon a future event (an adverse judgment being rendered) before becoming definite.

Contra-account   Any valuation account whose balance is subtracted from another account on the balance sheet. Examples include allowance for uncollectibles, accumulated depreciation, and receivables discount or bond discount.

Contra-asset (4)   A negative valuation account related to an asset account.

Contributed capital (10)   The amount of capital permanently invested or contributed by the owners. Normally, the sum of capital stock and paid-in capital accounts.

Control account (17)   An amount in the general ledger that shows the sum of the balances in individual subsidiary accounts kept in a subsidiary ledger.

Controller   The title often used for the officer responsible for all accounting and sometimes all information-systems activities within a firm.

Conversion index (16)   An index constructed from two representative prices, used to adjust groups of assets for changing price levels or replacement costs.

Convertible debenture (10)   A bond that may be exchanged by the bondholder for a given number of shares of capital stock.

Corporation   A legal entity authorized by a state to conduct business or perform some other function.

Cost   The amount paid, or to be paid, for the acquisition of goods or services.

Cost expiration (2)   The recognition by accountants of a decline in future usefulness or eventual recoverable value of an asset. *See* **Amortization, Depreciation,** and **Depreciation.**

Cost method (for investments) (11)   The measurement normally applied to all investments except for voting common stock representing more than 20 percent of outstanding shares. The investment is carried at acquisition cost, and revenue is recognized only when received or receivable—interest earned or dividends declared. Alternative to *equity method.*

Cost of goods sold (5)   The cost of inventory that has been sold to customers or that has otherwise disappeared—inventory expense.

Cost of sales (8)   *See* **Cost of goods sold.**

Cost or market, whichever is lower   *See* **LOCM.**

Cost principle   The measurement principle under GAAP which requires assets to be reported at adjusted original cost.

CPA (1)   Certified Public Accountant.

Cr (or Cr)   Abbreviation for **Credit.**

Credit (17)   In general business usage, refers to the privilege of purchasing or borrowing, with payment or repayment at a later date. In accounting, refers to the right side of an account or to record an amount on the right side of an account.

Creditor (1)   Someone who has a legal claim against the firm's assets resulting from supplying the firm with goods or services, lending funds, or some other commitment (customer claim for warranty, government claim for taxes, plaintiff claim for legally awarded judgment, or stockholder claim for dividends previously declared).

Credit sales (2)   Sales to customers on account.

Current assets (2)   Cash and any other assets that are expected to be converted into cash or consumed within a year or within the firm's normal operating cycle.

Current capital-lease obligations (2)   The present value of amounts owed within one year under leases qualifying as capital leases.

Current liabilities (2)   Those liabilities that are payable within one year or the firm's normal operating cycle, and which will require current assets in settlement.

Current ratio (3)   Total current assets divided by total current liabilities.

CVD (12)   *See* **Convertible debenture.**

DDB (9)   *See* **Double-declining-balance method.**

Debenture   A bond that is not secured by a prior claim against specific assets or income.

Debit (17)   Refers to the left side of an account, or to the recording of an amount on the left side of an account.

Debt   Any amount owed.

Debt conversion (7)   The exchange of a creditor claim for an ownership claim. Usually the result of bondholders exchanging their convertible bonds for stock.

Debt ratio (3)   Total liabilities divided by total equities. Often referred to as the debt-equity ratio.

Debt refinancing (7)   Arranging for the exchange of new debt for existing debt, with the new debt usually having a later maturity. In the case of bonds, may be called a *refunding*.

Declining-balance method (9)   A method of calculating depreciation or amortization by applying a constant percentage to the declining book value in successive periods.

Deferral (5)   The carrying forward to a subsequent period of appropriate matching purposes of any item which will ultimately be recognized as revenue or expense.

Deferred charges (2)   A noncurrent asset. Expenditures capitalized as assets to be amortized over future years. Similar to prepaid items but having a useful life beyond that which would qualify for current classification.

Deferred income tax (9)   A liability of indeterminate term (and, possibly, amount) representing taxes postponed through timing differences resulting from the use of different income accounting methods in tax returns and financial statements.

Deferred method (9)   One of the methods acceptable for accounting for the investment tax credit. Following the deferred method, the tax savings are taken as a reduction of fixed asset cost. The benefit is thus deferred and picked up in higher income over the asset's useful life through lower depreciation charges.

Deferred revenue   A liability representing advances from customers. *See* **Revenue collected in advance.**

Deficit (10)   Negative retained earnings shown as contra to stockholders' equity.

Depletion (11)   The amortization reflecting use of wasting assets—natural resources such as oil, minerals, and timber.

Depreciable base (cost) (9)   The cost of a tangible fixed asset to be depreciated over the asset's useful life—the cost less estimated salvage value.

Depreciate/depreciation (2)   The amortization of tangible fixed assets to allocate cost expiration over their useful life.

Discontinued operations (6)   Activities or segments of a business which are being phased out. Revenues, gains, expenses, and losses related to discontinued operations are required by GAAP to be classified on the income statement, together with extraordinary items following income from operations.

Discounted present value (11)   The value today of a future stream of cash flows with the assumed interest cost or benefit eliminated.

Discount on notes receivable (11)   A contra asset representing interest capitalized into the face amount of the receivable but not yet earned.

Discount on payables   A contra liability representing interest capitalized into the face amount of the liability but not yet owed.

Discount on purchases or sales   A price reduction granted for prompt payment.

Discounting a receivable   The practice of borrowing funds in exchange for a receivable or with the receivable essentially serving as collateral for the loan.

Discount rate   The interest rate assumed in the calculation of *discounted present value*.

Discretionary resource exchanges (7)   A term used to apply to flows of resources into and out of a firm which occur as a result of management decisions. Discretionary resource exchanges are reported on the SCFP. Resource losses and expirations not resulting from discretionary action are not reported on the SCFP.

Distributable income (16)   The amount of current income which, assuming adequate solvency, could be withdrawn by owners while still maintaining the firm's capital as variously defined.

Dividend (10)   A distribution of income to corporate stockholders.

Dividends per share (13)   The amount of dividends accruing to the benefit of the holder of a single share of the firm's currently outstanding stock.

Double-declining-balance method (9)   A method of calculating depreciation or amortization using the declining-balance approach and using a fixed percentage equivalent to twice the straight-line percentage (the percentage that would be used following straight-line depreciation).

Double entry   Any bookkeeping system where transactions and adjustments are recorded in such a way as to constantly maintain the balance equality.

DR (or **Dr**)   Abbreviations for **Debit.**

Drawing account   A temporary account used in partnerships and proprietorships to record individual owner withdrawals during the year (period).

Drawings (10)   Assets withdrawn by an owner during the year.

Dual-column statements (16)   Financial statements prepared showing two measurements for the same items. For example, statements prepared on an historical-cost (GAAP) basis and also on a current-cost basis could disclose the two measurements in two adjoining columns. Suggested as a means to facilitate changeover to a new measurement system if and when adopted.

Early debt retirement (12)   The repayment or other extinguishment of debt prior to scheduled maturity.

Earned surplus   An archaic and now improper term for *retained earnings*.

Earnings (4)   *See* **Income.**

Earnings multiple (10)   Stock prices are often expressed as a multiple of earnings per share; for example, "The XYZ Company is selling at ten times earnings."

Earnings per share (common stock) (10)   Net income available for common stockholders (net income minus preferred dividend) divided by the average number of common shares outstanding.

EBIT (13)   Earnings before interest and taxes. Used as the best earnings measure for calculating earnings on average assets employed. In use, means earnings before interest, taxes, and any extraordinary or discontinued-operation items.

Eliminations in consolidation (15)   As part of the preparation of consolidated financial statements, the amounts which are subtracted in the consolidated working papers from combined-statement totals. Eliminations are made to avoid duplication and to eliminate claims and transactions within the "consolidated family."

Ending inventory   The amount of inventory on hand at the end of the year (period) which will be carried forward on the balance sheet to the following year.

Entity   The economic organization or business unit being reported upon in the financial statement. May correspond to a legal entity in the case of a corporation, or represent an artificial legal entity in the cases of segments, proprietorships, partnerships, and consolidations.

EPS (10)   *See* **Earnings per share.**

Equities (2)   Claims against or sources of assets. The sum of all liabilities and owners' equity on a balance sheet.

Equity method (investments) (11)   A measurement principle required under GAAP for common-stock investments where the stock held (more than 20 percent) represents significant influence over the other firm. Following the equity method, the investor records, as an increase to investments and as revenue, its proportionate share of the investee's earnings each year. Any dividends are then treated as a collection of "future dividends receivable included in investments." Alternative to *cost method.*

Estimated liabilities (12)   Those liabilities where the precise amount and/or the specific creditor may not be known with certainty, but where the liability is not contingent. Examples would be accruals of service costs and estimated warranty repair or replacement costs.

Executory agreement (4)   An agreement where neither party has completed any (or some portion) of intended performance, and therefore no claim arising out of past performance exists.

Exogenous (8)   Outside of or resulting from occurrences beyond the control of the firm.

Expenditure (9)   The disbursement of cash to obtain goods or services.

Expense (4)   Any reduction in net assets (total assets minus total liabilities) not involving a distribution to owners. The use, expiration, or loss of an asset, or the incurrence of a liability, not matched by a new reportable asset. Unusual expenses are often referred to as losses.

External (outside) **source** (funds) (7)   A place or group from which a firm might obtain additional invested working capital or other resources. The two external sources are long-term creditors and owners (stockholders).

Extraordinary items (6)   An expense (loss) or revenue (gain) which is characterized as being both unusual in nature for the particular business and also not expected to recur in the foreseeable future. Extraordinary items are classified on the income statement following income from operations.

Face value (11)   The stated amount due at maturity on a bond or note exclusive of any separately stated interest.

Fair market value (2)   A price or cost arrived at in an arm's-length transaction or exchange, where both parties may be assumed to be acting in their rational self-interest.

FASB (1)   Financial Accounting Standards Board.

FICA   Federal Insurance Contributions Act. FICA employee and employer taxes are more commonly known as "Social Security."

FIFO (8)   First-in, first-out. One of several possible inventory cost-flow assumptions. FIFO assumes that earliest costs apply to inventory sold (cost of goods sold) and most recent costs apply to ending inventory on hand.

Financial accounting (1)   The accounting system for reporting a firm's financial position, income, and changes in financial position to outside investors and other interested parties. GAAP applies to financial accounting.

Financial activities (5)   Those activities of the firm primarily involved in the raising of new capital and the acquisition of noncurrent assets. Used to distinguish certain events from those involved in short-term operations of the business.

Financial leverage (13)   Refers to the degree to which the firm is *trading on equity;* that is, the degree to which the firm is using "less costly" creditor and preferred stockholder-invested capital to generate earnings for the benefit of the common stockholder.

Financial management (7)   The management of *financial activities* as distinguished from operations (*operating management*) and tax liabilities (*tax management*).

Financial statements (1)   Those accounting reports required by GAAP—the balance sheet, the income statement, the SCFP, the statement of retained earnings (owner's capital), and the necessary footnotes thereto.

Financial structure   *See* **Capital structure.**

Financial transactions (6)   Transactions involved with *financial activities.*

Financing activities (7)   *See* **Financial activities.**

Financing lease   *See* **Capital lease.**

Finished goods   An inventory account for a manufacturer representing the cost of products completed and ready for sale.

First-in, first-out   *See* **FIFO.**

Fiscal year (5)   A twelve-month reporting period for a firm. May or may not correspond to the calendar year.

Fixed assets (2)   Noncurrent assets including such items as land, natural resources, buildings, machinery, equipment, office furniture and fixtures, and property held under capital lease.

Flow of working capital (5)   A change in the balance of *net working capital.*

Flow-through method (11)   One method of accounting for the investment-tax credit, which reports all benefits of the credit in the year such benefits are realized.

Foreign operations (15)   Operations of a firm or of (one of its) subsidiaries conducted outside of the United States. If foreign operations are significant, certain supplementary information concerning same must be disclosed along with the financial statements.

Franchise   A legal right or privilege to use a name or to sell certain brand products or services.

Freight-in   *See* **Transportation-in.**

Freight-out   The cost of shipping inventory to customers as part of a sale. Freight-out is treated as a period cost (selling expense) as incurred.

Full-acquisition cost (8)   A term used to reflect the GAAP initial measurement basis for assets. All normal costs of acquisition, except for any interest cost, are properly capitalized for the asset.

Full disclosure (11)   A GAAP requirement that all material and relevant information to the investor concerning the firm be included in the financial statements or footnotes thereto.

Fully depreciated (9)   Refers to a depreciable asset whose book value is equal to its estimated salvage value, and for which no further expiration (depreciation) will be recorded.

Fully diluted EPS (13)   The smallest possible EPS figure that would have occurred had all possible outstanding potential dilution (convertible securities, warrants, and options) taken place.

Fund   In financial accounting, an asset or group of assets set aside for a specific purpose and classified as noncurrent. In governmental accounting, a designated accounting entity for a specific purpose.

Fund accounting   An accounting system different from financial accounting, used for government, governmental institutions, and many not-for-profit organizations.

Funds (5)   Usually used synonymously with working capital. May also refer to cash or cash plus marketable securities.

Funds from operations (5)   Working capital generated in operations—the difference between fund revenue (revenue involving an inflow of working capital) and fund expense (expense involving a reduction of net working capital).

Funds statement Used to describe the SCFP.

FUTA Federal Unemployment Tax Act. Provides for employer payroll taxes to cover costs of worker unemployment compensation.

GAAP (1) Generally Accepted Accounting Principles.

Gain Excess of proceeds over costs for a specific transaction. Usually applied to financial, as opposed to operating, transactions.

General ledger (4) The collection of all active nonsubsidiary accounts in the firm.

General partner An owner in a partnership who has unlimited personal liability for the debts of the partnership.

Going-concern assumption (2) The measurement assumption underlying financial statements prepared in accordance with GAAP. It is assumed that the firm will continue in business at least as long as the longest of its debt maturities or the remaining useful lives of its existing assets.

Goods in process *See* **Work in process.**

Goods available for sale (8) The sum of beginning inventory and net purchases (gross purchases plus transportation-in minus purchase returns minus purchase discounts) during an accounting period.

Goodwill (11) The excess of the cost over the fair market value of the net assets acquired in a purchase of control of another firm.

Gross margin (5) Net sales minus cost of goods sold.

Gross profit (5) *See* **Gross margin.**

Gross-profit method A method used for estimating ending inventory and cost of goods sold for interim reports and in the event of destruction of accounting records. Cost of goods sold is estimated as a percentage of sales, using prior period's gross-profit percentage. The gross-profit method is not acceptable for measuring inventory and cost of goods sold in the annual financial statements.

Gross-profit ratio (13) Gross profit divided by net sales.

Gross purchases (8) The total of all invoice prices for inventory purchased during the period, not including transportation in and before recognizing purchase discounts and purchase returns.

Gross sales Total of all sales at invoiced price before deductions for returns and allowances, and discounts.

Group depreciation (9) A method of calculating depreciation charges for assets taken as a group rather than separately.

Historical cost (9) *See* **Original cost.**

Holding company (15) A firm whose primary activity consists of holding the controlling stock of other operating companies.

Holding gain (8)   Difference between ending and beginning price of assets held during a period of inflation.

Imputed interest (11)   The difference between the face amount of an obligation and its present value discounted at an appropriate interest rate—the amount of interest that may be inferred as capitalized into the face value of an obligation.

Income (4)   Revenue minus expenses for a given period. Negative income is known as a loss.

Income from (continuing) operations (5)   All revenues and gains minus all expenses and losses during a particular period except those specifically qualifying as extraordinary, or related to discontinued operations, or the effect of accounting changes.

Income statement (1)   The final statement reporting all revenues, gains, expenses, and losses for the period, together with EPS data.

Incremental borrowing rate   The interest rate which would need to be paid by the firm for its next material long-term secured loan. The lessee's incremental borrowing rate is used as the discount rate in the original determination of the present value of a lessee's capital-lease obligations.

Independent accountant   The CPA engaged to audit and give a professional opinion on the firm's financial statements and supporting systems.

Insolvent   Unable to pay obligations when they are due.

Installment (sales) method (12)   A method of revenue and expense recognition where gross profit is recognized in proportion to collection of the related receivable.

Installment sales   Credit sales where payments are scheduled in specific amounts over a specific period.

Intangible and other assets (2)   A category of noncurrent assets including intangible assets, deferred charges, assets involved in discontinued operations, goodwill, and miscellaneous noncurrent assets.

Intangible assets (2)   Nonphysical noncurrent assets which are rights, claims, or other deferred expenditures. Examples include leasehold improvement, patents, trademarks, copyrights, franchises and goodwill.

Intercompany debt (15)   Refers to obligations between a parent and a subsidiary, which are eliminated in consolidation.

Intercompany investment (15)   The controlling interest of a parent (included in the parent's investments account) in the common stock of the subsidiary (included in the subsidiary's stockholders' equity) which must be eliminated in consolidation. Any intercompany ownership of preferred stock or bonds would also be eliminated.

Intercompany transactions   Transactions occurring between a parent and a subsidiary that are eliminated from income statements and SCFP's in consolidation.

Interest   The cost or rent for use of money.

Interest-bearing notes (11)   Promissory notes with interest explicitly stated separately from the principal of the note.

Interim reports (statements) (15)   Financial statements, often abbreviated, which are issued covering periods shorter than the firm's fiscal year or normal operating cycle.

Internal source (funds) (7)   Assets or activities from which a firm's management may obtain working capital or cash for nonoperational applications, without having to seek additional capital from long-term creditors or owners. Internal sources may be thought of as including funds from operations, sale of noncurrent assets, and reduction of net working capital balance.

Inventory (2)   A current asset representing goods and materials on hand ready for sale or which will be manufactured for sale to customers. "To inventory" means to physically count items in stock or to calculate the cost of items on hand.

Inventory-flow assumption   An assumption or arbitrary assignment relating specific purchase costs to specific items purchased. Necessary when specific identification of each unit in inventory with its purchase cost is not economically feasible. *See* **Average cost, FIFO,** and **LIFO.**

Inventory turnover (13)   A measure of the rapidity of movement of average inventory through the operating cycle. The cost of goods sold for a period, divided by the average inventory on hand during the period.

Investing activities (7)   *See* **Financial activities.**

Investment-tax credit (9)   A reduction in business income tax granted by the government in the year of acquisition of the qualifying assets to firms to subsidize replacement (modernization) of capacity assets.

Investors (1)   All those who commit goods or services to a firm. Investors include creditors, specifically including suppliers and employees, and owners.

Invoice (4)   A document registering a claim for payment as part of a sales transaction—a "bill".

IRS (1)   Internal Revenue Service.

Issued shares (10)   Shares of a corporation's authorized stock that have been distributed to stockholders.

ITC (9)   *See* **Investment tax credit.**

Journal (4)   A record in which entries reflecting transactions and adjustments are originally recorded in the order in which they occur.

Journal entry (4)   An instruction to change balances in certain accounts which is recorded in a journal to reflect the effect of transactions and adjustments.

Journalize (17)   To record an entry in a journal.

Labor (cost)   The cost of direct labor (hours worked in actual production) capitalized as part of product cost by a manufacturer.

Land (2)   A noncurrent asset recorded at full acquisition cost and not depreciated.

Last-in, first-out   *See* **LIFO**.

Leasehold improvement (2)   An improvement or betterment to property under operating lease, which is attached to the property and reverts to the lessor upon expiration of the lease.

Ledger   A group or collection of accounts.

Legal capital (10)   The amount of contributed capital which is required by law to be retained in a corporation for the protection of creditors.

Lessee   One who leases (uses) property belonging to another.

Lessor   One who owns the property (landlord) under lease to another.

Leverage   *See* **Financial leverage**.

Liability (2)   A legal obligation to provide resources to another as the consequence of a past event.

LIFO (8)   Last-in, first-out.   One of several possible inventory cost-flow assumptions. LIFO assumes that most recent costs apply to inventory sold (cost of goods sold), and earliest costs apply to ending inventory on hand. Under LIFO, balance sheet inventory amounts may reflect very old, unrealistically low costs.

Limited liability (10)   Refers to the fact that corporate stockholders (owners) are not personally liable for the debts of the company, whereas proprietors and general partners, as owners of their companies, have unlimited personal liability.

Limited partner   An owner in a partnership who has limited liability; he or she is not personally liable for the debts of the partnership.

Liquidation (2)   The payment of an obligation. Also the sale of all noncash assets and cash distribution to creditors and owners as part of terminating a segment or an entire business.

Liquidity (3)   A firm's ability to raise additional cash. Sometimes liquidity is used interchangeably with *solvency*.

Loss   The excess of expense or cost over revenue (proceeds) for a particular transaction; or an expiration, extinction, or disappearance of an asset with no matching revenue; or negative income for a period.

LOCM (8)   A GAAP requirement for inventory measurement and reporting, where inventory must be written down below acquisition cost if eventual net recoverable value is lower than cost.

Long-term   Noncurrent; ordinarily due beyond one year.

Long-term debt ratio (7)   The ratio of long-term debt to the sum of long-term debt and owners' equity.

Long-term investments and funds (2) A category of noncurrent assets including both noncurrent investments and also various special funds such as sinking funds.

Lower of cost or market *See* **LOCM.**

Major customer (15) A term designating a single customer (individual, firm, or government agency) responsible for 10 percent or more of a firm's revenue. GAAP requires supplementary disclosure, in the financial statements, of data related to any major customers.

Managerial accounting As distinct from *financial accounting*, refers to those systems and reports designed to provide accounting information for internal management use within the firm.

Manufacturing cost Factory costs—direct material, direct labor, and manufacturing overhead—included in arriving at full product costs for a manufacturer.

Manufacturing overhead Includes all manufacturing costs except direct labor and direct materials. Included as part of full product cost by a manufacturer.

Markdown The amount of reduction of a retail selling price below that which was originally established.

Marketable securities (2) A current asset classification for readily salable securities held as temporary investments of excess cash (will normally be sold as cash is needed). Most current marketable securities are in the form of short-term government paper and certificates of deposit. The term is also used to apply to stocks and bonds of other firms and governments which are readily salable. In this context, where marketable securities are held with no intention of selling within one year (period), they are classified as *noncurrent*, under investments.

Market price (of stock) (10) The price per share at which stock of a given firm may be traded.

Market value (of stock) (10) The current sale value of stock owned in a particular firm. The product of the number of shares owned times the market price per share.

Markup (7) The difference between cost and the originally intended retail selling price. Usually expressed as a percentage of *selling price* rather than of cost.

"Matched pair" (7) A term used in this text to identify pairs (matching sources and applications) of material resource flows required by GAAP to be included in the SCFP and not involving flows of working capital. The most common "matched pairs" involve a portion of a new noncurrent asset (application) obtained in exchange for new noncurrent debt (source); new noncurrent assets (application) acquired as a direct owner investment (source); or conversion of noncurrent debt (application) to new stock (source).

Matching (5)   The GAAP income-measurement principle involving the recognition of expenses on the income statement in the same period as that in which the related revenues are recognized (reported).

Material (cost)   The direct cost of raw material included by a manufacturer as part of full product cost.

Materiality (3)   The GAAP disclosure principle involving separate identification of only those events or statement effects where the result is significant in terms of total assets or net income.

Mature (4)   Having reached the date established for payment. *See* **Maturity.**

Maturity   The date when the principal of an obligation is due and payable. An obligation is said to "mature" when it becomes payable.

"Meeting the payroll" (14)   Slang for maintaining solvency.

Merge/merger (11)   The joining of two firms into a single economic entity. *See* **Business combination.**

Minority (15)   *See* **Minority stockholders.**

Minority interest (12)   An equity account appearing on a consolidated balance sheet representing the share in total assets attributable to stockholders who do not hold stock in the parent corporation. (*See* **Minority stockholders.**) Minority interests or claims against combined income are subtracted on a consolidated income statement so that the bottom line will represent income available to the parent's stockholders.

Minority stockholders (15)   Stockholders in a corporation where another individual or firm has controlling interest (more than 50 percent of the voting stock). Usually considered in the context of a subsidiary corporation which is not wholly owned. *See* **Minority interest.**

Monetary gain or loss   A firm's gain or loss in general purchasing power resulting from holding net monetary debt or net monetary assets during a period of general inflation (deflation). Monetary gain or loss is currently not measured and reported in financial statements.

Monetary items (2)   Cash and other assets and liabilities where claims (receivables and payables) in terms of dollars and time are fixed.

Multiple-step format (5)   One acceptable approach to classifying revenues and expenses on an income statement, involving subtotals for such items as gross profit and operating income (as distinct from income from operations).

NAA (1)   National Association of Accountants.

Net assets (2)   Total assets minus total liabilities, or the share of total assets claimed or contributed by owners.

Net current assets (5)   Another term for net working capital. Both equal current assets minus current liabilities.

Net income (4)   The difference between the total of all revenue and gains and the total of all expenses and losses for a period.

Net loss (6)   Negative net income.

Net purchases (8)   The net total acquisition cost of all merchandise or material acquired and accepted during the year. Gross purchases plus transportation-in minus purchase returns minus purchase discounts.

Net quick assets (3)   Quick assets (cash, marketable securities, and net receivables) minus current liabilities.

Net realizable value (8)   The amount of net cash that could result from disposition of an item. The selling price less costs of completion for sale and of selling.

Net sales (5)   Gross sales less sales returns, allowances, and sales discounts.

Net working capital (3)   The amount of working capital in the firm representing a necessary long-term investment by creditors and owners. Equals current assets minus current liabilities. *See also* **Working capital.**

Net worth (2)   A potentially misleading term sometimes used in place of net assets or owners' equity.

Nominal account (17)   A temporary account opened each year (or period) to accumulate desired detailed information. Nominal accounts are closed at year end to real or balance sheet accounts.

Noncurrent assets (2)   All assets that do not qualify for classification as current assets.

Noncurrent capital-lease obligations (2)   The present value of amounts owed beyond one year under leases qualifying as capital leases.

Noncurrent liabilities (2)   All liabilities that do not qualify for classification as current liabilities.

Noninterest-bearing note (11)   A promissory note with all interest capitalized in the face or maturity value. A note with no explicitly stated interest separate from principal.

Nonmonetary item   Any asset or equity which is not monetary.

Nonoperating revenue (5)   Revenue which is not derived from the firm's principal line(s) of business. Often designated as "other revenue."

Note payable (2)   An unconditional obligation in writing to pay a specific amount of cash at either a specific time or else on demand.

Note receivable (2)   An unconditional obligation in writing by another to pay to the firm a specific amount of cash at either a specific time or else on demand.

Objectivity   A GAAP measurement principle, which defers (perhaps indefinitely) recognition and recording of events and items until they can be reasonably measured in monetary terms, and the measurement is capable of independent verification.

Obligations under capital leases (12)   May appear as both a current and a noncurrent liability. The noncurrent portion represents the present value of all payments due *beyond* one year under capital-lease contracts. The current portion represents the present value of the currently maturing payment(s) plus accrued interest charges (incorporated in the payment) which have been earned.

Off-balance-sheet financing (9)   Refers to the practice of acquiring property under a long-term noncancellable lease, which may be (in substance) a purchase but which is accounted for as an operating lease.

"Omitted assets" (9)   A term used in this text referring to those intangible assets not presently considered capable of objective measurement, and therefore not included in the balance sheet. Examples include a firm's self-developed human resources or human capital, creditor goodwill, customer goodwill, and supplier goodwill.

On account (1)   Term referring to a purchase or sale where the privilege is extended of delayed payment and no promissory note as evidence of the debt is required.

On credit (1)   *See* **On account.**

On consignment   *See* **consignment.**

Operating   Refers to revenues and expenses related to the firm's primary line(s) of business.

Operating cycle (2)   The average time period involved for completion of the following series of events: Cash is converted into goods and services; goods and services are converted into receivables by a sale; and cash is collected on receivables. Also known as the *earnings cycle.*

Operating earnings (5)   *See* **Operating income.**

Operating expenses (5)   All expenses and losses for the period except extraordinary items and those related to discontinued operations. Often more narrowly defined to exclude also cost of goods sold, interest expense, provision for income taxes, and losses on financial activities.

Operating income (5)   Used interchangeably with income from operations, or often more narrowly defined to include only revenues and expenses directly related to the firm's primary line(s) of business and specifically excluding other revenue, gains and losses on financial activities, interest expense, and provision for income taxes (income tax expense). *See also* **Income from operations.**

Operating lease (9)   Any lease not meeting FASB criteria for identification as a capital lease. Operating leases are accounted for as executory contracts, no asset is recorded, and the liability and expense is only recognized *as earned* by the lessor.

Operating management (7)   Term used to describe day-to-day activities related to the firm's primary line(s) of business, as distinct from financial management and tax management activities.

Operating profit (5)   *See* **Operating income.**

Operating ratio (13)   Net income (or alternatively, income from operations) divided by net sales and usually expressed as a percentage.

Operational assets   *See* **Fixed assets.**

Opinion (auditor's) (1)   The auditor's report attesting to the financial statements, or disclaiming attestation.

Opportunity costs   The income that could have been earned or the cost that could have been saved, by using an asset in its next-best alternative use. Opportunity cost is not measured and reported in financial statements.

Original cost (9)   The initial (historical) cost(s) of an asset.

Other revenue (income) (5)   *See* **Nonoperating revenue.**

Outstanding (stock) (10)   Number of shares issued less any shares held as treasury stock.

Overhead (cost)   *See* **Manufacturing overhead.**

Owner withdrawal (4)   The transfer of assets (usually cash) from the firm to the owner(s). In a corporation, referred to as a dividend.

Owner's capital   Refers to that portion of total assets in a firm contributed (claimed) by owners. *See* **Owner's equity.**

Owner's equity (2)   That share of total assets not claimed by creditors; total assets minus total liabilities. Same as net assets.

Paid-in capital (10)   That portion of contributed capital in excess of amounts shown as par or stated value. Also may be used to refer to total contributed capital less donated capital.

Parent (company) (11)   A firm owning voting control (over 50 percent of voting common stock) of another firm which is known as a subsidiary.

Partnership (10)   A firm with two or more owners (general or limited partners) which is not incorporated. A partnership must have at least one general partner.

Partnership agreement (10)   The agreement among partners specifying the division of earnings, division of net assets upon dissolution, and procedures to be followed upon death or disability of a partner.

Par value (10)   The face value or the face amount of a security (bond, note, or stock).

Payable   Owed: past due, currently, or in the future.

Percentage-(of)-completion method (11)   An alternative method for recognizing revenues and expenses on a specific job under which revenues and expenses are recognized in proportion to the percentage of completion of the job.

Period cost   An expenditure, asset expiration, or incurrence of a liability regularly expensed in the period when incurred rather than being capitalized as an asset or included as part of product cost.

Periodic inventory (system) (8)   A system wherein cost of goods sold is not recorded perpetually throughout the year (period). Instead, it is calculated at year end by taking a physical inventory to obtain ending inventory, and then subtracting ending inventory from goods available for sale.

Periodic LIFO (8)   LIFO determined under the periodic-inventory method, wherein all shipments are presumed to have occurred at year end.

Permanent holding loss (investments) (11)   A loss of recoverable value on investments which is deemed permanent and is therefore recognized as a loss on the income statement.

Permanent investment (7)   A term referring to the long-term invested capital in a business, the sum of noncurrent liabilities and owners' equity or, equivalently, the sum of net working capital and noncurrent assets.

Perpetual inventory (system) (8)   A system in which inventory accounts are regularly updated to reflect purchases and shipments.

Perpetual LIFO (8)   LIFO determined under the perpetual-inventory method, wherein purchases and shipments are recorded as they occur. Strict perpetual LIFO maintains records of LIFO "layers" as far back as the last stock-out. Modified perpetual LIFO begins each period with a single opening "layer" at average cost, and only "layers" purchases during the year.

Physical inventory (4)   Refers to physically counting and determining the cost of inventory on hand.

PLAC (16)   *See* **Price-level-adjusted cost.**

Placed on C.O.D. (14)   A condition wherein a customer is denied credit privileges and is required to pay for purchases "cash on delivery."

Pooling of interests (15)   A business combination wherein two firms of similar size join together and operate as a single economic entity, with the original owners maintaining their proportionate voting shares in the new entity.

Pooling treatment (method) (15)   Accounting for a business combination which qualifies as a pooling by adding together the book values of assets and equities of the separate firms. Under the pooling method, there are no asset revaluations or purchased goodwill.

Posting (4)   Recording entries in the accounts.

Pre-emptive right   A stockholder privilege of first refusal on the purchase of any additional stock issued, which allows the stockholder to maintain proportionate interest and voting rights within the corporation.

Preferred stock (10)   Stock with preference over common stock as to dividends and assets in dissolution. Preferred stock is usually nonvoting.

Prepaid items (2)   Current assets that represent past expenditures for future benefits. Prepaid items can be thought of as current receivables for services rather than for cash.

Present value (11)   *See* **Discounted present value.**

Price–earnings ratio   The market price per share of the firm's common stock, divided by the previous year's EPS.

Price-level-adjusted accounting (statements) (16)   Financial statements containing measurements in dollars of uniform general purchasing power. Historical costs are adjusted to current amounts via general price-level indices.

Price-level-adjusted cost (16)   The valuation basis for nonmonetary assets in price-level-adjusted financial statements. Under price-level-adjusted cost, historical cost is adjusted to current purchasing power equivalence through the use of a general price index.

Primary EPS (13)   Earnings per share calculated under the assumption that, out of all possible dilutions, the more probable dilutions have occurred. Primary EPS will usually be less than simple EPS, and will always be equal to or greater than *fully diluted EPS.*

Prior-period adjustment (13)   Certain balance sheet adjustments for errors in earlier periods made directly to the ending balance sheet and bypassing the income statement. GAAP narrowly restricts items that may qualify for treatment as a prior-period adjustment.

Product cost   As distinct from period costs, which are expensed in the period incurred, product costs are all costs that are included (capitalized) in inventory and not expensed until sale occurs.

Profit   *See* **Income.**

Pro-forma (6)   Hypothetical or projected.

Pro-forma statements (10)   Hypothetical or projected statements.

Promissory note   *See* **Note payable** and **Note receivable.**

Property under capital lease (2)   A fixed asset indicating the unamortized balance of the present value of all payments required for property effectively controlled under a long-term, noncancelable lease, which qualifies as a capital lease.

Proprietorship (2)   A one-owner business, or the owner's equity of a one-owner business.

Purchase (of another company) (15)   A business combination where one firm acquires control of a subsidiary through giving subsidiary stockholders cash or debt instruments in exchange for their voting stock. Proportionate voting interest in the new economic entity is not maintained by the original owners.

Purchase discount (8)   *See* **Cash discount.**

Purchase method (treatment) (15)   Accounting for a business combination which does not qualify as a pooling, by recording the acquired firm's assets at the amounts effectively paid for them, with any payment in excess of fair market value of assets acquired being classified as *goodwill.*

Purchase returns (8)   Merchandise or material purchased from a supplier and recorded in the accounts, which are subsequently returned to the supplier for any reason.

Purchased goodwill (15)   *See* **Goodwill.**

Quick assets   Assets which are cash or can quickly become cash. Includes cash, marketable securities, and receivables.

Quick ratio (3)   Quick assets divided by total current liabilities. Also known as the acid-test ratio.

Raw material   A current asset representing inventory on hand and not yet used of material purchased by a manufacturer for use in manufacturing its product.

Real account (17)   Permanent or balance sheet account, as distinct from nominal or temporary account.

Receivables turnover (13)   Net credit sales (or, alternatively, net sales) divided by average net accounts receivable during the period.

Reconcile (6)   Explain how one amount is derived from another.

Refunding (12)   Refers to refinancing bonds payable with new bonds.

Replacement cost (16)   For an asset, the current cost of acquiring an asset of equivalent usefulness or productive capacity and in the same condition.

Reserve   As properly used in accounting, refers only to an appropriation of retained earnings. In accounting, a reserve is not a fund nor does it imply that assets have been set aside.

Reserve for depreciation   An inferior term for *accumulated depreciation.*

Restriction (of retained earnings) (10)   An amount of retained earnings not legally available for dividends as a result of contractual agreement with creditors or as a result of treasury stock acquired and not yet resold.

Retail inventory method   A method commonly used by retail firms for determining the cost of year-end inventory, and for estimating interim cost of goods sold. Inventory costs are estimated by using a percentage of selling price. The percentage is the weighted-moving-average percentage of goods available for sale at cost, to goods available at selling.

Retained earnings (10)   Net income not yet distributed to owners. The sum of net income since the start of the corporation, less all dividends declared (cash and stock). At any given time, equal to total stockholders' equity less contributed capital.

Retained earnings restrictions (10)   *See* **Restriction.**

Retained earnings statement   *See* **Statement of retained earnings.**

Retroactive depreciation (16)   In current-value accounting, applies to the amount of additional depreciation for prior years resulting from an increase in asset valuation in the current year. Also known as "catch-up depreciation."

Return on assets employed (13) EBIT divided by average total assets for the period.

Return on common equity (13) Net income (or income from operations after taxes) minus preferred dividend, divided by average common equity (total stockholders' equity minus preferred shares) for the period.

Return on investment The net earnings on any investment (rent, interest, dividends) for a period, divided by the average amount invested during the period.

Return on owners' equity (13) Net income (or income from operations after income taxes) divided by average total owners' equity for the period.

Revenue (4) An inflow of net assets not donated, or resulting from additional owner investment. Assets received from the sale of goods or services to customers and from investments, or net assets received from the sale of noncurrent assets.

Revenue collected in advance (2) Advances of cash from customers, where the goods or services purchased have not as yet been delivered.

Reversing entry (17) An entry which is the opposite of a previous entry, and which therefore cancels the effect of the previous entry.

Sale (5) A revenue transaction wherein goods or services are supplied to a customer in exchange for cash or a receivable.

Sales returns and allowances (5) A contra revenue item including merchandise returned for credit by a customer and reductions of previously invoiced prices made to compensate for damaged, defective, or otherwise undesirable items sold to and retained by the customer.

Sales discount *See* **Cash discount.**

Salvage value (9) The net recoverable cost (actual or estimated) of tangible fixed assets.

SCFP (1) *See* **Statement of changes in financial position.**

SCFP worksheet (14) A working paper used in the preparation of a SCFP from other financial statements.

Schedule of working capital changes (7) A supplementary listing of the changes in the balance of all current asset and current liability items during the period, which must accompany the SCFP as part of the financial statements.

SEC (1) Securities and Exchange Commission.

Security A document evidencing ownership or indebtedness.

Segment (of a business) (15) A portion of a business representing a line of business or type of activity distinct from others.

Self-liquidating (loan) (14) A loan made for the purpose of acquiring assets such as inventory which, in the normal course of business, will be converted to cash within a year.

Separately reportable segment (15)   A segment of sufficient size to require supplementary disclosure of certain summary data as required by GAAP.

Serial bonds (12)   An issue of bonds with staggered maturities, part of the issue maturing on one date and other parts on other dates.

Service life (9)   *See* **Useful life.**

Shareholder (10)   One who owns shares of a corporation's common or preferred stock. *See* **Stockholder.**

Short-term   Current: due within one year.

Shrinkage (5)   The difference between the balance of inventory shown after all transactions have been recorded and the *actual* quantity *on hand*. May result from theft, deterioration, loss, or clerical error.

Single-step (format) (5)   An alternative for the classification of revenues and expenses on the income statement, wherein all revenues are grouped and totaled, followed by all expenses, in arriving at income from operations before income taxes.

Sinking fund   An asset. A fund established to accumulate funds for the retirement of long-term debt.

Solvency (3)   The ability to pay obligations when due.

Sources of funds (7)   The places, activities, individuals, or groups from which a firm may obtain working capital for application elsewhere. Sources include operations, extraordinary gains, sale of noncurrent assets, new noncurrent debt, new owner investment, and reduction of balance of net working capital already on hand.

Specific (cost) **identification** (8)   One of the methods for measuring inventory costs, wherein items are each identified with their acquisition cost and an inventory cost-flow assumption becomes unnecessary.

Specific inflation/specific price changes   Changes in the prices of certain specific goods or services as distinguished from general price-level changes averaged for all goods and services. Specific price changes move independently, and can even move in the opposite direction to general inflation.

Stated value (stock) (10)   *See* **Par value.**

Statement of cash flow (14)   A statement indicating cash generated from operations during the period, together with all other sources and applications of cash during the period.

Statement of changes in financial position (1)   One of the four required financial statements under GAAP. A statement which discloses sources and applications of working capital (or cash), together with other major resource changes ("matched pairs") occurring during the year.

Statement of financial position   Another term for *balance sheet.*

Statement of owner's capital (6)   One of the four financial statements required for a proprietorship or a partnership. Reconciles owner's equity at the beginning and the end of the period.

Statement of retained earnings (1)   One of the four financial statements required for a corporation. Reconciles retained earnings at the beginning and the end of the period.

Statutory merger (15)   A business combination resulting from either a purchase or a pooling, when the resulting economic entity is organized as a single legal entity and the parent–subsidiary relationship no longer exists.

Stock dividend (10)   A pro-rata issuance and distribution of additional stock at no cost to existing stockholders. Usually limited to less than 20 percent of the shares previously outstanding.

Stockholder (10)   An owner of the capital stock of a corporation.

Stockholders' equity   The owners' equity of a corporation.

Stock split (10)   An issuance and distribution of additional shares of common stock on a pro-rata basis, to existing stockholders, at no cost to them. Generally limited to distributions in excess of 20 percent of shares previously outstanding.

Straight-line (depreciation) **method** (2)   A method of determining depreciation or amortization wherein the depreciable base (cost less salvage value) is expensed in equal amounts over the asset's useful life.

Subsidiary (11)   A corporation legally owned or controlled by another corporation (parent) which owns more than 50 percent of the subsidiary's voting common stock.

Subsidiary account (17)   A detail account carried in a subsidiary ledger. The subsidiary account's balance is combined with other like balances in a control account carried in the general ledger.

Subsidiary ledger (17)   A ledger combining like subsidiary accounts whose combined total is carried in a corresponding control account in the general ledger.

Sum-of-the-years' digits method (9)   *See* **Years' digits method.**

Supplies (2)   A current asset representing the cost of items acquired for consumption within one year as part of normal operating business activities.

SYD (9)   *See* **Years' digits method.**

"T account" (17)   A symbol used as an instructional device to portray an account. Debits and credits are shown on the two sides, and the account title across the top.

Take-home pay   Employee earnings less taxes withheld and other payroll deductions. The portion of total pay actually received in cash by the employee.

Tangible fixed assets (2)   Assets with future usefulness to the firm exceeding one year (noncurrent) which have physical form, such as land, buildings, equipment, and office furniture and fixtures.

Taxable income (6)   The amount of income used as the basis for computing income-tax liability. Taxable revenue and gains less tax deductions.

Rarely the same as accounting income before taxes because of both permanent differences and timing differences in the measurement of income between the two systems.

Tax accounting   The accounting necessary to satisfy the IRS. The maintenance of adequate supporting records and the preparation and filing of necessary tax returns.

Tax credit   A direct reduction of actual tax dollar liability, as distinct from a tax deduction.

Tax deduction   An amount specifically allowable as a deduction from taxable revenue and gain in the determination of taxable income. Similar to an expense in accounting; however, something that may logically be an expense may not be allowable under the tax code as a tax deduction.

Tax management (1)   The inclusion of "tax-consequence thinking" in the planning and execution of operating and financial decisions; and the preparation of required tax returns in such a manner as to minimize the firm's tax liability within the law.

Tax shield (12)   A tax deduction which does not involve a current outflow of working capital. For example, depreciation serves as a tax shield.

Temporary holding loss (investments) (11)   A loss in recoverable (market) value of a noncurrent investment which is deemed temporary; that is, it will be recovered at or before the intended time when the specific investment is to be liquidated.

Temporary revaluations of long-term investments   When a market loss is considered temporary, the asset "investment" is revalued (written down and written up but not *above* original cost) in the same manner as for current marketable securities. However, the corresponding temporary loss or gain is not included in the determination of net income. Instead it is reflected in a special valuation contra account included within owners' equity, which may be called "temporary loss on investments," or "temporary investments revaluation," or a similar title.

Terms of sale   Any conditions relating to payment connected with a particular sale transaction. For example, the terms "2/10, N/30" offer a two-percent cash discount if payment is made within ten days, and indicate full (net) payment is due within thirty days.

Times interest earned (13)   Suggested as a measure of a firm's potential ability to cover interest payments in the future. EBIT divided by annual interest expense.

Total assets (2)   The sum of all assets less all contra assets appearing on the balance sheet.

Trade discount   A reduction from a list price offered or given to customers of a given type, such as a wholesale discount. Note that trade discounts are not recorded in the accounting system. Sales are initially recorded **net** of trade discounts.

Trading on equity (13)   As an owner, earning money on the capital invested by others (noncurrent creditors and preferred stockholders). The objective of desirable debt financing. (*See also* **Financial leverage.**)

Trading profit (5)   The difference between the price obtained upon sale for an item and its current replacement cost—the "currently repeatable gross margin."

Transaction (4)   Any exchange between the firm and another entity that affects the firm's financial position as reported on its balance sheet.

Transaction entry (4)   A term used in this text to distinguish between entries recording the effect of outside exchanges (transactions) and those other internal adjusting entries.

Transportation-in (8)   The cost of delivering inventory from the supplier to the firm's selling locations (including to consignee's). If this cost is not already included in the invoice price for the inventory items, it is accumulated for inclusion in inventory-acquisition cost as part of net purchases.

Treasury stock (10)   A small portion of a firm's own stock previously outstanding which has been reacquired—repurchased—and is being held for some purpose. A firm's own treasury stock is not shown as an asset on the balance sheet. Instead it is classified contra within owners' equity.

Trend analysis (3)   In financial statement analysis, a term referring to the comparison of data for a given period and firm with like data for similar periods for the same firm.

Trial balance (17)   A summarization of all account balances with debits and credits separately totaled.

Turnover   The average number of times a particular asset, group of assets, or even total assets may be thought of as having been replaced during the year or period.

Unappropriated retained earnings (10)   The amount of retained earnings which the directors indicate may serve as a basis for future dividends, subject to any footnoted restrictions, and subject to adequate solvency to allow declaration of a dividend.

Unamortized cost (6)   The amount of the original cost of an intangible asset which has not yet been amortized to reflect expiration.

Unaudited financial statements (1)   Financial statements which have not been subjected to an independent audit by a CPA.

Undepreciated cost (2)   The current book value of a tangible fixed asset.

Undercapitalized   Refers to a state wherein a firm has insufficient invested assets to support its current or intended level of activity.

Units-of-production method (9)   One method of allocating depreciation over the useful life of a tangible fixed asset. The useful life is determined in terms of a usage measurement (e.g., a truck may have 200,000 miles of useful life). Annual depreciation is based on the proportion of current year's usage to useful life, times the depreciable base.

Units-of-service method (9)   *See* **Units-of-production method.**

Unlimited liability (10)   The legal status of proprietors and general partners (not true for limited partners or stockholders). Refers to full personal liability for all of the debts of the firm.

Useful life (9)   The period of time during which an asset is expected to provide benefit to the firm. The time period between date of acquisition and intended date of disposal.

Use of funds   *See* **Application of funds.**

Valuation account   An account, usually contra, which is used to modify the book value of another account. Examples include allowance for uncollectibles, discount on notes and bonds receivable and payable, accumulated depreciation, and treasury stock.

Verifiability   A principle of GAAP supporting the goal of objectivity in financial reporting. Verifiability requires that the transactions recognized in the financial statements must be supported by physical evidence such as receipts, cancelled checks, and so forth.

Voting stock (10)   The capital stock of a corporation (usually only the common stock) which entitles the holder to vote for the election of directors and make other ownership decisions.

Warranty   A commitment by a seller to repair or replace products sold which proved defective within some stated time limit following sale.

Wasting asset   A natural resource which is limited in amount and is therefore depleted as used. Examples include oil and gas, minerals, and timber.

Weighted average cost (inventory) (8)   *See* **Average cost.**

Wholly owned subsidiary   A corporation 100 percent of whose voting stock is owned by another corporation (parent), where there are no minority stockholders.

Withdrawals   Assets transferred from a firm to its owners.

Working capital (3)   In general business use and in this text, refers only to current assets. Current assets less current liabilities are then known as *net working capital*. Possibly because accountants are accustomed to using the term current assets, many accounting texts define working capital as current assets minus current liabilities, and therefore discard net working capital as redundant. Unfortunately, both definitions are in use, and you must be careful to identify the meaning of this term in each situation.

Working capital balance sheet (7)   An abbreviated balance sheet convenient in financial analysis for focusing attention on the permanent or long-term capital structure of the firm. A working capital balance sheet has total current liabilities eliminated from the assets and equities. It therefore consists of net working capital and noncurrent assets balanced by noncurrent debt and owners' equity.

Working capital funds-flow statement (7)   A statement of sources and applications of working capital during the period. Would not include "matched pairs"; therefore, if any "matched pairs" existed during the year, a working capital statement would require the addition of the matched pairs, in order to qualify as a SCFP.

Working capital funds from operations (5)   A partially redundant term focusing attention on funds as being net working capital and not cash or all resources. *See* **Funds from operations.**

Working capital percentage   A measure of the relative liquidity (composition) of a firm's assets. Current assets divided by total assets, converted to a percentage.

Work in process   A current asset representing, for a manufacturer, inventory on hand at year end in various states of partial completion. The cost of such items will therefore be greater than their material cost but less than the full cost of a finished good.

Worksheet (accounting) (17)   A multicolumn working paper for convenient and rapid completion of the process of adjustment, closing, and statement preparation.

Write off (down)   To reduce an asset account balance, and charge either expense or loss.

Write up   To increase an asset account balance not reflecting an actual transaction involving a flow of funds. GAAP currently allow write-ups in only three situations. Investments representing significant influence are written up to recognize proportional share of the other's earnings in advance of dividends. Current marketable securities may be written up, but not above original cost, to reflect market-value recovery of a previous write-down. Noncurrent investments previously written down to reflect a temporary loss may be written back up, but *not* above cost, to reflect recovery of market value.

Years' digits method (9)   One of the common methods of accelerated depreciation or amortization. The digits representing the useful life are summed and divided into the depreciable base to obtain a single portion. The asset is then depreciated each year by an amount equal to the year's digit times one portion, in inverse order—the highest digit is used the first year.

Yield method   A method of amortizing bond discount or premium involving maintenance of the book value of the liability at present value each year to maturity. The yield method is preferred under GAAP, but straight-line amortization is allowed where the differences are not material. Also known as the *interest method.*

D

SOLUTIONS TO ODD-NUMBERED ESSENTIAL AND SUPPLEMENTARY PROBLEMS

Chapter 1

There are no essential or supplementary problems in Chapter 1.

Chapter 2

EP 2.1

MR. SMITH

Personal Net Worth Statement	Dollar amount
Possessions:	
Balance in personal bank account	$ 1500
Personal possessions	500
Personal automobile	2000
($4,000 cost, less $2,000 depreciation)	
Balance of cash on hand in business	100
Business accounts receivable	200
Cost of merchandise on hand for sale	800
Total possessions	$ 5100
Debts:	
Amount owed on personal bills	$ 300
Amount owed by business to suppliers	400
Total debts	$ 700
Mr. Smith's net worth ($5100 − 700)	$4,400

EP 2.3

Current assets	$400	Current liabilities	$200
Noncurrent assets	$500	Noncurrent liabilities	$300
		Owner's equity	$400
Total Assets	$900	Total Equities	$900

$$\$900 - (\$200 + 300) = \underline{\$400}$$

Total assets − Total liabilities = Owner's Equity

EP 2.5

Cash
Marketable securities
Receivables (Notes and accounts)
Inventory
Supplies
Prepaid items

EP 2.7

Current Assets:

Cash		$100
Accounts receivable	$400	
Less allowance for uncollectibles	(50)*	350
Inventory		600
Prepaid items		200
Total current assets		$1,250

* $1250 - ($100 + 600 + 200 + 400) = \(50)

Chapter 3

EP 3.1

a) Pamela was more solvent as of 19X3, as revealed by higher current and quick ratios.

b) At the end of 19X3, Paul appeared to have a solvency problem with a quick ratio of only 0.5 to 1 and a current ratio of only 1.2 to 1.

c) At the end of 19X3, Paul appeared to have more apparent liquidity. The two firms had essentially the same proportion of capital tied up in noncurrent assets. However, Paul had proportionally less than half the debt (0.15 as compared to 0.4).

EP 3.3

a) Current ratio $= \dfrac{70,000}{40,000} = 1.75$ to 1;

b) Quick ratio $= \dfrac{70,000 - 15,000 - 6,000 - 2,000}{40,000} = 1.175$ to 1;

c) Debt ratio $= \dfrac{50,000}{135,000} = 37\%$;

d) Asset-composition ratio $= \dfrac{70,000}{135,000} = 52\%$;

e) Yes;

f) $6,667 additional borrowing theoretically possible.

$(1 - 0.4)X = \$85,000,$

$0.6X = 85,000,$

$X = \$141,667 =$ amount of total equity that would bring debt ratio to industry average;

$\$141,667 - \$135,000$ (current total equity) $= \$6,667.$

EP 3.5

Betty Company: Yes.

Current ratio $= \dfrac{84,600}{47,000} = 1.8 > 1.7$;

Quick ratio $= \dfrac{51,700}{47,000} = 1.1 > 1.0.$

Mary Company: No.

$$\text{Current ratio} = \frac{70{,}400}{32{,}000} = 2.2 > 1.7;$$

$$\text{Quick ratio} \ = \frac{28{,}800}{32{,}000} = 0.9 < 1.0.$$

Mary Company's quick ratio insufficient.

SP 3.7

PBFF COMPANY

Balance Sheet as of 12/31/X0 (000 omitted)

Assets		Equities	
Cash	$ 93	Current notes payable	$20
Marketable securities	27	Accounts payable	70
Accounts receivable (net)	30	Other current liabilities	25
Inventory	56	Total Current Liabilities	$115
Supplies	14	Noncurrent notes payable	177
Prepaid items	15	Total Liabilities	$292
Total Current Assets	$235	Owner's Equity*	
Noncurrent assets (net)	495		438
Total Assets	$730	Total Equities	$730

* Total Assets $730 less Total Liabilities $292 equals Owner's Equity $438.

a) $438,000

b) $120,000 ($235,000 Total current assets − $115,000 Total current liabilities)

c) 2.0 to 1 (rounded)

d) 1.3 to 1 (rounded)

e) 0.4 to 1

f) 0.3 or 30 percent (rounded)

SP 3.9

a) $18,608,000   d) 0.4 (rounded)

b) 2.3 to 1 (rounded)   e) 0.7 (rounded)

c) 1.1 to 1 (rounded)

SP 3.11

a) $571,027,000

b) 1.5 to 1 (rounded)

c) 0.8 to 1 (rounded)

d) 0.5 (rounded)

e) 0.4 (rounded)

Chapter 4

EP 4.1

a) NE

b) IA, IO

c) IA, IL

d) NE

e) IA, IO

f) IA, IO

g) IA, IL

h) IA, IL

i) IA, DA

j) IA, DA, IL

k) DA, DL, DO

l) DA, DL

m) DA, DO

EP 4.3

a) DA, DO

b) DA, DO

c) NE

d) IL, DO

e) IL, DO

EP 4.5

	Total Current Assets	Total Assets	Total Current Liabilities	Total Liabilities	Owner's Equity
a)	$14,800	$25,800	$ 9,000	$13,500	$12,300
b)	13,500	24,500	9,000	13,500	11,000
c)	16,000	24,200	9,000	13,500	10,700
d)	16,000	26,000	9,000	13,500	12,500
e)	16,500	27,000	10,500	16,000	10,500

EP 4.7

a) $500,000 total assets equal to the capital invested;

b) $100,000 provided by short-term creditors;

c) $ 25,000 provided by long-term creditors;

d) $375,000 provided by owner;

e) $215,000 share of total assets represents profits accumulated and not yet withdrawn ($375,000 owner's present share, less $160,000 capital originally contributed by owner).

SP 4.9

WADE COMPANY

19X3 Year-End Balance Sheet

Assets

Cash		$ 15,450
Marketable securities		35,000
Accounts receivable (net)		85,000
Inventory		110,000
Supplies		13,000
Prepaid items		5,000
Total Current Assets		$263,450
Investments		110,000
Land		60,000
Buildings and equipment	$510,000	
Less accumulated depreciation	130,000	380,000
Intangibles		28,000
Total Assets		$841,450

Equities

Accounts payable	$ 60,000
Taxes payable	10,000
Miscellaneous payables	3,000
Total Current Liabilities	$ 73,000
Long-term notes payable	175,000
Total Liabilities	$248,000
Owner's Equity	593,450
Total Equities	$841,450

Chapter 5

EP 5.1   Sales
Sales returns and allowances
Cost of goods sold
Wages expense
Utilities expense
Other operating expense

EP 5.3

Assets	Equities
Cash	Current notes payable
Accounts receivable	Accounts payable
Inventory	Accrued wages payable
	Other current liabilities
	Owner's Equity

EP 5.5

a) Neither	g) E, decrease
b) Neither	h) Neither
c) E, decrease	i) Neither
d) R, increase	j) Neither
e) R, increase	k) E, decrease
f) E, decrease	l) E, decrease

EP 5.7

Account	Statement	Effect on the account
a) Bad debt expense	E	Increase
Accounts receivable	B/S	Decrease
b) Supplies expense	E	Increase
Supplies	B/S	Decrease
c) Accrued interest receivable	B/S	Increase
Interest revenue	R	Increase
d) Accrued rent receivable	B/S	Increase
Rent revenue	R	Increase
e) Wages and salaries expense	E	Increase
Accrued wages and salaries payable	B/S	Increase
f) Telephone expense	E	Increase
Accrued telephone payable (or Accounts payable)	B/S	Increase

SP 5.9 Funds from operations would be $7,000, since all revenues and expenses involved current items and therefore represented flows of net working capital.

SP 5.11 a) 1975 income from continuing operations = $757,621,000
1976 income from continuing operations = $804,806,000

b) "Income before income taxes"

c)

	Percentage (rounded) of total revenue	
	1976	1975
Cost of rentals	14.6	16.5
Cost of sales	11.0	9.9
Research and development	5.1	4.9
General, selling, service, and administrative	49.7	48.1
Other income (revenue)	1.9	1.6
Other deductions	3.2	3.5
Income from operations before taxes	18.3	18.7

Operating revenues up 8.6 percent   (better)
Cost of rentals down 1.9%*   (better)
Cost of sales up 1.1%*   (worse)
G.S. and A up 1.6%*   (worse)

---

*   In proportion to total revenue.

Chapter 6

EP 6.1

RABBIT FUR COMPANY

Income Statement

Net sales		$600,000
Less cost of goods sold		400,000
Gross profit		$200,000
Less expenses:		
Bad debt expense	$ 7,000	
Capital-lease amortization	23,000	
Depreciation expense, equipment	8,000	
Insurance expense	5,000	
Property-tax expense	9,000	
Rent expense	11,000	
Supplies expense	3,000	
Utilities expense	4,000	
Wages and salary expense	80,000	150,000
Net income before extraordinary items		$ 50,000
Less extraordinary fire loss		(75,000)
Net Loss		$(25,000)

EP 6.3

a) Neither	e) REV	i) EXP	m) EXP
b) Neither	f) Neither	j) EXP	n) Neither
c) EXP	g) REV	k) REV	o) REV
d) EXP	h) EXP	l) EXP	p) Neither

EP 6.5

a) Not extraordinary	d) Extraordinary
b) Not extraordinary	e) Extraordinary
c) Not extraordinary	f) Not extraordinary, since not material

EP 6.7

TOMPKINS COMPANY

Statement of Owner's Capital
For the year ended 12/31/X2

Owner's Capital 12/31/X1	$38,000
Add: Net Income	32,000
	$70,000
Less: Withdrawals	20,000
Owner's Capital 12/31/X2	$50,000

EP 6.9

Sales	IFFO
Cost of goods sold	DFFO
Wages and salaries	DFFO
Rentals	DFFO
Utilities	DFFO
Insurance	DFFO
Supplies	DFFO
Extraordinary loss of inventory	NFFO

EP 6.11

BAUER COMPANY

	Amount	Percent of sales
Operating expenses:		
Cost of goods sold	$300,000	60.0
Wages and salaries	112,000	22.4
Rentals	20,000	4.0
Utilities	4,000	0.8
Insurance	6,000	1.2
Supplies	9,000	1.8
Depreciation on equipment	18,000	3.6
Amortization of leasehold improvement	22,000	4.4

$$\$191,000 \div 500,000 = 38.2\%$$

SP 6.13(a)

ALBERT COMPANY

Balance Sheet
As of 12/31/X6 (000 omitted)

Assets		Equities	
Cash	$126	Accounts payable	$ 85
Accounts receivable	150	Taxes payable	14
Inventory	85	Interest payable	3
Supplies	10	Wages payable	8
Prepaid insurance	4	Total Current	
Total Current Assets	$375	Liabilities	$110
Land	40	Noncurrent notes payable	120
Buildings	200	Total Liabilities	$230
Accum. depr. on bldgs.	(140)		
Equipment	175		
Accum. depr. on equip.	(145)		
Patents	9	Owner's Equity	290
Deferred charges	6		
Total Assets	$520	Total Equities	$520

ALBERT COMPANY

Income Statement
For the Year Ending 12/31/X6 (000 omitted)

Sales		$900
Cost of goods sold		590
Gross profit		$310
Operating expenses:		
Wages and salaries	$128	
Utilities	6	
Supplies	25	
Insurance	4	
Depreciation	24	
Amortization	2	
Interest	12	$201
Loss on inventory		20
Loss on patent		5
Gain on sale of equipment*		2
Income from operations before taxes		$ 86
Provision for income taxes		34
Income from operations		$ 52
Extraordinary earthquake loss		25
Net Income		$ 27

---

* Equipment cost $15,000, book value $5,000; therefore accumulated depreciation $10,000. Sale recorded by:

Increasing cash	$ 7,000
Decreasing accumulated depreciation	10,000
Decreasing equipment	15,000
Increasing gain on sale of equipment	2,000

ALBERT COMPANY

Statement of Owner's Capital
For the Year Ending 12/31/X6 (000 omitted)

Owner's capital 12/31/X5	$284
Add net income	27
Less withdrawals	21
Owner's capital 12/31/X6	$290

SP 6.13(b)

Determination of Funds from Operations

Net income		$27,000
Add: Depreciation	$24,000	
Amortization	2,000	
Loss on patent	5,000	
Earthquake loss	25,000	56,000
Subtract: Gain on sale of equipment		2,000
Funds from operations		$81,000

SP 6.15

Determination of Funds from Operations

Net income		$200,000
Add: Depreciation	$35,000	
Amortization	21,000	56,000
Subtract: Gain on asset disposition		14,000
Funds from operations		$242,000
Funds desired		$600,000
From operations		242,000
From asset disposition*		14,000
To be obtained from outside sources		$344,000

* Assumes noncurrent asset had zero book value at time of disposition.

Chapter 7

EP 7.1 Events **not** involving flows of funds (working capital):
(d), (e), (f), (h).

EP 7.3 a) Although Widget is acquiring $300 more of noncurrent assets than it is selling, information on asset expiration (depreciation and amortization) is required before this question may be answered affirmatively.

b) Definitely increasing or expanding. In 19XX long-term investment increased by $345.

Additional owner investment	$100
Retained funds from operations	270
Less net reduction in long-term debt	25
Increase in long-term investment	$345

c) Apparently decreasing as net reduction of long-term debt ($25) and increase in owner investment ($370).

d) Lower long-term debt ratio (see above) should increase potential borrowing capacity (liquidity). However, of $395 of new assets, $350 is committed to relatively nonliquid noncurrent assets.

EP 7.5 a) AJAX COMPANY—Abbreviated Balance Sheet as of 12/31/X2

Net working capital	$125,000	Long-term debt	$150,000
Noncurrent Assets		Owner's Equity	225,000
(net)	250,000		
Total	$375,000	Total	$375,000

b) Criteria:
Growth: industry, 20 percent; AJAX, 25 percent.
Balanced long-term debt/equity: 19X1 = 0.4; 19X2 = 0.4

Yes, Ajax should be considered an active candidate for future evaluation. The desirable long-term debt-to-equity balance is being maintained, and the firm's growth rate exceeds industry average.

EP 7.7

Sources		Applications	
Funds from operations[b]	$60	Purchase of equipment	$30
Sale of noncurrent assets	10	Owner withdrawals	20
New long-term debt	40	Retire noncurrent debt[a]	50
		Increase net working capital	10
	$110		$110

a) Beginning debt ($130) plus new debt ($40) = $170 of debt. If only $120 remained at year end, $50 was retired.

b) With $110 of total applications, total sources must have been $110 and funds from operations $60.

EP 7.9 a) Firm B was neither replacing nor expanding its capacity assets.

b) Firm B, since withdrawals exceed funds from operations.

EP 7.11

Sources		Applications	
Funds from operations	$45	Purchase new equipment	$100
New noncurrent debt	80	Owner withdrawals	10
		Increase balance of net working capital	15
	$125		$125

SP 7.13   a) Fong Company Pro-Forma 12/31/X1 Balance Sheet

Cash	$18,000	Accounts payable	$60,000
Accounts receivable (net)	75,000	Other current	
Inventory	45,000	liabilities	5,000
Supplies	7,500	Total Current	
Total Current		Liabilities	$65,000
Assets	$145,500		
Fixed assets	240,000	Long-term investment	
Less accum. deprec.	(90,000)	required	230,500
Total Assets	$295,500	Total Equities	$295,500

b) Additional net working capital   = $25,500
    Additional noncurrent assets   = 25,000
    Total required additional capital $50,500

c) 19X1 projected funds from operations $75,000
    Less necessary withdrawal   45,000
    40 percent balance available $30,000

Therefore, needing $50,500 (see above) and generating only $30,000 net, Mr. Fong will need to obtain $20,500 from outside sources.

SP 7.15   Net funds generated $130; $200 funds from operations indicates amount that would have been generated had extraordinary fund loss not occurred.

Chapter 8

EP 8.1

	Units	Cost	Total
Beginning inventory	200	$30	$ 6,000
Purchases: July	300	35	10,500
November	150	40	6,000
January	200	50	10,000
Goods available	850		$32,500

Weighted average cost = $32,500 divided by 850 = $38.24 (rounded).

a) Ending inventory = $11,472 (rounded);
b) Cost of goods sold = $21,028 (rounded).

EP 8.3

	Units	Cost	Total	Average cost
Beginning inventory	200	$30	$ 6,000	
July purchase	300	$35	10,500	
Available	500		$16,500	$33
September shipment	250 (@$33)		8,250	
October shipment	100 (@$33)		3,300	
November purchase	150	$40	6,000	
Available	300		$10,950	$36.50
December shipment	200 (@$36.50)		7,300	

Therefore, cost of goods sold = $8,250 + $3,300 + $7,300 = $18,850.

EP 8.5

B's cost of goods sold (FIFO)	$160,000
B's cost of goods sold (LIFO)	205,000
Increase in expense under LIFO	$45,000
B's income under FIFO	$70,000
Less increased LIFO expense	45,000
B's income under LIFO	$25,000

EP 8.7   Net purchases = $460,000.

EP 8.9   Ending inventory should be reported at $95,000 cost since "market" was $97,000. No adjustment is necessary, since $95,000 is lower of cost or market.

SP 8.11

	Cost	Selling
Beginning inventory	$ 22,000	$ 34,000
Net purchases	140,000	226,000
Markdowns	N.A.	(15,000)
Goods available	$162,000	$245,000
Ending inventory	?	40,000

Goods available cost percentage of selling = 66 percent (rounded).
66 percent of $40,000 = $26,400, estimated cost.

Chapter 9

EP 9.1

List price of machine	$260,000
Freight	4,000
Insurance while in transit	400
Installation of concrete base	500
Installation of power lines	1,600
Installation of machine	1,300
Total cost of machine	$267,800

Note. $900 maintenance excluded as not being part of cost of preparing machine for use.

EP 9.3

	A Straight-line	B Years' Digits	C Double-declining balance
Cost	$50,000	$50,000	$50,000
Salvage	5,000	5,000	N.A.
Depreciable base	$45,000	$45,000	$50,000
Estimated life	5 yrs.	5 yrs.	5 yrs.
First year's depreciation	$ 9,000	$15,000[a]	20,000[b]

Notes.   a) Sum of digits = 15; 5/15 × $45,000 = $15,000.
b) 40 percent of $50,000 = $20,000.

EP 9.5

Book value of assets sold =	$28,000
Realized gain =	2,000
Sale proceeds =	$30,000

EP 9.7 Let X = Original cost as of 1/1/X3.
Depreciation expense for 19X3 = $0.4X$.
Book value as of 1/1/X4 = $0.6X$.
Depreciation expense for 19X4 = $0.4(0.6X)$.
Accumulated depreciation as of 12/31/X4 = $0.4X + 0.4(0.6X)$ = $30,600.
X = $47,812 (rounded).

EP 9.9

12/31/X9 Book value	$28,125
12/31/X9 Accumulated depreciation	21,875
Original cost	$50,000
First-year depreciation (25 percent)	12,500
Book value, end of first year	$37,500
Second-year depreciation (25 percent)	9,375
Book value, end of second year	$28,125
Therefore, asset was acquired	1/1/X8

SP 9.11

Depreciable base	$48,000
Third-year straight-line depreciation	12,000
Third-year SYD depreciation (2/10)	9,600
Higher third-year depreciation under straight-line	$2,400

Therefore, for comparison, Hatch should mentally increase his reported operating income by $2,400.

Chapter 10

EP 10.1

	Pat	Mike	Total
Average investment	$60,000	$20,000	$80,000
Step 1: 10 percent distribution	6,000	2,000	8,000
Remaining to be distributed			8,000
Step 2: Percentage distribution	5,600	2,400	8,000
Total distribution	$11,600	$ 4,400	$16,000

EP 10.3 Total Assets − Total Liabilities = Total Stockholders' Equity

$400,000 − $150,000 = $250,000

Total contributed capital	+	Total retained earnings	=	Total Stockholders' Equity
$200,000	+	?	=	$250,000

Retained earnings = $50,000.

EP 10.5

Beginning retained earnings	$200,000
Net loss	50,000
Dividends	10,000
Ending retained earnings	$140,000

EP 10.7

Capital stock	$100,000
Retained earnings (deficit)	(8,000)
Total Stockholders' Equity	$92,000

EP 10.9

ABLE CORPORATION

Balance Sheet as of 12/31/X1

Assets		Equities	
Cash	$250,000	Total Liabilities	$220,000
Other assets	840,000	Capital stock*	440,000
		Paid-in capital	190,000
		Retained earnings	240,000
Total		Total	
Assets	$1,090,000	Equities	$1,090,000

* $5 par; 88,000 shares issued and outstanding.

EP 10.11 Total book value to common shareholders of Charlie Corporation equals Total Owners' Equity ($5,900,000) less preferred shareholder claim ($500,000 + 20,000 = $520,000) equals $5,380,000.

EP 10.13

Unappropriated retained earnings 12/31/X0	$1,670,000
Add net income for 19X1	400,000
Subtract preferred dividend (5,000 shs × $12)	60,000
Subtract common cash dividend	300,000
Subtract stock dividend (10,000 shs × $40)	400,000
Add reduction (return) of appropriation	400,000
Unappropriated retained earnings 12/31/X1	$1,710,000

SP 10.15

DAWE CORPORATION

Owners' Equity Section of 12/31/X1 Balance Sheet

Capital stock ($5 par 40,000 shares issued)	$200,000
Paid-in capital	62,000
Appropriated for treasury stock restriction	28,500
Unappropriated retained earnings	321,500
Treasury stock (500 shs)	(28,500)
Total Stockholders' Equity	$583,500

Chapter 11

EP 11.1   a) As of 12/31/X1: $90,000 (not reported above cost),
   As of 12/31/X2: $80,000 (loss recognized),
   As of 12/31/X3: $88,000 (partial recovery recognized).

   b) In year 19X1   : No income effect,
   In year 19X2   : Income would reflect $10,000 loss,
   In year 19X3   : Income would reflect $ 8,000 gain.

EP 11.3

Note receivable	$8,400
Less discount on note receivable*	400
	$8,000

---

* Principal $+ \left(\text{Principal} \times \dfrac{6}{12} \times 0.10 \right) = \$8,400,$

Principal $= \$8,000.$

EP 11.5   a) Property held under capital lease $98,181
              b) Current obligation under capital lease   4,909 (rounded)
              c) Noncurrent obligation under capital lease   93,272

EP 11.7   The $40,000 should not be treated as an expense in the year the bonds were sold. Instead it should be capitalized under Deferred Charges and amortized to Interest Expense over the 20 years of the bonds' life.

EP 11.9   a) Equipment cost   = $100,000   ($30,000 cash plus $70,000 present value of note)

              b) Noncurrent note payable $105,000
                 Less discount on note
                    payable   (35,000)
                                           $70,000

SP 11.11   a) Mike's investments account:
                  Beginning balance (12/31/X0) $412,000
                  Add share (40 percent) of Nice
                     Corporation's net income   60,000
                  Subtract dividends received   30,000
                  Balance 12/31/X1 $442,000
              b) Investments revenue $ 60,000

SP 11.13   a) $20,000 annual depreciation expense
              b) $33,000 provision for income taxes (less $20,000 ITC)
              c) $13,000 taxes payable ($33,000 less $20,000 ITC)
              d) $20,000 ITC expense reduction offset against provision for taxes
              e) $120,000 net income after taxes

SP 11.15   a) Transactions or adjustments from group which represents revenue or gain: (1); (2), (4), and (15) if sold above book value; (14); (23); (24); and (31).

              b) Transactions or adjustments from group which represent expense or loss: (11); (2), (4), and (15) if sold below book value; (16); (26); (28); (29) is a contra-expense; (37); and (38).

              c) Transactions and adjustments from group which have no effect on the income statement: (2), (4), and (15) if sold at book value; (3); (5); (6); (7); (8); (9); (10); (12); (13); (17); (18); (19); (20); (21); (22); (25); (27); (30); (32); (33); (34); (35); and (36).

SP 11.17   Transactions and adjustments which involve flow of working capital funds: (1); (2), (4), and (15) if gain or loss; (5) where loan is noncurrent; (7); (8) where noncurrent asset purchased; (10) where retiring noncurrent debt; (11); (12); (14); (16); (23); (24); (26); (28); (29); (31); (36); (37); and (38).

Chapter 12

EP 12.1   a) C   b) D   c) C   d) C
              e) E   f) C   g) D   h) D

EP 12.3   Increase cash $320,000
             Increase bonds payable   300,000
             Increase bond premium   20,000

EP 12.5   Interest Expense $23,000

$$\left(\text{Stated interest of } \$24{,}000 - \frac{1}{20} \text{ Bond premium} = \$1{,}000\right)$$

EP 12.7   a) Property under capital lease $102,796 ($125,640 original cost less $\frac{10}{55}$ amortization of $22,844)

b) Current obligation under capital lease $35,465 ($25,000 delayed first-year payment + $10,465 present value of second-year payment)

c) Noncurrent obligations under capital lease $46,226 ($56,591 original noncurrent liability less $10,465 maturing portion)

d) 19X2 lease interest expense $6,051 ($25,000 payment less principal portion $18,949)

SP 12.9

	Income statement	Tax return
Income before depreciation	$175,000	$175,000
Depreciation	25,000	50,000
Income after depreciation	$150,000	$125,000
Provision for taxes at 40 percent	$ 60,000	N.A.
Actual tax liability at 40 percent	N.A.	$ 50,000

a) $50,000 of taxes payable

b) $10,000 of deferred income tax

c) $60,000 of provision for income tax

SP 12:11   a) $300,000

b) $ 40,000

c) $1,275,000 (300 bonds × 25 shares × $10 par added)

d) $585,000*

---

* $300,000 less $40,000 discount = $260,000 book value of CVD's converted. $260,000 less $75,000 par value of shares exchanged equals $185,000.

SP 12.13   a) $624,000 (600 bonds × $1040)

b) $104,000 loss on extinguishment ($624,000 cash paid less $520,000 book value of debt extinguished)

SP 12.15   Shares before conversion = 120,000 shares
19X0 earnings = $120,000 (120,000 shs × $1.00)
19X0 earnings before taxes = $200,000 ($120,000 = 0.6X)
19X0 earnings before interest and taxes = $240,000 ($40,000 of bond interest)
19X1 earnings before taxes = $240,000 (no interest after conversion)
19X1 earnings after 0.40 tax = $144,000
Shares after conversion = 184,000 shares
19X1 EPS = $.78 per share (rounded)

SP 12.17 a) Transactions and adjustments from group involving revenue: none.

b) Transactions and adjustments from group involving expense: (89); (91) if goods or services purchased have no future usefulness; and (97).

c) Transactions and adjustments from group involving neither revenue nor expense: (83); (84); (85); (86); (87); (88); (90); (91) if goods or services are assets; (92); (93); (94); (95); (96); (98); (99); and (100).

SP 12.19 a) No working capital flow and neither revenue nor expense: (83) if not involved with noncurrent assets; (85); (86); (88); (90) if not involved in refunding to noncurrent debt; (91) if goods or services are current assets; (92); (93); (94) if not involved with noncurrent debt; (98); and (100).

b) No working capital flow but do involve either revenue or expense: none in this group.

c) Represent working capital flow but do not involve either revenue or expense: (83) if involved with noncurrent asset; (84); (87); (90) if involved in refunding to noncurrent debt; (91) if goods or services are noncurrent assets; (94) if involved with noncurrent assets (95); (96); and (99).

d) Involve both working capital flow and revenue or expense: (89); (91) if goods or services have no future usefulness; and (97).

CHAPTER 12 APPENDIX (CA 12): Selected solutions for parts of selected problems.

CA 12.1 a) $3,000   e) $6,000
c) $3,565 ($5,000 × .713)   g) $4,984 ($8,000 × .623)

CA 12.2 a) $2,164 (rounded) ($500 × 4.329)
c) $12,830 (rounded) ($400 × 12 × 2.673) if discounted annually. Also could be discounted over 36 periods (months) at one-half percent per month.
e) $12,960 ($4,000 × 3.240)

CA 12.3 a) Note PV = $5,000 face value; no discount or premium
c) Note receivable $7,000
Discount on note receivable   1,158
PV future payments $5,842

$7,000 × .340 = $2,380
  420 × 8.244 = $3,462 (rounded)
                        $5,842

CA 12.4 b) Bonds payable $10,000
Bond premium   2,115
PV future payments $12,115

$10,000 ×   .258 = $ 2,580
    900 × 10.594 =   9,535 (rounded)
                        $12,115

Chapter 13

EP 13.1 a) 3.1 to 1 (rounded)   c) .3 to 1 (rounded)
b) 1.6 to 1   d) 17.6 times (rounded)

EP 13.3
a) 1.9 times (rounded)
b) 9.0 times
c) 40.6 days (rounded)
d) 4.0 times
e) 91.2 days (rounded)
f) 23.8% (rounded)

EP 13.5
a) 19.1% (rounded)
b) 20.0% (rounded)

EP 13.7
a) $3.87 (rounded)
b) $1.27 (rounded)
c) 6.5% (rounded)
d) 2.1% (rounded)

EP 13.9
a) No, it has been decreasing:

19X0 = 58%
19X1 = 56%
19X2 = 54% (rounded)

b) Yes, using EBIT/Sales as the preferred method of calculating operating ratio, the ratio has definitely improved:

19X0 = 21%
19X1 = 21.9% (rounded)
19X2 = 25%

c) An owner/manager might wish to investigate further both the significantly declining gross-profit ratio and also the rapidly declining expenditure for maintenance. All other expenses appear reasonably in control in comparison to other years.

EP 13.11
a) No, it appears to be reducing its capacity:

	19X0	19X1	19X2
Depreciation	$ 60	$ 55	$ 50
Asset Dispositions	0	30	100
Asset Acquisitions	70	40	0

b) No, the owners are divesting:

	19X0	19X1	19X2
Earnings retained	$ 50	$(100)	$(400)
Additional owner investment	10	0	0

Dividend policy appears to be to declare substantial dividends regardless of earnings.

c) No, the evidence given indicates that the firm is becoming less solvent:

	19X0	19X1	19X2
Increase (decrease) in net working capital	$ 20	$ (35)	$(100)

d) The firm is radically increasing its debt proportion:

	19X0	19X1	19X2
Additional debt-net	$ (30)	$ 20	$ 150
Additional Owner's Equity	60	(100)	(400)

SP 13.13
a) Return on investment data is not provided. Independent of assets invested, Sugarman appears to be doing a slightly better job. Both have the same EBIT/SALES of 21% for 19X0. However Sugarman's gross profit and bottom line are significantly better.

b) Sugarman is significantly better than Tilamook with respect to gross profit. Assuming both firms follow the same inventory-flow assumption, Sugarman might be purchasing more advantageously than Tilamook and/or Tilamook might be discounting more prices. Other items are either not significant or not controllable (taxes).

c) If Sugarman were using FIFO, and Tilamook LIFO, then Tilamook could be doing a better job, depending upon the rate of inflation.

SP 13.15 a) Ultrasound is investing in capacity assets more than Victoria is in 19X0.

b) In 19X0, Victoria distributed only 20% of earnings reinvesting 80%. Ultrasound distributed 90% of 19X0 earnings in dividends and reinvested only 10%.

c) In 19X0, Ultrasound improved its solvency more than Victoria did. It added $20,000 to its balance of Net Working Capital as compared to a $5,000 decrease for Victoria.

d) In 19X0, neither firm had a net increase in noncurrent debt. Victoria, with a net reduction of $185,000, was reducing its indebtedness more than Ultrasound was, with only $30,000 of debt reduction.

SP 13.17 a) For each of the first 11 items, the better firm during 19X0 was:

1) Nan	2) Nan	3) Oboe
4) Oboe	5) Oboe	6) Oboe
7) Oboe	8) Oboe	9) Oboe
10) Nan	11) Nan	

b) Oboe would be preferable, since it is earning 10% on the cost of the stock, and paying a 6.7% (rounded) return in dividends. Nan is only earning 9.1% (rounded) and paying 4.1% (rounded).

c) Oboe would appear a safer investment for both an owner and a creditor, since it has only half Nan's debt ratio and 1.5 times the coverage of interest (times interest earned).

d) Nan is doing a better job of financial management and trading on equity. Oboe appears too conservative.

SP 13.19 For 1976:

		Xerox	Addison-Wesley
1)	Current Ratio	1.9 to 1	2.6 to 1
2)	Quick Ratio	1.2 to 1	1.3 to 1
3)	Debt Ratio	.46 to 1	.4 to 1
4)	EBIT	$924,628,000	$6,475,000
5)	Times Interest Earned	7.7 times	8.4 times
6)	Asset Turnover	.97 times	1.1 times
7)	Receivables Turnover	7.2 times	4.1 times
8)	Inventory Turnover	1.0 times	1.6 times
9)	Return on Assets Employed	20.4%	13.4%
10)	Return on Owner's Equity	18.4%	10.8%
11)	Return on Common Equity	17.6%	10.8%

EP 14.1   *Hodge Company for year ending 12/31/X1:*

Funds from operations	$30,000
Minus: Net increase in noncash current assets	5,000
Decrease in total current liabilities	10,000
Cash generated from operations	$15,000

EP 14.3   *Hodge Company Matched Pairs (000 omitted)*

Source		*Application*	
New noncurrent debt	$ 50<----->New fixed assets		$ 50
New stock	5<----->New intangible asset		5
New stock	100<----->Retire debt		100

HODGE COMPANY

Working Capital Funds-Flow Statement
For year ending 12/31/X1 (000 omitted)

Sources:	
Funds provided by operations	$ 30
Disposition of equipment	38
New noncurrent debt	50
New stock	50
Total Sources	$168
Applications:	
Acquire new buildings	$ 20
Retire noncurrent debt	83
Dividends	15
Increase balance net working capital	50
Total Applications	$168

EP 14.5

HODGE COMPANY

Statement of Cash Flow for 19X1

Sources:

Funds from operations	$ 30,000
Less: Net increase in noncash current assets	5,000
Decrease in total current liabilities	10,000
Cash generated from operations	$15,000
Disposition of equipment	38,000
New noncurrent debt	50,000
Sale of stock	50,000
Total Sources	$153,000

Applications:

Acquire noncurrent assets	$20,000
Retire noncurrent debt	83,000
Dividends	15,000
Increase balance of cash on hand	35,000
Total Applications	$153,000

EP 15.1   a) zero

b) $40,000

c) $600,000

EP 15.3   a) $30,000   (Q not consolidated or eliminated)

b) $30,000

c) $50,000   (25% of subsidiary book value including earnings)

d) $950,000

EP 15.5

P AND S CONSOLIDATED BALANCE SHEET

Cash	$400	Accounts payable	$ 660
Accounts receivable		Other cur. liab.	500
(net)	860	Total Cur. Liab.	$1,160
Inventory	800	Bonds payable	300
Total Current		Less bond discount	(30)
Assets	$2,060	Minority interest	200
Investments	$210	Capital stock	1,000
Fixed assets	1,200	Retained earnings	540
Less accum. deprecia-			
tion	(500)		
Goodwill	200		
Total Assets	$3,170	Total Equities	$3,170

EP 15.7

P AND S CONSOLIDATED INCOME STATEMENT

Sales		$1,300
Cost of goods sold		600
Gross profit		$ 700
Other operating expenses:		
Wages and salaries	$400	
Depreciation	130	
Interest	5	
Rent	140	
Other revenues		80
Operating income		$105
Less income taxes		40
Net Income		$ 65

EP 15.9   a) $170,000 (equivalent to S's contributed capital)

b) (1) $170,000 (intercompany ownership)

(2) $100,000 (intercompany ownership)

(3) $70,000   (intercompany ownership)

(4) None

c) $400,000   (combined total)

EP 16.1   Under GAAP: Inventory $45,000; Fixed assets $250,000.
Replacement cost*: Inventory $61,875; Fixed assets $337,500
Holding gain: $104,375

---

* Adjusted by indices constructed from representative data.

EP 16.3   a) $16,200   (5% of ($300,000 times 1.08))

b) $10,800

c) $28,800

d) $18,000

SP 16.5

PROGRESSIVE CORPORATION

Balance Sheet as of 12/31/X1 Prepared on Replacement Cost Basis
(000 omitted)

Cash	$ 60	Accounts payable	$100
Accounts receivable		Other current liabilities	25
(net)	120	Total Current	
Inventory	94.5	Liabilities	$125
Other current assets	30	Noncurrent liabilities	100
Total Current		Total Liabilities	$225
Assets	$304.5	Contributed capital	300
Investments	50	Retained earnings	75
Fixed assets	575	Holding gains	42
Less accumulated			
deprec.	(287.5)		
Total Assets	$642	Total Equities	$642

Income Statement for 19X1 Prepared on a Replacement Cost Basis
(000 omitted)

Sales		$720
Cost of goods sold		400
Gross profit		$320
Depreciation	$ 57.5	
Other operating expenses	200	257.5
Operating income before taxes		$62.5
Income taxes	$30	
Retroactive depreciation	30	60
Distributable income		$ 2.5
Holding gains		79.5*
Total income and gains		$82

---

*Inventory $4.5 plus fixed assets $75.

SOLUTIONS TO ODD-NUMBERED PREPARER PROBLEMS

Chapter 5

PP 5.1

		DR	CR
1)	Cash	$ 450,000	
	Sales		$ 450,000
2)	Accounts Receivable	1,000,000	
	Sales		1,000,000
3)	Sales Returns and Allowances	130,000	
	Accounts Receivable		130,000
4)	Cash	850,000	
	Accounts Receivable		850,000
5)	Inventory (or Purchases)	815,000	
	Accounts Payable		815,000
6)	Rent Expense	96,000	
	Cash		96,000
7)	Utilities Expense	17,250	
	Accounts Payable		17,250
8)	Bookkeeping Expense	18,000	
	Accounts Payable		18,000
9)	Accounts Payable	849,000	
	Cash		849,000
10)	Wages Expense	267,440	
	Wages Payable		267,440
11)	Wages Payable	285,440	
	Cash		285,440
12)	Incidental Expense	9,500	
	Cash		9,500
13)	Cash	61,000	
	Rental Revenue		61,000
14)	Owner's Equity (or Withdrawals)	135,000	
	Cash		135,000
15)	Cost of Goods Sold	800,000	
	Inventory		800,000
16)	Wages Expense	19,000	
	Accrued Wages Payable		19,000
17)	Bookkeeping Expense	2,000	
	Accrued Fees Payable		2,000
18)	Utilities Expense	1,750	
	Accrued Utilities Payable		1,750
19)	Accrued Rent Receivable	5,440	
	Rent Revenue		5,440

PP 5.3

	DR	CR
Adjusted Trial Balance		
Accounts payable		$ 75
Accounts receivable	$ 300	
Accrued wages payable		25
Cash	100	
Cost of goods sold	900	
Current Notes Payable		50
Inventory	500	
Other current liabilities		25
Other operating expense	225	
Owner's Equity		600
Sales		1,900
Sales returns and allowances	100	
Utilities expense	150	
Wages expense	400	
Totals	$2,675	$2,675

PP 5.5

		DR	CR
a)	Bad Debt Expense	$ 800	
	Accounts Receivable		$ 800
b)	Supplies Expense	4,500	
	Supplies		4,500
c)	Accrued Interest Receivable	750	
	Interest Revenue		750
d)	Accrued Rent Receivable	600	
	Rent Revenue		600
e)	Wage and Salaries Expense	1,700	
	Accrued Wages and Salaries Payable		1,700
f)	Telephone Expense	300	
	Accrued Utilities Payable		300

Chapter 6

PP 6.1

		DR	CR
3)	Utilities Expense	$ 114	
	Cash		$ 114
4)	Janitorial Expense	200	
	Accounts Payable		200
5)	Accounts Receivable	40	
	Sales		40
7)	Cash	70	
	Interest Revenue		70
8)	Depreciation Expense	800	
	Accumulated Depreciation (office equipment)		800

		DR	CR
9)	Wages Expense	900	
	Wages Payable		900
10)	Insurance Expense	400	
	Prepaid Insurance		400
11)	Accounts Receivable	142	
	Bookkeeping Services Revenue		142
12)	Fire Loss of Inventory	4,000	
	Inventory		4,000
13)	Wages Expense	4,000	
	Wages Payable		4,000
15)	Accounts Receivable	14,000	
	Sales		14,000

PP 6.3   a) Albert Company T accounts showings (b) opening balances, (d) all temporary accounts closed, and (e) ending balances.

Cash				Accounts Payable	
$ 80,000	$120,000			$ 75,000	$ 75,000
	6,000			500,000	585,000
100,000	142,000				$ 85,000
782,000	500,000				
7,000	21,000			Taxes Payable	
	25,000				
	9,000			$40,000	$40,000
	20,000				14,000
$126,000					$14,000

Accounts Receivable				Other Current Liabilities	
$132,000	$782,000			$27,000	$27,000
800,000					
$150,000					

Inventory				Noncurrent Notes Payable	
$110,000	$ 20,000				$120,000
585,000	675,000				
$ 85,000				Owner's Equity	

Supplies					
$ 35,000	$ 35,000			$ 21,000	$284,000
$ 10,000					27,000
					$290,000

Prepaid Insurance	
$ 8,000	$ 4,000
$ 4,000	

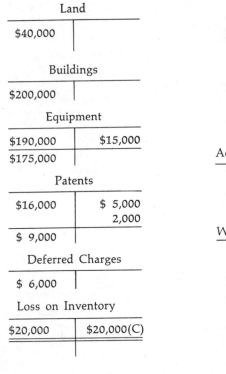

Land

$40,000	

Buildings

$200,000	

Equipment

$190,000	$15,000
$175,000	

Patents

$16,000	$ 5,000
	2,000
$ 9,000	

Deferred Charges

$ 6,000	

Loss on Inventory

$20,000	$20,000(C)

Sales

$900,000(c)	$900,000

Accum. Depr. on Bldgs.

	$131,000
	9,000
	$140,000

Accum. Depr. on Equipment

$ 10,000	$140,000
	15,000
	$145,000

Wages and Salaries Expense

$120,000	
8,000	
$128,000	$128,000(c)

Utilities Expense

$ 6,000	$ 6,000(c)

Loss on Patents

$ 5,000	$ 5,000(c)

Extraordinary Earthquake Loss

$ 25,000	$ 25,000(c)

Cost of Goods Sold

$675,000	$ 85,000
$590,000	$590,000(c)

Insurance Expense

$4,000	$4,000(c)

Gain on Sale Equipment

$2,000(c)	$2,000

Supplies Expense

$35,000	$10,000
$25,000	$25,000(c)

Depreciation Expense

$24,000	$24,000(c)

Amortization Expense		Interest Payable	
$2,000	$2,000(c)		$3,000

		Accrued Wages Payable	
Interest Expense			$8,000
$12,000	$12,000(c)	Income Summary	

Provision for Taxes			
		$128,000	$900,000
$34,000	$34,000(c)	6,000	2,000
		20,000	
		5,000	
		25,000	
		590,000	
		25,000	
		4,000	
		24,000	
		2,000	
		12,000	
		34,000	
		$ 27,000(c)	$ 27,000

c) Albert Company journal entries:

	DR	CR
Cash	$100,000	
Accounts Receivable	800,000	
Sales		$900,000
Cash	782,000	
Accounts Receivable		782,000
Inventory	585,000	
Accounts Payable		585,000
Wages and Salaries Expense	120,000	
Cash		120,000
Utilities Expense	6,000	
Cash		6,000
Accounts Payable	75,000	
Taxes Payable	40,000	
Other Current Liabilities	27,000	
Cash		142,000
Accounts Payable	500,000	
Cash		500,000
Loss on Inventory	20,000	
Inventory		20,000
Loss on Patents	5,000	
Patents		5,000
Owner's Equity	21,000	
Cash		21,000

Cash	7,000	
Accumulated Depreciation on Equipment	10,000	
Equipment		15,000
Gain on Sale of Equipment		2,000
Extraordinary Earthquake Loss	25,000	
Cash		25,000
Cost of Goods Sold	675,000	
Inventory		675,000
Inventory	85,000	
Cost of Goods Sold		85,000
Supplies Expense	35,000	
Supplies		35,000
Supplies	10,000	
Supplies Expense		10,000
Insurance Expense	4,000	
Prepaid Insurance		4,000
Depreciation Expense	24,000	
Accum. Depr. on Bldgs.		9,000
Accum. Depr. on Equip.		15,000
Amortization Expense	2,000	
Patents		2,000
Interest Expense	12,000	
Cash		9,000
Interest Payable		3,000
Wages and Salaries Expense	8,000	
Accrued Wages Payable		8,000
Provision for Taxes	34,000	
Cash		20,000
Taxes Payable		14,000

Chapter 8

PP 8.1

		DR	CR
a)	Purchases	$50,000	
	Accounts Payable		$50,000
b)	Accounts Payable	4,000	
	Purchase Returns		4,000
c)	Transportation in	5,000	
	Accounts Payable		5,000
d)	Accounts Payable	46,000	
	Cash		45,080
	Purchase Discounts		920

Chapter 9

PP 9.2

		DR	CR
	Land	$ 30,000	
	Building	260,000	
	Cash		$ 20,000
	Noncurrent Note Payable		270,000

PP 9.3

	DR	CR
Depreciation Expense	$ 66,000	
Accumulated Depreciation		$ 66,000

PP 9.5

	DR	CR
Depreciation Expense	$ 4,000	
Accumulated Depreciation		$ 4,000
Cash	40,000	
Accumulated Depreciation	194,000	
Equipment		230,000
Gain on Sale of Equipment		4,000

PP 9.7

	DR	CR
Depreciation Expense	$ 1,650	
Accumulated Depreciation		$ 1,650
Equipment	17,350	
Accumulated Depreciation	8,650	
Cash		6,000
Note Payable		5,000
Equipment		15,000

Chapter 10

PP 10.1

			DR	CR
b)		Dividends (or Retained Earnings)	$ 80,000	
		Dividends Payable		$ 80,000
		Dividends Payable	80,000	
		Cash		80,000
c)		Retained Earnings	180,000	
		Capital Stock		40,000
		Paid-in Capital		140,000
d)		No entry required. Footnote changed to read "$5 par; 88,000 shares issued and outstanding."		

PP 10.3

			DR	CR
b)		Unappropriated Retained Earnings	$360,000	
		Dividends Payable		$360,000
c)		Unappropriated Retained Earnings	400,000	
		Capital Stock		100,000
		Paid-in Stock		300,000
d)		Appropriation for Self-Insurance	400,000	
		Unappropriated Retained Earnings		400,000

		DR	CR
PP 10.5			
	Cash	$22,000	
	Treasury Stock		$20,000
	Paid-in Capital		2,000
	Reserve for Treasury Stock Restriction	20,000	
	Unappropriated Retained Earnings		20,000
	Treasury Stock	28,500	
	Cash		28,500
	Unappropriated Retained Earnings	28,500	
	Appropriated for Treasury Stock Restriction		28,500

Chapter 11

PP 11.1	19X1	(No entry required)		
	19X2	Loss on Marketable Securities	$10,000	
		Marketable Securities		$10,000
	19X3	Marketable Securities	8,000	
		Gain on Marketable Securities		8,000
PP 11.3		Notes Receivable	$8,400	
		Discount on Notes Receivable		$ 400
		Accounts Receivable		8,000
PP 11.5		Property under Capital Lease	$98,181	
		Current Capital Lease Obligation		$ 4,909
		Noncurrent Capital Lease Obligation		93,272
PP 11.7		Equipment	$100,000	
		Discount on Note Payable	35,000	
		Cash		$ 30,000
		Note Payable		105,000
PP 11.9		Cash	$30,000	
		Investments		$30,000
		Investments	60,000	
		Investments Revenue		60,000

Chapter 12

PP 12.1	Sales (current year)	$7,000	
	Unearned Revenue		$7,000
	Unearned Revenue	7,000	
	Sales (following year)		7,000
PP 12.3	Interest Expense	$24,000	
	Interest Payable		$24,000
	Interest Payable	24,000	
	Cash		24,000
	Bond Premium	1,000	
	Interest Expense		1,000

PP 12.5

Property under Capital Lease	$125,640	
Current Capital-Lease Obligation		$68,949
Noncurrent Capital-Lease Obligation		56,691
Current Capital-Lease Obligation	50,000	
Cash		50,000
Interest Expense	6,051	
Current Capital-Lease Obligation		6,051
Noncurrent Capital-Lease Obligation	10,465	
Current Capital-Lease Obligation		10,465
Amortization Expense	22,844	
Property under Capital Lease		22,844

PP 12.7

Provision for Taxes	$60,000	
Taxes Payable		$50,000
Deferred Income Tax		10,000

PP 12.9

7% CVD's Payable	$300,000	
Discount on Debentures		$ 40,000
Capital Stock		75,000
Paid-in Capital		185,000

PP 12.11

7% CVD's Payable	$600,000	
Loss on Early Debt Extinguishment	104,000	
Discount on Debentures		$ 80,000
Cash		624,000

PP 12.13

Salaries Expense	$60,000	
Withholding Taxes Payable		$12,000
F.I.C.A. Taxes Payable		3,600
Union Dues Payable		300
Salaries Payable		44,100
Salaries Expense	10,800	
F.I.C.A. Taxes Payable		3,600
F.U.T.A. Taxes Payable		2,400
Health-Plan Costs Payable		4,800

PP 14.1

WAHOO CORPORATION

SCFP Worksheet Column 1 and Column 2
(000 omitted)

	Column 1	Column 2
	12/31/X0	12/31/X1
Net working capital	$130	$259
Investments	90	92
Land	105	80
Tangible fixed assets (net)	180	150
Capital lease	80	72
Total Assets	$585	$653

	Column 1 12/31/X0	Column 2 12/31X1
Bonds payable (net)	$110	$108
Noncurrent capital-lease obligations	40	35
Deferred income tax	10	20
Total Liabilities	$160	$163
Capital stock and paid-in surplus	325	375
Investments revaluation	(10)	(15)
Retained earnings	110	130
Total Equities	$585	$653

PP 14.3

WAHOO CORPORATION

Ten SCFP-Irrelevant Entries for 19X2

		DR	CR
a)	Bond Premium	$ 2	
	Interest Expense		$ 2
b)	Investments Temporary Revaluation	5	
	Investments		5
c)	Retained Earnings	30	
	Reserve for Contingencies		30
d)	Depreciation Expense (bldg.)	20	
	Accum. Deprec. (bldg.)		20
e)	Deprec. Exp. (equip.)	25	
	Accum. Deprec. (equip.)		25
f)	Lease Amortization	8	
	Property under Capital Lease		8
g)	Investments	7	
	Investments Revenue		7
h)	Loss on Sale of Equip.	15	
	Equipment (net)		15
i)	Income Taxes	10	
	Deferred Income Tax		10
j)	Extraordinary Flood Loss	25	
	Land		25

PP 14.5

WAHOO CORPORATION

1971 SCFP Worksheet (000 omitted)

	Column 1	Column 2	Column 3	Column 4	Column 5
	12/31/X0	12/31/X1	Reversals	Revised 12/31/X1	Net changes during Year
Net working capital	$130	$259		$259	$ +129
Investments	90	92	$ + 5 (b)* − 7 (g)	90	0
Land	105	80	+25 (j)	105	0
Tangible fixed assets (net)	180	150	+20 (d) +25 (e) +15 (h)	210	+ 30
Capital lease	80	72	+ 8 (f)	80	
Total	$585	$653		$744	0
Bonds payable (net	$110	$108	+ 2 (a)	$110	0
Noncurrent lease obligation	40	35		35	− 5
Deferred income tax	10	20	−10 (i)	10	0
Contributed capital	325	375		375	+ 50
Investments revaluation	(10)	(15)	+ 5 (b)	(10)	0
Retained earnings	110	130	− 2 (a)	224	+114
Total	$585	$653	+20 (d) +25 (e) + 8 (f) − 7 (g) +15 (h) +10 (i) +25 (j)	$744	

* Letters in parentheses refer to SCFP-irrelevant entries listed under PP 14.3.

PP 14.7

a) Retained earnings changes (after reversals) $114,000
    Add: Cash dividends   25,000
    Equals: Funds from operations $139,000

b) Net Income $45,000

Add: Depreciation (bldg.)	$20,000	
Deprec. (equip.)	25,000	
Lease amortization	8,000	
Dfd. inc. tax incr.	10,000	
Loss on equip.	15,000	
Extraordinary flood loss	25,000	103,000
		$148,000
Subtract: Amort. (bond) premium	$ 2,000	
Nonfund investment rev.	7,000	9,000
Equals: Funds from operations		$139,000

PP 14.9

WAHOO CORPORATION

SCFP for Year Ending 12/31/X1

Sources		Applications	
Net income	$ 45,000	Purchase fixed assets	$ 30,000
Add: Deprec. (bldg.)	20,000	Dividends	25,000
Deprec. (equip.)	25,000	Maturing lease obliga-	
Lease amortization	8,000	tions	5,000
Dfd. tax increase	10,000		$60,000
Loss (equip.)	15,000	Incr. in Bal. Net Work-	
Loss (land)	25,000	ing Cap.	129,000
	$148,000		
Subtract: Amort. bond			
prem.	2,000		
Nonfund reve-			
nue	7,000		
Funds from operations	$139,000		
Sale of stock	50,000		
Total Sources	$189,000	Total†	$189,000

† Following unbalanced format, total applications would be $60,000, and $129,000 increase in the balance of net working capital would be shown as reconciling the difference between total sources and total applications.

PP 14.11

COLUMBIA CORPORATION

SCFP for Year Ending 12/31/X1

Sources		Applications	
Net income	$ 91,000	Additional investments	$ 5,000
Add: Depreciation	35,000	Purchase fixed assets	10,000
Bond discount		Dividends*	87,000
amort.	1,000	Incr. bal. net working	
Funds from operations	$127,000	capital	25,000
		Total Applica-	
Total Sources	$127,000	tions	$127,000

* Retained earnings 12/31/X0 =	$122,000
Net income for 19X1 =	91,000
Total	$213,000
Retained earnings 12/31/X1 =	126,000
Therefore, Dividends =	$ 87,000

PP 14.13

NAOMI CORPORATION

SCFP for Year Ending 12/31/X1

Sources		Applications	
Net Income	$168,000	Purchase land	$ 30,000
Add: Depreciation	50,000	Purchase other fixed	
Intangibles		assets	174,000
Amort.	6,000	Dividends	101,000
	$224,000	Increase in Bal. Net	
Subtract: Bond Premium		Working Cap.	47,000
Amortization	2,000		
Funds from operations	$222,000		
Sale of Bonds	50,000		
Sale of Stock	80,000	Total Applica-	
Total Sources	$352,000	tions	$352,000

		DR	CR
PP 17.1 b)	Cash	$10,000	
	Owner's Capital		$10,000
c)	Cash	5,000	
	Note Payable		5,000
e)	Cash	2,000	
	Sales		2,000
f)	Accounts Receivable	3,000	
	Sales		3,000
g)	Inventory	1,500	
	Accounts Payable		1,500

			DR	CR
h)	Supplies		600	
	Accounts Payable			600
i)	Cash		2,500	
	Accounts Receivable			2,500
j)	Leasehold Improvements		4,000	
	Cash			500
	Current Note Payable			3,500
k)	Note Payable		5,000	
	Interest Expense		400	
	Cash			5,400
l)	Accounts Payable		1,000	
	Cash			1,000
m)	Owner's Capital (Drawings)		500	
	Cash			500
PP 17.3 a)	Extraordinary Burglary Loss		$ 1,200	
	Inventory			$ 1,200
b)	Bad Debt Expense		2,500	
	Accounts Receivable			2,500
c)	Loss on Investments		2,800	
	Investments			2,800
d)	Repairs to Bldgs. & Equip.		1,000	
	Cash			1,000
e)	Legal Damages		3,000	
	Current Settlement Payable			1,500
	Noncurrent Settlement Payable			1,500
PP 17.5 1)	Cash		$ 50,000	
	Accounts Receivable		550,000	
	Sales			$600,000
2)	Cash		540,000	
	Accounts Receivable			540,000
3)	Marketable Securities		10,000	
	Cash			10,000
4)	Cash		5,450	
	Note Receivable			5,000
	Interest Receivable			450
5)	Inventory		400,000	
	Accounts Payable			400,000
6)	Supplies		5,000	
	Cash			5,000

		DR	CR
7)	Prepaid Items	3,000	
	Accounts Payable		3,000
8)	Notes Payable	15,000	
	Accounts Payable	90,000	
	Taxes Payable	14,000	
	Other Current Liabilities	6,000	
	Cash		125,000
9)	Accounts Payable	350,000	
	Cash		350,000
10)	Other Operating Expenses	100,000	
	Cash		100,000
11)	Cost of Goods Sold	390,000	
	Inventory		390,000
12)	Supplies Expense	20,000	
	Supplies		20,000
13)	Expirations of Prepd. Items	5,000	
	Prepaid Items		5,000
14)	Depreciation Expense	60,000	
	Accumulated Depreciation		60,000
15)	Amortization Expense	12,000	
	Intangibles		12,000
16)	Service Expense	7,000	
	Accounts Payable		7,000
17)	Tax Expense	10,000	
	Taxes Payable		10,000
18)	Miscellaneous Expense	3,000	
	Other Current Liabilities		3,000

INDEX

INDEX

[*Note:* Italic numerals indicate Glossary pages. Accounting language has many synonyms. Only those synonyms that are very widely used are included in this index; others can be found in the Glossary, pp. 577–609.]